ROUTLEDGE LIBRARY EDITIONS:
THE HISTORY OF ECONOMIC THOUGHT

Volume 1

ESSAYS ON PIERO SRAFFA

ESSAYS ON PIERO SRAFFA

Critical Perspectives on the Revival of Classical Theory

Edited by
KRISHNA BHARADWAJ AND
BERTRAM SCHEFOLD

Routledge
Taylor & Francis Group
LONDON AND NEW YORK

First published in 1990 by Unwin Hyman Ltd

This edition first published in 2017
by Routledge
2 Park Square, Milton Park, Abingdon, Oxon OX14 4RN

and by Routledge
711 Third Avenue, New York, NY 10017

Routledge is an imprint of the Taylor & Francis Group, an informa business

British Library Cataloguing in Publication Data
A catalogue record for this book is available from the British Library

ISBN: 978-1-138-29250-5 (Set)
ISBN: 978-1-315-23288-1 (Set) (ebk)
ISBN: 978-1-138-23010-1 (Volume 1) (hbk)
ISBN: 978-1-138-23011-8 (Volume 1) (pbk)
ISBN: 978-1-315-38694-2 (Volume 1) (ebk)

Publisher's Note
The publisher has gone to great lengths to ensure the quality of this reprint but points out that some imperfections in the original copies may be apparent.

Disclaimer
The publisher has made every effort to trace copyright holders and would welcome correspondence from those they have been unable to trace.

ESSAYS ON PIERO SRAFFA

Critical Perspectives on the Revival of Classical Theory

Edited by

KRISHNA BHARADWAJ
BERTRAM SCHEFOLD

London
UNWIN HYMAN
Boston Sydney Wellington

Published by the Academic Division of
Unwin Hyman Ltd
15/17 Broadwick Street, London W1V 1FP, UK

Unwin Hyman Inc.,
8 Winchester Place, Winchester, Mass. 01890, USA

Allen & Unwin (Australia) Ltd,
8 Napier Street, North Sydney, NSW 2060, Australia

Allen & Unwin (New Zealand) Ltd in association with the Port Nicholson Press Ltd,
Compusales Building, 75 Ghuznee Street, Wellington, New Zealand

First published in 1990

British Library Cataloguing in Publication Data

Essays on Piero Sraffa: critical perspectives on the revival of classical theory.
1. Economics. Theories of Sraffa, Piero, 1898–1983
I. Bharadwaj, Krishna II. Schefold, Bertram
330.15'5

ISBN 0–04–445254–3

Library of Congress Cataloging in Publication Data

Essays on Piero Sraffa.
Bibliography: p.
Includes index.
1. Sraffa, Piero—Congresses. 2. Classical school of economics—Congresses. I. Sraffa, Piero.
II. Bharadwaj, Krishna. III. Schefold, Bertram, 1943–
HB109.S73E87 1989 330.15 88–27998
ISBN 0–04–445254–3 (alk. paper)

Typeset in 10 on 11 point Sabon by Phoenix Photosetting, Chatham and printed in Great Britain by the University Press, Cambridge

Contents

Preface

This volume presents papers that were given at a conference held in Florence, 24–27 August 1985, to celebrate the twenty-fifth anniversary of the publication of Piero Sraffa's *Production of Commodities by Means of Commodities.* Sraffa's remarkable little book has opened up debates on fundamental issues in economic theory whose full implications and ramifications are yet to be drawn. The theoretical approach Sraffa sought to revive and develop in the book, as also in his earlier works (prominently in his monumental edition of Ricardo), and the critique he advanced of contemporary mainstream theory have been the focus of active discussion and controversy. The purpose of the conference was to elucidate some of the basic issues in theory and at the same time to assess the efforts that are under way to develop the classical approach to economic analysis and to extend it into the applied and policy fields. The conference invited the main participants in these debates to contribute papers in which they could elaborate their interpretations of Sraffa's work and evaluate its impact on present economic theory. In order to generate a critical and forthright appraisal, care was taken to invite scholars representing various positions and schools. Although not all the major contributors to the debates could be present at the conference, there was a very encouraging response, judging by the interest in continuing the discussions shown by the large body of participants prior to as well as during and after the conference.

The conference was organized in seven sessions, with key papers invited from authors belonging to different streams of theory dealing with critical interpretations of Sraffa and with extensions into the theory of effective demand and structural change. Two round tables were organized, one on 'Accumulation, Effective Demand and Distribution' and another on 'Development and Policy'.

In this volume most of the papers and the discussants' comments have been included – after editorial revision. The discussions from the floor during the sessions were most lively and have been recorded. However, for reasons of space, this volume confines itself to the written comments. Some of the papers offered at the conference could not be included; others were substantially revised for this publication. Some have been added later, notably that of Professor Samuelson who had been unable to attend the conference. The discussions continued and are reflected in comments and replies submitted until the autumn of 1988.

We regret the untimely death of Professor Fausto Vicarelli before this volume was edited: his contribution has been reprinted here without revision.

Among the participants at the conference we had the lively presence of

Professor Nicholas Kaldor, who made up for failing to contribute a paper by his active participation in discussions. He too is no more with us.

We are grateful to Professor John Hicks who had expressed his wish to participate more actively but who could not be present because of the death of his wife at the time of the conference. In spite of his personal loss he sent his paper on time. (He helped us with the proofs of his contribution shortly before he also passed away in May 1989.)

The papers and discussions have covered a surprisingly broad range of issues. To assemble and order this material has not been an easy task. In view of the length of the volume, the editors have decided to refrain from providing their own interpretations in an introduction. In any case, we hope that the issues that have been raised here, which are by no means resolved, will continue to be debated fruitfully to advance our understanding of theory and lead to further explorations. That alone can be a tribute to the indefatigable spirit of enquiry of Piero Sraffa.

Since these papers have emerged from the Florence conference, we should like to thank the organizing committee, which consisted of Krishna Bharadwaj, John Eatwell, Pierangelo Garegnani, Luigi L. Pasinetti, Bertram Schefold and Paolo Sylos-Labini, ably supported by Roberto Ciccone. We should like to extend our thanks to the contributors of papers and the participants in the Conference who made active and rigorous exchanges of ideas possible. H. Reich and P. Weihrauch, and later K. Carstensen helped to edit the manuscript. We should also like to thank the editors of Unwin Hyman who have shown a great deal of patience in seeing this book through the press. A grant from the Italian Research Council (CNR) is gratefully acknowledged.

Krishna Bharadwaj
Bertram Schefold
London
July 1988

PART I

1

Sraffa's Critique of the Marshallian Theory of Prices

Paolo Sylos Labini
Rome

Although our conference is devoted to an appraisal, after twenty-five years, of the most important of Sraffa's works, I think that it is worth while to reconsider, too, the critique of the Marshallian theory of prices expounded in the articles of 1925 and 1926, not only to understand better the intellectual journey behind *Production of Commodities*, but also because they contain hints that, in my opinion, have not yet been fully developed.

1 *The origin of the heterogeneity of the two laws of returns: Adam Smith and David Ricardo*

According to Sraffa, at the root of the inconsistencies in Marshall's theoretical construction and especially in his treatment of the supply curve we find the heterogeneity of the two laws of returns, those of increasing and of diminishing returns. The former represents largely the consequences of the process of the division of labour and was originally considered in relation to the problems of economic growth; the latter, which presupposes one of the factors of production as given, was originally considered in relation to the problems of income distribution. Now, such heterogeneity appears even sharper if we consider separately the two great classical economists whose works can in many respects be considered to be the basis of those two laws or tendencies: Adam Smith and David Ricardo.

The differences are great indeed. Smith was almost exclusively interested in the conditions governing the economic growth of nations and very little in income distribution; Ricardo, in contrast, was almost exclusively interested in the relations between prices and income distribution and very little in economic growth. Their theories of value are correspondingly different: Smith needed a standard of value to be used mainly in intertemporal comparisons, to understand how economic progress was affecting the different commodities; Ricardo needed a standard of value that could be relied upon to measure the exchange ratios between commodities. In Sraffa's words: 'the problem of value which interested Ricardo was to find a measure of value which would be invariant to changes in the division of the product' (Sraffa, 1951, p. xlviii). It is true that Ricardo, in company with all the other classical economists, attributed the greatest importance to the process of economic growth; in fact, he was interested in income distribution in order to understand how a change in this distribution could hinder or, conversely, favour accumulation. However, it is also true that Ricardo's analytical apparatus is basically different from Smith's since it is concerned with different problems.

Let us consider, first, the division of labour. According to Smith, this process goes on at different speeds, depending on the peculiarities of the different products; moreover, in the case of certain goods, it encounters special obstacles or limitations. This, for instance, is the case with cattle and minerals. As long as there is uncultivated land, cattle cost little more than the labour of catching them and their real price is stable. But when cultivation is extended over the greater part of the land of a given country, then to supply increasing consumer demand it becomes necessary to breed cattle by cultivating land to raise food for them and by tending them; in such circumstances the real price of cattle tends to increase, although certain improvements in breeding cattle can, for certain periods, counteract such a tendency (Smith, [1776] 1961, pp. 166–8). Minerals, too, tend to become dearer and dearer, since mines are limited and 'the discovery of new mines is a matter of the greatest uncertainty' (pp. 262–3).

According to Smith, then, the real price of these products tend to become dearer and dearer. Such tendencies have little in common with Ricardo's diminishing returns relating to agriculture as a whole. This tendency takes place when, with the increase of population, land of less and less 'fertility' is brought into cultivation. Contrary to widespread belief, Smith's views concerning a great and important part of agricultural products, that is, corn and other vegetable products, are very different from those of Ricardo. Smith believes that in vegetable products the division of labour meets with no appreciable obstacle, so that it tends to determine an improvement of the productive powers of labour and thus a progressive fall in the real price of such products. But since 'the nature of agriculture does not admit of so many subdivisions of labour, nor so complete a separation of one business from another, as manufactures', then 'the improvement of the productive powers of labour in this art does not always keep pace with their improvement in manufactures' (ibid., pp. 9–10). (Observations of this type are probably at the origin of the view that associates Smith and Ricardo in relation to the tendency to diminishing returns in agriculture). Thus, according to Smith, in agriculture too the tendency to increasing returns due to the division of labour operates, with the proviso that in vegetable products it is slower than in manufactures and that in cattle products such a tendency is likely to be reversed and increasing costs are likely to prevail when there is no more uncultivated land and when even the improvements that are introduced in cattle breeding are not such as to offset the tendency to increasing costs. As far as corn is concerned, Smith's position is a peculiar one. Corn is a vegetable product and, as such, its real price should fall in the course of time; but corn is produced with the help of cattle, the real price of which tends gradually to increase. On the basis of this reasoning Smith assumes that in the very long run ('from century to century'), the algebraic sum is not far from zero, so that the real price of corn is approximately constant. Now, such reasoning can be accepted or refuted, but it cannot be ignored; and this is precisely what Ricardo does when he criticizes Smith on this score. Here is the relevant passage:

> How, then, can it be true, that 'if you except corn, and such other vegetable, as are raised altogether by human industry, all other sorts of rude produce – cattle, poultry, game of all kinds, the useful fossils and minerals of the earth, & c., naturally grow dearer and dearer as the society advances' (Smith, [1776] 1961, p. 241). Why should corn and vegetables alone be excepted? Dr. Smith's error throughout his whole work, lies in supposing that the value of corn is constant; that though the value of all other things may, the value of corn can never be raised. Corn, according to him, is always of the same value because it will always feed the same number of people. In the same manner it might be said, that cloth is always of the same value, because it will always make the same number of coats. What can value have to do with the power of feeding and clothing?
>
> (Ricardo, [1817–21] 1951, p. 374; see also p. 14)

According to Smith, corn tends to be always of the same value, not because 'it will always feed the same number of people', but because he considers it reasonable to assume that the two contrasting forces mentioned above tend to offset each other. Smith, it is true, points out that he concentrates his attention on corn since 'it constitutes the principal part of the subsistence of the labourer' (Smith, [1776] 1961, p. 208); but nowhere does he make the statement that Ricardo attributes to him. It should be said that Smith is aware of the uncertain character of his assumption; he justifies it with the practical argument that a better alternative seems to be lacking. In fact, the data on wages necessary for constructing the preferable standard (that is, labour commanded, given by the ratio between the price of a certain commodity and the wage rate) often are lacking and therefore we have to content ourselves, *faute de mieux*, with the corn standard, given by the ratio between the price of the commodity considered and the price of corn, on the assumption that the real price of corn changes relatively little in the course of time. Here, again, two relatively long quotations are in order to clarify Smith's point of view, which Ricardo misinterpreted:

> In such a work as this, however, it may sometimes be of use to compare the different real values of a particular commodity at different times and places, or the different degrees of power over the labour of other people which it may, upon different occasions, have given to those who possessed it. We must in this case compare, not so much the different quantities of silver for which it was commonly sold, as the different quantities of labour which those different quantities of silver could have purchased. But the current prices of labour at distant times and places can scarce ever be

known with any degree of exactness. Those of corn, though they have in few places been regularly recorded, are in general better known and have been more frequently taken notice of by historians and writers. We must generally, therefore, content ourselves with them, as being the nearest approximation which can commonly be had to that proportion. I shall hereafter have occasion to make several comparisons of this kind.

(ibid., p. 43)

In every different stage of improvement . . . the raising of equal quantities of corn in the same soil and climate, will, at an average, require nearly equal quantities of labour; or what comes to the same thing, the price of nearly equal quantities; the continual increase of the productive powers of labour in an improving state of cultivation being more or less counterbalanced by the continually increasing price of cattle, the principal instruments of agriculture.

(ibid., p. 208)

These passages make it clear that Smith needs a standard of value with which to make intertemporal comparisons, since the growth of nations and the improvements in labour productivity are the main preoccupation of his inquiry: the corn standard represents an approximation to labour commanded, which is the standard to be used when the data of wages are available. Intertemporal comparisons of the value of commodities of different kinds are discussed in detail in the long 'Digression on Silver', which constitutes the largest part of Chapter XI, Book I, and which could be more accurately described as a digression on the price of corn over time.

2 *Two standards of value*

Ricardo was so convinced of the inevitability of diminishing returns in agriculture that he does not seem to be aware that Smith's position concerning the conditions of production of corn was completely different from his. Thus, when he finds statements pointing in a different direction in the *Wealth of Nations*, he attributes them simply to errors – for Ricardo, the corn standard is absurd because it is bound to be upset by diminishing returns. Ricardo was probably influenced in this belief by the experience of his time: owing mainly to the consequence of the French Revolution and of the Napoleonic wars, the price of wheat increased considerably during the last decade of the eighteenth century and during the first two decades of the nineteenth century. (In the following decades that price first went back to a level not much different from the previous average and then fell considerably.)

If we distinguish the two standards of value mentioned above – that is, the standard to be used in intertemporal comparisons and the one to be used to measure the exchange ratios between commodities in a given time – then we realize that, contrary to a long-standing indictment (which goes back to Ricardo, and was repeated by Marx and then by a host of other economists)

Smith is not guilty of confusing labour commanded and labour embodied, as he conceives it. According to Smith, labour commanded should be used both for intertemporal comparisons and to measure the exchange ratios between commodities. For the latter measure only labour commanded is to be used, since labour embodied can afford a rule for exchanging different commodities only 'in that early and rude state of society which precedes both the accumulation of stock and the appropriation of land' (Smith, [1776] 1961, p. 53). (When Smith refers to the question of exchange ratios between commodities he speaks of exchangeable value, and when he refers to the question of intertemporal comparisons he speaks of real price and real value.) However, if we assume a constant wage share in total product, the two standards are, in fact, equivalent for the intertemporal comparisons in the sense that they give the same results. The indictment is thus not really justified and arises from the failure to properly understand the two standards of value (see the Appendix). Labour commanded by a given commodity is the ratio between the price of that commodity and the wage rate (*P/W*); its inverse is the purchasing power of the wage rate in terms of that commodity, a purchasing power that is bound to increase hand in hand with the productivity of labour. Labour commanded is a standard that, as Smith said, can be used to measure the value of a particular commodity not only at different times but also in different places, particularly when prices are expressed in different money units. By necessity, such a standard is not and cannot be absolutely precise. In contrast, such precision can, and must, be the prerogative of the standard to be used in measuring the changes in relative prices arising from changes in the distribution of income, at a given technology. In looking for such a standard, Ricardo started with labour embodied, but then modified his position by introducing, as a measure of value, an abstract money 'produced with such proportions of the two kinds of capital as approach nearest to the average quantity employed in the production of most commodities' (Ricardo, [1817–21] 1951, pp. 44–5). The final step along this route has been Sraffa's standard commodity, which is, in fact, rigorously 'invariant to changes in the division of the product' in terms of its own means of production. (There is a third standard of value, which, by necessity, is even less precise than the one proposed by Smith, that is, a price index to be used as a deflator to measure the variations over time of total income and of other aggregates.)

3 *The laws of returns and the statical assumption: statics and dynamics*

The heterogeneity of the two laws of returns, then, is an expression of the radically different approaches of the two great classical economists, differences that in my opinion have not been and are not properly appreciated. This heterogeneity has not only contributed to those inconsistencies of Marshall's theory of prices that Sraffa has so incisively denounced, but has also had other damaging effects on economic theory, among which we find a confusing ambiguity in regard to the boundaries between static and dynamic assumptions.

Marshall's theory of prices belongs to partial equilibrium analysis, presupposes competition and is based, at least in principle, on static assumptions. Sraffa shows that some elements of this theory (internal economies) are incompatible with free competition, others (diminishing returns) with partial analysis, still others (external economies) with static assumptions and, again, with partial analysis. I will consider, in particular, the inconsistencies in which the static assumptions are involved.

The preliminary question is: can the two laws of returns be used in static models, as not only Marshall did, but many contemporary economists still do? If we consider the versions of those laws as they were proposed by the two great classical economists, the answer is necessarily 'No' – as I shall explain in greater detail in a moment.

But is it possible to modify those laws in such a way as to make that use logically acceptable without seriously altering their nature? Here the answer must be more articulated. But, first, we have to give a definition, as precise as possible, of statics and dynamics – a very difficult task indeed.

A static model is one that embodies a series of logical possibilities, independent of time. Correspondingly, a static curve represents a series of alternative hypotheses, that is, of virtual variations of the phenomena considered; reversibility is a necessary property of such a curve. A dynamic model is one in which quantities (and decisions) must be dated; a dynamic process is inconceivable outside time. It should be added that a stationary process is still a dynamic process, which, however, repeats itself always in the same way. (A stationary process lends itself easily to static analysis; in principle, however, we have to be well aware of the distinction.) A dynamic analysis tends to isolate certain groups of phenomena in order to explain their relations and their behaviour over time. In this analysis, time appears in a purely abstract way; when we consider it in its actual terms, that is, when we engage in an historical inquiry, then we have to record a given set of phenomena as they appear in reality, using dynamic models to interpret their behaviour.

Now, there is no doubt that, for Smith, the tendency to increasing returns is a dynamic process, behind which we find the division of labour. In its turn, the division of labour is the result of the growth and of the increasing differentiation of the economy as a whole and not simply of individual industries or, even less, of individual units of production. After studying the conditions and the main features of this process on an abstract plane, Smith considers its real (that is, historical) behaviour with reference to different countries. Indeed, often it is difficult, if not impossible, to separate the theoretical from the historical analyses in the *Wealth of Nations*. This may be a tribute to Smith's realism, but it is also a criticism of what appears, at several points, to be a lack of rigour. Smith's increasing returns, then, represent a dynamic process. The only case of increasing returns consistent, at least in a first approximation, with static assumptions is the case of economies of scale that presuppose technology as given – we may call them 'static economies of scale'. Those economies of scale that depend on technological progress and that can be obtained only by firms of an increasing size we call 'dynamic economies of scale'. In Smith's times, all kinds of economies of scale were largely absent; if anything, only the dynamic kind can be found, in an embryonic way, in the *Wealth of Nations*. Thus, it remains true that, in Smith, the whole process of the division of labour should be considered in dynamic terms. It should be added that, today, dynamic economies of scale are probably much more important than static economies.

Ricardo's tendency to diminishing returns also properly belongs to the realm of dynamic analysis. In fact, according to Ricardo it is the increase, over time, of population that calls into cultivation land of inferior quality or less advantageously situated and thus gives rise to rent. Ricardo recognizes that improvements in agriculture can counteract the tendency to diminishing returns. But he believes that in the long run it is the natural tendency that is bound to prevail. The consideration of improvements in agriculture belongs, again, to the realm of dynamic, not static, analysis. Yet, if one considers the increase in population as a virtual variation and if one neglects improvements in agriculture by assuming that their influence is secondary, then it is not so illogical to include the tendency to diminishing returns in a static model. Yet, as Pasinetti (1960) has shown, the proper approach to be adopted in interpreting Ricardo in modern terms is a dynamic approach.

Marshall was worried about the problems of logical consistency between increasing returns and static assumptions. He made considerable efforts to interpret Smith's process of the division of labour in such a way as to make it compatible with statical assumptions; the 'internal' and the 'external' economies of scale are the result of these efforts. Let us consider in greater detail the two types of economies of scale.

(1) Internal economies of scale are those determined by large-scale production, which, in its turn, is the consequence of the increase in the size of firms. Large-scale production makes possible the application of new methods and the introduction of new machines. These are new either (a) in the sense that, though already known from the technological standpoint, they were not previously used because the scale of production was not large enough, or (b) in the technological sense: the increase in the scale of production favours the subdivision of operations and thus stimulates the invention of new machines. (Only internal economies of type (b) are considered by Smith, and then very briefly.)

(2) External economies of scale are those arising from the concentration of specialized industries in particular localities. Such economies do not depend necessarily on the size of individual firms; they are a special case of economies arising from the development of the economy as a whole. External economies, then, are (a) those due to a process of specialization favoured or determined by the geographical concentration of industries of various kinds and (b) those due to the introduction of technologically new machines favoured or determined by the development of the economy as a whole. (Only external economies of type (a) are discussed by Marshall, who gives only brief and vague hints as to type (b) economies; in a certain sense, the opposite is true for Smith.)

It is clear that the only case of economies of scale compatible with static assumptions is that of economies that can be achieved with a given technology (internal economies of type (a)). There can be little doubt that all the others are incompatible with those assumptions (static economies of scale, however, are incompatible with competition as conceived by Marshall; on the other hand, external economies are incompatible not only with static assumptions, but also with partial analysis).

In a relatively long appendix (H) to his *Principles* ([1920] 1949) Marshall discussed the 'Limitations of the use of statical assumptions in regard to increasing returns'. Many years later Dennis Robertson reconsidered the whole matter. Owing to the importance of his observations, a fairly long quotation is justified:

> It will be seen that in many of the economies of both main classes (i.e. external and internal), the element of time is of supreme importance. This fact has raised many doubts as to whether in such cases it is sensible to attempt to think at all in terms of a 'true' or 'conditional sentence' supply curve. Can we really, even if we are careful to correct for the effect of major inventions which clearly did not depend on the scale of the industry, ever hope to get beyond what is really simply an historical record of the way costs have fallen as output has risen? Certainly Marshall was very much alive – more so than several of his more mathematically minded but less mathematically competent successors – to the perils of the whole method (see Marshall, [1920] 1949, Bk V, Ch. 12, especially pp. 460–1 and Appendix H). We must, I think, concede that any curve we can construct is not perfectly reversible, i.e. that the cost per unit set against an output x should properly be less if output has shrunk to x from some higher figure y than if it has reached x for the first time, since not all the economies of specialization won in passing from x to y will be lost in passing back from y to x. And the prospect of deriving such curves with success from the confused data of real life seems to be more remote than in the case of demand curves. Nevertheless, after a period of revolt,[1] I am now of the opinion that the concept of a true long-period supply curve is one which we cannot do without, though we must handle it carefully.
>
> (Robertson, 1957–9, I, pp. 118–19)

The most serious problems of logical consistency are those related to technical progress. Both Marshall and Robertson suggest that at least the effects of 'major' innovations should be excluded from a static supply curve. We have just seen how Robertson tries to dispose of those effects (though he does not exclude other economies in spite of his recognition that the element of time is of 'supreme importance' in many of them). The following is the way out suggested by Marshall: 'We exclude from view any economies that may result from substantive new inventions; but we include those which may be expected to arise naturally out of adaptations of existing ideas' (Marshall, [1920] 1949, p. 381).

Marshall is aware of the uncertain and vague character of these considerations and warns the reader that 'such notions must be taken broadly. The attempt to make them precise over-reaches our strength'. More generally, he is aware of the many problems that arise when, in constructing a static supply curve, one takes account, among other things, of the tendency to increasing returns. However, instead of changing his approach, he tries to dodge these problems by appealing to the conditions of real life (ibid., p. 382) or by emphasizing the 'imperfections of our analytical methods' (ibid., p. 667). Thus, in spite of all the warnings and caveats, both Marshall and Robertson conclude that increasing returns can, after all, be considered in a static long-run supply curve. And yet those warnings are so serious that the only correct conclusion would have been to reject the long-period supply curve. It seems that those warnings are issued only to exorcise the ghost of inconsistency – which remains.

4 *Constant returns, increasing returns and market conditions*

Marshall was much more worried about the problems of logical consistency arising from increasing returns than about those arising from diminishing returns; and the same applies to his successors, like Robertson. Yet Sraffa's criticism – that diminishing returns cannot be invoked for constructing a supply curve of an individual industry since they are incompatible with partial analysis – seems irrefutable. Sraffa concluded in his 1925 article that only constant costs are compatible with static competitive conditions. In his 1926 article, he emphasized that, in fact, a great number of commodities, and the majority of manufactures, are produced at decreasing costs and suggested that one should 'abandon the path of free competition and turn in the opposite direction, namely, towards monopoly' (Sraffa, 1926, p. 542). As Roncaglia (1978, p. 14) has pointed out, however, Sraffa came to the conclusion, probably after a period of uncertainty, that the two suggestions could not be amended and thus salvage the Marshallian theory with its apparatus of supply and demand curves. Indeed, a few years later (that is, at the 1930 symposium on increasing returns), Sraffa stated quite clearly that in his opinion Marshall's theory should be discarded. We now know, from the Preface to *Production of Commodities* (Sraffa, 1960), that the main propositions put forth in this book had taken shape even before 1930. It seems that Sraffa was already convinced that the problem could be solved satisfactorily not at the level of partial analysis, but only at the level of general analysis. However, this was to be done by adopting, not Pareto's point of view, but the classical point of view, that is, by conceiving of economic activity not as an arch, but as a circle or, better, as a spiral. Yet, the 1925 and 1926 articles are not to be left only to the historian of economic thought. Though limited in their scope, they have contributed indirectly to the development of what we may call the dynamic partial analysis of the firm and of market forms; a type of analysis, moreover, that does not close the doors to the consideration of all kinds of market forms in models of general analysis. In fact, we have to recall that the inclusion of non-competitive market forms in the traditional models of general analysis has proved to be extremely difficult if not impossible.

In working out dynamic models of partial analysis, the starting point is to recognize that in our times competitive conditions are largely restricted to agriculture and to a small number of manufactures; in the majority of industrial production, as well as in the majority of services, non-competitive conditions are the rule, either because of the process of concentration associated with dynamic economies of scale due to special forms of technical progress, or because of the process of product differentiation, related to the rising standard of living and all sorts of sales efforts and advertising, or for both reasons.

It is fitting to point out, however, that for the classical economists – and here there is no difference between Smith and Ricardo – competition is a dynamic process, characterized by free entry and therefore, considering the economy as a whole, by a tendency towards a uniform rate of profit. For the marginalist economists, competition is a situation characterized by a great number of small firms, the output of each firm being so small that its variations cannot affect the price. In his 1925 article, Sraffa mentions this definition of competition and quotes Pareto;[2] since his main purpose is to criticize the traditional model of competition, he does not enter into a comparison between the classical and the marginalist conceptions. Yet, if we want to develop some of his critical hints positively, we would be better advised to adopt the classical conception – if we accept the suggestion mentioned above concerning the element of monopoly that we find in a great number of productions, especially in manufacturing. In this connection, the works of Joan Robinson (1933) and Edward Chamberlin ([1933] 1947) are often mentioned. It should be observed, however, that these works meet only one of Sraffa's criticisms. Basically, they do not depart from the marginalist tradition; moreover, they do not go beyond a static framework. Kalecki's works, especially those published in 1937, 1938 and 1943 (Kalecki, 1937, 1938, 1943a), are much nearer to Sraffa's point of view, which conceives the widespread monopoly elements in terms of obstacles to entry and make possible a dynamic analysis.

From the 1926 article the following picture emerges clearly: many firms, especially in manufacturing, in the short run produce at constant marginal costs and, correspondingly, at falling total costs per unit; in the long run, again, total costs per unit are falling. This is precisely the behaviour of costs that Kalecki assumes in his 1938 and 1943 articles, in both of which he presents interesting empirical testing that employ those assumptions. And this is exactly the picture that emerged, first of all from the empirical inquiry conducted by Hall and Hitch (1939) and other economists in Oxford and, subsequently, from a great number of investigations, whose results are very carefully collected by Edwin Mansfield (1975, Table 6.4 and Figure 6.2.2). It should be observed that Mansfield's faith in the traditional curves is not shaken by the impressive list of findings, which almost all agree with the picture sketched by Sraffa and are in sharp contrast with the picture presented by traditional theory (which assumes that, after a point, both short-run and long-run marginal costs are rising) – an interesting illustration of the persuasive (I should say, hypnotic) power of a theoretical paradigm, which can blind us to even the most evident facts. It is to be observed, too, that the picture sketched by Sraffa is wholly consistent with the findings presented by John G.

Dunlop in 1938 to show that the belief expressed by Keynes in his *General Theory* (1936a, p. 10), that when money wages are rising real wages tend to fall, is unfounded – a belief that, as Keynes pointed out in his reply to Dunlop's criticism, 'was widely held by British economists' (1936b), p. 34) and was implicit in the view that, after a point, marginal costs tend to rise when output expands. Today, in most empirical and econometric analyses of prices, short-run marginal costs implicitly or explicitly are assumed to be constant (and therefore equal to direct costs), at least, as is usually added to avoid controversy, 'in the relevant range of output'.

It is important to notice that, once we abandon the static framework, the monopoly elements no longer appear necessarily as a source of waste or as an obstacle to growth. Sraffa emphasizes that the limit to output expansion is, as a rule, to be found not within the individual firm, as the traditional theory suggests (the limit being given by a rising marginal cost), but in demand. This thesis is worth reflection: it implies that, provided demand increases, output can expand and, as a rule, can expand even at decreasing costs. It becomes important, then, to study the conditions that make possible a widespread increase in demand – a question that in many ways is related to the much wider problems of the management of aggregate demand discussed by Keynesian and post-Keynesian theories.

In my opinion, other suggestions from Sraffa's 1926 article are still to be developed. Thus, Sraffa points out that the limits to bank loans that a given firm can obtain are due, not simply, or not at all, to the level of the rate of interest, but to the fact that it is known that that firm is unable to increase its sales outside its own particular market without incurring heavy marketing expenses. Now, this issue could be usefully discussed in connection with Kalecki's 'principle of increasing risk' to explain the distribution between internal and external means devoted to the financing of the investment of firms. In fact, this important problem has not yet been adequately explored.

5 The classical conception of production and Sraffa's model: the question of uses of the surplus

In the conception of the marginalists, including Marshall, the fundamental problem of economic theory is to find the conditions of equilibrium and, in particular, the equilibrium prices, determined by demand and supply curves – each price appearing as the keystone of an arch. In the classical conception the fundamental problem is to find the conditions of reproduction of the system.

In *Production of Commodities* Sraffa works out a rigorous formalization of the classical conception. He assumes an annual cycle of production and an annual market and studies the conditions of reproduction of this cycle. Such conditions are represented, first of all, by that 'set of exchange-values which, if adopted by the market, restores the original distribution of the products and makes it possible for the process to be repeated; such values spring directly from the methods of production' (Sraffa, 1960, p. 3).

In sharp contrast with the traditional theory, then, Sraffa views the prices of production as directly determined by the methods of production: there is no room for demand and supply curves and for their intersection. In this respect, however, the distinction between basic and non-basic commodities has a special relevance. The prices of basic commodities contribute to the determination of the general price system and the rate of profits, whereas non-basic commodities are passive: their prices are determined by the methods of production as well as by the prices of basic commodities but they do not contribute to the determination of the price system and the rate of profits (or the rate of wages if the rate of profits is taken as the independent variable).[3] Non-basic commodities enter into the surplus: in a given productive cycle, the surplus is free and the commodities constituting it have no role in reproduction. This poses the problem of the quantities of such commodities to be produced: since these are not determined by the necessities of reproduction, they are produced in relation to the possibilities of selling them. Such possibilities depend on consumers' preferences, which originate, in their turn, not in the psychology of the individuals, considered among the ultimate data, but from the stage and the type of development of the society as a whole. This is a problem of demand, which is very different from the problem of demand of traditional theory and which does not contradict at all the logical framework of Sraffa's model: the fundamental role in price determination always belongs to the technology of basic products. This question enters into the wider question of the different uses of the surplus.

Sraffa's model is a dynamic one, in the sense previously defined; it represents a stationary economy. In fact, it is a model worked out not to study a growth process, but, fundamentally, to explain how relative prices change when income distribution varies – exactly the problem in which Ricardo was mainly interested. Moreover, that model presupposes competition since it assumes a single rate of profit. Those who intend to use Sraffa's model to analyse a growth process under both competitive and non-competitive conditions should introduce several important modifications; these, however, can be such as not to alter its logic (Pasinetti's suggestion of adopting a vertically integrated sectoral analysis – see Chapter 8 in this volume – represents a line that seems to be complementary with that of Sraffa). Non-competitive market forms can easily be introduced by exploiting the possibility of considering the rate of profit, or a range of profit rates, as an independent variable. Even the consideration of a growth process at constant inputs is easy, although the constancy of inputs does not at all exclude technical progress but, on the contrary, presupposes innovations capable of offsetting exactly the tendency to diminishing returns from land and from mines.[4] Naturally, in such an analysis it would be necessary for at least a part of the surplus to be used productively, i.e. accumulated. The maximum rate of growth would depend on the availability of the surpluses of the basic products – the minimum surplus would fix the limit to growth. If even one of the basic products were to be produced without surplus, then reproduction would be possible, but not growth. (The surplus can consist of both basic and non-basic commodities: the latter can only be consumed, as hinted above, whereas in the case of basic commodities the alternative is between productive and non-productive uses.)

If we introduced the hypothesis that a part of the surplus of a given period were to be used to produce additional means of production of a new type – for instance, technologically new machines – then we would be analysing a process of growth propelled by technical progress corresponding to that most frequently observed in reality. At this point considerable difficulties arise, since changes in production methods imply changes in the standard system if basic commodities are involved (Sraffa discusses the case of the switch in the methods of production of one of the commodities in Chapter XII of *Production of Commodities*). However, in analysing a process of growth the main problem becomes that of measuring the changes in the value of individual commodities over time, so that we can put on one side the problem of the changes in relative prices depending on changes in income distribution (Ricardo's problem) and use Smith's standard, i.e. labour commanded. In any case, it is as well to remember that there are several models that, although not deliberately or formally linked to that of Sraffa, yet are fully consistent with the classical approach. As far as Sraffa's model is concerned, the view has hitherto prevailed that it was necessary to develop the implications of the pure model first, deliberately avoiding other analytical developments – like the one concerning technical progress and growth – that would create dangers of confusion. As far as I was able to understand, Sraffa himself was of this view. I think that such an attitude, fully justified twenty or even ten years ago, nowadays needs to be reconsidered. The conclusion will probably be reached that there is room for both kinds of analytical work – the development of the theoretical problems of the original model and the consideration of the most appropriate way to use it in order to examine the essential features of a growth process, which, after all, directly or indirectly was the main concern of the classical economists.

6 *Concluding remarks*

The heterogeneity of the two laws of returns, which Sraffa considers as the main reason for the inconsistencies of Marshall's theoretical construction, depends, in the final analysis, on fundamental differences in the approaches adopted by Smith and Ricardo. The former is almost exclusively interested in economic growth; the latter in the relations between the distribution of income and relative prices. Even the two standards of value – labour commanded and labour embodied – have different purposes: labour commanded being useful in intertemporal comparisons of a given commodity, labour embodied in measuring the exchange ratios of two or more commodities in given technological conditions. Now, economic growth is, *par excellence*, a dynamic problem, whereas the problem of income distribution and relative prices, as well as that of diminishing returns, can be treated with reference to a stationary process that lends itself to a static analysis. This is true, however, only in a first approximation, since a stationary process is a dynamic process of a particular kind.

The inconsistencies of traditional theory denounced by Sraffa with reference to the Marshallian theory can be avoided only by building models that can allow us to analyse markets under competitive and non-competitive conditions, on the basis both of static and of dynamic assumptions, without necessarily being confined to partial analysis. I think that significant progress has been made in this direction during the last sixty years as far as the theory of the firm and the theory of market forms are concerned. Certain important steps have also been taken in the direction of dynamic models of general analysis; it is here, however, that most of the theoretical work is still to be done.

Appendix I
On Smith's alleged confusion between labour embodied and labour commanded

1 *The two standards: difference and equivalence*

To make clear why the two standards as a rule give different results when considering the exchange ratios between different commodities in a given moment and under which conditions they are equivalent in the intertemporal comparisons of value of the same commodity, we might examine a simple numerical example, beginning with the first question – exchange ratios between different commodities.

If the production of commodity A requires 1 hour of labour, whereas commodity B requires 2 hours, then, according to labour embodied, the two commodities should exchange according to the ratio 2 to 1 (2 units of A for 1 unit of B). However, if, for reasons related to the techniques of production, the share of wages per unit of price (let us call it Y) in B is twice that in A, then the two commodities will command the same labour and the exchange ratio so measured would be 1 to 1.

If we call H labour embodied in 1 unit of a given commodity, P the price of the same commodity, W the wage rate, we have

$$Y = WH/P \quad \text{or} \quad P = WH/Y.$$

According to labour embodied, the exchange ratio between the two commodities is

$$H_B/H_A = 2$$

(two units of A for one unit of B).

According to labour commanded, the exchange ratio is

$$\frac{P_A/W}{P_B/W} = 1.$$

This is because

$$P_A/W = H_A/Y_A = 1/0.25 = 4$$
$$P_B/W = H_B/Y_B = 2/0.50 = 4.$$

Similar reasoning and a similar example can illustrate why the two standards – the wage share remaining stable – are equivalent in the intertemporal comparisons of value of the same commodity.[5]

2 *The relative stability of the wage share in Smith*

Although the assumption that the wage share remains stable over time is not explicitly made by Adam Smith, it seems to be consistent with his views of what happens in the progressive state of a country's evolution. Indeed, according to Smith, when the wealth of a nation increases, the share of rent tends to increase and the share of profits tends to decrease, leaving the share of wages relatively stable – so it seems. As for profits, Smith speaks of a decline in their rate, not in their share. However, considering that, for him, the principal part of capital is given by the labourers' consumption goods, and in any case assuming (as is reasonable) that total capital and national income increase in the same proportion, then the share and the rate of profits tend to behave in the same way.

The following specific quotations can be of help:

(a) *Rent*: 'The landlord's share of the produce necessarily increases with the increase of the produce' (Smith, [1776) 1961, p. 275).

(b) *Wages*: 'It is not the actual greatness of national wealth, but its continual increase, which occasions a rise in the price of labour' (ibid., p. 78).

(c) *Profits*: '. . . the rate of profit does not, like rent and wages, rise with the prosperity, and fall with the declension, of the society. On the contrary, it is naturally low in rich, and high in poor countries' (ibid., p. 277).

These remarks and quotations are concerned with the overall shares of the three categories of income. As for the individual commodities, the shares can be different from the overall shares, but the trends are not necessarily different. In fact, even in those commodities in which increases in productivity are particularly rapid, as in the great majority of manufactures, both the absolute and the relative prices can vary considerably, but the share of wages can remain relatively stable; in such branches, wages can increase without pushing up the share of wages if the changes in relative prices are proportional to the changes in the cost of labour per unit of output (see the quotation at the end of section 4 of this Appendix).

Smith's assumption will not seem so far-fetched if one thinks of the vast literature that aims to explain the relative stability of the wage share over national income pointed out by several statisticians with reference to a very long period – say for the hundred years preceding the Second World War.

3 *Ricardo*

I will limit myself to what I consider the most important statements:

> Adam Smith, who so accurately defined the original source of exchangeable value, and who was bound in consistency to maintain that all things became more or less valuable in proportion as more or less labour was bestowed on their production, has himself erected another standard measure of value, and speaks of things being more or less of this standard measure. Sometimes he speaks of corn, at other times of labour, as a

> standard measure; not the quantity bestowed on the production of any object, but the quantity which it can command in the market: as if these were equivalent expressions, and as if because a man's labour had become doubly efficient, and he could therefore produce twice the quantity of a commodity, he would necessarily receive twice the former quantity in exchange for it.
>
> (Ricardo, [1817–21] 1951, pp. 13–14)

4 Marx

To quote Marx:

> Many examples can be given to show how often in the course of his work, when he is explaining actual facts, Smith treats the quantity of labour embodied in a given commodity as value and as an element determining value. Some of these examples are quoted by Ricardo. His whole doctrine of the influence of the division of labour and improved machines on the price of commodities is based on it. Here one passage will be enough to cite. In ch. XI, 1.1 Adam Smith speaks of the cheapening of many manufactured goods in his time, as compared with earlier centuries, and he concludes with the words:
>
> > 'It cost a greater quantity of labour to bring the goods to market. When they were brought thither, therefore, they must have purchased or exchanged for the price of a greater quantity.
> >
> > [Smith, [1776] 1961, vol. I, p. 273]
>
> . . . [T]his contradiction in Adam Smith and his passing from one kind of explanation to another is based upon something deeper, which Ricardo, in exposing this contradiction, overlooked or did not rightly appreciate, and therefore also did not solve.
>
> (Marx, [1862–3] 1969–72, p. 71)

Marx then goes on to discuss certain aspects of labour embodied. At the beginning of the above quotation Marx states that one can find several examples of the said 'contradiction'. Another such example, given its importance, is worth quoting:

> It is the natural effect of improvement . . . to diminish gradually the real price of almost all manufactures. . . . In consequence of better machinery, of greater dexterity, and of a more proper division and distribution of work, all of which are the natural effects of improvement, a much smaller quantity of labour becomes requisite for executing any particular piece of work; and though, in consequence of the flourishing circumstances of the society, the real price of labour should rise very considerably, yet the great dimininution of the quantity will generally much more than compensate the greatest rise which can happen in the price.
>
> (Smith, [1776] 1961, vol. I, p. 269)

Even in this passage we find the 'confusion' that we are discussing, since by 'real price' Smith invariably means labour commanded and since the 'quantity of labour' cannot but refer to labour embodied. From this and from several other passages it is clear that, in the intertemporal comparisons of value, Smith considers the two expressions as equivalent. As is argued in the text, however, this is neither a confusion nor an error.

Why, then, in the said comparisons does Smith reason in terms of labour embodied rather than in terms of labour commanded? Because changes in the 'productive powers of labour' over time are measured by changes in labour input, i.e. by labour embodied; but the only practical way to measure these changes is to follow the changes in the ratio *P/W*, i.e. labour commanded, granting that the assumption of a stable wage share can be taken as sufficiently realistic. In fact, data on labour embodied are extremely difficult to find, whereas those on prices and wages as a rule are easy to find (if data on wages are not available, then Smith suggests using the price of corn as a substitute). Thus, labour commanded cannot be dispensed with in the intertemporal comparisons and the said procedure seems to have no alternative.

In short: labour embodied is the standard to be used in intertemporal comparisons, but, for practical reasons, labour commanded is to be adopted; the latter is the only standard to be used for the exchange ratios.

Appendix II – (see p. 555)

Notes

1 Robertson is here referring to an article of his published in January 1924 in the *Economic Journal.*

2 The reference is to V. Pareto, *Cours d'économie politique*, para. 46 and footnote.

3 Without fully realizing it, in the second part of my monograph on oligopoly, in which I tried to proceed from the partial analysis of the first part to a very simplified form of general analysis, I came across with non-basic products having the characteristics mentioned in the text (Sylos Labini, [1956] 1962, p. 143, fn 15).

4 At a seminar in 1968, in order to criticize a view that at that time was gaining ground among the young members of the Institute of Economics of the Faculty of Statistics of Rome, I presented a paper intended to show: (a) how non-competitive market forms could be introduced into Sraffa's model and (b) how, in a first approximation, a growth model could be examined on the basis of this model. Although that paper had some circulation in a mimeographed form, I did not publish it; I only summarized the first section, concerning non-competitive market forms, in Sylos Labini (1971); this was then reproduced, with modifications, in Sylos Labini (1984b). The reason is that I intended to develop and enlarge my rudimentary analysis of a growth process by also considering the case of changes in inputs due to technological progress; but for several reasons since then this remained only a project.

5 I worked out the above argument in my report to the Glasgow Conference for the Bicentenary of the *Wealth of Nations*, recently reprinted in Sylos Labini (1984a).

Comment

Peter Groenewegen
Sydney

Measure of value, laws of returns, empirical content and taxation conundrums

Professor Sylos Labini's title indicates that his stimulating paper comments on the heartland of Sraffa's work: the critique of the marginalist theory of price with special reference to its Marshallian variant. However, the paper does more than this. For example, there are some very interesting comments on important differences between Smith and Ricardo as regards the laws of returns and the standard of value. The paper also provides useful reflections on statics and dynamics in the context of classical and Marshallian economics, comments on the relevance of the hypothesis of constant returns and the connection between Sraffa's model (Sraffa, 1960) and the classical conception of production, and finally raises questions on productive and unproductive uses of the surplus as a crucial issue for the classical economists when they investigated the problem of economic growth.[1]

A major part of Sylos Labini's paper is clearly intended as a reminder of the continuity of development in Sraffa's critique of Marshallian price theory, which is particularly useful when attention is focused on his last major work with its emphasis on a 'Prelude to a Critique of Economic Theory'. The key features of this part of Sylos Labini's paper are easily summarized. Sraffa's critique of marginalist (including Marshallian) price theory started in his 1925 paper with its careful examination of 'the theoretical foundations of the laws of variation of costs' in the context of 'the determination of the particular equilibria of individual products under a regime of free competition' (Sraffa, 1925, p. 280). In 1926, part of this criticism was further developed – in the process being made far more accessible to the economics profession. Among many other things, it contained the famous but at the time largely ignored plea for the relevance to value of 'the old and now obsolete theory of value which makes it dependent on the cost of production alone' (Sraffa, [1926] 1953, p. 187). One important implication of this statement is its role as a devastating critique of Marshall's own interpretation of his value theory as the *completion* of the theory of Ricardo and the older economists (Marshall, 1961, Appendix 1, esp. pp. 813–14; Shove, 1942, esp. pp. 295–6). By the end of the 1920s Sraffa was ready for unambiguous and very explicit rejection of the Marshallian value theory, and did so unmistakably in his comments contributed to the famous symposium on increasing returns and the representative firm with Shove and Robertson (Sraffa, 1930, p. 93). This important step was undoubtedly facilitated by Sraffa's formulation over the preceding few years of the 'opening propositions' for a theory of value *independent* of a law of returns. He had shown a draft of this theory to Keynes as early as 1928, even though the final elaboration of these propositions was not to be published for more than three decades in the book now being celebrated (Sraffa, 1960, p. vi).

By focusing on these links between Sraffa's earlier and later work, Sylos Labini draws attention to what may be described as the construction-through-criticism aspects of Sraffa's work whereby the negative process inherent in removing the logical foundations of Marshallian price theory progressed within a relatively short time period to a new theory designed to avoid the conundrums of the rejected theoretical approach. This may be briefly elaborated. Sraffa's critique of Marshallian price theory, inspired by his well-informed suspicions of the spurious symmetry introduced into supply and demand theory by the hypothesis that the cost of production of every unit of the commodity under consideration changes with variations in the quantity produced – in short, the hypothetical foundations for the U-shaped cost curves of the text books – induced his systematic review of the relationship between cost and quantity produced (Sraffa, 1925) and eventually brought him to reject the relevance of this type of thought experiment for the theoretical work whose appraisal is the objective of this conference. Coquetting a little with Hegel, Sraffa's work (1960) can be seen from this perspective as a new theory's constructive transcendence through destructive criticism of the old, a negation of the negation. In this way, Sylos Labini's excursus into the disputes over Marshallian price theory and the laws of returns re-emphasizes the immanent critique of marginalism that lies at the heart of Sraffa's theoretical work.

This dialectical emphasis on the laws of returns in Sraffa's work also enables Sylos Labini to comment on aspects of classical economics whose rehabilitation is such an important component of Sraffa's contribution. In the first place, it allows an essential separation of Smith and Ricardo from each other with respect to both the laws of returns and the, in some ways, associated matter of the standard of value.[2] One aspect of this linking concerns the difference between Smith and Ricardo on secular tendencies in the real price of corn. Sylos Labini clearly demonstrates that Ricardo had misunderstood Smith's strange arguments about its stability and the purpose to which Smith put his standard of value. His proof of the conditions for formal equivalence of labour commanded and labour embodied (Sylos Labini, 1976, pp. 212–16) can be usefully supplemented by Bladen's far too little known interpretation (Bladen, 1975) that Smith in a quite fundamental sense regarded labour embodied as a synonym for labour commanded, when the labour commanded from a purchased commodity is depicted as the labour saved by the purchaser in not having to produce the commodity himself (Smith, [1776] 1976, I, v, 2). Such identification is indispensable when solving the problem of distinguishing monetary influences on secular price movements from those induced by changes in the method of production or the quantity of labour applied before using trends in secular price movements of particular classes of commodities as an index of the 'progress of improvement' of society (Smith, [1776] 1976, esp. I, xi, e.9, I.xi.i.3 and, most importantly, I.xi,n.9–10). Sylos Labini's Appendix demonstrates this point clearly.

One other aspect of Sylos Labini's comments on classical political economy and its relationship with Sraffa's economics may be explored briefly. This arises from his views on the statics and dynamics of the laws of returns (Sylos Labini, 1985a, esp. pp. 56–60). There he argues correctly that static increasing and decreasing returns are conceptually possible as a thought experiment represented by 'a series of alternative hypotheses' which embody complete reversibility because of their total independence of historical time. The classics did not have this static notion; for them, increasing and decreasing returns were part of the dynamic behaviour of costs and prices over time and hence able to accommodate technological change. Marshall as usual had a foot in both camps: he realized that what was really valuable in these laws was the dynamic part but that the static part was crucial for the coherence of the theory he was constructing. Marshall prevaricated on this in Appendix H; Robertson (in the long quote given by Sylos Labini) correctly reiterated that these difficulties belong to the problem of time.[3] Sraffa's rejection of the need for the static laws in constructing a price theory at the same time clears the way for using these concepts in the dynamic manner of the classics.

Finally, I would like to comment on two minor aspects of Sylos Labini's paper, both of which are incidentally associated with subsequent criticism and developments from Sraffa's (1960) work.

The first deals with his perceptive aside on the ambiguous attitudes of conventional economics to empirical invalidation of theoretical propositions made in the context of his remark on Mansfield's 'faith in the traditional curves' despite his careful collection of contrary evidence. He presents this as 'an interesting illustration of the persuasive (I should say, hypnotic) power of a theoretical paradigm can blind us even to the most evident facts' (Sylos Labini, 1985a, p. 62, see also Garegnani's contribution in this volume for more optimistic expectations about responses to changes in the facts).

It is appropriate to compare Sylos Labini's observations on Mansfield with the *obiter dicta* in Blaug's famous trial of the Cambridge Revolution (Blaug, 1974, esp. pp. 41–3) on the anti-empirical implications of a Cambridge 'methodology of "essentialism"'. Lest it be said that such inexactitudes are excusable in a 'political' tract produced for the Institute of Economic Affairs, it should be noted that Blaug has reproduced this passage almost verbatim in his *Methodology of Economics* (Blaug, 1980, pp. 204–8, esp. p. 207). The passage, which occurs in Blaug's empirical[4] critique of reswitching and capital reversing, is so brief it can be quoted in full:

> Take the simplest possible example of a neo-classical prediction: a tax on butter producers will raise the price of butter because it will shift the butter supply curve to the left. Let us take a look at butter prices to verify this prediction, making sure by all means at our disposal that the demand curve for butter has not shifted during the time-period of observation.
>
> (Blaug, 1974, p. 42)

Leaving aside his 'non-Popperian' remark on 'verification' of theory, the passage suffers from some important difficulties in demonstrating the empirical content of what Blaug himself describes as simple 'neoclassical orthodoxy'. The prediction can be supported from empirical observation since data on pre-tax change and post-tax change butter prices are generally readily available. Imposition of a tax change is also empirically confirmable. The theory, in my view, *cannot* be empirically supported from observation. I know of no empirical technique for assessing whether the supply curve of butter has shifted to the left – the alleged *theoretical* justification for this prediction. Even more strongly there is no way of observing Blaug's second theoretical postulate, that is, whether a demand curve for butter has or has not shifted during the unspecified 'time-period of observation'. Furthermore, the prediction that following a tax on butter the price of butter will rise is not the exclusive neoclassical prediction Blaug implies it is. It is, for example, quite consistent with physiocratic tax theory, Ricardo's taxation theory, the Kaleckian theory of taxation based on a substantially different theory of price determination and, for that matter, the Sraffa (1960) propositions on the effects of commodity taxation on prices. At best, empirical standards in neoclassical methodology discussion are not superior to those in other branches of economic discourse.

The subject of taxation introduces my final comment on Sylos Labini. This arises from the problems of application of Sraffa's theory to which he explicitly refers in the final pages of his paper – for example, his remarks to those intending 'to use Sraffa's model to analyse a growth process under both competitive and non-competitive conditions' and the plea for both 'the development of the theoretical problems of the original model and the consideration of the most appropriate way to use it in order to examine the essential features of a growth process, which, after all, directly or indirectly was the main concern of the classical economists' (p. 66). Less explicitly, they arise from his remarks on Kalecki's assumptions about 'the behaviour of costs' and the modest reference (p. 64, n. 15) to his own independent discovery of the characteristics of non-basics (in Sylos Labini, 1969, p. 143, n. 15, in the very classical context of an investigation of machinery, income and employment).

Let me first wholeheartedly endorse his, and also Roncaglia's, plea for greater attention to the application of classical postulates, especially as refined by Sraffa, to solving practical problems (see Roncaglia's contribution to this volume). In spite of the successes of Sraffa's (1960) prelude to a theoretical critique and their subsequent developments, applied economics continues to be largely dominated by marginalist or conventional economics. This is perhaps nowhere better illustrated than in the theory of public finance and fiscal incidence, which featured so prominently in the older classical literature by the physiocrats, Smith and, particularly in respect to taxation, Ricardo. Contemporary public finance and fiscal incidence theory is almost exclusively produced by the theory of value and distribution Sraffa tried to replace (see Eatwell, 1980, pp. 165–6). Apart from one page, Sraffa (1960, p. 55) himself was silent on tax theory.

Two examples of the potential for applying Sraffian economics to taxation problems can be given. The first derives from the classical question about the uses of the surplus, whence it can be argued that a distinction between productive and unproductive uses of the surplus (which for Sraffa included the part of the surplus going to labour) can be usefully applied to both enhance and analyse the growth-inducing potential of specific tax instruments (Groenewegen, 1988). Such an application has considerable relevance to the tax debate relating to capital gains, the ownership of wealth and the taxation of income from capital and consumption taxation. It was applied by Kaldor (1964, p. 261; 1980, pp. 200–9, esp. pp. 224–6, 227–9) in advocating selective taxation of luxuries in developing countries and service employment in low-growth developed countries with full employment (Eatwell, 1982a, p. 82). The second is to develop at the theoretical level the insights obtainable from Eatwell's (1980) framework for the analysis of taxation, distribution and effective demand and, more importantly perhaps, some empirical applications to demonstrate their practical significance.

The second point also brings to the fore tensions between Kalecki and Sraffa-inspired analysis, partly in evidence at this conference and present in Eatwell's paper itself (1980, esp. pp. 165–7). It is well known that Kalecki discussed taxation incidence in some detail with radically different results from those in neoclassical work. Kalecki's work has been developed with great insight by Asimakopulos and Burbidge (1974, 1979) and given further support in Mair (1984) on local taxation. This type of work has challenged neoclassical theory and its behavioural assumptions in its all too infrequently disputed realm of applied taxation economics. Further challenges of this nature should be the aim of all those involved in the reconstruction of political economy in the classical manner to which Sraffa has shown the way. The practical fulfilment of his 'Prelude to a Critique of Economic Theory' is the most fitting tribute that can be paid to his work.

Notes

1 Since the Sraffa conference, I have developed aspects of this in the context of taxation and public finance in (Groenewegen, 1988).

2 In the classical literature both laws of returns and standard of value are associated with labour productivity or the quantity of labour required per unit of output. The dichotomy in attitudes to laws and returns between Smith and Ricardo (see Sylos Labini, 1984d) relates of course to different expectations about labour productivity trends in agriculture, particularly the production of wages goods. A discussion of the Smithian side of the problem is given in Groenewegen (1977).

3 It may be noted here that *time* likewise creates havoc in the law of marginal utility, which is so important for the final construction of Marshall's demand curve. In an unusually candid passage in the *Principles* (Marshall, 1961, I, p. 94) he indicated the completely static nature of the law, here again exhibiting the symmetry of demand theory with the static laws of production and cost. Groenewegen (1982) investigates aspects of Marshall's conflict over time versus equilibrium which underlies the whole construction of the *Principles*.

4 It may be noted that Blaug omitted any explicit discussion of the distinction between logical proof and disproof and rejection of a theoretical proposition because it does not conform with observed facts.

Comment

Fausto Vicarelli†
Rome

In the preface to *Production of Commodities by Means of Commodities* Sraffa declares that the fundamental ideas contained in his book matured towards the end of the 1920s. This statement has aroused much academic curiosity concerning the ties between the theoretical model, developed in *Production of Commodities*, and the author's previous contributions to economics, and thus in his intellectual development, which spanned thirty years among the most fascinating in the history of economic thought.

Professor Sylos Labini's paper is based on an analysis of the link between Sraffa's critique of Marshall's theory of price determination under competition and his proposal to rebuild the theory of value on classical, neo-Ricardian foundations. In this way he fills a gap that might otherwise have exerted a negative influence on the interpretation of Sraffa's work and the debate surrounding it.

Sylos Labini places great emphasis on the difference between the two laws of increasing and decreasing returns on which Marshall based his theory of price determination, making special reference to the theoretical position these laws occupy in Smith's and Ricardo's thought. Smith believed that increasing returns are the fruit of the division of labour and of its diffusion through the economy as a whole. Increasing returns are thus a dynamic phenomenon, essential for the growth of national wealth; its effects are felt throughout the economic system and are therefore not open to analysis by partial equilibrium methods. In Ricardo's conception of the relationship between profit and rent, on the other hand, decreasing returns are seen as a consequence of the falling fertility of the additional land brought into use in response to economic and population growth. Here too then we have a dynamic phenomenon which, via the shift it determines in the distribution of income, exerts an effect on economic development – this time a negative one.

The dynamic general equilibrium nature of the laws of increasing and decreasing returns are seen to be incompatible with Marshall's static, partial equilibrium analysis. The fact that even relatively small firms can achieve decreasing costs leads Sraffa to suggest, among other things, the abandoning of the idea of perfect competition as the normal market regime. This did not lead him, however, to reformulate the theory of price determination in terms of monopoly or monopolistic competition. After initial doubts, at the beginning of the 1930s, he became convinced that it was necessary to abandon Marshall's model of supply and demand and conceived the idea of a return to the classical approach.

Sylos Labini makes it very clear how the shift from a partial to a general, classical rather than Walrasian equilibrium was crucial in the development of Sraffa's thought. In *Production of Commodities* Sraffa supplies us with a

† Deceased.

rigorous formulation of the classical vision of the fundamental problem in economic theory, which is not, to use Sylos Labini's words, to find 'the conditions of equilibrium and, in particular, the equilibrium prices, determined by demand and supply curves – each price appearing as the keystone of an arch' but rather that of identifying 'the conditions of reproduction of the system' (page 12 above).

Sraffa's system, whose uniqueness derives from the direct determination of values from methods of production, represents a stationary economy governed by competitive forces powerful enough to ensure a uniform profit rate. Sylos Labini believes, however, that with modifications 'such as not to alter its logic' it would be possible to extend the model's application to include the analysis of growth, with or without competition. This is the central point in his paper. If it were accepted it would provide an element of continuity between Sraffa's observations concerning the dynamic nature of the laws of increasing and decreasing returns and the model developed in *Production of Commodities*. At the same time it would open new analytical prospects which up to now have been hindered by the conviction 'that it was necessary to develop first of all the implications of the pure model' (page 14 above). In my opinion, however, there exist reasons, which I will attempt to explain, that make it difficult to accept this view if the theoretical specificity of Sraffa's contribution, namely his 'standard system', is to remain valid.

Sraffa attaches great importance to the classical idea that the joint effect of the division of labour, of growing markets and consequently of the general expansion of production is to increase productivity. What he criticizes is the use of this idea by the marginalists when they attempt to establish a non-proportional relationship between costs and quantity produced for a single commodity. In the classics 'the intensification of the division of labour is not generally conceived as a phenomenon strictly dependent upon the increase in the quantity to be produced but rather as an effect of general progress' (Sraffa, [1925] 1964, p. 179).

From the tone of this critical observation we can already catch a glimpse of the direction in which Sraffa thought it necessary to move: the dynamic action of the forces underlying economic progress has no analytical connection with the partial equilibrium relationship between the cost and the quantity produced of a single good. Rather it derives from the whole complex of relations which, in general equilibrium, link the costs and prices of every good to that of every other. This approach is reflected in the model developed in *Production of Commodities*. Here the effects of a change in productive processes as a consequence of the 'general progress of the economy' are expressed as decreased technical coefficients.

If Sraffa, in the journey that took him from the critique of Marshall's 'scissors' to the reconstruction of a classical system, had maintained his interest in the analytical representation of the defining feature of the capitalist system, namely the increase in its productive potential, he would have concentrated, in *Production of Commodities*, on the effects of generalized increases in productivity on the system of relative prices and on the distributive variables. This would probably have forced him to face up to the problem of the determination of levels of activity and of the mechanisms of accumulation. The only history that matters, however, is the history that has actually been written and, in practice, *Production of Commodities* contains a quite different theoretical message.

At the centre of the book we do not find a classical refoundation of the explanation of capitalist development but rather a rigorous demonstration of how it is logically possible to conceive of a measure of the value of commodities that is invariant with respect to distribution.

If one is to achieve an improved comprehension of the significance of what Sraffa actually chose to do, as opposed to what he might have done, it is useful to consider his critique of von Hayek at the beginning of the 1930s (Sraffa, 1932). Hayek had attacked the fundamental ideas put forward by Keynes in his *Treatise on Money*. Sraffa joined the debate with a strongly negative review of *Prices and Production* (1931), Hayek's book containing the concepts of monetary economics on which his critique of Keynes was founded.

Hayek's aim, Sraffa observes, is the perfectly acceptable – and ambitious – one of studying the effects of variations in the quantity of money on relative prices. As his analysis proceeds, however, he forgets this initial goal, concentrating, rather, on the search for a monetary policy that would allow decisions to save and invest to be effective as in a barter economy. Hayek considers money exclusively in its role as a means of exchange, paying no attention to the existence of variables fixed in nominal terms, and thus denying any importance to the notion of a general price level and to that of changes in this level. He thus reaches the conclusion that the only 'neutral' monetary policy – that is, a policy that does not distort the sort of individual decisions that would be taken in a non-monetary economy – would consist in maintaining the quantity of money constant. This conclusion is based on the concept of an 'equilibrium rate' (corresponding to Wicksell's 'natural' rate) capable of balancing real savings and investment and which may differ with respect to the market or money rate established by the banks. An increase in money supply – which Hayek sees as an excess flow of credit with respect to the flow of savings deposits – causes a fall in the money rate below the equilibrium rate, leading in turn to an excess of demand for goods. In a non-monetary economy in which loans are in kind and the rate of interest is expressed in terms of goods, this kind of disequilibrium can never occur.

Sraffa objects that for this argument to be valid it is necessary to assume that the non-monetary economy is in a state of permanent equilibrium. If money is to be seen as the cause of disequilibria in monetary economies, one has to suppose that in a non-monetary economy interest rates, in terms of every commodity, are equal. In practice, however, the rate of interest on loans expressed in terms of a given commodity is affected by the gap between the current price for the good and its expected future price. At the same time, the expected price for each good is affected by short-term disequilibria between supply and demand: short-term excess demand will lead to an increase in the good's price above the equilibrium level and create expectations of a future drop; the opposite applies in the case of excess supply. If, in a barter economy, we are going to talk in terms of a single interest rate, we have to posit that there will never be excess demand for or supply of any good. In an economy characterized by capital accumulation, such as the one Hayek was considering, this is not the normal situation; on the contrary, such an economy is marked by persistent gaps between supply and demand caused by continual shifts in demand for and production of certain goods with respect to others.

In such a situation a non-monetary economy has no *single* natural interest rate, but rather a whole *set* of rates: one for each good. What point is there, Sraffa asks, in comparing these to the rate formed on the credit market in a monetary economy?

What is most interesting here is Sraffa's conviction that in a capitalist economy with accumulation – even a hypothetical barter economy – a gap between supply and demand is *normal.* It is thus even more obvious that in a monetary economy it is *normal* that different commodities will have different interest rates and that these will differ from the money rate. As is well known, in Chapter 17 of the *General Theory* Keynes returned to Sraffa's notion of a 'commodity rate' and used it to explain the logic underlying the demand for different assets, in particular for capital goods. Within the framework of Keynes' thinking the demand for new capital goods, and thus the level of investment, is regulated by means of the equilibrium established among these goods' 'own rates' and between the latter and the money rate. The volume of investment in each good is determined by expectations concerning quasi-rents. It follows that for Keynes the levelling of the rates for different goods plays a fundamental role in determining the key component in effective demand.

In the model of price determination assumed in *Production of Commodities* Sraffa presupposes a uniform rate of profit. He gives us no hint of how to interpret this hypothesis in the light of the position he took in the debate with Hayek. The dominant interpretation is that Sraffa's model refers to a stationary equilibrium economy in which gaps between expected and current prices have been eliminated as a result of a long period of stationary conditions of production. Let us think, however, in terms of accumulation, which under capitalism must be considered as *normal.* In an economy with accumulation, what would be the impact of the levelling of commodity rates on the composition of effective demand and thus on technical coefficients of production?

It is hard to believe that Sraffa would have denied the importance of this kind of question. What seems more likely is that the thrust of his analytical interests was now in other directions and that he did not feel it was his job to supply an answer. Sraffa's active defence of Keynes' *Treatise on Money* and his failure to write a single line in support – or even concerning – the *General Theory* supports this view. Probably as early as the first half of the 1930s he had set himself the goal of solving Ricardo's problem of finding an invariant measure of value; as a result his attention was concentrated on identifying a model of production that might allow him to achieve this goal.

What are the difficulties that hinder the extension of the specific analytical model – that is, the specific theory – developed in *Production of Commodities* to cover the problems of accumulation and growth? The specific nature of the work is summed up in the one sentence of Sraffa's brief preface: the 'investigation is concerned exclusively with such properties of the economic system as do not depend on changes in the scale of production or in the proportion of factors'. He believes this kind of approach to be typical of the standpoint of the 'old classical economists'. Questions concerning changes in production or in factor proportions belong to the realm of 'marginal' theory.

One might observe that in reality the old classical economists were highly interested in changes in production and in the composition of the capital advanced to achieve them – in other words, in accumulation. They were convinced that economic development was tied to capital accumulation. Their interest in the problem of distribution – as Sylos Labini himself reminds us – stemmed from the way in which this influenced and interfered with accumulation. In historical terms, however, accumulation is not without influence on distribution: for Ricardo, the cultivation of steadily less fertile land was determining a fall in the rate of profit; for Marx, the rise in the organic composition of capital led to the same result.

It thus seems hard to accept Sraffa's interpretation of the classical 'standpoint', at least in so far as this concerns the importance of shifts in levels of production. If one is to evaluate the possibility of 'dynamizing' Sraffa's model, what one has to consider is the plausibility of the independence of production coefficients with respect to shifts in distribution. Such an assumption is only plausible if accumulation is taken to be independent of the rate of profit. As recent and more ancient history has most amply demonstrated, however, technological innovations, in their various forms, depend on investment: it follows that technical coefficients shift in line with changes in the intensity and direction of accumulation. If accumulation is stimulated by a high profit rate, this will have an effect on technical coefficients: the technical coefficients matrix will be modified, not in Sraffa's sense that the choice among *given* productive methods will depend on the rate of profit, but in the sense that the rate of profit will affect the range of productive methods *available*.

Why should abandoning the independence between production coefficients and distribution – an inevitable consequence of the 'dynamizing' of Sraffa's model – be seen as incompatible with the specific theory contained in *Production of Commodities*? In Pasinetti's words, the specificity of the theory lies in the fact that 'the system of prices and the system of physical quantities are two separate systems, each of which exerts no effect upon the other' (Pasinetti, 1981a, pp. 138–9). Closely connected with this characteristic of Sraffa's model is a second feature of his system which is of fundamental importance to the search for an invariant measure of value, namely the attempt to define a standard system as a 'logic construct involving only physical quantities with no relevance for the system of prices' (Pasinetti, 1981a, p. vi).

The consequences for Sraffa's theory of the interdependence between technical coefficients and distribution can be very simply seen if one examines the linear relationship between wage and profit rates in a system where prices are expressed in terms of the standard commodity. This relationship is defined in terms of a parameter – the 'standard ratio' – which corresponds to the maximum eigenvalue of the technical coefficients matrix and constitutes the basis for the interdependence of the measure of value with respect to distribution. If changes in distribution lead to changes in the technical coefficients, the result will be changes in the eigenvalues of the matrix: the linear relationship between the rate of wages and the rate of profit will no longer apply.

I have no intention of claiming that Sraffa was unaware of this kind of difficulty. Rather I agree with Roncaglia that his aim was simply to resolve the first of the two problems raised by Ricardo: the search for a measure of value, invariant, in the case of the first problem with respect to distribution, in the case of the second with respect to changes in productive techniques (Roncaglia, 1978, p. 78).

The extension of Sraffa's model to dynamic analysis proposed by Sylos Labini makes it necessary, however, to take a position with respect to the second of Ricardo's problems. Given that the difficulty arises from the functional relationship between the technical coefficients matrix and distribution in an economic system where accumulation is influenced by the profit rate and where technical progress is incorporated in investment, it cannot be resolved by inventing a new standard commodity for each individual matrix. This relationship reflects, in practice, the tie between the destination of surplus (consumption and investment) and the availability of differing sets of technical coefficients. The importance of the composition of demand is not, in other words, that it invalidates the 'non-substitution theorem' – which states the independence of the composition of demand with respect to choices among *given* techniques – but rather that it determines the *availability* of techniques among which to choose.

If one abandons the idea of the theoretical specificity of *Production of Commodities*, these observations may be seen as irrelevant. This, however, is equivalent to seeing Sraffa's model as a simple set of accounting relationships, applicable, after suitable manipulation, to differing lines of analysis. This minimizes Sraffa's real importance. What indeed does it leave of his original objectives?

In any event, one definite consequence of the interdependency between technical coefficients and distribution is that dynamic extensions of Sraffa's original model can no longer be seen in terms of a 'natural economy'. When such extensions have been made (see, for example, Pasinetti, 1981b), assuming investment decisions to be independent of the rate of profit and technical progress to be independent of accumulation, the 'natural' character of the economy described derives from the exogenous nature of the technical coefficients, which become the final determinants of the system of prices and of physical quantities produced. As soon as techniques are seen as depending on investment decisions and these as depending on distribution (as well – as Keynes taught us – as on a whole range of institutional factors of which the most important is money), assuming a 'natural' economy becomes impossible.

Reply

Vicarelli correctly states that the central point of my paper is that, with modifications such as not to alter its logic, it would be possible to extend the scope of Sraffa's model to include the analysis of growth with or without competition. Vicarelli believes, however, that 'there exist reasons . . . that make it difficult to accept this view if the theoretical specificity of Sraffa's contribution, namely his "standard system", is to remain valid'.

It seems that the main reason is that production coefficients are not independent from distribution. Thus, 'if accumulation is stimulated by a high profit rate, this will have an effect on technical coefficients: the technical coefficients matrix will be modified . . . in the sense that the rate of profit will affect the range of productive methods *available*'.

But, in principle, we can assume a stable rate of profit and a constant matrix even in a process of accumulation. This assumption would be legitimate anyhow on theoretical grounds, but we are entitled to qualify it by pointing out that, precisely because of Ricardo's diminishing returns, a constant matrix of coefficients *presupposes* technical progress, conceived to be such as exactly to offset diminishing returns from land and mines. It can be maintained that this is a very abstract hypothesis, but not that it is logically untenable. On the other hand, accumulation does not require a high, even less an increasing, rate of profit (which would imply a change in income distribution); it simply requires a rate of profit, neither increasing nor decreasing, but sufficient to provide the stimulus to accumulation.

Thus, in a first approximation it seems fully justified to assume a constant matrix and a stable distribution of income. But we can use a modified version of Sraffa's model in the analysis of growth even allowing for a change in the matrix and in the distribution of income. It is true that in this case we would not be able to make use of the 'standard system'; fortunately, however, we do not need to use it. This analytical tool is essential to study the relationship between changes in distributive shares and in relative prices (the principal problem of political economy in the conception of David Ricardo), but it is not essential in the analysis of growth (the principal problem in the conception of Adam Smith).

2

Reflections on Marx and Sraffa

Suzanne de Brunhoff
C.N.R.S., Paris

Examining the influence of Marx and Sraffa on the theory of money may at first seem paradoxical. In Sraffa's principal work, *Production of Commodities by Means of Commodities* (1960), the role of money in relation to the 'real' economy of production is nowhere mentioned. He introduces the monetary rate of interest as determining rates of profit without investigating either its origin or the role of money as a price standard. Several of Sraffa's disciples have nonetheless presented analyses of the monetary interest rate, which will be discussed below (in section 2).

As for Marx, many of his thousands of pages on the subject of money have not been adequately discussed, not even by his disciples. In the Marxist tradition only Hilferding's *Finance Capital* ([1910] 1981) stands out. He concerns himself primarily with the role of banks as centralizers of funds and with the dominant forms of monopolistic capital. Otherwise, the analysis of money in the Marxist tradition most often centres on the analysis of 'fetishism', a social relationship in which relations between men appear as relations between things.

Although Marx may have said a great deal about money, his disciples have not. Sraffa merely pointed out a path concerning monetary interest rates, but few of his disciples have ventured down it. This suggests that Marx had need of a concept of money to develop his 'Critique of Political Economy' (the subtitle of *Capital*), whereas Sraffa, in his 'Prelude to a Critique of Political Economy' (the subtitle of *Production of Commodities*), did not. And this difference influences the divergences in the theory of money after Marx and after Sraffa.

1 *Money as Marx's tool for making a critique of Ricardo*

Marx admired Ricardo as 'the economist par excellence of production' and distribution of the social product among different social classes (capitalists, wage-earners, landowners). Yet he profoundly disagrees with Ricardo –

Marx's conception of money being one of the ways he broke with classical political economy. Marx's disagreement with Ricardo is important in two ways: (1) it places Marx as a theoretician outside the bounds of the classical school; (2) it promotes a notion of money different from the quantity theory then dominant, and, in some aspects, still used today.

Any comparison of the opening of Ricardo's *Principles of Political Economy and Taxation* and that of Marx's *Capital* shows the dissimilarities to be more evident than the similarities, despite both authors' treatment of the notion of labour built into reproductive commodities. Marx introduces money at the same time as the commodity, both being, in Marx's view, the expression of society divided into producers, who not only are differentiated through use values and techniques, but also are separated socially from one another. The relationship between these producers is that of the exchange of 'commodities for money'.

Most of the analyses of fetishism in Marx begin here. Thus P. M. Sweezy (Sweezy, [1942] 1968, pp. 34–40) devotes several pages to the 'fetish character of commodities', showing that the social form of economic relations is important. 'This fetish character of the commodity world has its origin . . . in the peculiar social character of the labor which produces commodities', says Marx, as cited by Sweezy. Yet Sweezy neglects to present any notion of money, as if the subject mattered little.

Marx, on the other hand, takes issue with 'quantity' theories of money, most notably with Ricardo's establishment of a relationship between an increase in the quantity of money in circulation and an increase in the general level of prices. Marx proposes the inverse relation, going from the needs of circulation to the quantity of money in circulation. He also criticizes the reduction of the role of money to a mere means of exchange. For Marx, money has varied roles: price standard, means of circulation, value reserve. It also has different aspects: gold, banknotes issued by the state and convertible (or not) into gold, bank credit. The articulation of these functions and forms is not static; it is done through various mechanisms in which both private economic agents and the state play a role. Thus Marx's designation of money as a 'general equivalent', or form of value, does not correspond to a single good (as, for example, the famous gold pieces of the nineteenth century), but to a set of articulated elements that vary according to fluctuations in the economy and to measures taken by the state.

Quantitative theories, however, emphasize one form of money: gold in the nineteenth century and the so-called high-powered money issued by central banks in the twentieth century. The reductionist approach to the role of money, the quantitative variations of which act directly on prices, influences any characterization of money. The quantitativists' reference is the 'real' distribution of the *product*, according to the relative prices of the goods. Their goal is thus to conceive of a way to neutralize any possibly perturbing role a change in the quantity of money might play. They cannot show money's qualitative role in a capitalist market society, a role that Marx sought to establish.

By not introducing money into the economic process, quantitative conceptions separate 'real' goods from the quantity of money making these goods circulate as commodities. Marx takes the opposite view: 'the commodity form' of the products of labour is inseparable from the money form, as illustrated in the circulation schematic C–M–C (commodities–money–commodities). The distribution of the product among social classes in a capitalist market society is effected in relation to the monetary forms the product takes. An advance of money capital opens the production cycle, a monetary receipt becoming capital closes it, as in the scheme of circulation and reproduction, M–C . . . C^1–M^1; money capital, purchase of the means of production C (including wages paid to workers as the price for the use of their labour), sale of the commodities produced with a surplus ($M^1 = M + m$) to the capitalist investor.

The wages paid to workers are here an advance of capital that is, necessarily, in monetary form and represents a social and economic relation of production. According to Marx, we must study seriously the money form of wages and go beyond what 'the monetary relation conceals' (Marx, [1894] 1967a, p. 539). For 'the wage form ... extinguishes every trace of the division of the working day into necessary and surplus labour, into paid and unpaid labour. All labour appears as paid labour.' This distinguishes the capitalist wage-labourer from the slave or serf. Workers receive, in the form of a monetary wage, only a portion of the value they produce, the other part, the 'surplus value', going to capital.

Whatever the difficulties in Marx with the notion of the value of the *labour force*, the idea must necessarily take monetary form. Marx raises objections both to the classical economists' idea of 'wage funds' – whereby a more or less fixed portion of real overall production is distributed to workers – and to Proudhon's idea for monetary reform – whereby a system of coupons for products, allotted as a function of work hours, would be set up. In either case, distribution loses its monetary form, while production continues to be impelled by money capital, and reproduction retains a monetary form.

Another aspect of the same relation between 'real' and 'monetary' in Marx consists in the idea of 'the possibility' for economic crisis, which is related to the duality of commodity and money or to the 'polarity' of the two complementary and different notions.

The ability to produce value is a property of what Marx terms 'abstract labour' which is 'socially necessary'. Such labour is validated in the exchange of commodities for money, that is, in circulation. This understanding of value only makes sense if one links production and circulation. Any dissociation of these two leads to the idea of a 'real' economy in which the specificities of money, as an expression of the relation between private actions and social labour, lose their importance. Marx's critique of Say's Law, as adopted by such classical economists as Ricardo, implies a distinction, as well as a link, between money and commodities.

According to Say's Law, supply creates its own demand. 'The argument for Say's Law begins with the tautological observation that if all the commodities produced in a given period could be sold for money at given prices, the resulting money revenues would suffice to buy the commodities at these same prices' (Foley, 1986, pp. 183–4). Marx, on the other hand, believes that there can be 'a general overproduction due to the separation of sale and purchase'

(Foley, 1986, p. 185). And this separation implies a separation of money and commodities from each other. Thus 'the possibility for crisis' is inscribed within the money/commodity relation found in Marx's work: neither commodity without money nor money without commodity in economic and social relations; yet also a polarity between money and commodities, and a possibility for crisis, within these same relations. This is an application derived from the preceding analysis, in which monetary circulation reacts to the needs of transactions, contrary to the quantitative conception. Thus at the very start of *Capital*, in conjunction with a theory of money, the possibility for economic crisis is established. This is an important aspect of Marx's heterodoxy as regards classical economists.

The division of capitalist incomes into profit and interest rate has yet to be treated in this brief study of Marx's theory of money. The subject will receive attention in the section devoted to Sraffa's disciples, who believe that Marx contradicts himself on this point. For the moment we should review Marx's idea of the division of the surplus value as a capital income (founded on 'surplus labour') between an industrial capitalist and a financial capitalist. When a financial capitalist advances money to an industrial capitalist, he receives special remuneration – interest – which is a form of share in the surplus value. Its level at a given market price depends, according to Marx, on a power relationship between lenders (financiers) and borrowers (entrepreneurs/industrialists), given the particular conditions of the economic situation.

The schematic of the social reproduction of capital, outlined above, is thus completed: $M^*–M–C \ldots C^1–M^1–M^{1*}$ (M^{1*} indicating the return to the capitalist lender, M^*). Marx links money, money capital and credit in a way that strikes me as merely suggestive; none the less, he is the object of much criticism on this point, not least from Sraffa's disciples, whose objections will now be examined.

2 *Money, finance, and the rate of interest in the works of Sraffa's disciples*

Sraffa himself leads the critique of the marginalist theory without recourse to a theory of money. The suggestions he makes in 1932 (Sraffa, 1932) are not developed in his fundamental work of 1960 (Sraffa, 1960). In the latter he merely points out the need to have a price standard such that the set of commodities becomes, necessarily, one of $n-1$.

However, another indication is given when the rate of profit is chosen as an independent variable to 'close' the system of prices of production: 'The rate of profit, as a ratio, has a significance which is independent of any price, and can well be 'given' before the prices are fixed. It is accordingly susceptible of being determined from outside the system of production, in particular by the level of money rates of interest' (Sraffa, 1960, p. 33). This comment does not lead into any elaboration of a theory of money. Sraffa's disciples, however, have taken it as a starting point for examining the determination not only of the level, but also of the nature of the money rate of interest. Through their efforts, elements of a theory of money are grafted on to Sraffa's system of prices of production.

Garegnani criticizes the orthodox theory, which holds that interest rates are the payment for savings invested in capital (Garegnani, 1978a). This forms part of his overall critique of marginalism and of the distribution of income in terms of supply and demand concerning production factors. In the case of the rate of interest, Garegnani criticizes the idea of a function of investment demand being elastic according to the interest rates (Garegnani, 1978a, p. 351). He believes that the basis of his critique cannot be, as it is with Keynes, a concept of demand for money as reserve of value, nor, more generally, a monetary analysis of the economy. 'If it is so, the conflict between the traditional thesis and that of Keynes, concerning the dependence of the investment on the propensity to save, cannot be resolved only on the terrain of monetary theory, which Keynes chose for his critique. Rather, this conflict leads us back to the questions of "real" theory . . .' (Garegnani, 1979a, p. 79).

The problem is that Garegnani gives us no definition of 'monetary', whereas Sraffa spoke of 'money rates of interest'. For Garegnani, what counts is determining 'the nucleus' of a theory of distribution, derived from Sraffa's prices of production. Here, the level of the rate of interest is the effect of monetary policy, which, of course, according to Garegnani, 'is not conducted in a vacuum', especially when the 'wage bargain' is considered. That there is no theory of money simply shows that it isn't necessary, since it does not belong to the 'nucleus' of economic theory, which is fundamentally 'real'. Doubtless for this reason Sraffa had no need of a theory of money to make an authoritative critique of the marginalist idea.

None the less, by transferring the fixing of the rate of interest onto monetary policy Garegnani advances a hypothesis that can be neither proved nor disproved, for the tools of analysis of money and its mode of economic insertion are lacking:

> Now, money is not dealt with in *Production of Commodities* because logic does not allow for it. The relations studied in *Production of Commodities* are these of the 'core' which are also those necessarily entailed by the fact that under competition (or any other market form) the price of a commodity entails a distribution of the social product among the participants in the production of the commodity in question. Money cannot therefore enter into those relations . . .
>
> (earlier version of Garegnani, Chapter 5 in this volume)

But as the rate of profit depends on the *monetary* rate of interest, an analytical link seems to be missing. What about the work of other disciples of Sraffa?

At first glance, Pivetti's analysis (in Chapter 15 of this volume) seems to take up where Garegnani left off: 'in order to explain distribution and its variations in actual experience, the analysis of the factors influencing and/or conditioning the interest policy adopted by a country should come to the forefront' (earlier vision of Pivetti, Chapter 15 in this volume). But the method used differs profoundly from Garegnani's, so much so that conflict rather than continuity comes to mind.

Pivetti thinks that the rate of interest is a 'monetary phenomenon' that is at the heart of government monetary policy, itself defined first as public debt management. This rate would have a regulatory role in the monetary wages/ price ratio if it could be integrated into an analysis of capital and profit. Interest is a production cost in the sense that it is 'the price for the use of capital – the "pure" remuneration of capital, whatever the form of its employment, whether financial or real' (Chapter 15 below, p. 438). As an element of long-term normal cost, the interest rate influences variations in prices, as well as the relation of prices to monetary wages. Thus a rise in the interest rate pushes up prices, which lowers real wages.

The relationship between interest and profit is not, according to Pivetti, the reverse of what was established by Marx and Ricardo, who proceed from the rate of profit to the rate of interest. Thus Pivetti considers what he believes are the *two* components of the normal rate of profit in every sphere of production: 'The long-term rate of interest (i) or "pure" remuneration of capital, plus the normal profit of enterprise' (Chapter 15, p. 439).

This conception leads to the search for influences that affect freedom of action for monetary policy (as a policy for fixing the level of the rate of interest) – in particular the influence of wage bargaining, which can affect the level of prices for an unchanged rate of interest. However, monetary policy cannot be thought of as passive; and, in Pivetti's view, the relationship between classes (workers and capitalists) is determined, in part, through the determination of the level of the rate of interest (Pivetti, Chapter 15, section 5).

Problems arising from this analysis concern the nature of interest as a 'monetary phenomenon', although it is disconnected from money and credit and conceived of as 'pure' remuneration of capital as capital. It seems equally difficult to understand in a system of prices like Sraffa's, where 'the price' of the utilization of capital is not spelled out – it is neither production price nor market price. Is it then a purely political price, owing to its role in monetary policy? The problem of the nature of interest is exacerbated by the absence of a definition of 'capital' other than as a group of real and financial assets. In any event, we leave the scope of *Production of Commodities* without really knowing where we're heading.

Another method of integration of the monetary interest rate is used by Panico. Two aspects of this are studied here. First, Panico wishes to establish 'the relationship between the general rate of profits and the average rate of interest' (Panico, 1980) from the perspective of Garegnani and Pivetti regarding the determination of the level of this rate by monetary policy. At the same time he thinks it possible to arrive at a compromise with Marx: 'Some elements of Marx's analysis can . . . be formalised within a Sraffian price-system which explicitly includes the banking sector and establishes links between the rate of interest, the rate of profit, and the wage rates.' The point is to incorporate the rate of interest into the distribution of business revenues from the overall product, which was what Pivetti attempted, using a different method, while Garegnani did not attempt it at all.

Here, credit appears as a particular commodity, produced by a banking sector in its relations with an industrial sector that borrows and deposits simultaneously, depending on particular prices and interest rates on financial transactions. This would set up a *production of commodities by means of commodities and credit*, using a Sraffian price system and resolving what Panico considers to be a contradiction in Marx.

Marx contradicts himself, Panico maintains, when he makes the rate of interest a price that 'is not regulated by the natural laws of capitalist production' (Panico, 1980). Doubtless Marx is right in conceiving a relative autonomy for the interest rate, but wrong in making it a price 'outside the sphere of production' to be subjected to purely empirical analysis and institutional determination (Panico, 1980, pp. 368–9). According to Panico, this arises in part from Marx's scant study of capitalism's credit system. Panico, on the other hand, develops this study, in terms of Sraffian relative prices, and treats 'money capital', an inheritance from Marx, as a banking sector that produces the means of circulation (a particular commodity) for the industrial sector.

Panico's proposed system can only function in the long term if the bankers do well from it; hence the interest rate they earn from loans to entrepreneurs must be inferior to the general rate of profits for all business activities, including those of the banking sector (Panico, 1980, p. 377). Another condition is that the interest paid by the banks to enterprises in the industrial sector on their deposits must be inferior to the rate of profit – otherwise, industry would bank all industrial capital (ibid., p. 377).

Here Panico is straying far from Marx, at the very beginning when the idea of capital comes into play. He attributes the revenues of capital, profit and interest to *capital as such*, which is not at all in line with a Marxist approach. Marx considers the different forms of capital – money capital, productive capital, commodity capital – to be meaningless unless considered in relation to the rate of surplus value and to the production of value by a special commodity, the labour force. Thus the owner of money becomes a capitalist only when his funds are used, by himself or by a borrower, in the purchase of a labour force producing more than its inherent value. The relationship among capitalists as regards the use and allotment of the profit born of surplus value is something grafted on to the original production relationship (capitalist–worker). Thus funds become capital only through the purchase of the labour force producing more value than it originally possessed in the form of monetary wages. Neither industrial profit nor interest as financial income arises from capital as a real or financial 'asset'. This is why, for Marx, there is no more a 'natural rate of interest' than there is a 'natural' profit. Thus, if Panico wishes to retain a Marxist notion of capital, his critique of Marx goes too far. If Panico wishes to analyse credit as a market product of the banking business, paid for by an interest rate, his critique doesn't go far enough – it should give up the Marxist idea.

The latter course seems to be adopted by Panico in a later work (Panico, 1985). The crux of his argument remains the same, yet this time Marx is replaced by Keynes. Panico takes inspiration from Keynes in analysing movements of interest rates (particular prices) on capital markets. It is a question no longer of Marx's 'money capital' or lender money capital, but of 'assets' – financial (including money) or real – which are objects of arbitrage between the economic agents concerned. 'What gives consistency to the operation of the market forces is the fact that investors allocate their resources towards those assets which offer the highest benefits. These benefits were the yield of the assets and the convenience offered by holding them (in terms of security and liquidity)' (Panico, 1985, p. 39). Marx's money capital is thus replaced here by assets subject to market forces. Panico's analysis follows that of Chapter XVII of Keynes' *General Theory* (Keynes, 1936a) while trying to purge the latter of its marginalistic aspects (Panico, 1985, p. 52).

Panico seeks, without resorting to marginalism, to determine the markets' role in establishing stable prices for financial assets in such a way that these prices can affect a system of Sraffian production prices. Any disequilibrium in the markets for assets is offset by the action of these markets, whose result – stable prices – affects the rate of profit as defined in the production prices system.

At the same time, monetary policy, as a policy of interest rate levels, affects individual assessments of actors in the financial market (Panico, 1985, p. 47). However, here we find the same model as his one of 1980, which concerns the prices of financial assets and their being grafted on to a Sraffian price model. This calls into question the coherence of the analysis, which combines two price systems: stable market prices in relation to financial assets, and production prices based on the productive activity of commodities. Furthermore, Sraffian production prices might well be 'overdetermined' in the analysis if the intervention of monetary policy in interest rate levels is taken into account.

In Panico's analysis the notion of money is somewhat fragmented and, in any event, is not used in relation to the problem of account units; confused with bank credit (Panico, 1980) or with liquid assets (Panico, 1985), this notion fails to appear in either the text of 1980 or that of 1985. From this perspective Panico echoes Garegnani, who concludes by saying that money is not at the heart of any economic analysis. The circle is complete.

Conclusion

The study of the theory of money after Marx and Sraffa has led us to emphasize the difference between the two writers. Many Marxist authors borrow part of Sraffa's analysis in order to overcome the obstacle that Marx encountered with the transformation of value into prices. This is impossible when considering money in relation to commodities and capital. Whatever ingenuity Sraffa's disciples may show in their attempts to integrate interest into the revenue generated by the productive activity of a particular commodity, the concept of money used by Marx – and still partially valid today – is lacking.

Note

Translated from the French by Stephen O'Shea. For a sample of recent writings on the theory of money and finance in the Marxist tradition, see the works by S. de Brunhoff, Jim Getty, Duncan Foley, R. Pollin.

Comment

Ian Steedman
Manchester

Suzanne de Brunhoff is surely right to insist on the importance of a theoretical analysis of money, on the fact that money looms large in the work of Marx and on the fact that, the famous §44 reference to the rate of interest aside, money is practically invisible in Sraffa's *Production of Commodities*. The latter fact, of course, does not enable one to infer that Sraffa considered money to be unimportant. As a matter of historical record, Sraffa contributed several works on monetary questions during the period 1920–25, as well as the famous 1932 article to which de Brunhoff refers (Roncaglia, 1978, p. 151). And as a matter of logic, Sraffa's virtual silence with respect to money in the 1960 work is sufficiently explained by the assumption that Sraffa took money to be irrelevant *to the particular task in hand* – that of providing the basis for a critique of the marginal theory of value and distribution (Sraffa, 1960, p. vi). One does not necessarily consider unimportant everything to which one does not refer within a specific context. That said, writers inspired by Sraffa must indeed move on to develop monetary analyses, but I shall leave it to those more competent than myself to assess de Brunhoff's observations on the writings of Garegnani, Pivetti and Panico. Rather, I should like to draw attention to one particular role that money plays in Marx's analysis.

As is well known, Marx relates the 'values' of commodities not to the amounts of heterogeneous, concrete labour-times embodied in these commodities but to the amounts of 'abstract labour' that they contain. (Or, at the very least, to the relative amounts of abstract labour contained.) But since the production of each commodity has required, directly and indirectly, the use of various amounts of different concrete labour-times, this at once raises the question how these heterogeneous labour-times are to be reduced to a single amount of 'abstract labour' for each commodity. (Note that this problem arises even if no form of concrete labour is particularly skilled; unskilled concrete labours are still heterogeneous.) A simple and obvious way would, of course, be to aggregate heterogeneous labours with weights proportional to their respective money wage rates, as Sraffa did (Sraffa, 1960, §10). Now, although they never referred to the concept of 'abstract labour', many classical economists did refer to *the* quantity of labour required to produce a commodity, meaning precisely the wage-rate aggregated quantity of various kinds of labour. This usage is found, for example, in Cantillon, Smith, Ricardo and James Mill; Samuel Bailey explicitly objected to it. (For a detailed discussion, see Steedman, 1985, §III.) Marx, it need hardly be said, was thoroughly conversant with the relevant works of these authors but, so far as I know, he never repudiated this use of the term 'quantity of labour', notwithstanding his readiness to be critical. Moreover, and whether he realized it or not, Marx *needed* to derive 'abstract labour' per unit of a commodity from the corresponding amounts of concrete labour by aggregating these latter by means of weights proportional to the corresponding money wage rates. For three of his most fundamental propositions depend on the vector of 'amounts of abstract labour per unit of concrete labour', call it α, being *exactly proportional to* the vector of 'money wage rates per unit of concrete labour', call it μ.

First, if the rows of the matrix of labour use are linearly independent then the vector of zero-profit prices is proportional to the vector of abstract labour uses per commodity if and only if α is proportional to μ. Second, whether or not the labour use matrix has linearly independent rows, every group of workers performs zero surplus abstract labour, in a zero-profit economy in which all workers consume goods in the same proportions, if and only if α is proportional to μ. Third, in a positive-profit economy, the *rate* of surplus value (abstract labour) is the same for every group of workers if and only if α is proportional to μ. (For far greater detail, see Steedman, 1985, §II). Whether he knew it or not, then, Marx's vaunted 'abstract labour' and 'value' constructions amounted to nothing more (and nothing less), in relative terms, than relative direct and indirect – or vertically integrated – money wages bills per unit of net output.

Since Marx treated money as a produced commodity, gold – at least in his basic theory – it was then but a small step to link 'abstract labour' and 'value' with the 'universal equivalent', money being the 'social incarnation' of 'value' or 'abstract labour'. Indeed the link is complete if the gold values of commodities are thought of as their vertically integrated, or direct and indirect, gold wages bills, per unit of output, marked up by a uniform 'rate of exploitation' (where the latter is nothing more (and nothing less) than the profit/wage ratio in the vertically integrated gold-producing sector; see Steedman, 1985, §V.) Marx's 'deep' analysis of the 'essence' of value, abstract labour and the universal equivalent amounted to little more than a mysterious and complicated way of talking about the aggregation of heterogeneous, concrete labours via their gold money wage rates. In this respect, at least, money played a very central *but undesirable* role in Marx's analysis. This conclusion leaves entirely open, of course, the question whether Marx's discussions of interest, banking, credit, etc. do or do not still contain valuable lessons for us. But it does mean that no one can escape the implications of the Sraffa-based critique of the labour theory of value merely by insisting on the importance of 'abstract labour' in Marx's version of that theory.

Comment

Giancarlo de Vivo
Naples

On Marxists and political economy

In order to understand some distinctive features of the traditional Marxist attitude to political economy, it is of some interest to go back to the early debates on Marx's economic theory, which appear to have had a great influence on the development of the Marxist tradition.

The crucial years were in my view the 1880s, when socialism experienced a great revival at both the practical and the theoretical level. The huge success of Henry George's agitation, with its specifically economic character, in this decade drove large numbers of people to question the existing economic order, and especially the laws of distribution under the capitalist system, on which Henry George had concentrated his onslaught. George, however, as the Webbs put it (Webb and Webb, 1920, p. 376), gave only the 'starting push'.[1] This was bound to thrust many into Marx's arms – though for most of them (as for the Fabians) it proved only a short-lived idyll.

It was in the 1880s that many important critiques of Marx's theory appeared (in particular, of his theory of value), which were to set the stage for later debates. Among these critiques, those of Wicksteed and of Böhm-Bawerk's *Capital and Interest* were the most important ones from the marginalist camp. It is to be noticed that these critics, in great contrast with the attitude often adopted by later economic critics of Marx, spoke with respect of Marx's 'great work' (Wicksteed, [1884] 1944, p. 705), and that some of them, like Wicksteed,[2] were themselves socialists. Even Böhm-Bawerk, of course no sympathizer of socialism, was far from giving to Marx the offhand treatment that later became common among respectable economists.

The formal moderation shown by marginalist critics of Marx in this period may at least in part be ascribed to the state of turmoil and uncertainty then prevailing in the orthodox camp.[3] The 1880s in fact, no less than the 1870s, saw political economy in a state of virtual chaos, mainly as a result of the fierce struggle between the marginalist and historical schools. The complacent picture later established by marginalists, of their theory arising in 1870 and quickly sweeping the ground from under both the classical and the historical schools, is a gross misrepresentation: it was only in the 1890s that marginalism really carried the day.[4] This means that Böhm-Bawerk and Wicksteed, writing in 1884, were not the mouthpieces of an established doctrine.

The unemotional attitude shown by the critics of course made it more difficult for Marxists to shut their ears to them completely. The fact that some of them were even socialists, who published their critiques in leading socialist journals,[5] seemed to many as sensational as 'a Roman Catholic impugning the infallibility of the Pope', according to Bernard Shaw (Shaw, [1885] 1944, p. 724).

Notwithstanding the great sensation, much time passed without any real answer to the critics. Shaw, who was then regarded as a Marxist scholar who had defended Marx 'against all comers in and out of season', as he wrote (Shaw, 1925, p. 275), published a comment on Wicksteed's article, declaring however that he had not 'the slightest intention . . of defending Karl Marx against Mr. Wicksteed' (Shaw, [1885] 1944, p. 725). Instead, he invited other, better equipped, defenders of Marx to step forward.[6] But nobody did so. The issue was raised time and again (in particular by the Fabians) during the following years in the same journal, but Marx found only weak, dogmatic defenders like H. M. Hyndman, the head of the Social Democratic Federation. In the meantime Shaw (and with him the other Fabians, and many others) had put himself 'into Mr. Wicksteed's arms, and become a convinced Jevonian' (Shaw, 1925, p. 276).

That the Marxists should have been unable to produce a reply to the critics of Marx's theory of value is not surprising, if one thinks of the situation in which they found themselves. They only knew (if they could read German or French or Russian) the first volume of *Capital*, with its strict adherence to the labour theory of value; at the same time, the problem of the inconsistency between the exchange according to labour embodied and the uniformity of the rate of profit had been well known since Ricardo's times: Böhm-Bawerk himself had written that he was venturing 'on a field already traversed many a time, and by distinguished writers' ([1884] 1890, p. 375), and accused Marx of having 'ignor[ed], without expressly denying it', Ricardo's discussion of the 'exceptions' to the labour theory of value (ibid., p. 386).

In 1884, the only person to know how Marx had tackled the problem of those 'exceptions' – with his 'transformation of values into prices of production' – was Engels, who chose to keep aloof from the debate. That he was concerned by it, however, is shown by the fact that when he published volume 2 of *Capital* in 1885, he promised that a solution to the 'contradiction of the law of value' would be contained in volume 3, to be published in a few months (Engels, [1885] 1977, p. 19). As a matter of fact, volume 3 was only published nine years later, in 1894. Until then, Shaw wrote, 'Scientific Socialism' meant 'cashing a promissory note of Mr Engels' (Stigler, [1959] 1965, p. 272n).

The situation was undoubtedly an awkward one for would-be defenders of Marx. It is hardly surprising that they should have either abandoned the arena or taken refuge in dogmatism – they did not know the answers.

When volume 3 of *Capital* at last appeared, much damage had been done. Most important of all, marginalism had consolidated its position, and was now *the* economic theory. It no longer needed to take much notice of its opponents: as Hilferding wrote ([1904] 1949, p. 121), 'The publication of the third volume of *Capital* has made hardly any impression upon bourgeois science'. An exception to the lack of reaction was of course Böhm-Bawerk's essay, *Karl Marx and the Close of his System* ([1895] 1949), which was published the year after Marx's third volume. Böhm-Bawerk had asserted in 1884 that the promise to solve the 'contradiction' in Marx's system could not be fulfilled,[7] and must therefore have felt duty bound to criticize the solution provided (as Sweezy, 1949, p. vii, remarks). Böhm-Bawerk's essay was far from unanswerable,[8] but the decisive battle had been fought and won by him in the previous round. Hilferding's reply, which came only nine years later, and was far from effective, did not elicit from Böhm-Bawerk more than a dismissive footnote in the next edition of *Capital and Interest* ([1914] 1959, p. 472). Böhm-Bawerk was now the champion of the established doctrine, while Marxism had been pushed into a world of its own that was in effect removed from the economics profession – an 'underworld', as Keynes put it. For a long time afterwards, Marxism and political economy – or 'economics', as it now became[9] – virtually ignored each other, except for some reciprocal scoffing every now and then.[10] The Marxists' retiring attitude, coupled with the fact that 'revisionism' soon stepped in and took a heavy toll on the younger generation of Marxists, could not but strengthen a tendency to dogmatism that must have been fairly strong even in the earlier days of Marxism.[11]

A critical attitude towards Marx's theory of value was a crucial point in the 'revision' of his doctrine. Bernstein ([1899] 1909) for instance started the central chapter of the book that was the fountainhead of revisionism with a section on Marx's law of value, which amounted to its virtual repudiation. He even wrote that Marx's theory of value 'had brought disaster upon almost every student of Marx'. (Bernstein, it will be remembered, was living in London, and had been much influenced by the Fabians[12].) It is no wonder that a denial of the existence of any difficulty in Marx's theory of value must have become an article of faith for Marxists.

A tendency to adhere strictly to the letter of Marx's writings was perhaps also encouraged by Engels' conscientious attempt, as Marx's literary executor and editor of his posthumous works, to make use as much as possible of Marx's own words in the reconstruction of his positions. Unfortunately, adherence to the letter of a text does not necessarily prevent a loss of meaning. Such a loss appears to have happened for one of the points that has traditionally been regarded by Marxists as a hallmark of their theory, distinguishing it from all bourgeois economic theory: the concept of 'labour power'.[13]

The most authoritative (and perhaps the first) interpretation of the importance of the distinction between labour and labour power was the one given by Engels in his 1891 introduction to *Wage Labour and Capital*, where he argued that this distinction could avoid the 'contradiction' into which 'economists' fell when they 'applied the determination of value by labour to the commodity "labour"'. The contradiction would have been that 'for twelve hours' labour the worker receives as an equivalent value the product of six hours' labour. Either, therefore, labour has two values, . . . or twelve equals six! In both cases we get pure nonsense' (Engels, [1891] 1977, pp. 199–200). But this nonsensical conclusion merely derives from a confusion between the value of labour (the wage) and the value of its product. No such confusion is to be found in Ricardo, or in those works of Marx – like *The Poverty of Philosophy* and the 1849 article that Engels was now editing as *Wage Labour and Capital* – where Marx had not made the distinction between labour and labour power at all. In *The Poverty of Philosophy* he had quite simply stated that 'Labour . . . is a commodity like any other commodity, and has, in consequence, an exchange value' (Marx, [1847] 1978, p. 52), and that 'If the relative value of a commodity is determined by the relative quantity of labour required to produce it, it follows naturally that the relative value of labour, or wages, is likewise determined by the quantity of labour needed to produce the wages' (ibid., p. 44). There is nothing here of the contradiction attributed by Engels to authors not using the concept of labour power.

It is certainly true that Marx regarded the introduction of the concept of labour power as important in order to solve a problem that Ricardo had not seen, but Engels' reconstruction fails to indicate any serious problem to be solved. The problem, which was clearly and repeatedly spelled out by Marx in *Theories of Surplus Value*, can be formulated as follows. From the point of view of the production of surplus value, materialized labour and living labour have different values. Indeed,

> surplus value . . . arises . . . from the fact that commodities or money (i.e., materialised labour) are exchanged for *more* living labour than is embodied . . . in them.
>
> (Marx, [1862–3] 1969–72, vol. 3, pp. 15–16)

On the other hand:

> the value of a commodity is equally determined by the quantity of *materialised* (*past*) labour and by the quantity of *living* (*immediate*) labour required for its production.

Marx therefore asks:

> If this difference [between *materialized* and *living* labour] is of no significance in the determination of the value of commodities, why does it assume such decisive importance when past labour (capital) is exchanged against living labour? Why should it, in this case, invalidate the law of value, since the difference *in itself*, as shown in the case of commodities, has no effect on the determination of value? Ricardo does not answer this question, he does not even raise it.
>
> (Marx, [1862–3] 1969–72, vol. 2, pp. 398–9)

Thus the problem was that 'labour has two values', as Engels had written, but in a sense wholly different from the one envisaged by him: it has two values *with respect to materialized labour*. In the determination of the value of commodities it has the same value as materialized labour; in the capital/labour exchange it has a different value. This is the contradiction Ricardo had not even seen.

Marx's solution to this contradiction was provided in Chapter XIX, volume 1, of *Capital*, which opens with the question: 'How is . . . the value . . . of a 12 hours' working day to be determined?' (Marx, [1867] 1954,

p. 501). Marx soon faces the problem of explaining why 'the labourer . . . receives for 12 hours' labour . . . less than 12 hours' labour', and writes:

> This equalisation of unequal quantities not merely does away with the determination of value. Such a self-destructive contradiction cannot be in any way enunciated or formulated as a law. It is of no avail to deduce the exchange of more labour against less, from the difference of form, the one being realised, the other living.

After a sentence that reinforces this statement, he writes:

> That which comes directly face to face with the possessor of money on the market is in fact not labour, but the labourer. What the latter sells is his labour power . . . Labour is the substance and immanent measure of value, *but has itself no value.*
>
> (Marx, [1867] 1954, pp. 502–3)

Thus, Marx seems to think that it is possible to escape the contradiction he had noticed by distinguishing between 'labour' and 'labour power', the former not being a commodity but merely the 'substance' of value, which does not itself have any value. The problem of the relative value of living and materialized labour seemed therefore to disappear.

We may pause here in order to notice three things. The first is how Engels' reconstruction of Marx's problem, though made by using virtually Marx's own words, had really missed the point, and Engels had accused 'economists' of non-existent contradictions. The second is that Marx really had seen a problem in Ricardo's theory that Ricardo had not seen – a problem that had even been one of the causes of the 'disintegration' of the 'Ricardian school'. The question whether 'accumulated labour' was more valuable than 'living labour' had in fact given rise to many difficulties for the Ricardians, and had led to the abandonment of the labour theory of value.[14] The third point is that the contradiction was not really overcome by Marx. The real issue behind the problem was that of the correctness of determining values by summing labours embodied at different times. The very fact that we must distinguish between 'antecedent' and 'present' labour in the capital/labour exchange – i.e. the very fact that there is a profit – implies that we must also distinguish between 'antecedent' and 'present' labour when determining values. Marx's determination of the rate of profit, in his 'transformation', is instead still based on the incorrect summing of labours of different dates.

Engels' reconstruction of the role of the concept of labour power has of course been endorsed by Marxists for decades. It is to be noticed, however, that Marxists have often gone far beyond what Marx and Engels ever maintained about the significance of the concept of labour power, and have accordingly put an exaggerated emphasis on the split between Marx and bourgeois economics.

Perhaps the most extravagant claim is the one put forward by Mandel in his book on the formation of Marx's economic thought. He asserts that without the concept of labour power it is impossible 'to make a scientific analysis of surplus-value', and therefore maintains that works like *The Poverty of Philosophy*, or *Wage Labour and Capital*, do not even contain 'the idea of surplus-value' (Mandel, [1967] 1971, p. 81). He of course implies that this must be the case for the works of all other authors who do not use the concept of labour power.[15]

Marx and Engels never wrote that without the concept of labour power there could be no theory of surplus value. On the contrary, in his preface to volume 2 of *Capital*, Engels quoted *The Poverty of Philosophy* and the articles later republished as *Wage Labour and Capital* as proof that already in the 1840s Marx 'had known very well not only whence but also *how* "the surplus-value of the capitalist" came into existence' (Engels, [1885] 1977, p. 7). And Marx never claimed to have been the first to have a theory of surplus value: he credited Smith with having 'recognised the true origin of surplus-value' ([1862–3] 1969–72, vol. 1, p. 80), and Ricardo with having 'express[ed] the true theory of surplus-value' (ibid., vol. 3, p. 33). What Marx attributed to himself was simply to have treated surplus value independently of its special forms of profits, interest, land rent, etc., while 'classical political economy . . . lumps them together with the general form' (Marx to Engels, 24 August 1867, in Marx and Engels, 1983, p. 111).[16]

It seems to me that it has been not uncommon in recent times for Marxist writers who wish to emphasize the differences between Marx and Ricardo actually to make points that lack any basis in Marx's writings, and are sometimes in direct opposition to them.

A rather striking example of this is to be found in Rowthorn's paper on the 'neo-Ricardians', in which he levels at Ricardo's 'modern followers' the charge of regarding distribution as 'the only level at which social relations occur', and of treating production as 'an asocial or natural process' (Rowthorn, [1974] 1980, p. 31). This is no minor matter for Rowthorn. Such a conception would, according to him, bring the 'neo-Ricardians' very close to 'vulgar economy', one of the characteristics of which is, according to Rowthorn, that 'it sees production as an asocial or natural process'. It is well known that the conception of production as governed by natural, eternal laws, and of distribution as governed by social, and therefore changeable, laws, was J. S. Mill's conception, which Marx condemned as 'absurd' (Marx, [1862–3] 1969–72, vol. 3, p. 84).[17] Marx regarded the laws of production and distribution as 'the same laws under different forms' (Marx, [1857–8] 1973, p. 832), and attributed basically the same conception to Ricardo. He even favourably contrasted Ricardo's conception with Mill's 'absurd' ideas, in the following terms:

> Economists like Ricardo . . . have regarded distribution as the exclusive object of political economy, for they have instinctively treated the forms of distribution as the most precise expression in which factors of production manifest themselves in a given society . . . Ricardo, the economist of production *par excellence*, whose object was the understanding of the distinct social structure of modern production, for this very reason declares that distribution, *not* production, is the proper subject of political economy. This is a witness to the banality of those economists who

> proclaim production as an eternal truth, and confine history to the domain of distribution.
>
> (Marx, [1859] 1977, pp. 201–2)

Of whatever vices one may wish to accuse Ricardo's 'modern followers', the one that Rowthorn chooses is a most un-Ricardian one – at least for Marx.

De Brunhoff, in her paper for this conference, rightly stresses the difference between Ricardo and Marx on monetary theory. Ricardo was, of course, a staunch advocate of the quantity theory of money, whereas Marx consistently opposed it. But she fails to notice that Sraffa's suggestion that the rate of profits, rather than the rate of wages, can be regarded as the independent variable in his theory of distribution, and that the rate of profits 'is . . . susceptible of being determined . . . by the level of the money rates of interest' (Sraffa, 1960, p. 33), is inconsistent with the mechanism envisaged by Ricardo to explain the variations in prices engendered by variations in the quantity of money (on this, see the section on money in de Vivo, 1987). Indeed, as shown by the paper contributed by Pivetti (Chapter 15 in this volume), to develop Sraffa's suggestion brings one into the camp of Tooke – the great opponent of Ricardo's monetary theory: being Ricardian on value and distribution does not at all entail being Ricardian on money.

It seems to me that de Brunhoff shares with many Marxist writers a misunderstanding of the scope of *Production of Commodities*. These authors appear to think that Sraffa's book is intended as a substitute for Marx's *Capital*, and they therefore find fault with it because a number of problems that they regard as vital are entirely left out of Sraffa's book. It seems even too obvious to me that Sraffa's slender book could not (and did not) aim at covering the whole field covered by the bulky volumes of *Capital*. Indeed, Sraffa addresses himself to virtually one problem: that of building a logically coherent wage–profit–price relationship. This was of course a crucial problem for both Ricardo and Marx – such a relationship is a cornerstone of a surplus theory of value and distribution. It is most striking that de Brunhoff, in the conclusion of her paper, appears to reject Sraffa's solution to this problem, and yet she seems to admit that there are difficulties in Marx's transformation. Unfortunately, she does not say what the solution ought to be, according to her. Her attitude is similar to that of the Marxists of the 1880s, who refused to face up to the critique of Marx's theory of value. In the 1880s, this attitude was to a certain extent justified. Today, it appears wholly unwarranted.

Acknowledgement

I should like to thank A. Campus for helpful suggestions on an earlier draft of this paper.

Notes

1 This was of course especially the case in English-speaking countries. As Beer writes, 'Four fifths of the socialist leaders of Great Britain had passed through the school of Henry George' (Beer, 1929, p. 245).

2 Wicksteed himself apparently used to say that he was often taken for a socialist by friends who were not socialists, but generally rejected as one by friends who were (Hutchison, 1953, p. 97). Shaw, for one, regarded him as a socialist (Shaw, [1885] 1944, p. 724). Also Wicksteed had been strongly influenced by George, and it was *Progress and Poverty* that drew him to the study of political economy (Herford, 1931, p. 197).

3 Hobsbawm ([1956] 1964) overlooks this as one of the causes of the 'calm and impartiality' which he notices among the Victorian critics of Marx. Correspondingly, he appears to put too much weight, as a cause, on the British lack of concern, at that time, for an anti-capitalist movement.

4 See also Hutchison (1953, p. 6). It may also be mentioned that when in 1885 a new edition of *Encyclopaedia Britannica* appeared, the article on political economy was signed not by a marginalist, but by J. K. Ingram, one of the leaders of the historical school in Britain. Ingram was himself of socialist tendencies, and used to send complimentary copies of his works to Marx (Kaiser, 1967, p. 103).

5 *To-Day*, the journal where Wicksteed's paper appeared, had as its subtitle 'The Monthly Magazine of Scientific Socialism'. Its contributors included virtually all the leading characters of British socialism at that time. Marx's daughter Eleanor was also a regular contributor.

6 It is to be noticed that, even before Wicksteed's article, Shaw had doubts about Marx's theory, which he had formulated in a letter to the organ of Hyndman's Social Democratic Federation (Shaw, 1884), under the allusive pseudonym 'G.B.S. Larking'. He 'expected that some more expert socialist economist would refute me' (Shaw, 1925, p. 275), but his doubts were instead enhanced by Wicksteed.

7 Loria too, in his obituary of Marx (Loria, [1883] 1902), had maintained that the promise to solve the problems left open in the first volume of *Capital* could not be fulfilled. He even surmised that such a promise was only 'un ingegnoso spediente' (an ingenuous trick) invented by Marx in order to make people think that the weak points in his theory derived from the incompleteness of the argument, and could disappear in a more thorough treatment (Loria, [1883] 1902, p. 24). Loria's 'humbug' of course elicited an irate reply from Engels in the preface to volume 3 of *Capital* ([1894] 1977, pp. 16 ff.). Loria retorted that volume 3 was only a 'miscellanea di note scucite' (a miscellany of unconnected notes), and the chapter on the transformation a 'mistificazione', which he doubted Marx could have wished to publish (Loria, [1895] 1902, p. 155).

8 For a more detailed discussion of Böhm-Bawerk's essay, and Hilferding's reply, see Garegnani (1981, pp. 67 ff).

9 On the change from 'political economy' to 'economics', see Cannan ([1929] 1964, ch. 2).

10 The only attempt at a full-scale critique of marginalism in the Marxist tradition is Bucharin ([1919] 1966). It was remarkably ineffective. Bucharin had attended Böhm-Bawerk's courses at Vienna during his exile in Austria.

11 The famous sentence which, according to Lafargue, Marx uttered, 'Moi, je ne suis pas Marxiste', must have reflected something of the sort. In his comment on Wicksteed, Shaw wrote that 'Socialists often dogmatise intolerably on the subject of what Marx taught, or what they suppose him to have taught, on the subject of value' (Shaw, [1885] 1944, p. 724).

12 E. R. Pease, the official historian of the Fabian Society, even went so far as to write that 'Revisionism . . . is but a German version of the English school of Socialism, as expounded by the Fabian and I.L.P. thinkers and leaders' (Pease, 1913, pp. 314–15). However, in his memoirs, Bernstein seems to play down his relations with the Fabians during his London exile (Bernstein, [1915] 1921, p. 226).

13 For a more detailed discussion of the origin of the notion of labour power, see de Vivo (1982), p. 92 ff.

14 On this, see de Vivo (1984), ch. 2.

15 It is curious that while in this book Mandel writes that the distinction between labour and labour power was established by Marx after the 1840s, in his previous book, *Marxist Economic Theory*, he had written that 'Ricardo soon arrived at the distinction between labour and labour-power' (Mandel, [1962] 1968, p. 703).

16 Mandel ([1962] 1968, p. 705) asserts that in the letter quoted in the text Marx had declared that 'his working out of the theory of surplus value . . . [was] his greatest achievement'. This is due to an inaccurate reading of the letter, because nothing more is claimed by Marx than what is reported here in the text.

17 It should be remembered, in contrast to Rowthorn's characterization of Mill's conception as a hallmark of vulgar economy, that Marx thought that 'to put J. S. Mill among vulgar economists would be very wrong' (Marx, [1867] 1954, p. 572n).

Reply

G. de Vivo does not treat the subject discussed in my paper until the end of his presentation, using a critical approach that I found questionable. I. Steedman, on the other hand, directly treats a problem concerning the role of money in Marx, which leads me to demonstrate that the problem is incorrectly posed.

De Vivo's commentary surprised me as regards both the questions raised in my text and, more generally, to the method he uses.

First, it is a commentary . . . but not really. It could be used in a discussion of any contemporary Marxist author, as is evident in the criticisms it makes concerning the papers of Mandel and Rowthorn before briefly treating my remarks on the theory of money. De Vivo's reproach of my discussion – i.e. that it does not directly address the debate on labour value – can be applied to his own paper, which sidesteps an analysis of the subject I attempted to discuss in my work.

In addition, the reference to the works of Pivetti on money[1] is used by de Vivo as an argument from authority rather than as an introduction to further development. So too with the reference to the object of Sraffa's book. According to de Vivo, '[I share] with many Marxist writers a misunderstanding of the scope of *Production of Commodities*', which is not a substitute for Marx's *Capital* but addresses one problem – the construction of 'a logically coherent wage–profit–price relationship'. Yet the only coherent attitude is Gagegnani's (which I treat in my paper): 'money is not dealt with in *Production of Commodities* because logic does not allow for it.' Either de Vivo should examine the logical steps that allow him to introduce money without breaking with 'the core' of Sraffa's theory of prices, or, as in his commentary, he must content himself with referring to the problem without dealing with it.

Second, the greater part of de Vivo's paper is made up of a discussion of the difficulties encountered by Marxists of the 1880s, 'who refused to face up to the critique of Marx's theory of value', an attitude that is allegedly shared by 'many Marxist writers' of the 1970s and 1980s (the principal targets here being E. Mandel, R. Rowthorn, and myself). The choice of historical period of reference is not neutral. First of all, it allows the author to measure all 'the Marxists' of the earlier period by the yardstick of the critiques of Böhm-Bawerk and Wicksteed and, far more tellingly, to reveal in this way their theoretical insignificance at a time when the criticisms made of Marx were moderately formulated. Further, the weaknesses of the 1880s are supposed to anticipate the later fate of Marxism, most notably the problems encountered by Engels. These problems, according to de Vivo, have their very roots in the work of Marx.

De Vivo's approach is unconvincing. Either the attitude of the Marxists of the 1880s can be put down to their dogmatism (which arose from what de Vivo sees as extenuating circumstances, the first volume being the only one available and then 'only' in German, Russian or French) or it resulted from contradictions that Marx himself could not reconcile, and that Engels' editions of the second and third volumes of *Capital* could only adopt unchanged. In this case, de Vivo's discussion of the Marxists of the 1880s serves only to emphasize Marxist dogmatism of the 1970s and 1980s. The text does not resolve anything.

This second sidestep reinforces the first. They lead me to think that the 'fundamentalism' of Sraffian economists inhibits theoretical discussion to the same extent as Marxist dogmatism.

Steedman also chooses to put aside the developments on money and credit proposed by Pivetti and Panico. However, he raises the question of the role played by money as a 'general equivalent' in Marx's analysis of abstract labour and value, a 'central *but undesirable*' role, he writes, for the three notions under consideration are linked in Marx. Marx has made a mysterious detour through the notions of value, abstract labour and general equivalent, whereas the correct method, suggested by his own research, 'would, of course, be to aggregate heterogeneous labours with weights proportional to their respective money wage rates, as Sraffa did.'

According to Steedman, who here conforms to the tradition of political economy, labour can only be represented through wages, which play the role of the 'key in sharing out the net product'. On this point, there is a break between Marx's and Sraffa's ideas. Marx analyses merchant relations that do not fall into the categories of 'labour commanded' as outlined in the price system constructed by Sraffa.

Steedman also assumes that a problem in his own approach – the status of money in relation to the wages structure – has been resolved. For this reason, the idea of 'money wage rate' used by him is unclear. The monetary characteristic of a 'real wage' implies the use of a price 'numéraize', yet the articulation of this with the idea of money is left undefined. Here 'the burden of proof' must rest with Steedman. Either money (the introduction of which can alone allow us to speak of 'monetary wages') is identified with the commodity standard, which is manifestly not the case in Sraffa, or it can well be introduced into a Sraffian price system by new developments that await description. Or, perhaps, money has no place at the 'core' of the system and the idea of monetary wages (like that of a monetary interest rate) denotes some other reality that Steedman fails to describe.

Note

1 K. Bharadwaj has indicated that my presentation of these works and those of Panico should be carried further, a suggestion I willingly accept.

3

Sraffa's Return to Classical Theory

Krishna Bharadwaj
New Delhi

In the preface to his *Production of Commodities* (1960), Sraffa revealed his dual objectives in that work (subtitled 'Prelude to a Critique of Economic Theory'): one was a return to the approach of the old classical economists from Adam Smith to Ricardo, and the other was to provide the basis for a critique of marginalist theory. A unique and impressive feature of the book is that he develops a set of basic propositions designed to serve both these tasks and they effectively reveal the contrasting structures and standpoints of the two theoretical – 'classical' and 'marginal' – approaches.

Sraffa himself identifies his return to the classical ways of thought thus:

> The investigation is concerned exclusively with such properties of an economic system as do not depend on the changes in the scale of production or in the proportions of 'factors' (Sraffa, 1960, p. v); or, that it examines 'the conditions of production in a given situation irrespective of whether constant or variable returns prevail'.
>
> (Sraffa, 1960, cover text)

Sraffa adds:

> This standpoint ascribed to the old classical economists has been submerged and forgotten since the advent of the 'marginal' method. . . . [this] approach required attention to be focussed on change, for without change either in the scale of an industry or in the proportions of the factors of production there can be neither marginal product nor marginal cost.
>
> (ibid., p. v)

The second feature of the return to the classical standpoint is to regard production as a circular process in which the same kinds of commodities appear both among the means of production and among the products – rather than as a process beginning with 'factors of production' and ending with consumption goods, a 'one-way avenue' of the 'modern' theory (see Sraffa, 1960, Appendix D, p. 93).

The particular standpoint adopted by Sraffa in this investigation of properties of an economic system that do not depend upon change has often been misinterpreted (prompted by the habitual modes of marginalist thought) as connoting an avowed admission of the assumption of 'stationarity', which rules out *a priori* changes in the system, or else as presuming 'invariance' in the face of exogenous changes. The latter is evident in the reading of the Sraffa system as a particular case of general equilibrium under conditions when the 'non-substitution theorem' is applicable. It has also prompted a number of authors to look upon Sraffa's theory as an abstract 'intellectual experiment'. At the same time, the marginalist theory, with its focus on 'changes', apparently bestows generality and flexibility on the conditions defining the system. Notwithstanding this, paradoxical as it may seem, there have been a growing unease, ambivalent admissions and sometimes protests against the sterility of the neoclassical (demand-and-supply-based equilibrium) theory even among its practitioners; in particular, against its inability to handle effectively even descriptive interpretations of historical experience, let alone predictions based thereupon. This state of affairs points to the need for a clear comprehension of the implications of Sraffa's distinction between the 'classical' and the 'marginal' methods and the originality of his critique.

Criticisms of the mainstream theory have arisen from various quarters and viewpoints.[1] My attempt, in this paper, will be to argue that the analytical inadequacies, as well as the ahistoricity that appears to plague the mainstream theory, arise from the specific structure of the theory of value and distribution based on demand and supply. I also note that writers of very different persuasions have acknowledged that Smith, Ricardo and Marx incorporated elements of historical change into their theoretical schemes, particularly in their analysis of accumulation, technical change and distributive relations. I attempt here to trace these differences in perspectives to differences in the *structures* of the surplus-based classical theory and of the supply-and-demand-based equilibrium theory, following certain suggestive hints and ideas from Sraffa's constructive and critical writings.[2]

My discussion on the distinctiveness of the *structures* of theories concentrates on the theory of value and distribution, which also appears to be the central theme in Sraffa's critical and constructive writings. The theory of value, for very different reasons, acquired analytical importance in the two theories. The particular *structure* of neoclassical theory, in which all *prices* (including 'factor prices') *and quantities* were simultaneously determined, led to the 'value theory taking the centre of the stage'. In the classical theory, an explanation of value that was consistent with the surplus-based explanation of the rate of profit acquired critical importance.[3] The contrasting structures of the two theoretical approaches are best revealed in their theories of value and distribution which are the foundation of the theory of accumulation. I also note the crucial significance of the theory of distribution in the history of economic theories: it acted as a prime mover that propelled them in new directions, leading to the acceptance of some, and the abandonment of other, frameworks – sometimes even prematurely.[4]

In the following I explore the differences in the structures of the two theories. In Section 1, I discuss briefly some developments in the formation of neoclassical theory that, in fact, constituted radical departures from the earlier classical theory, although they often appeared covertly as modifications or extensions. While not attempting to offer here a comprehensive account of all the changes in theory during the transitional stage, I focus particularly on those that seemingly maintained a semblance of 'continuity', thereby creating a false appearance of gains in generality and rigour. These radical departures rendered the theory increasingly rigid and incapable of dealing with the complexity and diversity of the nature and causes of changes in economic activities.

A continuity in theoretical developments was vehemently asserted by Marshall.[5] It is in Marshall that we see attempts at reconciling elements drawn from the two theories leading to contradictions. In him we also note an awareness of the alternative theoretical positions that he attempted to forge together and an occasional recognition – even if veiled and cautious – of the theoretical troubles so concealed. Sraffa's critical attacks on Marshall's theory appear mainly to be due to Marshall's strategic position in the theoretical transition.[6] For this reason, I too will make frequent references to Marshall in the following when I attempt to trace how the domain of the demand-and-supply-based theoretical model was progressively extended to cover all economic spheres and, consequently, led to the dictatorship of the relative-price-based scarce-resources-allocational scheme. In particular, I shall attempt to trace how the 'reductionist' approach (i.e. reducing all collective or 'market' phenomena to individuals' choices) and the quantity-price-response mechanisms presumed in the demand-and-supply-based equilibrium theory were progressively extended to cover all spheres of economic decisions and all phenomena of economic change.

In Section 2 I shall outline some consequences of such analytical extensions and of attempts at constructing symmetries on theoretical notions such as 'change', 'competition' and 'equilibrium'. In Section 3 I shall briefly consider the relatively more open character of the classical structure, which renders it more flexible and able to deal with a wider range of historical changes. I shall also indicate some of the misinterpretations that have crept in because of an insufficient appreciation of the distinctive character of the classical structure.

1 *The two structures and the transition*

The classical approach to which Sraffa seeks a return is centred on the processes of generation, appropriation and distribution of the surplus and its accumulation, mainly in the context of a competitive capitalist economy, where competition is characterized by the active tendency towards a uniform rate of profit and wages.[7] The theory of prices emerged in this approach as an important prerequisite for a consistent explanation of the rate of profit.[8] Proceeding to make an important distinction between 'temporary' or 'accidental' and 'persistent' or 'stable' economic forces influencing prices, the classical writers distinguished between 'market prices' (or, actually observed prices), and 'natural prices' (or the central prices around which 'market prices' oscillate). 'Natural prices' (or 'prices of production' – the form in which they occur in Sraffa's *Production of Commodities*) are those prices compatible with the condition of a uniform rate of profit and wage, under given 'effectual demand', the observed methods of production in use and given wage. Without going over rather well-known ground,[9] I shall only point out some features relevant to our purpose.

First, it is the material and social conditions of production (as reflected in the observed methods of production), along with the level of wages (determined by social and historical conditions), that determine prices. This is consistent with the rule of surplus distribution (here, the rule of uniformity of the rate of profit) among the surplus sharers (here, the capitalists). The level and composition of social output, as well as methods of production, are determined prior to prices, in the sense that it is acknowledged that the factors determining output levels and composition, the methods of production in use and the pace of accumulation are not entirely subsumed within the domain of price determination. This is not to deny or even undermine the interdependence and interaction between levels of output (and changes therein), distribution and technology, but to recognize that such interrelations are considered diverse and complex enough to require deeper analysis outside the core of the price theory.[10] This implies, in the first instance, a sequential separation of the analysis of quantities from that of prices.

In contrast, the currently dominant supply-and-demand equilibrium theory simultaneously explains prices of commodities, as well as distribution ('factor prices') and quantities (output and factor utilizations that, in equilibrium, are fully utilized). It does so within the theoretical structure of given supplies of 'factors of production', given technological transformation possibilities, and given the structure of preferences. Under certain assumptions, the required kinds of price–quantity relations are expected to be generated through a choice behaviour resting on the relative-price-guided principle of substitution. First, all economic magnitudes are thus determined through the interplay of the forces of demand and supply leading to an equilibrium. Second, economic forces operating to determine these are taken to be reducible, comprehensively and consistently, to domains of individual choices.

Many proponents of the general equilibrium theory would consider their theoretical scheme to be the most general and rigorous one and the classical scheme to be a subsystem. They thus propose a common theoretical structure. It will be interesting, therefore, to turn to the evolution of the present theory and its radical departures from the older framework.

Generalization of the rent principle

The classical theory of rent (Malthusian in origin and adopted by Ricardo)[11] became the fountainhead for most basic marginalist ideas. The idea of differential rents, cast in the mould of 'the principle of diminishing marginal returns' (accruing to the 'doses of capital and labour' applied to a fixed 'factor', i.e. land), was extended into directions and put to theoretical purposes different from those envisaged by the classical originators of the theory. As Sraffa points out (1925, 1926), in the classical approach the theory of rent appeared under distribution, where land, 'a non-reproducible social asset was taken as fixed in supply to the whole community', in the sense that land of uniform quality was limited.[12] Further, 'it had always been perfectly obvious that its operation (i.e. of diminishing returns) affected not merely rent but also the cost of the product: but this was not offered as a cause of variation in the relative prices of individual commodities' ([1926] 1953, p. 182). To the extent that diminishing returns were reflected in the difficulty of production (requiring higher labour input per unit of output), the value increased. But no general and functional association between output and cost was derived therefrom that was applicable to all commodities.[13]

The general notion of the law of decreasing returns appeared to have been derived in two steps. First, the distinction between the 'extensive' and the 'intensive' case was virtually eliminated and the latter eventually dominated as a generalized principle. The classical theory, which was directed to the explanation of rents rather than the prices of individual commodities, rested more predominantly on the extensive case of the simultaneous cultivation of lands of different fertilities or qualities. No doubt, the intensive case was also referred to but only with some hesitation (see Sraffa in Ricardo, 1951–73, vol. 4, pp. 3–8). While the differential productivities of lands of different qualities were directly observable in a single situation, the 'marginal product' of the marginal dose referred to an incremental output attributable to a potential additional 'dose', requiring a hypothetical 'change' in the situation. The marginal dose, no different from any other, was identified as such owing to its ordered position in successive application, involving thus a change in the situation.[14]

Secondly, this subtle shift towards intensive margins implied an important change in the method of analysis – a shift from 'observable' to 'potential' or hypothetical changes. This facilitated the illegitimate generalization and construction of symmetry between land and other factors, and an analysis in terms of potential changes and variable proportions of factors. The generalization proceeding from the case of land as a fixed 'factor' led to the general assumption of given factor endowments, thus extinguishing a distinction, crucial to the classical writers, between non-reproducible and reproducible resources. 'The Ricardian law of rent . . . is the first great example of the marginal method, later to become the key-stone of the entire system of economic theory', remarks J. M. Clark (1931; quoted by Sraffa in Ricardo, 1951–73, vol. 4, p. 6). Jevons, who was critical of Ricardo's system and announced its closure, conceded:

> There are many portions in economical doctrines which appear to me as scientific in form as they are consonant with facts. I would especially mention the themes of population and rent, the latter a theory of a distinctly mathematical character which seems to give a clue to the correct mode of treating the whole science.
>
> (Jevons, [1871] 1971, p. 43)

The laws of returns and the supply schedule

Another instance of altering an inherited notion so as to force it into the straitjacket of a supply schedule, functionally linking unit costs and output, was Marshall's attempt to co-opt and co-ordinate the law of increasing returns along with that of decreasing returns. This process led to a drastic change in the content and scope of the law of increasing returns itself. As Sraffa ([1926] 1953, p. 182) comments: 'The position occupied in classical economics by the law of increasing returns was much less prominent as it was regarded merely as an important aspect of the division of labour and thus rather as a result of general economic progress than of an increase in the scale of production.' For Adam Smith, division of labour was an important source, as much as a consequence, of technical change and of extensions of the market (or of accumulation, putting it more generally). This meant that the notion of increasing returns could no longer be confined to the scale of an individual industry, but would be connected with a whole group of interrelated industries; and the unit cost of output in an industry could not be linked to changes in its output alone. Marshall himself devoted much attention to this aspect of the problem in his early work, *Pure Theory* ([1879] 1930), where he saw the more significant economies arising from the localization and geographical conglomeration of industries, but he put increasing returns on a different footing in his later work (see Bharadwaj, 1972).

Marshall introduced the notion of externalities; Sraffa (1926) demonstrated how logic would then confine increasing returns to the implausible case where there were 'external economies', external to the firm and internal to the industry. The tortuous course of these attempts did not lead to a satisfactory resolution, and Sraffa's trenchant critique of Marshall's supply curve demonstrated the contradictions they ran into (see Sraffa, 1925, 1926, and 1930). Furthermore, there was the problem of irreversibilities. Economies once achieved through such general economic progress (or even expansion of the industry) could hardly recede, even if the output of the individual industry were to decline. This implied, as Marshall himself realized, the impossibility of moving backwards and forwards on the same supply curve and suggested a redrawing of the curve whenever 'great additional economies are introduced' (Marshall, [1879] 1930, p. 30). If such advice was to be followed, however, the supply schedule could be only a 'historical curve', describing events *ex post facto* (see Bharadwaj, 1972) and could not remain a predictive theoretical supply curve as required for the determination of equilibrium. Thus the phenomenon of increasing returns created a number of logical hurdles, jeopardizing the assumption of competition, challenging the meaningfulness of the supply curve for the industry, and endangering the mechanistic postulate of reversible movements along the supply curve. Marshall, aware of the problems, remained more cautious about his supply curve than about his demand curve, about which he also had certain reservations (see, Bharadwaj, 1972).

In the theory of the firm, the notion of monopolistic competition attempted to meet only a part of the difficulty – namely, that created by the irreconcilability of increasing returns with competition. But, as is well known, the easier way adopted was to assume away increasing returns and postulate convexity conditions, which Koopmans (1957) concedes:

> Such assumptions can lay no general claim to realism . . . The principal

> reason for making a convexity assumption lies not in its degree of realism but in the present state of our knowledge . . . [it] enables us to state minimum assumptions for the validity of important parts of existing economic theory thus helping to reduce this part of our knowledge to its logical and mathematical essentials.

We must note here, however, that Sraffa's critique is directed not so much against the lack of realism of the theory, but against its logical consistency (see Sraffa, 1930, p. 93).

Symmetrical theory of demand

The notion of a demand schedule – in which, given the preferences of the consumer and his budget constraint, quantities of a good demanded are obtained as a function of prices – did not exist in classical theory. Adam Smith's 'effectual demand' was a 'central' position depicting the average state of social demand in the economy. The first deviant but uncertain steps towards a functional relation between price and quantity demanded were taken by J. S. Mill when he tried to relate use values and exchange values quantitatively, following De Quincy's suggestion (see Bharadwaj, 1978a). The demand and supply schedules so constructed as symmetric but opposite forces provided the foundation for a new theory of equilibrium.

While the principle of diminishing marginal utility appears to have been prompted by a recourse to the individual's psychology, its use as one blade of a pair of scissors appears to have been strengthened, as by Marshall (Marshall, 1920, pp. 356–7), on the analogy of diminishing returns on land. For example, while Marshall held that the demand function rested on the 'self evident' 'fundamental and universal' principle of diminishing marginal utility, he wrote:

> This law [of satiable wants or of diminishing utility] holds a priority of position to the law of diminishing marginal returns from land which however has the priority in time: since it was the first to be subjected to rigid analysis of semi-mathematical character. And if, by anticipation, we borrow some of the terms, we may say that the return of pleasure which a person gets from each additional dose of a commodity diminishes until at last a margin is reached at which it is no longer worthwhile to acquire any more of it (Ibid., p. 93, fn. 1)

Marshall, however, also claimed that the tendency of diminishing utility had its roots in the qualities of human nature, while that of diminishing returns had its roots in the technical conditions of industry (ibid., p. 70). Sraffa (1925) questions the apparent dichotomy. Is it not strange, he asks, that two such heterogeneous elements as human nature and industrial technology should bring about results so similar and, even more improbable, that the tendency towards diminishing returns reflecting technical conditions should operate alike in a large number of very different industries and even in the 'production of utility'! The resemblance arises from the common premise about the behaviour of individuals and the presumed operation of the 'substitution' principle. Diminishing returns and diminishing utility both presuppose the operation of the principle of substitution when the individual (producer or consumer), optimizing his returns (profits or utility), ranks the alternatives open to him according to returns and allocates his limited, given resources. This ranking of alternatives does not arise as a result of material/technical necessity for which the uses must follow a particular sequence. They call into question difficult problems of *a priori* ranking of value magnitudes: in fact, as Sraffa (1960) was to demonstrate, no such ranking of methods of production according to 'factor intensities', invariant with respect to distribution, could be made because it involved the reckoning of capital as a value magnitude.

In his introduction of the demand schedule, Marshall expressed some equivocation, both in the text of *Principles* and, characteristically, in the footnotes and appendices. Unlike Jevons, who declared that the introduction of utility-based demand was a break with earlier tradition, Marshall tried to present a semblance of continuity. He explained: 'Until recently, the subject of demand or consumption has been somewhat neglected' (Marshall, 1920, p. 86). In the first edition (1890) he continued the text with the following sentence (dropped from the second edition onwards): 'The prominent place which consumption has received in the programme of the science has not been justified by any attempt to examine it carefully. Nor has this neglect been altogether accidental'; and to this was appended the footnote: 'James Mill indeed called a large part of his *Elements of Political Economy* by the title "consumption" but it is really occupied exclusively with an enquiry into the principles of taxation.' This indicates, we may observe here, that what dominated the analysis was the effects of changes in individual prices on consumption that were consequent upon, say, a tax, but that there was no generalized theory of demand, functionally linking demand to prices. Indeed, 'effectual demand' did play a significant role in their analysis, so that the 'neglect' or 'absence of the demand factor' is to be understood only as the absence of a neoclassical demand function.

Marshall explains the 'comparative neglect' thus: 'For important as is the enquiry how to turn our resources to the best account, it is not one which lends itself, so far as the expenditure of individuals is concerned, to the method of economics.' He believed that 'the common sense of a person who has had a large experience of life will give more guidance in such a matter than he can gain from subtle economic analysis . . .' In fact, the three reasons that Marshall offers to explain the prominence acquired later by demand theory do not relate to this difficulty at all. The first is the growing belief that 'harm was done by Ricardo's habit of laying disproportionate stress on the side of cost of production when analysing the causes that determine exchange value'.[15] Secondly, the growth of exact mathematical habits of thought is mentioned and, thirdly, Marshall writes:

> The spirit of the age induces a closer attention to the question whether our increasing wealth may not be made to go farther than it does in promoting the general well-being; and this again compels us to examine how far the exchange value of any element of wealth – whether in collective or individual

use – represents accurately the addition which it makes to happiness and well-being.

(Marshall, 1920, p. 87)

It is this last question of welfare through price-guided resource allocation (which was not a question that concerned the classicals) that appears to have been important to Marshall. He was to construct the doctrine of 'maximum satisfaction', attained through the balancing of real costs and utilities by individuals. Thus the introduction of demand was an important element in the reductionist programme, seeking to demonstrate that efficient resource-allocation is achieved through the individual choices of the profit-maximizing producers and utility-maximizing consumers. The theoretical demand schedule was based not so much on observation as on hypothetical attributes of demand behaviour and, if Marshall ultimately reduced consumption behaviour to utility calculus, despite his strong reservations (see below), it appears to have been dictated by the theoretical need to construct a demand schedule that, in conjunction with the 'symmetric and opposite' supply schedule, would yield equilibrium prices and outputs.

Nevertheless, as in other instances, Marshall was not very comfortable with the break in tradition. He devoted quite a few pages to describing 'the variety of human wants, considered in their relation to human efforts and activities'; he made a verbal obeisance to civilization's 'desire for variety for its own sake', its 'craving for distinction and excellence', and its wants resulting from activities, habits and customs which were prompted by class distinctions, etc. He also gave an explicit warning against the sweeping tide in favour of the prominence of the 'demand' side.

> It is important still to assert the great truth on which they [the classicists] dwelt somewhat too exclusively: viz, that while wants are the rulers of life among lower animals, it is to the changes in the form of effort and activities that we must turn when in search for the keystones of the history of mankind.
>
> (Marshall, 1920, p. 85)

He was to repeat his warning again, [16] maintaining that 'much that is of chief interest in the science of wants is borrowed from the science of efforts and activities'. But, as was characteristic of Marshall, he proceeded with his theory of demand – 'an elementary analysis of an almost purely formal kind'. Occasional warnings were given in short hints (e.g. in the Appendix on notes on statistics of consumption) referring to the importance of changes in incomes rather than prices in explaining changes in consumption. It is well to remember that the classical writers did indeed put more emphasis on the influence of income changes on demand than on effects of variations of relative prices.

Marshall's substantive contribution remained one of 'the purely formal kind'. For example, despite reservations, he proceeded to the construction of the notion of consumer's surplus. A rigorous extension of his theory of the doctrine of maximum satisfaction in the hands of Pigou[17] could not but expose the vulnerability of the theoretical construction. Similarly, in the case of the extension of Marshall's 'representative firm' into the 'equilibrium firm', Pigou drew out the rigorous consequences of what Marshall had left tentative and vague. Marshall's biological analogies could not be integrated into his formal theoretical constructions, which prompted Sraffa to conclude his debate on the 'representative firm' thus:

> I am trying to find out what are the assumptions implicit in Marshall's theory: if Mr. Robertson regards them as extremely unreal, I sympathise with him. We seem to be agreed that the theory cannot be interpreted in a way which makes it logically self-consistent and, at the same time, reconcile it with facts it sets out to explain. Mr. Robertson's remedy is to discard mathematics, and he suggests that my remedy is to discard the facts. Perhaps I ought to have explained that, in the circumstances, I think it is Marshall's theory that should be discarded.
>
> (Sraffa, 1930, p. 93)

It would seem, therefore, that the new theory of demand, which constructed the demand schedule as symmetric and opposite to the supply schedule, moved away from the richness and variety of consumption behaviour. Moreover, the theory was prompted not by practical observation but by theoretical necessity. Akin to the redefinitions, modifications and increasingly restrictive assumptions that have accrued on the supply side, similar developments are occurring in the demand theory in the form of 'income effects', 'demonstration effects', 'hysterisis effects', 'process of learning', 'quality of life', etc.

The new structure of value and distribution theory

The marginalist theory thus created an altogether new structure for the explanation of value and distribution. Both relative prices of commodities and prices of 'factors of production' resulted from the equilibrium between the forces of demand and supply, which also determined, simultaneously with prices, the quantities of output and the (full) utilization of the factors. The theory assumed as its data the factor endowments, technological possibilities and preferences. In conceiving the existence of such an equilibrium, the theory had to stipulate appropriate restrictions on the supply and demand relations. *The theory needed to hypothesize properties of the system at the equilibrium position in terms of 'marginal' magnitudes of quantities and thus invoke hypothetical changes in the system. Further, these changes were supposed to be entirely governed by the economic principle of substitution. In particular, the substitution principle must so operate that 'well-behaved' supply and demand relations are generated.* In some cases (such as the prevalence of increasing returns) the difficulty was set aside by suitable assumptions or, in other cases, by hypothesizing particular conditions (such as the dominance of substitution effects over income effects in demand).

The difficulty could not be avoided in the case of the demand function for capital. Capital which constituted heterogeneously produced means of production could not be conceived, as the neoclassical theory required, as a *magnitude* given independently of distribution (i.e. of the rate of profit). The operation of the principle of substitution among 'factors' consequently failed to ensure the required demand function for capital, inversely relating capital-intensity to the rate of profit. These difficulties on the demand side were sufficient to demolish the explanation of the rate of profit, even ignoring additional difficulties that could also arise on the 'supply side'. The difficulty arose not only in the more obvious case (which has been conceded more readily in recent controversies) in the versions of marginalist theory explaining distribution by means of an aggregate production function (à la J. B. Clark) but also in the general case of many commodities and general equilibrium. In the latter case, a measurement of capital endowment as a value magnitude is equally required (as in Wicksell) to make the assumption of capital endowment as a datum consistent with long-period equilibrium characterized by the uniform rate of profit (see Garegnani, 1960). I shall not enter into a detailed discussion of the subject here, but I will mention as germane to my theme of transitions in theory, the attempts of the Austrians and Fisher to resolve the question of the rate of profit. Some of the novel elements they introduced or highlighted within the overall structure of the marginalist theory have been used by later writers as grounds for introducing further radical conceptual shifts to a new notion of equilibrium (see below).

The Austrian approach: the one-way avenue

The Austrian approach was characterized by two elements. First, the notion of the supremacy of demand, as reflected in the hierarchical ordering of commodities in relation to final consumption – the explicit one-way avenue of production. By essentially reversing the logic of classical theory that the price of a commodity is built up from the requisites of production, the Austrians derived the value of intermediate goods (and 'factors') from their contribution to final utility. Thus a 'time structure' entered into their valuation process.

The second element was their attempt to reduce capital to invested land and labour, which also introduced a 'time structure' in the depiction of their production process. However, a central question to which they addressed themselves was the determination of the rate of profit within the supply and demand framework. While the reduction of capital to invested land and labour allowed them to avoid the use of capital as a value magnitude in the representation of the production possibilities (as Wicksell did), the requirement of having to represent capital endowment as a datum independent of distribution could not be avoided or consistently resolved by either Böhm-Bawerk or Wicksell. Böhm-Bawerk's attempt to isolate the period of production as a unit of time independent of distribution was simply a search for a proxy for capital-intensity. Sraffa (1960) demonstrated that such a measure could not be constructed, even in the case of capital consisting entirely of circulating capital.[18]

Extension of the principle of substitution to intertemporal analysis

It was, however, in Fisher that the attempt to represent all commodities and 'factors' as congealing 'events' or 'flows of incomes' was fully extended to supplant the notion of costs of production altogether, with each 'good' merely a depository of 'income flow' over time.[19] Fisher's view, like the

Austrians', emphasized the subjective or 'psychological' elements in value[20] and treated time as 'the great independent variable of human experience'.[21] Fisher insistently denied the existence of the 'cost of production in its objective sense and offers instead the principle of "present worth" which made the value of any article of wealth or property dependent on the future alone'. He argued: 'When prices find their normal level at which costs plus interest are covered, it is not because the past costs of production have determined prices in advance, but because the sellers have been good speculators as to what prices would be' (1906, p. 188). Thus Fisher shifted all economic accounting to the future. Fisher's concern, however, like the Austrians', was with the explanation of the long-run rate of profit as the rate of return, and his attempt also met a capital-theoretic difficulty (see Pasinetti, 1969). *In terms of the arena of supply and demand relations, this view extended their operation freely into the future.* In fact, it was a complete reversal of the classical causation, as Fisher himself put it.[22] What needed to be anticipated here was to envisage the entire stream of future incomes and equilibrium as being established *through the substitution principle operating intertemporally.*[23]

My focus in the above rapid review was on indicating how the demand and supply approach was successively extended so that it could be applied to economic activities and spheres of diverse kinds. Consequently, analytical symmetries were illegitimately imposed through choosing assumptions that were *not derived on the basis of historical observation, but were merely postulates required for theory*. Not only was the choice problem of allocating given resources to alternative uses generalized to all spheres, but the 'reductionist' programme was adopted simultaneously. With the theory of distribution co-opted within relative pricing, the choice model was presented entirely in terms of individuals' intentions and decisions, and was presumed to generate consistent 'market' (collective) behaviour at the macrolevel. The capital theory debate has brought out the fallacy of explaining the general rate of profit in terms of the supply and demand framework through merely inverting the choice-of-technique problem posed for the individual producer, for whom prices and wages are assumed to be parametrically given. Keynes, as is well known, exposed the 'fallacy of composition' when he questioned the theory's result that competitive equilibrium would lead to the equalization of savings and investment at full employment.

2 *Altered scope and content of concepts within a different structure of the theory*

Apart from these important problems which the theory faced in preserving its internal consistency, the new structure of the theory connoted changes in the scope of certain central concepts now placed within a different structure. This has clouded a clearer understanding of the structure of classical theory, and the constructive role of Sraffa's *Production of Commodities* (1960), in particular. By way of illustration, I shall discuss two such notions: 'competition' and 'equilibrium'.

The notion of competition

To the classicists, competition signified mobility of capital and, to a certain extent, of labour, which manifested itself in a tendency towards uniformity of the rate of profit and wages. It was, however, allowed by Adam Smith that there could be a vector of rates of profit and of wages, with more or less stable differentials, not greatly or systematically affected by the movements of the economy. Furthermore, this uniformity was seen as a tendency since it was never implied that, in practice, one could observe the uniform rate of profit or that any individual industry could actually achieve it, just as it was not envisaged that the 'natural price would be attained' actually and necessarily.[24] It was, in fact, through the restless movements of capital (investment) that the tendency would manifest itself.

With the shift to marginalist theory, with its choice behaviour extended to demand and collective market behaviour rendered reducible to individuals' (quantity-adjusting and price-taking) choices, the characteristics attributed to competition became more stringent. The stipulation of a large economy with agents who have no influence on prices, have perfect knowledge of commodities and markets, have unrestrained access to them and who do not intervene directly in each other's choices (i.e. no externalities) became the content of competition.[25] Such competitive conditions not only set the environment for the price formation of commodities, but also characterized 'factor-markets'. Given the availability of resources or factor supplies, the working of competition would drive the economy toward full utilization as a consequence of the full play of competitive demand and supply forces. Adam Smith, in contrast, had no problem in recognizing a 'combination of masters' (the unequal bargaining strength of labour and capital), nor did Marx have any difficulty in allowing a fluctuating but permanent reserve army of labour. Faced with the reality of persistent unemployment, the neoclassical theory, attempting to synthesize Keynes, could only revert to imperfections and rigidities in the system as explaining deviations from the full employment equilibrium (see Garegnani, 1983b).

The notion of equilibrium: long-period position in classical theory

Another important notion that was reinterpreted and acquired changed connotations is that of equilibrium. While, strictly speaking, 'equilibrium' is a misnomer in the context of classical theory, the notion of a 'long-period' or 'natural' position as an organizing concept is used in classical theory as much as in neoclassical theory (see Garegnani, 1976a). The method lay in trying to identify relations that appear to be fairly persistent, so that they may be viewed as dominant tendencies at work in the economy.[26] Adam Smith's distinction between the 'natural' and 'market' price of a commodity illustrates this method of analysis. The 'market price', or the actually observed price, could deviate from the 'natural price', which was defined as the price that is just sufficient to cover costs – namely, wages, rents and profits – all paid at their natural rates. Whenever the actual supplies in the market fell short of, or exceeded, 'effectual demand' (itself defined as the quantities demanded by those who were willing to pay the 'natural price'), 'market prices' would deviate from 'natural prices', setting up a tendency for supplies to adjust to 'effectual demand'. 'Effectual demand' was thus a state or a position of demand that could itself be seen as a central or average position of social demand.[27] A distinction was made between 'persistent' or 'stable' shifts in 'effectual demand', and 'temporary' deviations. When the former were identified, the position of 'effectual demand' would be suitably altered. The 'natural price', or a long-period position, was thus obtained, given 'effectual demand', the dominant methods of production and wage. It was not essential that the actual observed positions of the system should comply exactly with this position. Thus, in actual practice, methods in use could differ from firm to firm: the actual rates of profits could also differ from firm to firm, or from industry to industry. It was required, however, that there would be underlying tendencies for the system to move towards the 'dominant' methods of production and towards uniformity of the rate of profit.

It was not necessary, therefore, to view the long-period position as a 'static' position or one that should be, in effect, attained. The distinction between a 'market' and 'natural' position was not made in terms of a temporal division as such, and hence the use of a 'long-run position' for the latter could itself be misleading. The distinction was rather in terms of the character of causal forces and of their effects. For example, a tax on a commodity could have a 'temporary' or 'persistent' effect on its price and the quantities of it which were demanded or supplied. The effects would be considered permanent and affecting the 'natural position' of the system only if they invoked changes in the 'givens', that is in 'effectual demand', 'the dominant method of production', or the 'wage' (appropriately defined as constituting the basis for the 'natural position'). For example, the corn tariff became an important issue, affecting the 'natural position' of the economy, because corn entered significantly into the 'natural wage' and also, under extended cultivation, connoted changes in the methods of production following upon changes in output. The temporary effects could, in turn, be distinguished from the purely 'accidental' – the latter referring to short-lived causes, illustrated by Adam Smith's allusion to the sudden spurt of demand for black cloth in the event of the death of a queen. The effects of a drought could be 'accidental', 'temporary' or 'persistent', depending upon the nature of the output, the severity of the drought and its duration over production cycles and the nature of the consequent effects upon methods of production and the natural wage. The forces forming 'market values' were not considered suitable for exact analysis of a *general* kind: the actual forces at work and the manner of adjustments they invoked or entailed could be historically diverse and specific, requiring concrete specification of the events. While 'accidental' causes were too fickle to be analysed at all, a short-period analysis of 'temporary' events was not ruled out. In the analysis of taxation, for example, Ricardo distinguished between cases where a tax on a commodity led to price changes of particular commodities without altering the general rate of profit, and cases where it did alter the rate.[28] The former involved effects confined to changes in the conditions of a specific commodity that did not affect the natural position. Marx's analysis of the various circuits of capital and their failure to be co-ordinated, giving rise thereby to disproportionalities and periodic crises, illustrates the distinction he maintains between long-term tendencies and cyclical movements or irregularities. A 'short-period' realization crisis could arise through the temporary disjunction between sales and purchases due to the intervention of money, disrupting the continuous circuit of exchange. There could also be a 'long-period' realization crisis due to a chronic failure of demand consequent upon a very low or declining share of wages. The distinction, as illustrated here, between 'market' and 'natural' conditions and 'short' and 'long' periods appears to have been drawn on the basis of the qualitative nature of causes and effects, rather than on the basis of 'duration' of calendar time.

Long-period equilibrium in the demand and supply theory
With a different theory explaining value and distribution, the explanation of the 'long-period position' as 'long-period equilibrium' changed. What is germane to our immediate purpose, is to note first that Marshall's – or, for that matter, Wicksell's or Walras's – 'long-period equilibrium' was not a 'stationary state', as suggested by recent associations of equilibrium with the latter concept. It was more akin to the classical notion, in that it was presumed neither that the economy was in equilibrium already, nor that equilibrium connotes absence of change and, in particular, a zero rate of savings. As Robertson (1957, pp. 92–3) explains:

> Trends in the long run to equal does not mean equals . . . We must not think of the long-run value of a thing as something which will be attained after so many months or years and then stay put. It is more nearly legitimate to think of it as a norm around which actual values oscillate . . . yet even that conception though helpful may be too clear-cut for application to a changing world. It may be that in such a world, long-run equilibrium is never attained. It is the state of affairs which would be attained if all the forces at work had time to work themselves out.

Thus the notion of equilibrium did not imply that the economy would achieve equilibrium. However, the fact that it may never be achieved in practice was not considered sufficient to deny a tendency towards it.

Robertson also noted a growing tendency towards mathematical formalization, which was likely to make concepts such as perfect competition more precise than Marshall had intended. Harrod (1948, pp. 6–8) also noticed some conceptual changes that have occurred: 'As an instance of the eroding process, tending to narrow down the static economics, taking the life out of it and departing widely from the intentions of its authors, may be cited the notion that it has to make such assumptions as perfect mobility, perfect knowledge and perfect foresight.' He noted the tendency to narrow the scope of statics by imposing even more numerous and rigorous restrictions on the alleged sphere and validity of the branch, 'making static assumptions so far reaching that a law based upon them seems incapable of having any application to the world of reality'. However, this development seems to have been inevitable – *not because of the mathematical formalization*, as such, but because the logical difficulties that the theory faced were overcome by recourse to assumptions and axioms that were increasingly distant from observed reality. Marshall's early writings maintained the significance of the classical distinction between 'temporary' and 'permanent' effects much more assiduously.[29] The new price theory, however, had a radically different structure. The explanation of prices and outputs, as well as of distribution, rested on the symmetrical influence of opposite and balancing forces of supply and demand, so that the 'causal forces' were now grouped into 'demand' and 'supply'. Marshall introduced 'a classification of problems of value by the periods to which they refer' (Marshall, 1920, p. 378; see Bharadwaj, 1978a). In elaborating the notion of equilibrium and emphasizing 'the great element of time' (Marshall, 1920, p. 347), one of Marshall's important and explicit concerns was to interpret and limit 'this doctrine that the value of a thing tends in the long run to correspond to its cost of production' (p. 348), and to establish that 'every plain and simple doctrine as to the relations between cost of production, demand and value is necessarily false' (p. 368). He thus treated both Ricardo and Jevons as being at the extremities of his own position.

Marshall's classification of 'periods'

Marshall proposed a four-fold classification. First, in the case of 'market prices', supply is a fixed stock 'in sight'. Secondly, normal prices in the short period 'of a few months or a year' relate to the situation where supply adjustment is limited by what can be produced 'for the price in question with the existing stock of a plant, personal and impersonal, in the given time'. Thirdly, long-period normal prices refer to the situation 'when supply can be produced by a plant, which can be remuneratively produced and applied within the given time'. Fourthly, secular movements in normal prices are caused by 'the gradual growth of knowledge, of population and capital and in changing conditions of supply from one generation to another' (Marshall, 1920, p. 368). While Marshall insistently refers to a broadly specified calendar period of time with regard to each classification, the distinctions rest on what conditions are imposed on the elasticity of supply, that is, what is held in *ceteris paribus*.

> In the relatively short period problem, no great violence is needed for the assumption that the forces not specially under consideration may be taken for the time to be inactive. But violence is required for keeping broad forces in the pound of *ceteris paribus* during, say, a whole generation, on the ground that they have only an indirect bearing on the question in hand.
> (ibid., p. 379, fn. 1)

In the illustrative example of the fishing industry (pp. 369–70), Marshall refers to the accidental oscillations in 'market prices' due to weather conditions. The short-period 'normal price' rests on the adaptability of supply to demand (given the existing capacity of fishing boats, number of sailors, etc.), while the long-period 'normal price' is governed by a 'different set of causes, with different results', with productive capacity and labour, as well as methods of production, suitably adjusting to the long-term demand conditions. All supplies are governed by expected demand, and the short-period utilization of capacity is influenced by the expectations concerning immediate changes in demand (which could also be expected to be short-lived). Decisions as to changes in productive capacity, on the other hand, rest on long-term expectations of demand that take into account changes in income, population, tastes, living standards, etc. Once these different causes affecting supply (or investment decisions) are classified, Marshall applies the same theory of supply and demand to trace their effects on price and quantities in each case. His reference to 'the period of time over which the forces work themselves out' is given no further analytical expression, since the process of the 'cause' producing the 'effect' is not analysed as a dynamic sequence. The differences in each case are entirely defined by the identification of different causes.

It is evident from Keynes that this distinction between the 'short period' and the 'long period' (with the former referring to existing capacity and the latter to changes in productive capacity), as well as that between short- and long-term expectations of demand, could be fruitfully used in the analysis of investment. Marx also distinguished between investment decisions pertaining to circulating capital (or to fluctuations in short-term capacity utilization), and those concerned with 'machinery' or capacity-generating investments (Marx, [1885], 1956, vol. 2, p. 262). The two types of decision could be influenced by different causal considerations. It may, however, also be noted that the causal structure of this part of Keynes's theory of output, particularly the multiplier process, is closer to the spirit of the classicals and bears an affinity to their separation of the analysis of prices and quantities.[30]

Marshall was concerned, however, with establishing that 'the general theory of the equilibrium of demand and supply is the Fundamental Idea running through the frames of all the various parts of the central problem of Distribution and Exchange' (1920 p. viii), and probably, for that reason, insisted that there was no sharp analytical line dividing short and long periods.

> In both use is made of the paramount device, the partial or total isolation for special study of some set of relations. *In both opportunity is gained for analysing and comparing similar episodes . . . and for ordering and coordinating facts which are suggestive in their similarities and still more suggestive in the differences that peer out through their similarities.*
>
> (ibid., p. 379, fn. 1; emphasis added)

The 'principle of continuity', which he staunchly advocated, was used by him, on the one hand, to argue that the element of time was continuous (and hence that the short and long periods shade into one another by 'continuous gradation'). This was an aspect of his 'statical method'[31] that he considered noteworthy:

> The forces to be dealt with are however so numerous that it is best to take a few at a time; and to work out a number of partial solutions to our main study. Thus we begin by translating the primary relations of supply, demand and price in regard to a particular commodity. We reduce to

> inaction all other forces by the phrase 'other things being equal' . . . In the second stage, more forces are released from the hypothetical slumber.
>
> (ibid., p. xv)

On the other hand, Marshall used the periodisation to extend the domain of analysis; he saw the 'dynamical problem' becoming larger with changes in the conditions of demand and supply of particular groups of commodities coming into play; and, finally, reaching 'the central problem of Distribution among a vast number of different agents of production'. Thus 'fragmentary statical hypotheses are used as temporary auxiliaries to dynamical – or rather biological – conceptions' (p. xv). The analytical use to which Marshall puts his device of 'periods' in his 'statical' method is clear from the following examples. He argues that, 'as a general rule, the shorter the period which we are considering, the greater must be the share of our attention which is given to the influence of demand on value; and the longer the period, the more important will be the influence of cost of production on value' (p. 349). The reason he gives for this is that 'the influence of changes in cost of production takes as a rule a longer time to work itself out than does the influence of changes in demand' (ibid.). It is not clear, however, what 'time to work itself out' means in this context, nor why it should take a longer time in the case of changes in costs of production than of changes in demand.

Another example of the 'notion of time' being brought into use is when Marshall argues for the symmetrical treatment of land, labour and capital. In the classical theory, the role that land, labour and capital play in the production process and the explanation of their revenues is different in each case. Marshall, while treating rent in the classical fashion (as 'not entering costs' and as a residual), treats efforts of labour and waiting of capital as entering, on par, into the costs of production. He attempts to bolster up the symmetry argument by the suggestion that 'the greater part, though not the whole of the distinction between Rent and Interest on capital turns on the length of the period which we have in view . . .'. For land, labour and capital, though having peculiarities of their own in respect of supply and demand, could all be treated as 'fixed' or 'variable', depending upon the length of time; so that 'even the rent of land is seen, not as a thing by itself, but as the leading species of a large genus'. Thus Marshall supported his claim that the Fundamental Idea of demand and supply 'runs through all frames' of exchange and distribution. Another instance when the statical theory of particular commodities was threatened, and Marshall recurrently reverted to the 'element of time' and 'limitations of the statical method', was the case of increasing returns. Neither his device of 'external economies' nor that of the 'representative firm' could eliminate the difficulty created by 'increasing returns' for the construction of a supply curve for the industry that was consistent with competitive equilibrium (see 'Symposium', 1930; Bharadwaj, 1972).

Like the classicals, Marshall only used the long-period normal values for his analysis of distribution and investment of resources, etc. In fact, these were considered by him as 'dynamical extensions' of his statical method of determining the prices of particular commodities. However, Sraffa's critique of Marshall's supply curve (Sraffa, 1925, 1926), as well as of the representative firm (Symposium, 1930), demonstrated that Marshall's attempt to construct a 'normal supply curve' under statical assumptions, on the basis of the co-ordination of the laws of return, was not logically sustainable. He failed in his attempt to reduce thereby the Ricardian 'cost-of-production theory' of price to a special – and 'accidental' – case of his own. This also made it clear that the conditions impounded in *ceteris paribus* for the purpose could not be so contained and that it would become necessary to consider the supply and demand conditions of all commodities simultaneously (Sraffa, 1926). With the theory of supply and demand moving into the general equilibrium, the theory of distribution could no more lie in the background, as it did in Marshall's theory of prices. The determination of 'factor prices' now appeared simultaneously with that of commodities in the theory of general equilibrium.

'The element of time' and 'dynamical methods' in Hicks: a shift in the notion of equilibrium

The issue of 'the element of time' and 'dynamical methods' became the focus of discussion when the explanation of the rate of profit within the general equilibrium framework encountered difficulties and was taken up by Hicks in *Value and Capital* (1962), in which he introduced a change in the notion of 'equilibrium' (see Garegnani, 1976a). While the difficulty regarding capital arises from the structure of the neoclassical theory of value and distribution, which requires capital as a datum to be measured independently of distribution, Hicks viewed the problem as one concerning 'method' – the error, in his view, being that the earlier neoclassicals had no general dynamic theory in which all quantities are properly dated.[32] Hicks saw Marshall's position as rather ambiguous:

> Although Marshall raises at least a part of the general dynamic problem, it is curious to observe how reluctant he is to abandon static conceptions even in dynamic analysis. Statics and dynamics are very little separated in his work: his dynamics are not made easier by running in terms of very static 'equilibrium' and by the fact that their central passage leads up to the introduction of that 'famous fiction', 'the stationary state'.

In the case of the Austrians, too, Hicks considers their hallmark to be the stationary state (1982, p. 287), which 'is a dynamic state where tastes, techniques and resources remain constant through time'. The crux of the dynamic theory, according to Hicks, lay in the fact that current supplies (and, ultimately, demand too) are governed as much by expected prices as by current prices, and the assumption of stationarity is made possible by ignoring the vital distinction between price expectations and current prices. It may be observed here that by shifting the onus on to 'method', Hicks bypasses the logical difficulties that the theory encountered, even in its 'stationary or static state' version. For example, Marshall's statical theory faced difficulties even before the question of passing from a statical to dynamical theory could be taken up. Secondly, the 'changelessness' that Hicks associates with the stationary state of the Austrians or of Walras appears to have been, as noted earlier, a product of attempts to render the theory logically consistent and rigorous by moving away from the original conception.

Initially (in *Value and Capital*), Hicks proposed the route of 'intertemporal equilibrium', wherein the analysis was in terms of plans and realizations during a single period within which prices were expected to be determined by the usual equilibrium analysis, that is, prices varied adequately in the period so that demands over the periods would always be equal to the supplies over the period in terms of quantity. The windfall gaps between expectation and realization were to be entirely absorbed by price variations. Garegnani (1976a, p. 30) argues that this shift in method appears to have been prompted by an erroneous identification of the weakness of the underlying theory with another difficulty – namely, the influence of expectations. He states:

> This difficulty over the determination of the quantity of capital is independent of the divergence between current and expected prices. The same need to measure the capital would arise if we wanted to determine the long period equilibrium while assuming that tastes and techniques and resources are not going to change in the future.

Hicks's solution appears to be to abandon the traditional *method* while preserving the *theory* unaltered.

Hicks himself sees the limitation of this model in a very different light (1982, pp. 218–35). The model could work best only when there were two sorts of commodities – perishable goods and personal services – which could not be carried over in stocks and speculatively traded goods by merchants. Further, it needs to be assumed that, while prices are fully adjusted at the end of the single period, they remain constant throughout the period, so that either the equilibrating forces work instantaneously or not at all. Hicks's self-critical remarks thus remain focused on the method. The entire onus is now on 'expectations', for which no objective basis is provided.

In his later work, Hicks adopts alternative 'methods of dynamic analysis' (Hicks, 1982, pp. 217–35). He identifies the problem of capital as mainly its longevity, which inevitably brings in the element of time. Capital is created with the expectation of future returns in the minds of the investors and, once formed as fixed capital, the capital goods generate a flow of services over time. Hicks distinguishes two approaches to the dynamic problem: one based on the Lindahl-type, *ex ante/ex post* forward accounting, and the other based on stock/flow relations. In the first approach, expectations play an active role, with the deviations between *ex ante* and *ex post* quantities and prices directing the dynamics. In the second, the role of expectations is somewhat subdued and the accent is on the time structure of the relation between the stock of fixed capital and the flow of services. Hicks suggests that alternative methods of dynamic analysis may be appropriately adopted to suit the problem at hand, and may further be coupled with alternative assumptions regarding responses – one with flexible quantities and fixed prices, and the other with flexible prices and fixed quantities.

While this gives a neat taxonomy of methods, Hicks himself admits that 'these do not quite fit together into a single coherent whole' (1982, p. 219). This disintegration of the supply and demand theory into separate methods appears to be an indirect admission of the failure of a theory that attempts to be comprehensive in its scope. What Hicks tries to do is to salvage the theory by introducing special assumptions regarding the period over which the supply and demand relations are considered effective in establishing equilibrium, or regarding lags in the price–quantity responses. This shift to alternative methods does not in any way resolve the initial difficulty with capital in the theory of distribution. Expectations acquire new importance, although no new or objective basis is provided for them. The models also deal mainly with expectations about prices, while those that influence investment decisions appear mostly to relate to the general conditions of the state of the market and other systemic macro-level forces. These latter expectations were the predominant ones in classical discussions as well as in Keynes. The problems of the dynamics of change, of uncertainty and of expectations are important dimensions of economic processes that every worthwhile theory must aim to capture. However, the question of paramount importance is the structure of the theory forming the foundation.

3 *Structural contrasts: 'openness' of the classical structure*

In contrast to the structure of the neoclassical theory of value and distribution, the structure of the classical analysis keeps open the possibilities of allowing for a number of historical and social influences to enter the analysis. The broad methodological point may be put in the words of Sraffa, in the context of his critique of Marshall,[33] which illustrates the meaning we may put on 'openness'.

> The first approximation ['cost-of-production theory' of the classicals, as Marshall called it] as far as it goes, is as important as it is useful: it emphasises the fundamental factor, namely, the predominant influence of cost of production in the determination of the normal value of commodities, while at the same time it does not lead us astray when we desire to study in greater detail the conditions under which exchange takes place in particular cases, for it does not conceal from us the fact that we cannot find the elements required for this purpose within the limits of its assumptions.
>
> (Sraffa 1926, p. 187)

Unlike the marginalist theory (which, as we have seen, needed to presume *a priori* quantity–price relations in the form of the well-behaved demand and supply relations generated through the active principle of substitution), no such strict relations need be presupposed in the classical theory.

More explicitly, the two important distinguishing features of the classical, or surplus-based, theory of prices that allow this openness may be underlined here. First, the theory separates, in the first instance, changes in quantities from changes in prices, in the sense that the output levels and composition, methods of production and the wage are given or determined prior to prices; whereas in the marginalist theory, all quantities and prices are determined simultaneously and within the same framework of relations.

This 'separation', as a first step, may appear unduly restrictive. On the contrary, it opens up the possibility of introducing a wider range of determinants and the real dynamics of the process of change – precisely because the more complex, historically specific, institutional and social forces that govern changes (particularly in distribution, technology of production, and investment) can thereby be introduced. While prices may, in turn, influence quantities, it is recognized that there are even more significant factors directly influencing quantities that may be considered to operate fairly independently of changes in relative prices. This is illustrated, for example, in Adam Smith's treatment of the relation between the division of labour and the extent of the market; or in Marx's discussion of qualitative and quantitative changes in capital/labour relations influencing, and being influenced by, technical change. Keynes' analysis of the multiplier could be said to follow the same approach.

That wages (i.e. distribution) are influenced by various historical and social factors is amply evident from labour studies. A growing literature on the intricacies of the growth of technical knowledge, innovations, imitation and adaptation, etc., has over and over again demonstrated the importance of factors other than prices. The relationship between prices and quantities is asymmetrical in the force of their mutual determination, so that the relative prices of commodities may be derived uniquely on the basis of given quantities. We may even go a step further and state that the major influences on the determination of investment, distribution and technical change are not confined to relative prices alone; the real dynamics of economies is generated through direct interactions among these. It is this openness of Marx's prices of production that enabled him to account for 'historical tendencies' in the domain of production, distribution and accumulation. At any 'observed' position of the economy – given wage, methods of production and the principle of surplus sharing among the capitalists (say, the uniformity of the rate of profit) – it was possible to know simultaneously the rate of profit, the value of the surplus and prices, and the corresponding distributive shares. Prices are thus seen to conform to the rules of production and distribution of surplus appropriate to the particular mode of production.[34]

The second important distinctive feature of the classical structure is its view of production as a circular process. The one-way avenue of the neoclassical theory takes factor endowments as given. I have already noted the consequences of treating 'capital' as a given endowment in the theory of profit. Further, within this structure, the given endowments (along with given preferences and technology) determine outputs. In the circular view, changes in output might as well determine the availability and utilization of resources. To note one of the analytical implications of this difference: in the neoclassical theory, prices not only play the role of allocating scarce resources to different uses, but they also ought to lead to the full employment of resources. This indeed runs against the actual experience of capitalist economies.

Some misinterpretations of classical theory

We may here refer briefly to some misinterpretations of the classical theory prompted by marginalist habits of thought. The idea that the classical theory of value is 'incomplete' and requires the demand side to be provided occurs repeatedly in critical writings (e.g., Samuelson, 1971a, 1978). Indeed, following Marshall, it has sometimes been suggested that the demand analysis was incipiently present in Ricardo (see Hollander, 1979; see Bharadwaj, 1983a, for a detailed discussion). On the latter, my discussion above has indicated the difference between the notion of effectual demand in classical theory and the demand schedule of the marginalist theory. Further, as Garegnani has argued elsewhere (Garegnani, 1983a) the particular significance of the role that demand functions play in the marginalist theory arises solely from their explanation of distribution on the basis of the equilibrium between the demand for and supply of 'factors'. In other words, that theory has to rely on the complement of demand schedule, which is no longer necessary in the classical theory where wages are given by historical and other forces outside the price schema.

Hicks, too, imposes the marginalist structure on classical theory when he attributes a simple static model, relying on 'fixed technical coefficients', to Smith and Ricardo, and concludes that

> the range of problems to which such a model could be applied was nevertheless limited. For, in strictness it is only if there is just one original factor, into terms of which all costs are ultimately reducible (the 'labour theory of value') that the technical coefficients are sufficient to determine relative costs; if there is more than one factor, the relative prices of the factors must also play a part.
>
> (Hicks, 1979, pp. 47–8).

Hicks then goes on to define those conditions of factor prices that keep factor supplies from changing. All this is contrary to the way both Smith and Ricardo perceived the problem of distribution. In the classical theory the question of choice among known methods of production was not confined to the context of the changes in factor prices; nor were factor prices determined on the basis of the demand for and supply of factors.[35]

A common misunderstanding in relation to Sraffa's *Production of Commodities* (1960) arises from his statement that his investigation is concerned with those properties of the system that do not depend upon changes in the scale of production or in the proportions of factors. This has tempted some to look upon the system as one that is invariant under these changes, and hence to attribute to it such assumptions as would render the system invariant within the general equilibrium theory. Accordingly, constant returns to scale are considered an essential assumption. The system of relations is also seen as a changeless, and hence a stationary, state. I have attempted to clarify in what way change is an essential requirement for the marginalist theory, but not for Sraffa. However, the fact that the propositions in the book do not depend upon change does not imply the assertion that no changes would or could follow.

In the circular view of the economic process that Sraffa endorses in the very title of his book, the condition of self-replacement is not identical with self reproduction. Exact reproducibility occurs only in the system without surplus. Self-replacement refers to the viability of the system and does not indicate how the system would change in the next period. In fact, Sraffa takes an observed system of relations as given. When wages change, changes in other quantities may or may not follow. What Sraffa implicitly denies is the necessity of hypothesizing quantity–price responses, or of imposing conditions on the direction of these responses for his derivation of prices and the rate of profit. Thus a change in the wage may or may not induce a permanent shift to another method of production; even if it does, it may not be presupposed that the new method would replace a more (less) 'capital-intensive' method when the wage declines (rises). Similarly, not all changes in wage necessitate changes in output composition or level. *It is not therefore denied that changes take place, but it is not presumed that the scheme of relations determining relative prices is the exclusive and comprehensive domain in which to analyse changes in quantities.*

Sraffa's 'return' to classical theory

Sraffa's 'return' to classical theory lies in his attempt clearly to delineate the structure of the surplus-based theory of value and distribution. In *Production of Commodities* (1960), he had a specific constructive goal – to identify and resolve some central problems in the basic structure of that theory, so that the approach could be shown to survive the carry-over from the labour theory of value to prices of production. A much-needed clarification was to demonstrate the inessentiality of certain appendages to the theory which had been adopted for momentary convenience, especially by Ricardo. These not only crippled the theory, but they also led it into deviant directions by making it easily misinterpreted. Some of these misinterpretations had already been discarded by Marx – for example, Malthus' 'population dynamics' to explain the subsistence wage, which, with some hesitation, was used by Ricardo and subsequently criticized by Marx. Sraffa's 'given' and variable wage removed this association with the fixed subsistence wage, seen by some critics as a logical requisite of the classical theory.[36] In his chapter on land, Sraffa (1960) shows how the classical view of rents could be divorced from the traditional law of diminishing returns, and thence from the 'supply schedule' based on it. We have seen how powerful the rent theory was in the original construction of marginalism. In fact Sraffa shows, correcting the classicals, that differential rents as well as the identity of the 'no-rent' land depend on the rate of profit.[37] Similarly, the adherence to Say's Law, as in Ricardo, is no longer to be seen as an essential feature of the prices of production, as indeed Marx expressly recognized.[38]

4 *Conclusion*

My attempt in the above was to bring out the distinctive characteristics of the structures of the surplus-based classical theory and the marginalist theory of value and distribution, and to interpret Sraffa's 'return' to the classical theory as his being engaged in a dual task of criticizing the marginalist theory and clarifying the ground for the classical theory.

Acknowledgement

I am grateful to the participants at the Sraffa conference and to Professors Richard Arena and Harvey Gram for very useful discussions.

Notes

1 Although they reach similar conclusions, the various critiques have different focuses and bases. A major thrust of the criticisms – which were coincidentally voiced by three presidents of prestigious associations (Leontief, 1971; E. Phelps-Brown, 1972; Worswick, 1972) – had been the deficient observational basis and empirical support for assumptions in economic theory, their refutability and operational significance, as well as the limitations of the econometric techniques employed to 'test' the validity of the theory. Another critique of 'fundamental Keynesians' (see Coddington, 1976) concerns 'the equilibrium method', which argues that the logical conditions defining the notion of equilibrium connote a state of affairs either unapproachable or unattainable, unless the economy is already in it (see Shackle, 1972; Joan Robinson returned to this theme repeatedly, contrasting history with equilibrium). Hicks has been engaged in developing 'methods of dynamics', wherein he is mainly concerned with modifications required in the demand and supply mechanisms in order to consider the element of 'time' (Hicks, 1982, pp. 217–36, 282–301). Kaldor (1972), indicating the increasing arbitrariness of the assumptions imposed upon the theory by ever-more precise cognition of the need for logical consistency, considers that the setback in economic theory started when 'value theory' took the centre of the 'stage'. This 'meant focussing on the allocative function of the market to the exclusion of the creative functions as an instrument for transmitting impulses in economic change'.

2 For a review of Sraffa's work, see Bharadwaj (1984).

3 The problem appeared in Ricardo as one of finding a measure of value that was invariant with respect to a change in distribution; in Marx, it took the form of the 'transformation' problem. Sraffa's *Production of Commodities* (1960) focused on the resolution of this difficulty, which is at the very foundation of the classical theory.

4 Ricardo began his investigations in part because he was dissatisfied with the explanation of profit given by Smith in terms of 'competition of capital'. Marx criticized Ricardo for his 'neglect of constant capital' and his tendency to identify surplus value with profits. It was the controversy over the 'transformation problem' that was used by his critics to denounce the surplus approach. Recent attacks on the neoclassical theory have been prominently against their explanation of profit with the connected capital-theoretic controversies. The capital-theoretic critique also challenges the neoclassical theory of output and employment; prices and quantities being *simultaneously* determined within the *same* scheme of explanation in that theory.

5 Other pioneers of marginalist theory, like Jevons, stressed the break with the past. It is interesting that whereas this 'continuity' view has been revived in some recent discussions of the classicals (see Hollander, 1979; Hicks, 1979; Hicks and Hollander, 1977; and Samuelson, 1957, 1959, 1971a, among others), the theories of the classical writers, Adam Smith and Ricardo, have been viewed mainly as partial models of the later marginalist theory. Marshallian views have made their reappearance and have proved more long-lasting than was formerly believed.

6 On the constructive side, Sraffa's editorial commentaries on Ricardo brought out in clear form the significant features of the surplus approach to value and distribution that was being developed in the classical theory. Sraffa thereby helped dispel a number of misinterpretations.

7 Adam Smith considered the possibility of stable differentials in wages and profits, not greatly or systematically affected by advances in output, so that a *vector* of rates (of profits and wages) could be envisaged as 'given'.

8 The rate of profit, explained as the distribution of the total profits over the value of capital, necessitated the consistent measurement of heterogeneous aggregates and required the simultaneous determination of prices and the rate of profit, given wage (Sraffa, 1960).

9 See Garegnani (1960, 1984); Bharadwaj (1978a,b).

10 In other words, the nature of the causal forces, as well as the pattern of their interaction, determining *quantities* could be diverse in historically specific cases. This is not to rule out the possibility of their abstract analysis, but to suggest a wider arena of causal forces and determination than we find in the supply-and-demand-based theories, where it is coterminous with the ones determining prices.

11 See Sraffa in Ricardo (1951–73), vol. 4, pp. 3–8.

12 Land was 'fixed' in supply to the society as a whole, while individual producers could vary the land under their command and its utilization.

13 The first tentative attempt to relate unit costs to output occurs in J. S. Mill (see Bharadwaj, 1978a; de Vivo, 1980) where, following the suggestion of Bailey, Mill seems to have adopted a classification of commodities with their own respective Law of Value.

14 For this reason, Wicksteed (1914) considered the extensive case a spurious case of 'marginal' analysis (see Sraffa, 1925; 1960, p. vi). The intensive margin also raised the question of what 'equality of a dose' and its 'marginal product' meant (see Bharadwaj, 1978a).

15 Ricardo's 'onesided emphasis' on costs of production and relative neglect of demand has been a favourite argument for those who see, in Ricardo, a partial resource-allocational model of general equilibrium. Hollander's attempt (Hollander, 1979), to attribute 'demand mechanisms' to Ricardo are critically discussed in Bharadwaj (1983a).

16 'There is a special need to insist on this just now because the reaction against the comparative neglect of wants by Ricardo and his followers shows signs of being carried to the opposite extreme' (Marshall, 1920, p. 85).

17 Marshall expresses his grave concern about Pigou's overstepping the limits of the 'statical method' and shows awareness of the deeper troubles which he had skilfully tried to contain – and even conceal.

18 Hicks (1982, p. 98) quoting Sraffa, among others, points out that fixed capital cannot be reduced to invested land and labour. However, while mentioning this difficulty, he does not refer to the basic capital-theoretic difficulty that Sraffa poses, which arises even in the case of circulating capital. In fact, Hicks appears to pose the capital problem as one arising entirely from its durability (or its stock dimension in a stock/flow relation), and therefore from its irreducibility to 'land and labour' (see pp. 71–2 above).

19 'All wealth and property imply prospective services or desirable events. It is the desirability of these future expected services which gives meaning to all economic phenomena' (Fisher, 1906, p. 41).

20 'Wealth is wealth only because of its services: and services are services only because of their desirability in the mind of men and the satisfactions which man expects them to render . . . It is only in the interim between the initial desire and the final satisfaction that wealth and services have place as intermediaries' (ibid.).

21 'When values are considered, the causal relation is not from capital to income but from income to capital, not from present to future but future to present' (ibid., p. 328).

22 See note 21.

23 Another method of extending the scope of equilibrium analysis over time was to envisage complete future markets so that each commodity with the specific time-suffix is treated as a separate commodity – a procedure adopted in Debreu (1959).

24 The following rather well-known passage from J. S. Mill ([1871] 1909, p. 452) illustrates the argument:

> 'On an average of years sufficient to enable the oscillations on one side of the central line to be compensated by those on the other, the market value agrees with the natural value; but it very seldom coincides exactly with it at any particular time. The sea everywhere tends to a level: but it never is at an exact level; its surface is always ruffled by waves, and often agitated by storms. It is enough that no point, at least in the open sea, is permanently higher than another. Each place is alternatively elevated and depressed but the ocean preserves its level'.

25 Morgenstern writes (1972, p. 1164):

> 'In identifying the economic phenomena certain primitive concepts and terms have to be used . . . However, because of the freedom with which mind can move, it happens frequently that the relation with reality is lost, and that purely hypothetical notions are introduced. In addition there is often a change in the meaning of words. Consider 'competition': the common sense meaning is one of struggle with others, of fight, of attempting to get ahead, or at least to hold one's place . . . In current equilibrium theory, there is nothing of this true kind of competition, there are only individuals, firms or consumers, given prices, fixed conditions, each firm or consumer for convenience insignificantly small and having no influence whatsoever on the existing conditions of the market (rather mysteriously formed by *tâtonnement*), and therefore solely concerned with maximizing sure utility or profits – the latter then being exactly zero. The contrast with reality is striking'.

It may be added that this disjunction with reality is not so much because of 'the freedom of mind' as the necessity imposed by the nature and structure of the supply and demand theory, explaining quantities and prices in general equilibrium.

26 Marx, more than any other economist, recognized the importance of structuring theory on the basis of abstractions drawn from historical observations. He made a distinction between 'qualitative' changes that occur in social formations and the 'quantitative' changes that occur within the bounds of a particular formation: the 'laws of motion' that propel these quantitative changes (and eventually transform them into a qualitative transition) were particular to the social formation or the 'mode of production'. Each mode of production is therefore characterized by the dominant relations and forms of production and its corresponding rules of surplus extraction, distribution and of exchanges. The 'price of production' forms the rule of exchange under competitive capitalism.

27 As seen above, the classical economists had a much wider notion of social demand based on 'wants' generated by 'efforts and activities' (as Marshall called them), by custom, tradition and habits, by the class composition of incomes and levels of income. In particular, they were conscious of the effect of the availability of commodities on demand. Marx, in particular, emphasized the interaction between production and consumption (Marx, [1857–8], 1973).

28 Hollander (1979, p. 271) points to such a peculiarity, among others, in Ricardo and attempts to explain it on the basis of an attribution of an implicit assumption of identical factor proportions. Hollander's interpretation of reading 'demand and supply based allocative mechanisms' in Ricardo is critically examined in Bharadwaj (1983a, pp. 32–5): Ricardo's peculiarities are there explained along the above lines.

29 Marshall wrote to Edgeworth in 1902: 'You know I never apply curves or mathematics to market values. For I don't think they help much and market values are, I think, either absolutely abstract or terribly concrete and full of ever-varying (though individually vital) side issues' (see Pigou, 1925, p. 435). Even later, he wrote (Marshall, 1920, p. 291): 'The actual value at any time, the market value as it is often called, is often more influenced by passing events, and by causes whose action is fitful and short-lived, than by those who work persistently. But in long periods, these fitful and irregular causes in large measure efface one another's influence so that in the long run persistent causes dominate value completely.' An attempt was made to tone down this contrast by devising a classification of markets, denying at the same time that there is any sharp line of division between 'short' and 'long' periods and asserting that, in all cases, price is governed by the relations between demand and supply.

30 When the causal structure is complex, with sequential separation of the determination of interdependent variables, historical conditions and specificities can be introduced through a comparison with natural or normal positions, as indeed was done by the classical writers (and Keynes). The historical conditions enter into the determination of effectual demand, wage and methods of production.

31 Marshall's distinction between 'statical' and 'dynamical' must be seen as different from the usual 'statics' and 'dynamics', such as used by Hicks (1965). 'Statical' did not mean changeless, but implied that 'certain conditions remain the same'.

32 Hicks writes (1962), p. 116n):

> 'People used to be content with static apparatus, only because they were imperfectly aware of limitations. Thus, they would often introduce in their static theory 'a factor of production', capital and its 'price' interest supposing that capital could be treated like the static factors (cf. J. B. Clark's 'free capital' and Cassel's 'capital disposal'). That some error was involved in the procedure would not have been denied; but the absence of a general dynamic theory in which all quantities were properly dated made it easy to 'underestimate' how great the error was.

Thus, in *Value and Capital*, Hicks sought to lay the foundation of dynamic analysis.

33 It is worth recalling here that the 1926 article was directed mainly against Marshall's scheme of determination of prices of particular commodities in his partial equilibrium framework, although the point made here is more general. Sraffa, keeping to Marshall's terminology, calls the classical theory of prices the cost-of-production theory. He warns explicitly against such a usage in his later work, *Production of Commodities* (1960).

34 Forewarning that analogies are dangerous if interpreted too precisely, we may use one here. The statement that a train is moving – obeying, no doubt, its laws of motion – implies that the wheels are on the tracks at each moment as it moves. It is a statement of compatibility or consistency. The prices of production state similarly the set of prices consistent with the rules of surplus generation and distribution. Using this analogy, we may say that the marginalist theory, in order to generate consistent prices, requires not only that the wheels are on the tracks

but, additionally, that the tracks also turn in required directions (thus depending essentially upon hypothetical changes and having also to impose conditions, such as of convexity, on the feasible sets of choices).

35 Another misconception rests on treating the classical hypothesis of a *given* wage as being the fixed, subsistence wage so that, it is argued, the classical system of price equations was closed by determining the fixed wage through Malthusian population dynamics. Or else, it is maintained, the system would remain incomplete, requiring closure through the introduction of 'demand' (Samuelson, 1971a).

36 See note 35 above.

37 In this sense, under capitalist production rents become subordinated to profits, as Marx argued. Paradoxically, however, in the neoclassical theory an increasing temptation seems to be to treat capital as land.

38 It may be noted that Marx, too, comes to the realization problem sequentially separated from the problem of determination of prices, and that Say's Law is not implied in prices of production.

Comment

Richard Arena
Nice

In order to establish the originality of classical political economy as revived by Piero Sraffa, Krishna Bharadwaj (K.B.) attaches substantial importance to the notion of a long period or 'natural position'. The meaning of this notion constitutes one of the major differences between classical and neoclassical theoretical traditions and that is why I shall devote my comment to it.

K.B. considers the concept of 'natural position' from three perspectives: its methodological foundation; its theoretical content; and the nature of the relation between natural and non-natural phenomena.

A methodological opposition between classical and neoclassical approaches accounts for the presence of the concept in the former type of analysis and its absence in the latter. Classical analysis is indeed assumed to associate two types of analytical investigation: one has a general and purely logical character, and is developed inside the limits of 'the core of the price theory' (page 56); the other does not exhibit this generality, involves historical elements and takes place outside the 'core'. Now, 'natural' changes or changes in the 'natural' position of the system are identified with changes in the 'givens' of the 'core' (pages 165–66). Neo-classical analysis does not introduce such distinctions. Its 'reductionist approach' would have led it to replace 'assumptions . . . derived on the basis of historical observation' by 'postulates' (page 64) and then to render the theory 'increasingly rigid' and incapable of understanding the real world (page 55). In contrast, the possibility given to classical theory to develop a more flexible approach outside the core would induce its 'openness' (page 73).

The theoretical content of the notion of 'natural position' allows one to distinguish between 'persistent, 'temporary' and 'accidental' changes. The first correspond to modifications of the 'givens' of the 'core'. The second do not affect these 'givens' but can be analysed. The last are, in turn,' too fickle to be analysed at all' (page 66). Therefore, the differences between the three types of changes and, in particular, the isolation of changes in 'natural positions' are not so much rooted in 'temporal divisions' but rather lie in the 'nature' and 'effects' of economic modifications (pages 65–6).

As far as the question of the nature of the connection between natural and non-natural phenomena is concerned, K.B. supplies the significant example of the relation between 'natural' and 'market' prices. This relation is described as a 'tendency' for market prices to 'oscillate' around natural or production prices provided that 'observed techniques' become 'dominant', that profit and wage market rates tend to uniformity and that 'effectual demand' can be defined as 'a central or average position of social demand' (page 66).

Let us now consider the three perspectives specified by K.B.

I fully agree with the author when she emphasizes the fundamental opposition between the 'sequential separations' (page 56) of classical analysis, which allow one to deal successively with one economic phenomenon after the other, and the simultaneity of the determination of all the variables in neoclassical analysis (pages 56, 73). This, however, does not necessarily entail acceptance of the existence of a 'core' in classical theory and of a dichotomy between 'general' and 'concrete' approaches. In other words, noting that classical analysis includes more institutional or historical elements in its theoretical structure than neoclassical analysis does not prove this dichotomy. In my view, the origin of this fact lies not in methodology but in radical theoretical differences between classical and neoclassical conceptions.

The classical conception develops a production viewpoint according to which the main analytical scope is the explanation of the increase of social wealth in economies where the industrial division of labour is the simultaneous result of both technical specialization and private property.[1] In such a logical scheme, economic activities are assumed to take place in a *recursive and sequential order*. Every period is defined as 'an annual cycle of production with an annual market' (Sraffa, 1960, p. 10). As K.B. points out quite relevantly, 'self-reproduction' is more important and stringent than 'self-replacement' (page 75). Economies are here 'self-reproducible' in *two* fashions. In the production sphere, a surplus – i.e. an increase in material wealth – must be generated; this corresponds to Sraffa's 'annual production' and to the constraints of self-replacement'. In the market sphere, entrepreneurs are separated by the industrial division of labour and are compelled to convert commodities into cash, i.e. to transform an increase in material wealth into an increase in social wealth. This corresponds to Sraffa's 'annual market' as well as to K.B.'s 'circular view of the economic process' and renders economies 'self-reproducible'. Moreover, in a pure production scheme, agents are neither equal nor identical. They are distributed among social groups that play different but complementary parts in the production process. These correspond to a given social hierarchy that enforces an order of succession to the different economic activities (see Arena, 1982).

The neoclassical conception, in contrast, develops an exchange viewpoint according to which the main analytical purpose is the explanation of the optimal allocation of given resources between individual agents who can only be distinguished by their preference sets and their initial goods endowments (see Pasinetti, 1981b, 1986). In such a scheme, economic activities are assumed to be *simultaneous*, and the sole problem is to make the best social use of what is already available. This distribution involves equal and identical agents in an environment in which the only social hierarchy derives from individual choice. These features give the neoclassical approach its flavour of 'ahistoricity' (page 54).

The rise of neoclassicism may therefore be interpreted as a 'catallactic revolution'[2] inducing a new and different 'vision of economic life'[3] – neither more nor less 'abstract' than the previous one – rather than as the progressive replacement of empirically founded assumptions by general axioms. The Jevonian 'break' is here more significant than the Marshallian 'semblance of "continuity"' (page 55).

Such an interpretation of the opposition between classical and neoclassical theories obviously implies the negation of the distinction between an analytical 'core' and a non-analytical environment. In both traditions, all the problems dealt with are equally 'abstract' and have to be solved by means of economic theories, even if these are drastically different. The choice of 'givens' has therefore little to do with 'historical conditions' (page 80, n 30). It derives from the very logic of the particular theoretical problem one decides to cope with.

In turn, the resort to the notion of 'core' raises the critical problem of the definition and determination of 'givens'. It may be admitted that 'permanent' changes are those that affect the 'givens'. But how are we to choose between the 'givens' and the 'variables' if we are content with assigning a secondary role to temporal division and if we renounce purely logical criteria? One runs the risk of resorting to, at best, several arbitrary criteria (those relative to particular historical aspects of the problem), at worst, tautological criteria (what is 'given' is 'natural' and what is 'natural' is 'given').

On the other hand, how are 'permanent', 'temporary' and 'accidental' changes to be isolated? The example given by K.B., that of a Marxian '"short-period" realization crisis' (page 67) is very significant here. If such a crisis became cumulative, it would be interpreted as a long-period crisis, and if it affected market prices, as in the case of industrial' disproportionalities', we could hardly consider these price changes as 'accidental' and 'not suitable for exact analysis *of a general kind*'.

In contrast, if sequential determinations of variables are logically founded, it is then easier to solve problems in a progressive fashion by gradually introducing more and more complex theoretical problems[4] and also by isolating or combining different types of changes depending on the problem examined by the theory. In this framework, it is perhaps possible to avoid some of the imprecisions that derive from the concept of 'core' and the subsequent definition of a 'natural position', especially in the context of the gravitation problem of market prices around natural ones to which K.B. refers. For instance, 'dominant' and 'observed' techniques seem to be distinguished, by the author, depending on whether they are associated with natural or market prices. Some passages seem, however, to support the opposite idea.[5]

By the same token, the analysis of the relationship between natural and market prices is questionable. Natural prices are indeed defined simultaneously as theoretical variables (i.e. 'prices of production') and as empirical variables ('central prices around which "market prices" [i.e. 'actually observed prices'] oscillate') (pages 55–6). Market prices, in contrast, are purely empirical; they are not suitable for logical general analysis and give a good illustration of 'accidental' changes. Here the question is obviously that of two heterogeneous price concepts. It is not easy to conceive how it would be possible to characterize, to measure or, at least, to ascertain the existence of a 'tendency' or of 'oscillations'. Recourse to econometrics would lead to the usual problems of refutability and operational significance of empirical support, limitation of their observational bases as well as the econometric techniques employed to 'test' the validity of the theory (see page 77); besides, econometric studies could not integrate the characterization of 'prices of production' as theoretical variables. Recourse to analytical models would, in turn, exclude any reference to observed prices and, therefore, to market prices. From this viewpoint, nothing assures us of the theoretical or empirical existence of a tendency of market prices to oscillate around production prices. It is, however, impossible to consider this tendency as an obvious fact. As Steedman has indeed stressed, 'the moral' of the analysis of the 'gravitation' problem is 'simply that there is a genuine question at stake here, whose answer is not self-evident' (Steedman, 1984a, p. 137). Another solution is to consider both prices as theoretical in nature, but then it is necessary to deal with the gravitation problem in a purely analytical framework and its solution seems today far from being found.[6]

The foregoing suggests that my own reasons for upholding the thesis of Sraffa's return to classical theory might differ somewhat from those defended by K.B. I am, however, in strong sympathy with the author's project and conclusion and with her emphasis on what she identifies as the two important distinctive features of the classical structure, i.e. the separation between price and quantity determinations and the view of production as a circular process. These features indeed produce a clear distinction between classical and neoclassical approaches and so avoid some widespread interpretations of Sraffian theory. In this perspective, the present comment is nothing more than an invitation to the author to carry on with the rigorous, fruitful and substantial works she has already devoted herself to, thus providing us with inestimable help in rediscovering the classical roots of modern economic analysis.

Acknowledgements

I should like to thank the participants at the Sraffa conference for their comments, criticisms and suggestions and C. Dangel for her highly valuable help in the English translation of this comment. Remaining errors are mine alone.

Notes

1 This definition is very close to that of Pasinetti; see Pasinetti (1981b, Introduction) and (1986).
2 The expression is taken from Hicks (1976a), p. 212.
3 Ibid.; see also Baranzini and Scazzieri (1986a) and Quadrio-Curzio and Scazzieri (1986).
4 This is our understanding of the differences introduced by Pasinetti (1981b) between his 'short-run' model, his 'simple dynamic model' and his long-period 'general multi-sector dynamic model'.
In previous contributions (Arena, 1984; Arena and Froeschlé, 1986) I distinguished three types of economic changes on an 'analytical–temporal' basis: 'intra-periodic changes' inside the Sraffian 'annual cycle', deriving from the mere succession of economic operations (advances–production–market); 'inter-periodic changes' taking place at the beginning of each new period and corresponding to the 'annual' revisions of entrepreneurial decisions, parameters (methods of production and social demand pattern, essentially) being given; 'transperiodic changes', relative to modification of those parameters that constrain entrepreneurial behaviour. The three types of 'change' may be progressively combined in order to analyse their different and specific effects.
5 On pages 55–6, prices of production are associated with 'observed' methods of production; on page 66, with 'dominant' ones; on page 76, we read that 'Sraffa takes an "*observed*" system of relations as given' (emphasis added). On p. 353 of Bharadwaj (1986), the author uses the expression 'dominant observed methods of production'.
6 See Arena and Torre (1986) for a survey of the main attempts and problems.

Comment

Athanasios Asimakopulos
Montreal

Bharadwaj's treatment of Marshall's theory of prices is potentially misleading because it appears to identify 'market prices' in his analysis with 'short-period equilibrium prices'. Marshall, however, clearly distinguished between market prices and short-period equilibrium prices. He pointed to four 'classes' of price, with the first two being 'market' and 'short-period'.

> As regards *market* prices, Supply is taken to mean the stock of the commodity in question which is on hand, or at all events 'in sight'. As regards *normal* prices, when the term Normal is taken to relate to *short* periods of a few months or a year, Supply means broadly what can be produced for the price in question with the existing stock, of plant, personal and impersonal, in the given time.
>
> (Marshall, 1920, pp. 378–9)

The *normal* price in the short period is, of course, the short-period equilibrium price.

Bharadwaj's statement that Marshall's periods relate more to the distinction he makes in terms of what is held within the *ceteris paribus* clause rather than strictly to a duration of time or a chronological sequence of time does not do justice to the 'real' time dimension of Marshall's short period, a dimension that he himself drew attention to in the quotation given above. It is neoclassical textbook writers whose treatments give no recognition to the passage of time, who define 'short run' and 'long run' solely in terms of the variability of inputs. Marshall's short period – an interval of actual time 'of a few months or a year' – is the stage of Keynes's theory of employment and it provides a 'real'-time setting for that theory.

Comment

Harvey Gram
New York

Professor Bharadwaj's thesis is that the foundations of neoclassical theory have been developed from a narrow base: the classical theory of rent. Thus, the whole complex structure of general equilibrium theory is seen as a generalization of one basic principle: substitution in response to (hypothetical) changes in relative prices. She makes clear how this principle, the meaning of competition and the requirements of equilibrium have been made to fit the logical demands of the neoclassical theory of simultaneous price and quantity determination. A curious aspect of this development was the introduction of postulated symmetries between production and consumption, symmetries that never occurred to the classical economists. Odder still, and certainly more far-reaching in its implications, was a reversal in the classical treatment of time. In neoclassical theory, equilibrium actions are predicated upon the consequences of future events while the history of past actions is relegated to the limbo of 'initial conditions'. This leads to a rejection of the long-period method of analysis and therefore of the classical notion of a *tendency* toward the formation of *natural prices*.

An *intertemporal* equilibrium of supply and demand provides the most relevant starting point in drawing a contrast between neoclassical theory and the classical theory that Sraffa helped to revive. Irving Fisher played a prominent role in extending the concept of a balance of market forces to encompass future time. He denied the importance of the classical notion of cost of production, although he retained the idea of a long-run tendency toward equalization of the rate of profit (Garegnani, 1976b). Bharadwaj quotes the remarkable passage from *The Nature of Capital and Time*: 'When prices find their normal level at which costs plus interest are covered, it is not because the past costs of production have determined prices in advance, but because the sellers have been good speculators as to what prices would be' (Fisher, 1906, p. 188). Thorstein Veblen also remarked that 'the relation sought by [neoclassical] theory among the facts with which it is occupied is the control exercised by future (apprehended) events over present conduct. Current phenomena are dealt with as conditioned by their future consequences. . . .' (Mitchell, 1947, p. 158).

The Fisherian tradition inspired a large literature on optimal growth models. These rigorous formulations revealed an important feature of intertemporal equilibrium models, namely, the saddle-point property of the long-run solution (see Bruno, 1967). A saddle-point is not a centre of gravity relative to which prices and quantities fluctuate. Indeed, it can be reached only by *aiming* the system in a precise way. Initial conditions must therefore be *chosen* to make continuous market clearing consistent with an eventual long-period equilibrium. As Bharadwaj remarks, the assumptions of the theory are 'not prompted by practical observation but by theoretical necessity'.

Neoclassical theorists are ambivalent about the difficulties that follow from attempts to extend the notion of equilibrium to include the influence of future events over present conduct. Thus, Samuelson uses a metaphor to describe convergence to a saddle-point. He asks us to regard the rider of a bicycle as maintaining, perhaps unconsciously, the equilibrium of his vehicle. 'The rider . . . is the bulk of the market, a somewhat mystical concept to be sure – like its analogue, the well-informed speculator who gets his way in the end because his way is the correctly discerned way of the future; and those who think differently are bankrupted by their bets against (him and) the future' (Samuelson, 1967, p. 229). But Samuelson doubts the relevance of his metaphor: 'It is easier to identify the well-informed speculator *ex post* than *ex ante*, and the image can easily dissolve into an empty tautology.' He then retreats to a position that amounts to little more than an act of faith reminiscent of Irving Fisher's statement to the effect that, in equilibrium, sellers must have *been* good speculators: '[W]hen the system is led too far from the balanced-growth configuration, some entrepreneurs begin to foresee the shoals ahead . . . and they act to push the system back toward the turnpike.' This act of faith appears to lead Samuelson to reject the whole idea of an equilibrium path: 'Even if there is something valid in this heuristic reasoning, one must admit that the system need not – and, generally, will not – move from its present position to the golden age in the most efficient way: it will hare after false goals, get detoured, and begin to be corrected only after it has erred' (Samuelson, 1967, p. 229; cf. Joan Robinson, 1962d, pp. 23–9).

Like many of the early neoclassical economists, Samuelson regards equilibrium as a position (or path) around which the economy fluctuates. Thus, he readily admits the limited value of models whose coherence depends on the unexplained dominance of speculators with correct foresight. This analytical inadequacy arises, as Bharadwaj points out in other contexts, 'from the *specific structure* of the theory of value and distribution based on demand and supply'.

The unsatisfactory state of general equilibrium theory (of which optimal growth models constitute a sub-theory) is all the more remarkable for its enduring appeal. There appears to be a consensus among general equilibrium theorists that their framework of analysis remains the standard for acceptable theorizing (see Hahn, 1984b, p. 44). The Arrow–Debreu formulation, with a complete set of markets for all goods and services contingent upon all possible future states-of-the-world, is clearly regarded as unattainable. This is granted on theoretical grounds, not only because markets are costly to form, but also because some markets cannot exist if states-of-the-world depend upon actions taken. And yet, the general equilibrium ideal remains a central conception relative to which new ideas – even the Keynesian theory of effective demand – must ultimately bear a logical consistency.

The enervating effect of the general equilibrium standard is commented on by Kaldor (1972, p. 1238). It is evident in recent work on *temporary* general equilibrium theory (Hicks, 1946). This class of supply and demand models is intended to provide general equilibrium foundations for Keynesian theory. Markets are assumed to exist for all currently available goods and services, but not for goods and services that become available in the future. Current prices and expectations of future prices must be determined simultaneously in such a way that, although contingent future actions need not be mutually consistent, the actions taken in each time period are, in fact, market-clearing. The lack of co-ordination of plans for the future has been regarded by some as the distinguishing feature of Keynesian economics. But in the class of competitive temporary general equilibrium models, there is no *involuntary* unemployment. Rather, the theory emphasizes the logical difficulties created for a supply and demand model by the possibility of bankruptcy. Even when initial debts do not exist, some agents may perceive the possibility of unlimited profitable arbitrage. This is inconsistent with equilibrium because it leads to the taking of unlimited forward positions, and hence to bankruptcy. In dealing with this problem theorists have shown that 'a necessary and sufficient condition for the existence of [a sequence of temporary equilibria] is the occurrence of some agreement among agents about future spot prices' (Grandmont, 1982, p. 892). The need to postulate such agreement illustrates what Kaldor refers to as 'the increasing (*not* diminishing) arbitrariness of [the] basic assumptions [of neoclassical theory]' (Kaldor, 1972, p. 1238; cited by Bharadwaj, page 77, n 1).

Interpretations of temporary general equilibrium models bring out a further aspect of Bharadwaj's thesis, namely, the central importance of appropriately large substitution effects 'requiring a hypothetical "change" in the situation'. Bharadwaj notes the shift of emphasis from the *extensive* margin in agriculture – the central focus of the classical theory of rent – to the *intensive* margin of the neoclassics. Wicksteed went so far as to regard the extensive margin as a spurious case of marginal analysis. Defined as a *hypothetical* response to an *expected* price change, the intertemporal substitution effect takes the argument a stage further – at a point in time one can observe neither the dependent nor the independent variable. Nevertheless, Grandmont has argued that the existence of a sequence of temporary general equilibria depends on the dominance of intertemporal substitution effects over those wealth effects that may be associated with expected price changes (Grandmont, 1983, ch. 1). Even Hicks's *unitary elasticity of expectation* (Hicks, 1946, p. 205) may not be sufficient to guarantee an equilibrium.

The difficulties created by the need simultaneously to determine current prices and expectations of future prices have led theorists recently to embrace a remarkable expedient: the hypothesis of rational expectations. This is both the apotheosis and the nemesis of neoclassical theory. On the one hand, rational expectations is a logical development, applying the rationality principle to the formation of expectations as well as to the actions taken in response to current prices. It solves at a stroke the problem of ' "too many" potential disequilibria' (Fitoussi, 1983, p. 19). These are sequences of market-clearing prices that eventually lead to meaningless solutions, as in optimal growth models where initial conditions, if not restricted, lead prices and quantities away from their long-run equilibrium values. On the other hand, the rational expectations hypothesis, intended as a major theoretical advance, rules out disequilibria *even in the short run*: to allow *any* time for adjustment to unforeseen events is to allow *too much* time. Thus, it 'amounts to a steady-state equilibrium condition: expectations are rational when they lead to agents taking actions whose results do not contradict their expectatioins' (Fitoussi, 1983, p. 20). Within a stochastic framework of analysis, the rational expectations hypothesis serves the function of the mysterious bicycle rider invoked by Samuelson (1967), and is a further instance of 'the eroding process tending to narrow down the static economics, taking the life out of it and departing widely from the intentions of its authors' (Harrod, 1948).

Of course, the rational expectations hypothesis is not universally accepted. It is criticized by Axel Leijonhufvud who suggests that, under the hypothesis, 'fully informed agents have no need for a price mechanism to inform them about what is happening. Prices merely reflect what they already know' (Leijonhufvud, 1983, p. 80). And Frank Hahn contends that the hypothesis leaves unexplained the process by which agents learn about the stable elements in their environment (Hahn, 1984b, p. 82). However, the alternative ways of dealing with the problem posed by the need to solve simultaneously for market-clearing prices and their expectations are only partially satisfactory. Expectations can be taken as fixed data in each market period, shifting between periods in some exogenously specified manner. Such a procedure is *ad hoc* to some extent, for any model incorporating such rigid rules may be said to 'depend too much on the past and not enough on the future' (Fitoussi, 1983, p. 19). Alternatively, current prices can be fixed (Hicks, 1965, ch. 7). This approach has received much attention under the heading of temporary general equilibrium with *quantity rationing*, a question-begging label since, for the most part, the rationing schemes that determine how the short side of each market is allocated are insufficiently discussed. In Malinvaud (1977), for example, it is simply assumed that the government is served first when there is excess demand in the goods market. The theory also leaves unexplained the movement of prices between periods. This, of course, is recognized as one of its failings.

The intractable problems created by the effort to extend into the unobservable future the terrain over which the forces of supply and demand hold sway are somehow set aside as questions that will ultimately yield to a more sophisticated analysis. Meanwhile, the existence of an alternative framework of thought based on a revival of classical theory is denied. Certainly the critics of neoclassical theory committed a great heresy during the capital theory debate by proving false the analytical basis for the principle of substitution in so far as it affects the demand for capital and labour. Those who would defend neoclassical theory against any attack on its logical structure fail to see the significance of this result. This is because they have given up any causal claims for general equilibrium theory (Hahn, 1984b, p. 47), thus abandoning the traditional notion of equilibrium as a centre of gravity relative to which prices and quantities fluctuate. The revival of interest in classical theory is, in part, a revival of interest in this old-fashioned idea. It is also a revival of interest in a broadly based theory that does not presume to find the essence of all market phenomena in terms of the single principle of substitution.

Bharadwaj points out that a Sraffa model in which the rate of profit, the composition of output and the technique of production are all given is intended to be only one part of a general framework of analysis. It provides a theory of prices for final goods, produced inputs and non-produced factors consistent with the competitive drive towards equalization of the rate of profit. While not denying systematic links between prices and quantities, classical theory *does* deny the claim that substitution in response to relative price movements should be the overriding consideration in all economic analysis. Without committing itself to such a universal principle, and without the need to express all economic phenomena in terms of a market-clearing price vector, classical theory can more easily introduce an awareness of history into its conceptual apparatus. The social determinants of income distribution, the concept of effective demand and the independently evolving processes of technological and organizational change thus gain a hearing. Consideration of these matters neither over-determines the theory, which is constructed to have the appropriate degrees of freedom, nor contradicts the logic of the theory, as so often happens in attempts to incorporate Keynesian ideas and historical processes into the neoclassical framework.

Developments in neoclassical theory, however complex, are predictable. Like the works of an artisan, they conform to a paradigm and are reducible to re-expressions of a few basic ideas. The future course of developments in classical theory is more difficult to ascertain. Having adopted a theory that *requires* independent explanations of income distribution, the composition of output and the technology of production, followers of the classical tradition face the challenging task of resuscitating what Kaldor (1972, p. 1240) has described as the *creative* (as opposed to the *allocative*) functions of markets. Success in this endeavour will open up new and fruitful avenues of research, leaving behind the blind alleys that have come increasingly to characterize neoclassical economics.

Reply

I should like to thank Harvey Gram and Richard Arena for the care with which they have read my paper and offered their useful reactions. Professor Gram has presented my main position lucidly and accurately and has extended the arguments further to a critical consideration of intertemporal analysis in general equilibrium. I agree with his perception and standpoint on the theoretical developments and share with him the hope that the future course of development in classical theory will open up new and fruitful avenues of research.

Professor Arena's comment raises many difficult questions. However, many of his differences with me arise from a misreading of my critique, which is based on a comparison of the structures of the classical and neoclassical theories. Arena opens his comment by observing that I attach 'substantial importance' to the notion of . . . 'natural position' and that I see its *existence* in the classical theory as constituting a major distinguishing feature. He therefore proceeds to devote his comments entirely to that notion. Further he states his own position to be that the difference between classical and neoclassical economics lies not in the methodology but in radical theoretical differences. Arena's characterization of my position and of the difference between us rests on an important misunderstanding: it is nowhere suggested by me that the *existence* of the natural position in the classical theory is its distinctive 'methodological' feature; on the contrary, I explicitly state: 'While, strictly speaking, "equilibrium" is a misnomer in the context of classical theory, the notion of a "long period" or "natural" position as an organizing concept is used in classical theory as much as in neoclassical theory' (p. 65). I also say: 'With a different theory explaining value and distribution, the explanation of the "long-period position" as "long-period equilibrium" changed' (p. 67). Somewhat surprisingly, Arena appears not to notice when I observe, by way of criticism, that Hicks bypasses the logical difficulties created for the neoclassical theory by shifting the entire onus onto *method* and that I emphasize in various places that my own attempt is to trace the differences in perspective of the two theories to differences in their *theoretical* structures. Thus my critique is based not so much on differences in *methodology* as on those in the *theory*.

Having displaced the focus of my analysis, Arena interprets my discussion of the 'natural position' as carried out from 'three perspectives': 'its methodological foundation; its theoretical content; and the nature of the relation between natural and non-natural phenomena.' Before I counter Arena's arguments presented in the above sequence, I would like to make it clear that I do not consider the 'natural position' as a 'phenomenon', nor do I recognize, in opposition, 'non-natural phenomena'. A natural position is an analytical abstraction drawn on the basis of observation and thus, while founded on concrete observation, need not itself have a concrete existence.

Arena also gives an erroneous reading of my 'methodological foundation' of the natural position. I have already denied his interpretation that the presence of the natural position in the classical theory and its absence in the neoclassical amounts to a 'methodological opposition' between the theories. Further I *do not* maintain, as Arena ascribes to me, that the classical analysis involves 'two types of analytical investigation: one has a general and purely logical character, and is developed inside the limits of "the core of the price theory"; the other does not exhibit this generality, involves historical elements and takes place outside the "core"'. However, Arena fully agrees with me when he finds me emphasizing 'the fundamental opposition between the 'sequential separations' of classical analysis . . . and the simultaneity of the determination of all the variables in neoclassical analysis'. He further observes: 'This, however, does not necessarily entail acceptance of the existence of a "core" in classical theory and of a dichotomy between "general" and "concrete" approaches.' Arena grossly misreads me when he attributes this 'methodological dichotomy' to me. First, the sequential separateness needs to be understood as *not* separating the *different types of analytical investigations*. Prices and quantities are determined separately in the sense, to quote from my paper (page 74), that 'the relationship between prices and quantities is asymmetrical in the force of their mutual determination, so that the relative prices of commodities may be derived uniquely on the basis of given quantities. . . . The major influences on the determination of investment, distribution and technical change [in classical theory] are not confined to relative prices alone; the real dynamics of economies is generated through direct interactions among these.' This is not to suggest that the determination of prices from within the core has a general and purely logical character while the determination of quantities, which involves historical elements, is not 'logical' or 'analytical'. The latter is as much a logical and analytical investigation as is the former; however, the theory explaining 'quantities' and their dynamics is 'open' to capture (in its abstraction, and in contrast to the neoclassical theory) forms and mechanisms of their interaction that are historically specific to economies and their stage of development. Thus no methodological dichotomy is maintained by me in terms of the 'core' and the 'outside'. The distinction implies no more than the 'separation', in the sense above, of the explanation of prices and quantities.

As to the theoretical content of the 'natural position', Arena is mistaken about the interpretation of 'givens'. In a circular view of the production process (which both of us agree is indeed a most important characteristic of the classical approach), the 'givens' are also historically produced. And, in this sense, 'historical elements' enter the 'core' as well as the 'outside'. These are provisionally 'given', meaning that they are taken at their 'average' or 'central' values. Thus it is clear that I do not propose a distinction between the 'analytical core' and the 'non-analytical environment'. The 'givens' of the core are related to and originate in history, as are the elements 'outside the core'. I have also not proposed a distinction between theories on the grounds of greater or less abstraction. I am rather surprised that Arena should form this impression. At the very beginning of my paper and in note 1, I differentiate my critique from others in arguing that the 'lack of relevance' or the ahistoricity that appear to plague the marginalist theory arise from the specific structure of the theory and that it is the requirement of maintaining logical consistency within the structure that has necessitated the imposition of more and more restrictive assumptions.

Arena raises the problem of definitions and determination of the 'givens'. What is to be 'given' is defined by the theory. In the classical structure of causal relations, the basic elements determining prices and distribution are effectual demand, methods of production and wages at their 'natural' level. The determination of these 'givens' entails a conception of a system of social production that reproduces the production, exchange and distributive relations under which surplus is produced, exchanged, appropriated and distributed. The classical theorists' vision consisted in their belief that such a system could be conceptualized on the basis of observation. A distinction was then made by the classical authors among those forces of change that affect these structural elements and those that do not, and between those that affect these elements persistently enough to displace one or more of them from their average value(s) and those that do not. For example, a change in the method of production or in the quantity supplied of a 'luxury' good (a 'non-basic' in Sraffa's sense) would not affect the wage–profit relation (or the prices of the basics). Even in the case of a prime wage good like corn, if an accidental small shortfall in supply occurs it may not generate a change in the natural position if the methods of production do not permanently change. Ricardo, on the other hand, analysed the effects of restrictions on corn imports – precisely in terms of their persistent consequences. A new method of production may yield 'super profits' as analysed by Marx and affect the long-term relations of the system only when, under competition, it emerges as 'dominant' – to the extent that it is reproducible and eventually displaces the inferior methods. If it is not reproducible – or only to a limited extent – the method would earn 'quasi-rents'.

I do not rule out the 'short-period' analysis either – an example that Arena quotes from my paper being the short-period realization crisis. Nor do I rule out the possibility that a short-period phenomenon may develop into a change in the long-period situation. I agree with Arena that the possibility of sequential determination of variables may here prove an advantage. The interaction between the 'short' and the 'long' (which has appeared in the literature as discussions on relations between the 'trend' and 'cyclical fluctuations') not only is difficult but would have to be structured for specific situations and problematics.

Arena's last question about the relation between natural and market prices has, to my mind, no clear and definitive resolution. However, the interpretation that the oscillations of 'market' prices around the natural price can only be analytically explained in terms of systematic rules of price–quantity responses akin to the supply and demand relations seems to be misleading. It would be imposing an abstract structure of definite relations on a phenomenon that the classical writers evidently saw as a rough and ready outcome of 'competition'. I have already referred to the much more flexible notion of competition in the classical theory, which mainly allowed for mobility of capital and labour. The tendency of market prices to hover around the natural price appears to be based on the presupposition that, for each system of production (characterized by certain modes of production and appropriation of surplus and corresponding rules of surplus distribution and exchange), there exists a set of exchange values compatible with the reproduction of these conditions of production, distribution and exchange. Natural prices are not empirical, in the sense of being defined as statistical averages of market prices. (Arena also appears to agree with this.) However, when considered analytically, they do not necessarily lose their connection with observation, as he appears to argue on the basis of an analytical/empirical dichotomy. For, the system of production (which yields 'natural prices' as consistent conditions of exchange for the system's reproduction) is construed on the basis of historical observations, which reveal the more regular and permanent relations. (The need to do so, or its possibility, is not an idiosyncracy of the classical theory. Modern planning models or macroeconomic representations construct input–output systems and other transaction matrices on some such hypothesis of the possibility of identifying regularities.)

The classical theorists do talk about oscillations of market prices around natural prices and do suggest that the market price of a commodity deviates when the actual demands and supplies deviate from effectual demand. Some peculiarities of their discussion differentiate their analysis from the marginalist demand and supply analysis and must be taken into account. First, 'effectual demand' is a position (a vector) of the average level and composition of social demand. Whenever supplies exceed (or fall short of) effectual demand in any commodity, there is supposed to be a tendency for the market price to fall below (or above) the natural price. The force of competition induces adjustments of supplies to demand. However, the adjustment is not explained in terms of substitution in consumption and production being induced by relative prices, as is done in the supply and demand theory. No such mechanism of quantity adjustment is envisaged. In fact, John Stuart Mill even discusses situations where producers, perceiving shortages and excesses in the market, adjust their supplies without having to respond to or waiting for the price signals to arrive. This could be in expectation of a change in price; but such a change in fact may not even materialize. Further, it appears that, with the notion of 'effectual demand', it is not 'relative demand' but absolute shortfalls or excesses that appear to be relevant for the producer's supply adjustment. Thus we need to be wary about applying the logic of the price–quantity variations of neoclassical theory to the analysis of the oscillations of market prices around the natural price. The question of how precisely to relate market prices to natural prices and, in general, how to distinguish between transitory variations and variations in natural values, remains open and calls for more research.

Professor Asimakopulos in his two brief points has raised some questions that are significant for my purpose of distinguishing theories on the basis of their structure and noting differences in the scope and context that particular concepts acquire in their particular context. Asimakopulos is correct in stating that Marshall clearly distinguishes between 'market' and 'short-period' normal prices. This is evident from his four-fold classification of prices, given on page 68 above. A point I perhaps dwelt upon insufficiently is that Marshall's distinction between 'market' and 'normal' prices in his earlier works (particularly in *The Economics of Industry*, 1881, written with Mrs Mary Marshall) remained closer to the classical dichotomy between 'market' and 'natural' values. In his subsequent work, particularly in the *Principles* (which ran to eight editions between 1890 and 1920), the distinction underwent an alteration of some analytical consequence. In the *Principles*, he stressed 'the principle of continuity' in analysing 'the consequences of the element of time' and offered a periodization scheme – the four-fold division. I shall argue that Marshall attempted to use this relativist periodization to translate his analytical conviction that the Fundamental Idea of the equilibrium of demand and supply 'ran through all the frames' of value and distribution as well as investment and accumulation.

The distinction in classical theory between 'market' and 'natural' values rested on a qualitative distinction among the causal forces – 'accidental', 'temporary' and permanent or persistent – which was recognized by their influence on the basic constituents of the 'natural position' (namely, the level and composition of effectual demand, the dominant methods of production and the division of the surplus; see pp. 65–6 above). In his early writings, Marshall was inclined to stress the distinction, in qualitative terms, of the different causal factors:

> Normal results are those which would be brought about by competition; if it acted freely, and always had time to cause those effects which it has a tendency to cause. Market results are those which actually are brought about by the complex social and economic forces of the world in which we live.
>
> (Marshall and Marshall, 1881, p. 148)

Market values were discussed in that work mainly as arising in situations where competition is kept in abeyance, e.g. owing to combinations among buyers or sellers or owing to the prevalence of ignorance, inertia caused by rigid customs, etc., limiting the free action or choices of individuals. In addition, market prices were discussed in the context of supply factors not adjusting fully to changing conditions of demand. The latter featured prominently in the *Principles*. Marshall, like the classicals, stressed the significance of analysing 'normal action':

> The normal action of economic forces is hindered, or even overridden, but never destroyed by friction, by *combination* or by those passive events which exercise a restless influence on Market Values.
>
> (1920, p. vii)

Marshall's reluctance 'to apply curves or mathematics to market values' is evident throughout, although it is somewhat muted in the later editions of the *Principles* (see his letter to Edgeworth and the passage from the *Principles* quoted in n 29, p. 80 above; see also Marshall's letter to J. N. Keynes quoted in Bharadwaj, 1978a, pp. 260 and 265). In the first edition of the *Principles* (1890, p. 423n) he began with the suggestion that the diagram pertaining to the stable long-period equilibrium 'may be adapted to represent the oscillations of a market price' but added, 'But the causes which determine supply price for market bargainings are fundamentally different from those that determine normal supply price, whether for long periods or short. . . .' This footnote was dropped from subsequent editions of the *Principles*.

In the *Principles*, the distinction between 'market' and 'normal' prices was somewhat attenuated:

> Market prices and normal prices are alike brought about by a multitude of influences, of which some rest on a moral basis and some on physical; of which some are competitive and some are not. It is to the persistence of the influences considered and the time allowed for them to work out their effects that we refer when contrasting Market and natural price and again when contrasting the narrower and broader use of the term normal price. (1920, pp. 347–8)

What is evident is that Marshall had identified the uniformity of influences – namely the 'supply' and 'demand' forces – active in all cases (market, short-period normal, long-period normal, and secular; see 1920, pp. 378–9). They were differentiated on the basis of their 'persistence' and the time period allowed for their effects to be worked out. He insisted, however, that 'there is no impassable gulf between the two ['normal' values and current or market values]; they shade into one another by continuous gradations. For the element of time, which is in the centre of the chief difficulty of almost every economic problem, is itself absolutely continuous; nature knows no absolute partition of time into long period and short' (1920, p. vii). It may be noted here, however, that the 'continuity' that Marshall has in mind is not one pertaining only to 'time' in Nature, but is also the *analytical continuity* of superimposing a uniform analytical structure on all these cases.

Marshall proceeded to characterize and classify the causal forces on the 'demand' and the 'supply' side. On the demand side, 'the element of time' introduced difficulties of a short- and long-term nature: the purchasing power of money changes continuously; changes in general prosperity and total purchasing power influence 'normal' demand; changes occur due to the gradual growth of population; and changes occur in tastes and habits. Different time durations are required for these causes to produce their full effects. What is remarkable is that the illustrations of changes in demand that Marshall discusses are reminiscent of the classical discussions on the formation of effectual demand – its level and composition and the changes in it. These have very little to do with the sort of changes in (relative) demand that form the theory of consumption on which Marshall's demand curves are based.[1] The forces influencing demand mentioned by Marshall fall into what he originally described as the analysis of wants and activities, and their classification into short- and long-period causes appears problematic.

On the supply side, the distinction between short and long periods appeared much more practical and useful, being drawn on the basis of the material conditions of the organization of supply and centring on the kinds of investment decisions producers make. The influences acting on the supply side are here classified mainly on the basis of the elasticity of supply or the ease with which supply can accommodate changing conditions of demand. Thus, in the very short run, the stock in hand constitutes the entire supply. Short-run adjustments occur through the utilization of existing capacity. In the long run, the conditions of supply adjust in various ways: through creating new capacity, through technical changes, and, in the even longer run, the population, skills, information and knowledge themselves adapt.

Although Marshall classifies markets with regard not only to different causes but also to the time elapsing between the cause and effects, his analysis cannot be taken as occurring in 'real time', as Asimakopulos suggests in his comment. The first difficulty that Marshall faces is one shared perhaps by all dynamic analysis. In Marshall's own words:

> There are always occurring disturbing causes whose effects are commingled with, and cannot be easily separated from, the effects of that particular cause which we desire to isolate. The difficulty is aggravated by the fact that in economics the full effects of a cause seldom come at once, but often spread themselves out after it has ceased to exist.
>
> (1920, p. 109)

The analytical method that Marshall adopted was one of 'partial analysis', moving from simpler to more complex situations, working through shorter chains of reasonings. It was thus he hoped to work through particular cause–effect relations to the more general, through the analysis of particular commodity markets to the more interdependent systems and finally towards the problem of distribution and accumulation. The method was one of 'breaking up a complex question, studying one bit at a time, and at last combining [his] partial solutions into a more or less complete solution of the whole riddle' (1920, p. 336).

However, the method had its difficulties. In the real world, 'changes in the value of production, in its methods and its costs are ever mutually modifying one another; they are always affecting and being affected by the character and extent of demand. Further, all these mutual influences take time to work themselves out and, as a rule, no two influences move at equal pace' (p. 336).

The difficulty was not only in identifying and isolating the specific cause–effect relation in an interdependent system with mutual interactions but also in tracing the effects of a cause as a sequence through time. Marshall – as also Keynes – did not introduce the element of time (the short–long period division) for any analysis of sequential processes. The effective use of periodization has been made where the characterization represents certain conditions of production and investment. The 'short period', for example, refers to the existing capacity, while in the long period the installed capacity may be changed.

In the classical theory, too, it would appear, recognition of the complexity and variety of the causal mechanisms that mutually connect the social output, demand, methods of production and the division of the surplus prompted the separation of the determination of prices and of quantities. Thus the classical writers, Marx in particular (as well as Keynes later) have used distinctions akin to the Marshallian short and long period to analyse the basis and consequence of investment decisions. Classical writers also fruitfully used the method of analysing particular causal sequences, isolating 'persistent' from 'temporary' causes and effects.

Marshall, however, believed essentially in *analytical continuity*, in that he believed that the 'generating theory of the equilibrium of demand and supply is the Fundamental Idea running through the frames of all the various parts of the central problem of Distribution and Exchange' (Preface to the first edition of *Principles*, 1890). The 'element of time' was used by Marshall, as is discussed in my paper (pp. 69–70 above), to interpret and limit the classical cost of production doctrine to very long-run situations where the influence of demand was annulled, to stretch the theory of price formation of a particular commodity to the pricing of factors (i.e. to 'distribution') and to argue for a symmetry among factors of production.

Marshall's periodization was, and is, a useful device to the extent that it attempted to clarify analytically different causal forces and their influences that interconnect quantity and price changes. The device is particularly useful in the analysis of investment, as in Keynes. However, his own use of the device in the supply and demand theoretical framework was bound to lead to logical hurdles. Here again, it is the instance of a flawed theory rather than of the method.

Note

1 The identification of the 'role of demand' with the demand functions premised on the marginalist theory of consumer choice has misled some to interpret the classical theory as a cost of production theory that ignores or undermines the role of demand. Marshall himself was responsible for popularizing such a reading of the classical theory. This misidentification has also led some modern economists to treat the classical theory of prices as connoting an invariance with respect to changes in demand and therefore they see it as a limiting case of the general equilibrium theory. However, the classical theory presumes/connotes no such invariance if 'changes in demand' are interpreted, as they should be, as changes in effectual demand.

4
Ricardo and Sraffa

John R. Hicks[†]
Oxford

In 1984 I wrote a paper on 'Sraffa and Ricardo', which has appeared in a collection of essays, *The Legacy of Ricardo*, edited by Caravale (1985). That paper is more about Ricardo than about Sraffa. If fate had been kinder, I should like now to have presented a companion piece 'From Ricardo to Sraffa – and perhaps beyond'. But as it is, I am not able to do more than give a sketch of what I should like to have said.

In that former paper, I distinguished three differences between Sraffa's model and Ricardo's. First, Ricardo's is dynamic, at least in the elementary sense that he is concerned with directions of change; Sraffa's is deliberately static. As he says himself in his Preface, 'no changes in output are considered'.

Second, Sraffa's industries are fully interlinked, as is indicated in the title of his book. I don't believe that that is true of Ricardo. I believe that he thought of his 'industries' as vertically integrated. Their only inputs are labour (and in some cases, land); their only outputs are finished (consumable) products. That is why there is no *basic – non-basic* distinction in Ricardo. In mathematical terms, Sraffa's matrix of coefficients is indecomposable; Ricardo's is completely decomposed.[1]

Third, Ricardo's model is what would later have been called a perfect competition model. In equilibrium (and he usually thinks of his system as being in equilibrium), prices are equal to marginal costs. In his agricultural sector, marginal cost rises with output; thus, with given wages and given rate of profit, price rises with output. In non-agricultural industries, there are constant costs in terms of factors (the increasing returns that were so important to Smith were notoriously neglected by Ricardo). So marginal costs in these industries are equal to average costs. There is no reason why a perfectly competitive equilibrium, in such an economy, should not exist.

The Sraffa model, as I see it, was meant to be what Ricardo's would have become if one rejected the empirical assumptions of Ricardo. Sraffa did not want to have his non-agricultural industries producing at constant costs. He would have them producing at diminishing cost (as in Marshall). So his model

† Deceased.

cannot be in perfectly competitive equilibrium like Ricardo's. Prices are equal to average costs, including profit. Just how the (apparently uniform) rate of profit in Sraffa's system is established is rather a mystery. One must, I suppose, think of it as a mark-up, established by convention.

The interlinkages, which he proceeds to introduce, must presumably be supposed to attend to the agricultural, as well as to the other sector. So he does away with Ricardo's sectoral division. Prices, in all sectors, are formed in the same way.

Diminishing returns, in the agricultural sector, then become hard to deal with; but increasing returns, throughout, are hard to deal with. So now one sees why he had to insist on 'no changes in output being considered'. He is unable to deal with changes in output, which call forth either increasing or diminishing returns. So the only question he can deal with is 'if the (conventional) rate of profit were different, other things being equal, what would be the effect on wages?' For that he gets what is substantially Ricardo's answer; but Ricardo, at that point, did not have to stop.

I am myself most unwilling to stop. I want to go on to ask further questions. I want to set the model to work. I want to enquire how it is to respond to 'exogenous' changes.

In fact, at about the time Sraffa's book came out, I was myself engaged in the construction of a model that is formally quite similar to his. It is presented in chapters 12–16 of my *Capital and Growth* (1965). As a matter of presentation, I began with the simplest case, of one capital good and one consumption good (in his terminology, one basic and one non-basic); but I did go on (in my chapter 14) to generalize to many capital goods – a structure of 'basics' which resembles Sraffa's quite closely, and for which I did in fact derive a number of similar properties. So far, then, there was full agreement between us.

I was, however, anxious to place my model *in time* (like Ricardo, but unlike Sraffa). A model in which outputs are unchanging over time, from period to period, can only be a model of a stationary state. So Sraffa's appears as the stationary case of my model. I was not content with that. But once one leaves the stationary state, one is confronted with the scale economy trouble, which prevented Sraffa from pushing further on. I preferred to see what happened if, at the next stage of the argument, one abstracted from those economies, so that a steady state, maintaining proportions with a positive growth rate, would be possible. That state could maintain relations between prices, essentially the same as Sraffa's; there would be no reason why relative prices should change over time. Nor would there be any reason why prices should be different, as between one steady state and another, if the only difference between the economies was a difference in growth rate.

Relative quantities (of capital goods or basics) would also remain unchanged over time; but they would depend on the growth rate. If, as between the two steady states, the growth rate was different, relative quantities would be different.

I do not attach much importance to that steady-state theory, in itself; but I found that it throws up questions that are indeed important. How could one get from one such steady state to another? This I called the problem of '*traverse*' (see chapter 13 of my *Methods of Dynamic Economics*, 1985b).

I began by directing my attention to the case where the change was simply a change in the 'desired' growth rate. I defined this as the change that is needed to absorb a *given* labour supply, which, in a steady state, will be increasing at a given constant rate. Up to time 0, the system has been in a steady state, at growth rate g_0; but at time 0, the growth rate of labour increases, to g_1. Already, in the next period, there is more labour to be absorbed; and it is an excess that will go on increasing, if nothing is done, from period to period. Is there anything that can be done? Is there any way in which the system can get into a new equilibrium?

There is in principle a steady-state equilibrium, with the same coefficients as before; but how is it to be reached? The structure of the economy at time 0 is adjusted to g_0; for an equilibrium at g_1, things are in the wrong proportions. So if there were to be an immediate shift to production on a plan that was appropriate to g_1, not all of the (intermediate) goods that at that time were available could be fully employed. One may accept that it would usually be the case that a vector of goods appropriate to g_1 could be found *within* the existing vector; but to start from that on a path appropriate to g_1 would leave many of the existing goods underemployed – and in all probability labour also underemployed. And the unemployment of labour would go on, indefinitely, along the new growth path.

There is no way out of this by delaying the change-over. The same dilemma will arise whenever the change takes place.

Is there any other way out? I suppose that a 'neo-classical' economist, confronted with this problem, would have been sure of finding a solution through adjustment of prices. He would say that when a 'basic' good became surplus, its price would fall; that would make it profitable to change techniques, in the direction of making more use of the surplus products. That of course is the kind of adjustment that Ricardo himself had in mind for this agricultural sector. 'Neo-classical' economics, as is evident from its history (witness Longfield and Thünen), was an extension to the whole economy of the analysis that Ricardo had used for his agricultural sector. But that required to be justified.

For it might have been noticed – what is very clear in the model as just set out – that prices are due to be restored to what they were, when the new equilibrium is reached – if it is. So what is needed for the 'neo-classical' adjustment to be possible is that there should be a rapid adjustment of coefficients (of 'technique') in response to a *temporary* variation of prices. That is asking a good deal. I would accept that there may be sectors (such as Ricardo's agriculture) where such adjustment is not unrealistic. But that it can be sufficient to do the job, all along the line, is hard to swallow.

There is, however, another alternative, which does not depend on price changes. One need not interpret the production coefficients in the rigid sense that I have so far been giving to them. Instead of taking a_{ij} to mean the quantity of good i that is necessarily required to make a unit of j, one can make it the quantity that it is most convenient to use. In a growth equilibrium, or steady state, this would be the same as the quantity that was actually employed; so the steady-state theory is unaffected by this reinterpretation. But out of equilibrium, they need not be the same. Along the traverse, this gives additional flexibility.

It may well be said that by giving permission for discarding we have already introduced this reinterpretation; I do not need to argue that. For what I am now contending goes much further. We need not only permit underutilization along a traverse; overutilization also can be permitted. That makes quite a bit of difference. For, if scarce goods can be overused, surplus goods can be used more fully. Both overutilization and underutilization make traverse easier.

I am hopeful that extension, more or less in the direction I have been describing, would have had some appeal to Sraffa. He certainly believed in scale economies; he must have wanted to find a place for them in his system, though he did not succeed in finding it. It is a little easier to find it on my reinterpretation. For it will surely be the case, in any economy where indivisibilities are important, that opportunities for overutilization will be large.

Perhaps it was a pity that Sraffa leaned so much on Ricardo. There was another classical economist, a quite regular classical economist, who ought to have been allowed to put in a word. It was none other than John Stuart Mill. He said, quite explicitly:

> This perpetual non-employment of a large proportion of capital is the price we pay for the division of labour. The purchase is worth what it costs, but the price is considerable.
>
> (Mill, 1844, p. 70)[2]

There is a sequence from Mill to Marshall, to Sraffa and beyond.

I have two more points to make in conclusion. First, as seems to be implied, on my interpretation, if we make prices based on costs, not of actual outputs but of 'normal' outputs, the fact that actual outputs, at these volumes, must be such as cohere in a social accounting system gives no guarantee that normal outputs will similarly cohere. So there is no reason why a 'normal' system should cohere, and should thus be capable of being maintained over time. One is therefore left with doubts about those propositions in Sraffa that are based upon the possibility of such continuance. I think this applies to most of what he says about his 'standard commodity'.

The other point is another bit of historical perspective. Sraffa tells us that his book is based upon a paper that he gave in Cambridge in the late 1920s. This was the time that Keynes was writing the *Treatise on Money*. The curious thing about the formal part of the *Treaties* is that, just as in Sraffa, 'no changes in output are being considered'. A very few years later, Keynes had learned better (see Hicks, 1985b, ch. 6). But even now, the economics of Sraffa awaits its 'Keynesian revolution'.

Notes

1 The strongest evidence for this is the unpublished paper on 'Absolute value and exchangeable value' (Ricardo, [1823] 1951). This was discovered by Sraffa, but he did not see the significance of it.

2 See also my essay on Mill in Hicks (1983a), pp. 60ff.

Comment

Christian Bidard
Paris

Professor Hicks sees three main differences between Ricardo and Sraffa:

1 Sraffa's industries are fully interlinked, whereas Ricardo's industries are integrated, their only input being labour; this explains the absence of a distinction between basic and non-basic goods in Ricardo's works.
2 Ricardo's model is a perfect competition model, in which prices are equal to marginal costs; Sraffa ignores margins.
3 The most important point, and the most damaging, is that Ricardo's model is dynamic, whereas Sraffa's is not.

I fear I am not in agreement on these issues, which at least deserve a close examination.

Interlinkage of industries

On the point of fully integrated or fully interlinked industries, I shall try to clarify the debate by transposing it to the field of the theory of value. We can distinguish three levels in this theory:

The first level considers that the value of a commodity is the quantity of labour that directly or indirectly enters into the product. 'Dead' labour is then strictly equivalent to 'living' labour. Ricardo ([1817–21] 1951) refers to this conception when he examines questions of taxation or international trade, because he wants to derive clear conclusions; but he knows that this type of labour theory of value is only a simplification and, when he focuses on abstract questions as in chapter I, his conception is that of the second level.

The second level distinguishes between past and current labour. Past labour is for instance materialized in machines, and Ricardo is very aware of new elements thus introduced in the determination of value. This conception of dated labour is not only Ricardo's; it is shared by Austrian economists – though the role of demand, the one-way avenue of production, the attempt to define a period of production as an index of the quantity of capital are found only in the work of the Austrians.

The third and last level is Sraffa's theory (Sraffa, 1960). In chapter 6 on 'Reduction to dated quantities of labour', the reduction takes the form of an infinite series (it converges for $r<R$, i.e. the maximal profit rate is finite) and the coefficients depend on the whole technique, not on those of *one* industry. This property expresses the complete interlinkage between industries in Sraffa's model. For instance, a technical improvement in one industry has effects on the whole economy and, *a priori*, Sraffa's model seems to be an adequate tool to study the various aspects of such changes; it offers the correct framework for research on dynamics, to be discussed later.

In conclusion on this first point, I agree with Hicks if he wants to state that interlinkage is only partial in Ricardo's chapter I and complete in *Production of Commodities*; this is indeed a major difference between Ricardian and neo-Ricardian theories, but it does not put the latter at a disadvantage.

Basics and non-basics

Though the notions of basic and non-basic goods do not appear in Ricardo's works, there exists a patent distinction between 'luxury goods' and 'wage goods', for instance in the study of taxation.[1] Even when Ricardo refers to taxation on consumption, he has production in mind: a workers' basket of goods is, in some sense, fuel for production, and any taxation on it will increase costs and lower profits, whereas luxury goods are a 'very final consumption', which does not help production.[2] The distinction between basics and non-basics is not 'given', but Sraffa's reconstruction of Ricardo's reasoning throws light on the logical basis of a statement like: 'It is the profits of the farmer that regulate the profits of all the other trades', and identifies it as: 'Corn is the sole basic product in the economy under consideration' (Sraffa, 1960, Appendix D). While the general and abstract concept of a basic good is absent in Ricardo, its effects are present and, in my opinion, it is arbitrary to oppose Ricardo and Sraffa rather than to recognize their respective contributions to the theory. The link of continuity is moreover explicit on another point: the property that taxation on rents has the same effect as that on luxury goods ('taxes on rent fall wholly on landlords'[3]) suggests that land is, with regard to production, in the same position as luxury goods; Sraffa's counter-intuitive general definition of non-basics in joint production is justified by his wish to explain this similarity.

Returns to scale and 'margins'

An obvious requirement for a dynamic analysis is that it should allow for change either in produced quantities or in the way they are produced. Hicks quotes Sraffa: 'No changes in output . . . are considered, so that no question arises as to the variation or constancy of returns' (Sraffa, 1960, p. v) and he concludes that, by its very nature, Sraffa's model cannot but be static. He draws extreme conclusions from this interpretation: there is no marginal cost; it is not a model of perfect competition; it is impossible to examine how one moves from one state to another, etc. More briefly, 'Sraffa's model cannot be placed in time'. Before considering these conclusions, I would contest their basis and the interpretation Hicks gives to 'no changes in output'.

The question of returns and of changes in output in *Production of Commodities* is two-fold and has to be analysed in two stages.

First, one must remember that the book aims at being a 'Prelude to a Critique of Economic Theory'. With the subtitle in mind, the lesson of 'no returns to scale assumption' is: assume there is one and only one system of production that is able to satisfy given requirements for use. In spite of the absence of a neighbouring system, prices can be determined. Hence, these prices are not calculated by marginal variations, and no change in quantities is necessary.

Now, to consider that assumptions on returns to scale or even that marginal equalities *must* be excluded from Sraffa's (or Sraffian) analysis is a misinterpretation. For instance, when Hicks refers to a perfect competition model, he has in mind that capitalist rationality leads to profit-maximizing choices, which will be mathematically expressed by some equality between marginal magnitudes. But, as far as these equalities are the expression of capitalist rationality, they may perfectly well be derived from the Sraffian framework. For, if we drop the previous uniqueness assumptions on the available system of production, the system that will be finally chosen is the cost-minimizing one (and a market algorithm to determine it is studied in chapter XII entitled 'Switch in methods of production'); if there is a continuum of techniques, the cost-minimizing technique is the one satisfying some marginal equality. Moreover, the possibility of substituting one technique for another demands that both can satisfy the same requirements for use, hence, in part III of his book, Sraffa himself assumes – implicitly – constancy of returns.

Moreover, when Sraffa studies land and scarce resources in chapter XI, the scarcity of resources and the notions of extensive and intensive rents can be considered as formally equivalent to a diminishing returns assumption, especially if, following Hicks, we assume the existence of a historical sequence from Ricardo to the marginalists. Most economists will consider a statement like 'the price of corn rises with output' as correct in a Sraffian framework, with some qualification.

The analytical limits of this oecumenical position explain themselves by the ideological background of the modern theory, which considers diminishing returns on land as a pure law of Nature: extensive rent springs from the decreasing fertility of land as the cultivated area is increased, and intensive rent from the decreasing substitution between factors; the price of corn will rise along with margins, for technical reasons. Sraffa, in contrast, understands the law of diminishing returns as a law of diminishing profitability: farmers first cultivate the more profitable lands but, this quality being scarce (this is the technical factor), less profitable lands have to be ploughed, and the rent of the extensive kind is an expression of this juxtaposition. Intensive rent also appears when social demand forces up the costs of production. Two concrete differences between the neo-Ricardian position and that of modern theory are:

- The order of profitability is not reducible to a natural order of fertility, and changes with distribution.
- The price of corn in terms of wages will increase as a consequence of the scarcity of land *if* distribution is unchanged. But, for workers, a fall in the profit rate may counter-balance the growing difficulty of production.

Sraffa's position on changes in output therefore varies according to the question he is examining, but it does not appear ambiguous. The 'emphatic warning' of the preface has to be understood in its critical dimension, not as a general and necessary condition for the analysis to hold true. The only problem is not whether Sraffa is static, but whether Sraffians are dynamic in both senses of the word.

Dynamics

It is possible to contest Hicks' opinion simply by referring to the many works on dynamics already done in a Sraffian framework. Here I will mention only those of Garegnani on long-term fluctuations, and of Pasinetti and Schefold on changes in techniques; these authors can illustrate the point better than I could, and I prefer to dispute Hicks's premises on changes and returns rather than his conclusions. Hicks refers more specifically to the question of 'traverse'; I cannot see any theoretical obstacle that prevents its examination in a Sraffian framework, and many papers have been published on the neighbouring question of changes in prices and on the 'gravitation' of market prices around prices of production; this of course does *not* mean that Hicks's solution to the traverse problem may be immediately adopted or simply transposed to a neo-Ricardian framework. For, just as Hicks explains why he is in disagreement with what he calls the neo-classical solution to the problem, we have to check that his proposal is in accordance with the principles of classical economists.

As a general conclusion, I would stress that not everything is perfect and not everything has already been done in neo-Ricardian theory: J. S. Mill, to whom Hicks refers, is also famous for writing that the theory of value was completed in his time and that no new ideas on the question could still be formulated. As for Keynes, also quoted by Hicks, I am personally rather disappointed by the slow pace at which strong connections are being established between Sraffa's and his theory, though they are often considered as complementary. Hicks's pessimism on the scope of Sraffa's theory is ill-founded, but the only complete answer to his fears would be to work more on the genuine problems he raises.

Notes

1 Compare, for instance, the first sentences of chapter XV ('Taxation on profits') and chapter XVI ('Taxation on wages') in Ricardo ([1817–21] 1951).

2 One paradox of Sraffa's formalization is that 'the necessaries of consumption are relegated to the limbo of non-basic products' (Sraffa, 1960, ch II, §8),

3 Ricardo ([1817–21] 1951), ch X, first sentence; also quoted in Sraffa (1960), ch XI, § 5.

Comment

Fernando Vianello
Modena

'But even now,' Professor Hicks states at the very end of his paper, 'the economics of Sraffa awaits its "Keynesian revolution"' (page 102, above). The key to such a revolution is indicated by Hicks in the recognition that the productive system possesses a higher degree of flexibility than is commonly ascribed to it in long-run analysis. I shall submit that Sraffa's equations are fully compatible with the principle of effective demand, so that no further 'revolution' is needed to that effect. I shall also submit that Hicks's suggestion as to the flexibility of the productive system is, nevertheless, a really valuable one.

Indeed, in expressing the hope that the above suggestion 'would have had some appeal to Sraffa' (page 102, above), I think Hicks hits the nail on the head. For, I shall argue, in order to unlink distribution and growth (and to link the former to the money rate of interest), Sraffa cannot but have relied on the flexibility of the productive system, i.e. on its ability to accommodate changes in aggregate demand through over- or underutilization of productive capacity.

A suitable starting point for my argument may be the interpretation of Sraffa's equations as 'a model of a stationary state', put forward in Hicks's earlier essay on Sraffa and Ricardo (Hicks, 1985a, p. 307). According to this interpretation, it is the zero-saving hypothesis that makes 'equally possible' any rate of profits (the only restriction being that imposed by the limit below which the wage in no case can fall). The wage and the rate of profits, Hicks says, 'can be what they like, so long as they are tied together, *in his* [Sraffa's] *stationary state*'. But 'as soon as one admits a relation (*any* positive relation) between profits and saving, the picture looks very different' (ibid., pp. 308–9).

Now the rate of profits, Hicks argues, can no longer be what it likes. It must be what is required by the condition that the stock of capital should grow at a given rate, constant through time, which he assumes to be equal to the rate of growth of population (but no other part of the argument is affected if non-full employment growth is assumed instead). An 'extra equation' (ibid., p. 308) should therefore be added to the original system: the very well-known equation linking the rate of profits to the rate of growth of capital through the propensity to save of the capitalists (assumed to be the only savers) (see ibid., p. 310).

The reason why Sraffa did not write such an equation is, in Hicks's view, that in a steady-state model, where all quantities are expanding at the same rate, constant-returns must necessarily be assumed; and Sraffa was so unwilling to introduce the constant returns assumption that confinement to stationariness seemed to him the lesser evil (see ibid., p. 307; see also pages 99–100, above).

This, then, is 'Sraffa according to Hicks'. In order to see what 'Sraffa according to Sraffa' looks like, it may be appropriate to pay some attention to that so often overlooked aspect of *Production of Commodities by Means of Commodities*, the one-way causal connection between the rate of interest and the rate of profits established in § 44, where the rate of profits is said to be 'susceptible of being determined from outside the system of production, in particular by the level of the money rates of interest' (Sraffa, 1960, p. 33).

As is well known, the view that it is the rate of return on capital that tends to adjust to the rate of interest, rather than the other way round, is shared by Keynes. According to Keynes, a progressive reduction of the rate of interest (supplemented by other measures whenever necessary to maintain full employment) would cause 'changes in technique or in the direction of consumption which involve a . . . larger use of capital in proportion to output' (Keynes, [1937c], 1973b, p. 131), thus forcing down profitability. Unless population is growing too rapidly, 'a properly run community' – i.e. one consistently committed to the above policy – would find itself, within a single generation, 'so well equipped with capital that its marginal efficiency is zero and would become negative with any additional investment'; a state of affairs that would mean the 'euthanasia of the rentier' (Keynes, 1936a, pp. 220, 217 and 376).

Needless to say, the mechanism entrusted by Sraffa with the task of bringing the rate of profits into line with the rate of interest cannot possibly be the one just described, which is based on such changes in the methods of production and in the composition of national output as to make the latter produced with the appropriate proportion of capital to labour. Changes may of course occur both in the methods of production and in the composition of output. But the fall (or rise) in the rate of profits, as envisaged by Sraffa, is independent of any such change. It reflects only the fall that competition brings about (or the rise it does not prevent from taking place) in money prices relative to the money wage whenever, owing to a change in the terms on which finance can be raised, the ruling rate of profits comes to be regarded as a more (or, respectively, less) than sufficient inducement to hold physical assets and to use them in production (see Vianello, 1985, pp. 83–4; see also Garegnani, 1979a, p. 81, and Pivetti, Chapter 15 below).

This may help to explain how reference to the rate of interest as the regulator of the rate of profits can occur in a book where, as we are told, 'no changes in output and (at any rate in Parts I and II) no changes in the proportions in which different means of production are used by an industry are considered' (Sraffa, 1960, p. v).

Reverting now to Hicks's reading of the matter, it must be stressed that the above statement should not be taken to mean that the investigation is confined to those economic systems in which no changes in output do in fact take place, but that it is confined, as Sraffa makes clear, to 'such properties of an economic system as do not depend on changes in the scale of production' (ibid., p. v). It is in the analysis of this kind of properties – in particular of the relation between the rate of profits and the wage, and of the associated changes in relative prices – that the quantities produced are considered as already determined. No assumption of stationariness seems to be implied in assuming 'this standpoint, which', Sraffa contends, 'is that of the old classical economists from Adam Smith to Ricardo' (ibid., p. v).

Hicks's interpretation implies that Sraffa refers the causal connection between the rate of interest and the rate of profits to a stationary economy, being prepared to renounce it as soon as the zero-saving hypothesis is dropped (and refraining from giving any warning to that effect). Such a conclusion is, however, unjustified. For the opinion that between the rate of interest and the rate of profits there must be a close connection seems to have no less solid a foundation in a growing than in a stationary economy. And the same is true of the opinion that the rate of interest is determined 'from outside the system of production', care of it being taken by the monetary authorities. Indeed, if the causal connection between the rate of interest and the rate of profits is to have any meaning at all, it must hold true in a growing as well as in a stationary economy.

From this it is apparent that the reading of *Production of Commodities* as 'a model of a stationary state' is no less foreign to Sraffa's conception than the neo-Keynesian twist given to it by Mrs Robinson (1962d) who makes the rate of growth of capital, rather than the rate of interest, the regulator of the rate of profits. Here, however, we are faced by the question: what grounds are there for Sraffa's implicit (but not thereby less clear-cut) rejection of the link between distribution and growth?

To answer this question I shall avail myself of a two-commodity model, which bears some resemblance to the one presented in chapter XII of *Capital and Growth* (Hicks, 1965, pp. 131ff.; regrettably, this part of the book has not been included in Hicks, 1985b). Following Hicks, the two commodities (which are produced by two separate industries) will be called 'tractors' and 'corn', respectively. Tractors are employed as means of production in both industries and do not wear out with use. Wages are paid and the two commodities brought to market at the end of each year. Profits are entirely saved and wages entirely spent on the purchase of corn. Any change in demand is foreseen sufficiently in advance for production to be perfectly adjusted.

The rate of growth of capital can be expressed as $I/(T_1+T_2)$, where I is investment, or the newly produced quantity of tractors, while (T_1+T_2) is the pre-existing quantity, T_1 being employed in the tractor and T_2 in the corn industry. An equivalent expression, to which it may prove convenient to refer, is $(I/T_1)/(1+T_2/T_1)$.

The only possibility allowed for in steady-state models is that, the right quantities being produced with the right amount of equipment, the normal degree of capacity utilization prevails continuously. As this means that the ratio of T_1 to I is treated as a 'fixed coefficient' (see Hicks, 1965, p. 137), my second expression makes it apparent that a definite relation comes to be established between the rate of growth of capital (assumed to remain constant through time) and 'the proportion in which the stock of tractors is divided between the two industries' (ibid., p. 141): a higher rate of growth of capital is necessarily associated with a lower T_2/T_1 ratio. A definite relation also comes to be established between the latter ratio and the wage in terms of corn: if corn is to be produced, like tractors, with the normal degree of capacity utilization, then a lower proportion of tractors in the corn industry is necessarily associated with a lower wage.

The $I/(T_1 + T_2)$ ratio is equal to what Mrs Robinson (1962d, p. 29) has called the 'realised' rate of profits (of the economy as a whole), namely, to the ratio of overall profits (equal to the value of I) to overall capital (the total value of T_1 and T_2). In steady-state models the $I/(T_1 + T_2)$ ratio and the 'realised' rate of profits are also equal to the 'ordinary', or 'normal', rate of profits, as we may decide to call the (uniform) rate corresponding to the normal degree of capacity utilization (see Vianello, 1985, pp. 83–4).

As long, then, as one is concerned with comparing steady states, faster accumulation goes hand in hand with a higher normal rate of profits and a lower wage in terms of corn. From the harmonious and changeless world of steady-state models let us move, however, to a world closer to the real one, if only in one respect: faster accumulation does not need to take the form of an immutably higher $I/(T_1 + T_2)$ ratio and of a correspondingly lower proportion of tractors employed in the corn industry, but can be accommodated through a temporary rise in the degree of capacity utilization. In my expression this would show itself in a higher I/T_1 ratio. Unless a bottleneck is reached in the corn industry, its production rises in the same proportion as that of the tractor industry, and the wage in terms of corn has no reason to fall.

While productive capacity is overutilized, the 'realised' rate of profits is obviously higher than the normal rate. But the normal rate – the rate of profits that is considered a sufficient reward for the employment of capital in production, thus forming the basis for investment decisions – remains the same even if productive capacity is over- (or under-) utilized. It is *this* rate of profits that appears in Sraffa's equations, and is made to depend on the rate of interest.

Suppose that initially the normal degree of capacity utilization prevails in both industries, and the normal rate of profits is obtained. Suppose further that, after a period of overutilization, a moment comes at which productive capacity finds itself once more fully adjusted to the requirements of production. Both the I/T_1 ratio and (if the normal rate of profits and the wage in terms of corn have not changed for independent reasons) the T_2/T_1 ratio are equal in the old and in the new 'fully adjusted situations' (as I have proposed to call them in Vianello, 1985); and the same is true, therefore, of the $I/(T_1 + T_2)$ ratio.

Indeed, the $I/(T_1 + T_2)$ ratio observable in a 'fully adjusted situation' does not give us any information as to the speed at which the stock of tractors is growing over time. Be that speed high or low, if the economy is caught at a moment of its history when the normal degree of capacity utilization prevails in both industries, the $I/(T_1 + T_2)$ ratio (the ratio of overall profits to overall capital) will turn out to have come into line with the normal rate of profits.

From this it can be seen how misleading is the steady-state assumption according to which the economy does not depart, even temporarily, from the normal degree of capacity utilization, and the $I/(T_1 + T_2)$ ratio never gets out of line with the normal rate of profits. It is only in an economy subject to this (rather peculiar) rule that faster accumulation is compelled to go hand in hand with a higher normal rate of profits, a lower proportion of tractors in the corn industry and a lower wage in terms of corn. Not to commit oneself to the steady-state assumption is therefore, I submit, all that is required in order to achieve freedom from the link between distribution and growth.

By the same token, one achieves freedom from the necessity of assuming constant returns. Consider once more our two 'fully adjusted situations'. By taking as given in succession the two corresponding sets of quantities, two distinct curves will be drawn in the case of non-constant returns, each showing how the wage in terms of corn falls as the normal rate of profits rises from zero to its maximum value. If, then, the rate of interest and the normal rate of profits are kept constant by the action of the monetary authorities, increasing returns will show themselves in a higher wage in terms of corn in the new than in the old situation.

Flexibility is, I have argued, the key to the unlinking of distribution and growth implicit in Sraffa's claim that the (normal) rate of profits is determined by the rate of interest. For it is thanks to the possibility of over- or under-utilizing productive capacity that the interest-determined normal rate of profits and the corresponding wage are made compatible with the speed at which the inducement to invest, whether strong or weak, makes the stock of capital grow over time. That is why I appreciate so much Hicks's vindication of flexibility (which, however, is unnecessarily restricted to the case of the 'traverse' – namely, of an economy moving from one steady state to another – while obviously no such restriction is implied in my argument).

In favour of flexibility, Hicks invokes the authority of J. S. Mill (see page 100, above). Much in the same vein as Mill, S. Bailey refers to the unexploited potentialities of the productive system as a 'dormant power'. 'We may,' he writes, 'in reference to this dormant power, adopt the beautiful expression of the poet [T. Campbell] when he speaks of "the might that slumbers in a peasant's arm"; a might in this case ready to be put forth the instant it may be required. In the same way, there is always a greater or smaller quantity of capital lying inert, a quantity of food, tools, and raw materials not actually in request, which may at any time be called into activity when any demand arises for their employment' (Bailey, 1837, pp. 54–5).

Marx shares this view (see, e.g., Marx, [1867] 1967b, p. 571, n3). Ricardo obviously does not. 'Perhaps it was a pity', Hicks observes, 'that Sraffa leaned so much on Ricardo' (page 102, above), overlooking Mill and the flexibility issue. May I ask Hicks what makes him so sure that Sraffa leaned on Ricardo in matters other than those that form the argument of *Production of Commodities*?

5

Sraffa: Classical versus Marginalist Analysis

Pierangelo Garegnani
Rome

1 I believe that a wide agreement would exist on the fact that Piero Sraffa's central contribution to economic theory lies in two strictly related fields. The first is the rediscovery and revival of the approach to distribution and relative prices of the 'old classical economists from Adam Smith to Ricardo . . . submerged and forgotten since the advent of the "marginal" method' (Sraffa, 1960, p. v). The second is the criticism of the 'marginal' approach to the same problems.[1] Less agreement and, more importantly, less clarity seems to exist on the basic elements of that classical approach which Sraffa has brought back to life, and on the content of the criticism of the marginalist concept of capital that he has initiated and stimulated. The purpose of this paper will be to deal with the first of these two questions.[2]

2 Thus, most of the paper (sections 2 and 3) will be devoted to the basic elements of the classical approach and to some frequent misreadings of them. I have, however, thought it useful to precede this by a less analytical opening section, intended to bring into focus what I believe to be at stake in the debate on the work of Sraffa and of the classical economists. This first section will attempt to bring out in an intuitive fashion the implications, for the view taken of the economy, of the basic formal difference between the modern and the classical approaches to value and distribution – the determining role attributed to factor endowments in the modern 'marginal' or 'neoclassical' approach. The stimulus for this first section has in fact been offered by the opportunity to answer a recent allegation according to which Sraffa's analysis would be encompassed in 'neoclassical' theory as a 'special case' of it (see para. 6 below).

The question raised in section 1 will be taken up and developed in a more systematic fashion in the remaining sections. Section 2 will be concerned with the basic element of the classical approach. The first part will focus on the central feature of classical theories, namely the kind of explanation given for the division of the product between wages and profits. The second part will draw the implications of that explanation for the analytic structure of the classical theory. This structure is characterized by 'separate' logical stages and is deeply different from the 'simultaneous' determination of distribution, outputs and prices we find in 'neoclassical' theories (see para 3 below on the use of the term 'neoclassical'). Finally in section 3, I shall use the arguments of the preceding two sections to clarify misreadings of Sraffa's work. These misreadings appear to centre on: (a) the role played by consumer preferences and the demand for products in determining outputs; (b) the supposed need of the assumption of constant returns to scale for the significance of the analysis in *Production of Commodities*, and, finally (c), the radically different meaning from the modern one that demand and supply have in the classical economists and Sraffa. I shall also briefly discuss the meaning and implications of Sraffa's standard system.

1 *Classical and 'neoclassical' theories*

I Sraffa's analysis a 'special case' of neoclassical theory?

3 The claim that Sraffa is concerned with a special case of neoclassical theory has recently been put forward in Hahn (1982b) where, using Sraffa's *Production of Commodities* as his main reference for what is meant by 'neo-ricardian theory', he writes: 'There is no correct neo-ricardian proposition which is not contained in the set of propositions generated by orthodoxy' (p. 353). In particular, he argues that Sraffa's analysis constitutes the special case of 'neoclassical theory' dealing with a uniform rate of return over the supply price of the capital goods (Hahn, 1982b, pp. 363–4, 368).[3]

In order to examine this claim we must first try to be clear about what we mean by 'orthodoxy' or 'neoclassical theory' on the one hand, and by 'neo-ricardian theory' on the other. In his article, Hahn defines neoclassical theory as follows:

> I shall call a theory neo-classical if: a) an economy is fully described by the preferences and endowments of agents and by the production sets of firms; b) all agents treat prices parametrically (perfect competition) and c) all agents are rational and [at] given prices will take that action (or set of actions) from amongst those available to them which is best for them given their preferences. (Firms prefer more profit to less.)
>
> (Hahn, 1982b, p. 354)

However, of the three elements Hahn includes in this definition, it appears that only element (a) counts for the distinction between the two theories. Element (c), rationality in the sense there specified, is common ground for neoclassical theory and for what Hahn calls 'neo-ricardianism', but is in fact, I shall argue, the approach of the old classical economists.[4] Element (b) is also irrelevant since the basic formulation of both theories relates to conditions of free competition and, on the other hand, both appear capable of dealing with what are generally understood to be non-competitive cases.

4 We may therefore turn to element (a) alone. By saying that 'the economy is fully described by the preferences and endowments of agents and by the production sets of firms', Hahn clearly means that, given

(i) the 'preferences of agents' as consumers,
(ii) the 'endowments' of factors of production,
(iii) the technical conditions of production,

the theory determines the corresponding set, or sets, of equilibrium prices and outputs.

The forces that are supposed to determine that (unique or multiple) equilibrium position are the well-known ones of demand and supply as understood in the theory. Individuals' choice among consumer goods and the existence of alternative methods of production for each commodity would make it possible to 'substitute' the factor that is becoming cheaper for the remaining ones in the economy as a whole. In fact, a lower remuneration of the factor would entail:

(a) a lower relative price of the consumer goods requiring the factor in a higher proportion and, therefore, as a result of the analysis of consumer equilibrium, a higher relative output of these goods[5] and a higher proportional employment of the factor in question in the economy as a whole;
(b) the adoption in the several lines of production of methods requiring a higher proportion of that factor.

This inverse relation between the quantity in which the factor is employed and its rate of remuneration – given the quantities employed of the other factors – is then expressed as the 'demand function' for the factor, which, when coupled with its endowment (or the supply function based on such an endowment), would determine the price of the factor by means of the associated demand and supply equilibrium. Simultaneously, the equilibrium prices of all other factor services, for which a similar mechanism would be at work, would also be determined, together with the equilibrium prices and outputs for all products. (The concept here used of the demand function of a factor service is thus the one underlying a general equilibrium formulation of the theory: for a definition of this concept see, for example, Garegnani, 1978a, p. 346n.)

This decreasing shape of the demand functions for factors was in fact traditionally supposed to ensure the uniqueness and stability of the equilibrium in question and thus to provide a validation of the demand and supply mechanism postulated in the theory. Now, this decreasing shape rested in turn on the decreasing shape of the marginal product functions or their equivalents (covering also the case of a finite number of alternative methods) and of the functions of marginal utility or their equivalents. Hence the key role of the concept of 'margin' in these theories as the expression of a substitutability (that is, either directly or ultimately, between factors of production.) Hence, also, the reason for referring to these theories as 'marginal' or 'marginalist', whichever the specific mathematical tools by which that substitutability is then analysed. (I shall generally prefer the terms 'marginal' and 'marginalist' for such theories.[6] However, the meaning of the text would not be affected if these adjectives were replaced by the adjective 'neoclassical'.)

5 Thus, if Sraffa's propositions are to be contained in an 'orthodoxy', which as Hahn states has the endowment of factors among its data, such a datum should be present also in *Production of Commodities*. But how can Hahn trace it since that datum is not there?

6 Hahn attempts to do so when he introduces a simplified model of 'neoclassical theory' involving two commodities – wheat and barley – each of which is both a capital good and a consumption good. He asserts that, in order to obtain Sraffa's uniform rate of return on the two capital goods, the initial endowments of wheat and barley must bear some *particular proportion* to each other, because '*It cannot be part of the doctrine* of Sraffa that you are uninterested in whether there is enough . . . wheat and barley to meet demand' (Hahn, 1982b, p. 365; emphasis added). In other words, Hahn finds it inconceivable that the simple answer to the question he raises in that passage might be:

> Yes, it can, and it is, part of the doctrine of Sraffa that distribution and normal prices do *not* require the initial endowments of wheat and barley for their determination.

Clearly, Hahn has begged his question here. He has *assumed*, and not proved, that what constitutes a characteristic feature of 'neoclassical' theory by his own definition of it – the determining role of factor endowments – is present in Sraffa's analysis. To that extent he has *assumed* what he intended to prove, namely that Sraffa's analysis is a 'special case' of neoclassical theory.

In fact, as he tells us in his Preface[7], Sraffa's standpoint is that of 'the old classical economists from Adam Smith to Ricardo', and, as we shall presently see, this standpoint does *not* attribute a determining role to 'the endowment of agents'. Therefore, his analysis can hardly be a 'special case' of the 'neoclassical' theory, which *does* admittedly rest on such a role.

7 This independence of distribution from factor endowments in Sraffa may however surprise many readers whom received theory may incline to share Professor Hahn's belief that 'it cannot be the doctrine' of anybody to determine distribution without reference to factor endowments.[8] It may therefore be useful here to begin by questioning that tendency to view the demand and supply explanation of distribution as an immediate reflection of facts in a preliminary, intuitive way. I shall do this in the remainder of this section by enlisting a Voltairian Candide, and by asking the reader to share for a while the irrepressible tendency of that character to compare what he is told with what he can see.

8 Indeed, it seems that Candide, turned economist, would not be easily led by observation to the conclusions of modern theory. Candide might start by noticing the presence in general, in a market economy, of the phenomenon of labour unemployment, at times a considerable amount of labour unemployment, a phenomenon that is *prima facie* of doubtful compatibility with modern theory, since, as Candide will be quick to remark, wages show nowhere the tendency to fall to zero.

As for the possible counter-observation that experience shows some sort of long-run rough coincidence between labour employment and labour seeking employment, Candide might of course retort that such rough coincidence is only to be expected, to the extent that workers cannot live on air. That rough coincidence may in fact result from employment-seeking labour adjusting to employment opportunities rather than the reverse, with the labour 'endowment' being a determin*ed* rather than a determin*ing* magnitude of the system. Candide might indeed easily indicate the massive migrations of workers from country to country that have steadily accompanied the economic development of market economies in the last two centuries. He might also, more subtly, and even more importantly, point to the adaptation implicit in the so-called 'dualism' of many economies, in which a sector using advanced techniques coexists with sectors using the traditional methods, which provide much lower incomes to the producers and release labour in step with the needs of the advanced sector.

9 However, is not Candide being too innocent here? Is it not the case that much work has been done, above all recently (see para 18 below), to reconcile unemployment with received theory by resorting in particular to various kinds of wage 'rigidities'? Has not therefore neoclassical theory shown that it can allow for labour unemployment and for some 'institutional' or 'conventional' determination of wages, with 'endowments', and in particular the non-labour endowments, determining outputs and labour *unemployment*, rather than the real wage?

To this Candide might answer that observation does not seem to lead naturally to this second, less vulnerable position – where 'neoclassical' theory sheds some of its earlier most characteristic colours – any more than it led naturally to the first. This second position turns in fact on attributing a determining role to the non-labour endowments, and in particular to the capital stocks, on which both employment and outputs would depend. Now, the size of the capital endowment seems, if anything, even more susceptible of adaptation to its employment than the size of the labour force is. In fact, it might appear to Candide that, within the multiple interaction likely to exist between outputs and capital stocks, the size of the capital stocks may adjust to outputs at least as well as the outputs are ever likely to adjust to the capital stocks. Candide may remember that this has in fact been argued in comparatively recent economic theory and by a famous economist. In chapter 16 of the *General Theory*, Keynes has in fact written that if, for a rate of interest zero or close to zero, a tendency to net savings at full employment income were to persist, then inevitably 'the stock of capital and the level of employment will have to shrink until the community becomes so impoverished that the aggregate of saving has become zero' (Keynes, 1936a, p. 217)?

In other words, Candide makes out, the fall in output due to deficient aggregate demand can cause a shrinking of the capital stock until it adjusts to the lower aggregate output. Here, therefore, it is the level of aggregate demand and output that determines the level of the capital stock. Thus the 'endowment' (this time, the endowment of *capital*) is determin*ed* by output rather than determin*ing* it, contrary to what (in the above passage) Hahn implied had to be part of any theory.[9]

10 If unprejudiced observation would not aid Candide towards validating Hahn's certainties, Hahn might rightly claim that observation, though unprejudiced, may be superficial. Has not the result of a century and a half of post-Ricardian analysis been to arive at the marginalist explanation of distribution by demand and supply functions of factors or production and by the associated 'endowments of agents'? Is it not the case, then, that systematic analysis has brought to light other, less immediately visible elements which, to use Marx's famous distinction, go against the 'appearances', on which our Candide has so far relied?

Candide's answer to this may, however, be easily imagined, given today's theoretical situation. He might readily agree that neoclassical theory was *not* the result of any direct observation either of demand functions for factors or of a flexibility of wages and other renumerations capable of leading to the full utilization of any such factors. On the contrary, he will easily agree that the inverse relation between renumeration and quantity employed of each factor, on which those demand functions rest, was the result of pure logical deduction from the facts of producer choice among alternative methods of production, and of consumer choice among goods (para. 4 above). He will therefore also agree that the doubts he has raised, which do not refer to *those* facts, are by themselves inconclusive. He will, however, quickly add that it is certainly not on this purely *logical* side that the theory can be shown to be strong today – of all times. Has it not emerged in recent decades that those logical deductions were faulty as far as the division of the social product between wages and profits is concerned? And – Candide might ask – where are the other, less visible elements, indicated by pure analysis, that support Hahn's convictions?

11 It is now time to leave Candide – though the doubts raised by his reasoned observation will, I believe, find confirmation as the argument progresses. Indeed, as already mentioned, the old classical economists up to Ricardo – the historical example of such reasoned observation – had not been led, whether by direct facts or by deduction, to the modern demand and supply theory of distribution. The 'wage fund theory', to which we must probably resort to find the beginning of the modern demand and supply analysis of wages, was a later development, characteristic of politically more disturbed times when practical interests may have interfered with objective enquiry (see Cannan, 1967, p. 207; Bharadwaj, 1983b, pp. 60–8).

I must now support and develop my assertion that the classical economists and Sraffa did not explain distribution by means of demand and supply and therefore had no need to introduce factor endowments among their data.

2 *The classical approach to distribution and relative prices*

II Wages

12 I said Sraffa had no need to refer to factor endowments because the standpoint he was adopting was that of 'the old classical economists from Adam Smith to Ricardo [which] has been submerged and forgotten since the advent of the "marginal" method' (Sraffa, 1960, p. v). It is the standpoint that dominated the first century of systematic economic thought starting with the physiocrats – and it was a slow and laborious process lasting half a century that finally led to the 'marginal' theories and to their dominance.

As paras 8–10 above may have suggested, the explanation of the division of the product between wages and profits by an equilibrium between demand and supply is where the dissatisfaction with mainstream theory of distribution has found its focus. It is not only that the so-called 'reswitching controversy' impinges there;[10] it is also that, independently of that controversy, there is a growing awareness of and preoccupation with the contrast between the theory and phenomena like those I mentioned in section 1 (see para. 8 above). Now, significantly enough, it is in the theory of wages that we must trace the basic difference between the modern and the classical standpoints.

In the classical theories we find no idea of the distribution determined by the 'substitutability' between factors of production that we saw in para. 4. The basic idea implicit in these theories may be described rather as that of an explanation of the real wage,[11] in which institutional and customary elements play a central role, because they determine to a considerable extent the *present* bargaining position of the groups involved, while at the same time expressing the *past* bargaining position of those same groups. It appears to be to the extent to which they can affect that bargaining position, that factors like the speed of capital accumulation and population growth – often stressed in modern interpretations of the classical economists as primitive elements of the modern demand-and-supply analysis (cf. Garegnani, 1983a, p. 311) – can affect the wages for those economists.

I cannot enter into a detailed examination of the classical theories of wages – an issue to which I hope to be able to return in the not too distant future. However, since the view taken here of those theories differs from some current interpretations, I must attempt to clarify and support it, however briefly.

13 A convenient starting point for grasping the contrast between classical and modern theories of wages lies in that the classical authors had no difficulty in admitting the possibility of labour unemployment in the positions of the economy corresponding to normal or 'natural' rates of wages and profits. This is true for Adam Smith in the *Wealth of Nations*[12] and is equally true for the other early classical economists[13] – in particular for Ricardo

who, in his famous chapter XXX of his *Principles*, saw the possibility that the introduction of machinery would result in permanent labour unemployment.[14]

14 This allowance for long-run labour unemployment immediately poses a question for the modern economist: what about competitive wages in such a situation? Would they not tend to fall indefinitely so long as unemployment persists, and if not, why? In order to understand the kind of answer that the classical economists implicitly gave to this question, we must start from an important fact. This is that we do not find in those authors the idea described in para. 4 above that a sufficient fall of the real wage would lead to the full employment of labour through factor substitution. Lower wage rates could reduce unemployment in time, if at all, chiefly through the faster accumulation associated with higher profits, or through slower population growth.[15]

Now, the fact that these authors did not see the lowering of the real wage as capable of eliminating unemployment is important in that it prevented them from thinking of free competition as entailing an *indefinite* lowering of the wage so long as labour unemployment persists. Such an indefinite lowering of the wage would indeed have brought them to the absurd conclusion of wages tending to zero in a condition – that of persistent labour unemployment – recognized as frequent or even normal. It led them instead to a different conception of free competition. In the labour market the conception was that, at any given time and in any given economy, there is a *minimum* below which wages cannot fall under normal competitive conditions. In the words of Adam Smith: 'there is . . . a certain rate below which it seems impossible to reduce, for any considerable time, the ordinary wages even of the lowest species of labour' (Smith, [1776] 1960, Bk. I, ch. VIII, vol. 1, p. 60).[16]

15 This idea of a minimum below which wages cannot fall in spite of competitive conditions has in fact long perplexed the more attentive among modern interpreters. It appeared difficult to reconcile it with Smith's other basic idea that the tendency of wages towards a socially determined subsistence level results from the 'advantage' that employers have with respect to workers in the bargaining on wages.[17] And, above all, it appeared difficult to reconcile *both* these ideas with the free competition that Adam Smith seemed otherwise to assume in the labour market (for example, with respect to the tendency of wages for the same quality of labour to a uniform level throughout all trades).[18] I submit, however, that these perplexities are only the result of habits engendered by thinking in terms of demand and supply *functions*, which was altogether foreign to the old classical economists.

16 In order to understand this basic point we may start by considering more closely the 'advantage' that Smith saw the employers to have relative to the workers. In addition to several elements, among them the capacity to 'hold out longer' than workers in wage disputes, Adam Smith writes that employers are 'always and everywhere in a sort of tacit, but constant and uniform combination' not to raise wages. Of particular interest for our purpose here is the way in which Smith envisages such a 'tacit' combination

operating. He writes: 'to violate this combination is everywhere a most unpopular action, and a sort of reproach to a master among his neighbours and equals' (Smith, [1776] 1960, Bk. I, ch. VIII, vol. 1, p. 59) where social conventions, and the social sanctions attached to their violation, are seen to be the essence of that behaviour. I submit it would be incorrect to describe the behaviour here envisaged by Smith as monopolistic. This is indicated by the fact that it is to this behaviour that Adam Smith refers his general theory, which appears to be competitive with respect to distribution, no less than with respect to the prices of products (note also the adjective 'tacit' which he attached to the word combination).

If now we turn from the limits to a *rise* in the wage rate back to my original question of the limits to *a fall* in the wage, it seems natural to suppose that a similar constraint based on social sanctions and conventions would act even more strongly on labourers, and prevent them from lowering wages below the minimum that is held to be compatible with 'common humanity', to use Adam Smith's own expression. And even if the individual worker, especially in Smith's times, could be so desperate as to offer his labour at levels incompatible with the standard of living accepted 'among his neighbours and equals',[19] is it not clear that some such constraint will act on employers also? The idea of 'common humanity[20] is surely something that Adam Smith supposes each employer to share with the rest of the community, and that, in any case, he cannot violate without exposing himself to difficulties and sanctions, both within and outside his own enterprise.[21] Indeed, the habits, conventions or institutions here referred to as setting a lower limit to the wage possible in any given society at any given time would seem to be something that any community not possessing it already would quickly have to evolve, and find a way of enforcing upon the individuals, in order to ensure the maintenance over time of the conditions for a sufficiently orderly working of the economy and society (which of course does not mean that such conventions or institutions can be the result of some rational procedure leading to conscious agreements). Minimum wage legislation is a manifestation of that need, though generally not its most important expression.

17 Now, the constraints acting in this way on workers and employers alike are bound to be seen by them as largely *independent of their will*. It is natural for us to see these constraints as not in conflict with voluntary competitive behaviour and, therefore, as a part of all those written or unwritten rules within which free competition is only conceivable. Thus, it would be normal for workers to compete above that socially accepted minimum wage – and therefore, for example, to compete in a way that tends to realize a uniform wage for the same quality of labour.[22] It would however not be normal to compete so as to lower the entire wage structure below that corresponding to some minimum standard of living recognized as such at each given time in each given society.

What seems surprising is not so much that these ideas about unemployment and wages should be present in the classical economists, but that they should have disappeared from later theory – to reappear only under the sheer force of facts, in the somewhat artificial form of 'monopolies' and other restrictions to 'free competition' that are supposed to act in the labour market.[23]

At the root of the modern position there seems in fact to lie a highly specific concept of free competition in the labour market, which, as I indicated in paras 4 and 14, appears to be the product of the modern analysis of wages in terms of the intersection between the demand and supply *functions* for labour, and is in fact hardly distinguishable from that analysis. Without a twin – a theory, that is, allowing us to postulate a demand function for labour of negative elasticity, sufficient to ensure that some acceptable real wage does exist for which all the labour supplied would be employed irrespective of the stage reached by accumulation[24] – it would have been inconceivable to identify competition in the labour market with a tendency of the wage to fall indefinitely under a condition that would then be recognized as frequent or even normal.[25]

18 Indeed, today we should be better equipped than fifty, or even only twenty, years ago to understand the appeal to conventional and institutional elements implicit in Smith's theory of wages and, in particular, in his concept of a minimum wage. It is not only that the criticism of the marginalist notion of capital has thrown into doubt the 'twin' of that notion of free competition. It is also that the deep-rooted success of Keynes' theory has created the need to *explain* the persistence of labour unemployment – the need, that is, to reconcile that *fact* with an orthodox doctrine for which a sufficient flexibility of the wage would ensure the elimination of unemployment. Though arising from a belief in a questionable theory, this need seems to be slowly working its way towards imposing a rediscovery of just those conventions and institutions that were central to the classical theory of wages, and were exemplified in Adam Smith's concept of a limit to the fall of wages.

Thus, for example, Robert Solow has recently written:

> I think they [feelings about equity and fairness] also come into play as a deterrent to wage cutting in a slack labour market. Unemployed workers rarely try to displace their employed counterparts by offering to work for less; and it is even more surprising . . . that employers so rarely try to elicit wage cutting on the part of their laid-off employees, even in a buyer's market for labour. Several forces can be at work, but I think Occam's razor and common observation both suggest that a code of good behaviour enforced by social pressure is one of them.
>
> (Solow, 1980, p. 5; see also Solow, 1979, pp. 347–8)[26]

Solow is here taking his cue from other interesting work being carried out on social norms and the notion of a 'fair wage', which is now being brought to bear on the problem that unemployment constitutes in marginal theories. We may be beginning to witness one of the instances of the long-run force exerted by facts even in a non-experimental science like ours. The need to explain a fact – persistent unemployment – to which (I am quoting Solow again) 'the structure of modern economics is inhospitable',[27] – but which, it must be stressed, was taken for granted by Adam Smith and Ricardo – may be slowly leading back towards classical concepts of wages and, perhaps, also of free competition, which subsequent developments in economics have all but obliterated.

III The structure of classical analysis

19 From the above view of the real wage there follows the basic analytical structure of the classical theories of distribution and relative prices.[28] That view entails in fact that the real wage can be determined *separately* from the social product. This is due to the institutional and customary elements that directly set the minimum or 'subsistence' wage and contribute to determining the bargaining position of the groups involved and, therefore, the normal wage in the given situation. It is also due to the kind of other economic, political or more broadly social factors that influence that position and wage. The wage can accordingly be taken as known, prior to the social product and to the other shares in it.[29]

On the other hand, the absence of the modern demand and supply determination of the wage entails the absence of the necessary relations postulated by modern theory between wages and social product. The latter, taken as a physical aggregate, is accordingly also envisaged as susceptible of being determined *separately* from the wage, from the shares other than wages and from the relative prices, in the way and for the reasons we shall see in paras 28–33 below. Therefore, similarly to the wage, the social product is taken as a known magnitude when approaching the determination of those shares and prices. The technical conditions of production are supposed to be similarly known: that is, separately determinable. (As we shall see below, interactions between those three groups of circumstances are, of course, admitted but are not held to be representable in terms of functional relations allowing for the simultaneous determination of two or more of them.[30]) However, a given yearly social product and given technical conditions implied a known number of workers employed. (For the sake of simplicity we assume here that only one method is known for the production of each commodity.[31]) Given the rate of real wages, we then have a known yearly aggregate of wages (see Figure 5.1). Thus the shares other than wages had to result as the *difference* between a known net social product and the known part of the product that constitutes wages[32] – as the 'surplus', that is, that the social product shows over and above wages. This determination of the shares other than wages was on the other hand soon found also to entail that of relative prices.[33]

This simple analytical scheme can be described by taking 'shares other than wages' as the only unknown in the following equation

$$\text{Net social product} - \text{aggregate wages} = \text{shares other than wages} \qquad (1)$$

Equation (1) encloses in a nutshell the underlying logic of the theory, whichever the exact mathematical form that the determination of the 'shares other than wages' will then take – the 'simultaneous price equations' that we find in Sraffa's *Production of Commodities* or, alternatively, the 'surplus equations' (which are formally closer to equation (1)) of Ricardo, Marx or of

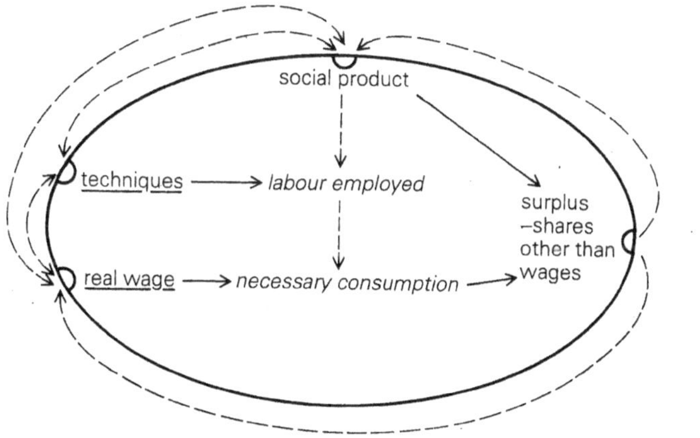

Figure 5.1 A diagram of the 'core' in the classical theories. Underlining distinguishes circumstances determined outside the 'core'. Continuous arrows point to dependent magnitudes inside the 'core'; discontinuous arrows indicate influences studied outside the 'core'.

Source: Garegnani (1984), p. 294.

Sraffa's standard system, or of the 'integrated wage goods sector' (Garegnani, 1984, pp. 311–20).

20 One point needs however to be stressed for a better understanding of the method and scope of economic theory for the classical economists. This is the concept of what may be called the 'core' of classical analysis, and the associated distinction between two different kinds of relationships that classical authors found in their analysis.

When the classical authors took the real wage and the social product as data or independent variables in determining the remaining distributive variables and the relative prices, they in no way implied that the social product would not depend in some respects on the real wage and vice versa. And when they took the technical conditions of production as their third independent variable, they did not assume these conditions to be independent of the wage and social product and vice versa. Similarly, by the structure of their analysis, the classical economists did not imply that profits and relative prices would have no reverse influence on wages, social product or technical conditions of production. Indeed, the study of such mutual relations and reverse influences occupied much of their theorizing.[34]

What the analytical structure summarized by equation (1) *did* imply was something quite different, something that modern economists, used to the ambitions of marginalist 'general equilibrium', may at first find difficult to grasp. This is the distinction between two fields of analysis: a field where general quantitative relations of sufficiently definite form can be postulated, and another field where relations in the economy are so complex and variable according to circumstances as to allow not for general quantitative relations of sufficiently definite form, but rather for a more inductive kind of analysis, continuously supported by what Marshall used to call 'specific experience' (Marshall, 1961, vol. 1, App. C, pp. 771–2).

21 Let us look more closely into this distinction. The first of the two fields of analysis is the one we find in what I called the 'core' of the theory. Here the necessary connection between the price of a commodity and the remuneration of the resources that have gone into its (direct and indirect) production entails general quantitative relations of well-defined properties. Thus the competitive tendency towards uniform rates of remuneration – or, if sufficiently definite, the corresponding conditions under non-competitive assumptions – entail exactly defined quantitative relations between the real wage (the independent variable) and the remaining rates of remuneration and the relative prices. These relations have to be studied on the basis of given methods of production and, therefore, on the basis of given levels of output when returns to scale are not constant.

Equally necessary and studied in the 'core' are (a) the influence of the technical conditions of production (the independent variable) on the rate of profits and prices; and (b) the relations between the levels of outputs and those same dependent variables, under non-constant returns to scale.[35]

(The logical fact of these relations following from the necessary connection between the price of a commodity and the remuneration of the resources used for its production should incidentally help to dispel the misunderstanding as a result of which it is at times alleged or implied that, since money is not discussed in Sraffa's *Production of Commodities*, that book is based on the pre-Keynesian dichotomy between monetary and real factors. However the pre-Keynesian dichotomy consists of the attempt to determine both the social product and its distribution among classes, independently of monetary factors. This is, of course, quite different from the determination of the relations of the classical 'core' with which Sraffa is concerned in most of his book and which are independent of money because of the above-mentioned logical fact.[36] Indeed, when he occasionally goes beyond those relations, Sraffa gives clear indications *against* any such independence of distribution and outputs from monetary factors, and in particular against any independence of distribution from them.[37])

22 Beyond these relations engendered by the necessary connection between the price of a commodity and resource remunerations there lay the second field of analysis where no similarly definite quantitative relations could be postulated about reality. (This did not exclude the possibility or usefulness of obtaining relations on the basis of *special hypotheses*. Because they were special hypotheses, however, these relations could not be applied to reality with the generality associated, for instance, with the equality between prices and costs in the price equations or, in marginal theory, with decreasing marginal products or, more generally, with the decreasing demand functions for factors described in para. 4 above.[38])

The relations pertaining to this second field had accordingly to be studied in their multiplicity and diversity according to circumstances. This field included, for example, the classical analysis of wages sketched in section 2 above. It also included the analysis of accumulation as carried out by Adam Smith, or David Ricardo or Karl Marx.

Now, the study of the *reciprocal influences* between real wages, levels of output and technical conditions of production, mentioned in para. 20 above and treated as independent variables in the core, were seen to pertain to this second field of analysis. And into this second field there would also fall the study (also mentioned above) of the reverse influence of the shares other than wages, or of relative prices, on those same independent variables. In this second field all those dependencies could be studied together with all the other factors influencing wages, the social product and technology – like social and political factors, independent monetary factors, or independent technical changes. The multiplicity of these dependencies, and their variability according to circumstances, made it necessary to study them *separately* from the relations of the core and not *simultaneously* with them.

23 This classical distinction between two kinds of relations and the associated separation of the analysis into successive logical stages (for example, the determination of the real wage by relations of the second kind, and *then* that of the other shares of the product by relations of the first kind), contrasts sharply with what we find in marginal theories. The demand and supply explanation of distribution we saw in para. 4 above is founded on a belief in the possibility of extending the field of necessary quantitative relations of sufficiently definite general properties *beyond* those between distributive variables and prices which we find in the 'core' of classical theory. As we saw there, relations between prices and the quantities demanded of commodities, taken jointly with analogous necessary relations following from the existence of alternative methods of production, were seen to entail the existence of decreasing demand functions, which provided the basis for a determination of both the wage and the quantities produced, and thus of most economic phenomena, by 'demand and supply'.

The resulting determination of the wage was, on the other hand, *simultaneous with, and symmetrical to*, that of the other shares of the product. It was also *simultaneous* with the determination of the volume and composition of the social product.[39] What I said above should make it clear why no such symmetry and simultaneity could be found in the classical theories: in this respect the two analytical structures could be no further apart.

24 An important implication of all this should now be explicitly considered. It has often been lamented that modern economic theory, as distinct from classical theory, has tended to ignore or underestimate the influence of the broader social and historical factors affecting many of the phenomena it studies.[40] What we saw above may be used to see why that shortcoming was not there in the early classical economist or in Marx, who followed and developed their approach, and why it appears instead to be inherent in the marginalist framework. Indeed, it seems that the particular analytical structure of classical analysis reflected an instinctive recognition of the role that broader social and historical factors necessarily play in the economy, while

the contrary is true of the analytical structure of marginalist analysis, which is built on the utilitarian doctrine and on the consequent analogy with mechanics.[41]

25 Let us look at the point in some more detail. By limiting the scope of the quantitative relations of known general properties to those of the core, the classical economists recognized the multiplicity of the factors affecting both distribution and accumulation, and allowed for the role of variable social and historical factors. In this way they also allowed the study of these social and historical factors to be an integral part of economics. For example, the separate determination of the wage outside the core of the theory allowed for a role for historical factors both with respect to the notion of subsistence that we find in the given economy and, more generally, with respect to all the other events that influence the relative bargaining position of the classes involved. These historical factors are often embodied, so to speak, in the conventions and institutions within the limits of which, and through which, competition must operate. Similarly, the separate consideration of the levels of output allowed for a determination of the outputs and of the speed of accumulation in which broader social and historical factors pertaining to the class structure and to the policies of the country could play an essential role (as a reading of the *Wealth of Nations* soon reveals[42]).

On the other hand, the belief of marginalist authors in the possibility of widening the scope of general quantitative relations of known properties to cover the determination of distribution and of the social product naturally tended to exclude from that determination all the social and historical factors that are inherently variable over time and space. Any role for them was in fact necessarily confined to influencing the data of the general equilibrium equations, that is, consumer preferences, capital endowment or tendential technical conditions.

This tendentious exclusion goes together with another subtler and deeper element acting in the same direction. The attempt of marginalist authors to widen the scope of general quantitative relations inevitably tended to shape the method of economics *as a whole* along those relationships. All those phenomena that, though recognized to influence the economy, were obviously refractory to a treatment in terms of quantitative relations, which should be both sufficiently general and sufficiently well defined in their properties, were excluded from economics and left to other sciences. The result was to leave outside economics altogether a large part of the study of the determinants of technical knowledge, of consumer 'tastes', and of factor endowments (in particular labour availability), to which the role of historical factors had been confined in the first place by the marginalist conception of the demand and supply mechanism.

Thus, the most influential definition perhaps of economic theory in its present marginalist shape – that given by Lionel Robbins ([1935] 1962) – completely left out of economics what determines 'the ends' (consumers' tastes) and 'the means' (techniques and endowments). Now these are factors whose study was thought by the old classical economists to be an important or even a central part of economics.

This difference between the two approaches is perhaps nowhere more clearly exemplified than in the attitude of the two schools towards the technical conditions of production, the only set of conditions that *both* approaches took as data when determining profits and prices. Classical economists like Adam Smith or Karl Marx thought that the technical conditions of production, and their evolution over time, were largely determined by phenomena with which economic theory had to deal, just as with wages and outputs, and therefore constituted one of its central concerns (think of the analysis of the division of labour in Adam Smith). The opposite attitude has prevailed among later theorists, who have tended to take technical conditions as exogeneous, no less than consumer tastes or labour and land endowments.[43]

3 *Preferences, returns to scale and Sraffa's analysis of prices*

IV *Relative prices and consumer preferences*

26 We now have the foundation on which to stand for attempting to clarify some aspects of the analysis of Sraffa and the classical economists that have been at the centre of controversy. These aspects are strictly connected and are: (i) the role of 'demand' and consumer preferences in the determination of relative prices and the dependent distributive variables; (ii) the irrelevance of the assumption of constant returns to scale in that determination; (iii) the meaning of demand and supply in classical theory.

Before proceeding to this, we may, however, take advantage of equation (1) to comment on another aspect that has also been an object of controversy and is of some importance for a correct understanding of Sraffa's book: the 'standard system'. This concept has often been looked at as if *there* lay the key to that puzzling box entitled *Production of Commodities by Means of Commodities*. However, Sraffa himself had warned that 'the standard system is a purely auxiliary construction' (Sraffa, 1960, p. 31) and, what seems to have often escaped attention, in his *Preface* he wrote that the standard commodity constitutes a 'particular point', which had come 'later', and was not one of those 'central propositions' of the book that had taken shape in the late 1920s (Sraffa, 1960, p. vi).

In order to understand the role of the standard commodity and standard system, we must in fact return to the formal basis of the classical theories and to the fact that the real wage and the social product are taken as given physical aggregates when approaching the determination of non-wage remunerations and relative prices. It is then natural that the theorist should attempt to measure aggregate wages and the social product of equation (1) – together with a third magnitude, the aggregate of the necessary means of production – independently of distribution, even when, with the determination of the rate of profits, these have to be expressed in value terms (see Garegnani, 1984, p. 309). The absence of the disturbances caused by changes in relative prices as the division of the product between wages and profits changes would in fact considerably simplify the reasoning and thus 'give transparency to a system and render visible what was hidden' (Sraffa, 1960, p. 23). Now these independent measurements are just what we are again able to achieve in Sraffa's 'standard system'.[44]

27 But let us proceed to the first of the three main points on which discussion of Sraffa's work has centered: the role of 'demand' and consumer preferences in Sraffa's analysis of relative prices.

Hahn e.g. writes: 'Sraffa's followers claim that Sraffa has established the irrelevance of the psychological theories of demand and, indeed, of demand to the determination of relative prices' (1982b, p. 359).[45] It was however Adam Smith and Ricardo who 'established' that independence, much before Sraffa. The essential terms of the question are indeed simple.

As was paradoxically to be rediscovered in recent years, in the form of a 'non-substitution theorem',[46] the system of relative prices is determined independently of demand conditions and consumer preferences, once the real wage – or the rate of profits (interest) – is given, and constant returns to scale are assumed. We saw how the classical economists could take the real wage (or, with Sraffa, the rate of profits) as given when approaching the determination of relative prices. The two things together mean that in classical theory, under the assumption of constant returns to scale (which is generally made in marginal theory), we shall have: (a) that demand conditions and consumer preferences are irrelevant for the determination of relative prices,[47] (b) that their irrelevance is due to a different theory of distribution.

The non-substitution theorem is of course generally known. What has engendered misunderstandings has been a failure to appreciate the different meaning that that proposition has in the two theoretical settings. In marginal theory, the proposition is a logical relation of no direct relevance for distribution theory, since the real wage itself is *not* given independently of demand conditions and consumer tastes. In modern theory, therefore, the relevance of the non-substitution theorem lies merely in making it clear that consumer preferences can affect prices only to the extent to which they affect distribution – which, of course, those preferences do, because they underlie the demand functions for the factors of production (as we saw in para. 4 above).[48]

The position is entirely different for the classical economists where the independence of prices and the residual distributive variable from what are today described as demand conditions and consumer preferences constitutes a fundamental aspect of the theory. This is because that independence follows from a theory of distribution where the real wage (or the rate of profits) can in fact be taken as known when determining relative prices.[49]

V *Variable returns and the determination of outputs*

28 However – and here we come to the second focal point of controversies over Sraffa's analysis – what happens when we abandon the assumption of constant returns to scale to labour and means of production? It could in fact be objected that when that hypothesis is abandoned – as we must do in classical theory in order to deal, for instance, with the rent of land – outputs, and therefore 'demand conditions', become relevant for determining prices also in a classical context. It could be argued further than these demand conditions in any case become relevant when joint production is introduced.

In response to this, we should start by noting that determining outputs need not at all be a synonym for introducing demand conditions as these are understood in modern theory. In his Preface Sraffa writes that he assumes outputs to be given, 'so that no question arises as to the variation or constancy of returns' (Sraffa, 1960, p. v). This passage has induced Professor Hahn, for example, to write that the claim reduces Sraffa's analysis to 'just a fancy way of presenting accounts ex post'. However, Hahn would be correct only if the modern *simultaneous* determination of prices and outputs by 'demand and supply' were the only conceivable way to determine outputs. Only then would taking outputs as data when determining prices be equivalent to 'presenting accounts ex post'. However, as we shall see, a *separate determination of outputs* is possible and was in fact associated with the different classical theory of distribution considered above – and this is precisely what underlies Sraffa's assumption of given outputs and the independence of his analysis from constant returns to scale.

29 In fact, let us consider, one by one, the circumstances on which it will be generally agreed the output of each commodity will depend. These will be, to begin with: (1) the level of aggregate income and activity; (2) the technical conditions of production (governing, among other things, the outputs of means of production); (3) the distribution of the social product among the social classes (and therefore, in terms of the classical theories, the level of the independent distributive variable), since different classes generally spend their income on different commodities. Now, we have seen that classical authors take all three circumstances as given when approaching the determination of relative prices and the dependent distributive variables (para. 19, above). The outputs can therefore, also be taken as given in that determination, in so far as they depend on those same circumstances.

30 Outputs, however, also depend on what is modernly described as consumer preferences. With respect to this *fourth* circumstance, it is essential to start by distinguishing between two aspects of consumer preferences, which are generally taken together. The first aspect is the *content* of these preferences – the fact, that is, that at some given relative prices one individual may consume, say, one of a commodity *A* and nine of commodity *B*, rather than nine of *A* and one of *B*. The second aspect is the *formal property* for which when the relative price of a commodity *A* falls, the quantity of it consumed would increase. In the terms of modern theory, the distinction might be seen to correspond to that between the 'position' of a demand curve and its 'slope'.

Now what is *principally* relevant in determining output is the first aspect of consumers' tastes, their 'content'. However, this is just what modern theorists leave to the analysis of psychologists or sociologists and take as given (under the guise of 'given tastes') when conducting their analysis of demand – which is exclusively concerned with the second aspect, the formal property.

It is therefore difficult to see why taking the 'content' of tastes as given should arouse objections when adopted in a classical context. The paradox, however, is that, unlike most modern theorists, classical authors considered the analysis of the 'content' of preferences to be an important part of economics (for example, in the analysis of the cultural elements affecting 'workers' necessaries', para. 12 above). This analysis was however conducted when dealing with wages and outputs and, to that extent, the outputs could be taken as given when determining prices.

31 The argument, however, is clearly not complete as yet. We have to answer an objection, which could be formulated as follows. It is true that, so far as consumer preferences are concerned, outputs chiefly depend on the *content* of tastes, and this can be legitimately taken as given by classical economists when determining prices, just as it is so taken by their marginalist successors. But it does not follow from this that the need for a simultaneous determination of prices and outputs on the basis of demand functions is confined to the marginalist demand and supply theory of distribution. For example, if we consider a change in the real wage, how can we determine the *new* normal prices independently of the *new* outputs on which the former will depend under variable returns to scale? And on the other hand, how could we determine the new normal outputs independently of the new prices on which, plausibly enough, the new outputs will to some extent depend?

My reply to these questions will proceed in two steps. I shall first note that the reciprocal dependence of outputs and prices can be dealt with by means other than the demand functions. In the second step, I shall indicate why this alternative treatment, which was that of the classical economists, seems to be the only one generally possible in a classical context.

As for the first step of the answer, we find here a basic instance of the procedure by separate logical stages that we saw in section 2 to be characteristic of the analysis in the classical theories. Where relevant, the dependence of outputs on prices can in fact be analysed in two successive stages:

(i) The effect on prices, and on the dependent distributive variables, of the change in one or other of the independent variables (for example, in the real wage) is conducted while supposing outputs to be constant – or to undergo the assumed *independent* change when the outputs themselves are the changing independent variable (think of Ricardo's analysis of the extension of the cultivation of 'corn' to inferior lands).

(ii) The effects on outputs of that change in relative prices can then be analysed in accordance with the circumstances of the case – together with the effects resulting *directly* from the initial change of the independent variable (for example, the changes in wage goods outputs resulting from the change in the real wage even if the relative prices of commodities were not to change). At this stage, it will also be possible to analyse the effects of the changed outputs on relative prices and on the dependent distributive variables, when non-constant returns to scale are assumed[50] – together with any further effects that the changed prices might have on the independent variables.[51]

32 The above procedure, which might at first appear less satisfying and

exact than the modern simultaneous determination of prices, seems to emerge as the better founded one when we proceed to some further considerations – and here we come to the second step of the answer to the question raised at the beginning of the previous paragraph.

Any demand function has to depend on individual incomes. Now, in marginal theories the condition relating to the equilibrium in the market for factors (or other equivalent conditions, for example, in the so-called 'disequilibrium' theories) ensures that, as the demand price varies, the associated constancy or variation in individual incomes can be simultaneously determined and that the influence of this on the quantity demanded of the commodity can accordingly be reckoned. But, as we abandon marginal theory, we no longer have any such condition relating to factor markets and therefore, it seems, no *sufficiently general* ground for determining the change in the quantity demanded associated with a given change in price.

More generally, once marginal theory is abandoned, it no longer seems possible to determine individual incomes, and therefore the quantities demanded, by means of functional relations having properties that are sufficiently definite and at the same time sufficiently general as to render the procedure meaningful at the level of a general theory, as distinct from special 'models' (see para. 22).[52] It would therefore seem inevitable to proceed by *separate* logical stages, as indicated above.

This conclusion is strengthened by a second consideration. The received general concept of a dependence of the quantity demanded of a commodity on its price may be seen to run the risk of falling between two stools. If the effect of the price on the quantity bought is not appreciable, then the effect can be ignored without great error. Alternatively, when the effect is important enough to need general consideration, it seems it will often be the case that the effect constitutes an *irreversible* change, which is incompatible with its treatment in terms of a demand function. That is, the effect will entail a permanent change in the habits of consumers, which even marginalist authors would have to treat as a change of 'tastes' and therefore by a stage of analysis *separate* from the 'general equilibrium' determination of prices and the associated demand functions, where tastes appear as given. (Think, for instance, of the increase in the demand for cars in the USA in the 1920s, as technical developments led to an appreciable fall in their price.)

33 If now I try to summarize the main conclusions of my argument on the two questions of consumer preferences and constant returns to scale (paras 26–32), I may say that:

(a) Because of the different theory of distribution, the formal properties of consumer preferences (concerning a decreasing demand function for the commodity) lose in classical theory the relevance they have in marginal theory for the determination of relative prices through distribution.
(b) Together with the importance of consumer tastes for determining relative prices, there disappears both the need for, and the possibility of, the traditional demand functions for products, with the associated simultaneous determination of outputs and prices. Outputs have,

therefore, to be studied separately from prices and have to be generally taken as data when determining prices.

(c) Important dependencies of outputs on prices can be considered by the two-stage procedure described in para. 31 above.

(d) The hypothesis of constant returns to scale, when inserted in Sraffa's price equations, appears, therefore, to add little or nothing to the significance of those equations. On the one hand, that hypothesis would *not* ensure the independence of prices from consumer tastes and from demand conditions, were it not for the different theory of distribution, which allows the real wage (the rate of profits) to be taken as an independent variable. On the other hand, this different theory of distribution makes it natural to treat outputs as known magnitudes when determining prices, and, therefore, renders irrelevant any hypothesis about returns to scale in that determination.

In conclusion, we may now see why the fact that Sraffa does not assume constant returns to scale does not reduce his theory to 'presenting accounts ex post' (para. 28). The outputs he takes as given are *ex ante normal* outputs just like the neoclassical 'equilibrium' outputs – though, of course, they are *not* determined in the marginalist way by an intersection between demand and supply *functions* based on endowments, techniques and consumer preferences.[53]

VI Classical versus 'neoclassical' concepts of demand and supply

34 The fact that the outputs Sraffa refers to, though differently explained, are *ex ante normal* outputs, no less than those marginal theory deals with, may be used to clarify an associated point on which frequent misunderstandings seem to occur. Thus, for example, Hahn writes of neoclassical theory as 'the fundamental approach of . . . market clearing prices' (Hahn, 1982b, p. 26),[54] apparently implying that the assumption of 'market-clearing' necessarily leads to 'neoclassical' prices. We might then legitimately ask what kind of prices can those of Sraffa and the classical economists ever be.[55]

However, 'market-clearing' is no criterion for a distinction between the two approaches. The prices to which Sraffa and the classical economists refer are no less 'market-clearing' than those of marginal theory. As Adam Smith argued in Chapter VII (Book I) of the *Wealth of Nations*, and as for example Ricardo, Marx – and Sraffa himself – repeated or implied, these 'natural' or 'necessary' prices (or 'prices of production') can rule only when the quantity of the commodity 'brought to market' is equal to its 'effectual demand' – that is, to the quantity demanded at that very 'natural' price, or 'price of production'. It follows that at the 'natural price' or 'price of production' the quantity demanded is equal to the quantity supplied and the market is supposed to be 'cleared', no less than it is supposed to be at the equilibrium prices of marginal theory.[56]

35 Thus, in Hahn's passage we seem to be again faced with an unwitting identification of marginal theory as the only possible theory of the phenomena

considered. The simpler and more basic idea of a normal price at which the quantity of a commodity demanded is equal to the quantity supplied – thus constituting 'a position of repose and continuance' (Smith, [1776] 1960, p. 51) – is identified with the modern idea of an intersection between demand and supply *functions*.[57] However, that simpler and more basic idea is in fact susceptible of being developed in a direction quite different from that of the marginalist demand functions – in particular, in the direction of the classical conception of 'effectual demand' defined as the quantity demanded at the natural or normal price (coinciding with the normal outputs determined in the way I described in paras 29–32).

The reference here to a 'natural' or 'normal' price, or 'price of production', known when defining 'effectual demand', is made possible by the classical theory of distribution and by the procedure I described in para. 31 for dealing with any interactions between normal outputs and normal prices to scale. All the classical economists needed then to add was the immediately plausible postulate that, when the supply falls short of 'effectual demand', the price will exceed the normal price, and vice versa when the quantity supplied exceeds 'effectual demand' (Smith, [1776] 1960, pp. 48–51). There is no need to define the individual points of a demand function.

This alternative conception of 'demand and supply', where these are always confronted as two *quantities* and not two *functions*, is then used by the classical authors in order to claim a tendency of the actual or market price towards the 'natural' price (Smith, [1776] 1960, ch. VII; see also Garegnani, 1983a). It is not and it could not be used to determine either the 'natural' price or the normal output, which are known independently of 'demand and supply' as there conceived, owing to the theory of distribution and outputs I described.

36 What seems to emerge in the identification of market-clearing prices with those determined by marginalist theories as well as in the belief in the inevitability of the reference to factor endowments for determining distribution, or in the presumption of a simultaneous determination of prices and outputs, is an unwitting tendency to take marginal theory as the only conceivable explanation of the facts in question. I hope I have succeeded in showing in this paper that marginal theory is no such thing and that Sraffa has unearthed for us the altogether different theory that had been developing and had been dominant over more than a century from William Petty up to David Ricardo.

Notes

1 Sraffa's contributions to the theory of the firm and to the analysis of the Marshallian 'laws of returns' may in fact be seen as part of an earlier stage of his criticism of the dominant theory.

2 Much of the material for the present paper comes in fact from a more comprehensive work, where the second of the two questions indicated in the text is also treated.

3 I am not concerned here with some difficulties in Hahn's treatment of such a uniform rate of profit.

4 The maximization of entrepreneurial profits (minimization of costs) by an individual firm taking prices as given should not be confused with any maximization of satisfaction obtainable from given amounts of factors of production. Whereas the first proposition is common to both theories, the second is specific to neoclassical theory, depending as it does on the idea of a given fully utilized factor endowment. In this connection we may notice how frequent reference to Adam Smith as the originator of modern 'allocation theory', of which the second proposition above would evidently constitute an essential part (see, e.g., Arrow and Hahn, 1971, pp. 1–2), appears to be misleading. What Smith argued by his 'hidden hand' argument was only the 'mode in which the division of labour tended to be kept in equilibrium by the mechanism of relative prices' (see, Robbins, 1935, p. 68) – that is the spontaneous tendency to adjust the several outputs to the quantities demanded at the respective natural prices or 'effectual demands' (on this concept, see para. 28 below). Smith's argument therefore regards the *proportions* of outputs, and differs from any 'maximizing' of outputs or satisfactions, with which modern theory deals.

5 For example, assume an economy with only two factors, homogeneous labour and homogeneous land, and two consumption goods, 'corn' and 'cloth', such that corn requires more land relative to labour than cloth in order to be produced. Any fall in land rent in terms of either product would lower the relative price of corn. The analysis of consumer preferences would then allow the conclusion that, in general, the relative output of corn would increase. A higher proportion of the available labour will then be used for producing corn, with a consequent increase in the total land entrepreneurs would wish to employ with a given amount of labour.

6 For the reasons favouring this choice, see, e.g., Aspramourgos (1986).

7 The passage by Hahn I quoted above begins: 'I want to emphasise that this question [the role of endowments in determining distribution] must be faced whether you are a neo-ricardian or not', and he continues 'yet Mr Sraffa does not consider this matter'. It is overlooked here that the question might be faced in a way other than the one that modern theorists have grown used to.

8 Today some authors admit that distribution in the economy may have to be explained by conditions other than the *equilibrium* between those demand and supply forces (see, e.g., contemporary 'disequilibrium' theory). There, however, the above demand and supply forces continue to constitute the basis of explanation – with the addition of whichever other forces prevent the former from working themselves out to equilibrium. (See also para. 9 below.)

9 In neoclassical theory, even in states of 'stationary' or 'balanced growth' equilibria, where the capital stocks are quantities to be determined, the demand and supply determination of prices entails that the output levels continue to be determin*ed*, rather than determin*ing*, quantities – the ultimate determinants being the individual preferences governing capital accumulation and thus the (variable) capital endowment.

10 That controversy turns essentially on the legitimacy of envisaging a downward-sloping demand for labour (or for 'capital', i.e. investment) and therefore, like the broader 'capital controversy' of which it constitutes one main focus, it bears on the validity of the modern explanation of distribution between wages and profits. (These questions will be dealt in the comprehensive work mentioned in para. 1, n. 2.)

11 I am following the classical authors in supposing a sufficient persistence of the *ratio* between the normal wages for labour of different qualities, enabling us to use those ratios to render labour homogeneous, and to refer to a single real wage rate (see Garegnani, 1984, p. 293, n5).

12 Thus, e.g., Adam Smith writes with reference to a 'declining state of society':

> the competition for employment would be so great . . . as to reduce the wages of labour to the most miserable and scanty subsistence of the labourer. *Many would not be able to find employment even upon these hard terms*, but would either starve, or be driven to seek a subsistence either by begging or by perpetration of the greatest enormities.
>
> (Smith, [1776] 1960, Bk. I, ch. VIII; vol. 1, p. 64; emphasis added)

See also Hollander, who notes (1973a, p. 193) Smith's concern for the employment-generating capacity of alternative kinds of investment, and remarks that 'it is common for 18th century writers to assume the existence of a reserve of unemployed or underemployed labour' (Hollander, 1973a, p. 245).

13 As I noted in section 1 (para. 11), the situation appears to have changed very rapidly in this respect in the period immediately after Ricardo's death, with McCulloch's wage fund theory (see Cannan, 1967, pp. 206–7 and Bharadwaj, 1983b, pp. 60–8). It is also interesting to note that, while the shallowness of the wage fund theory is nowadays generally recognized, the idea it appears to have originated, that of a 'full employment' wage, has been preserved through marginal theory.

14 Ricardo (1951–73), vol. 1, p. 390. The unemployment was permanent in the sense that its elimination could result only from further accumulation or from a decline in population (see para. 14).

15 I have noted elsewhere (Garegnani, 1970a, p. 527) how this contrast between classical authors and later theorists on persistent unemployment finds an interesting expression in Wicksell's criticism of Ricardo's position on the effects of the introduction of 'machinery'. According to Wicksell, Ricardo would have ignored the fall in wages, and the consequent tendency to return to the full employment of labour with lower wages but a higher social product (Wicksell, 1934, p. 137). What Wicksell forgets is that no such idea of a quantity of labour demanded and employed regularly increasing as the wage falls is to be found in Ricardo.

16 The passage continues as follows

> A man must always live by his work and his wages must always be sufficient to maintain him. They must even upon most occasions be somewhat more, otherwise it would be impossible for him to bring up a family and the race of such workmen could not last beyond the first generation.

For the population problem to which Smith refers here, see n19 below.

17 Thus, in his well-known study of classical distribution theories Edwin Cannan wrote, referring to the 'advantage' in bargaining that Smith attributes to the 'masters':

> if the combination of masters has the power of depressing wages with which it is credited, why should it leave the labourers enough to support a family? Doubtless if it did not, then 'the race of such workmen could not last beyond the first generation': but why should the masters of the present generation concern themselves about that? . . . That Adam Smith himself felt that his doctrine was rather weak on this point, we may infer from the prominence he gives to the irrelevant fact that wages sufficient to support such a family as is required to keep up the population are the lowest consistent with common humanity.
>
> (Cannan, 1967, p. 185)

In his perceptive article 'The Ricardian theory of distribution', Frank Knight objects to the same passage of Smith: 'since workers are not actually slaves by inheritance, there is no reason why the individual employers should provide the worker with maintenance for a family' (Knight, 1956, p. 81n).

Samuel Hollander mentions the difficulty and postulates an 'arbitrary decision' of monopsonystically organized employers who would choose to act in accordance with 'common humanity' (Hollander, 1973a, p. 185n).

18 Thus, for example, Knight (1956) refers to Adam Smith's analysis (which he correctly sees as common to Ricardo and the other old English classical writers) and, in particular, to Smith's belief in the 'advantage' the 'masters' have in wage bargains, as implying 'that the employer-capitalist makes the division by arbitrary . . . fiat' (Knight, 1956, p. 81), implying, that is, 'the absence of any impersonal mechanism of market competition fixing wages' (ibid., p. 80).

Knight seems puzzled by failing to find in those authors the *modern* analysis in terms of demand and supply functions, which he clearly identifies with 'the impersonal mechanism of market competition'. He finds this in contrast with other aspects of the analysis of wages by the classical authors, and, in particular with what he sees as the idea that 'wages are controlled by a "standard of living" through the tendency of population to increase or decrease whenever they are above or below workers' psychological requirements' (ibid., p. v).

The same contrast is felt by Samuel Hollander, who attempts to deal with it by distinguishing in Smith two quite separate theories of wages. The first is applicable only to a stationary situation, where for otherwise unexplained reasons Smith would contemplate a 'breakdown of competitive processes in the labour market', and the second is applicable to the case of a progressive or a declining society, where competitive processes would come back into their own (Hollander, 1973a, pp. 185–6).

However, I submit, this contrast between a wage determined by competition and a wage dependent on the bargaining position of the parties involved begins to disappear as soon as we stop identifying competition with the interplay of demand and supply functions and look at it as a force acting within a set of conventions universally shared in that society. In particular, the contrast between a wage determined on the basis of the speeds of accumulation and of population growth and a wage dependent on the relative bargaining position seems to be due to thinking of the former elements in terms of demand and supply functions for increments of labour employment along the lines of the so-called 'canonical classical model' (see Garegnani, 1983a, p. 311), rather than looking at them as factors (perhaps, with Ricardo, the main factors) affecting the relative position of the two classes, and, therefore, the level of the normal wage around which competition will act.

19 As Smith put it:

> By necessaries I understand not only the commodities which are indispensably necessary for the support of life, but whatever the custom of the country renders it indecent for creditable people, even of the lowest order, to be without.
>
> (Smith, [1776] 1960, Bk V, ch. II, art. IV, vol 2, pp. 351–2)

In Torrens' phrase, later taken up by Ricardo (1951–73, vol. 1, p. 94), workers' 'necessaries' are determined by those 'habits of the country . . . which it is found difficult permanently to alter' and, therefore, become 'a second nature' (Torrens, 1815, pp. 57, 58; quoted in Cannan, 1967, pp. 191–3).

20 Smith ([1776] 1960), Bk I, VIII, p. 86, where he defines that minimum wage as 'the lowest consistent with common humanity'.

21 In this respect, see, for example, the passage from Solow (1979), quoted in para. 18 below.

22 See Smith ([1776] 1960), Bk. I, ch. X, vol. I, p. 117.

23 Samuel Hollander's reference to a 'monopsony' of employers in order to account for Smith's theory of wages is interesting in this respect (note 17 above).

24 On the link between the two ideas, see Garegnani (1983b), pp. 70 and 73. For the different classical notion of demand and supply, see below para. 35.

25 The difference between the classical and modern conceptions of free competition may extend beyond the labour market. Suffice it to remember here Marshall's need to introduce in his theory the 'fear of spoiling the market' in order to attempt to reconcile his demand and supply analysis of the market for a product with the facts.

26 Elsewhere in the article Solow specifies that the 'substantive mystery that employers do not more aggressively push for wage reductions in a buyers market' should be answered by referring to the fact:

> that they may fear reputation as a bad employer with a consequent deterioration of morale among the firm's workers, reduced productivity, shoddy workmanship, mild sabotage with the quality of his labour pool degenerating when market improves and he needs to take up more workers.
>
> (Solow, 1979, p. 347)

It is interesting to notice how a writer like Pigou (whose observation of reality tended to go beyond what his theory would easily allow for) referred to the existence of a minimum wage, the level of which is 'derived half-consciously [by "Public Opinion"] from a knowledge of the actual standards enjoyed by more or less "average" workers' (Pigou, 1933, p. 255; quoted in Solow, 1980, p. 5). Now, this minimum level would evidently depend on the bargaining position achieved by wage-earners over the historical past, but at the same time it would influence their present bargaining position by establishing a minimum beyond dispute, for the time being (see para. 14 above).

27 The fuller passage by Solow deserves reporting:

> The structure of modern economics is inhospitable to the idea of persistent unemployment and is always trying to extrude it. Only the stubborn refusal of the brute fact to go away has kept the analytical problem alive.
>
> (Solow, 1985, p. 1)

28 For a more detailed consideration of some of the points here raised on the structure of classical theory, see Garegnani (1984) and (1987).

29 As an attentive student of the classical authors put it: 'The foundation of modern political economy . . . is the conception of the value of labour power as something fixed, as a given magnitude . . .' (Marx, [1862–3] 1969–72, vol. 1, p. 45).

30 The mutual dependence thus admitted among the circumstances taken as independently variable in determining the shares other than wages raises a problem, of course. The problem is that of the 'coherence' between the values attributed to those independent variables in the positions of the economy that are being studied (e.g. the 'coherence' between the level and composition of the real wage and the commodity composition of the social product, or that between Adam Smith's natural price of a commodity and its 'effectual demands', for which see para. 25 below). Here it is important to distinguish between the two positions that are being compared whenever analysing a change: the one before and the one after the change in the data. As for the position of the economy *before* the change, that 'coherence' is inherent in the reality from which the data are

taken. As for the situation *after* the change, that coherence will be ensured by the procedure I shall indicate below (paras 25–26).

31 The consideration of alternative methods of production would imply that the real wage is also relevant for ascertaining the number of labourers employed.

32 To face this problem consistently was, however, no easy task when, after Quesnay, and with Adam Smith and his determination of the rate of profits, the aggregates in question had to be expressed in value terms. The natural price envisaged by Smith as the sum of natural wages, profits and rents lent itself to the 'popular' view that such rates could vary independently of each other (Sraffa, 1951, p. xxxv). It was only with Ricardo's 'corn' measurements, and then with his labour value measurements, that the constraint linking the rates of remuneration could again be brought to light (on this point see, e.g., Garegnani, 1984, pp. 300–3).

33 In Quesnay's '*produit net*' the surplus was identified with what society could dispose of without impairing the 'subsistence' of its 'productive' class (which Ricardo was later to call 'necessary consumption') and, therefore, the conditions of its survival. In the later development of the theory, the notion has tended to become co-extensive with the shares other than wages, even when wages could not be identified with subsistence, as they indeed could not in the case of authors like Adam Smith or Marx.

34 For some examples (which could easily be multiplied) of such interactions studied by the classical economists, see Garegnani, 1984, pp. 296–8.

35 See, for example, Ricardo's analysis of the fall in profit rate as cultivation is extended to less fertile lands.

36 This point seems to have been overlooked when Minsky writes 'Both neoclassical and Sraffian theory stand mute when it comes to money' (page 368 below).

37 See the indication of the monetary rate of interest as the determinant of the rate of profits in Sraffa (1960), p. 33. See also Garegnani, (1978a), pp. 390–1, the analysis of deficiencies of 'effective demand' within a classical approach.

38 An example may be provided by Marx's analysis of simple and extended reproduction (Marx, [1885] 1956, chs xx–xxi). Those quantitative relations had a quite definite form, but were not meant to determine the actual speeds of accumulation of the economy or to express in any way approaching completeness the factors on which that speed depended. They expressed only the conditions that the quantities involved had to fulfil in order to satisfy the hypothetical conditions of an equilibrated simple or expanded reproduction.

39 See Garegnani (1983a), p. 312, (1984), pp. 236–7. The simultaneity in the determination of the several variables concerns the basic structure of marginal theories and is not by itself in contrast with the attempts to achieve *approximate* solutions of particular problems by means of a 'partial equilibrium' analysis within marginal theory. Alfred Marshall's attempts in this direction are a recognition of the fact that, in economics, as he himself put it, 'the function of analysis and deduction is not to forge a few long chains of reasoning, but to forge rightly many short chains' (Marshall, 1961, p. 773); and these attempts contributed greatly to rendering the theory acceptable and capable of achieving dominance at the end of the last century. However, any such partial equilibrium analysis essentially rests on its general equilibrium counterpart for any assessment of the degree of approximation achieved, and for the determination of the basic distributive variables.

40 An aspect of this dissatisfaction can be traced in a writer like Schumpeter who is otherwise close to orthodoxy. Thus Schumpeter has stressed the importance for economics of 'the question how the economic system generates the force which necessarily transforms it', and therefore of 'a purely economic theory of economic

change which does not merely rely on external factors propelling the economic system from one equilibrium to another. . .' (Schumpeter, [1912] 1961, n.1, pp. 158–60; see also pp. 82–3).

41 In Marshall's apt image:

> The nominal value of everything, whether it be a particular kind of labour or capital or anything else, rests, like the keystone of an arch, balanced in equilibrium between the contending pressures of its two opposing sides. The forces of demand press on the one side, those of supply on the other.
>
> (Marshall, 1961, vol. 2, p. 593)

42 See, for example, Book III of the *Wealth of Nations* ([1776] 1960, vol 1). Thus the fact that, as Harcourt puts it, 'there is no history in Sraffa' (Harcourt 1975, p. 370) has to do with *Production of Commodities* being exclusively concerned with the relations in what I have here called the 'core' of classical theory, and is not due to the theoretical approach he is reviving there. That is revealed in the few instances in which we are allowed a glimpse into the wider theoretical background, as in connection with a wage specified in part or entirely in terms of necessaries determined 'by social conditions' (1960, p. 33; also pp. 3, 9), or in connection with the idea that it might instead be the rate of profits to be determined from 'outside the system of production' by the level of the money rates of interest, and therefore with an intervention of the monetary authorities.

43 Thus, for example, Robbins asked himself 'is it not possible . . . by including in our conceptions of endogenous change, changes such as . . . induced inventions . . ., to provide a formal outline of probable developments which shall be useful?' (Robbins, [1935] 1962, p. 132). After analysing the question, his conclusion is 'from the point of view of economics there are certain things which must be taken as ultimate data', among which he puts the technical conditions of production (ibid., p. 135).

44 See above para. 19, on the 'surplus equation' method for determining the dependent distributive variable (see also Garegnani, 1984, pp. 311–12 and 320–3, where the role attributed to the rate of profits as an independent distributive variable is discussed in its relevance for Sraffa's construction of the standard system). It seems on the other hand natural that those who fail to see the exact terms of the classical approach to distribution that Sraffa is adopting should find the 'standard system' 'almost incomprehensible' (Hahn, 1982b, p. 358); but at the same time, and paradoxically, that they should view it as the main or only new point in *Production of Commodities*. See, in this respect, Burmeister (1975), p. 456, Hahn (1982b, p. 362), Kaldor (1985), p. 634.

45 Hahn says a few lines later that no such claim is found in Sraffa's book. However, no reference to consumer preferences for determining profits and prices is found there either. On the contrary, references are to be found to a real wage determined by subsistence or alternatively to a rate of profits determined by the money rate of interest, either of which is sufficient to determine relative prices in Sraffa's book without any reference to consumer preferences.

46 Samuelson (1967), p. 528. We may take the occasion to point out a misediting in Garegnani (1983a), p. 310, where the sentence 'This proposition would have seemed less novel had it been clear that the pattern of demand can only affect relative prices' was left incomplete by dropping the last phrase 'to the extent in which it affects distribution', thus radically altering the sense of the passage.

47 This will perhaps become clearer for people used to envisaging the determination of prices in the partial equilibrium terms of the demand for and supply of products once it is remembered that the upward slope of a supply curve, necessary in order

to make the equilibrium price depend on demand conditions, is but an expression of the dependence of distribution on the output of the commodity in question (an expression, that is, of the rise in the relative price of the services required in a higher proportion in the production of that commodity; see Garegnani, 1983a, p. 310).

48 It is argued at times as if, once constant returns to scale are granted, the possibility to determine prices independently of consumer preferences were generally admitted in current economic theory (see, e.g., Hahn, 1986b, p. 362; Roncaglia, 1978, p. 16). This is not correct, as should on the other hand be evident from the simple fact that consumer preferences are relevant in any modern general equilibrium system, where constant returns to scale are assumed. (For the different significance of the independence of prices from consumer preferences in Sraffa, and in the non-substitution theorem, see Eatwell, 1977, p. 66.)

49 This, together with the assumption that the number of processes is equal to the number of commodities (on the justification of which, see Schefold, 1985a, pp. 23ff), also takes care of the case of joint production.

50 This aspect would evidently imply returning to the relationships in the 'core'. Thus, whereas the first stage of the above analysis would be carried out within the 'core' of the theory, the second stage would imply moving in both the fields of analysis I mentioned in para. 17 above.

51 Thus, in case these further effects were appreciable enough to be considered, we would have a sort of iterative analysis. (The 'convergence' of such an analysis seems the same question as that of the existence of a normal position of the economy corresponding to this new data. This question of convergence was raised by M. Piccioni and Professor B. Schefold in the course of a discussion at the Trieste summer school of 1987.)

52 To avoid misunderstandings, it may be useful to note that my discussion of 'demand functions' or 'curves' applies exclusively to the traditional relations between the quantity demanded of a commodity and its *price*, and does not in any sense apply to the possibility or opportunity of referring to other *relations*, involving quantity demanded and consumer preferences like, for example, 'Engel curves', etc. resulting from 'specific experience' as Marshall put it (para. 26 above; see also what we saw there about 'intellectual experiments').

53 For the question of the 'coherence' of the data among which a form of dependence is admitted – as e.g. between real wages and the levels of the outputs – see para. 22 above.

54 The full passage refers to 'the fundamental neoclassical approach of rational choice and market-clearing prices'. We saw above (para. 3 and note 4) that 'rational choice' in the sense there specified by Hahn is present in the classical economists no less than in the marginalist ones; just as now is the case for 'market-clearing prices'.

55 Indeed, a theory aiming to explain observable prices must aim to determine prices that we have reason to suppose constitute a position of rest for actual prices and therefore, necessarily, prices for which the quantity demanded is equal to the quantity supplied.

56 It has been claimed, on the contrary, that 'there is no reason to suppose that [Sraffa's] prices of production should equate quantity demanded with quantity supplied' (Roncaglia, 1978, p. 16), Sraffa, however, stated explicitly that his prices could properly be referred to 'by such classical terms as necessary price, natural price or price of production' (Sraffa, 1960, p. 9) though, he adds, 'value and price have been preferred as being shorter and in the present context (which contains no reference to market prices) no more ambiguous' (*ibid.*). Here Sraffa clearly identifies his treatment of prices with that of the classical economists and

with their distinction between 'market prices' and 'prices of production'. Now prices of production and, therefore, Sraffa's own prices do imply the equality between quantity supplied and 'effectual demand'.

The possible roots of Roncaglia's remarks emerge in a second passage: 'There is no reference, implicit or explicit, in any of Sraffa's assumptions to an aggregate equality between the quantities produced and supplied on the one hand, and the quantities demanded and sold on the other (ibid., p. xvii). There is no sense in which Sraffa's theory could be said to imply Say's law'. In this passage the problem of the equality between 'effectual demand' and quantity supplied of an individual commodity, implicit in the notion of its price of production, does not seem to be sufficiently distinguished from the quite different question of aggregate demand, and in particular of Say's law (which of course we have no reason to think Sraffa assumes verified). The question of Say's law has in fact two aspects, neither of which appears to involve the relation between prices of production and market prices. The first aspect of deficiencies of aggregate demand concerns the *long period*, where aggregate demand can affect the levels of productive capacity. This aspect clearly regards the determination of the 'effectual demands', that is of the normal outputs. It cannot, therefore, emerge as a divergence between quantities supplied and 'effectual demands'. The second aspect is the *short-period* one, which is reflected in the degree of utilization of a given productive capacity. It has to do with the relation between what we could define as a short-period normal output, determined by aggregate demand, and the output we would have in the industry if aggregate demand allowed for normal capacity utilization throughout the economy. This short-period problem may emerge in short run oscillations of the price *level* (of the value of money), but not in long run deviations of *relative* market prices from *relative* prices of production, which are the only issue in the question of 'natural' and 'market' prices.

57 As I contend elsewhere (Garegnani, 1983a, p. 309), a particular and very complex theory – marginal theory – is required in order to provide a foundation for the idea that the quantities demanded of a commodity can be determined also at prices which are not the normal or average price, and cannot therefore be observed.

Comment

Geoffrey Harcourt
Cambridge

In December 1982, the *Cambridge Journal of Economics* published a paper by Frank Hahn entitled 'The neo-Ricardians' (Hahn, 1982b). The paper itself had been around since the early 1970s; it was in fact a technical blow-up of the arguments that Hahn had set out in 1975 in the *Economic Record* in his note 'The wrong issues and the wrong argument' (Hahn, 1975). It was hoped that the publication of Hahn's 1982 paper would bring forth an authoritative reply to his argument to the effect that Sraffa's propositions were all derivable from orthodox, neoclassical general equilibrium theory, provided that the correct (but not always the most interesting) assumptions were made. So, said Hahn, what is all the fuss about, we can all be Sraffians now; or, rather, all Sraffians can be general equilibrium theorists. In the meantime, 'The neo-Ricardians' has been an influential paper in the profession, helping considerably the sort of development whereby, when a great figure is no longer around, the profession to which he/she belonged proceeds to behave as though they never existed. Thank goodness this process may now be halted in Sraffa's case by the appearance of a paper by Pierangelo Garegnani from the first part of which, I understand, the present paper draws very heavily. In the best Sraffian tradition it has been a long time a'coming but it was well worth a'waiting for.

It is not, of course, that Garegnani has not addressed many of these issues before. Most of the arguments in his paper may be found somewhere or other in his previous papers. What is important about this paper is that he has tried to bring the various arguments together and that, in particular, he has addressed himself to the important conceptual issues. Though I think his satirical first section resembles more the swipes of a sabre than the lightning thrusts of a rapier, I think it very effectively gets to the basic point, namely, that the overlap of theorems (i.e. of the mathematical analysis) as between different approaches does *not* imply that the same approach to economic analysis must have been taken, as Hahn argues. Garegnani has reminded us very forcefully that the view of economic life contained in Sraffa's work (and in that of the classical economists' approach which he was attempting to revive) differs fundamentally from that of the part of modern economics of which Hahn is in some ways a typical representative. (It must be said that Hahn makes far less grandiose claims for the scope and achievements of general equilibrium theory than do other, less careful, practitioners, or even the co-author of *General Competitive Analysis* – Arrow and Hahn, 1971 – Kenneth Arrow, in, for example, his Nobel Prize Lecture – Arrow, 1974.) Garegnani gets right to the heart of the matter when he quotes Hahn as saying, in effect, that it is inconceivable that factor endowments should be other than determinants of distribution (p. 115). Hahn has been so accustomed to seeing economic life within the neoclassical approach, and to specifying his models accordingly, that he has forgotten that a specified model, as far as its mathematical structure goes, is just mathematics (as Maurice Dobb always told us), and that it only takes on economic meaning when the conception of the economic process of the author is known. That is to say, while we may be able to deduce the formal analytical structure of a system by knowing an author's conceptual presuppositions, this is *not* a reversible process – we cannot deduce a person's conceptual stance, their 'vision', from a knowledge of their mathematics alone. That I take to be the most important general lesson from the first part of his paper.

The specific point that Garegnani stresses is a very interesting and persuasive one, namely, that endowments, far from being the determinants of the system as we understand it, should be regarded rather as the things themselves to be determined. I like very much his idea that in capitalist economies labour adjusts to the employment that the system tends to offer, that levels of capacity too show similar tendencies, and that this is part of the 'vision' that we inherited from the classical economists' work which Sraffa was trying to revive and to part of whose system he gave analytical content in his 1960 book. (As with all great economists, Sraffa and Garegnani look for empirical generalizations before they start theorizing.) Garegnani stresses the fact that Sraffa's book belongs to a tradition whereby there are different levels of abstraction according to the issues being discussed; that, while simultaneity is not ruled out in the analytical discussion of one issue, we can nevertheless explore more the possibility of taking one issue at a time, and so take as given the values of variables in other parts of the system. The values themselves will have to be determined in a full analysis, but perhaps at a different level of abstraction. Moreover, they may not be able to be dealt with in a general way but, rather, according to the concrete historical situations in which they occur.

Next, I was very pleased to see that Garegnani gave more content to the theory of wage determination, the outcome of which was to be introduced into the classical/Sraffian core in order to determine the classical/Sraffian natural prices/prices of production and the rate of profits. It was also fascinating (and amusing) to see him take as a most unlikely bed fellow Bob Solow, whose recent work on unemployment and wages has been most interesting – and courageous; see, for example, Solow (1980). While the bulk of the American profession became 'pure' Walrasian, supply and demand analysts in their theory, and extremely vulgar Smithians in their policy views, Solow, with a few other hardy souls, has fought in terms the profession could understand against treating the labour market as equivalent to the market for peanuts, in particular that excess supply does not imply continuous pressure for wages to fall, and even if they did in money terms (which is the only thing they *can* do in a capitalist economy) that it would necessarily do any good. I also applaud Nicky Kaldor's aside at the conference that he has *never* heard a monetarist call for a *rise* in real wages as the cure for generalized excess demand. While we are on the subject of Nicky Kaldor, we could also note an idea that occurs in his 'Keynesian' theory of distribution (Kaldor, 1955/6), which is similar to Pierangelo Garegnani's discussion of the social forces that tend to create upper and lower limits to the level of wages. As a result, free competition, as understood by the classical economists, could operate to determine the level of the natural wage (or levels of natural wages) only somewhere in between these limits. Kaldor, it will be remembered, argued that his distributional mechanism applied only within a range of values of the share of profits, the upper limit of which implied such low real wages as to lead wage-earners to revolt and the lower limit of which implied such poor returns to capital that capitalists would cease to invest.

I was glad that in his presentation to the conference Garegnani reasserted the simple but profound proposition that *if* the basic 'vision' of the economy is that prices are indexes of scarcity, depending on the relative quantities obtained or supplied, and that *if* distribution is viewed analytically as *just* an aspect of pricing, there is no way that neoclassical economists can get away from the need rigorously to define, *before* they start the analysis, what they mean by a 'lot' or a 'little' amount of 'capital' (relative to labour).[1] Sraffa was always explicit about this and regarded it as a central object of his critique. He mentioned it not only several times in *Production of Commodities* but also in his intervention at the Corfu conference on Capital Theory in 1959 (Lutz and Hague, 1961), and in his reply, which was carefully thought out and phrased, to Harrod's review (Harrod, 1961) of his 1960 book. Thus: 'One can only wonder what is the good of a quantity of capital or a period of production which, since it depends on the rate of interest, cannot be used for its traditional purpose, which is to determine the rate of interest' (Sraffa, 1962, p. 479).

Finally, had there been time, I would have asked Garegnani to spell out whether he is principally concerned with existence or stability problems in his critique, for I have always thought that he and Bliss did not get to grips in 1970 (Bliss, 1970; Garegnani, 1970b) because of a certain incoherence about this distinction at least as each understood the other, as opposed to being clear about what they were doing themselves. I found Heinz Kurz's recent paper (Kurz, 1985a) particularly helpful in sorting out these issues as I also found helpful Alessandro Roncaglia's comment at the conference to the effect that it was important to make clear whether a tendency towards, or a tendency to fluctuate around, a centre of gravitation (or both) was what was being discussed in long-period analysis.

Note

1 This particular set of arguments is now to be part of the more comprehensive reply to Hahn referred to above.

Comment

Alessandro Roncaglia
Rome

There is much in Garegnani's paper with which I agree. First of all, I fully share the main thesis of the paper – the antithesis of the classical and marginalist analysis. Second, I am also in agreement with some points referring to debates internal to the classical–Sraffian approach, such as the standard commodity not being the main element in Sraffa's analysis. The interested reader can check my own appraisal of these issues in Roncaglia (1978).

Within this basic common ground, there are also some differences of opinion. While these are 'differences of the second order', for the sake of discussion in this comment I will concentrate attention on some of them: specifically, on the relationship between 'the core' and the rest of economic analysis, and on the related issue of the interpretation of the level of commodity output in Sraffa's analysis given in sections 2 and 3 of Garegnani's paper.

My common point of departure with Garegnani is the stress laid on the different vision of the working of the economic system of classical and marginalist economists. Sraffa (1960, p. 93) refers to the counter-position of 'the circular process of production and consumption', which characterizes the classical approach, and the 'one-way avenue' of marginalist economists, whose analysis relies on demand and supply forces stemming from the confrontation of initial resource endowments (the side of supply) and economic agents' preferences (the side of demand); in other terms, the counter-position of the 'spiral' and the 'arch', as Sylos Labini (1985b) says.

Because of their vision of the economic problem, marginalist economists are led to conceive as the object of economic analysis the determination of equilibrium positions, where quantities and prices – including employment and distributive variables – are simultaneously determined. In contrast, the circular flow vision of classical economists lends itself quite naturally to the distinction of a series of related analytical issues, which can be subjected to separate treatment; and this *analytical separability* opens the way to the use of *different levels of analysis* for dealing with the various issues. (On this, see Roncaglia, 1978, ch. 7; and my contribution to this volume – ch. 16 below.)

Within this context, Garegnani (pp. 123 above) stresses 'the separation between two fields of analysis'. The first is 'the "core" of the theory' (i.e. the set of issues analysed in Sraffa, 1960), which Garegnani considers to be the only field of analysis 'where general quantitative relations of sufficiently definite form can be postulated'. The second field comprises all remaining economic issues, 'where relations in the economy are so complex and variable according to circumstances as to allow not for general quantitative relations of sufficiently definite form, but, rather, for a more inductive kind of analysis'.

In my opinion, this dichotomy between the 'core' and the rest of economic analysis, as stated by Garegnani, goes too far. Many would agree that the theory of value and distribution is important in economic analysis, because it is the field of analysis where differences in the underlying vision of the economy are better and more precisely expressed. (Thus any other piece of analysis, referring to any other economic issue, must be conceptually consistent with the 'core', in a sense that I tried to exemplify in my paper at the conference.) But the importance of the 'core' from this point of view should not suggest that it be considered as 'superior', in the sense of being both necessary and logically prior to any other piece of analysis (Garegnani, p. 125, speaks in this context of 'successive logical stages' of analysis) and of being the only one based on 'general' rather than on 'special hypotheses'.

Also, the importance of the 'core' does not imply that the main line of causality in the economy runs *from* the relations analysed within the 'core' *to* all other relations; say, from income distribution to technical choice. On the contrary, a greater openness to possible alternatives in the search for main lines of causality may prove very fruitful. (For a survey of some examples, see Roncaglia, 1986b, which also contains a discussion of the ideas of 'successive logical stages of analysis', and of the 'gravitation of market prices to/around prices of production', as set out by Garegnani in his paper.)

The sharp dichotomy Garegnani poses between 'two different fields of analysis' (the 'core' and the rest of economic analysis) raises a basic unsolved methodological issue, which is not explicitly dealt with in his paper.

There is common agreement on the fact that Sraffa's 1960 analysis provides a precise quantitative representation of the main forces in action in an economic system (in short, technology and competition) affecting relative prices and their relationship with income distribution. But here, too, we must be careful not to go too far. Theoretical analysis can provide the formal representation of the outcome of the action of certain forces, considered in isolation from all sorts of complicating factors present in reality. Thus, once logical consistency is ensured, theoretical analysis only expresses the implications of our selection of the forces to be considered within the analysis, and of our hypotheses about the way such forces operate *in vacuo*. However, such a theoretical analysis cannot by itself prove that the forces selected for analysis are the main forces in action in reality. To support this selection, we must refer to our 'vision' of economic reality, and to the fruitfulness of such 'vision' and of the theoretical work stemming from it for our understanding of economic events.

There is some sort of reference to an underlying 'vision' of the economy, in the way in which Garegnani justifies his emphasis on the 'core'. This is revealed by the stress on the 'persistency' of the forces determining prices of production, which can thus be described as 'centres of gravity' for actual (market) prices. Here 'persistency' means that techniques and income distribution (the forces determining prices of production) are rather stable, or change slowly; but 'slowly' in this context must mean 'at a speed which is of a lower order of magnitude than the speed of change of other economic variables'. In section 2 of Garegnani's paper the qualitative jump between the 'necessity' and 'generality' of the relations among variables within the 'core', and the 'multiplicity and diversity' of the relations among variables outside the 'core', is simply asserted. However, while this idea may have an intuitive appeal to economists trained in the classical approach to value and distribution, no proof is provided for it.

In this respect, we might recall, for example, the neat formal way in which Harrod expresses the interaction and the balancing of the forces making for the growth of aggregate demand and of productive capacity. In what sense could it be said that these latter relations are less 'general' and less 'definite' – when the difference is seen not as one of degree, but as a qualitative one: a *quantum leap* – than the relations depicted by Sraffa's price equations?

This discussion leads to the relevance of the debate on the 'gravitation of market prices to/around prices of production' for the all-dominating role attributed by Garegnani to the analysis of the 'core'. I have considered this point elsewhere (Roncaglia, 1986a). Here I shall briefly comment on one aspect of this issue, namely, on how Garegnani interprets the outputs, which are taken as data in Sraffa's analysis.

According to Garegnani, 'the outputs [that Sraffa] takes as given are *ex ante normal* outputs just like the neoclassical "equilibrium" outputs' (p. 132). Moreover, 'these "natural" or "necessary" prices (or "prices of production") can *rule* [my italics] only when the quantity of the commodity "brought to market" is equal to its "effectual demand"' (p. 132). This point of view is attributed both to classical economists and to Sraffa. However, Sraffa states that his analysis 'contains no reference to market prices' (Sraffa, 1960, p. 9), and hence no reference to any issues pertaining to the realization of produced quantities or to prices ruling in the market. Sraffa carefully avoids taking up an issue that for classical economists was inextricably connected to the theory of value and distribution; perhaps this can be interpreted as a sign of the change in methodological views that intervened in the meantime.

Moreover, when defining 'effectual demand' as 'the long-run magnitude emerging from an average of booms and slumps', Garegnani refers to 'normal output' – a physical magnitude. But I shall now argue that he should rather refer to the 'normal degree of capacity utilization', which is a percentage independent of dimensions.

The idea of 'effectual demand' as a 'long-run magnitude' risks stimulating the search for a 'long-run theory of output', as some papers at the conference testified. The reconstruction of a non-neoclassical analysis of output and employment should rather concentrate on integrating short-run and long-run aspects, which are both essential and mutually interact. For instance, whenever the current and the normal degree of capacity utilization differ, *ex post* realized profits will be affected, and this will affect financing conditions, which in turn may affect investment expenditure, and hence the expansion of productive capacity; on the other hand, the current level of investment expenditure will affect aggregate demand, and hence the current level of capacity utilization.

To repeat: the idea that productive capacity and demand must adapt to one another if we consider averages over long spells of time should be replaced by the idea that the current percentage degree of capacity utilization oscillates around the 'normal' *percentage degree* of capacity utilization. At the same time, we must admit that available productive capacity is constantly changing, however short the period to which we refer, because of investment decisions taken in the past. Therefore a series of booms and slumps implies that the quantities produced oscillate not around a long-period average, but around a (very likely irregular) trend, which we can interpret as Steindl's (1981) 'semi-autonomous trend' (where an exogenous element, 'the emergence of new know-how', and the endogenous elements embedded in 'the economic growth of the past' 'are reacting on one another and between themselves produce the trend').

I do not maintain that the above account is the best interpretation of what Sraffa (let alone classical economists) had in mind. All I have tried to do, in commenting on Garegnani's carefully framed paper, is to suggest that his ideas on the role of the 'core', as compared with the rest of economic analysis, and the connected interpretation of Sraffa's outputs (and, possibly, the underlying methodological views of the relationship between theory and reality) stop far short of making full use of the idea, on which Garegnani agrees, of the 'separability of issues' and of 'different levels of analysis'. A different interpretation of Sraffa's analysis might thus bring us nearer to a conceptual coherence of the (Sraffian) analysis of prices of production and income distribution with the (Keynesian–Kaleckian) analysis of output and growth and the (Steindl–Sylos Labini-like) analysis of market forms.

Reply

1 *Wages*

1. I am glad to find that Dr Harcourt's agreement with what I wrote in my paper is not limited to the general point that the main contribution of *Production of Commodities* lies in clarifying and developing the classical approach to distribution, while providing the spring-board for a criticism of marginal theory. What matters most, the agreement extends to the essential terms of that classical approach.

2. Dr Harcourt appears in fact to agree on the importance today of the approach to wages of the classical economists, with its underlying recognition of the possibility of labour unemployment and the associated conception of free competition in the labour market. The latter had to differ from what developed later in parallel with the idea of a demand *function* for labour and, therefore, of a 'full employment' wage – an idea that (as I argued in my paper) was absent until the time of Ricardo and appears to have originated with the wage fund theories.

As Harcourt indicates, when we take up and develop today the classical approach to wages we should start by recognizing that there are two levels of the real wage which are relevant. The first is the 'normal' level in the given situation. This will generally change over time depending on the extent to which the bargaining position of workers allows them to participate in the sharing of the fruits of technical progress. The amount of unemployment will play an important role in that evolution, though jointly with other factors pertaining to the broader political and social situation (which might, for example, for a time, give a faster rise in real wages, even while labour unemployment is increasing, as has happened in the recent past). And this will be so, whether these factors act directly on the real wage, or rather act indirectly through their effects on monetary policy and the structure of the rates of interest.

However, Sraffa's suggestion is that, jointly with that 'normal' level of the real wage (which will generally include an element of 'surplus') it will be important to consider the level below which real wages could not fall in the economy in question – the level which is indicated by Sraffa (and by Smith) as the subsistence wage. This second level, whose indirect influence on the behaviour of the normal wage, under modern conditions, may easily be underestimated, is likely to change considerably over time (though more slowly and evenly than the normal wage) in response to a number of economic and social factors, among which the dominant influence would seem to be the trend of the 'normal' wage and its effects on consumption habits.

Somewhat more open to doubt I find instead the idea that Harcourt reports from Kaldor of a minimum rate of profits (maximum wage) symmetrical to that of a minimum wage. Reflection seems to show that owners of capital are in a fundamentally different position from workers. Keynes's idea of the 'euthanasia of the rentier' may already indicate how symmetry might be misleading here (Keynes, 1936, p. 376, also 221).

3. I was thus pleased to find Harcourt also in agreement on the associated question of a rejection of the role of factor endowments postulated in post-classical theory (my paper, para. 11) – and on the importance of the several complex mechanisms (about which economists would stand to learn from economic historians and demographers) by which 'endowments' may adjust to the long-period growth of output and effective demand (as Sir John Hicks, Professor Vianello and others stressed at the Conference), rather than constrain it.

Of course, what I have just said about labour unemployment shows that the rejection of a determining role of factor endowments in distribution does not mean that the growth of the labour force and the speed of capital accumulation have no independent relevance for the distribution between wages and profits. However, clearly, Marx's theory of the 'reserve army' of unemployed labour is different from a theory of wages based on the intersection between a demand function for labour, determined by factor substitution, and the corresponding supply – though both theories have something to do with comparative speeds of capital accumulation and of growth of the labour force.

4. Finally, I found Harcourt's stress on the conceptual rather than the formal aspect of theories very refreshing. This is particularly so in the present conditions of our discipline, which imposes a re-examination of long-dominant ideas.

This stress on the conceptual rather than the formal aspect of theories is not however in conflict with the fact that the significant conception of the economic system by an author cannot but be embodied in the logical structure of his theory, whether or not the author is aware of it (Adam Smith or Ricardo were, for instance, largely unaware of how their theory of the distribution between wages and profits could entail the recognition of class conflict in the workings of the economy and society. It was left to later socialist writers to bring that implication to light, when historical events posed the issue. The impact this had on the dominant stream of economic theory, may still be seen as late as Foxwell, [1899] 1962, e.g., pp. xl–xlii).

Thus, in the case more immediately to hand here, the difference between the conception of the economic system we find in Sraffa and that which Hahn attributes to him when viewing Sraffa's analysis as a special case of neo-classical theory is objectively recorded in the fact that the equations relating to the demand for and supply of factors are not present in Sraffa and correspondingly the real wage (or the rate of profits) is taken as determined 'outside the system of production' (Sraffa, 1960, p. 33).

However, I must ask Dr Harcourt to wait for the more comprehensive work to which I referred in my paper for an answer on whether the focus of my criticism on capital lies on what Hahn calls 'adjustment theories', rather than on what he calls 'equilibrium theory' (Hahn, 1986, p. 373). A short answer would be that I see the two aspects as indissolubly related, as they were when Marshall would qualify as 'real' a stable equilibrium only (Marshall, 1890, Appendix H, 2, p. 806, n.; cf. also Pigou, 1933, p. 195). A basic theoretical difficulty emerging in one form in a version of the theory, will emerge in a different form in another version. Thus the criticism on capital which can be directed to the general equilibrium system as originally formulated by Walras, regards the existence of those equilibria. However, the phenomena of 'reverse capital deepening' and 'reswitching', in so far as they affect the demand for investment and the productive factors, impinge upon what would be regarded as 'adjustment theories'. But the main point seems here to be that the kind of instability which may be caused by those phenomena contradicts experience, and to that extent calls into question the theory as a whole. When in the continuation of the above passage, Marshall admitted an unstable equilibrium merely as a 'dividing boundary' between two *stable* equilibria, he showed how aware he was that 'unstable' equilibria and, therefore, the *possibility* of 'equilibria' with zero prices for commodities or productive services known to have a positive price, would call into question the validity of a demand-and-supply explanation – unless it could be convincingly argued that should those equilibria arise, they would not lead to such results or, more generally, to results too greatly at variance with experience. To my knowledge no such argument has been advanced so far with respect to the phenomena in question.

2 *On the 'core' of classical theories*

5. I am equally pleased with Professor Roncaglia's agreement with the main points of my paper, and I am convinced that the differences between our two standpoints will be considerably narrowed after a clarification of what appear to be some misreadings of my position, undoubtedly due to my failure to be sufficiently clear. I shall now consider in turn the two groups of issues raised by Roncaglia:

(i) the relations between the 'core' and the rest of the analysis of the classical economists;
(ii) the meaning of the prices and quantities which we find in Sraffa.

6. Roncaglia argues:

> In my opinion, this dichotomy between the 'core' and the rest of economic analysis, as stated by Garegnani, goes too far. Many would agree that the theory of value and distribution is important in economic analysis, because it is the field of analysis where differences in the underlying vision of the

economy are better and more precisely expressed . . . But the importance of the 'core' from this point of view should not suggest that it be considered as 'superior', in the sense of being both necessary and logically prior to any other piece of analysis (Garegnani, par. 18, speaks in this context of 'successive logical stages' of analysis) . . . (page 145 above).

However, my view is in fact that it would *not* be correct to argue that the relations analysed in the 'core' are in some definable sense of 'superior' importance with respect to those analysed outside it (see par. 7 below). The passage on par. 18 referred to by Roncaglia states rather the opposite, since it relates to 'successive logical stages (for example, the determination of the real wage [outside the "core"] and *then* that of the other shares of the product [in the core]', where what is 'logically prior' is the determination of the wage, which lies *outside* the 'core', and not within it.

Even less would I argue that those relations are 'superior' on the ground Roncaglia indicates, according to which 'differences in the underlying vision of the economy are [there] better and more precisely expressed'. As I have argued elsewhere (e.g. Garegnani, 1981, pp. 84–8), and have just recalled, the conception of the economic process characterizing a theoretical approach is embodied in the logical structure of the theory as a whole, independently even of the awareness of its originators or practitioners. It therefore needs to have little specifically to do with the way in which the relative prices of commodities are determined. (The substantive part of the theory of distribution to which Roncaglia also refers in his passage lies in any case outside the core.) This of course does not mean denying that in the last three quarters of the last century, and beyond, the theory of value was often used as an ideological tool. However, we would all agree that the possible ideological use of scientific concepts does not mean that science does not exist. (I have in fact used the term 'conception' instead of Roncaglia's, and Schumpeter's, more subjective term 'vision', to avoid any implication that economic theorizing can *by its nature* be legitimately made to suit our preconceptions, political or otherwise.)

7. To conclude now on the 'superiority' Roncaglia thinks I ascribe to the relations in the 'core' of classical theory, in a paper published after the Conference, I had in fact written:

> To avoid misunderstandings, it should be noted that the distinction between the part of the theory to be found in that core and the part outside it, has to do with a difference only in the nature of the relationships studied. It has therefore little to do with the comparative interest or importance which one wished to attach to those two kinds of relationships, as should be evident from the fact that questions as central as distribution, aggregate demand, accumulation or technical change fall largely outside the core.
> (Garegnani, 1987, p. 562)

As I continue in that passage, the relationships studied in the core are simply a step, though generally a necessary step, in the analysis of those central questions dealt with outside the core. (For example, Ricardo needed to clarify the relation between the rate of profits and the wage in order to reach his conclusions about the tendencies of accumulation, or about the effects of a tariff on corn in Britain.)

Thus there seems to be a misreading when Roncaglia thinks that in my opinion 'the main line of causality in the economy runs *from* the relations analysed within the 'core' *to* all other relations' (page 145). On the contrary, the lines of causation, in so far as they do not run *within* each of the two fields, will rather tend to run from *outside* to *inside* the core, as is implied by the fact that the independent variables of the core are determined *outside* it.

8. Still in connection with the 'core', Roncaglia writes in his comment

> There is some sort of reference to an underlying 'vision' of the economy, in the way in which Garegnani justifies his emphasis on the 'core'. This is revealed by the stress on the 'persistency' of the forces determining prices of production, which can thus be described as 'centres of gravity' for actual (market) prices. Here 'persistency' means that techniques and income distribution (the forces determining prices of production) are rather stable, or change slowly; but 'slowly' in this context must mean 'at a speed which is of a lower order of magnitude than the speed of change of other economic variables'.
>
> (page 146)

However, the persistency referred to by the classical economists and Sraffa (and all other theorists as well, as I shall presently argue) for their data is not relative to that of 'other economic variables' in general. That would not be possible, because the forces whose persistency is in question are those that determine the other variables – the speed of change of which cannot therefore be any faster than that of the forces that determine them. The persistency referred to is on the contrary relative to the forces that continuously cause, say, differences between the rates of remuneration for different units of the same resource, or between the prices of different units of the same commodity, etc. – the persistency, that is, is relative to those 'fitful and irregular causes' that, over a sufficient period of time, will 'efface one another's influence' (Marshall, 1920, p. 281). This is quite general and applies to Keynes's 'short-period' equilibria or to Marshall's short-period partial equilibria, no less than to the 'long-period' positions of the marginal theorist and of the classical economists.

When this meaning of the persistency in question is clear, it will appear that its assumption is not due to any desire of mine to emphasize the core in classical theory:[1] the assumption is in fact implicity done whenever economic theorizing is carried out (see my comment on Asimakopulos's contribution to this volume, par. 3 below). Indeed, when any theorist refers to, say, an amount of investment or to a money rate of interest, or to an amount of money loans, of course they are not referring to that quantity as it is on a *particular* day or week – when the quantity is likely to be strongly influenced by accidental factors altogether different from those they are considering. They clearly refer to the quantity as it can be observed over a period of time sufficient to allow elimination of the effects of those accidental causes. It follows that the forces they are referring to, are in fact assumed to be persistent enough not to change appreciably over such a period.

Roncaglia's disagreement seems, however, to refer particularly to the persistence of the forces that should determine the long-period 'normal' values – though one can now see that what is peculiar to these 'long-period' normal positions is simply that the 'persistency' of the determining forces has then to be relative *also* to the forces that cause disproportions between the productive capacities of the various sectors, or more generally disproportions between the availabilities of the several capital goods.[2] That this is in fact Roncaglia's more limited target is confirmed by what he writes on page 147, where he seems to criticize the very idea of a *long-period* theory of outputs. However, what he writes there about 'integrating short-run and long-run aspects' and about a 'semi-autonomous trend' appears to be in fact an indication of possible lines for a *particular* 'long-period' theory of outputs. The 'irregularity' of the trend to which he refers seems to me to be a way of saying that the trend does not follow the kind of rules we economists have often expected it to follow – which does not mean that it does not follow *other* rules (see my comment on Asimakopulos's contribution to this volume, par. 4).

It seems therefore that Roncaglia's disagreement on 'persistency' is not really present, and that what he is rejecting is not the possibility of a long period analysis of accumulation, and of the associated persistent forces, but rather some *particular* kind of long-period analysis. (What is rejected in the post-Keynesian literature to which Roncaglia appears to refer is in fact the marginalist long-period theory with its conclusion about a tendency to the full employment of labour, implicitly viewed in that literature as the only possible long-period theory.) On the other hand, I have attempted to illustrate elsewhere[3] the reasons why the long-period normal positions – and the corresponding persistency of the forces determining them – have long and unanimously been deemed essential for a general theory of distribution and relative prices and, therefore, essential for the determination of the variables in the core.

9. The 'persistency' of the determining forces relates to the analysis conducted outside the 'core' no less than to that conducted inside it. It therefore constitutes an issue that is different from that of the 'core', and of the corresponding distinction between two kinds of analysis I refer to in my paper. However, Roncaglia addresses himself more properly to the 'core' when he continues the passage above as follows:

> In section III of Garegnani's paper the qualitative jump between the 'necessity' and the 'generality' of the relations among variables within the 'core', and the 'multiplicity and diversity' of the relations among variables outside the 'core', is simply asserted. However, while this idea may have an intuitive appeal to economists trained in the classical approach to value and distribution, no proof is provided for it.
>
> (page 146)

A central issue is in effect raised here. The proof that Roncaglia asks for, appears to lie in the surplus principle itself, which Roncaglia elsewhere admits to be at the centre of the classical theories (in, for example, Roncaglia 1978). We could not otherwise explain the possibility of taking the wage, social product and technical conditions of production as independent variables when determining prices and the residual distributive variables – while at the same time admitting reciprocal influences between those 'independent' variables, and also influences on them of the dependent variables. Clearly, if relations of sufficiently definite properties and of the same generality as the price equations could be postulated between wages and quantities produced – or between both of them and still other variables – it would not make sense to determine 'shares other than wages' as the difference of equation (1) in my paper (par. 19). We should rather have a *simultaneous* determination of the social product, prices and the dependent distributive variables, *given* the real wage – or, even, a simultaneous determination of those same variables *and* of the real wage, given some other parameters.

The latter case is in fact that of marginal theory, which postulates the existence of relations of precisely that definiteness and generality (the demand and supply functions for factors), and accordingly arrives at a simultaneous determination of wages, prices and the rate of profits (interest) on the basis of consumer tastes and factor endowments.

10. This reference to the surplus principle may also indicate more precisely the sense to be attributed to what Roncaglia describes in the above passage as the 'qualitative jump' that I would envisage between the relations that the classical economists studied in the 'core' of their theory, and those they saw as prevailing outside it. The basic point is that, unlike what happens in marginal theory, the relations between wages, outputs and technical conditions of production do not prevent their treatment as independent variables.

This, it might be observed, does not by itself prevent the possibility of other formal relations outside the core. It does not prevent, for example, the existence of formal relations between investment, social product and aggregate savings. In fact, Roncaglia writes in the continuation of the above passage (p. 146):

> In this respect, we might recall, for example, the neat formal way in which Harrod expresses the interaction and the balancing of the forces making for the growth of aggregate demand and of productive capacity. In what sense could it be said that these latter relations are less 'general' and less 'definite' . . .?

Harrod's equation, however, is perhaps not a good example in favour of Roncaglia's thesis because it is clearly difficult to see it as *determining* the rate of growth of an economy in the same sense in which the price equations may be said to determine prices and the dependent distributive variables in the classical theories. A more favourable example for Roncaglia's thesis would perhaps be Keynes's multiplier $\Delta Y = \Delta I/s$ which can be viewed as determining an observable phenomenon (the increment in social product resulting from an increment in investment) not unlike the price equations of the 'core'.

However, when the two cases are considered closely enough, I believe that some important differences become apparent.

The relation between distributive variables and relative prices has the same degree of rigour and generality as our assumptions concerning the definition of the distributive variables. Now, in the case of competition, for example, it has been beyond dispute in both marginal and classical theories that the market will tend to realize a uniform rate of remuneration for the same kind of resource, wherever employed.

In the case of the multiplier, however, it would seem that the increment of output determined by the equation will follow only when a number of assumptions are satisfied, which are additional to those concerning the definition of the variables involved. Moreover, we have no reason to expect those assumptions to be tendentially realized by the market and, therefore, they are of the nature of simplifying hypotheses which, at best, can only be realised as approximations. Among these assumptions we have, for example (a) that the consumption function is independent of the amount of investment; (b) that the consumption function is also independent of the physical composition of investment; (c) that the system of relative prices and the rates of remuneration can be taken as given. Even without going into a detailed examination of the question, it would seem evident that, even if (c) could perhaps be separately dealt with, on an analogy with the quantities produced in the classical 'core', there is no reason to expect conditions (a) and (b) to tend to be realized in the same sense in which, for instance, equal rates of remuneration for the same kind of resource tend to be realized under free competition.

It thus appears that whereas the price equations can be held to provide a rigorous representation of reality, the multiplier equation can be seen (even when its basic Keynesian theoretical premise on the independence of investment from savings is accepted) as being either an approximate representation of real phenomena, or alternatively as something that is rigorously valid only under very special simplifying assumptions. In either case, it would seem that a relation like that of the multiplier and similar ones, far from contradicting what I argued concerning the distinction between the two fields of analysis, would confirm that distinction. The possibility of formal relations in fields of analysis like the determination of outputs, accumulation and distribution appears to exist only under special assumptions, and in that sense either as approximate (though of course highly useful) descriptions of reality or, alternatively, as intellectual experiments intended to analyse the logical implications of particular hypotheses.

3 *On prices and outputs in Sraffa's analysis*

11. Some misreading of my position seems on the other hand to occur in connection with the second group of questions raised by Roncaglia. On page 147 of his comment Roncaglia refers to the passage in my paper where it is stated that 'these natural or necessary prices (or prices of production) [of the classical economists and Sraffa] can rule only when the quantity of the

commodity brought to market is equal to its effectual demand' (par. 34). He then continues:

> this point of view is attributed [by Garegnani] both to classical economists and to Sraffa. However, Sraffa states that his analysis 'contains no reference to market prices' (Sraffa, 1960, p. 9), and hence no reference to any issues pertaining to the realization of produced quantities or to prices ruling in the market.

There can be no question, I believe, about the presence of that point of view in the classical economists – as a reading of, say, the chapter 'On the natural and market price of commodities'[4] of the *Wealth of Nations* (Book I, ch. 7) or of chapter XXX of Ricardo's *Principles* quickly reveals. Roncaglia's doubts must therefore refer exclusively to Sraffa. However, when examined more closely, the passage in Sraffa on which Roncaglia rests his doubts appears to state the opposite of what Roncaglia takes it to mean. The full passage (already quoted from in note 56 of my paper) reads as follows:

> A less one-sided description than costs of production seems therefore required. Such classical terms as 'necessary price', 'natural price' or 'price of production' would meet the case, but value and price have been preferred as being shorter and, in the present context (which contains no reference to market prices) no more ambiguous
>
> (Sraffa, 1960, p. 9)

The bracketed clause 'which contains no reference to market prices' is there to explain why Sraffa felt that no adjective like 'natural' etc. was required – though it would be quite appropriate, as he tells us. Thus, what Sraffa is in effect saying is that, if he had chosen to treat 'market prices', he would have done so on the same lines as the classical economists – so much so that he considers the prices he is referring to as properly described by the other term in that indissoluble analytical couple of classical theory.

12. Moreover, when in the above passage Roncaglia says that Sraffa is not concerned with 'market prices', readers used to modern terminology and unaware of the exact classical meaning of 'market price' used by Sraffa (the actual price at a particular time and place, influenced, as it inevitably is, by accidental circumstances) might be excused for taking it to mean the price that 'market forces' tend to establish and, therefore, as the normal price observable on an average in the economy. The same readers may therefore be excused if they understand the opposite of what Sraffa says – that he is *not* concerned with prices as established in the reality of a market but rather with prices of some different nature.

What might so far be the result only of a misreading of Sraffa's expression 'market price' begins to take a different nature when we see it in conjunction not only with the passage from Roncaglia (1978 p. 16) that I quote in my paper (note 56), but also in the light of what Roncaglia writes when he takes Sraffa's passage about 'market price' as a sign of the 'change in methodological views that intervened [since the classical economists]' (page

147) or as referring to some specific new 'methodological views of the relationship between theory and reality' (ibid.). These methodological views are those he indicates as follows:

> Theoretical analysis can provide the formal representation of the outcome of the action of certain forces, considered in isolation from all sorts of complicating factors present in reality. Thus, once logical consistency is ensured, theoretical analysis only expresses the implications of our selection of the forces to be considered within the analysis and of our hypotheses about the way such forces operate *in vacuo*. However, such a theoretical analysis cannot by itself prove that the forces selected for analysis are the main forces in action in reality. To support this selection, we must refer to our 'vision' of economic reality, and to the fruitfulness of such 'vision' and of the theoretical work stemming from it for our understanding of economic events.
>
> (page 146; see also Roncaglia, 1978, p. 21)

I am not sure I fully understand what Roncaglia is arguing here. However, it would seem clear that if the classical economists and Sraffa treated the social product and the wage or the rate of profits as independent variables in their determination of profits and prices it was *because of their theory of distribution and outputs*, and not because of any arbitrary selection of the independent variables – equally possible for an economist believing in a marginalist demand-and-supply explanation of distribution and prices. It would also seem that such a classical analysis of distribution was the result of a series of reasoned observations carried out by a succession of authors over centuries – with the 'vision' in the head of any individual economist being either a result of such reasoned observations by past generations or a stimulus for further ones.

Whatever we may think about these wider methodological questions, it would seem that, in the case in hand, we do not need to go far into a discussion of them. Sraffa seems to have made clear that his position is in that respect the same as that of the classical economists, last but not least in the very passage about market prices that Roncaglia has quoted (see also Sraffa, 1960, p. v).[5]

13. I am also not sure that I understand what Roncaglia means when he writes:

> When defining 'effectual demand' as 'the long-run magnitude emerging from an average of booms and slumps', Garegnani refers to 'normal output'. . . But I shall now argue that he should rather refer to the 'normal degree of capacity utilization', which is a percentage independent of dimensions.
>
> (page 147)

In the note to which Roncaglia refers, I used the expression 'effectual demand' as the classical economists did, to mean 'the demand of those who are willing to pay the natural prices of the commodity', (Smith, [1776] 1960, Bk. I, ch. VII, vol. 1, p. 49), which is clearly a quantity of the commodity and, not a 'percentage of capacity utilization[6]. As is shown by the argument he refers to in his passage and which he develops after it,[7] Roncaglia appears to be mixing the classical question of 'effectual demand' pertaining merely to the adjustments of *relative* outputs with the altogether distinct question of aggregate demand – just what I have claimed in that very note of my paper, on the basis of some passages in Roncaglia (1978).

14. The questions Roncaglia has raised on the 'core', and on the meaning of outputs and prices in Sraffa's analysis and that of the classical economists are obviously complex questions, made even more complex by the long dominance of marginal theory. They need discussing in order to consolidate the basis of further constructive work. We should all be grateful to Professor Roncaglia for his contribution to this discussion.

Notes

1 In fact the question was raised in Garegnani (1976a) only in order to point out a shift in the concept of equilibrium that had occurred in marginal theory, as a result, I argued there, of the difficulties with the concept of capital underlying that theory.

2 So that the normal position of the economic system will include a 'normal' relation between the rates of return on the supply prices of the capital goods (in particular the equality of those rates, in the benchmark case of free competition).

3 Garegnani (1976a), pp. 26–9, also (1989), pp. 355–6, and n. 19, 21, 22.

4 On the meaning of natural and market prices, see my paper, par. 30.

5 See also Sraffa (1960) p. 9.

6 It is on the other hand clear that for the classical authors adjustments to 'effectual demand' involve movements of capital and therefore changes in what we would today describe as the proportion between the productive capacities of the several industries. It follows that those relative outputs are 'long-period normal outputs' in that specific sense.

7 I have dealt in par. 8 above with Roncaglia's conclusion on that argument about the 'irregularity' of the trend likely to emerge from the development of aggregate demand over time. I might add here that when, in connection with aggregate demand, he writes:

> the idea that productive capacity and demand must adapt to one another if we consider averages over long spells of time should be replaced by the idea that the current percentage degree of capacity utilization oscillates around the 'normal' percentage degree of capacity utilization.
>
> (page 147)

I have difficulty in seeing the difference between the two kinds of oscillations he mentions there. To say that the current percentage degree of capacity utilization oscillates around a 'normal' degree of utilization appears to me not to differ from saying that current output oscillates around a 'normal' output. The second way of putting it has the advantage of reminding us that we also have to explain the *size* of that productive capacity (on the question of the average degree of utilization of capacity over time, see Garegnani, 1982, p. 10).

6

The Sraffa Model, Constant Returns to Scale and Empirical Implications

Larry Levine
New Brunswick

> . . . I do not . . . want to suggest that the *essence* of Sraffa's book lies in [his] rehabilitation of the classical approach: Sraffa's primary concern is not to show that there's life in old dogs yet, but to build a 20th-century model to deal with 20th-century problems.
>
> (Meek, 1961, emphasis in original)

> In a quasi-realistic world of many different capital goods, a proper description of its operations must be in terms of its technological properties . . .
>
> (Samuelson, 1966, p. 524)

Some years ago, in the course of discussing the 'transformation problem', Paul Samuelson made passing reference to what he desccribed as 'this age of Leontief and Sraffa' (Samuelson, 1971a, p. 400). He was referring of course to the notion of a set of relative commodity prices determined by techniques of production. We have come a long way since Samuelson's characterization of 'this age', but not far enough to have put paid to a continuing debate on whether or not the Sraffa system 'fails' without an assumption of constant returns to scale. (See, for example, Burmeister, 1975, 1977, 1984; Eatwell, 1977; Levine, 1974, 1975, 1977, 1983; Samuelson, 1971b.) But this question is merely a curtain-raiser for a larger debate that has both an 'open' agenda and a 'hidden' agenda. The open agenda features such hardy perennials as the question of whether the contents of Sraffa's 'standard commodity' (his composite commodity numéraire) should or should not have any relevance to actual consumer preferences; the treatment of capital and joint production in Sraffa's model; the twinning of Sraffa and Leontief. The 'hidden agenda' – it is not really very well hidden – offers such items as whether or not the Sraffa system should be equipped with a production function (not a surprising offering this, in view of the dispute centering upon constant returns to scale), and some speculation concerning what 'equilibrium' is all about in the Sraffa system. (Should Hicks's dictum, 'Discussion of equilibrium conditions is always a means to an end' – Hicks, [1939] 1946 – always be trump in such speculation?)

But a set of unsettled questions can also have more 'positive' components. Thus, one may test the credentials of the late Ronald Meek's claim that the 'essence' of Sraffa's *Production of Commodities* lies in a presentation of a '20th-century model' to deal with '20th-century' problems by, for example, extracting theory-of-the-firm implications from the Sraffa model, and (taking seriously Samuelson's 'description' of a 'quasi-realistic' world) by considering whether the Sraffa model provides a suitable vantage point for examining the consequences of experiments in various countries in the 1970s in price freezing, price guidelining and wages and incomes policies. (For this bit of 'positive' economics, I even would go one better than Samuelson and say that the world that Samuelson depicted – paramountcy of technological properties, etc. – is not a 'quasi-realistic' one but a most *realistic* one.)

Section 1 will provide a brief (overview) note on what the Sraffa system is really all about. Section 2 will conduct what I hope will be the final inquest into the question of the need or non-need for a CRS assumption in the Sraffa model. Section 3 will present the items of the 'open agenda': consumer demand phenomena and the Sraffa model; joint production and capital inputs; and Sraffa and Leontief. Section 4 will unveil the 'hidden' agenda; namely, the production function and equilibrium. Section 5 will attempt to avoid the polemics of some of these agendas and will consider what may be actually *done* with the Sraffa model. Thus, the first part will be an exploration of theory-of-the-firm implications of the Sraffa model, and the second part will expose the Sraffa model to characterizations of various prices and incomes 'planning' episodes of the 1970s.

1 *A note on what the Sraffa system is (and on what it is not)*

Obviously, Sraffa's is, among other things, a model of the determination of *relative* commodity prices, and not of the absolute level of prices. In short, the model is homogeneous of degree zero in prices. Furthermore, the determinants of these price relatives are supply-side or essentially technological phenomena: demand considerations do not intrude in any *price-determining* role. But the Sraffa model is also a view of the structure of economic reality: a 'technological interdependence' view of structure. As regards *distribution*, the wage/profit share-out of the economy's net product is determined exogenously to the determination of commodity prices. However, the Sraffa model does display a concern with one important problem of distribution; namely, how an alteration in distributive shares may bear upon the set of commodity price ratios. This it does by that elaborate exercise to construct a composite commodity numéraire that brings into being Sraffa's 'standard commodity'. Again, levels of activity, the factor mix and the technologies in use are all exogenously given data.

So much for what the Sraffa model *is*. Just as important must be an understanding of what it is *not*. The array of given 'data' listed above provides an inkling. Thus, it is not at all about change in activity levels, in factor proportions or in technologies (Sraffa, 1960, p. v).[1] And along with that expurgation there departs some additional matter – the notion of a production function and the principle of returns to scale (of which, more later).

What remains is Sraffa's 'technological interdependence' model of economic structure and of commodity price determination. To characterize it as 'static' is to evoke a conventional static-dynamic distinction and to provide an infelicitous rendition of intentions. Actually, it is a 'snapshot', as it were, taken at a census moment of real time (see Roncaglia, 1978, pp. 21–2) – a representation of aspects of a real economy, given certain parameters (data) that obtain at that point of time, which is represented by the equations of production of Sraffa's supra-subsistence model.

2 *The Sraffa model and constant returns to scale: the never-ending debate*

Does the Sraffa model 'fail' without an assumption of constant returns to scale (CRS)? Debate over the need or non-need for such an assumption in the Sraffa system persists. It has now become like a debate between religionists and atheists. One side says, 'I believe!' the other says, 'I don't believe.' There is no middle ground.

Edwin Burmeister's comment on 'The irrelevance of Sraffa's analysis without constant returns to scale' may be singled out as the *locus classicus* for the view that without a CRS assumption the Sraffa system collapses into irrelevance ('I conclude that constant returns to scale is irrelevant for Sraffa's analysis only if one is content to pose somewhat irrelevant questions' – Burmeister, 1977, pp. 69–70) or into meaninglessness, if one may cite Burmeister's 'Comment' on 'This age of Leontief . . . and who?: 'Of course, one may deny constant returns to scale, but it is crucial then to determine what meaningful propositions remain valid?' (Burmeister, 1975, p. 545). Burmeister has stuck to his guns, albeit somewhat less obtrusively and less polemically, in his recent 'Sraffa, labour theories of value, and the economics of real wage determination' (Burmeister, 1984).

But the blow that may leave one reeling comes from Samuelson's 1971 paper on 'Sraffa's returns and post-Ricardian analysis'. Here one is treated to a list of 106 'places' in the *Production of Commodities by Means of Commodities* in which a CRS assumption is required if Sraffa's analysis is to be permitted to stand without '[re]consideration' (Samuelson, 1971b, p. 49, footnote 20).

I should like to introduce some of Samuelson's prose back-up for his census of places of vulnerability (without CRS) in the *Production of Commodities*, commencing with the note of Samuelsonian disbelief that was prompted by Sraffa's prefatory caveat, 'no such assumption [i.e. CRS] is made', and also by Sraffa's characterization of what he had set out to do: 'The investigation is concerned exclusively with such properties of an economic system as do not depend on changes in the scale of production or in the proportions of "factors"' (Sraffa, 1960, p. v). Here is Samuelson's expression of disbelief:

> as the mathematician knows and as Professors Henry Schultz and Yntema had to rediscover years ago in the attempt to understand Pareto and Walras, the postulated fact that there exist *invariant relations regardless of scale* is itself a covert form of the axiom of first-degree-homogeneous-functions.
>
> (Samuelson, 1971b, p. 4; emphasis in the original)

Samuelson comes on even stronger in the Mathematical Appendix to the same paper, writing that:

> I have now completed a compact summary of the conventional Sraffa system. But, it cannot be stressed enough, *every part of my discussion did explicitly presuppose constant-returns-to-scale technology* . . .
>
> Be it emphasized that it is not just the neoclassical fairy tales . . ., which Sraffa manifestly does not accept, that require constant returns to scale. It is every relation that I have taken from Sraffa or from anti-neoclassical writers which requires constant returns to scale in order to preserve relevance and/or avoid logical error or triviality.
>
> (Samuelson, 1971b, p. A21; emphasis in original)

If one is to remain undaunted by Samuelson's list of 106 instances of a need for CRS in *The Production of Commodities*, what is one to do? Do we not have any licence to grant the tenability of Sraffa's expressed concern with 'such properties of an economic system as do not depend on changes in the scale of production or in the proportions of factors'? Samuelson claims that Sraffa in effect abandoned this concern (e.g. Samuelson, 1971b, p. 5, including footnote 4). My retort (hinted at in the previous section) is that Sraffa's objective – besides that of developing a model of commodity price determination – was to present a view of the structure of economic reality. To repeat, Sraffa offers a snapshot taken at a census moment of time (see Roncaglia, 1978, pp. 21–2 and Harcourt, 1982, p. 259). I honestly do not know how much beyond John Eatwell's 'Since the size and composition of output and the technique in use are *data*, the issue of returns to scale does not arise' (Eatwell, 1977, p. 63) one can go, except to point out (yet again) that Sraffa presented an analysis of the determination of relative commodity prices, *given* a particular regime as regards technology, distributive shares and activity levels (see Levine, 1985, pp. 347–8).

Still on CRS: some of those who reject Sraffa's position on the dispensability of the assumption allege that the assumption is *in*dispensable to the 're-scaling' that is part of Sraffa's composite commodity numéraire construction exercise (e.g. Collard, 1963, 1964) and, also, to Sraffa's suggested 'changes' in the scalar multiples (my description, not Sraffa's) or proportions of some of the industries of the system in order to ensure that the latter will be in a self-replacing state (Sraffa, 1960, p. 5, footnote 1) or fulfil the Hawkins–

Simon condition, if you will (for example, see Samuelson, 1971b, p. 10). The re-scalings and proportion changes are purely notional (Eatwell, 1977), purely logical, or of the nature of algebraic *Hilfskonstruktionen* referred to by Newman (1962, p. 71). Data remain data.

But back to the *generic* phenomenon – the principle of returns to scale. I have already insisted that to push Sraffa *there* is to push him where he did not want to go. Incidentally, it is indeed a *strange* destination for critics to want to push Sraffa in the first place; that is, those critics who will not accept Sraffa's disclaimer about *change*. After all, the conventional neoclassical principle of returns to scale is a notoriously *static* principle that takes (almost) everything as *given*, including composition of output and factor proportions. Are the critics, then, shifting the ground from 'change' to *comparative statics* (alterations in some of the data, which now simply become shift parameters with no questions asked about the how's and the why's of the new regime), which, surely, was another place where Sraffa did not wish to go?

3 *The 'open agenda'*

Consumer demand phenomana and the Sraffa model

Burmeister (1984) and others remain unpersuaded about Sraffa's 'neglect' of consumer preferences in working out weights for the contents of the consumption basket that will constitute the real wage, calibrated in terms of the standard commodity numéraire, or, what amounts to the same thing, weights for the contents of the standard commodity itself. However, given the purpose of the latter, it *must* be constructed from technological considerations alone, without the intervention of consumer preferences; that is, in order to make the standard commodity numéraire (which is turned out by a standard system) invariant to the (internal) price effects of different regimes as regards distributive shares. The invariance is achieved by conferring upon the standard system the *technological* property that the output mix of that system will be the same as its commodity input mix (see above and, also, Sraffa, 1960, pp. 12–25).

But reality is reality. How *may* preferences – consumer demand considerations – be said to enter the Sraffa model? Consider the equations of production of the single-product variant of Sraffa's system. The levels at which the various industries perform or the implicit scalars of each of the equations of production could be regarded as reflecting consumer preferences. And, of course, precisely the same point may be made with respect to Sraffa's joint-product model.

Joint production and heterogeneous capital goods in the Sraffa model

Burmeister has insisted that the Sraffa system can handle neither joint production nor heterogeneous capital goods (Burmeister, 1984, pp. 516, 517, 522). On the question of joint production, Burmeister's objection rests upon a familiar bottom line; namely, Sraffa's 'neglect' of consumer demand, with the (inevitable) accompanying neglect of the possible existence of more than one steady-state equilibrium. More precisely, according to Burmeister, where it is a case of *intrinsic* joint production (e.g. wool and mutton), the answer to the question of which of the steady-state equilibrium price vectors that can obtain at a particular rate of profit will actually obtain will depend upon the final demand mix (Burmeister, 1984, p. 516). Therefore, since there can be, potentially, many different final demand bills at each rate of profit, there can exist, potentially, many different equilibrium price vectors associated with a particular rate of profit. But *intrinsic* joint production, or joint production in the 'strict' sense, is surely the exception rather than the rule. Furthermore, even if there *were* joint production in the strict sense, and even assuming that variable rather than fixed (product) proportions were the rule where there was joint production – thereby giving Burmeister's joint-production point its most favourable context – Burmeister's critique here must still be rejected, unless one wishes to dish Sraffa *entirely* (which, we surmise, Burmeister is not willing to do). The grounds for rejection here remain the same: the determination of activity levels and other Sraffa-system *data* remain unexplained as to magnitude, etc., in the exogenous beyond. And, to paraphrase – and extend – Samuelson (1966a, pp. 524–5), whether or not these magnitudes are determined prior to, or as a result of, 'confrontation with market forces' in that beyond is a question that is totally outside the intended scope of Sraffa's analysis.

There is perhaps a more telling argument to bring in at this juncture – and here we enter upon the question of heterogeneous capital goods in the Sraffa system. One wonders whether Burmeister forgot about Sraffa's principal *raison d'être* for having introduced the joint-production case in the first place. Let Sraffa speak for himself: 'The interest of Joint Products does not lie so much in the familiar examples of wool and mutton, or wheat and straw, as in its being the genus of which Fixed Capital is the leading species' (Sraffa, 1960, p. 63).

Recall that the inputs on the left-hand sides of Sraffa's (joint-product) equations can include installations of durable capital equipment, and what remains of them (physically) at the end of the 'period of production' will appear among the outputs of product on the right-hand sides. Sraffa, then, deals with inputs of fixed capital in the same way as in the von Neumann equilibrium growth model (von Neumann, 1945–6, p. 2) and, long before that, as in the classical treatment of Robert Torrens.[2] And the joint-product version of his model not only permits Sraffa to handle inputs of fixed capital, but it also enables him to deal with depreciation (see Sraffa, 1960, pp. 64–6).

Sraffa and Leontief

Some of the difficulties in interpreting Sraffa may stem in part from an insufficiently nuanced twinning of Sraffa's analysis with that of Leontief and, also, from the placing of Leontief as well as Sraffa within the key aspect of the Walrasian system that is the mutual determination of the prices of goods *and* of factors of production. In neither the Sraffa nor the Leontief system is there a mutual determination of commodity and factor prices. In both, the set of relative commodity prices is determined by supply-side phenomena – the technological properties, once again, of the system. However, in the Sraffa system these same technological properties do not obscure *all* problems of distributive shares as they do in the Leontief. Thus, the way in which a different regime as regards the wage–profit split can bear upon the commodity price set is an important feature of Sraffa's analysis. Specifically, keep in mind Sraffa's composite commodity numéraire construction exercise. In contrast, profit or, indeed, anything having to do with distributive shares, can scarcely be said to feature very prominently in the Leontief system. Thus, consider this equation, which depicts an open Leontief model (Zarnowitz, 1955/6, p. 111):

$$X_j p_j = \sum_{i=1}^{m} a_{ij} X_j p_i + a_n X_j p_n \ (j = 1, \ldots, m),$$

where X is output, p is price, a_{ij} is the i'th resource requirement for a unit output of product j, and the subscript n denotes all labour inputs including 'entrepreneurial services'. Here profit is not explicitly represented but conceivably could be buried in $a_{nj}X_jp_n$ to be spent as part of final demand ($\sum_{j=1}^{m} a_{nj}X_jp_n$). But, again, distributive shares do not have much of a part to play in the Leontief system. Furthermore, this is more than a mere matter of nuance.

4 *The 'hidden agenda': the production function and equilibrium*

The production function

In one other key respect the Sraffa–Leontief distinction goes beyond nuance. In the course of his straying 'a long way from Sraffa's analysis' (Burmeister, 1984, p. 524), Burmeister equipped his variation on a Sraffian theme with a production function (ibid., pp. 519, 521) – with Joan Robinson's 'powerful instrument of miseducation' (Robinson, 1962a, p. 114) – as had Samuelson before him (1971b, p. 4). In Burmeister's case, the production function becomes a vehicle for describing experiments in choice-making along an intertemporal consumption transformation locus (pp. 518–20). Moreover, this production function is endowed with the usual properties – concavity, etc. – *and* homogeneity of degree one. Now, those who work with the Leontief system *do* think in terms of a production function, although, because the Leontief function has fixed technical coefficients, it may not appear to be much of a 'production function'. Still, to many who work with it, production function it is. It is, moreover, linearly homogeneous. But to equip the Sraffa system with a production function is, most assuredly, to take Sraffa where he did not intend to go. *A fortiori*, as has been argued above, this applies to constant returns to scale. *Ab initio*, Samuelson wished to equip Sraffa with a production function (e.g. Samuelson, 1971b, p. 4). Perhaps Samuelson's twinning of Sraffa's name with that of Leontief in order to characterize 'this age' (Samuelson, 1971a) may have had, among other things, a production function objective. Samuelson's reference to 'this age' was, as we have seen, primarily to supply-side-determined sets of relative commodity prices. And, once again, there is such a thing as a Leontief production function, and it is

CRS to boot! Note that this business of affixing a production function to the Sraffa model is presumably made more palatable by Samuelson with the warning that 'partial derivatives in the form of everywhere definable marginal productivities . . . definitely do not exist in this model' (Samuelson, 1971b, p. 19).

Equilibrium

Here we return to the snapshot, to Sraffa's view of the structure of economic reality at a census moment of time – with all the 'data' being what they are. Mrs Robinson has referred, not entirely complimentarily (as we shall see below), to the Sraffa model as a system 'of equations expressing equilibrium relationships' (Robinson, 1971, p. 72, footnote 8). There is indeed such a thing as a Sraffa or Sraffa-like view of equilibrium in an economy: it is that of an open but bounded set of mutual consistencies (Hahn, 1973, pp. 2, 28; Weintraub, 1977, p. 20). More particularly, the mutually consistent set of phenomena includes both endogenous variables (relative commodity prices) and data (inputs, outputs, input–output relations; and distributive shares). This set of consistencies appears to be a 'tight' one. However, it is 'open' with respect to levels of activity in the different industries. Specifically, activity levels can assume different magnitudes, subject to the additional 'equilibrium' requirement that the system be in a 'self-replacing' state (or, more technically, fulfil the Hawkins–Simon condition), without disturbing commodity price relatives. The latter will of course change if input–output relations (technologies) and/or distributive shares change. This is a view of equilibrium at what we have referred to as a census moment of time. It has nothing to do with Marshall's conceptual time periods or with any sort of static/dynamic distinction. It is merely a representation of aspects of a real economy, given certain parameters (data) that may obtain at a particular point of time – which brings us back to Roncaglia's snapshot. Obviously, it is sited somewhere in the passage of *real time*. Of course, key 'parametric' aspects can change over time, but such change will not *necessarily* be equilibrating.

5 Beyond polemics: what to do with the Sraffa model?

Implications of the Sraffa model for the theory of the imperfectly competitive firm, especially oligopoly

When Samuelson wrote that constant returns to scale provide the only instance in which 'industry has no need for any *theory of firms' structure*' (Samuelson, 1971b, p. 48, emphasis in original), the implication was that the Sraffa model too – since here as elsewhere Samuelson brings the Sraffa model within the ambit of CRS – contains 'industries' that generate no need for a 'theory of firms' structure'. By 'theory of firms' structure' Samuelson would appear to be referring to the theory of firms' decision-making behaviour and decision-making style rather than to structure *per se* – this on the evidence of a reference in the same place to programming, planning, optimality conditions, etc. CRS aside, let us remind ourselves once again that the Sraffa model belongs to the genre identified by Samuelson when he wrote of 'this age of Leontief and Sraffa' – the 'age' of supply-side-determined relative commodity prices – and it is this entire genre, no doubt, that, to Samuelson, depicts 'industries' that have no need for a theory of the firm. Although there is a considerable consensus on Samuelson's side on this issue, I would nevertheless contend that the genre, including Sraffa's contribution, *does* have important implications for the theory of the firm.

The neoclassical heritage did not provide us with a legacy of analytical tools for the study of economic process and behaviour at the level of the firm (see McNulty, 1968; and Cyert and March, 1963, p. 15). Rather, this heritage, and especially its Walrasian variant, provided us – and this in abundance – with a *framework* for analysis (see Friedman, 1955, p. 908), with a 'state' theory that centred mainly upon market structure (see McNulty, 1968) and with a theory of the firm that was merely a corollary, in logic, of a theory of market structure. It is true that when the heritage is scrutinized more closely, this judgement stands in need of modification. Certainly in the case of the Marshallian species – one thinks of a paper like Alchian's 'Costs and outputs' (Alchian, 1959) – this judgement is not wholly apt. (Arguably, the master himself should be exempted from the full force of the judgement; see Loasby, 1978, p. 12, and Levine, 1982.) Moreover, there is that vast literature on mathematical programming, which can scarcely be considered as lying outside the neoclassical heritage. Still, to the extent that our heritage is Walrasian, and to the extent, too, that the Marshallian part of that heritage – or, more specifically, the Marshallian theory of the firm – is not long on *detailed* analysis of firm-level decision-making behaviour, the charge must stick.

On the other hand, because decision *rules* may be deduced from the neoclassical theory of the firm (of whatever species) – from the lore of maximization – this theory has of course provided *implications* for firm-level decision style and decision behaviour.

What, however, of that other heritage – the classical one, the legacy of David Ricardo? Again, we find an absence of specifics for process and for problem solving at the level of the firm. And, of course, there is also an implicit motivational assumption similar in kind to the neoclassical one – an assumption that surfaces in the perception of shadowy figures who operate the decision-making mechanisms in the manner of maximizing 'global rationalists' (to borrow a phrase from Herbert Simon). But do we also draw a blank when it comes to implications for a flesh-and-blood theory of the firm, and do these implications differ from those of neoclassical theory? 'A Ricardian system', wrote Edward Nell, 'shows the interlocking of possibilities and necessities, rather than of motives, plans and information' (Nell, 1967, p. 18). And, '. . . [in] Ricardian models no reference need ever be made to choices or to motives, and prices are determined without anything being maximized' (ibid., p. 22; how, though, to square the Ricardian assumption of a uniform rate of profit with the absence of profit-maximizing behaviour?). And, again, '. . . in a "Ricardian theory of value" firms . . . are never mentioned; only industries are shown – or, rather, only the techniques of production appear, each industry being defined by the technique it employs' (ibid., pp. 16–17). Strictly speaking, much of this is true. But this concatenation of industry-level techniques and 'interlocking . . . possibilities', in that it is a view of key aspects of the structure of economic reality, has important *implications* for micro-level behaviour and decision style.

Does the Sraffa model have implications for decision-making behaviour and process at the level of the firm, or must it be viewed, as Mrs Robinson did (Robinson, 1971, p. 72, footnote 8), as a system 'of equations expressing equilibrium relationships . . . [that] cannot be used to discuss the behavior of the human beings who inhabit [it]'? Secondly – this query is really antecedent to the first – may the Sraffa perception of economic structure be regarded as being empirically relevant on any level of aggregation? There surely has to be an affirmative reply to the first part of the first of these queries. As to the second query, it should be borne in mind that the Sraffa system is, like the Ricardian, both a view of economic structure and a model of commodity price determination. The Sraffa view of structure is relevant to advanced industrial economies if there is in such economies a 'preponderance of commodities locked into a technological interdependence with each other' (Levine, 1974, p. 880; see Bose, 1965; Frankel, 1955) and, also, series of institutional interfaces that have very little to do with the marginal productivity principle and that play a determining role as regards wages and profits (Levine, 1974). Finally, to complete this brief description of a perceived reality: in that the Sraffa model is, among other things, that of a set of relative commodity prices determined by techniques of production, it may also be said to suggest a hypothesis concerning micro-level activity that is relevant to the kind of oligopoly and other imperfectly competitive markets that appear to obtain in reality. More specifically, Sraffa's 'technological interdependence' view of economic structure with its accompanying technique-of-production-determined commodity price set and his view of distribution as a process could imply some of the canon of the behavioural theories of the firm or of managerial theories of the firm or both. The generation of these implications is furthered when the Sraffa model is brought into touch with Okun's model of customer markets and cost-determined pricing (see Okun, 1981, ch. 4).

In brief, what is at issue here is a decision style that in logic may be associated not only with a technological interdependence view of structure and concomitantly with Sraffa's model of commodity price determination and with the Okun model, but with the exogeneity of distributive-share determination that is part of Sraffa's system.

Here are some particulars. The Sraffa (or Sraffa–Okun) universe would seem to imply (i) a propensity for imperfectly competitive firms to attempt to 'arrange' their 'vertical' external environments (relations with suppliers), which in turn conduces to a stability and routinization of decision processes and a de-emphasizing of reliance by the firm upon anticipatory data; (ii) in so far as the 'horizontal' environment (i.e. relations with customers and the firm's position *vis-à-vis* competitors) is concerned – a propensity to attempt to 'arrange' that environment, too, with a consequent relative absence, in the oligopoly case, of the mutual interdependence that is conventionally associated with oligopoly (Baumol, 1959, ch. 4).

Admittedly, it might *appear* that the Sraffa model is entirely bereft even of implications for any sort of theory of firm-level process and behaviour, let alone a theory of oligopolistic behaviour. First, there is Sraffa's prefatory caveat (cited above) that his is an 'investigation [that] is concerned exclusively with such properties of an economic system as do not depend on changes in the scale of production or in the proportions of "factors"'. This might seem to preclude any kind of search for micro-level implications. Secondly, although the assumption of a uniform rate of profit suggests profit-maximizing behaviour, details concerning the latter are nowhere provided by Sraffa, not even in the numéraire construction exercise in which a scenario is described for the appearance of profit as a phenomenon and in which a particular wage–profit locus is postulated. Thirdly, the assumption of a uniform rate of profit, in that it suggests profit-maximizing behaviour and hence an implicit assumption of perfect competition, would seem to preclude any relevance to oligopoly.

As to the first of these difficulties: Sraffa's self-denying ordinance concerning changes in scale and the like should not be regarded as an insurmountable barrier to a search for implications for process and decision style, because, once again, Sraffa's perception is also that of an *economic structure* that *has* such implications. (It would surely be difficult to imagine any perception of structure that had absolutely no implications for behaviour.) As to the absence of details in the Sraffa system concerning profit-maximizing behaviour: our exploration for theory-of-the-firm implications does not yield anything that is *irreconcilable* with such behaviour. Finally, as regards Sraffa's uniform rate of profit with its implied perfectly competitive regime, both the assumption and the implication may be dispensed with, and still leave Sraffa's perception of structure and of commodity price determination intact. As Roncaglia has pointed out, the substance of the Sraffa model remains inviolate if a different rate of profit should be postulated for each industry or activity. In this way, the Sraffa system can be accommodated to an oligopoly regime replete with the kind of barriers to entry postulated by Bain and Sylos Labini (Roncaglia, 1978, p. 29) and, also, with the notion of potential competition.

Income and prices policies from a Sraffian vantage point[3]

With the aid of a modified joint-product Sraffa model, consider the problem of a prices board that has been given the task of attempting to control the rate of increase of the absolute level of prices. To get some additional insight into the board's problem, it will be helpful to put Sraffa's equations of production into matrix form (the modification is that profit as a rate is computed on the basis of the value of the commodity *and* labour input, and also – following Roncaglia – a different rate of profit is assumed for each industry):

$$\pi\ \mathbf{Ap} + \pi\ \mathbf{w} = \hat{\mathbf{A}}\mathbf{p} \tag{2}$$

or

$$\mathbf{p} = [\hat{\mathbf{A}} - \pi\ \mathbf{A}]^{-1}\ \pi\ \mathbf{w}, \tag{2'}$$

where π is the $k \times k$ diagonal matrix of profit factors, $1 + \rho_1, \ldots, 1 + \rho_k$

$(=\pi_1, \ldots, \pi_k)$; $\rho_1, \ldots, \rho_k$ are the rates of profit for each of the k industries; **A** is the square matrix of commodity inputs of order k (some of the columns of **A** may consist entirely of zero elements, since not every commodity will necessarily be used as an input); $\hat{\mathbf{A}}$ is the square matrix of outputs of order k; **w** is the column vector of labour incomes, $w_1 \ldots, w_r$; and **p** is the solution vector or column vector of commodity prices unknowns, $p_1, \ldots, p_k$. (Observe that with the equations of production in matrix form, what was previously noted now becomes even more obvious: that is, given the technique of production, as mirrored in the matrices of inputs and outputs, the absolute level of prices is determined by the exogenously given rates of profit and labour incomes. In this respect, a relevant comparison would be with an open Leontief model. See Allen, 1965, p. 351.)

To get closer to the actual activities of the prices board, assume that the board attempts to fulfil its price control mandate in the manner of the now defunct Anti-Inflation Board of Canada; that is, by attempting to control rates of increase of factor incomes. Specifically, assume that the board decrees new magnitudes – that is, magnitudes other than the presently observed ones – for the elements of the matrix of profit factors, π, and for the components of the vector of labour incomes, **w**. The solution set of relative prices generated by equation (2′) would also change, unless – a most unlikely happening – the board's choice of factor incomes (elements of π and **w**) were such as to produce no change in the relative magnitudes of the solution set of prices.

Two problems immediately arise: (i) Will there be a unique solution for the k commodity price unknowns? (ii) Will the new solution set of prices be strictly positive?

The answer to (i) should be 'yes' for the same reason that it is in the Sraffa model. That is, if we can assume that the matrix of differences, $(\hat{\mathbf{A}} - \pi\,\mathbf{A}]$, of equation (2′) will be non-singular, there will exist a unique solution vector (of relative commodity prices) for (2′).

As regards question (ii), the solution set of prices could fail to meet a strict positivity condition if the matrix of differences, $[\hat{\mathbf{A}} - \pi\,\mathbf{A}]$, were not indecomposable. An in-principle solution to this problem should lie at hand if the prices board made use of Sraffa's distinction between basic and non-basic commodities, and confined its activities solely to the basic sector. That is, given Sraffa's definition of basic commodities, only basic commodities are price determining. Furthermore, to address, specifically, the strict positivity condition, and, again, given Sraffa's definition of basic goods, the matrices of coefficients and of 'differences' for the basic sector will be indecomposable; and, on the presumption that the matrix of differences will, in addition, be square and non-singular, the solution vector of prices will be strictly positive.

Notes

1 Unless, of course, one is prepared to believe that Sraffa's chapter XII on 'Switch in methods of production' was intended to be a *full-blown* analysis of that issue, including an analysis of changes in factor prices and choices of production techniques. There is surely nothing in that chapter to support such a belief.

2 Sraffa (1960, pp. 94–5) provides the relevant quotation from Torrens' 'Strictures on Mr. Ricardo's doctrine concerning exchangeable value', *Edinburgh Magazine*, October 1818, p. 336.

3 For a detailed consideration of this issue, see Levine (1983).

Comment

Fabio Petri

Siena

Professor Levine's paper addresses so many important issues that I will be obliged to leave some out of my comment. I will briefly discuss the following ones:

(1) Is there a notion of equilibrium in Sraffa? And how is it connected with the analysis of change?

(2) Is the difference between Sraffa's analysis and neoclassical analyses adequately characterized by speaking of Sraffa's prices as supply-side determined or techniques-of-production determined, and of Sraffa's 'technological interdependence' view of economic structure?

(3) Do Sraffa's results need an assumption of constant returns to scale (CRS)?

(4) Does Sraffa's model have implications for the theory of the firm?

On the first question, I find it surprising that Levine should not have started from Sraffa's explicit identification of his own standpoint with that of Smith and Ricardo – and, I may add, of Marx, as implicitly acknowledged by Sraffa himself in the 'References to the literature' at the end of his book. Now, one finds in these authors a definition of natural prices or prices of production (terms Sraffa finds appropriate for the prices he studies) as – to quote from Smith, but Ricardo and Marx use almost identical words – 'the central prices, to which the prices of all commodities are continually gravitating', a gravitation due, as is well known, to competition and in particular to capital mobility.

This conception appears to be hardly reconcilable with Levine's use of the term 'snapshot' (his rendition, I understand, of Roncaglia's 'photograph' in Roncaglia, 1978) and with the associated idea that Sraffa's data are actual observations at a certain instant in the given economy. In order to be centres of gravitation of market prices, the prices of production must be determined on the basis of relatively persistent data. The conditions of production must therefore be the normal ones rather than those at one instant (on this Roncaglia, 1978, agrees; see also Adam Smith, who writes of the need – in order to ascertain the natural price of agricultural products – to consider the average productive results of agricultural activity over a number of harvests). And if the quantities produced influence techniques, the quantities taken as given when determining the prices of production cannot then be the ones observed at any instant either, influenced as these may be by transitory or accidental causes. It would seem that they must be interpreted in the way indicated by Adam Smith, as in their turn the centres of gravitation of the quantities produced, i.e. the 'effectual demands', the *normal* quantities demanded at the prices of production (a conception also implicit in Marx's notion of 'socially necessary labour' as the labour necessary to supply – under normal conditions of production – the *social need*). The metaphor of the 'snapshot' or 'photograph', suggesting reference to observed rather than to normal magnitudes, is therefore misleading.

Actually, the same idea that day-by-day prices should be explained as gravitating towards 'normal' prices guaranteeing a uniform rate of profits is also found in the other main tradition in value and distribution theory, the marginalist one (often nowadays inappropriately called neoclassical): Böhm-Bawerk, J. B. Clark, Wicksell, Marshall and Walras also tried, although within a different approach, to determine the prices (which they called equilibrium prices or – Marshall – long-period normal values) associated with a uniform rate of profits and having the role of centres of gravitation of day-by-day prices. In fact both traditions shared what Garegnani (1976a) has called a *method* which consists in trying to analyse the effects of changes by means of comparisons of what can be called the 'long-period, or normal' positions of the economy; positions that are determined according to different theories in the two approaches, but sharing the uniform rate of profits element and having the role of centres of gravitation of actual prices and quantities. Only in recent times has this method been partially abandoned and obfuscated, owing to the shift towards neo-Walrasian notions of equilibrium; but there is no evidence (rather the opposite) that Sraffa had abandoned it. It is therefore also misleading to say that Sraffa's analysis is not about *change* at all: it is about normal positions, and one of the purposes of the study of normal positions is to understand change – see below, on CRS.

Analogously misleading is to say, as Levine does, that in Sraffa the composition of demand does not influence prices, these being determined by 'the structure and technical relations of production' (Levine, 1974, p. 873) independently of consumer choices, just as in Leontief models. In his 1974 article, Levine says this is one fundamental distinguishing aspect of the classical tradition.

One is given to suspect here a double misunderstanding. First, to take quantities as given does not mean to deny that they may have an influence on prices – they no doubt do, for instance, if there are scarce natural resources; it only means that this influence can be studied *separately* (the contributions by Garegnani, Schefold, Bharadwaj and Roncaglia to this volume discuss the issue in greater detail). Second, marginalist theory, when it attempts to determine long-period prices (i.e. prices yielding a uniform rate of return on the supply price of capital goods) in disaggregated models, determines prices that are 'techniques-of-production determined' as much as Sraffa's.

Let us for example imagine an economy that produces two goods in yearly cycles, corn and bread, each with a fixed-coefficients CRS technique, with corn and labour the only inputs, and no technical choice. The uniform-profit-rate price equations:

$$(1 + r)a_{cc}p_c + wa_{lc} = p_c = 1$$
$$(1 + r)a_{cb}p_c + wa_{lb} = p_b$$

(where the a's are the unit input coefficients of, in order, corn and labour in the production of, respectively, corn and bread, and wages are assumed to be paid at the end of the production cycle) would be written in this way by a marginalist as well as by a classical (Sraffian) economist (although only since Sraffa has this point been clearly perceived). So, given r or w, relative prices are determined in either approach in the same way. It is not here that the two approaches would differ in analysing price formation in this economy, but rather in the way *distribution* is determined; and it is through its influence on distribution that the composition of demand would influence prices in the marginalist approach. In the present example, with no choice of techniques, in order to determine distribution the marginalist approach would rely precisely on demand, i.e. on the *indirect* factor substitution mechanism, based on consumer choice. The argument is well known: if, for example, there is labour unemployment and hence w decreases, the relatively labour-intensive good will become relatively cheaper and consumer choice will (apart from perverse cases of, it is argued, little relevance) shift in its favour, thus decreasing the average capital–labour ratio in the economy, i.e. – with a given employment of corn-capital – increasing the demand for labour. It is therefore the tastes of consumers that determine the position and slope of the labour demand curve, and thus consumer demand enters the determination of the equilibrium wage and hence of prices. The possibility of choice of techniques does not alter the situation: consumer tastes will affect long-period equilibrium relative commodity prices only because and to the extent to which they enter the determination of distribution (Garegnani, 1983a) – a role they do not have in the classical approach, where distribution is determined by a different, complex set of forces, only partially evoked by the umbrella term 'class struggle'.

By stressing the presence of technological interdependence in Sraffa's model, Levine means perhaps to remind us that only with models such as Sraffa's have we become capable of fully grasping the way prices are influenced by the fact that commodities are produced by means of commodities; one can then only agree with him. Sraffa's analysis has, for example, meant a significant advance in the treatment of fixed capital and has dispelled many confusions about the implications (for the theory of prices and of the rate of profits) of intermediate products: these were usually completely excluded from capital (no profit or interest rate being computed on them) in the literature of the 1950s and early 1960s on the Leontief model (see, for instance, Dorfman, Samuelson and Solow, 1958, p. 288). But it would be wrong to infer that, simply owing to the attention given to technological interdependence, Sraffa's equations present 'a view of the structure of economic reality' different from the dominant marginalist one. For example,

Wicksell knew quite well that commodities are produced by means of commodities (as shown by his awareness that in general his 'reduction' of capital to dated labour and land will give rise to infinite terms) – and with him all marginalist economists who tried to tackle the problems posed by heterogeneous capital. A different 'view of the structure of economic reality' does emerge, but from the advances Sraffa makes in the analysis of the implications of this interdependence for price and distribution theory. As the previous example may have helped to make clear, in so far as the rate of profits is uniform (and, as said before, this assumption is also present in traditional marginalist value theory), prices *cannot but* satisfy Sraffa's equations. In fact, Samuelson, Ferguson, etc. have not disputed the correctness and relevance of Sraffa's equations, and have been shocked by the results emerging from them precisely because those results derive from assumptions they themselves would have made.

In other words, Sraffa's price equations by themselves (i.e. simply by the way they are written) do not discriminate between the two alternative approaches. As stressed by Roncaglia in his contribution to this volume (Chapter 16), they can be interpreted as internal either to a classical framework (i.e. with as data the magnitudes – conditions of production, quantities, real wage or rate of profits – taken as given by the classicals in their study of what Garegnani, 1984, has called the 'core'), or to a marginalist framework (i.e. seen as one part of a marginalist long-period general equilibrium model). No particular Sraffian 'view' of the structure or functioning of the economy can therefore emerge simply from the way the equations are formulated (apart from the central importance attributed to the uniformity of the rate of profits, which sets them apart only from the neo-Walrasian versions of marginalist theory, not from Wicksell or Pigou, etc.). It is the *results* emerging from them that discriminate between the two approaches.

It is perhaps useful briefly to summarize the import of those results, in order to highlight the *double role* of Sraffa's analysis. When interpreted as internal to a classical framework, Sraffa's equations rehabilitate the classical approach by showing that, if one takes as given what the classicals took as given when attempting to determine prices and the rate of profits, then prices and the rate of profits *can* be determined. When interpreted as internal to the marginalist framework, Sraffa's equations destroy the logical consistency of its attempt to determine a long-period equilibrium, by showing that 'capital' cannot be measured independently of distribution, and that there is no ground for faith in the existence of the substitution mechanisms between 'capital' and labour on which marginalist theory rests for its determination of distribution (and hence also for its determination of quantities).

Therefore, for a positive, constructive analysis or 'vision' of capitalism, Sraffa sends us back to the classical tradition and to Marx; in this he is quite different from Leontief, who, although clearly influenced by that tradition and sympathetic to many elements in it, has never, as far as I know, rejected the marginalist view of 'capital' as a factor of production and of relative factor scarcity as a main determinant of distribution.

The double role of Sraffa's analysis – constructive *vis-à-vis* the classical approach, critical *vis-à-vis* the marginalist one – is also important when we come to the role of CRS in Sraffa. Levine, like Burmeister (1977) and Eatwell (1977), has discussed the issue only with reference to the first role (I will not discuss the paper by Samuelson quoted by Levine because I have not read it).

It may none the less avoid misunderstandings to make it clear that, when interpreting Sraffa's equations as internal to a marginalist framework in order to criticize it, then an assumption of CRS appears both legitimate and necessary – necessary, because marginalist theory needs it, as shown by Sraffa himself in 1925; legitimate (given the critical aims), because marginalist theory, if inconsistent when one assumes CRS, certainly is not salvaged by non-constant returns.

Coming to Sraffa's positive contribution, and to the *Journal of Economic Literature* controversy, I must admit that I find the replies given there to Burmeister unsatisfactory. In particular, it seems to me that Levine's reply (extended but, I think, unchanged in its essentials in Levine, 1985, and in his contribution to this volume) suffers, again, from his conception of Sraffa's analysis as a 'snapshot'. Burmeister had argued that, realistically, changes in distribution change outputs; unless the conditions of the non-substitution theorem are assumed to hold, the change in outputs will cause techniques to change; but then Sraffa's analysis of the $w-r$ curve (or outer envelope) is of no use, since the curve (or outer envelope) may shift, so that e.g. its downward slope does not exclude the possibility that w and r may rise together. Levine's reply has been: 'Why bring in anything about change? . . . Sraffa's price-determining apparatus is about reality at a "moment" and not about *change*' (Levine, 1985). Thus he appears to concede, perhaps unwillingly, that Burmeister is right in arguing that Sraffa's $w-r$ curve cannot be used for the study of the effects of changes in, say, the real wage. In that same article, Levine continues: 'an account of actual change . . . must center upon change in technique and other essentially dynamic phenomena' and in his paper in this volume he writes *against* 'shifting the ground from "change" to *comparative statics* . . . which, surely, was another place where Sraffa did not wish to go'.

But Sraffa locates himself in the classical tradition; and classical authors did use their theories of value – their analyses of the 'core' – to predict the effects of changes of w and r in real economies. There is no evidence to suggest that Sraffa did not intend his analysis to be used in the same way; thus Eatwell's 'Since the size and composition of output and the technique in use are *data*, the issue of returns to scale does not arise' (Eatwell, 1977, p. 63) does not meet Burmeister's objection.

A more satisfactory reply to Burmeister appears to require an analysis of the way in which the classical approach can legitimately use 'comparative static' exercises in the 'core' as a basis for the analysis of change, in spite of not necessarily assuming CRS or the absence of scarce natural resources. The main point is that these exercises do not exhaust all that is necessary for the analysis of change, but are only one part of it (cf. also see 7 and 9 below).

I would put it as follows. Only the marginalist approach requires the simultaneous determination of outputs and techniques for the determination of the rate of profits, relying as it does on the action of substitution mechanisms that operate precisely through variations in the proportions between outputs and/or 'factors'. Only in this approach, therefore, are general and persistent functional relationships between prices and quantities necessary to determine distribution.

The different explanation of distribution in the classical approach – the possibility of taking one of the two main distributive variables as given or as autonomously changing when trying to determine outputs or the other distributive variable – makes it possible to admit a (possibly irreversible) dependence of, for example, investment, or consumer tastes or technology on a variety of factors (for instance, the political climate), which it may be impossible to formalize into a set of general functional relationships. It remains possible to adopt a procedure – in order to analyse e.g. the effects of changes of w on r – consisting of separate stages in logical succession. First, in the 'core', one may take the quantities produced and techniques adopted as unchanged. (This may actually give a good indication of the first-impact effect of a change in real wages on relative prices in a world – which might be ours – where relative prices adapt rapidly because the tendency towards a uniform rate of profits requires, to assert itself, only *potential* capital mobility, the simple *threat* of entry.) In a second stage, still inside the 'core', one may derive indications of whether the price changes have altered the optimal techniques, assuming free entry and CRS. In a third stage, outside the 'core', one may analyse the probable effects on the quantities produced, in connection with the specific circumstances of the case under consideration. In this third stage, the time horizon of the analysis may indicate which changes in techniques made convenient by the changes in distribution should be considered to alter the price-determining matrix, and which (requiring a long gestation) should be left to only influence investment and hence outputs. Now one may consider whether there will be relevant effects on techniques, owing to relevant changes in the utilization of scarce natural resources, or possibly to joint production. Back to the 'core', one may then study how these changes in techniques alter the first-impact effect of the change in w on r. At a still more concrete level, one may then try to take into account the existence of non-constant returns to scale at the firm level, whose effects, as argued by Sylos Labini, are not necessarily predictable, and depend on the form taken by investment in an industry – for example, a new medium-sized firm forestalling the possible expansion (and cost reduction) of an existing firm. Thus, no doubt the 'dynamic' elements Levine insists upon will enter the analysis, but the 'comparative static' exercises in the 'core' preserve a fundamental importance too.

I come to Sraffa and the theory of the firm. Levine argues that the Sraffian stress on technological interdependence, when viewed against the importance implicitly assigned to institutional elements in the determination of distribution, suggests a view of firms as attempting to 'arrange' their environment both 'vertically' and 'horizontally', i.e. attempting to establish some kind of collusive agreements with suppliers, customers and competitors. This may well be a fruitful approach, but I doubt whether one can read it in Sraffa. I have already argued against singling out technological interdependence as a key feature distinguishing Sraffa's analysis from marginalist theory. One may add that the assumption of a uniform profit rate is normally associated with free competition.

Sraffa's analysis does have implications for the theory of the firm, I think, but these implications are indirect, connected with the new strength Sraffa gives to the classical approach. As said above, within this approach there is no need to establish general and persistent functional relationships between prices and quantities in order for these variables to be determined – a need that makes it very difficult to allow for strategic behaviour, irreversible increasing returns, etc. in the marginalist approach. In the classical approach, such phenomena appear to cause no comparable problem, allowing analysis to become more realistic. Thus, for example, Marxist analyses have no difficulty in admitting that the squeeze in profitability caused by considerable wage increases will often cause a speed-up of the processes of capital concentration and of the search for and introduction of innovations. And Sylos Labini's contribution to this volume (Chapter 1) has stressed the compatibility of a classical framework with realistic analyses of industrial structure and price-setting behaviour, admitting product differentiation, demand constraints facing individual firms, mark-up pricing, quantity adaptations with rigid prices, etc. (Actual or potential entry appears to be anyway usually quite powerful in enforcing a tendency of profit rates towards uniformity. Differences in barriers to entry may be used, at a second approximation level, to explain persisting differences in rates of profits. These differences should not in any case be exaggerated – very high profit rates attract competitors very quickly and do not seem to last very long.)

It is in this much greater compatibility of the classical approach with realistic analyses of firm behaviour that the implications, for the theory of the firm, of Sraffa's rehabilitation of the classical approach appear essentially to lie.

7

On Changes in the Composition of Output

Bertram Schefold
Frankfurt/M.

Introduction: preferences and needs

It has often been remarked that 'demand' is missing from the Sraffa system. If the level and composition of output change, the input–output coefficients change so that there seems to be no room for a consideration of demand. If, on the other hand, distribution is given and there are constant returns to scale, prices are determined independently of the levels of output in the different sectors. It would then seem that demand conditions can be freely introduced, but they only fix the quantities. The latter case can clearly only serve as an introduction; yet it is erroneously regarded as the main case by neoclassical interpreters.

The difficulties surrounding such notions as 'demand' and 'composition of output' are connected with the specific classical methodology. It is a theory that, given technology, uses separate approaches to:

(1) the determination of output (effective demand regulating the level of activity and socioeconomic factors affecting its composition),
(2) the analysis of distribution (the forces governing distribution are subject to historical change),
(3) the theory of value (it shows how relative prices are determined if one of the distributive variables is fixed and if the structure of production and consumption is given).

It is the purpose of this paper to show how the classical methodological distinction can be maintained in the face of changing conditions of demand. The solution is, broadly speaking, that (within certain ranges) the separation of the theory of value from the theory of output can be kept beyond the limits set by the so-called 'non-substitution theorem' and that, where this is not possible, characteristic interactions between the determination of the level of output and the determination of prices take place that are in some cases quite different from those discussed in neoclassical theory.

In order to make room for a classical treatment of demand, it is necessary first to review some of the neoclassical assumptions critically and to remind the reader of some logical objections to the neoclassical mode of reasoning. After perusing the traditional objections, i.e. the hypothetical character of preferences outside the equilibrium point (a), I want to argue that 'compromises' between neoclassical and classical approaches are problematic if they are based on a neoclassical theory of distribution and a classical theory of prices (b). This will lead me to ask what we should mean by neoclassical theory: not a research programme but a closed and coherent account of how the economy is supposed to work (c). It will be shown that the logic of the neoclassical theory of equilibrium requires a high degree of substitutability (if not homogeneity) of both the 'factor' capital (d) and of goods (e), and the conditions that are necessary to guarantee uniqueness of equilibrium are very stringent (f). The neoclassical theory of preferences necessarily provides an inadequate representation of the stratification of needs (g) and must conceal the conflicts between different social roles played by individuals (h). It usually emphasizes tastes, not the rationality of domestic production in the determination of private consumption (i).

On the basis of this critique, a reconsideration of the classical theory will be proposed (j). It is very simple in its formal representation and does not give rise to the objections raised against the neoclassical theory. The main sections (sections 1–3) following upon this introduction will explain its use. After a discussion of causes and effects of changes in the composition of output in single-product systems with constant returns to scale (section 1), the crucial analytical step taken in the paper will be to extend this approach to joint production (section 2) and the case of variable returns (section 3).

(a) Criticism of the assumption that utility functions or preferences are defined outside equilibrium is older than the developed forms of neoclassical theory themselves. One usually does not know – not even using introspection – what one's preferences would be if one had to choose in an economic situation quite different from one's own. Even if preferences are fairly homogeneous within given income classes, one has first to learn the consumption pattern, the behaviour, in short the 'lifestyle', of a higher stratum before one can move freely within it. Few people know how they would behave if their income were curtailed significantly. In particular, one knows very little about what one's preferences would be at different levels of employment and the associated states of the economy.

(b) This presupposes the adoption of the methodological principle of dividing the classical theory into one of output, distribution and value (and not, like the neoclassical, into that of partial and general equilibrium). Once the principle is accepted, one might be tempted to use the neoclassical theory of demand in order to provide a theory of the composition of output. But, on the one hand, such a theory is not missing in Smith, Ricardo or Marx (see Schefold, 1981). On the other, the neoclassical theory of demand cannot be taken over because it is linked with the neoclassical theory of distribution.

For, according to an argument stressed by Garegnani (1983a), demand functions act on commodity prices through their influence on factor prices.

To see this, it suffices to consider the long-period equilibrium of a single-product system exhibiting (as is usual in neoclassical theory) constant returns to scale, with an unlimited supply of each factor at constant factor prices. Prices are then equal to cost of production (the supply curve is horizontal) and demand determines the quantities to be produced. Only because factors are scarce, demand for them (as derived from the demand for commodities and augmented by the own demand by owners of the endowments) will cause higher factor prices to be associated with higher levels of output, and this will affect commodity prices, both directly through the cost of the factors employed as well as indirectly through the influence of the level of factor prices on the choice of technique.

The neoclassical theory of demand thus affects prices essentially through changes of factor prices, which reflect scarcity and determine technology. The non-substitution theorem proves the point for a rather trivial special case *e contrario*: prices do not depend on demand if the supply of labour, the only non-produced mean of production, is not limited and if the rate of profit is given.

However, if the neoclassical theory of the demand for goods acts primarily through influences on factor prices, it is difficult to see how it could be maintained without accepting the neoclassical theory of distribution and employment. Since the latter are the chief object of criticism both on theoretical and on empirical grounds from the classical side, the neoclassical theory of demand is difficult to maintain.

It might be concluded that preferences affect prices of goods through effects on factor prices in general equilibrium, but that a dissociation of the neoclassical theory of distribution and of the neoclassical theory of the determination of demand through preferences remains logically possible, as long as one accepts the assumptions of the so-called non-substitution theorem. However, the usefulness of such an approach for a general theory may be doubted. Suppose, for example, that a Sraffa-type model with constant returns is given, that the wage rate rises with the productivity of labour, and that all technical progress takes the form of reductions in labour requirements. Rising incomes will cause shifts of the composition of output determined by Engel elasticities. It then follows that the share of wages and the level of employment will change – unless Engel elasticities are, as in Morishima (1964, p. 138), quite arbitrarily assumed to be equal to one – so that, even in this simple case, tensions may develop that put existing wage agreements into question. In a changing economic environment, they are likely to lead to changes of preferences. It will therefore be more appropriate to focus on the specific content of consumer demand directly; for it will be sufficiently difficult to predict consumer demand in a given state of prices, distribution and employment, even without formulating hypotheses about what consumer demand might be in a different state.

A faithful neoclassical like Schumpeter will consider preferences as fixed and as pertaining to one and the same long-period equilibrium, which remains fixed as employment fluctuates around the normal state (Schefold,

1986a). But it is not plausible to extend the idea of given preferences to a theory of accumulation along classical lines, with a non-neoclassical theory of distribution and a neoclassical determination of the composition of output, if the economic environment changes.

(c) We are thus not concerned here with models that might allow an *ad hoc* combination of classical and neoclassical elements for the analysis of special situations. By neoclassical theory we mean the body of economic theory, derived from the marginalist revolution, that explains distribution and employment in terms of supply of, and demand for, factors of production in a general equilibrium, which is meant to be used in the analysis of concrete economic problems, by means of the familiar method of comparing equilibrium states. The equilibria therefore have to be stable and to be essentially unique.

A firm belief in the working of the neoclassical equilibrium mechanism in this traditional, narrow but relevant sense is perhaps not often admitted today. Yet, this concept of neoclassical theory is appropriate for our discussion. In a similar vein, I shall interpret the analysis of preferences in the liberal tradition of individualism and am here not interested in formal extensions such as the consideration of externalities in consumption using interdependent utility functions.

It is then the purpose of the paper to defend the determination of the composition of output according to the classical tradition against the treatment of demand according to the neoclassical view. To do so, however, it would not be appropriate to confine the discussion to great authors in the neoclassical tradition (such as Marshall, Wicksell or Schumpeter). Modern Walrasian models (following Debreu, 1959) and other works on demand by – if the expression is permitted – enlightened neoclassicals will also be used (sometimes, perhaps, against the intentions of their authors) to indicate limitations of the comprehensive neoclassical theory and to collect tools towards a reconstruction of the classical theory. Whether the same tools and models might provide a sufficient basis for some other new theory or a true generalization of neoclassical theories will not be discussed.

(d) Modern neoclassical theorists usually consider the intertemporal equilibrium as paradigmatic. If the equilibrium is intertemporal, competition will ensure that the rate of return (in terms of a given commodity) will be uniform for all activities used and equal to the own rate of interest of the numéraire commodity. The own rate of interest is, for this purpose, defined as the maximum rate of remuneration of a commodity, in terms of itself, to be obtained by investing or by holding it; hence it is equal to $(X_{t+1}/X_t) - 1$ if the quantity X_{t+1} of the commodity is the promised pay-back of the commodity in the next period and X_t the quantity available in period t, and $X_{t+1}/X_t = p_t/p_{t+1}$ where p_t, p_{t+1} are discounted prices of the intertemporal equilibrium such that $X_t p_t = X_{t+1}/p_{t+1}$).

This leads to a difficulty concerning the endowments, which is easier to understand in a special case. If some reproducible endowments (capital goods i) are available in excess, their services will not be used and their own rates of interest $p_{o,i}/p_{1,i} - 1$ will be zero or low relative to their cost of reproduction, which would be positive. They will thus partly be used but (initially) not be reproduced, which may violate the condition of the uniformity of the rate of profit with respect to traditional notions of long-period equilibrium. Moreover, the corresponding stocks had once been acquired in order to use them profitably later and if they now yield no or very low returns, expectations are deceived, and these deceived expectations are not treated in the model (Schefold, 1985b).

The extent to which this will happen varies with the assumptions made. As Garegnani has shown in his discussion of Walras's model of capital formation, the difficulty disappears if capital is conceived of as a homogeneous magnitude (Garegnani, 1960). Similarly, if all goods available as endowments are consumption goods as well as capital goods, or if the time horizon is sufficiently long and if there is free storage of goods, none of the endowments can be free in the modern intertemporal model because they will be shifted through time so that they will either directly or indirectly be consumed (assuming no satiation). If turn-pike properties (see e.g. Bewley, 1982) hold, the intertemporal equilibrium will eventually converge towards a long-period equilibrium in which rates of return are equal; the effect of the unequal scarcities of different reproducible capital goods in the initial period then diasappears. But if capital goods are not objects of consumption (such as plant) and if they are subject to wear and tear, the being in excess of endowments represents – like that of excess capacities – an unpleasant surprise for their owners: they are not needed now and cannot be held without cost to be used tomorrow. Hence they are conceptually proof of a disequilibrium with respect to the situation prior to the initial period (Eatwell, 1975a). Even if their prices do not fall to zero but are low in comparison with their cost of reproduction, expectations are deceived and may, according to economic logic, lead to a fall in effective demand that is not reflected in the data of the model (preferences). From a normative point of view, it might be said that past mistakes should be irrelevant to the valuation of assets, but the experience of mistakes alters expectations in a dynamic process, and this is not taken into account in the modern neoclassical theory of intertemporal equilibrium.

Differences of rates of return in terms of different commodities are another aspect of the same phenomenon in models with a constant linear technology. To achieve one uniform rate of return that is the same in terms of any chosen numéraire, and to exclude zero prices of endowments of capital goods, a high degree of substitutability on the input side may thus be necessary in the neoclassical model, which, in the limit, entails that all means of production are of one kind. The problem does not appear in classical theories of the long period since they consider the relative amounts of capital goods and labour required for production as unknowns.

(e) We cannot discuss here the difficulties associated with a reallocation of misguided investment according to the neoclassical theory of supply of and demand for factors of production. But it may be observed that one obtains a similar result regarding the substitutability of consumption goods if the stability of equilibrium in *tâtonnement* processes is examined. The most meaningful sufficient condition (not capable of significant extensions according to Hahn, 1982a) guarantees that an equilibrium is stable provided that all commodities are gross substitutes (one extension is provided by Morishima, 1970). But, at least according to classical thinking in the interpretation presented below (section 3), goods that are gross substitutes fulfil the same need and are, for the purposes of classical theory, conveniently treated as one and the same good (commodities should be defined according to their economic properties). Hence, in a sense, neoclassical theory is able to obtain a stable equilibrium by assuming that endowments and consumption goods are each reduced to one commodity. The problem of the neoclassical theory of capital and that of stability both disappear in a one-commodity world.

To present the matter in this way implies a simplification. But the importance of the argument concerning stability is now much better understood because of Sonnenschein's and Debreu's proofs that, to virtually every arbitrary system of excess demand functions, an artificial exchange economy fulfilling the usual axioms can be constructed (with endowments and preferences for as many commodities as there are consumers) that approximates those excess demand functions to any given degree (Sonnenschein, 1972; Debreu, 1974). Therefore, if one wants to preserve one of the most fundamental neoclassical assumptions, i.e. that the free choice of individuals is given by independent preference orderings, one has to accept that unstable equilibria may result. Attempts to single out those systems of preferences (in terms of some property relating to needs and their satisfaction) that would exclude unstable excess demand functions have not been successful – and if they were, neoclassical theory would lose part of its claim to generality with respect to the possibilities of choice of individuals.

(f) The application of equilibrium analysis is problematic unless the equilibrium is determined uniquely. For one can otherwise not say with certainty what the effect of a change in one of the parameters will be on the final equilibrium position. The long-period positions considered by Sraffa are in this respect definitely superior to the neoclassical general equilibrium because they are always uniquely determined, except for some cases in the theory of joint production (Salvadori, 1982). The criterion of profit maximization will lead to the choice of a unique technology in single-product Sraffa systems. But, as Kehoe (1985) has recently shown by using an index theorem, a (in general finite) number of equilibria may result in an economy with given preferences and endowments for each consumer in the neoclassical case even if joint production is ruled out. Kehoe has analysed the extension of known results from pure exchange economies to economies with production and found that gross substitutability is *not* sufficient to ensure uniqueness in economies with single production involving more than three consumers. The weak axiom of revealed preference ensures uniqueness, but to postulate it is to postulate that the economy behaves like a single consumer. Or it has to be assumed that the technology is given by an input-output system. Hence, it would seem that attempts to define those general equilibrium systems that are both stable and unique lead back time and again to one-commodity worlds or to assumptions close to those of classical analysis. Perhaps this insight will induce some of those educated in the neoclassical tradition to follow the path traced below.

(g) The high degree of substitutability required for the working of the neoclassical equilibrium mechanism contrasts with the complementarity of needs emphasized (implicitly) by classical authors and with the structure ascribed to needs in modern psychology. Gross substitutability in systems of excess demand functions also involves the supply of (or the own demand for) endowments. Ignoring this for simplicity, one may use a diagrammatic representation at the level of the individual consumer. Neoclassical theory assumes that between any two goods there is a definite relationship in that a price rise of the first leads to an increase (gross substitute) or a reduction in the consumption of the second (complementary good). The corresponding points in Figure 7.1 are P and Q_1, Q_2, Q_3 respectively, where the reduction of good 2 is more (Q_2) or less (Q_1) than the proportional reduction of good 1. An increase in the consumption of good 1, relative to the initial position A, is also possible (Q_3). Strict complementarity (proportional reduction in the consumption of both goods) is accidental (point Z). Note that only point P fulfils the condition of gross substitutability.

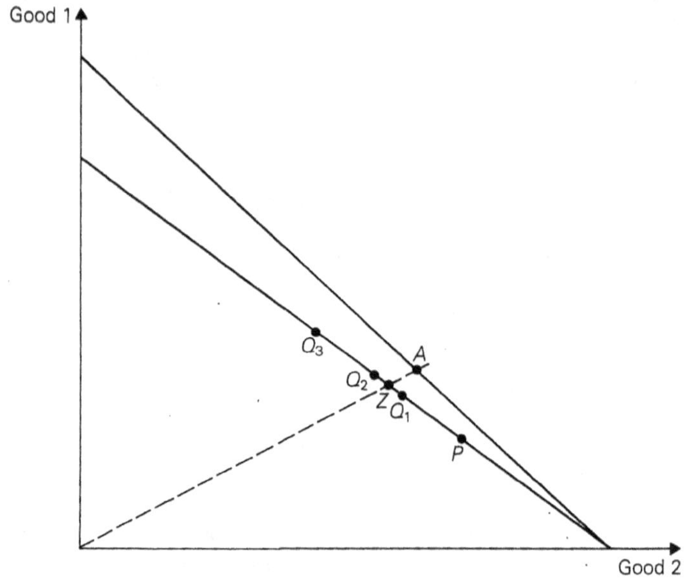

Figure 7.1 Substitutability and complementarity

However, as far as I can see, all theories of wants and their satisfaction (except the neoclassical) negate the generality of substitution and postulate hierarchies of needs and their satisfaction. The modern view of psychologists is that only the satisfaction of basic needs is tantamount to the reduction of an arousal in the nervous system. There is a want, associated with a desire to reduce it, in the case of 'existence needs' such as the want for food, shelter and security. But there are also 'relatedness needs' such as the want for love and recognition. The second category of needs may be different from the first even at the physiological level in that they are not satisfied by a reduction of the arousal of the nervous system, because they are motivated by the growth of the cognitive, aesthetic and social abilities, the enlargement of the consciousness and the perfection of movements, actions and the minds of people. Such personal growth has, unlike the famous narrow capacities of the human stomach in Adam Smith, in principle no bounds (Maslow, 1970; Scherhorn, 1984).

The belief that these complex wants can be reduced to a system of preferences is mistaken because, to the extent that there is a hierarchy of wants, a system of preferences allowing the construction of a utility function with the appropriate properties of substitutability does not exist (Georgescu-Roegen, 1966). For a hierarchy of wants implies a lexicographic ordering: first, elementary needs have to be fulfilled before there comes the turn of higher needs; in the extreme, there is no substitutability whatever between them (though there may be a substitutability between goods fulfilling the same need). Given a minimum level of nutrition, music and bread are complementary (although they are hardly gross substitutes). Below that, near the subsistence level, there is no substitutability at all.

(h) The system of needs is further complicated because one and the same person may fulfil different roles in society (Krause and Steedman, 1984), so that there is a Faustian conflict about what one should do with one's time: should I dedicate it to my children as a father or to my students as a teacher?

To the extent to which there is no established hierarchy of my needs according to which I live, the conflict between roles is inevitable. If I assume boldly that the set of potential objects for consumption is ordered according to a consistent set of preferences for each of a finite number of such roles, any individual consumer consists, as it were, of several systems of preferences. It can then be shown that it may not be possible to aggregate those systems of preference to one 'higher' preference ordering for the individual, much in the same way as it may not be possible to obtain a welfare function for a group of decision-makers according to Arrow's impossibility theorem (Arrow, [1951] 1963).

The customary answer to conflicting demands resulting from the several roles played by individuals in society is to cling to *habits* and *conventions*. This I regard as the justification for taking the needs of individuals in classical theory as given at the atomistic level. The hypothesis fits in well with the assumption that groups of individuals attempt to fulfil needs mainly according to hierarchical order and that substitutability between needs is of lesser importance. At the same time, the roles one can play and the means at one's disposal to satisfy one's needs are embedded in a *given structure of production and consumption*, and the satisfaction of needs – even the needs themselves – are conditioned by *institutions* at the macroscopic level.

Different combinations of roles are thus associated with different economic environments or *lifestyles*.

However, the economic conditions under which the habits and the structure of consumption once were formed may change, for example because incomes rise and individuals assume new roles; they then 'learn' to behave according to a new pattern. Some of the changes so engendered may have to be treated simply as exogenous because they represent unique historical events. But others may have a more systematic character and find an explanation by dividing the mass of individuals and the roles they play into social groups with economic characteristics, and by analysing the changing economic conditions of those groups.

(i) The task is now to show how these elements can be combined to introduce a theory of consumption in a classical framework. It is clear that the distinctions provided lead to important economic effects. For instance, the price elasticity of demand may be generally low for goods directly related to the fulfilment of basic needs. Income elasticities of demand may be explained in terms of migrations of people between income classes. Snob-effects (Veblen-effects, Giffen paradox) must be explained in terms of the sociological dynamic of attempted transitions to upper-income classes and role conflicts may help to explain uncertain behaviour (do I save or dissave in a slump?).

Marketing analysts use these categories rather than preferences, which is perhaps sufficient proof for the operational character of the approach. But there is also the task of providing theoretical underpinnings for well-established and useful concepts of applied economics such as elasticities, which are the testing ground for any theory of consumption. We assume that households work to transform the commodities bought on the market in order to obtain goods that satisfy their needs. To the extent that the rationality of capitalistic production penetrates households, they minimize their costs. This assumption leads to definite conclusions regarding reactions to changes in prices and incomes. Price elasticities can be calculated if there are several processes to satisfy given needs.

In particular, one may use the assumption to propose a theoretical explanation of elasticities that have been measured empirically. To do the same, neoclassical theorists have to face the difficulty of relating aggregate empirical market data (elasticities) to the data required by the theory, which are individual preferences. A similar difficulty exists here in so far as the valuation of domestically produced goods and of domestic labour seems to be merely subjective and not tested on the market. But in those areas where hypothesis (5) below is applied (for instance, the theory of joint production in section 2 below), the goods produced domestically compete with commodities sold on the market as substitutes, and domestic labour may be valued using wage rates, so that the hypothesis is then based on magnitudes, which are more accessible to observation than preferences.

(j) Five hypotheses should be retained from these considerations, which may be useful in the reconstruction of an alternative approach:

(1) There are hierarchies of needs, from basic needs up to higher needs such as the need for self-fulfilment. The needs are taken as given in a given economic environment.
(2) There are segments in the population that correspond to income classes (they have some sociological unity as well as economic properties in common but they need not be classes in the traditional sense of the difference between wage-earners and capitalists). They are further to be differentiated according to the environment, upbringing and cultural background. To different segments there correspond different patterns of consumption to satisfy the hierarchies of needs.
(3) There are conflicts in the roles one plays so that an individual may, as it were, belong to different segments at the same time.
(4) There are learning processes associated with transitions between such segments.
(5) Households are units that produce the goods required to satisfy needs by means of commodities bought on the market and by means of domestic labour.

Most of these ideas are present in works of classical authors and related ones in reformulations of the classical theory (see e.g. Parrinello, 1982). There are also neoclassical parallels (Weizsäcker, 1983). Household production is discussed in Gershuny (1981), Lancaster (1966) and Becker (1976). Pasinetti (1981b) has used Engel-curves to represent learning processes in his theory of growth and structural change. The tool can be reinterpreted to describe a migration from lower to higher income classes as suggested above.

The changes in social values that accompany a process of accumulation cannot, however, be completely subsumed under a concept of Engel-curves, if those who will be rich tomorrow decide – because their cultural outlook has changed – to follow a consumption pattern that is different from that of people who own the same riches already today. If, for instance, it should be true that concern for environmental problems increases with the advances of a modern industrial society, the income elasticities for certain positional goods such as motorcars will diminish and those for health foods will increase. This change of the hierarchy of needs can be represented (as we have tried to show in a project relating to energy; see Dickler, 1983) by letting the demand curves shift accordingly, with election results serving as indicators for the change in social values. The new role conflicts associated with new threats to the environment should be obvious.

In this paper, the principal idea will be to consider the household as a producing unit that uses the commodities bought on the market for consumption to produce goods to fulfil needs. Different needs will be regarded as complementary, and, where there is substitutability between goods, it will be regarded as due to the possibility of using different goods to fulfil the same need. While neoclassical economists have sometimes attempted to reduce the criterion of profit maximization to that of the maximization of utility, I thus go here in the opposite direction (Lowe, [1965] 1983). To the extent that households are tradition-oriented, they are assumed to buy commodities for consumption in fixed proportions that they 'need'. To the extent that the principle of opportunity costs has penetrated their private lives, members of households are assumed to behave rationally and to produce the satisfaction of their given needs by choosing the cheapest method of transforming commodities for consumption into the objects they desire. As a result, they will, even with given needs, be responsive to changes in relative prices.

Apart from the 'objective' factors determining consumption, there are others that remain outside the scope of this theory. They should not be ignored from a humanistic point of view. Choice is here seen in terms of transitions between segments (learning processes or role conflicts) and the rationality of domestic production. But if it is true that taste exists and cannot always be reduced to social conditions, it is also true that neoclassical theory summarizes too many diverse influences under this heading. The need to stress the opposite point of view would be a sufficient cause to at least tentatively pursue the approach proposed here, even if we did not find additional, and perhaps decisive, reasons in the theoretical difficulties surrounding the concept of preferences itself and its implications for the theory of distribution and employment.

1 *Single-product systems and constant returns*

The case of single-product systems with constant returns and with a given distribution seems to present no problems; quantities are given in terms of social needs and expand with accumulation. Prices are given independently of the levels of output so that various explanations of demand are compatible with a given structure of production and distribution. Morishima (1964) has shown how preferences may be introduced without affecting a Cambridge-type theory of income distribution with given savings propensities on a balanced growth path. His assumption of Engel elasticities equal to one precluded an influence of demand on factor prices and hence the operation of the neoclassical interrelation between demand and distribution. To represent demand by means of given needs in a given period is, from a formal point of view, then even more trivial.

But how are income effects associated with growth to be treated? If incomes change because of a change in the distributive variables such as a rise in the real wage rate associated with a change in productivity, wage-earners get the opportunity to buy commodities that were not part of their habitual consumption basket. If they exercise their option, they acquire what at least initially must be considered as luxury goods; if they do not, they save. This shows that in this view the budget constraint must be assumed to be weak in that there is no necessity to spend incomes fully, and that there is a symmetric possibility of spending (slightly) more than current income. In the absence of perfect foresight there can be no definite commitment to the purchase of specific future consumption goods. On the other hand, there may be a pattern to the way in which people climb a social ladder as they receive higher incomes. Their behaviour can then be predicted on the basis of an ordering of consumers according to income classes. This yields an explanation of income elasticities of demand.

It is natural to order these three possibilities and to assume a social process by which rises in incomes are first saved, then spent on luxury goods, and these luxuries tend after some time in turn to be regarded as conveniences in a habitual standard of life. The classical distinction between luxuries and necessaries could thus be maintained for modern applications, although the social framework has lost much of its former rigidity. Instead of saying that the necessaries of the rich become the luxuries of the poor, we might differentiate and observe that the consumption pattern of the upper middle class is imitated by upwardly mobile individuals of the lower middle class, etc.

Next we come to price changes. Among the possible causes we may mention that the cost of production may rise in particular industries according to the theory of differential rent and that there may be reductions in prices with technical progress. After the change, there may again be constant returns within a certain range, as we shall see in section 3. The income effect of individual price changes on the standard of life of households is usually negligible because of the weak budget constraint.

The macroeconomic effects become important if there is a series of such changes. We take the case of a fall in the relative price first. With rapid technical progress in many sectors, which proceeds sufficiently evenly so as not to disturb steady accumulation, the savings so obtained may help to finance the process of investment. The increase in the disposable income of households also allows the acquisition of more or new luxury goods. Effective demand is then increased, and the budget constraint is observed in that additional income is spent.

If, on the other hand, some prices rise significantly more than others because diminishing returns are operating within the system, the surplus tends to get reduced and there results a threat to the existing state of distribution. Ricardo had such a case in mind when he spoke of a reduction in the general rate of profit and a redistribution in favour of the landlords. He assumed that the money wage of workers rises with the price of corn so as to keep the real wage constant. Ricardo's assumption eliminated the problem of effective demand but, *a priori*, price rises may work either way: if households try to maintain their level of consumption, effective demand is increased since costs have risen, but, if purchasers are discouraged and renounce the satisfaction of their needs, effective demand falls.

Generally, households will try to limit the impact of a fall in the real wage by substituting other methods of domestic production. If, for instance, the price of oil rises, they will start by wearing sweaters, then use gas and insulate houses, so as to maintain, as well as they can, a certain level of comfort. In doing so, households rarely revert to previous forms of behaviour; the fall in the price of oil in the 1950s and 1960s and the later rise did not lead to a return to the consumption patterns of the 1950s. It is therefore not illuminating to represent such a process of substitution as a substitution according to given preferences; it is more pertinent to analyse technical progress in the methods of domestic production that depend on the availability of consumption goods. Changes in methods of production are easier to observe while needs remain relatively stable, and if they are transformed their change should be traced back to definite causes.

Processes of substitution of the same type take place with all kinds of domestic activities: if grapes are expensive, one substitutes apples in order to have fruit. The formal treatment can be very simple. If (a_i, l_i) denotes a vector of consumption goods a_i and the input of domestic labour l_i necessary to fulfil a given need in a household, and if there are n such domestic processes of production possible with $i = 1, \ldots, n$, the household maximizes its 'profits' by minimizing its costs, given the costs of the consumption goods and a value attributed to the domestic labour. The wage rate used to measure domestic labour is, under conditions of perfect rationality, equal to the wage rate obtainable by the working members of the household, and a rate of profit on costs can in principle also be charged. It must be stressed that this form of rationality penetrates the household only slowly; other forms of rationality not only exist by virtue of the forms of tradition but are also re-created by obvious other social forces, which need not be discussed here.

If one wishes, therefore, one may list the inputs in terms of consumption goods to be bought on the market (and this includes, for instance, the material for insulation of houses) with the associated inputs of domestic labour. To each set of prices and a wage rate there corresponds a demand for inputs to the domestic processes of providing heat (or saving energy) of any given household under ideal conditions (absence of habits, ignorance, instantaneous adaptation, etc.). This is a demand associated with prices. One can then work out how demand changes with changes in prices, taking complications such as the diversity of households, speeds of adaptation, etc., into account, and thus work out short-run and long-run demand schedules.

The analysis of the methods of domestic production is subsequent to the analysis of the methods of industrial production. Or, if one prefers, some methods resembling those of an ordinary Sraffa system are reinterpreted as groups of methods of domestic production and added to it. Each group represents domestic production according to the lifestyle associated with a segment of the population and the income that finances the purchase of the inputs necessary to those processes. Sraffa has excluded them from the core of his theory since his definition of the wage as a share in the surplus leads to the interpretation of consumption goods as non-basics that cannot enter his standard system.

Changes in domestic methods of production and elasticities are thus analysed, given distribution and the basic system. Large deviations from the existing state of affairs are not compatible with the general approach presented here, so that the schedules obtained are not really full demand curves in the neoclassical sense but are indications of what the elasticity of demand might be in the neighbourhood of existing situations, i.e. of what is actually observable. The short-run elasticity indicates what the reaction would be to changes in market prices, while a long-run elasticity is an expression of how the demand of households might shift in a process of accumulation involving changes in relative normal prices. Movements of demand are reversible if the needs and the means for their satisfaction are constant. An exact formulation is not necessary here and perhaps not appropriate because it might conceal the importance of the other factors mentioned above, i.e. the weakness of the budget constraint and the importance of cultural factors in the explanation or, rather, phenomenological description of the evolution of consumption according to different lifestyles.

We can thus see how the methodological separation of the theories of output, of value and of distribution can be maintained to some extent with single-product systems because, with constant returns, prices are determined and remain the same with small changes in the output composition while larger changes, especially if they affect the budget constraint significantly, lead to a consideration of the interaction of the theories of output, distribution and effective demand, so that the quantity system and the distributive variables, which together determine prices, undergo a transformation. Under the conditions stated, the methodological separation of the theories and a sequential consideration of change are therefore not incompatible.

The crucial question is whether this methodology can also be pursued in those cases that have traditionally been considered by neoclassicals as their special domain: joint production and variable returns to scale. For the neoclassicals have (starting with Jevon's critique of Mill) habitually thought that under those circumstances the classical theory of value must fail and concluded (but it is a *non sequitur*) that 'value depends on utility'. They thought that relative prices of joint products could not be ascertained through a cost of production approach (which is how they saw the classical theory) without taking into account what John Stuart Mill called 'the antecedent forces of supply and demand' (Mill, [1871] 1909). But we shall now show – and this is, analytically speaking, the testing ground for the idea of this paper – that Sraffa has found a way to extend the classical methodology. It has been explored elsewhere (Schefold, 1980, 1985a); here, I shall present a summary that stresses the link with classical views of consumption. The key idea is to analyse change sequentially: if, for example, technological change is to be considered, the vector of final demand (which includes domestically produced consumption goods) is regarded as given as in Schefold (1978b), while methods of production are regarded as fixed if we want to analyse (small) changes in demand. Large changes in demand may necessitate technological changes (in the case of joint production), and this may be a more complicated matter, especially if there are effects on distribution.

2 *Joint production*

As is well known, Sraffa assumes that the number of commodities produced is equal to the number of processes used, i.e. that his system is 'square'. This equality seems problematical to the ordinary economist for at least three reasons:

(1) Casual observation suggests that multi-product industries are frequent and single-product industries are rare. Against this, Sraffa's suggestion is that multiple-product processes coexist in sufficient number so that the equality between the number of commodities (goods with positive prices) and processes used can be established. But in many cases there seem to be too few processes and an abun-

dance of commodities (for instance, oil refineries) while on the other hand there is often a multiplicity of methods for the production of the same commodity (for instance, there are several competing methods for producing steel).

(2) Sraffa' procedure is not immediately reflected in the literature on business administration. On the contrary, in those markets where prices can be set by producers, procedures for ascribing costs to individual products in order to charge a mark-up are difficult because of the presence of joint costs, i.e. because of joint production. Conversely, in those markets where prices should be regarded as given, it is difficult to ascribe the profit contributions to individual products as long as the problem of joint costs has not been solved. Accounting is for this reason nowadays often seen as a strategic tool of management rather than as a rational procedure for measurement according to impersonal standards.

(3) In modern theory, overproduced goods are free and unprofitable activities not used. It can be shown that neoclassical versions, using preferences or utility functions, do not necessarily yield 'square' solutions, i.e. solutions where the number of commodities (goods with positive prices) equals the number of activities used.

The reasoning of the marginalists can be illustrated by means of the simple diagram in Figure 7.2. Assuming a linear technology with constant returns to scale (therefore 'rigid' joint production for any given method), the transformation curve is spanned by a (finite) number of activities for the production of two goods. The equilibrium will be found at the point where an indifference curve touches the transformation curve. If this happens at a corner of the transformation curve, two commodities will have been produced by one method and the relative price will be determined by the rate of substitution as in Figure 7.2a.

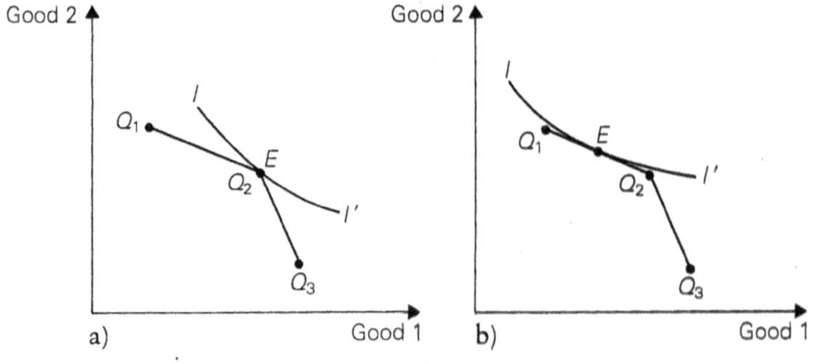

Figure 7.2 Transformation curve spanned by three processes Q_1, Q_2, Q_3; equilibrium E determined by indifference curve II'. The two commodities may be produced by one (Q_2 in Figure 7.2a) or by a linear combination of two processes (Q_1, Q_2 in Figure 7.2b)

But if the equilibrium lies on a linear segement spanned by two activities, we can, from a neoclassical point of view, conclude that the relative price is also equal to the rate of transformation (Figure 7.2b). It is easily seen that this will be equal to the corresponding price ratio obtained in a Sraffa system of the form:

$$(1 + r)\,\mathbf{Ap} + w\mathbf{l} = \mathbf{Bp},$$

with **A, B** being square matrices. Under suitable assumptions (Schefold, 1971, 1978b), the price vector of such a Sraffa system will be determined and positive for a given rate of profit, and the price of any two commodities can be represented in a diagram analogous to Figure 7.2. Let b_{ij} be the output of commodity j in process i. Without loss of generality, we consider the first two commodities produced by the first two processes. If they happen to have the same cost of production (which is, of course, not a necessary assumption but a convenient one for the use of this graphic technique), their relative price is given by (p_1, p_2). The vector (p_1, p_2) will be orthogonal to the difference of the vectors (b_{11}, b_{12}) and (b_{21}, b_{22}) (Figure 7.3).

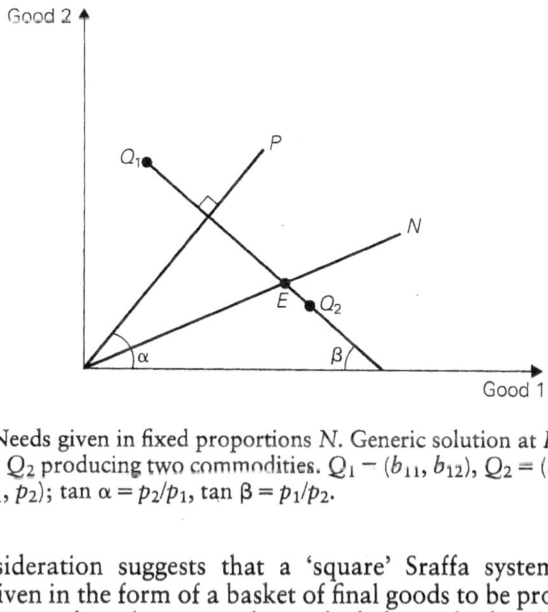

Figure 7.3 Needs given in fixed proportions N. Generic solution at E involves two processes Q_1, Q_2 producing two commodities. $Q_1 = (b_{11}, b_{12})$, $Q_2 = (b_{21}, b_{22})$. Price vector $\mathbf{p} = (p_1, p_2)$; $\tan \alpha = p_2/p_1$, $\tan \beta = p_1/p_2$.

This consideration suggests that a 'square' Sraffa system emerges if demand is given in the form of a basket of final goods to be produced and if there is a large number of processes from which the methods to be used can be selected. If needs are given in rigid proportions (for the reasons mentioned above), at least as many processes will in general be needed as there are commodities to be produced in the required proportions (without overproduction). But, on the other hand, not more processes can be used in an equilibrium with a uniform rate of profit, for otherwise prices would be overdetermined.

The idea has here been illustrated by means of diagrams based on a simplifying assumption. It has been assumed that costs of production are given, so that the interdependence has been neglected between the 'demand side' of the Sraffa system (output prices on the right-hand side) on the one hand and the 'cost of production aspect' (supply-side, left-hand input prices) on the other.

It can be proved rigorously that a 'square' Sraffa system will emerge with probability one on a golden rule path, if a vector of final demand is given. Among all square systems that can be obtained from a finite set of feasible alternatives and that allow the production (or partial overproduction) of the given basket of goods, the one will be chosen that yields the highest real wage, given the rate of profit. The envelope of these wage curves is monotonically decreasing. The problems in extending this result to the more plausible case where the rate of profit is larger than the rate of growth or to non-proportional growth has not been explored fully yet, but the substance of the argument seems to be valid from a mathematical point of view (Schefold, 1978b; Salvadori, 1982; Bidard, 1984). It was shown after the conference (Schefold, 1988a) that square solutions emerge with probability one even if golden rule conditions do not obtain, i.e. if the rate of growth is smaller than the rate of profit.

Sraffa, however, does not approach the problem of joint production from this angle. Instead of optimizing and looking for an equilibrium among a number of feasible alternatives, he takes a square system as given and performs his thought experiment of observing what happens to relative prices as distribution changes. This leads to many complications because of the possible occurrence of negative prices (to be eliminated by means of truncation) and other effects, which have been studied extensively in the literature. But the main interest in the model is elsewhere.

First of all, Sraffa's method corresponds to the classical approach to the problem of accumulation: the system is taken as given and one examines the conditions under which it may reproduce itself. The question of how other methods may be chosen is to be treated subsequently (in particular, the idea of having a long list of blueprints is problematical because it is difficult to assess and to compare the costs of actual and of potential techniques). It is of particular interest to observe the effects of changes in one method of production on prices and quantities in a square joint-production Sraffa system, for there may be effects that are qualitatively different from those observed in single-product systems. For instance, an increase in the productivity of labour in one sector of the economy leads always to a fall in all prices in terms of the wage rate in a basic single-product Sraffa system, whereas the same need not be true for joint production (Schefold, 1978a). Or, if there is a profit contribution from the selling of a by-product that had previously not been a commodity, it will generate a revenue such that all prices fall if the new commodity is produced in indispensable processes, but some prices may rise and some fall if the process is not indispensable.

This indicates that it would be desirable to construct square joint-production output matrices so as to enlarge input–output analysis in order to detect such effects, which will always remain concealed as long as joint production is eliminated by means of aggregation procedures in applied economics.

It is clear, at any rate, that alleged difficulties with 'demand' are no reason to reject the classical theory of value from a theoretical point of view. By assuming an equality of the number of processes with the number of commodities, Sraffa has indicated a way to determine relative prices in the case of joint production in exactly the same way as in single-product systems, i.e. by taking as given the needs and the methods of production to satisfy them. Changes in the system can be analysed in consecutive steps. In particular, small changes in needs do not have to lead to an immediate change in the methods of production employed, while exogenous changes in the method of production are compatible with a satisfaction of the same needs. Thus, one can analyse continuous changes in the composition of output, arising from the growth of incomes, with gradual (stepwise) changes in methods of production in response to shifts in demand or engendered by technical progress. For example, it is possible to increase the proportion of wool to mutton continuously by raising the average age of a flock of sheep. Since live sheep of age t can be treated as fixed capital yielding wool and $t + 1$-year-old sheep as joint products, with the T-year-old sheep being transformed into mutton, this can be achieved by increasing T by one step for an increasing number of sheep.

If this settles the question of the logical consistency of the classical approach at least provisionally, in that it has been shown that square systems determine prices and are compatible with changes in the composition of output, there remains the contrast between the main hypothesis of an equality of the number of commodities produced and the number of processes used on the one hand and the apparently frequent occurrence of an inequality on the other. It may be due either to an overdetermination of prices because of competing processes or to an apparent underdetermination in those cases where there is one process yielding multiple products and no other processes are visible that might help to determine the relative prices.

In my view, such cases of overdetermination or underdetermination are quite real and frequent, and the practice of business administration would not be explicable otherwise. But both overdetermination and underdetermination can be explained in terms of a classical theory of disequilibrium; they are aspects of processes of gravitation of market prices towards prices of production. The thesis is illustrated systematically and by means of concrete examples in Schefold (1985a); the result can be summarized as follows.

The normal case (even with single-product industries) is that of a multiplicity of methods of production which compete in one or, in the case of joint production, in a restricted number of separate markets. The prices are then formally overdetermined. The practical result is that rates of profit differ. The multiplicity of processes may persist if surplus profits are consolidated as rents and accrue to those who control the causes of the permanence of the multiplicity of methods. Not only land, but also patents or even certain components of wages are cases in point. The surplus profits are temporary and will tend to disappear in the case of technical progress with unrestricted competition. But the principle extends beyond the sphere of industrial commodity production; in some cases a limit to prices may be provided by the costs of domestic production (for instance, processed industrial vs.

homemade food). Many phenomena of the neoclassical theory of imperfect competition have here their logical place in a classical system. For instance, product differentiation can – but need not be – a way to legitimate unequal prices due to unequal costs of production, and it is then formally compatible even with equal rates of profit in a high-cost and a low-cost firm.

There are therefore many interesting forms of overdetermination that can be analysed by means of various models. However, the problem of overdetermination as such is by no means new; it has always been present in the classical vision. The converse case, where there seem not to be enough processes to determine prices according to Sraffa's method, is more intriguing. It is best to look at this matter by assuming that there is one method of production, producing a single commodity, and that then a by-product is discovered that had previously been disposed of as a waste but that now can be used either as an input to some other processes or as a consumption good. It can then only rarely be expected that another process is discovered in which the roles of the by-product and the main product are reversed so that they can be combined to yield the appropriate quantities. Often, additional processes will use one of the products as an input and thereby determine its value. The main possibilities are:

(1) Either the original process, run at its original level, provides more than enough of the by-product so that this will not acquire a price and become a commodity if disposal is free (case 1a). If disposal is costly, the producer of the by-product pays for the service of a firm that is prepared to take it over. Part of it is still disposed of; that amount for which there is a social need will be processed and sold at a price that is normally equal to the cost of processing the amount used *minus* what it would have cost to dispose of it (case 1b).

(2) Or the original process, run at its original level, does not provide enough of the by-product. It is then either expanded to the level required by the need for the by-product. In consequence, one should expect the orginal product to be overproduced and to receive a zero price or to result in a disposal cost (case 2a). However, the cheapening of the original product, with its established market, may also lead to the discovery of new uses for it in industrial (case 2b) or in domestic processes of production (case 2c). Or, finally, the original process is not expanded; the excess demand for the by-product will then have to be satisfied by an additional process (case 2d).

In formulae, one obtains for case 1b:

$$K_1 = Mp_{\mathrm{M}} + B_1p_{\mathrm{B}}$$

$$K_2 + (1 + r)\, B_2p_{\mathrm{B}} = 0$$

$$K_3 + (1 + r)\, B_3p_{\mathrm{B}} = Cp_{\mathrm{c}},$$

where K_1, K_2, K_3 respectively are the costs (including wages and profits) of the original process (producing the main product M at price p_{M} and the by-product B_1 at price p_{B}), of the waste-disposal process (which produces no commodity by means of the quantity B_2 of the by-product to be disposed of) and of the process yielding a useful commodity C at price p_c, manufactured from the quantity $B_3 = B_1 - B_2$ of the by-product. If costs are given, the number of unknowns (p_M, p_B, p_c) is equal to that of equations. Note that p_B is negative, while p_c and p_M are positive if coefficients K_1 and K_3 are sufficiently large. K_3 is the cost of producing C, $-B_3p_B$ that of disposing of B_3. The analysis transcends the conventional approach in so far as truncation is ruled out (the pollution abatement process is imposed so that a negative price obtains).

Case 2a is similar. The point of the theory now, however, is that the fall in the market price of the main product, owing to the necessity of expanding the original process above the level at which it had previously been run, in cases 2b and 2c, is an incentive to introduce new processes that will eventually lead to the determination of the unknown price unless the solution, according to case 2d, makes such an expansion unnecessary. If, to illustrate 2d, the importance of a by-product of a large industrial process is discovered, it is possible that it – or a close substitute – can also be manufactured directly, and this cost of manufacturing will then determine the price at which the by-product and, consequently, the main product can be sold.

But if the original process is expanded and the market price of the main product falls, its price may also be determined on the input side, for if its new use is to produce by a new method some other commodity that had already been produced in some other process at known costs, its price may fall from its original level to the point at which it will make the new process profitable (2b). If the demand for steaks increases relative to that for other forms of meat used in more traditional cooking, more cattle will be slaughtered, more meat will be processed and more hamburgers will have to be marketed. (The hamburgers represent the additional process.) Or, if more gas is to be produced from coal, coke will be processed to briquettes.

It is possible that the additional process is introduced by the households themselves, and this is perhaps the less familiar case (2c). Increased consumption of a commodity thanks to its reduced price does not have to lead to a change in needs or habits. If, for instance, the price of electricity at night is lowered because of new forms of power stations, the answer of households may be to introduce domestic storage heating that allows the accumulation of heat at night and its release during the day. Since the cost of direct (central) heating by means of oil is given, this activity determines the value of night-time electricity to households. In such cases, a domestic method of production may, by contrast with what has been said in section 2 about single-product systems, influence the basic system. In the example, the value of storage heating influences the price of night-time electricity, the latter that of day-time electricity, and both forms of electricity are basic commodities.

The answer to cheaper electricity at night is not to start cooking at bedtime but to store heat if electricity cannot be stored. We do not have to postulate that needs are responsive to price changes. Indeed, if the original good and the by-product were immediate substitutes for the same need, like big and small apples, they could be treated as the same good.

The multiplicity of potential methods of production, which has here been invoked to explain how prices of production can be determined in the face of an apparent underdetermination, is greatly enhanced if we remember the fact that most processes of production are not rigid, in that some substitution between outputs is possible. In order to take this into account, one could allow the input–output coefficients to vary continuously as a function of some parameter, but it seems more convenient to use a linear approximation, by means of a finite number of separate activities, to transformation curves (where they exist).

It follows that the tendency towards an underdetermination of prices is replaced by one towards an overdetermination, with many methods competing against each other and with a differentiation of rates of profit. The square Sraffa system may be regarded as the result of the corresponding competitive process. But, for theoretical as well as applied analyses, it is often better to take it as the starting point and to regard the methods employed in the system, from which one starts, as given and socially necessary, either by using averages between existing techniques or by taking least-cost techniques as the point of departure. One may then consider how the socially necessary technique shifts, or which other methods might become socially necessary, according to projections about productivity growth, expected changes of distributive parameters and other outside influences such as policies for research and development.

We may conclude that, in spite of specific effects, changes in the composition of output can be discussed in the presence of joint production in essentially the same way as in single-product systems.

3 *Variable returns and technical progress*

I return to single-product systems in order to investigate how my considerations are affected by variable returns. I want to show that the dependence of the cost of production on the scale of output does not require a different consideration of the role of demand. In particular, variable returns do not lead to supply schedules to be matched by demand curves.

As is well known, Sraffa discussed diminishing returns, taking the familiar example of land in a Ricardian setting. As in Ricardo, there is not only differential rent of the extensive kind, owing to the extension of cultivation from better to inferior lands – ordered using prices at a given rate of profit – but also intensive rent owing to the coexistence of two different methods of production for one commodity on one and the same land. In the latter case, one method is, at the given prices, more land-intensive, the other more cost-intensive (where costs include wages and capital with normal profits). An extension of cultivation may now take place if the cost-intensive technique (which must have a higher productivity per unit area to be eligible) is gradually extended at the expense of the land-intensive technique (which has lower costs but requires more land per unit of output). As soon as the more productive technique covers the entire area, a new, yet more productive technique comes in. In this way, production may rise continuously, while rent rises spasmodically. For each step, there are constant returns with a given technology, but total unit costs rise as production expands and techniques change (Schefold, 1971). Sraffa emphasizes that the order of fertility of different lands in the case of extensive rent and the ordering of techniques according to cost-intensity in the case of intensive rent cannot be given independently of prices, hence of distribution.

If several crops can be grown on different lands, curious patterns of specialization of lands are possible at a given rate of profit (Schefold, 1971), and the superposition of joint production can cause rents to fall as well as to rise with the expansion of production on one particular piece of land because of the interrelationships with other lands (Saucier, 1981).

If there is only one crop to be grown in a single-product system, there results, at the given rate of profit, a stepwise rise of the price of the crop. It can be drawn in a diagram, with its discontinuities, as a function of output (Figure 7.4). The graph looks very much like a neoclassical supply curve to be matched by a demand curve, but it is a different construction.

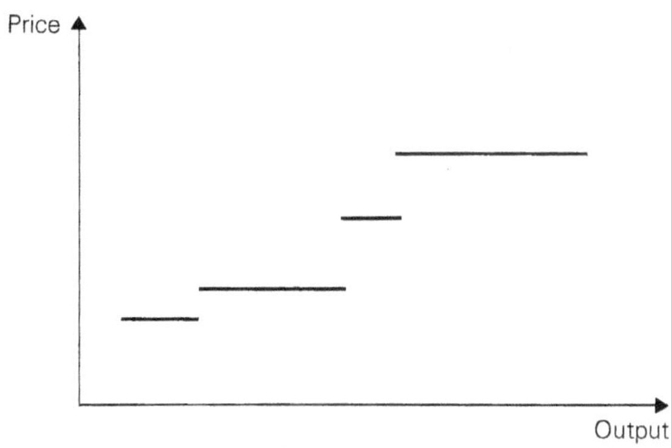

Figure 7.4 Output of crop and price with extension of cultivation over different types of land for a given rate of profit.

A neoclassical supply curve is *either* drawn as a partial equilibrium curve. Factor prices must then be considered as given in order to calculate the costs associated with different levels of output of the good under consideration. The marginal cost curve so constructed is matched with a demand curve to obtain the equilibrium in one market. However, the demand curve and the supply curve are, strictly speaking, interdependent because, with different levels of demand, there might be associated different factor prices. For instance, if the good under consideration is a consumption good, a higher price for it may change the supply of labour (Sraffa, 1925).

Or the full interdependence of markets is taken into account and the general equilibrium of demands and supplies of all goods is considered. But then, the supply curve usually disappears from the argument because there is, ideally, only one equilibrium point to be determined in the space of all quantities and prices. This point may shift if an exogenous parameter of equilibrium such as population changes. If population increases, the equilibrium point will follow a trajectory (as in the neoclassical one-sector growth model), and to this the construction in Figure 7.4 may be compared better than to a partial equilibrium supply curve. For the change in the composition of output discussed by Ricardo and reflected in Sraffa's more formal consideration concerns a particular scenario: population increases, accumulation goes on and output is expanded. Ricardo showed (first in his essay on corn – Ricardo [1815] 1951) that the rate of profit will fall if the real wage contains agricultural products, if methods of production are not improved over time, if overall productivity diminishes with an expansion to inferior lands, and if the real wage is given. Sraffa's treatment, dissociated from this historical context, takes the rate of profit as the independent variable. The interaction of markets can be taken into account (the good considered need not be a non-basic) and yet the rising curve can be derived, under simple assumptions, because full employment is not assumed and distribution is taken as given. The curve is therefore not a supply curve in the sense of the neoclassical textbooks, because the theory as a whole has not been subdivided into that of partial and of general equilibrium as in neoclassical theory but into that of a theory of value, given outputs and techniques of production on the one hand, and into theories of output, of technical progress and of distribution on the other. Whether the case is a legitimate representation of a rise in price in a process of growth therefore depends on the extent to which the supposed conditions regarding distribution and demand (and of course the technologies available) remain unchanged (Ricardo's point, of course, was simply to show that they eventually had to change – he could not say exactly how).

The neoclassical equilibrium trajectory for such a Ricardian scenario would be much more difficult to obtain because full employment would have to be assumed as the exogenous parameter (population) changes so that factor prices would be affected. For instance, the increase of population relative to a given factor endowment of land might lead to a fall in real wages that would counteract rising land rents, with an uncertain overall result on the price of agricultural products even in the absence of the more complicated effects discussed in the capital theory debate.

Matters are different in the case of technical progress and also in that of increasing returns (the latter are really inseparable from the former). A curve showing prices, at outputs corresponding to successive long-period positions, depicts only a specific, irreversible historical process and will in general not be expected to hold if accumulation were to be reversed because of an exogenous destruction of capital or in a depression. Yet, a schedule can be drawn as an *ex post* description of the development of the price of production in any one market or as an estimate even in the presence of technical progress; to this extent, Figure 7.5 is analogous to Figure 7.4 (the fall in the price might also occur in steps).

The increasing returns to scale traditionally associated with an increase in the division of labour are difficult to distinguish from other forms of making labour more productive by reducing the direct input. Economists of the classical and the historical school have attempted to give phenomenological

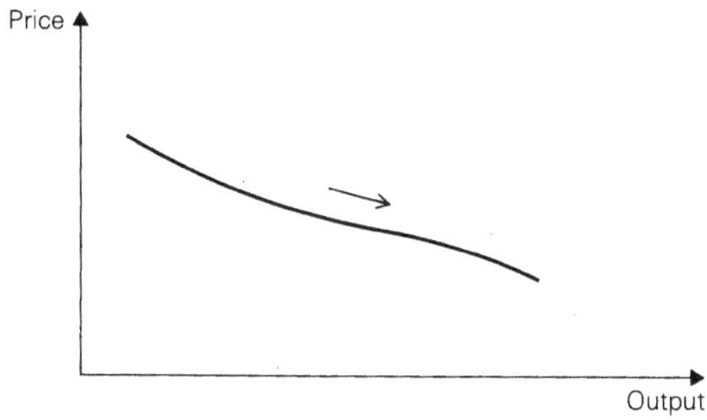

Figure 7.5 Increasing returns causing falling price of production with output expanding in a given industry at a given rate of profit.

descriptions of different forms of the division of labour; Adam Smith's pin factory and the chapter on the production of relative surplus value in Marx are the standard references, but Karl Bücher ([1893] 1926) provided perhaps the most extensive account. The price of production at a uniform rate of profit can in principle be calculated even if the firms enjoy advantages of scale. It may well be that the rates of profit in the corresponding sectors, calculated as some average of the market prices, will tend to be higher. But, according to classical arguments (which have reappeared in the theory of contestable markets), full monopolies are not likely to develop and any form of competition that results can be discussed with reference to the prices of production. As was stressed earlier, it is possible that mark-ups are such that prices set by firms are equal to prices of production, that short-run disturbances are smoothed through changes in stocks and orderbooks and that competitive pressures are exerted more through product differentiation, marketing, and research and development than through price cutting.

A more formal treatment of how the price of production changes with increases in output can be obtained if it is assumed that the changes in technology are known or can be projected at the level of the input–output coefficients. Various research institutions publish forecasts of changes in direct labour productivities for the important sectors of the economy at the level of aggregation of input–output analysis. Searching for the relevant coefficients by means of sensitivity analysis, one can also try to obtain estimates by experts of individual industries of expected changes in key input–output coefficients and take those into account at some intermediate level of aggregation. Speaking more theoretically, different forms of technical progress can be distinguished conceptually (Schefold, 1976a), and the effect of a steady flow of technical changes can be expressed by calculating the impact on normal costs.

I suggest that classical analysis provides a theoretical rationalization of what economists mean when they talk, for instance, about the future price of grain, cars or computers some years hence, be it in terms of educated intuitive guesses or aided by statistics and econometric models. For they will want to talk about future prices in relation to some 'normal' level of profitability and output. They will probably not want to hazard guesses about the consequences of a change in the distribution of income, but, if they do, they will discuss such a change by considering the unusual circumstances that bring it about, along with other important institutional factors that may have to be taken into account. Hence they will follow the classical methodology of estimating normal prices, given the expected changes in quantities, in particular in the technology, and they will not be following a strict neoclassical methodology because that would involve a simultaneous consideration of changes in factor prices at full employment.

It follows that increasing and diminishing returns do not give rise to supply curves to be matched by demand curves but that to each stage in the process of accumulation there corresponds a level of output of each industry that allows demand to be satisfied. Changes in the relative composition of output will accompany the expansion; their macroeconomic consequences may be diverse, as discussed in section 1. In a given normal position, prices are calculated, given distribution, the levels of output and the technology. If output expands and technology changes, the associated changes in prices due to changes in technology and varying returns to scale may induce changes in the demand for goods. The relevant factors affecting demand as such dynamic changes take place were those listed as hypotheses 1–5 in the Introduction.

Conclusion

I have now analysed the interaction between the theories of value and of output in several steps. It was first argued that individual choice is likely to be often inconsistent but that there are social roles to be fulfilled. I have regarded needs as given because they can be associated with social groups, because individuals are likely to stick to habits and conventions in the face of conflicting influences and because there is a structure to the system of consumption. We saw how households, having different methods to produce the goods they require to satisfy their needs, adapt to exogenous changes in prices and incomes, and what macroeconomic consequences might follow according to the surplus approach. I then showed that extensions do not alter the conclusion, although they give rise to special phenomena such as (in the case of joint production) the search for methods of production to adapt the composition of output to given needs and (in the case of variable returns) the (false) appearance of supply curves.

The approach allows one to focus on the needs in a stratified society directly, without the intervention of utility functions or preference systems. The underlying methodological separation of the theories of value, distribution and output will not easily be overcome in a unified, formally closed theory, but this is no drawback if a sequential analysis is best suited to grasp the essential traits of historically changing economic problems. In particular, the economics of welfare will then again be concerned with the well-being of concrete social groups, and with the question of what output we want and by which means it is to be produced. The focus is, to use an old concept, on wealth, not on utility and on representatives of social groups, not on individuals.

From an analytical point of view, the key contention of the paper has been that changes in the composition of output can, in a classical theory, be analysed not only if the conditions of the non-substitution theorem are fulfilled but also if there are joint production and variable returns. There is no reason to identify the classical theory with an analysis restricted to 'balanced growth' or 'steady states' (as Hahn, 1982b, does). To do so would exclude the possibility of changes in the composition of output that accompany development. The classical theory is not a special case of the neoclassical (Schefold, 1985b). It was clearly conceived to deal with fundamental economic transformations of the type of the Industrial Revolution, involving non-proportional growth and changes in the composition of output. The theory of value was designed to provide a conceptual foundation for the corresponding social and technical transformations, with the theory of demand being based on an assessment of the cultural change associated with the material progress of the economy.

Acknowledgements

A different version of this paper has been published in Schefold (1985c). I should like to thank G. Orosel, P. Garegnani, S. Parrinello and others for helpful comments.

Comment

Edwin Burmeister
Charlottesville

Joint production, technological change and the evolution of economic systems

How does the sociological development of households within a given culture interact with the evolution of the economic system? That is Professor Schefold's sweeping question, and it is clearly one of importance and interest. But such a general question cannot have any single 'answer', and the issue becomes whether or not one can identify a set of precisely defined problems whose solutions provide useful insights. Schefold's paper contains a sequence of propositions in an attempt to reveal such insights; the ambitious goal set out in this paper is to be admired.

Schefold chooses to attack his problems using a classical methodology with distinct approaches to (a) the determination of output, (b) the analysis of distribution, and (c) the theory of value. In the extended conference version of his paper he states,

> The classical theory is made up of these constituent parts, and it varies considerably according to the assumptions made about, e.g., distribution. Neoclassical theory, on the other hand, is based on the unifying principle of supply and demand which determines prices simultaneously with distribution and the composition of output.
>
> It is the purpose of this paper to show how this methodological distinction can be maintained in the face of changing conditions of demand.

A priori it is not obvious that the neoclassical approach should be discarded so quickly. In fact, all theories are wrong, for otherwise they would be facts and not theories. Theories are caricatures that attempt to capture some aspects of reality and to yield interesting predictions. Whether or not a particular theory, along with its specific assumptions, constitutes a 'good' theory depends upon what questions are being asked and how well they are answered.

For example, a model in which friction is ignored is useful if one is interested in the motion of a small spherical object rolling down an inclined plane, and in school we all learned how such a model yields useful predictions about terminal velocity, the relationship between velocity and the angle of inclination, etc. But clearly this model is foolish if instead the questions we wish to address involve how long it takes to stop an automobile by applying the brakes.

This observation illustrates how difficult a task Schefold has set out for himself: the more general the set of questions one wants to address, the more unlikely it is that any one theory will prove adequate. Why, then, is the neoclassical approach rejected out of hand? Is it not conceivable that some blend of classical and neoclassical approaches would provide a more satisfactory methodological framework? I shall discuss selected aspects of Schefold's paper that bear on these points.

1 *Criticism of neoclassical assumptions*

There is no single neoclassical model; each economist working in the neoclassical tradition introduces special assumptions to address specific issues. Thus, while Schefold may object to certain typical neoclassical assumptions, it does not follow that the whole of neoclassical methodology need be rejected; he could instead have opted to modify or drop objectionable assumptions to suit his own needs.

I am sympathetic to his criticism of utility maximization, and in fact wish to add to his list of objections. The typical assumption of a 'representative' utility-maximizing agent is particularly inappropriate in combination with models addressed to macroeconomic questions. Even if one believes that heterogeneous agents maximize their individual utility functions subject to their own budget constraints, at the macroeconomic level this implies only the existence of market demand curves for commodities; there is no reason to suspect that these market demand curves could have been generated by a single utility-maximizing individual.

But what assumption is more reasonable? That question cannot be answered without knowing what questions and what predictions we judge useful. Like the assumption of no-friction, utility maximization may be a useful approximation for some purposes, a disaster for others. On page 187, Professor Schefold postulates that, 'Households are units that produce the goods required to satisfy needs by means of commodities bought on the market and by means of domestic labour.' This assumption seems to beg the issue of what are 'needs' and what is 'required' to satisfy these needs. Causal observation suggests that individuals have wide variations and there is no accounting for a person's tastes.

On page 182 Schefold observes that competition ensures that own-rates of return on produced commodities are equalized. If some commodity is in excess supply, its price (and hence own-rate of return) will be zero in equilibrium. There is nothing wrong with this; in fact, the above conditions are precisely what one wants for intertemporally efficient allocation of resources. The fact that some initial endowments are inconsistent with long-run equilibrium prices should come as no surprise, and it certainly is not a 'logical contradiction'.

As to full employment, I merely note that a great many economists working in the neoclassical tradition consider it an unacceptable assumption when addressing most macroeconomic questions; there is no disagreement with Schefold here.

2 *Deviations from prices of production*

Below I follow that Sraffian tradition and use the term 'prices of production' to mean those prices associated with a long-run equilibrium at a uniform rate of profit, i.e. in obvious notation 'prices of production' are given by the price vector satisfying

$$\begin{aligned} P &= a_0 W + (1+r)P\mathbf{A} \\ &= \text{(under suitable assumptions)} \\ &\quad a_0 W[\mathbf{I} - (1+r)\mathbf{A}]^{-1}. \end{aligned}$$

Schefold finds it useful to use P as a benchmark from which to measure deviations due to imperfect competition, technological change, etc. If such deviations are of interest, then why not build a model that explicitly takes them into account?

3 *Joint production*

Schefold and I share the belief that joint production is a crucial complicating feature. I will use joint production to illustrate my earlier point that assumptions cannot be separated from the questions one wishes to ask.

Let us first consider the no-joint-production assumption in connection with Sraffa's standard commodity. Then it is well known that there exists a consumption basket with fixed weights $C^* = (C_1^*, \ldots, C_n^*)$ such that the 'standard commodity wage' is

$$\omega = \frac{1}{PC^*} = 1 - \frac{r}{r^*} \tag{1}$$

where $P = (P_1, \ldots, P_n)$, r is the uniform rate of profit, and $r^* > 0$ is the maximum rate of profit (see, e.g., Burmeister, 1968, 1980).

Now allow joint production, so the model becomes:

$$\sum_{i=1}^{n} P_i b_{ij} \leq a_{0j} W + (1+r) \sum_{i=1}^{n} P_i a_{ij} \tag{2}$$

with $x_j = 0$ if $<$ 0 holds, and

$$\sum_{i=1}^{m} b_{ij} x_j \; - \; C_i \geq (1+g) \sum_{i=1}^{m} a_{ij} x_j \tag{3}$$

with $P_i = 0$ if $>$ 0 holds (see Burmeister, 1974, pp. 451–3). We thus have the national income relationship

$$P(1+g)\mathbf{A}x + PC = P\mathbf{B}x = \mathbf{A}_0 W x + P(1+r)\mathbf{A}x \tag{4}$$

where $P = (P_1, \ldots, P_n)$, $\mathbf{A}_0 = (a_{01}, \ldots, a_{0m})$, $\mathbf{A} = [a_{ij}]$, $\mathbf{B} = [b_{ij}]$, $C = (C_1, \ldots, C_n)'$, and $x = (x_1, \ldots, x_m)'$. Now assume that there exists a $\lambda^* > 0$ such that

$$[\mathbf{B} - \lambda^* \mathbf{A}]x^* = 0 \tag{5}$$

has a solution with $x^* \geq 0$, $x^* \neq 0$. Under these conditions there exist consumption weights C^* such that (1) holds, exactly as it did without joint production; a proof is sketched in the Appendix.

Moreover, there is equal organic composition of capital with relative prices constant for all $r \in [0, r^*)$ if, and only if, there exists a scalar function $\alpha(r)$ such that

$$P\mathbf{B} = \alpha(r)\mathbf{A}_0 \qquad \text{for all } r \in [0, r^*), \tag{6}$$

exactly as in the no-joint-production case; again a proof is sketched in the Appendix.

Consequently, for questions involving Sraffa's standard commodity or equal organic composition of capital, the assumption of no joint production is innocuous; the central conclusions, namely (1) and (6), are essentially unaltered. (Of course, with no joint production $m = n$ and $\mathbf{B} = \mathbf{I}$.)

On the other hand, suppose we are interested in technological change, and again suppose we first exclude joint production. Consider two goods, 1 and 2, which are produced by themselves and one unit of labour in one period. Also assume that neither of these goods is used as an input in any other production process. (These assumptions are merely to focus on the problem and are not essential.) Initially the economy is in a steady-state equilibrium at profit rate r with prices $P = (P_1, P_2)$:

$$\begin{aligned} P &= W + [1 + r)P\mathbf{A} \\ &= W[\mathbf{I} - (1 + r)\mathbf{A}]^{-1}. \end{aligned} \tag{7}$$

Now suppose a new technology, $\mathbf{A}_N$, becomes available and that

$$W + (1 + r)P_N\mathbf{A}_N \equiv P_N \leq P, \qquad P_N \neq P. \tag{8}$$

The new technology will be introduced because positive profits can be earned initially with

$$P \geqslant W + (1 + r)P\mathbf{A}_N \geqslant P_N = W + (1 + r)P_N\mathbf{A}_N \tag{9}$$

where $>$ holds for at least one of $i = 1, 2$.

Consider now the same story when joint production exists and the original technology is $(\mathbf{B}, \mathbf{A})$ with prices P and the new technology is $(\mathbf{B}_N, \mathbf{A}_N)$ with prices P_N, all at the uniform profit rate r. The conclusions might be the same as before. But they might not, as the following illustrates.

It is easy to show that cases arise for which *neither*

$$P \gtrsim P_N$$

nor

$$P \leq P_N$$

holds. Should the new technology be introduced? *We cannot tell without an appeal to preferences*. To see how the question may be answered for a very special case, let us imagine homogeneous utility-maximizing consumers, all with indirect utility functions

$$U = U(P_1, P_2) \equiv U(P).$$

Then the new technology should be introduced if, and only if,

$$U(P_N) > U(P).$$

Alternatively, suppose

$$U = C_1{}^{\beta}C_2{}^{1-\beta}, \qquad 0 \leq \beta \leq 1.$$

For a given β and technology $(\mathbf{B}, \mathbf{A})$, there is a U-r frontier as in Figure 7.6, with the golden rule point of maximum utility at $r = 0$. In Figure 7.7 the new technology $(\mathbf{B}_N, \mathbf{A}_N)$ is superimposed. For any given $r \in [0,r^*)$ in Figure 7.7, the technology preferred (the utility-maximizing technology) is that associated with the highest U-values, and r_1 and r_2 designate switchpoints between the two technologies. In general, with joint production, r_1 and r_2 are functions of the taste parameter β; in fact, the U-r frontiers shift with β. Accordingly, given a value of r, we cannot even conclude which technology is 'best' without recourse to tastes.

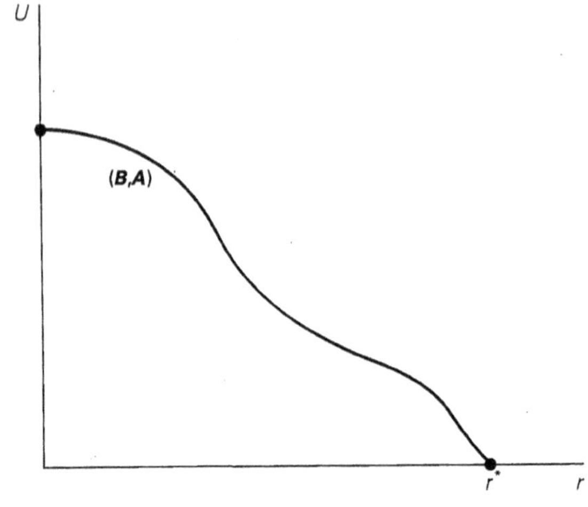

Figure 7.6

Note that for the particular value of β corresponding to Figure 7.7, the new technology ($\mathbf{B}_N$, $\mathbf{A}_N$) is strictly preferred to the old only for $r \in (r_1, r_2)$. *Thus for this second example joint production introduces essential differences from the simple no-joint-production case.*

What about heterogeneous tastes for this second example? Evidently matters are even worse in the sense of not being able to draw precise conclusions. People with certain tastes will prefer the old technology, those with other tastes the new technology. What will prevail will depend in part upon the

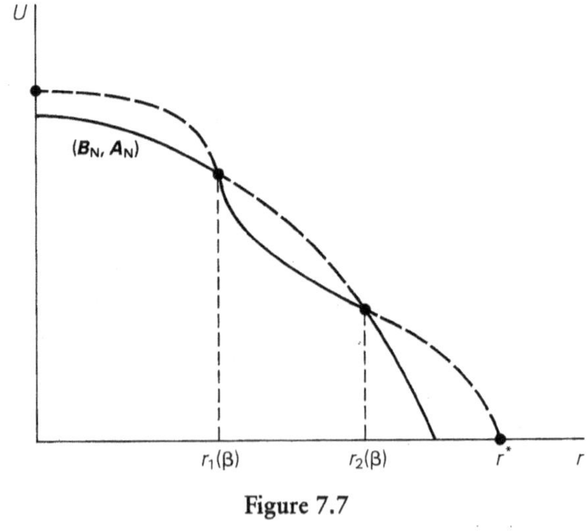

Figure 7.7

distribution of income across agents with heterogeneous tastes. A complete characterization of the possible outcomes appears intractable.

Schefold states (page 198). 'We may conclude that, in spite of specific effects, changes in the composition of output can be discussed in the presence of joint production in essentially the same way as in single-product systems.' My reaction is, 'Perhaps, but definitely *not* when both joint production and technological change exist.'

4 *Intertemporal prices*

Schefold is concerned with '. . . fundamental economic transformations of the type of the Industrial Revolution, involving non-proportional growth and changes in the composition of output.' (page 203). But it is precisely under such circumstances that prices will change over time, and the properties of the intertemporal price path are fundamental for the questions to be studied. Why should we ignore them?

The dynamic properties of models with heterogeneous capital goods is a difficult problem that has received considerable attention. The correct summary of some known facts are these:

(i) The conditions required to assure a unique long-run steady-state equilibrium are themselves restrictive.
(ii) Even when the dynamic system has a unique rest point, in general more than one dynamic path will converge to it from given initial capital stocks.
(iii) When the unique rest point of the dynamic system is a regular saddlepoint, for given initial capital stocks there exists a *unique* initial price vector, $P(0)$, for which the system converges.

References to proofs of (i)–(iii) can be found in Burmeister (1980).

5 *Concluding remarks*

Schefold is interested in fundamental questions involving the evolution of an economy over time. In my opinion many of these questions could be better answered by combining classical and neoclassical methodologies; for example, in Burmeister (1984) I showed how it was possible to have a real wage rate versus profit rate indeterminacy that leaves room for worker versus capitalist conflicts.

More seriously, I doubt whether or not we will ever have satisfactory answers to the type of important questions posed by Schefold until uncertainty is explicitly taken into account. The future is unknown, including future technologies, and hence every investment project has associated risks: Will new innovations make the project obsolete? Will taste changes reduce the rate of return? Will the project be viable if the equilibrium rate of return increases? etc. I do not pretend to have even tentative ideas about how uncertainty could best be introduced, but I do feel strongly that it is essential if we are to derive meaningful predictions about the future evolution of economic systems.

My own preference would be to try a blend of neoclassical and classical methodologies, attempting to derive a general equilibrium model that captures a few essential features of decision-making with an uncertain future. Obviously Schefold prefers quite a different approach. But, then, as I stated earlier, there is no accounting for tastes.

Appendix Sraffa's standard commodity and equal organic composition of capital with joint production

Consider the joint-production technology described by (2), (3) in the text, and assume the condition stated as equation (5) holds. Let $\lambda = (1 + r)$, and assume there are no regime changes for all $\lambda \in [\underline{\lambda}, \lambda^*)$, i.e. that for all λ such that $0 \leq \underline{\lambda} \leq \lambda < \lambda^*$, neither (p, W) nor $(\mathbf{B}, \mathbf{A}, x)$ change.

We then have

$$\mathbf{B}x^* = \lambda^* \mathbf{A}x^* \qquad \text{[from (5)]}$$

$$P\mathbf{B}x^* = \mathbf{A}_0 W + P(1 + r)\mathbf{A}x^* \qquad \text{[from (4)]}$$

which imply

$$P\mathbf{A}x^* = (\lambda^* - \lambda)^{-1}$$

and hence

$$P\mathbf{B}x^* = 1 + \lambda(\lambda^* - \lambda)^{-1}$$

(using the labour constraint $\mathbf{A}_0 x^* = 1$). It follows that

$$PC^* \equiv P[\mathbf{B} - \mathbf{A}]x^* = 1 + \lambda(\lambda^* - \lambda)^{-1} - (\lambda^* - \lambda)^{-1}$$

$$= \frac{\lambda^* - 1}{\lambda^* - \lambda}.$$

Consequently Sraffa's standard commodity wage is

$$\omega \equiv \frac{1}{PC^*} = \frac{\lambda^* - \lambda}{\lambda^* - 1} = 1 - \frac{r}{r^*},$$

exactly as in equation (1) in the text for the no-joint-production case.

To generalize the equal organic composition of capital concept to joint-production cases, we shall assume that $m \geq n$ and that $\mathbf{B}$ is of rank n. Define

$$Z \equiv \mathbf{B}'(\mathbf{B}\mathbf{B}')^{-1}$$

so that

$$\mathbf{B}Z = \mathbf{I}_n,$$

where $(\mathbf{B}\mathbf{B}')^{-1}$ exists because $\mathbf{B}$ is of rank n.

Then condition (6) in the text may be written as

$$P\mathbf{B} = \alpha\mathbf{A}_0 = \mathbf{A}_0 + P\lambda\mathbf{A}$$

or

$$P\mathbf{B} = \frac{P\mathbf{B}}{\alpha} + P\lambda\mathbf{A}$$

or

$$P[\mathbf{B}(\mathrm{I} - \frac{1}{\alpha}\mathrm{I}) - \lambda\mathbf{A}] = 0,$$

where here α denotes the scalar function $\alpha(r)$.

The condition

$$P\mathbf{B} = \alpha(r)\mathbf{A}_0$$

may be written as

$$P = \alpha(r)\mathbf{A}_0\mathbf{B}'(\mathbf{B}\mathbf{B}')^{-1}$$

with

$$P^* = \alpha(r^*)\mathbf{A}_0\mathbf{B}'(\mathbf{B}\mathbf{B})^{-1};$$

hence

$$P = P^*\alpha(r)/\alpha(r^*).$$

Accordingly,

$$P[\mathbf{B}(\mathrm{I} - \frac{1}{\alpha}\mathrm{I}) - \lambda\mathbf{A}] = \frac{P^*\alpha(r)}{\alpha(r^*)}[\mathbf{B}(\mathrm{I} - \frac{1}{\alpha}\mathrm{I}) - \lambda\mathbf{A}] = 0,$$

and thus

$$P^*[\mathbf{B}(\mathrm{I} - \frac{1}{\alpha}\mathrm{I}) - \lambda\mathbf{A}] = 0.$$

But since λ^* is the unique solution to $P^*[\mathbf{B} - \lambda\mathbf{A}] = 0$, we see that

$$\lambda^* = \frac{\lambda}{1 - \frac{1}{\alpha}}$$

or

$$\alpha(r) = \frac{\lambda^*}{\lambda^* - \lambda} = \frac{1 + r^*}{r^* - r}.$$

We conclude that all relative prices P_i/P_j are constant for all $r \in [r, r^*)$ or $\lambda \in [\lambda, \lambda^*)$ if, and only if,

$$P\mathbf{B} = \alpha(r)\mathbf{A}_0$$

where $\alpha(r) = \frac{1 + r^*}{r^* - r}$, exactly as in the no-joint production case.

Comment

Neri Salvadori
I.U.N., Naples

Bertram Schefold follows a long and established tradition in interpreting the classical economists as dealing with three separate but interconnected theories to determine distribution, normal prices and outputs, respectively. Whilst I basically agree with him, I think that a more detailed qualification is necessary in order to be able to advocate this methodology nowadays.

In my opinion what really characterizes the classical methodology is the separation between the determination of one distributive variable on the one hand, and the determination of quantities and prices of production on the other. In the neoclassical view, prices, quantities *and* distribution are determined simultaneously since endowments of all inputs are given. The classicals considered the real wage as independently determined; nowadays it is perhaps more appropriate to consider the monetary interest rate as independently determined, as Sraffa himself has suggested, or the growth rate, as Kaldor and Pasinetti have suggested. This characteristic feature of classical methodology should definitely be preserved. Yet I think that the separation between the determination of outputs and the determination of prices of production is difficult, if not impossible, to sustain.

Before I try to drive home my point, let me stress immediately that I do not think that the separation between the determination of quantities and the determination of prices of production constitutes an essential element of the classical approach in the sense that if this element is removed the whole approach is to be abandoned. Schefold is not of this opinion; he defends the idea of this separation. I will try to provide some arguments in support of my view.

In section 1 of his paper, Schefold has provided us with several suggestive ideas concerning changes in consumption in response to changes in prices and distribution; however, since no formalization of these ideas is provided, I prefer not to enter into a discussion of them. In the same section, it is also pointed out that, if single production and constant returns to scale are assumed, then there is no problem with the 'methodological separation' of the theory of the determination of prices, since the latter are definitely and unequivocally determined irrespective of the former.

I think that serious difficulties arise with regard to some of the propositions in the last two sections of Schefold's contribution. Take joint production first. Clearly, the older marginalist economists (such as Jevons) were not right to claim that, if there is joint production, then the number of processes operated is necessarily smaller than the number of products and that, therefore, prices can be determined only by introducing 'utility functions'. It is true that the number of processes *may* be *equal* to the number of products, as Sraffa assumed in Part II of *Production of Commodities by means of Commodities*. Nevertheless, we know today that the number of processes operated does *not* need to be equal to the number of products. Many examples have been provided that reflect this fact. Moreover, it has been shown that these examples do not require a neoclassical theory of demand in order to determine relative prices. An example can be easily constructed on the assumption that capitalists and workers consume commodities in fixed but different proportions, so that there is no substitution effect for each consumer, each commodity is strictly complementary to all the others for each consumer, and social class structure is strictly connected with consumption decisions.[1]

I think that there are also problems with respect to the existence and uniqueness of prices of production associated with the cost-minimizing technique. Existence and uniqueness can be proved in special cases, but they cannot be proved in general, as many examples have clearly shown. Moreover, even if only square systems are considered, the 'requirements for use', as Sraffa calls the outputs in demand, must be known in order to prove, when possible, both existence and uniqueness.

Finally, I am not sure I have understood correctly the meaning of Schefold's argument (page 193) that a number of processes larger than the number of commodities produced can be operated *if* the profit rates may differ. If each process may have its own rate of profit, which may differ from each of the others, and which, of course, is not given from outside but is endogenously determined, then the number of equations does not suffice to get a solution. If only *some* are free to have their own rate of profit, then an economic rationale for this choice must be provided, and the choice must be such that the number of processes whose rates of profit are set as uniform are equal to the number of commodities. Thus, to regard the square Sraffa system as a result of the competitive process between overdetermination and underdetermination (page 198) appears to be inadequate.

Now, let us turn to variable returns. I do not intend to comment on increasing returns since the issue is still fairly unexplored. With respect to diminishing returns, the problems are not substantially different from those just dealt with. D'Agata (1983) has shown, by means of examples, that even if only intensive rent is allowed, existence and uniqueness of prices of production cannot be proved in general.

Moreover, only special rent cases have been fully analysed up to now, and when some rather strong assumptions commonly held are dropped, then there is no way to prove that the number of processes is equal to the sum of the number of commodities produced plus the number of qualities of land yielding a rent. Again, it is not just that no such a proof has been yet found, but that examples have shown that such a proof *cannot* be found.

The relevance of these remarks is perhaps better understood if we look at Figure 7.4 of Schefold's paper on page 199, and ask ourselves to which kind of output and which kind of price the axes refer to. Indeed, the 1925 Sraffa paper suggests that such a diagram can be constructed only if there is *one* industry utilizing land (the scarce input). Moreover, even if corn is assumed to be the unique agricultural commodity, so that on the axis we have the net output of corn and the price of corn, the curve does need to be a (step) function, because, as I have previously pointed out, uniqueness of solutions is not ensured. I agree, of course, with Schefold that Figure 7.4 cannot be interpreted as a supply function, and indeed my remarks reinforce this opinion. Nevertheless, it is necessary to take into account the interplay between distribution, prices and quantities demanded in order to determine prices (one distributive variable being independently determined, obviously). Therefore the separation of quantity determination from price determination is inappropriate when diminishing returns are taken into account.

Of course, I know that Bertram Schefold is very well aware of all the problems that I have been raised. Therefore, I am prompted to believe that he thinks that they are of only negligible importance. However, such a standpoint appears to be sustainable only if it can be shown that the mentioned examples are flukes.

To conclude, let me emphasize again that it would be a complete *non sequitur* to argue that taking into consideration interdependences between distribution, prices and quantities demanded involves acceptance of the neoclassical theory of demand. The first section of Schefold's contribution has not only made it clear that the standard neoclassical treatment of consumer demand is inadequate, but it has also introduced new and suggestive ideas that contribute to an exploration of consumption analysis along classical lines of thought. It goes without saying that there is still a lot of work to be done; but Schefold deserves the credit for having made a substantial step in this direction.

Note

1 Let six units of commodity 1 and three units of commodity 2 be produced by five units of commodity 1 and one unit of labour; workers consume only commodity 1 and do not save; capitalists consume only commodity 2. Then

$$6p_1 + 3p_2 = 5(1+r)p_1 + w$$

$$w = (1-5g)p_1$$

$$5rp_1 = 5gp_1 + 3p_2$$

where p_1 and p_2 are the prices of commodities 1 and 2 respectively, w is the wage rate, r is the profit rate, and g is the growth rate. Simple calculations give (the numéraire has been chosen in such a way to avoid fractions):

$$p_1 = 3$$

$$p_2 = 5(r-g)$$

$$w = 3(1-5g).$$

Comment

Stefano Zamagni
Bologna

In his important and rich paper Schefold sets himself the task of showing 'how the classical methodological distinction can be maintained in the face of changing conditions of demand' (page 178). In what follows I shall discuss three specific points of Schefold's ambitious research programme. The first deals with Schefold's criticism of neoclassical theory of demand: "In order to make room for a classical treatment of demand, it is necessary first to review some of the neoclassical assumptions critically and to remind the reader of some logical objections to the neoclassical mode of reasoning' (page 179). The second point addresses the question of the adequacy of the linear production model as the proper analytical structure for studying the process of accumulation of a capitalist economy – the subject matter of Schefold's paper. Finally, I will raise some doubts concerning the appropriateness and relevance of the method suggested by Schefold for studying change over time: 'Changes in the system can be analysed in consecutive steps' (page 195).

(1) It is well known that the common ground for both classical and Marxian economics is the *assumption* that the conditions of the markets are dominated by the conditions of production and reproduction of commodities. In other words, contrary to the neoclassical view, these conditions are more important than market structure and demand. A fundamental consequence of this assumption is that there are centres of gravity for prices and profits given by the long-run conditions of social reproduction that regulate market phenomena. What is the rationale for such a central assumption? The fact that the classicals' mode of explanation is not methodological individualism.

A common feature of all modes of explanation is the careful distinction between exogenous and endogenous variables, where the former are taken as given and are part of the explanans, while the latter constitute the explanandum. Methodological individualism – the common mode of all the versions of neoclassical thought[1] – differs from other types of explanations (such as functionalism or holism) precisely in what it postulates as exogenous variables. What are exogenously given are individual preferences (together with endowments and technology), while social facts such as the price level and the existence of collective entities, such as markets, the legal system and other social institutions, have to be explained by reference to individual action stemming ultimately from such preferences.

The familiar description of agents identifies them with the goals they pursue, i.e. with their preferences or utility functions. To ask why people have the preferences they have is beside the point (in fact, they are exogenous), as it is to inquire into the possibility of endogenous changes of preferences.

Indeed, if one were to start analysing the origin of preferences – or, as Garegnani (1983a, p. 311) says, 'the content of (these) tastes' – or whether it is possible for preferences to change endogenously, one would have to explore the role of institutions in shaping people's preferences and needs. Thus one would have to exogenize institutions in order to be able to refer to them in explaining the genesis of needs. This, however, would plainly run counter to the methodological individualist's problem.

So, a good deal of the criticism levied in the first ten pages of Schefold's paper against the neoclassical theory of demand is, in this specific sense, beside the point. The neoclassical economist would simply react by stating that it is his fundamental assumption to take individual preferences as given and defined over all possible conceivable states of the world. Rather, there are two appropriate levels of critique. The first deals with the fact that, because of the assumption of exogenously given preferences, the explicative worth of the neoclassical theory of demand is too modest. Three claims can be advanced in this regard: (i) the existence of incomplete preferences destroys the notion itself of demand function, since changes in prices and/or in income may generate irreversible changes in demand even though preferences stay the same; (ii) orthodox theory provides no theory of beliefs that can support its own claim that explanations of demand choices are explanations in terms of preferences and beliefs; (iii) the notion of choice accounted for by orthodox theory poses problems when one tries to accommodate important phenomena such as regret, precommitment, preferences for preferences, and so on. The second and more fundamental level of the critique has to show the substantial incompatibility of the doctrine of methodological individualism and the principle of rational action as used by mainstream neoclassical theory to explain consumers' choices.

In view of the above, it surprises me that Schefold finds Lancaster's and Becker's approaches (Lancaster, 1966; Becker, 1976) to the theory of consumer behaviour a reasonable starting point capable of 'supporting' a long-run theory of effective demand. I cannot really see how the arguments he himself forcefully develops in the Introduction to his paper against the orthodox theory vanish once he comes to apply the Lancaster–Becker approach: 'In this paper, the principal idea will be to consider the household as a producing unit that uses the commodities bought on the market for consumption to produce goods to fulfil needs' (page 187). Moreover, 'to the extent that the principle of opportunity costs has penetrated their private lives, members of households are assumed to *behave rationally* and to produce the satisfaction of their given needs by choosing the cheapest method of transforming commodities for consumption into the objects they desire' (pages 187–8; emphasis added). But which notion of rationality is here being presupposed? On page 190 we read: 'under conditions of perfect rationality'. What should we take this to mean – epistemic rationality or simply practical rationality? And in the latter case are we sure that such a notion of rationality is consistent with the classical paradigm and in particular with the classical way of tackling consumer demand? I doubt it.

(2) *What* determines the classical long-run prices are conditions of social

reproduction (structure of production and distribution), but *how* are they determined? Neo-Ricardian theory utilizes the apparatus of linear economic models to give an answer. It is taken that the centres of gravity are the solutions of linear production models. Because of the similarities of the properties of production prices to the properties of prices in linear production models with constant returns to scale, the latter are being used to interpret classical theory.

This has greatly helped our understanding of many properties of production prices. At the same time it has contributed to increasing the formal rigour of the whole analysis. However, as is often the case, this reductionist move has managed to impoverish the classical representation of the accumulation process. Indeed, the linear approach, by assuming constant returns to scale and by visualizing the productive process in a *horizontal* manner, is not the proper vehicle for extolling the potentialities of the classical vision. In particular, the classical theory of manufacturing production has been put to one side and neglected because it does not fit into the formal structure of neo-Ricardian theory.

The classicals – it should be recalled – did not dwell much on machinery as one of the 'causes of wealth'. Instead they made the division of labour their grand theme. Smith and Marx, in particular, treated the role of machinery as important but as secondary and subsidiary to the 'increasing division of labour' in their accounts of economic progress. As Sraffa [1926, p. 536] comments: 'The position occupied in classical economics by the law of increasing returns was much less prominent as it was regarded merely as an important aspect of the division of labour and thus rather as a result of general economic progress than of an increase in the scale of production.'

Now, as one proceeds with the study of the classical theory of the division of labour, it increasingly escapes the analytical categories of the linear production model. A fundamental characteristic of productive activity involving the use of durable means of production is that events are causally linked in temporal sequences. This implies that, to be useful, a study of the evolution of the material structure of an economy must, on the one hand, visualize production as an essentially joint process and, on the other hand, pay due attention to the complementarity relationships among technical possibilities belonging to different moments of time. The linear approach, while it is capable of tackling the first aspect – an aspect that expresses the 'synchronic' heterogeneity of capital – is clearly inadequate to deal, in a direct and explicit way, with both the duration and timing of production, i.e. to deal with the 'diachronic' heterogeneity of capital (see Zamagni, 1984).

Just because classical theory is a theory of an evolutionary process rather than a theory of the rational choice between known alternatives, one is not doing the classical vision a service if one continues to look at it through the lens of the linear production model. Needless to say, this does not mean that one cannot use this analytical tool to interpret certain aspects or to solve specific problems of classical theory. Indeed, this is the case with the problems posed and solved by Sraffa himself in his book. What it does mean is that for a study of the process of accumulation of a capitalist economy – the subject of Schefold's paper – the linear approach, at best, is not the most convenient instrument to adopt, and, at worst, pushes the researcher to look for the 'wrong facts' or to pose the 'wrong questions'.

This state of affairs is very common in our discipline, where too often it is the availability of the formal tool that dictates what should be done. Yet Sraffa himself rejected such a methodological stance, according to which logic and mathematics are syntactically neutral and univocal languages. Incidentally, it is because of its acceptance of such a position that neoclassical theory can support the myth of an economic science as a pure technique, neutral in its means even though non-neutral in its extra-logical ends. For Sraffa, in contrast, the distinction between syntaxis and semantics cannot lead to a subsumption of the one by the other with the result that even at the level of formal systems there is a co-penetration of the two, in the sense that the choice of a formal apparatus of inquiry is not independent of its own uses.

(3) 'Changes in the system can be analysed in consecutive steps . . . thus, one can analyse continuous changes in the composition of output, arising from the growth of incomes, with gradual (stepwise) changes in methods of production in response to shifts in demand or engendered by technical progress' (page 195). Now the difficulty I see in adopting Sraffa's analytical approach – as Schefold does in his paper – in order to treat the problems of accumulation and changes in the composition of demand is due to the fact that such an approach, while it is well suited to comparative static or comparative dynamic analyses, cannot cope with the problems of a truly dynamic analysis, as is certainly the case with the problems emerging in an investigation of 'change over time'. In fact, what characterizes a comparative dynamic type of inquiry is that one is dealing with a *given* number of productive methods, and the problem of the choice of techniques is solved once one knows one of the distributive variables, say the rate of profit. In such a framework, it is therefore legitimate to postulate that the matrix of coefficient does not depend on the rate of profit and to assert that the determination of output is independent of distribution.

However, this is no longer the case in a truly dynamic context, for the simple reason that the methods of production are no longer given from the start. The methods that become *available* over time depend on the path taken by accumulation, in particular by the intensity and direction of investment. The latter, in turn, depends crucially on the rate of profit, as well as on other factors such as expectations. It follows that the distribution and production structure can no longer be kept separated, as is the case in the Sraffa system. Indeed, a certain pattern of distribution, by determining how the surplus is divided between consumption and investment, has a direct effect on the availability of productive processes. This means that the change in productive techniques is related to the pace and pattern of accumulation.

Of course, the above is no objection at all to Sraffa's work, for the very reason that, in his book, he does not deal with the effects of the 'general progress of the economy' and the implied changes in its productive potential on relative prices and on distribution. Rather, he chooses to deal – and with good reason – with those properties of an economic system that do not depend on changes in the scale of production or in the proportions of factors.

But this does not mean that the system is 'invariant' under these changes. Sraffa's system does not presuppose 'changelessness'. Indeed, whereas the propositions that are discussed in the book do not depend on change, they are not to be taken to imply the assertion that no change could follow. The conclusion I draw is that the 'analytical core' – to use Garegnani's expression – of Sraffa's system, while it is adequate for studying the relationships between relative prices and distributive variables, is not the right analytical level at which to tackle the fundamental idea of classical thought: the idea of the link between the division of labour, growth of markets and productivity increases.

There is a second reason that makes the method suggested by Schefold inadequate for an understanding of change over time. I am referring to the fact that, after a structural change, a new long-run position – defined with respect to the particular composition of demand – can only be achieved, *if ever*, when the *transmutation* of the capital stock to the proportions required by the new situation has been completed. In turn, this might require a modification of the mode of behaviour of the capitalists, who do not simply adapt themselves but *react* to the new situation. Now, the study of these 'turbulent' not-so-short periods poses new and interesting problems. By way of example, suppose that, owing to a change in the composition of output, the input coefficient matrix changes. (Ricardo and Marx knew quite well that a change in effectual demand can lead to a change in the 'facility' or 'difficulty' of production.) How can we conceive the market process to establish the new centres of gravity? Which behavioural assumptions should we introduce for the proper working of such a process? Clearly, if such an adjustment process does not exist, the new production coefficients cannot determine the new long-run prices.

To give it a name, this is the problem of *transition* from an 'old' to a 'new' long-run position, a problem that has nothing to do with the usual problems of stability or gravitation analysis. In fact, while the 'new' position is time-dependent in the sense that it depends on the path followed by the economy during the transition itself, the familiar process of gravitation is conceived of as 'an adaptation to quantities *already fixed*, i.e. determined in another part of the theory' (Garegnani, 1976a, p. 29; emphasis added). I believe that if one is interested in studying, in a classical mode, the historical dynamics of technical change and of changes in the composition of output, a method for analysing transitions in the above sense becomes a theoretical necessity.

A final general comment. It seems to me that a good deal of the recent neo-Ricardian literature has ended up by unconsciously accepting the same kind of methodological stance as neoclassical theory – the stance being represented by the idea that there should be a unique analytical core to tackle any problem whatsoever. Of course, this is not surprising. When a theoretical paradigm becomes dominant it also establishes a standard for correct theorizing, in the sense that it fixes the canons of rational validation for any theoretical inquiry. This produces a dangerous distortive effect since one starts formulating one's meta-theory of a given domain with an already formed model of valid reasoning. This model then makes the researcher quite incapable of seeing how reason does and can really function in the domain to the degree that it does not fit the procrustean bed of that model of validation. In his rich and stimulating paper, Schefold has not completely resisted this temptation, in so far as he seems to believe that it is possible to fruitfully apply what he calls the classical methodology to studying changing conditions of demand. However, this attitude might lead, if generalized, to a progressive immiseration of the classical paradigm.

Note

1 See Hahn's manifesto in the Introduction to Hahn (1984).

Reply

The heterogeneity of the comments on my paper allows me to reply to each of them in turn, taking up the arguments one by one.

Professor Burmeister has raised some interesting questions. He sympathizes with my critique of utility maximization but doubts whether real needs can be identified. In a way, this is my point. The formal structure of a theory that introduces given needs is necessarily simple, even if one adds household processes that produce goods to satisfy those needs. But the question of what needs there are, how they develop, why they belong to a given social environment, has to be discussed with reference to a concrete historical situation; it cannot be done without making reference to social values. Needs therefore cannot be identified merely by observing quantities and outputs. At best such observations yield a determination of elasticities. Whether elasticities should be explained in terms of preferences, in terms of the theory presented in my paper, or in still other terms, cannot be decided on the basis of quantitiative evidence; the explanation requires an understanding of the social and psychological processes involved.

The assumption of given needs not only is comfortable from an analytic point of view when discussing the theory of value, it is also appropriate from the point of view of the theory of output. The theory of output is qualitatively different from the theory of value: it is mainly descriptive and not analytic. It would run counter the doctrine of methodological individualism to question whether what somebody has bought is really useful to them. Of needs, it is legitimate to ask whether they are, for example, an outgrowth of a natural need like that for basic food, whether its satisfaction constitutes a social necessity according to the legal norms that define poverty standards, or whether it is associated with a more recent cultural development. I certainly do not set myself the task of covering this entire field, but I think that economists should not shy away completely from a reasoned, liberal and tolerant discussion of such issues. They were addressed not only by the classical economists, but also by members of the historical and instutitionalist schools. A growing world population and environmental pressures will make it inevitable to order needs somehow and in some degree according to importance; nobody can deny it. Why, then, do we put so much emphasis on a theory that makes choice dependent on utility maximization and presupposes general substitutability.?

I certainly do not reject utility maximization 'out of hand'; I value greatly the mathematical and many of the other intellectual tools forged by neoclassical economists, Burmeister among them. I regard a general equilibrium, and within it especially the method of factor pricing, as the core of neoclassical theory. Burmeister's remarks on intertemporal equilibrium suggest that he is a neoclassical in that he believes that the intertemporal theory is essential for the determination of factor prices. But then I find it difficult to understand his eclectic attitude when he also writes 'as to full employment, . . . a great many economists working in the neoclassical tradition consider it an unacceptable assumption when addressing most macroeconomic questions' (p. 205). Is the treatment of the endowment of labour in general equilibrium irrelevant to macroeconomic questions? Are the criticisms of Keynes and Sraffa really peripheral?

The main interest of Burmeister's comment lies in his contribution to joint production. It is a well-known fact that the technique to be chosen in joint-production systems depends on the composition of output. I have worked on this problem for nearly twenty years. Only recently have I been able to prove the existence of a solution to my own satisfaction. Given the composition of net output, the rate of growth and the rate of profit, a dominant technique will exist that maximizes the real wage in terms of that output and that will use exactly as many processes as there are commodities (goods with positive prices) to be produced (Schefold, 1988a). Golden rule conditions need not hold. This dominant technique minimizes costs, in that other processes, not being part of the dominant technique, will all show losses if evaluated in terms of the process of the dominating technique. The criterion for the choice of technique thus is neither the minimisation of prices nor the maximisation of utility (as Burmeister suggests on p. 207) but, given needs and distribution, simply profitability.

The dominant technique may change with changes in the rate of profit, the rate of growth or the composition of output. However, it will in general be possible to change any of the positive components of final demand, the rate of growth or the rate of profit in a possibly small but not infinitesimally small – neighbourhood without having to change any of the processes of the dominant technique, so that we obtain, in neoclassical language, a kind of local non-substitution theorem under conditions of constant returns to scale. Burmeister does not seem to be aware of this result, or of the work that preceded it, for he would otherwise have known that only square joint-production systems qualify for the dominant technique, and his proofs of the existence of the standard commodity and of a condition guaranteeing the uniformity of the organic composition of a capital (Schefold, 1971, p. 29) would then have been much simpler.

However, my main concern is with the fact that he regards the results obtained for joint production as substantially different from those obtained for the single-product case. He can believe that the dominant technique does not depend on the composition of output in single-product systems only because he assumes, as a matter of course, that constant returns prevail. But Sraffa has not only asserted that constant returns need not to be assumed, he has also shown how the dominant technique does depend on the composition of output in the case of diminishing returns in agriculture, with also a kind of local non-substitution theorem – if the demand for wheat diminishes and that for barley increases, the proportion in which each is grown on the marginal land will change (supposing, for simplicity, that both grow on it), and hence the price of production of these commodities will stay constant unless the change is large enough to cause a change of the marginal land or pattern of cultivation itself. The problem of the dependence of the dominant technique on the composition of output therefore precedes the treatment of joint production in the classical approach. It can be handled if either the composition of output is treated as completely exogenous, or if special models for a dependence of the composition on prices and incomes are made that capture some aspect of the classical views as to the forces determining that composition.

Burmeister's analysis of technical change in terms of utility leads to the conclusion that a 'complete characterisation of the possible outcomes appears intractable' (p. 209). Classical analysis in terms of given needs and distribution fares better by considering feedbacks of technical change on distribution, and possibly also on needs in subsequent steps. Similarly, I should like to invite him to consider whether his problems with the intertemporal theory (p. 209) could not best be tackled by using the classical method of comparing long-period positions (cf. also p. 304 below concerning the regularity assumption).

I am grateful for Burmeister's thoughtful and challenging critique. My problem is not so much to account for our difference in tastes but to communicate with someone whose intellectual development has been shaped by the reading of different texts.

Professor Salvadori's doubts concerning my interpretation of the classical approach again centre around the problem of joint production. He wishes to link the theories of prices of production and of output, and to treat only distribution as exogenous when approaching the determination of value. I believe, however, that this methodological stance will quickly lead him also to integrate the theory of distribution in a model, which is then bound to be special. And attempts to generalize it are likely to lead in the neoclassical direction.

To show this, it is convenient to start from the seemingly only formal problem of whether the dominant technique will be 'square'. Consider first a square solution with as many processes used as there are commodities produced (goods with positive prices). Such solutions are known to exist for given rates of growth and of profit, and for a given composition of output (Schefold, 1988a). If this (in general unique) solution with n commodities and $m = n$ processes is given, one can easily see that up to n 'spurious' solutions will exist that produce the same n commodities with $n-1$ processes and such that prices will nevertheless be determined (though different from that of the main solution) through the presence of demand equations (as illustrated by the example given by Salvadori in the note to his paper, where the main solution would be given – if the composition of output was fixed – with $n = m = 1$ or by $n = m = 2$ in the presence of another process).

Since Salvadori wishes to distinguish between consumption out of wages, consisting of a basket of wage goods $\mathbf{c}_w$, and consumption out of profits, given by a basket of luxuries of $\mathbf{c}_p$, there will be a vector of activity levels $\mathbf{q}$ and a square joint-production system $\mathbf{A}$, $\mathbf{B}$ (possibly a truncation) such that the output for consumption $\mathbf{d}$ can be produced at rate of growth g:

$$\mathbf{d} = \mathbf{c}_w + \mathbf{c}_p = \mathbf{q}[\mathbf{B} - (1+g)\mathbf{A}], \tag{1}$$

as I have proved in Schefold (1988a). There will also be a price vector $\mathbf{p}$ and a labour vector $\mathbf{l}$ of order n such that

$$[\mathbf{B} - (1+r)\ \mathbf{A}]\mathbf{p} = \mathbf{l}. \tag{2}$$

Moreover, the general results show that a budget equation

$$\mathbf{dp} = \mathbf{ql} + (r-g)\mathbf{qAp} \tag{3}$$

will hold: the value of consumption (expressed in terms of the wage rate) is equal to the wage plus consumption out of profits (there is saving only out of profits).

But if we have a budget constraint for the workers, too, the equation

$$\mathbf{c}_w\mathbf{p} = \mathbf{ql} \tag{4}$$

must also hold. It implies, together with the overall budget equation,

$$\mathbf{c}_p\mathbf{p} = (r-g)\mathbf{qAp}. \tag{5}$$

Since it is now known that equations (1)–(3) hold for the dominant technique for essentially arbitrary values of r and g, the additional equation (4) can be introduced only if one degree of freedom is abandoned. It is, of course, distribution that is thus determined by a given real wage. To simplify matters, we may assume here that the value of workers' consumption in terms of the wage rate, $\mathbf{c}_w\mathbf{p}$, is a rising and continuous function of the rate of profit, so that equation (4) holds exactly for one value of r, which is thus determined.

It follows that, with this approach of assuming separate consumption vectors for the two classes, not only employment will be determined (through the effective demand for investment and the consumption of capitalists) but distribution will be determined, too.

However, in order to make room for separate theories of distribution, aiming at a determination of the rate of profit, demand for consumption goods must be made variable, and this leads Salvadori to adopt the special hypothesis that workers' consumption is proportional, with a factor t_w, to a basket $\mathbf{c}_w$, therefore that it is equal to $t_w\mathbf{c}_w$, and similarly capitalists' consumption equals $t_p\mathbf{c}_p$. Since we now have two additional degrees of freedom, the level both of the rate of profit and of employment can be left undetermined, opening up the question of what determines either. However, since consumption is not likely to be a linear function of anything – except of employment, in the workers' case – this treatment of consumption leads either back to equation (4) and a classical model with a given real wage per worker, or to the task of making demand truly endogenous, hence dependent on prices and incomes. If demand and prices depend on distribution, why should distribution not depend on prices and demand? So I doubt whether Salvadori's suggestion of abandoning the principle of treating consumption as exogenous in the theory of value is really a happy one.

As to his 'spurious' solutions, consider the equation

$$t_w \mathbf{c}_w + t_p \mathbf{c}_p = \mathbf{q}^* [\mathbf{B} - (1+g)\mathbf{A}]. \tag{6}$$

In general, there are up to n non-negative solutions, in t_w, t_p and $\mathbf{q}^*$, to equation (6), given g, depending on which component of $\mathbf{q}^*$ is arbitrarily set to zero, and leaving one degree of freedom (e.g. t_w). This we may eliminate by assuming that employment is given, hence that we have

$$\mathbf{q}^* \mathbf{l} = L. \tag{7}$$

Prices $\mathbf{p}^*$ of this solution will now be determined by an equation, with r given,

$$[\mathbf{B}^* - (1+r)\mathbf{A}^*]\mathbf{p}^* = \mathbf{l}^*, \tag{8}$$

where $\mathbf{A}^*$, $\mathbf{B}^*$, $\mathbf{l}^*$ are the input and output matrices and the labour vector obtained from $\mathbf{A}$, $\mathbf{B}$, $\mathbf{l}$ by deleting that row for which the corresponding component of $\mathbf{q}^*$ has arbitrarily been set to zero in equation (8). There is thus one degree of freedom left in the determination of relative prices in terms of the wage rate. This is eliminated by the budget equation for workers

$$\mathbf{q}^* \mathbf{l} = t_w \mathbf{c}_w \mathbf{p}, \tag{9}$$

and the corresponding equation for profits, analogous to (5), then follows from a budget equation analogous to (3). (We assume that the process omitted is not profitable in terms of prices $\mathbf{p}^*$.)

It is thus not difficult, at least in terms of the counting of equations, to construct the solutions proposed by Salvadori which are not square. I call them 'spurious' because I regard them as admissible only for special short-period situations. The normal positions, with which we are really concerned, must be stable in that they allow small perturbations; in particular, perturbations of quantities must be allowed. The system of production must be capable of adapting to small fluctuations of demand in any direction. This means that, if the demand vector $\mathbf{d}$ is replaced by some demand vector $\mathbf{d}^*$, with all positive components changed by small amounts, $\mathbf{d}^*$ must also be producible at non-negative activity levels by means of the same methods as before. This requires that the number of processes in operation is not smaller than the number of commodities to be produced and rules out the 'spurious' solutions, which are one process short.

To develop the consequences of a short-run disturbance, a corresponding short-run model would have to be developed. Since this cannot be done here, let us consider, as a proxy, a slight displacement of the long-period position, assuming a rise of some components of c_p because capitalists decide to increase spending. One would expect a direct effect on employment and possibly on distribution but the straightjacket of Salvadori's equations leads, with constant employment (7), to ups and downs of activity levels, and of t_w and t_p, and to changed prices of production at given r via equation (9). Would it not be much more plausible, since existence generically is guaranteed, to start from equations (1), i.e. from a square system, with causality running from changes in effective demand to employment, and to discuss alternative assumptions about effects on distribution as in Schefold (1988a, Appendix 2, containing my critique of Salvadori's examples mentioned on p. 213), if special assumptions about different consumption patterns of classes are to be made?

The square dominating technique determines the prices of production. It is natural to think of it as the latest technique. If the process of diffusion of new techniques is slow, old techniques are still in existence that will earn subnormal profits. Salvadori's doubts in this regard are justified to the extent that it is not always easy to identify this dominant technique in the real world, though the formal solution is straightforward: it is the system yielding the highest real wage for any given rate of profit, among all conceivable cost-minimizing systems. I also agree that there may be obstacles to the gravitation of market prices to the prices of production so defined. I agree with Salvadori that my Figure 7.4 represents a very special case – indeed, that was my point. But it illustrates that the classical method allows the discussion of the dependence of prices on distribution in an interesting case without neglecting the interdependence of industries. Concerning rent, cf. my comment on Samuelson below.

Salvadori has helped a great deal to solve the formal problems deriving from Sraffa's proposal for a new foundation of the classical theory of value. The remaining problems are, I believe, mainly conceptual, and only conceptual advances may one day generate new formal problems.

I agree with many of Professor Zamagni's thought-provoking observations. I shall, however, not easily allow him to prevent me from contrasting the consequences of the assumptions of methodological individualism with the implications of what reasonable economists are likely to think about the world, or from pointing out inconsistencies between what neoclassical economists apparently intend to prove and what has been shown. Joan Robinson's postulate that one should state one's assumptions does not imply that one is allowed to assume what one pleases. The insistence on the fact that a satisfactory neoclassical microeconomic foundation of macroeconomics has not been found up to now provides the main reason for making economists who are inclined to methodological individualism question their beliefs.

But I do not agree that methodological individualism is the main issue anyway. Profit maximization is as much at the root of classical economics as it is part of neoclassical theory. I am interested in the household as a producing unit precisely because that allows us to visualize the penetration of the capitalist spirit into the sphere of consumption. Not all production is profit oriented, or, what amounts to the same thing, aimed at the minimization of costs. Production may also be creative, an end in itself, or it may be directed by the forces of tradition and habit, which may, but need not, be wasteful in comparison with cost-efficient procedures. Profit maximization is part of the definition of capitalism, but not all production is capitalist in this sense.

Now it is an interesting fact that capitalism may exist without capitalist rationality having permeated households; capitalists are perfectly happy to sell to 'irrational' buyers. I therefore do not assume one type of rationality for the household. On the contrary, I am interested to expose its ambiguity, where that obtains. (This implies, by the way, that I do not adopt the utilitarian stands of Lancaster and Becker. I only borrow the idea of goods characterized by properties to fulfil needs from the former, and household production from the latter.)

Cost minimization in household production then is a principle that, to the extent that it applies, allows one to explain utilitarian behaviour within a framework that is institutionally given. In particular, my proposal for explaining price elasticities in terms of the substitution of household processes to fulfil needs holds only if households are profit oriented. Institutions, on the other hand, like the given needs and traditional constraints in household behaviour, are not in turn to be derived from other exogenous data in an enlarged theoretical framework – at least not in general – but they are objects of a phenomenological description that makes use of an understanding of cultural forces. Such a 'description' is 'theory' of a different kind. It may be that in this I am more inspired by the historical school than by the classical, properly speaking.

Adam Smith, of course, analysed an analogous transformation within the sphere of production when he described the division of labour, and he has had many followers. He also had predecessors: the idea of an alienation of work in commodity production, if it is undertaken under the dominance of the profit motive, can be traced back to Aristotle, as I have shown elsewhere (Schefold, 1988b). Zamagni is undoubtedly correct that such considerations are outside the linear production model – although there is a concept that may provide another bridge: the concept of the socially necessary as opposed to that of the dominating technique.

Indeed, the description of forms of technical progress by means of linear models is more explicit and more accurate than in terms of the old labour theory of value as employed by Ricardo and Marx. Marx justifies his postulate of a rising organic composition of capital by arguing, on the basis of a long series of phenomenological descriptions and of sociological considerations of the implications for the labour process, that the amount of raw materials used must increase per unit of output produced if machinery is introduced to save labour. This argument could be made rigorous only by using Sraffa's theory (Schefold, 1976a). It is true that the description of modern technologies in linear models is not so simple. For example, the cost escalation of nuclear power stations in the United States and Germany may be explained as being the consequence of a repeated redesigning of individually planned (as it were 'hand-made') plants in reaction to an increasing awareness of risk, while hopes for a future for solar technology are based on the mass production of solar cells. When translated into the language of linear systems, such observations result in rather trivial statements: some coefficients go up and some go down.

However, it turns out that, having introduced the grand theme of progress and the division of labour, Zamagni has something more technical in mind. He refers to the temporal structure of production. But this can be analysed better by treating fixed capital as a joint product than in any other model. This linear approach provides the best-known compromise between a unifying principle of description and the greatest possible diversity in the representation of different temporal structures of capital.

I am of a different opinion regarding the question of transition. *If* I believe that I know what the socially necessary technique is going to be in the future (for instance, electricity from nuclear power), then the problem of transition does reduce to an explanation of gravitation, where gravitation involves an adaptation of market prices, quantities and methods of production, and is necessarily influenced by institutional considerations, at least to the extent that the socially necessary technique does not coincide with the dominant one. Capital stocks never adapt completely in reality; there always remain 'fossils'. Nevertheless, comparison of the corresponding normal positions provides the best insight for assessing the consequences of the transition from an old to a new technique. It is true that market prices, quantities and methods may not adapt fast, but then there is hope that actual quantities do not deviate too much from the normal ones. The comparisons may thus lead to 'mistakes' since the introduction of new technologies, whose normal prices deviate only a little from that of old ones, may not be introduced at 'false' (market) prices although they are advantageous. However, such mistakes, which would make the outcome dependent on the transition, may be disregarded in the most relevant cases if the two techniques to be compared are 'far apart' in their structure while the two normal positions are not too distant in time. Path-dependence in the gravitation process will be the more important, the more distant the comparison, the slower the gravitation and the more the techniques are similar. The possibility of this kind of path-dependence limits the reliability of applications of the theory, but I do not believe that there are sufficiently general models of gravitation that would fare better.

The remark that the development of the new techniques depends on 'the intensity and direction of investment' is a correct observation on the method rather than an objection, for this refers to a different kind of path-dependence. Anyone who has tried to assess the potential of future technologies will try to assess just that by making several alternative assumptions about the investment behaviour of the industries concerned, and perhaps of the state, in order to get the best possible view of what the future spectrum of techniques might be. The entire discussion regarding the potential of solar cells, for instance, centres around the question of how much investment will be undertaken, and under what conditions, such that it would lead to a degree of mass production that allowed the price of solar energy to be lowered to the point where it would be competitive with, at least, the price of fossil fuels (in turn expected to be rising). Path-dependence in this sense is a fact of life. Everybody deals with it in practice, and usually not by working out ever more elaborate models of transition, but by multiplying the comparisons of normal positions so as to compare the present and a spectrum of possible outcomes. ('Normal' here means, of course, including knowledge about market imperfections and institutional data. After twelve years of researching the area, I still have doubts as to what really constitutes the socially necessary technique in the field of energy production, but matters are simpler for other industries. And even in the case of energy the difficulty has not been to generate reasonable visions of future normal positions in the form of scenarios that could be regarded as plausible by many; rather, the main difficulty has been a different type of path-dependence: to trace the social, political and institutional influences, and changes of normal prices rather than market prices, that might determine the outcome.)

Zamagni ends by expressing the fear of 'a progressive immiseration of the classical paradigm', which I should associate with a simplified interpretation of the theory. The simplicity of the formal structure has admittedly led to mistaken beliefs in some cases – that it would be easy to change distribution under capitalism or to plan the economy under socialism, once the inter-industry structure has been understood. In fact, the theory of value is only a subordinate aspect of classical economic theory, which emphasizes historical change in the conditions of economic life. Historical factors, as opposed to a simple utility maximization principle, have particular importance in the determination of the composition of output. My concern has been to reconcile this view with the given classical theory of prices by providing some intermediary concepts.

8

Sraffa's Circular Process and the Concepts of Vertical Integration

Luigi L. Pasinetti
Milan

Piero Sraffa's *Production of Commodities by Means of Commodities* (PCMC) is not the only work at the root of the recent revival of interest in classical economics, but, from an analytical point of view, it is probably the most solid one. Twenty-five years after its publication, it insistently reveals itself as what the author claimed: a necessary *prelude* to further work; and in two directions: as a critique of current economic theory, and as a reconstruction of economics along the lines of 'the old classical economist'. PCMC thus emerges as one crucial piece in what is still regarded by many as the great puzzle of an approach to economic reality that, by going back to the foundations of classical economics, can reasonably claim to be an alternative to the approach that has become prevalent among economists since the end of the nineteenth century.

Sraffa's PCMC is centred on theories connected with the price system (mainly theories of value and income distribution). It does not deal with the economics of physical quantities, which are taken as given. This is its major point of differentiation from the theories that, from Keynes (1936a) to the post-Keynesians, have (quite independently of Sraffa) shared the same critical attitude to prevailing theory and have pursued the same aim of reconstructing economic theory along the lines of the old classical economists. Keynes and the post-Keynseians, in striking contrast to Sraffa, have concentrated on movements of macroeconomic magnitudes through time, while neglecting relations at the inter-industry stage and normally taking the price structure as given.

This situation seems to cry out for a clarification, on the one hand, of what has (improperly) been referred to as the micro-foundations of Keynesian analysis and, on the other hand, of the macro and dynamic implications of the type of analysis that Sraffa has revived.

Modern economic analysis has revealed that, even on purely analytical grounds, any elaboration concerning the theory of prices has a (dual) counterpart in an elaboration concerning the theory of physical quantities, and vice versa. Hence, although as a first step it may be legitimate to concentrate on only one of the two sides, it sooner or later becomes inevitable to consider also the other (dual) side.

In this paper, I am going to adopt an approach to economic reality that is the same as Sraffa's, but I am aiming at considering an economy that is moving through time. I shall therefore put myself *beyond* Sraffa's assumption of given physical quantities and reach out for a link, and a harmonization, along classical lines, with the economic theory that has stemmed from Keynesian and post-Keynesian analysis.

1 *A sharp break with the 'marginal' method*

A striking feature of PCMC, which emerges in the very first passages of the Preface, is Sraffa's deliberate intention to set himself in opposition to 'modern theory', which is explicitly identified with the 'marginal method', and to go back to the 'standpoint which is that of the old classical economists' (Sraffa, 1960, p. v).

This attitude is further elaborated in the 'References to the Literature', given at the end of PCMC. In a section entitled 'Production as a circular process in the Physiocrats and Ricardo',[1] Sraffa specifies the sense of 'The connection of this work with the theories of the old classical economists'. He reminds us that 'It is of course in Quesnay's *Tableau Economique* that is found the original picture of the system of production and consumption as a circular process', and he goes on to point out the similarity of this approach to the 'method devised by Ricardo . . . of singling out corn as the one product which is required both for its own production and for the production of every other commodity' (p. 93). This method, he adds, 'stands in striking contrast to the view presented by modern theory of a one-way avenue that leads from "Factors of production" to "Consumption goods"' (p. 93). But this assertion cannot be taken lightly; it must be investigated very carefully.

2 *Circularity of the production process*

The title of Sraffa's mentioned section is '*Production* as a circular process in the Physiocrats and Ricardo'. But already in his reference to Quesnay (and *a fortiori* to Ricardo), Sraffa adds something else – he talks of a 'picture of the system of production *and* consumption as a circular process' (p. 93, emphasis added). There seems to be a certain ambiguity here that must be cleared up, and it may be useful to distinguish two stages.

The circularity of the production process emerges in its purest form in chapter I of PCMC, which deals with 'production for subsistence'. All commodities are, directly or indirectly, necessary to the production of all other commodities, and all of them return, at the end of each year, to the production process, either as necessary technical requirements or as necessary means of subsistence for the labourers. (In this context, there really is no difference between the two.)

The same circularity may be looked at from the price system point of view. There is a unique set of rates of exchange among commodities that is determined by technology alone and that must be adopted in order to keep the system in a self-replacing state. Sraffa points out that these rates of exchange might indifferently be called 'natural prices', or 'prices of production', or 'values' (he prefers the latter term for shortness), but he objects to the term 'cost of production', because of the circularity. He explains that it would be inappropriate to call them 'costs of production', because what appears on the left-hand side of each equation (the 'price') depends on what appears on its right-hand side (the 'cost'), no less than the other way round.

At this stage, both from a physical system point of view and from a price system point of view, there is perfect circularity.

3 *Production with a surplus*

Chapter II of PCMC is devoted to 'Production with a surplus', and a complication immediately arises. Sraffa warns,

> one effect of the emergence of a surplus must be noticed. Previously, all commodities ranked equally, each of them being found both among the products and among the means of production . . . But now there is room for a new class of 'luxury' products, which are not used . . . (p. 7)

At least as far as these 'luxury' products are concerned, the circularity is broken. There also immediately appears one degree of freedom as to the distribution of these 'luxury' consumption goods. No longer must they go necessarily to the labourers (since they emerge *above* subsistence). They might be divided, in a proportion to be determined from outside the production relations, between profits and 'surplus' wages.

But let us return to the main point. When there is a surplus (all made up of luxury goods) a very clear distinction can be made, in physical terms, between the production process and the surplus – more specifically, between the commodities making up the means of production (all basic commodities, in Sraffa's terminology) and the commodities making up the surplus (all non-basic commodities, *ex hypothesi*, in our case). The former are produced within a perfectly circular production process; the latter emerge from this production process without re-entering it.

A parallel, equally clear, distinction can be made between the natural prices of the means of production and the natural prices of the consumption luxury goods. The former are still characterized by complete circularity, while the latter are no longer so characterized. The 'prices' of the consumption goods, in this case, are clearly and unambiguously distinguishable from their 'costs'. Sraffa does not bring out this distinction explicitly; on the contrary, he seems to minimize it. Perhaps he is afraid that the reader might be confused with what he had earlier called the 'one-way avenue [of traditional economics] . . . from "Factor of production" to "Consumption goods"'.

But the distinction deserves attention.

One can see very clearly the circularity of the production process concerning the means of production. But equally clearly one can see, on each side of it, the emergence of a surplus of consumption goods at one end and the inflow of a physical quantity of labour at the other end.

A relation between the two seems to suggest itself in a natural way. It may be useful to note that such a relation is *not* of the type traditional theory has suggested. First of all, there certainly is no direct, or broad, 'avenue' between the two. In between labour on the one side and consumption goods on the other, there is a very intricate and complicated circular process concerning all the commodities making up the means of production. This process in fact represents the main object of Sraffa's investigation. Second, the relation does not go (even in a very complicated way) from labour (or for that matter from the means of production) to consumption goods; if at all, it goes the other way round. For any given (or externally determined) physical set of final consumption goods, the inter-industry coefficients determine the set of physical commodities required as means of production and the required amount of labour.

In a precisely parallel way, the relation in the price system does not go – as traditional marginal analysis would have it – from final consumers' preferences to 'imputed' costs. As classical analysis has always claimed, it goes from costs of production (which are unambiguous in the case we are considering) to 'natural' prices. At least in the case of a surplus made up of consumption (luxury) goods, Sraffa's scheme therefore implies an overturning of the causal links that were traditionally considered, both in the physical quantity system and in the price system.

But what about the case of a surplus made up of basic commodities? In this case, the whole question becomes more complicated.

If one looks at the economic system in physical terms, one can still distinguish very clearly, as in the previous case, the consumption goods that make up the surplus on one side of the circular process (concerning the means of production), and the labour inflow on the other side of it. The price system, however, does not reveal such a clear distinction. The natural prices of the (basic) consumption goods depend on the natural prices of their means of production, no less than the other way round. We are back to circularity.

There is however an analytical device that allows us to separate in an unambiguous way what pertains to the surplus from what pertains to the circular process. I am referring to what Sraffa, by looking at the economic system from an inter-industry point of view, has called the method of the 'subsystems'; and what I myself, by looking at it from a final demand point of view, have called the method of the 'vertically integrated sectors'.

4 *Subsystems*

The method of the subsystems is presented by Sraffa, in a three-quarter-page appendix, simply as a device to 'show at a glance' the amount of labour that directly and indirectly goes into producing each commodity. It is interesting to note that Sraffa, having objected to the term 'cost of production' when he presents the price system (§ 7), resorts to such a term precisely when he faces the problem of the direct and indirect quantities of labour that go into producing each commodity. He talks, in this respect, of a 'cost of production aspect' of prices (§ 45). And in order to analyse this aspect he uses two alternative analytical devices: the device of the 'reduction to dated quantities of labour' (in Chapter VI) and the device of the subsystems (Appendix A, recalled in § 14). However, the first device is subject to severe limitations – it can be adopted only in the case of single production. The second device, on the other hand, can be used in general, both for single and for joint production.

By taking advantage of an analysis already carried out elsewhere (see Pasinetti, 1973) and by using the same symbols, an economic system in which m commodities are produced may be represented, in a particular period of time (a 'year'), as follows:

$$(\mathbf{B} - \mathbf{A})\mathbf{X} = \mathbf{Y}, \qquad (1)$$

$$\mathbf{a}_n\mathbf{X} = L, \qquad (2)$$

$$\mathbf{AX} = \mathbf{S}, \qquad (3)$$

where **B** and **A** are the output and the input inter-industry matrices respectively, $\mathbf{a}_n$ is the input direct labour coefficient (row) vector, **X** is the (column) physical quantity vector, **Y** is the (column) net product vector, **S** is the (column) means of production vector, and L is the (scalar) quantity of labour. All matrices are m-order square matrices and all vectors have m components.[2] Equation system (3) might in fact appear redundant, as is already implied in (1), and simply gives a definition of that part, **S**, of physical production, **X**, that will have to go back to the production process to replace the used-up means of production. Sraffa does not pay particular attention to this system of equations and does not consider it explicitly. But (3) will be seen in a moment to play a crucial role.

The price system, for its part, may be represented as:

$$\mathbf{pB} = \mathbf{a}_n w + \mathbf{pA} + \mathbf{pA}\pi, \qquad (4)$$

$$w = 1, \qquad (5)$$

where **p** is the (m-component, row) price vector, w and π are scalars for the wage rate and the rate of profits respectively, and w is expressed in terms of 'labour commanded' ($w = 1$).[3] For simplicity, I shall suppose that physical units have been chosen in such a way as to make the main diagonal of **B** a list of ones. I shall also suppose that technical coefficients are given and constant (constant returns to scale) within the period concerned. Moreover, to avoid complications, I shall suppose that technical coefficients are such as to be economically meaningful at all levels of π between zero and its maximum.

This economic system may now be partitioned into m subsystems defined as follows:

$$(\mathbf{B} - \mathbf{A})\mathbf{X}^{(i)} = \mathbf{Y}^{(i)}, \qquad i = 1, 2, \ldots, m, \qquad (6)$$

where $\mathbf{Y}^{(i)}$ is a (column) vector the components of which are all zeros except the i'th one, Y_i, which is the i'th component of vector $\mathbf{Y}$, and $\mathbf{X}^{(i)}$ is the (column) vector of the physical quantities corresponding to it. By 'solving' each particular subsystem i with respect to its $\mathbf{Y}^{(i)}$, we obtain:

$$\mathbf{X}^{(i)} = (\mathbf{B} - \mathbf{A})^{-1}\, \mathbf{Y}^{(i)}, \tag{7}$$

and, by substituting into (2), (3), we have:

$$L_i = \mathbf{a}_n(\mathbf{B} - \mathbf{A})^{-1}\, \mathbf{Y}^{(i)}, \tag{8}$$

$$\mathbf{S}^{(i)} = \mathbf{A}(\mathbf{B} - \mathbf{A})^{-1}\, \mathbf{Y}^{(i)}, \qquad i = 1, 2, \ldots, m, \tag{9}$$

where $\mathbf{X}^{(i)}$, L_i, $\mathbf{S}^{(i)}$ represent those particular magnitudes, defined by systems (1)–(3), that would correspond to a particular net national product made up of the single physical (scalar) quantity Y_i. Linearity of course ensures that:

$$\Sigma\, \mathbf{Y}^{(i)} = \mathbf{Y}; \qquad \Sigma\, \mathbf{X}^{(i)} = \mathbf{X}; \qquad \Sigma\, \mathbf{S}^{(i)} = \mathbf{S}; \qquad \Sigma\, L_i = L, \tag{10}$$

i.e. all subsystems exactly add up to the original economic system.

As may be observed, equation system (7) represents the familiar Leontief solution of a hypothetical economic system that produces as final product only the single physical quantity Y_i. Equation (8) takes us one step further by giving us the amount of labour that is directly and indirectly required in the whole economic system to produce the single final good Y_i. This amount of labour now appears 'at a glance', as Sraffa says. Finally, equation system (9) takes us yet one step further, by giving us the set of physical quantities of commodities 1, 2, . . ., m, that are directly and indirectly required in the whole economic system to replace the means of production used up to obtain the single final good Y_i. It should become clear at this point that it is for this purpose that equation system (3) was formulated to begin with.

Thus, each subsystem i essentially is an analytical construct that represents a self-contained economic system that produces physical quantity Y_i, as net product, and absorbs physical quantity L_i of labour as net input, while at the same time reproducing all the means of production (no less and no more) necessary for this purpose, through a self-replacing circular process.

If we turn to the price system, it can be seen immediately that, when $\pi = 0$, p_i the price of commodity i, is simply equal to L_i/Y_i. In other terms, we can see that $p_i\, Y_i$, i.e. the value of Y_i, is L_i,[4] which indeed represents the physical quantity of labour of subsystem i, or physical quantity of labour that has directly and indirectly gone into the production of Y_i.

For each subsystem, therefore, the relation of labour to final goods emerges immediately. The partitioning of the economic system into m subsystems allocates a particular quantity of labour to each final good. The final goods produced by the m subsystems exhaust all the produced final goods and the quantities of labour allocated to the m subsystems exhaust all the available labour.

Each physical quantity of final good (independently of whether it is a non-basic or a basic commodity!) is unambiguously related to a physical quantity of labour; and the two have, in between them, a physically defined self-replacing circular process of means of production, which simply reproduces, at the end of the 'year', exactly those means of production (no more and no less) that were inherited at the beginning.

5 Vertically integrated sectors

On purely analytical grounds, the elaborations reviewed in the previous section open up entirely new horizons. The singling out of a relation between each physical final good and a physical quantity of labour offers us another point of view from which to look at, and consider, the whole economic system. To be more specific, an economic system may be considered from two different points of view.

One point of view is that of the circularity of the production process, which has already been analysed above. From this point of view, one can investigate the interconnections among the various production processes and the numerous complications that they entail, both in physical terms (fixed capital, joint production, natural resources, etc.) and in terms of prices (relations of value and distribution, ways of making them simple through devices such as the standard commodity, changes in income distribution and changes in relative prices, and switching, or reswitching, of techniques, etc.). Inevitably, when adopting this point of view, the need to concentrate the analysis on those aspects that pertain to circularity leads one to minimize all the other aspects. This is the point of view chosen by Sraffa. The labour/consumption relation is kept in the background. Final demand is taken as given, or assumed to be unchanged, so as to cause a minimum of complications. The technique of production itself is taken as given or is supposed to be unchanged. The analysis must be carried out either as referring to one single period of time, considered in isolation, or as referring to a (stationary) economic system that exactly reproduces itself without any change from period to period.

Another point of view from which to look at the whole economic system is that of final demand. From this point of view, in any economic system one can investigate the final product and immediately relate it to its direct and indirect requirements, quite independently of what is going on inside these requirements. The purpose is normally that of setting the stage for a dynamic analysis concerning the movements of the final product through time. From this standpoint, the circular process, however complicated it may be, appears of secondary importance, as it simply reproduces those means of production that existed already at the beginning of each period. It can therefore be taken for granted and kept in the background.

When I first came to adopt this approach, I thought of so minimizing the complications of the circular process of production as to explicitly reduce it *ex hypothesi* to a single quantity of intermediate labour. The analysis was then carried out no longer in terms of 'industries', or production processes, as they may immediately be observed when one looks at them as operating in the real world, but in terms of 'vertically integrated sectors', i.e. of 'sectors' that take all the intermediate processes for granted, however complicated they may be, while bringing into relief precisely the final goods, on one side of the process, and their ultimate requirements (labour quantities), on the other (see Pasinetti, 1965).

In terms of the analysis carried out above, a vertically integrated sector i may be represented simply by one physical unit of final good i, one physical unit of vertically integrated productive capacity for final good i, and one physical quantity of labour for final good i ($i = 1, 2, \ldots, m$). In simple terms we may represent each vertically integrated sector i, when operating at unit activity, by the elementary vector:

$$[1, 1, v_i], \qquad i = 1, 2, \ldots, m, \tag{11}$$

where the first component refers to the physical final good i, the second component to the physical vertically integrated productive capacity for final good i, and the third component to the physical quantity of (vertically integrated) labour for final good i. As may be observed from (11), the remarkable feature of the concept of a vertically integrated sector is that, complex though it may be (behind the scenes, so to speak) in its composition, it is simply reduced to two ones and to a further single number representing a physical quantity of labour.

The prices relating to each vertically integrated sector i may correspondingly be represented by the vector:

$$[p_i, p_{k_i}, w, \pi], \qquad i = 1, 2, \ldots, m, \tag{12}$$

where w and π are the scalars already defined, p_i is the price of one physical unit of final good i, and p_{k_i} is the price of one physical unit of vertically integrated productive capacity for good i. The latter synthesizes in one single number the whole complicated circular process.

Within each period of time, for the same economic system, the relation between its expression in terms of the m vertically integrated sectors (11) and (12) and its expression in terms of the usual inter-industry formulation (1)–(5) is given by the m subsystems (6)–(10) considered in the previous section. As may be realized, each unit of final commodity i is the same both in the inter-industry formulation (1)–(3) and in the vertically integrated formulation (11). Each unit of vertically integrated productive capacity, on the other hand, extremely simple as it is in (11), appears as very complicated in formulation (1)–(3); for it is constituted by a composite commodity corresponding to each column h_i ($i = 1, 2, \ldots, m$) of a matrix $\mathbf{H}$, defined as:

$$\mathbf{H} = \mathbf{A}(\mathbf{B}-\mathbf{A})^{-1}. \tag{13}$$

And each physical quantity of vertically integrated labour appears in (11) as the compact component v_i ($i = 1, 2, \ldots, m$) of a vector $\mathbf{v}$ defined as

$$\mathbf{v} = \mathbf{a}_n(\mathbf{B}-\mathbf{A})^{-1}. \tag{14}$$

Each v_i synthesizes in itself all physical quantities of labour directly and indirectly required in the whole economic system for the production of one unit of commodity i.

Similarly, p_i, w and π are the same both in fomulation (4) and in formulation (12). But the price of each unit of vertically integrated production capacity p_{k_i} ($i = 1, 2, \ldots, m$) emerges from a linear combination of all the prices of the means of production. Setting all p_{k_i}'s together in one single vector $\mathbf{p}_k$, whose components are the m prices of the vertically integrated units of productive capacity, their relation to the price vector of equation system (4) is defined by the expression:

$$\mathbf{p}_k = \mathbf{p}\mathbf{A}(\mathbf{B}-\mathbf{A})^{-1} = \mathbf{p}\mathbf{H}. \tag{15}$$

There exists therefore, at each particular time, a one-to-one correspondence between expressing an economic system in terms of 'industries' and expressing it in terms of vertically integrated sectors, both with reference to physical quantities and with reference to prices. And this one-to-one correspondence is evinced by the two linear operators $\mathbf{H} = \mathbf{A}(\mathbf{B}-\mathbf{A})^{-1}$ and $\mathbf{v} = \mathbf{a}_n(\mathbf{B}-\mathbf{A})^{-1}$, which refer to productive capacities, i.e. to the means of production, and to labour, respectively.

However, precisely these analytical expressions very clearly evince also the exact nature of this one-to-one correspondence. As will be realized, the one-to-one correspondence refers to given matrices $\mathbf{A}$, $\mathbf{B}$, $\mathbf{a}_n$, i.e. it is relative to a given technique. But techniques change as time goes on! Therefore, from an analytical point of view, one might say that the one-to-one correspondence breaks down with time. Or rather, it may be more appropriate to say that there is a particular one-to-one correspondence specific to each particular period of time. As time (t) goes on, each particular period of time will be characterized by a particular set $\mathbf{A}(t)$, $\mathbf{B}(t)$, $\mathbf{a}_n(t)$, and thus by a particular set $\mathbf{H}(t)$, $\mathbf{v}(t)$. This means that, from the point of view of inter-industry analysis – i.e. of the circularity approach – all relations are upset and have to be recomposed from one period of time to the next, when technical change takes place.

Yet this creates no complication from the point of view of the vertically integrated sectors. The first and the second components of vector (11) are unity, *quite independently* of technical change! This is obvious for the definition of one unit of final good i. But a remarkable property of vertically integrated sectoral analysis is that it is also true of a unit of vertically integrated productive capacity for good i. The concept of a unit of vertically integrated productive capacity is entirely independent of its composition. In other words, the composition may well change, even dramatically (i.e. the corresponding subsystem may well break down and be recomposed in an entirely different way), and yet, conceptually, a unit of vertically integrated productive capacity remains a unit of vertically integrated productive capacity, quite independently of its changed composition. This is precisely what gives relevance to the concept of vertically integrated sectors.

It should be noted for example that, when there is technical change, it would be quite impossible – outside the framework of vertically integrated sectoral analysis – to say anything about what the circular process should reproduce. It is the concept of vertically integrated productive capacity that gives us the precise specification (through its new technical relation to the various physical commodities expressed by a new subsystem) of the physical means of production (quite different from those that have been used up) that have to re-enter the production process in order to ensure self-replacement.

The vertically integrated concepts thus emerge as becoming essential precisely at the point of going over to dynamic analysis, i.e. precisely at the point where inter-industry analysis would otherwise become useless, and hopeless. There is therefore complementarity (not incompatibility!) between vertically integrated sectoral analysis and inter-industry analysis. The foregoing arguments seem to me to indicate quite clearly that the appropriate combination of the two approaches, or, more specifically, the finding of an appropriate way of switching back and forth from one approach to the other, can pave the way for a truly modern version of classical economic analysis – an economic analysis that may encompass, at the same time, the circular process of production and the evolution of the economic system over time.

6 *Sraffa and Keynes – a meeting point*

The conclusions reached at the end of the previous section – through a chain of arguments starting from Sraffa – can also be reached by starting from the other end (i.e. from Keynesian analysis).

If we go back for a moment to the statements made at the beginning, it is not difficult to realize that what has allowed Keynesian and post-Keynesian analysis to deal with technical change (in striking contrast with inter-industry analysis) is precisely the fact that, by being conceived in macroeconomic terms, it had necessarily to leave out all intermediate relations, which means that it had necessarily to be conceived in vertically integrated terms. By the same token and in the opposite direction, it is not difficult to realize that what has made it impossible for inter-industry analysis to absorb technical change is precisely its requirement of sticking to the same technical coefficients. Very wisely, Sraffa has stopped his analysis short of allowing changes in physical quantities. But the two other well-known authors who have attempted a 'dynamization' of the inter-industry scheme – Leontief (1953) and von Neumann (1945–6) – have been compelled to develop models of a hypothetical economy that expands only in size (due to population growth), with no development. By keeping technical coefficients absolutely constant, the steady dynamic path, to which their models lead, implies that all per capita magnitudes remain absolutely constant, thus yielding perfectly proportional growth with no change in structure. Such models – I have argued elsewhere (Pasinetti, 1981a) – can only be considered as intermediate analytical steps. If taken at face value, they would represent the negation of what is called progress. It is also doubtful whether they should be called 'dynamic' at all. More appropriately, they have in fact sometimes been called 'quasi-stationary'.

Unfortunately Keynesian analysis, though capable in principle of overcoming the limitations of given technical coefficients, when extended to the long run has not been carried beyond the stage of macroeconomic analysis. It is therefore paradoxical that, while being able to absorb technical change, it has come to share the defects of Leontief/von Neumann models, owing to the fact that – by being macroeconomic – it had to be interpreted as referring to a structure (of prices and quantities) that remains constant through time. The consequences for long-run analysis have been even worse than those following from the proportional dynamics of Leontief/von Neumann models; for, it is contradictory (as I have argued elsewhere – Pasinetti, 1981a, esp. ch. IV) to assume a constant structure over time when per capita incomes are increasing.

But there is no need for Keynesian dynamic analysis to be carried out only in macroeconomic terms. The singling out of the concept of vertically integrated sectors allows the possibility of a complete disaggregation of the economy into as many sectors as there are final goods. And this allows the possibility of building up a complete scheme of structural dynamics.

Here therefore is the clear way to analytical development. It has become commonplace that Keynesian analysis must be developed beyond its original macroeconomic conception. However, most attempts have been made in terms of a merger with Walrasian economics. The arguments above indicate that the way forward is in an entirely different direction. The Keynesian macro-magnitudes must be broken down into as many vertically integrated sectors as there are final commodities. The analytical device of the subsystems can then complete the relations so much sought after and links with the field of investigation concerning the circular process of production.

We thereby arrive – from another route – at the same conclusions reached by the end of the previous section. Starting from Keynesian macro-dynamic analysis, one can see the way to a disaggregation into vertically integrated sectors. Then one can see the analytical links with the subsystems, i.e. with Sraffa's circular process analysis. From another point of view, this appears as a quite clear and logical way to accomplish an integration of the two types of economic analysis, associated with the names of Sraffa and Keynes, which stemmed from the same preoccupations (inadequacy of traditional marginal economics) and built on the same common ground (classical economics), but have not so far been merged into a unified research programme.

Notes

1 The title of the section does not appear explicitly in the text (on p. 93), but (as for all sections of PCM C) can be found in full in the Table of Contents (on p. xii).

2 The easiest way to look at equation system (1), (2) and (3) is to consider it as an open Leontief model. The m final physical quantities in vector $\mathbf{Y}$ are considered as given. Then the $2m + 1$ equations (1), (2) and (3) determine the $2m$ physical quantities $\mathbf{X}$ and $\mathbf{S}$ (two m-component vectors) and the (scalar) physical quantity of (required) labour L.

3 We may follow Sraffa and leave the price system open (i.e. indeterminate) as to the distribution of income between wages and profits. All prices can be determined relative to any particular level of the rate of profits, to be fixed from outside the equation systems (4)–(5).

4 From (4) and (5), when $\pi = 0$, we have:

$$\mathbf{p} = \mathbf{a}_n(\mathbf{B} - \mathbf{A})^{-1},$$

i.e. from (8),

$$p_i = L_i/Y_i.$$

Appendix: Growing (or hyper-)subsystems and vertically hyper-integrated sectors

The analytical device of partitioning an economic system into subsystems (and correspondingly of constructing vertically integrated sectors) can be taken one step further into dynamic analysis, with remarkable implications.

In fact, if one looks carefully at the physical quantity side, as against the price side, of the usual equations representing a production economic system, one may notice a formal asymmetry. In the physical quantity system, the means of production are specific to each particular subsystem or, to put it another way, there is a specific vector of means of production for each particular subsystem. In a sense, the physical quantities of the means of production appear to play a sort of ancillary role with respect to the physical quantities of final demand; the former being, so to speak, 'at the service' of the latter. By contrast, no similar feature emerges for the price system. There is absolutely no difference, in the scheme earlier proposed, between the prices of the means of production and the prices of the final goods. The vector of prices is exactly the same in all subsystems.

I shall show that this asymmetry disappears when the scheme is further generalized.

1 Growing or hyper-subsystems

Suppose an economic system of the type already sketched out above. When growth is considered explicitly, the physical quantity system, in each particular unit of time t, is represented by:

$$\mathbf{AX}(t) + g\mathbf{AX}(t) + \mathbf{C}(t) = \mathbf{BX}(t), \qquad (A.1)$$

$$\mathbf{a}_n\mathbf{X}(t) = L(t), \qquad (A.2)$$

$$\mathbf{AX}(t) = \mathbf{S}(t), \qquad (A.3)$$

where $\mathbf{A}$ and $\mathbf{B}$ are the input and output inter-industry matrices respectively, $\mathbf{a}_n$ is the input direct labour coefficient (row) vector, $\mathbf{X}(t)$ is the physical quantity (column) vector, $\mathbf{C}(t)$ is the consumption goods (column) vector, $\mathbf{S}(t)$ is the means of production (column) vector, $L(t)$ is the (scalar) quantity of labour and g is the (scalar) percentage rate of growth of the labour force (for simplicity's sake no distinction will be made between labour force and population, which will be taken as coincidental). All matrices are m-order matrices and all vectors have m components. The physical units are so chosen as to make the main diagonal of $\mathbf{B}$ a list of ones. The technical coefficients are supposed to be such as to be economically meaningful at all levels of the population percentage rate of growth, g, from zero to its maximum, i.e. in the interval $0 \leq g \leq G$, where G is the maximum rate of growth allowed by existing technology.

Suppose, to begin with, constant technical coefficients and population growth. It is also convenient to assume immigration. Immigrant labour is supposed to be available in a practically unlimited amount. When the growth of demand is very strong, workers are allowed to come in, and when the growth of demand slackens the foreign workers are invited to leave the country, so that there is always full employment, as a result of adapting the labour force to the requirements of production (rather than the other way round)[1]. It is also convenient to assume that the consumption tastes of the immigrants are different from those of the indigenous population, so that the per capita rates of growth of demand for commodities 1, 2, . . ., m, are all different from one another. This means that if g, defined above, is the proportional rate of growth of the labour force (whether by natural growth or by immigration) and if r_i (which may be positive or negative) is defined as the per capita rate of growth of consumption demand for each commodity i, then the rate of growth of consumption demand for each commodity i will be $(g + r_i)$, and in general will be different from one consumption good to another (i.e. $r_i \neq r_j$ in general).

Let us now proceed to partition the economic system into as many such newly defined subsystems as there are consumption goods. Since the economic system is growing, these newly defined subsystems are more comprehensive than those considered in section 4 of my paper, because they include not only the labour and the means of production for the reproduction of each subsystem, but *also* the labour and the means of production necessary to its *expansion* at its particular rate of growth $(g + r_i)$. I shall call these newly defined subsystems the *m growing subsystems* or, more compactly, the *m hyper-subsystems* of the economic system under consideration.

We may denote by $C_1(t)$, $C_2(t)$, . . ., $C_m(t)$ the m consumption goods produced in period t, making up the m components of the already defined consumption goods (column) vector $\mathbf{C}(t)$. Each $C_i(t)$ is expanding through time at its particular rate of growth $(g + r_i)$, which we assume to be steady for the time being:

$$C_i(t) = C_i(0)\, e^{(g+r_i)t}, \qquad i = 1, 2, \ldots, m. \tag{A.4}$$

We may now proceed in a way perfectly analogous to the one used in defining the earlier subsystems but with the essential difference of now including in each hyper-subsystem *all* gross investments (both replacements *and* net investments). We thereby obtain:

$$\mathbf{X}^{(i)}(t) = [\mathbf{B} - (1 + g + r_i)\mathbf{A}]^{-1}\mathbf{C}^{(i)}(t), \tag{A.5}$$

$$L_i(t) = \mathbf{a}_n[\mathbf{B} - (1 + g + r_i)\mathbf{A}]^{-1}\mathbf{C}^{(i)}(t), \tag{A.6}$$

$$\mathbf{S}^{(i)}(t) = \mathbf{A}\,[\mathbf{B} - (1 + g + r_i)\mathbf{A}]^{-1}\mathbf{C}^{(i)}(t), \quad i = 1, 2, \ldots, m, \tag{A.7}$$

$$\Sigma\mathbf{C}^{(i)}(t) = \mathbf{C}(t); \quad \Sigma\mathbf{X}^{(i)}(t) = \mathbf{X}(t); \quad \Sigma\mathbf{S}^{(i)}(t) = \mathbf{S}(t); \quad \Sigma L_i(t) = L(t), \tag{A.8}$$

where $\mathbf{C}^{(i)}(t)$ is a (column) vector the components of which are all zeros except the i'th one, which is the scalar C_i, i.e. the i'th component of vector $\mathbf{C}(t)$; and $\mathbf{X}^{(i)}(t)$, $\mathbf{S}^{(i)}(t)$, $L_i(t)$ are the particular corresponding magnitudes that, in a self contained expanding economic system, are necessary to produce over time that physical (expanding) quantity $C_i(t)$, and at the same time to produce all the means of production necessary both to maintain in operation such an economic system and to expand it at the required rate of growth $(g + r_i)$.

In this way, each hyper-subsystem i is characterized by: (a) production of one single consumption good i, expanding over time at its particular rate of growth $(g + r_i)$; (b) absorption of a physical quantity of labour $L_i(t)$, expanding over time at whatever rate is required by the technical coefficients (in our case, clearly, at rate $(g + r_i)$); and (c) maintenance of a circular production process that *both* reproduces all (no less and no more than) the means of production that are absorbed by the production process for consumption good $C_i(t)$ *and* also produces those means of production that are strictly necessary to expand this circular process at rate of growth $(g + r_i)$.

Since $i = 1, 2, \ldots, m$, there are m such hyper-subsystems, and the sum of the physical magnitudes of these m hyper-subsystems (see (A.8)) add up to the physical magnitudes of the actual economic system, while the (A.1) takes up the more general form:

$$\mathbf{AX}(t) + g\mathbf{AX}(t) + \mathbf{C}(t) + \mathbf{A}\Sigma r_i \mathbf{X}^{(i)}(t) = \mathbf{BX}(t). \qquad \text{(A.16)}$$

For convenience, we may define the following vectors and matrices:

$$\mathbf{l}^{(i)} = \mathbf{a}_n [\mathbf{B} - (1 + g + r_i)\mathbf{A}]^{-1}, \qquad \text{(A.9)}$$

$$\mathbf{M}^{(i)} = \mathbf{A}[\mathbf{B} - (1 + g + r_i)\mathbf{A}]^{-1}, \qquad i = 1, 2, \ldots, m. \qquad \text{(A.10)}$$

Unlike what happened for Sraffa's subsystems, each hyper-subsystem i is now characterized by a particular vector $\mathbf{l}^{(i)}$ and by a particular matrix $\mathbf{M}^{(i)}$, $i = 1, 2, \ldots, m$.

It should be noticed, however, that not all columns of matrix $\mathbf{M}^{(i)}$ are relevant, but only the i'th column, which we may denote by a star:

$$\mathbf{m}_i^{(i)} = \mathbf{m}_i^*. \qquad \text{(A.11)}$$

This is a vector that defines a particular composite commodity, which may be called *a unit of vertically hyper-integrated productive capacity*, for commodity i. Similarly, not all components of vector $\mathbf{l}^{(i)}$ are relevant, but only the i'th component, which we may equally denote by a star:

$$l_i^{(i)} = l_i^*. \qquad \text{(A.12)}$$

This scalar defines what may be called the *vertically hyper-integrated labour coefficient* for commodity i.

We may ask of course what is the meaning of any other column $\mathbf{m}_j(i)$ of each matrix $\mathbf{M}^{(i)}$ and of any other component $l_j^{(i)}$ of vector $\mathbf{l}^{(i)}$; $j \neq i$; $i, j = 1, 2, \ldots, m$. The answer is that their meaning takes a *hypothetical* connotation. Each vector $\mathbf{m}_j^{(i)}$ (each component $l_j^{(i)}$) in matrix $\mathbf{M}^{(i)}$ (in vector $l^{(i)}$), where $j \neq i$, has the meaning of a unit of vertically hyper-integrated productive capacity (of a vertically hyper-integrated labour coefficient), *if* commodity j were to be produced as a consumption good (though it is not) in hyper-subsystem i.

Therefore, in each matrix $\mathbf{M}^{(i)}$, we may call the relevant column $\mathbf{m}_i^*$ the *actual* unit of vertically hyper-integrated productive capacity and all the other columns $\mathbf{m}_j^{(i)}$ the *hypothetical* units of vertically hyper-integrated productive capacity in hyper-subsystem i. Similarly, in each vector $\mathbf{l}^{(i)}$, we may call the relevant component l_i^* the *actual* vertically hyper-integrated labour coefficient and all the other components $l_j^{(i)}$, the *hypothetical* vertically hyper-integrated labour coefficients; $j, i = 1, 2, \ldots, m$; $j \neq i$.

The generalizing features of this analytical construction should now be evident. In the very particular case in which all $g + r_i = 0$, $i = 1, 2, \ldots, m$ (i.e. in the particular case of a perfectly stationary economic system), all matrices $\mathbf{M}^{(i)}$ coincide with one another and moreover they come to coincide with matrix $\mathbf{H}$ defined by (13) above. Similarly, all vectors $l^{(i)}$ coincide with one another and moreover they come to coincide with vector v of my paper. In other words, when $g + r_i = 0$, the m hyper-subsystems reduce to the simpler subsystems previously defined. The latter thereby emerge as particular cases of the former. Or, to put it the other way round, the growing or hyper-subsystems represent a truly general notion, of which Sraffa's subsystems are particular cases.

2 *The natural price subsystems*

We may now turn to the system of prices. Here the general attitude (which has also been followed by Sraffa) has been so far that of accepting a uniform exogenously given rate of profits. In this case we would be back at the usual price system (4)–(5) of my paper; and that would be the end of the story (but at the same time we would be back to the asymmetry pointed out at the beginning).

The relevant, and significant, alternative is to depart from the traditional assumption of a uniform rate of profits. Following the approach already taken elsewhere (Pasinetti, 1981b), I shall therefore introduce the notion of a natural rate of profits. A *natural* rate of profits, denoted by a star, π^*, is defined as a rate of profits that is equal to the rate of growth of demand for the corresponding consumption good. This means that in general we shall have, in the whole economic system, m different *natural rates of profits*:

$$\pi_i^* = g + r_i, \qquad i = 1, 2, \ldots, m. \tag{A.13}$$

More specifically, this means that there will be a particular natural rate of profits for each hyper-subsystem.

It follows that there will also be a specific set of *natural prices* for each particular hyper-subsystem. In total, there will be m sets of natural prices, each one concerning the corresponding hyper-subsystem.

A crucial distinction emerges at this point, which did not arise before. The distinction is between the natural prices of the consumption goods and the natural prices of the means of production.

In each hyper-subsystem i, we can see that its specific set of natural prices refers, to begin with, to the means of production (which may well include the particular good i, which is also used as consumption good). Calling this specific set of natural prices $\mathbf{p}^{(i)}$, we have the particular price vector:

$$\mathbf{p}^{(i)} = \mathbf{a}_n[\mathbf{B} - (1 + \pi_i^*)\,\mathbf{A}]^{-1}w, \tag{A.14}$$

or, from definition (A.9) and (A.13),

$$\mathbf{p}^{(i)} = \mathbf{l}^{(i)}w. \tag{A.14b}$$

But $i = 1, 2, \ldots, m$, i.e. there are m hyper-subsystems. It follows that there exist m sets of natural prices for the same means of production, each set of natural prices being specific to a particular hyper-subsystem.

The situation is remarkably different for the m consumption goods. Each consumption good *only* appears in one hyper-subsystem and therefore only has *one* natural price. The consumption good natural price is the i'th price in each price system (A.14). By calling it p_i^*, it clearly emerges as:

$$p_i^*(t) = \mathbf{a}_n\,[\mathbf{B} - (1 + \pi_i^*)\mathbf{A}]^{-1}\mathbf{e}_i w = l_i^*(t)w, \quad i = 1, 2, \ldots, m, \tag{A.15}$$

where $\mathbf{e}_i$ is the unit (column) vector and $l_i^*(t)$ is the corresponding actual vertically hyper-integrated labour coefficient, defined by (A.12).

In all hyper-subsystems taken together, i.e. in the whole economic system, each good therefore has only one natural price as a consumption good, although it may have up to m different natural prices as a capital good.

Notice, from (A.15) and (A.6) that, since $\pi_i^* = g + r_i$, when we put $w = 1$, the price p_i^* of commodity i, $i = 1, 2, \ldots, m$ (i.e. its price as a consumption good), is simply equal to $L_i(t)/C_i(t)$, which means that $p_i^* C_i(t)$, the value of $C_i(t)$, is simply equal to $L_i(t)$. The value of the physical quantity of each consumption good that is produced turns out to be equal to the physical quantity of labour that has directly, indirectly and – as I have called it elsewhere (Pasinetti, 1977, 1981b) – hyper-indirectly been required for its production. Because of linearity, the consumption goods produced by the m hyper-subsystems exhaust all the produced consumption goods, and the quantities of labour allocated to the m hyper-subsystems exhaust all the available labour.

This is a complete generalization of the pure labour theory of value. Each physical quantity of any consumption good is unambiguously related to a physical quantity of labour; and the two have, in between them, a physically defined self-replacing, and expanding, circular process.

In terms of the compact notation defined by (A.9), each p_i^* is simply proportional – and, in the case in which w is used as *numéraire*, it is exactly equal – to the corresponding actual vertically hyper-integrated labour coefficient l_i^*, which precisely represents the quantity of labour that is necessary directly, indirectly and hyper-indirectly to its production.

However, the interesting result that follows immediately from this compact notation is that the natural prices $\mathbf{p}^{(i)}$ of the corresponding means of production have exactly the same meaning, though assuming a *hypothetical* connotation. As emerges from (A.14), (A.14b), these prices are proportional (or actually equal, in the case in which w is used as *numéraire*) to the quantity of labour that *would* be necessary – directly, indirectly and hyper-indirectly – to produce them as consumption goods, *if* they were produced as consumption goods in the corresponding hyper-subsystem (though in fact they are produced as capital goods, and not as consumption goods). In other words, they are proportional to the corresponding *hypothetical* vertically hyper-integrated labour coefficients, as defined in the previous section.

At this point, the whole set of natural prices of the means of production appear as performing a sort of ancillary role in each hyper-subsystem with respect to the corresponding price of the consumption good. Formal symmetry has been re-established perfectly between all aspects concerning physical quantities and all aspects concerning prices.

3 *A complete generalization of the pure labour theory of value*

The elaborations of the previous section, which provide a complete generalization of the pure labour theory of value, may be further illustrated by taking an alternative route.

Let us start from the general price system (4) of my paper, in which there is a uniform rate of profit, π. We can always rewrite it as:

$$\mathbf{pB} = \mathbf{a}_n w + \mathbf{pA} + (g + r_i)\,\mathbf{pA} + (\pi - g - r_i)\,\mathbf{pA}, \qquad \text{(A.16)}$$

where $(g + r_i)$ is the rate of growth of demand for any one of the consumption goods, which we have called i. Of course, since $i = 1, 2, \ldots, m$, there are m *different* ways, expressed by (A.16), of rewriting *the same* general price system (4) of my paper, each one with reference to the particular consumption good i, $i = 1, 2, \ldots, m$, whose rate of growth $(g + r_i)$ is explicitly introduced. But let us proceed with one of them – the one that we have called i. By re-arranging, and by using previous notation, we obtain:

$$\mathbf{p}[\mathbf{B} - (1 + g + r_i)\mathbf{A}] = \mathbf{a}_n w + (\pi - g - r_i)\mathbf{pA}, \tag{A.17}$$

$$\mathbf{p} = \mathbf{a}_n[\mathbf{B} - (1 + g + r_i)\mathbf{A}]^{-1} w + (\pi - g - r_i)\, \mathbf{pA}[\mathbf{B} - (1 + g + r_i)\mathbf{A}]^{-1}. \tag{A.18}$$

This is a remarkable expression. On the right-hand side, the first addendum contains the vector of the vertically hyper-integrated labour coefficients for hyper-subsystems i, and similarly the second addendum contains the matrix of the hyper-integrated units of productive capacity for the same hyper-subsystem i. Using definitions (A.9) and (A.10), expression (A.18) may simply be rewritten:

$$\mathbf{p} = \mathbf{l}^{(i)} w + (\pi - g - r_i)\mathbf{pM}^{(i)}. \tag{A.18b}$$

Clearly, in the very particular case in which

$$\pi = g + r_i, \tag{A.19}$$

the second addendum, on the right-hand side of (A.18b), disappears and the expression comes to coincide with $\mathbf{p}^{(i)}$ in (A.14b) – the natural prices for hyper-subsystem i.

It is important to stress that, since we can write expression (A.16) in m different ways, with reference to each specific r_i – i.e. to the rate of growth of per capita demand for consumption good i; and in general $r_i \neq r_j$, for $i, j, = 1, 2, \ldots, m$ – then it follows that, if it were to happen that (A.19) is satisfied for consumption good i, it would *not* in general be satisfied for any of the other $(m - 1)$ consumption goods.

In general, therefore, if π is uniform, the second addendum on the right-hand side of (A.18b) does not vanish, and we will be able to rewrite (A.18b) as:

$$\mathbf{p} = \mathbf{l}^{(i)} [\mathbf{I} - (\pi - g - r_i)\, \mathbf{M}^{(i)}]^{-1} w; \qquad i = 1, 2, \ldots, m, \tag{A.20}$$

(which of course reduces to

$$\mathbf{p} = \mathbf{l}^{(i)} w, \qquad i = 1, 2, \ldots, m, \tag{A.21}$$

coinciding with the natural prices for hyper-subsystem i, only in the very particular case in which $\pi = g + r_i$).

We can see now, in another way, i.e. from the point of view of the solution of the price system, that there are m different ways expressed by (A.20) – each one with reference to each of the consumption goods and therefore to each of the particular hyper-subsystems – of writing the *same* general price system (4) of my paper in which there is a uniform rate of profits.

It also emerges very clearly at this point that expression (A.20), when $w = 1$, can also be regarded as providing a complete generalization of Marx's 'transformation problem'.[2] It 'transforms' the physical quantities of labour $\mathbf{l}^{(i)}$

into the prices **p** of an economic system in which there is a uniform rate of profit π.

There are *m* expressions (A.20) for any given uniform rate of profit π, which means that there is a particular 'transformation', carried out by the corresponding hyper-subsystem, for each particular consumption good produced in the economic system. This transformation concerns *both* the price of the consumption good *and* the prices of the corresponding means of production.

We should now be able to look from yet another point of view at the meaning of the complete generalization of the labour theory of value emerging from the foregoing elaborations.

In a hypothetical economic system in which we were able to *actually separate* the various hyper-subsystems, it would be possible at least in principle to envisage *m* different natural price subsystems, which would embody a perfectly general pure labour theory of value. Such a labour theory of value would be general in the sense that it would realize, for an advanced society, the fundamental characteristic of the pure labour theory of value originally proposed by Adam Smith with reference to a primitive society: namely a set of values that realize a universal equality of 'labour commanded' and 'labour embodied'. The analytical step that allows the achievement of this result is of course a redefinition of the concept of 'labour embodied', which must be intended as the quantity of labour required directly, indirectly *and* hyper-indirectly to obtain the corresponding commodity as a consumption good.

In any economic system in which the analytical process of deriving the various hyper-subsystems is to be taken only as a *conceptual* (not a real) process, any rule of price determination inevitably entails a 'transformation' process, no matter whether the economic system itself is organizationally centralized or decentralized. In such a context, the general labour theory of value that has emerged from the foregoing elaboration has to be taken as providing a logical frame of reference – a conceptual construction that defines a series, actually a family of series, of ideal *natural* prices, which possess an extraordinarily high number of remarkable, analytical, and normative, properties.

4 *Choice of efficient techniques*

There is a further normative property of the natural prices, that emerges with reference to the problem of choice of techniques.

In the previous sections, all analysis has been carried out with reference to an economic system with a *given* technique, represented by the technical triple $[\mathbf{a}_n, \mathbf{A}, \mathbf{B}]$. In general, however, many alternative techniques of production, which we may call $\alpha, \beta, \ldots \omega$, may be available. More specifically, alternative technical triples:

$$[\mathbf{a}_n, \mathbf{A}, \mathbf{B}]^{(\alpha)}, [\mathbf{a}_n, \mathbf{A}, \mathbf{B}]^{(\beta)}, \ldots [\mathbf{a}_n, \mathbf{A}, \mathbf{B}]^{(\omega)} \qquad \text{(A.22)}$$

may be open to choice. A criterion of choice becomes necessary. Now, if the criterion of choice to be adopted is the usual one of minimization of costs, then it follows that the natural system of prices, by virtue of expressing physical quantities of labour (directly, indirectly and hyper-indirectly required), has the normative property of leading to the choice of the technique that entails the minimization of labour inputs. This means that natural prices possess the normative property of being *efficient prices*.

But in a growing economic system, as has been shown, the quantities of labour that are required directly, indirectly and hyper-indirectly for the corresponding commodities are *different* (for the same commodities) in the various hyper-subsystems, just as the corresponding natural prices are different in the various hyper-subsystems.

It follows that the efficient technique – i.e. the technique the choice of which entails the minimization of labour inputs – may turn out to be different from one hyper-subsystem to another. If it is technique α that minimizes labour inputs for hyper-subsystem 1, it may well be that another technique, let us say technique β, is the technique that minimizes labour inputs for hyper-subsystem 2, and so on.

A further consequence will now be noticed. The actual choice of different techniques in different hyper-subsystems will *a fortiori* entail different natural price systems. In other words, the natural prices, in general, will turn out to be different from one hyper-subsystem to another, not only because of the differences in the natural rates of profit, which would be the case even if the efficient technique were to remain the same for all hyper-subsystems (as has been considered up to this section), but also, and more fundamentally, because of differences in the efficient techniques themselves. For, as a consequence of cost minimization, the efficient technique may well turn out to be different from one hyper-subsystem to another.

Notice, again, that the differences in the natural prices concern the prices of the means of production, not the prices of consumption goods. Each consumption good continues to have one single natural price – the one that emerges as reflecting the physical quantity of labour directly, indirectly and hyper-indirectly required in the corresponding hyper-subsystem. Of course the same physical good, to the extent that it is also used as capital good in other hyper-subsystems, may also have other natural prices *as a capital good*. But its natural price as a consumption good is unique.

This property further enhances *the ancillary role*, already pointed out, of the natural prices of the capital goods with respect to the natural prices of the consumption goods.

But of course, at this point, it becomes necessary to go back to consider the meaning to be attributed to the logical construction of the hyper-subsystems. The partitioning of the whole economic system into *m* hyper-subsystems has been presented, since the beginning, as a *logical* operation, *not* as a *factual* one.

In practice, that is the way in which hyper-subsystems will have to be considered, that is, as *logical* constructions. Thus the foregoing analysis allows us to state that, if it were actually possible to separate the various hyper-subsystems from each other, then a whole series of families of natural prices could actually come into existence, with the normative properties that have been brought into evidence by the foregoing analysis. It goes without saying that, when actual separation is not possible, the choice of technique induced by current prices (which may deviate from natural prices) will entail deviations from efficient positions. An interesting point to stress is that this will be so in any economic system, whether market oriented (i.e. decentralized) or centrally planned.

More specifically, two distinct obstacles to the achievement of efficient positions through the choice of efficient techniques have emerged from the foregoing analysis. The first obstacle is represented by the difficulty of applying differentiated rates of profit in the various hyper-subsystems. The second obstacle is represented by all those factors that are opposed to actually carrying out a particular choice of technique in each growing hyper-subsystem. While the first obstacle is typical and specific to decentralized (e.g. market-oriented) economies, the second obstacle is common to both decentralized and centralized economic systems.

5 *Vertically hyper-integrated sectors*

There remains one further aspect to be explored, and that is the relation of the hyper-subsystems with the concept of vertically integrated sectors defined in my paper.

In fact, the generalization of my previous analysis to vertically hyper-integrated sectors has become obvious and immediate at this stage. If we return, for clarity of exposition, to the case of a single technique $\mathbf{a}_n$, $\mathbf{A}$, $\mathbf{B}$, in the whole economic system, and thus common to all hyper-subsystems, we can distinguish very clearly the two points of view from which any production economic system may be looked at.

The point of view of the circularity of the production process is evinced by the construction of the hyper-subsystems (which now acquire completeness by inclusion of the relations concerning the expansion of the means of production, besides those concerning their replacement). The point of view of final demand is evinced in an even sharper way. Even in a growing economic system, *consumption* appears at one extreme of the production process and labour appears at the other extreme; and the two are immediately and directly put into relation with each other. The complex circular (expanding) production process, which is in between, is taken for granted, as it is closed onto itself and fulfils a merely intermediate and ancillary function.

From the point of view of final demand, all intermediate circular processes fulfil an ancillary role. The economic system appears simply as made up of as many vertically hyper-integrated sectors as there are consumption goods. Each vertically hyper-integrated sector i, when operating at unit activity, may simply be represented by the elementary vector:

$$[1, 1, l_i, (g + r_i)], \qquad i = 1, 2, \ldots, m, \tag{A.23}$$

where the first component refers to one unit of consumption good i, the second component to one unit of vertically hyper-integrated productive capacity for consumption good i, the third to the physical quantity of (vertically hyper-integrated) labour for consumption good i and the fourth to the growth rate of demand for consumption good i.

The corresponding magnitudes in the price system continue to be represented by the simple vector:

$$[p_i, p_{k_i}, w, \pi_i], \qquad i = 1, 2, \ldots, m, \tag{A.24}$$

where p_i is the price of one physical quantity of consumption good i, and p_{k_i} is the price of one unit of vertically hyper-integrated productive capacity for consumption good i (while w and π_i are, as usual, the wage rate and the rate of profit). All asymmetries have now disappeared: vectors (A.23) and (A.24) are perfectly symmetrical.

One should note the extreme simplicity with which the unit of vertically hyper-integrated productive capacity in (A.23) and the corresponding price p_{k_i} in (A.24) have been introduced. They have been introduced without any specification of the composition of the unit concerned. In fact, at any point in time, t, given the technique $\mathbf{A}(t)$, $\mathbf{B}(t)$, $\mathbf{a}_n(t)$, the relation of the unit of vertically hyper-integrated productive capacity to the physical commodities of which it is composed, and correspondingly the relation of the natural price p_{k_i} to the natural price p_i of the various commodities measured in physical ordinary units, are rather complicated. The former is obtained directly from (A.7) while the latter is obtained after multiplying (A.14) by (A.10), i.e.:

$$\mathbf{p}_{k_i}(t) = \mathbf{p}^{(i)}(t)\,\mathbf{M}^{(i)}(t) = \mathbf{l}^{(i)}(t)\,\mathbf{M}^{(i)}(t)\,w(t),$$

or, by expansion,

$$\mathbf{p}_{k_i}(t) = \mathbf{a}_n(t)\,[\mathbf{B}(t) - (1 + \pi_{(i)}{}^*)\,\mathbf{A}(t)]^{-1}\mathbf{A}(t)[\mathbf{B}(t) - (1 + \pi_{(i)}{}^*)\mathbf{A}(t)]^{-1}w(t) \tag{A.25}$$

Now, the crucial point to notice is that this relation will continually be upset, over time, because of technical change.

Yet, essential though these complicated relations are for any analysis concerning the interrelations of the circular (expanding) process at any given point in time, they become irrelevant for all those dynamic analyses that concern the movements through time of the final consumption goods and of the corresponding physical quantities of labour, as well as for all those relations that follow therefrom – think for example of the analyses concerning the evolution of sectoral employment and income distribution.

As far as the analyses of these problems are concerned, complete emancipation is obtained from the constraints of fixed technical coefficients. The analysis becomes open to the absorption of technical progress in whatever form it may take place.

Notes

1 This is simply an analytical device to avoid inconsistencies in assuming differentiated growth rates for different consumption goods, in the presence of constant technical coefficients.

2 This complete generalization concerns the version of Marx's transformation problem as presented in Pasinetti (1973, pp. 9, 13, 17n).

Comment

Donald J. Harris
Stanford

Professor Pasinetti has forcefully shown here, and elsewhere, the power of his idea of vertically integrated sectors as an analytical device.

The crucial point is that it permits us logically and systematically to relate an analysis in terms of quantities of net product (final demand), taken item by item, to the respective quantities of labour and stock of means of production 'ultimately' required to produce each and every one of those items of final product. The exact relation between final product and the labour and means of production that produce it is explicitly seen to be constituted by the complex circular process of interdependent production lying, so to speak, in the background. As such, this relation cannot therefore be conceived in terms of a single one-way avenue from factors of production to final product that characterizes traditional marginalist theory. There are as many such avenues as there exist final products, and each goes through a complex structure of inter-industry relations. Similarly, prices of final products can, by the same mediation, be reduced to ultimate costs consisting of labour required for final output and a single unit of vertically integrated productive capacity, so that the meaning of those prices as cost-determined prices immediately becomes transparent.

The essential feature of the device that permits this operation is that it 'synthesizes in one single number the whole complicated circular process of production'. In its construction, it is analogous with and uses the same information as Sraffa's subsystem and the Leontief inverse. But it has the advantage of giving a more compact or consolidated expression of production conditions than either of these and, unlike the Leontief inverse, is capable of taking explicit account of joint production and hence the use of fixed capital in production. The computations involved are, however, no less laborious and would for any actual economy require computers with an enormous capacity.

Provided that production conditions do not change in the period of the analysis, which is an important and crucial proviso, the main advantage of this device is one of economy of analytical effort. This comes from being able to relate changes in final demand directly to changes in 'ultimate' input requirements using the one-time calculation of vertically integrated sector coefficients. In this way, also, the device allows a direct and immediate link between the usual Keynesian macro-analysis set out in terms of national income aggregates and a micro-analysis of prices, production conditions and employment, at the level of individual commodity sectors.

But what if production conditions do change? Then, the computations have to be performed all over again, and for each successive change, using the new information about the individual technical coefficients as data generated by the process of technical change. For the Sraffa and Leontief system this recomputation would result in a wholly different set of numbers each time to represent the productive structure of the economy. Not so for Pasinetti's concept of vertically integrated sectors. In this latter construction, the synthetic unit of vertically integrated productive capacity (constituted by a composite commodity) which ultimately produces one unit of final good i is conceptually invariant to changes in its composition. Its production coefficient therefore remains the same, at unit level of output, regardless of the actual underlying pattern of technical change. The only change registered is in the production coefficient of vertically integrated labour (see his equation (11)).

Pasinetti evidently regards this feature of his method as its great merit. But that depends on what one is trying to achieve. The fact that 'the concept of a unit of vertically integrated productive capacity is entirely independent of its composition' means that it is wholly insensitive to the actual pattern of technical change as it affects the underlying structure of material inputs. Consequently, this concept must fail to yield a quantitative representation of the actual character of technical change except and only in so far as technical change is labour augmenting. In this respect, it does little better than the existing inter-industry models of constant proportional growth in which by default it must be assumed that technical change is always purely labour augmenting. With Pasinetti's method, the actual rate of labour augmentation is of course captured separately for each specific sector so that the *uneven* pattern of labour productivity growth can be directly represented. This is certainly a valuable feature of the method.

To get a closer picture of the actual sources of technical change and the changing pattern of input use one must refer back to the inter-industry data. Moreover, in making the calculations that this method uses to derive the vertically integrated sector coefficients, one must necessarily start each time from the new information contained in the set of inter-industry data that technical change generates. This means that the inter-industry analysis is both logically and in reality prior to the scheme of vertically integrated sectors. It is not clear, therefore, what is gained from taking the additional step of vertically integrated analysis, at least from the standpoint of analysing the sources of technical change.

What the vertically integrated analysis successfully accomplishes is the remarkable conceptual feat of homogenizing the heterogeneous structure of production, considered as a complex circular process, by aggregating the diverse material inputs up to a single composite commodity for each sector through an appropriate linear transformation. In this respect, it provides a new analytical device (a composite commodity) for expressing the idea of an aggregate capital–output ratio in the context of heterogeneous capital goods without resorting to prices as weights for aggregation. To some, this may uncomfortably evoke shades of the now defunct surrogate production function or the long-dead average period of production. This would not be an unwarranted association so far as the mere goal of aggregating diverse inputs is concerned, but the method of aggregation used here is quite different and, of course, the theoretical purposes are also different.

Pasinetti's special method of aggregation makes sense, and indeed is an indispensable logical basis, for the limited purposes of a macroeconomic analysis carried out under unchanged technical conditions. However, his strong claims to the contrary notwithstanding, it does not seem well suited for analysis of certain aspects of the dynamic properties of technical change except in the most summary fashion. The reason for this, I think, lies in the very success of the method in accomplishing the feat of aggregation, which turns out to be an obstacle in the way of capturing essential properties of the process of technical change. In other words, because of the homogenization of the production process that this method entails, there is much that goes on in terms of the actual dynamics of the process of technical change that escapes the net of this method.

Let me illustrate this point. A large and growing body of concrete studies now allows us to identify a number of salient ingredients of the process of technical change. Among these is worth mentioning the fact that the process is inherently and intrinsically a *localized* phenomenon, occurring in the first instance at the level of particular industries, firms and production techniques. Even though its direct and indirect effects may ultimately be far reaching across the whole economic structure, it is only through a systematic and time-intensive process of *diffusion* that these effects operate. In so far as technical change is congealed in particular physical products, the product itself does not immediately take a fixed form but undergoes successive transformations as it goes through the diffusion process. Moreover, there are 'spillover effects', which operate between different production units and sectors of the economy so as to influence significantly the rate and pattern of technical change, quite independently of the inter-industry flows of physical products.

Because of the existence of these and other notable features of the actual process, not only is the quantitative representation of technical change at an aggregative level fraught with deep conceptual problems, but all such aggregative quantities have the unfortunate consequence of obliterating essential ingredients of the phenomenon being represented. This is so in the case of the commonly used growth-accounting framework. It is so, moreover, in the case of measures of the 'factor-saving bias' of technical change. I might add that the concept of an aggregate organic composition of capital, as commonly used in some versions of Marxian theory to represent technical change, fares no better in this regard. Compared with these alternatives, Pasinetti's method has some unique advantages already noted. But it still leaves us groping for elements of the process that are profoundly significant for analytical purposes.

The preceding comments relate only to the purely formal and technical uses of the method of vertical integration. But there are larger and deeper issues concerning Pasinetti's claim of providing with this method a substantive link, or a 'way to accomplish an integration', between the different analyses of Sraffa and Keynes. This claim is highly problematical and it would have been useful to have the underlying argument developed in the paper. As it stands, no attempt is made to engage the issues. But this is certainly where the discussion must go in seeking to advance the analysis beyond the work of Sraffa and, of course, beyond Keynes.

Comment

Stephen A. Marglin
Cambridge, Mass

Pasinetti's paper is particularly welcome because it marks the passage of the Anglo-Italian school from a destructive to a constructive stance, from a repetitive insistence on the logical shortcomings of Walrasian economics to an attempt to build an alternative framework of analysis. There may be disagreement about the merits of this alternative or that; but there is no disagreement about the need to go beyond the recital of the logical deficiencies of the reigning orthodoxy. Sraffa subtitled his book 'Prelude to a Critique of Economic Theory'; as Pasinetti indicates in his opening paragraph, it is now – after a quarter of a century – high time to get beyond the Prelude.

Pasinetti's contribution to this enterprise lies in his formulation of 'vertically integrated sectors' as a bridge between Keynesian macroeconomics and Sraffian microeconomics. The basic idea, as I understand it, is to provide a means for short-cutting the links from a unit of final demand for good i to the labour input required to produce this output on a sustainable basis, that is, the labour required to produce the output and replace the intermediate goods used up in the production process. For each good i there is a vector listing the gross outputs required to sustain one unit of final good production. There is also a scalar measure of the direct and indirect labour requirements, defined by the vector product of a labour requirement vector $\mathbf{a}_n$ and the gross output vector. As long as we confine our attention to linear systems, we can add the vectors of gross outputs and the scalar measures of labour inputs to obtain system-wide output and input requirements. This defines a mapping $\mathbf{Y}\rightarrow\mathbf{X}$ from an arbitrary vector of final demand $\mathbf{Y}$ to its corresponding vector of gross outputs $\mathbf{X}$ and simultaneously a mapping $\mathbf{Y}\rightarrow L$ from final demands to corresponding quantities of labour L. If we denote the inverse of the mapping by $\mathbf{Y}\rightarrow\mathbf{X}$ by $\mathbf{B}-\mathbf{A}$, that is, if in the usual Leontief–von Neumann fashion we write (cf. p. 233)

$$(\mathbf{B}-\mathbf{A})\mathbf{X}=\mathbf{Y}, \tag{1}$$

then the original mapping is written

$$\mathbf{X}=(\mathbf{B}-\mathbf{A})^{-1}\mathbf{Y}.$$

We can also write

$$\mathbf{S}=\mathbf{AX}=\mathbf{A}(\mathbf{B}-\mathbf{A})^{-1}\mathbf{Y}$$

as the capacity requirements of the vector $\mathbf{Y}$, 'capacity' being understood as the pre-existing stocks of goods required to produce a given vector of final demand. The matrix $\mathbf{H}$, defined by the equation

$$\mathbf{H}=\mathbf{A}(\mathbf{B}-\mathbf{A})^{-1},$$

is a matrix of 'integrated productive capacities'. Its columns represent the vectors of input requirements for one unit of final demand for each commodity. Finally, we can write the labour requirements for **Y** as

$$L = \mathbf{a}_n\mathbf{X} = \mathbf{a}_n(\mathbf{B} - \mathbf{A})^{-1}\mathbf{Y}.$$

The vector **v** defined by the equation (14, p. 236)

$$\mathbf{v} = \mathbf{a}_n(\mathbf{B} - \mathbf{A})^{-1}$$

is the vector of 'vertically integrated labour', that is, the labour required to produce one unit of each component of final demand on a sustained basis.

This, I think, represents the heart of Pasinetti's construction, but closer examination is necessary to appreciate its economic significance. Pasinetti, it should be observed, follows convention in taking final demand as exogenous and the means of production as well as gross outputs as endogenous. One starts with a given final demand vector **Y** and computes the outputs **X** necessary to produce that vector *and* replenish the inputs used up in the production process. It is simply *assumed* that the physical stocks required to initiate the production process, that is, the means of production **AX**, are in place. In historical time, however, to use Joan Robinson's phrase, we start with a vector of stocks **S** and produce a vector of outputs $\mathbf{X} = \mathbf{A}^{-1}\mathbf{S}$, which, when added to what remains of the original stocks, gives a new vector of stocks **BX**. The matrix **B** can be thought of as the sum of the identity matrix **I** and a matrix of depreciated capital goods $\bar{\mathbf{A}}$:

$$\mathbf{B} = \mathbf{I} + \bar{\mathbf{A}}.$$

In the extreme case in which capital goods are infinitely durable and lose none of their technical efficacy over time, we have $\bar{\mathbf{A}} = \mathbf{A}$ and $\mathbf{B} = \mathbf{I} + \mathbf{A}$. At the other extreme, in which all capital is working capital completely used up within a single production period, as in a model in which corn is produced from seed corn and labour, $\bar{\mathbf{A}}$ is the null matrix and $\mathbf{B} = \mathbf{I}$.

Having obtained the new stocks **BX**, we must now set aside the original stocks $\mathbf{S} = \mathbf{AX}$ so as to be able to repeat the process next period. The residual $(\mathbf{B} - \mathbf{A})\mathbf{X}$ represents the net output of the system. That is, as in equation (1),

$$(\mathbf{B} - \mathbf{A})\mathbf{X} = \mathbf{Y}.$$

Observe that the temporal sequence is just the opposite from the analytic logic. Period by period, we start from **S** to produce **X** and **Y**, but the analysis starts from **Y** to calculate **X** and **S**. There is no contradiction here, but it is important to understand the difference between the two perspectives.

One final concept completes the picture. Pasinetti introduces the price vector $\mathbf{p}_k$, the *i'th* component of which represents the price of a unit of vertically integrated productive capacity. By definition (cf. p. 236)

$$\mathbf{p}_k = \mathbf{pH} = \mathbf{pA}(\mathbf{B} - \mathbf{A})^{-1}, \tag{15}$$

where **p** is the price vector corresponding to the technology $(\mathbf{B}, \mathbf{B}, \mathbf{a}_n)$ and the profit rate π, with the wage rate normalized at $w = 1$. The significance of $\mathbf{p}_k$ can perhaps be better understood if we multiply the two sides of equation (15) by $(\mathbf{B} - \mathbf{A})\mathbf{X}$, which gives

$$\mathbf{p}_k(\mathbf{B} - \mathbf{A})\mathbf{X} = \mathbf{pAX}$$

or

$$\mathbf{p}_k\mathbf{Y} = \mathbf{pS}.$$

This last equation indicates that the price vector $\mathbf{p}_k$ is defined so as to make the value of the final demand vector – evaluated in terms of the capacities required to produce it – equal to the value of the pre-existing stocks.

To illustrate, consider the two extreme cases of zero depreciation, that is, of infinitely durable capital, $\mathbf{B} = \mathbf{I} + \mathbf{A}$, and of 100 per cent depreciation, that is, where capital consists of working capital only, in which $\mathbf{B} = \mathbf{I}$. In the first case we have $\mathbf{p}_k = \mathbf{pA}$, so that the value of a unit of productive capacity for good i is the value of the gross stocks required to produce one unit of gross output of good i. At the other extreme, we have

$$\mathbf{p}_k = \mathbf{pA}(\mathbf{I} - \mathbf{A})^{-1} = \mathbf{pA}\,(\mathbf{I} + \mathbf{A} + \mathbf{A}^2 + \ldots),$$

which is to say that the value of a unit of productive capacity for good i is the value of the gross stocks A, augmented by the quantities of goods required to reproduce these stocks.

We can generalize to the case of an intermediate but still uniform rate of depreciation by writing

$$\mathbf{B} = \mathbf{I} + (1 - d)\mathbf{A}$$

where d represents the rate of depreciation. Since now

$$\mathbf{p}_k = \mathbf{pA}\,(\mathbf{I} + d\mathbf{A} + d^2\mathbf{A}^2 + \ldots),$$

it can be seen that the value of a unit of productive capacity is a positive function of the rate of depreciation. In other words, the more durable the equipment, the lower is the cost of capital relative to output.

However, Pasinetti claims more for his notion of vertically integrated sectors than that they are a useful way of thinking about the effects of depreciation on the value of capacity relative to output. There is, he suggests, 'a one-to-one correspondence between expressing an economic system in terms of "industries" and expressing it in terms of vertically integrated sectors' (page 237) Evidently Pasinetti means something different by 'one-to-one correspondence' from what I have always understood this term to mean; for we cannot go backwards from vectors $\mathbf{v}$ and $\mathbf{p}_k$ to an underlying industrial structure. To any $\mathbf{v}$ and $\mathbf{p}_k$ corresponds a whole continuum of technologies $(\mathbf{A}, \mathbf{B}, \mathbf{a}_n)$. Perhaps what Pasinetti means to do is to establish an *equivalence* among all technologies $(\mathbf{A}, \mathbf{B}, \mathbf{a}_n)$ that correspond to the same vectors $(\mathbf{v}, \mathbf{p}_k)$; all these technologies may be said to be equivalent in terms of their labour and capacity requirements.

There is however an important asymmetry, which must be recognized. The labour requirement $\mathbf{v} = \mathbf{a}_n(\mathbf{B}-\mathbf{A})^{-1}$ is defined solely in terms of technology. By contrast, the price vector $p_k = p\mathbf{A}(\mathbf{B}-\mathbf{A})^{-1}$ depends both on technology and on the price vector p, which in turn (assuming $w = 1$) depends not only on technology but also on the rate of profit π, a result that seems to vitiate the usefulness of summarizing the economic structure in terms of $(\mathbf{v}, \mathbf{p}_k)$. To use this formulation to deal with technological change would require us to be able to separate out the effects of changes in the rate of profit from the effects of technical change. As a conceptual or empirical matter this separation appears difficult.

There is a deeper problem, however. I frankly do not understand why coming to grips with technical change – granting for the sake of argument that Pasinetti's formulation does so – is the key to integrating Keynes and Sraffa. Pasinetti sees Sraffa as an alternative to Walras and his research programme is proposed as an alternative to the mainstream attempt to merge Keynes with Walras. As I have indicated at great length elsewhere, my own view is somewhat different (Marglin, 1984a). I see Keynes as an alternative to Walras and both of them as compatible with Sraffa: each provides a way of closing the basically indeterminate framework provided by Sraffa, its indeterminateness being, in this view, the main point of the Sraffian story.

A Walrasian closure operates by means of complete competitive markets, for labour and capital as well as for goods, with utility maximization directing the allocation of given endowments. By contrast, a Keynesian closure posits inherently imperfect labour and capital markets and substitutes exogenous effective demand for exogenous endowments. In my view, technical change, the focus of Pasinetti's analysis, is not central to the theoretical differences between Keynes and Walras, however important it may be to understanding the process of economic development. In point of fact, neither Keynesian nor Walrasian theory has much to say about technical change.

The foregoing is evidently cryptic, so let me expand. Both Sraffa and Keynes admit of many interpretations and it may be unreasonably reductionist to insist on any one of these as 'True Sraffa' or 'True Keynes'. Let us start with Sraffa, to whom at least six different projects have been attributed. First, his intention has been said to have been the development of an economic theory that was independent of demand, that is to say, of household preferences (Robinson, 1961). Second, his project has been taken as an attack on capital aggregation (Dobb, 1970). Third, the Sraffian goal has been argued to have been the reconstruction of Marx without the labour theory of value (Garegnani, 1987, pp. 567–70). Fourth, it has been suggested that the point was to lay the foundations for an economics without counterfactuals (Sen, 1978; Velupillai, 1980, 1982). Fifth, Sraffa has been understood as offering a theory of distribution in which the rate of profit is 'determined from outside the system of production, in particular by the level of the money rates of interest' (Sraffa, 1960, p. 33; see Pasinetti's paper, page 233, n3). Finally there is my own view, elliptically stated above: for me, the point of Sraffa's exercise is the incompleteness, nay the irrelevance, of marginal analysis as a theory of distribution. This point is made by effectively assuming fixed proportions (despite the disclaimers) and showing that distribution is indeterminate in such a model. In this view Sraffa's challenge to orthodox theorists was this: 'if you have a theory of distribution, it should work in a simple model in which there are no margins to vary. But distribution is incompletely determined by production in such a model. So what is your theory?'

It is a measure of the richness (as well as of the opaqueness) of Sraffa's work that it can be given so many interpretations. It would perhaps be the better part of wisdom to admit that we do not know what Sraffa's point was and to speak rather of the lessons different people have drawn from it. In my own case, Sraffa's work had an importance beyond measure because it, as well as the surrounding debate, obliged me to examine both orthodox and heterodox theories in an attempt to understand each theory's analytic core. The work alluded to earlier on (Marglin, 1984a) was largely a result of that effort.

Candour however compels me to temper this praise: to the extent that the lesson I have drawn from Sraffa was in fact any part of his intent, I believe his project to have been based on a serious misunderstanding of orthodox theory and therefore fundamentally misconceived. Orthodox theory, at least as it has evolved in the dominant Anglo-American strain (Hicks, Samuelson, Arrow, Hahn, etc. – all looking more to Walras than to Marshall), is not fundamentally 'marginalist'. Its essence is rather complete markets and the allocation of exogenous endowments by means of utility maximization. From a purely logical point of view, one can close the basically indeterminate Sraffa (or Leontief) model by assuming exogenous endowments, utility maximization, and complete markets. That is, one can marry Walras to Sraffa. But the marriage is a difficult one to consummate, and is extremely unlikely to bear any fruit. The problem is not one of logical inconsistency or incompleteness, but one of empirical irrelevance. Walrasian theories and other theories stemming from the neoclassical dispensation describe a logically possible world, but not (alas!) the one we inhabit.

Keynes, like Sraffa, is open to many interpretations. Indeed, the mainstream sees Keynes as complementary to neoclassical theory rather than as an alternative. Neoclassical theory putatively describes the long run in which there is ample time for adjustment to take place; Keynesian theory describes the short run in which inertia, friction and incomplete adjustment are central features. My own view once again is somewhat different. I see Keynes not as offering a theory of the short period, which leaves the long run to Walras and his ilk, but as offering a novel way of viewing the capitalist economy in the long run as well as in the short run. The centrepiece of this theory is effective demand, and in the long run the key exogenous element is investment demand. I have expanded on the distinctive elements of this theory elsewhere (Marglin, 1984a, b, 1987) and will not elaborate the argument here. Where I differ from others is that I see Keynes as implying a theory of relative prices and income distribution as well as a theory of output and growth.

I should, however, give notice to doubts that echo my reservations about neoclassical theory. Keynesian theory also poses problems, problems of an empirical rather than a logical order. But these problems are not as fundamental as in the case of Walrasian theory. The problems with Walras lie with the story itself, whereas the problem with Keynes is with what the story omits. To be specific: I have no doubt that exogenous effective demand is a crucial element in the explanation of how a capitalist economy functions. But this is not the whole story. In two words, the problem with the Keynesian analytic framework is the absence of Marxian concerns: the role of *class conflict* in the determination of real wages and the organization of production and hence in the determination of income distribution, economic growth, the price level and the structure of relative prices. In my view, the central problem in working out a suitable theory of the capitalist economy lies precisely in bringing Keynes and Marx together.

Reply

I should like to thank both Donald Harris and Stephen Marglin for their words of appreciation and for their efforts to present the essentials and the usefulness of the concept of vertically integrated sectors. With a limited space for my reply, I shall concentrate on answering their objections.

Let me start with Harris's Comment. In his concluding paragraph, Harris complains that I have made 'no attempt . . . to engage the issues'; these issues being those of 'providing . . . a substantive link . . . between the different analyses of Sraffa and Keynes'. But this contradicts what he says earlier when, after an explanation of what vertical integration can achieve, he concludes precisely that '. . . In this . . . way the device allows a direct and immediate link between the usual Keynesian macro-analysis set out in terms of national income aggregates and a micro-analysis of prices, production conditions and employment, at the level of individual commodity sectors' (p. 250).

All his other objections can be reduced to one single point, namely that the device of vertical integration does not catch the detailed and localized sources of technical change. I agree: but the analytical device of vertical integration *is not meant* to catch the detailed and localized sources of technical change; on the contrary, it is meant to synthesize the overall *effect* of technical change (whatever its sources, or nature, or remote localization in the economic system) on the final stage of production, in order to single out its ultimate consequences on the structure of production, of prices and of employment. As is said explicitly in section 5 of my paper, it should be stressed that the analytical tool of vertical integration must be considered, and actually used, as complementary to – not as alternative to, or, even less, as excluding – input–output analysis, diffusion analysis, or *any* microeconomic analysis of technical change.

Turning now to Marglin's Comment, let me start with his objection (on page 255) to my using the terminology 'one-to-one correspondence between expressing an economic system in terms of "industries" and expressing it in terms of vertically integrated sectors'. Marglin objects that 'we cannot go backwards from vectors $\mathbf{v}$ and $\mathbf{p}_k$ to an underlying industrial structure'. But this is not so. He has missed the crucial bit at the very beginning of the quotation, namely 'at each particular time'. For, *at any given point of time*, the $[\mathbf{A}, \mathbf{B}, \mathbf{a}_n]$ are *given* and known. Therefore it is indeed as possible to go from $[\mathbf{A}, \mathbf{B}, \mathbf{a}_n]$ to $[\mathbf{H}, \mathbf{v}]$, as it is to go back from $[\mathbf{H}, \mathbf{v}]$ to $[\mathbf{A}, \mathbf{B}, \mathbf{a}_n]$. For any given π, it is also as possible to go from $\mathbf{p}$ to $\mathbf{p}_k$, as it is to go back from $\mathbf{p}_k$ *to* $\mathbf{p}$: the correspondence is indeed one-to-one. It is only when time goes on, and technical coefficients change, that the correspondence breaks down.

Marglin's statement that there is an asymmetry between the physical quantity system, which depends only on technology, and the price system, which depends also on π, is not a peculiar feature of the vertically integrated concept: it is a *general* feature. What is true of prices $\mathbf{p}_k$ is also true, in *exactly* the same way, of prices $\mathbf{p}$. This means that, when the price system is considered, the difficulties of separating changes due to technical progress from changes due to variations in the distribution of income represent a problem that cannot be eluded in *any* context. We have known this since Ricardo's time. What the device of vertical integration does is to provide units of productive capacities that are unambiguously defined *in physical terms* at the vertically integrated level, and moreover to provide the appropriate system of prices $\mathbf{p}_k$.

Marglin seems to have lost his way through these relations when he multiplies both sides of (15) by $(\mathbf{B}-\mathbf{A})\mathbf{X}$ and then writes the result as:

$$\mathbf{p}_k\mathbf{Y} = \mathbf{p}\mathbf{S}.$$

He interprets this as meaning that 'the value of the final demand vector, *evaluated in terms of the capacities* required to produce it, [is] equal to the value of the pre-existing stocks'.

But this makes no sense. Vector $\mathbf{Y}$ contains physical quantities of final commodities. These physical quantities cannot but be evaluated at *their* prices, namely $\mathbf{p}$. It is meaningless to evaluate them at prices $\mathbf{p}_k$, which are the prices of the vertically integrated units of productive capacities. As I have shown in my original elaboration (see Pasinetti, 1973, p. 10), the result should be written as:

$$\mathbf{p}_k\mathbf{K} = \mathbf{p}\mathbf{S},$$

where $\mathbf{K}$ is the vector of the m physical quantities of vertically integrated productive capacities. Of course, in equilibrium, $\mathbf{K} = \mathbf{Y}$, i.e., in equilibrium, the physical quantities of the m vertically integrated productive capacities *numerically* (owing to their definition) coincide with the physical quantities of final demand. Their meanings, however, are completely different and should not be confused.

When the result is written in this way the meaning of the equality becomes evident and revealing. Both the left-hand side and the right-hand side represent an evaluation, at current prices, of *the same* physical capital stocks, which are however classified according to two different criteria, i.e. are measured in terms of two different physical units. On the right-hand side, the capital stocks are measured in ordinary physical units, multiplied by their (ordinary) prices $\mathbf{p}$; on the left-hand side they are measured in physical units of vertically integrated productive capacities, multiplied by the corresponding prices $\mathbf{p}_k$. The results of both multiplications are, obviously, exactly the same.

The last and, to me, the most interesting part of Marglin's Comment concerns his interpretation of the relations between Keynes, Walras, Sraffa and Marx. It is a pity that these remarks were not presented to the conference. They would have deserved wide discussion, which is obviously not possible here. I should like, however, warmly to welcome them as a concise statement of Marglin's own position, duly supplemented with the appropriate references to his book (Marglin, 1984a).

As to myself, I prefer to remain with the presupposition behind my paper. In other words, I continue to consider (like Marglin) both Keynes and Marx, but (unlike Marglin) also Sraffa as alternatives to Walras. True, both Keynes's and Sraffa's analyses (and for that matter Walras's) had little concern with technical progress. But my point is that it is precisely the opening up to the problems of technical progress, i.e. to dynamic analysis, that strikingly brings out the affinities of both Sraffa's and Keynes's analyses with that of the classical economists (including Marx) and their overall incompatibility with that of Walras.

The claim, by Marglin, that 'one can marry Walras to Sraffa' is very weak even in a static context, if he is compelled to add immediately that 'the marriage is a difficult one to consummate, and is extremely unlikely to bear any fruit'. In a dynamic context, it seems to me the difficulties are compounded by so high a factor as to make any such attempt positively harmful to both.

PART II

9

Revisionist Findings on Sraffa

Paul A. Samuelson

Piero Sraffa was a great economist whom I remember with warm admiration. He wrote too little, which is our loss. His reputation tends to get tied up with ideological jockeyings within our profession. Perhaps this is inevitable but I regret it – for, ideology aside, mainstream economists of the mathematical or literary persuasion can benefit much from Sraffa's contributions and also from the problems that his works pose for further investigations.

By chance the *New Palgrave* (Eatwell, Milgate and Newman, 1987) contains two articles on Sraffa, both of some length. The one by me originated accidentally: I was not the editors' natural choice for this topic, but they wanted my participation and were willing to indulge my preferences to write out some views on Wicksell and also on Sraffa. The other *Palgrave* article on Sraffa, by John Eatwell and Carlo Panico, is seen to have some overlap with mine; still readers of this valuable new reference will, I daresay, benefit from the differences in viewpoint registered by the different authors. (It should be said that, until the finished volumes appeared, I could not benefit from the thoughtful Eatwell–Panico treatment; that is perhaps all for the better since differences can be more interesting than agreements.)

Here, also by invitation of hospitable editors, are some further thoughts on Sraffa. They are neither listed in strict chronological order nor ranked by relative importance.

1 *Scholar as young man*

One yearns to know more of Sraffa's early Italian years. Schumpeter, in his graduate lectures at Harvard in the mid-1930s, referred to Sraffa as unfortunately spoiled by having been born too affluent. No doubt Schumpeter was expressing regret that Sraffa did not write more, but this diagnosis as to cause for that seems quite unwarranted. (Rumour has it that Sraffa did die well off, leaving behind him gold in Swiss vaults for Trinity College. According to Kaldor's obituary piece on Sraffa for the British Academy, this legacy seems to have been the fruit of a daring coup in which Sraffa staked his all on the comeback of Japanese bonds after that country's defeat. What theory of inductive inference, I wonder, could have persuaded me to make a like investment?)

2 *Writer's block*

The myth of Sraffa as dilettante gained from such stories as I heard in the 1930s (perhaps from Robert Bryce, the Canadian John the Baptist who brought Keynes's message to America in 1935). Sraffa is supposed to have begged off being named director of research at Cambridge when he learned this might require his attending an occasional before-noon meeting; as assistant director he could avoid that risk, and for many years the 'graduate' curriculum at Cambridge was reported to involve attending a seminar with other non-Englishmen at which Sraffa presided while classmates presented papers in turn.

Several times I have heard the following sample of Keynes's wit. When Maynard was told that a mysterious ailment of Nicky Kaldor's was diagnosed as athlete's foot, he is reported as saying: 'I don't believe it. Next you'll be telling me Piero suffers from writer's cramp.'

Sraffa's block against lecturing was even more pathetic than his writer's block. The story used to be repeated in Cambridge of a series of lectures Professor Pigou had arranged on great economists. Sraffa of course was to speak on Ricardo. But as the day approached, he could not face the ordeal, pacifying Pigou by a gift of gooseberry jam and the promised substitution of Kaldor, who cheerfully agreed to volunteer as substitute. Posterity is grateful to the incident for Kaldor's brilliant 1955 article in which Ricardo's model is artfully presented as one alternative to neoclassical Clarkianism. (Since writing these words I have read the 1984 Italian interview with Kaldor – Christina Marcuzzo, 1986 – where a definitive version of this incident is told.)

3 *Thursday conversations at Trinity*

One yearns to know more about Sraffa's precise influences on Wittgenstein.

4 *The spectacles one peers through*

Sraffa's relationship to the Communist Party and to various Marxian factions, whatever its biographical interest and testimony for Italian intellectual history, has little bearing on his scholarly economics. Sraffa's general interest in Marxian economics is quite another matter. He was 50 when I first knew him; and the puzzlement this sophisticated intellectual engendered in me by orally defending such a notion as Smith's concept of *productive* labour (whereby concrete *goods* are given a primacy over ephemeral *services*) suddenly evaporated when I came to hypothesize that this sophisticated mind had a penchant for Marxian notions. This paradigmatic insight for understanding Sraffa served the observer well.

5 *Monetary insights*

One should constantly nominate suspicions in economics. Marx's legacy is valuable in this regard. But of course nomination and election are quite distinguishable procedures in any empirical science, and in this regard the algebraic worth of Karl's value-added is problematic.

Eatwell and Panico (1987, pp. 448–9) point out that Sraffa's early monetary writing – his 1920 Italian thesis and 1922 work for Keynes – sided with the angels (Cassel, Keynes and Hawtrey, as against Wicksell and Einaudi) in opposing a return to pre-war gold parities with the entailed deadweight losses from deflation. So far, so good. But one hopes that the following paraphrase of Sraffa's 1920 thought is taken out of context: '. . . the *normal* value of a currency is completely "conventional", i.e. it can be at *any* level that common opinion expects it to be.' Chancellor Churchill made his 1925 boo-boo in part because the current ephemeral belief that the pound would be restored to its 1914 value made it float *temporarily* and misleadingly near to that disastrous level of overvaluation. Of course, Wicksell was wrong and Cassel was right on post-war restorations of parity. *Any* absolute price level can obtain (if the right things are done to sustain it); but Couéism is silly monetary economics.

Also, Sraffa's nominated suspicion that class interests shape price-level policy decisions and achieve significant alterations in income distribution fares poorly under the test of economic history. To be sure, the industrialist Hugo Stinnes was splashed in the 1920–3 inflation and Heidelberg University was permanently penalized. But, as Schumpeter used to say, the rooms of capitalism's hotel are fully occupied, albeit, with a *changing* set of people. Even Keynes's eclectic view of the 1923 *Tract*, that long waves in the price level generate systematic changes in the terms of trade between risk-taking entrepreneurs on the one hand and rentiers on the other, has had to be attenuated in this century. What is surprising is not how much *hysteresis* there is of the type Sraffa suspected, but rather how little! One capitalist gains when waves move sand to his Florida beach; another loses. But this speaks little for a Marxian model of oceanography.

6 *Reproduction models of Quesnay–Marx*

Sraffa's 1960 input/output economics, like that of Leontief in the 1925–39 years (and that of Adolph Löwe and Fritz Burchardt in Kiel around 1930), one had supposed was influenced by Marx's Volume II tableaux of steady and expanded reproduction. It is useful to learn from Eatwell and Panico (1987) that Marx's reproduction schemes were indeed the source of the initial notes that Sraffa showed to Keynes around 1927 and from which the 1960 Sraffa classic evolved. There seems no evidence that Sraffa knew the related 1898 works of the Russian V. K. Dmitriev; although von Bortkiewicz was Leontief's Berlin mentor, he tells me he knew Marx's work but not Dmitriev's. For the Metzler *Festschrift* (Samuelson, 1974), eschewing the puffery in which Morishima (1973) declared Marx to be the peer of Walras as *mathematical* (!) economist, I pronounced Marx's most important *analytical* contribution to economics to be those reproduction models from Volume II, which gets least read.

Marx's admiration (merited admiration) for Quesnay stemmed from his own struggle with reproduction tableaux. Marx's successful struggle – which was purely arithmetic rather than mathematical and which avoided groping (successfully or otherwise) with the so-called 'transformation' problem – was motivated by Marx's erroneous belief that Adam Smith cheated in claiming to break down a good's price and a society's national income into the eclectic triad of wage component, land-rent component and interest (or, sans uncertainty, profit) component. Marx suspected that a *fourth* component of used-up capital goods somehow escaped appropriate inclusion: in a world where iron needs coal input and coal needs iron input – indeed where corn needs as input corn itself – Marx suspected Smith of perpetrating on his reader a value-added calculus that involved the swindle of an *infinite* regress. In tens of thousands of words and repeated MSS bequeathed to Engels, Marx grappled with this perplexity – which has naught to do with a category of income that involves 'surplus' since it arises in a zero interest, zero rent model.

Paradoxically, Marx's successful depiction of tableaux of *stationary reproduction* and (geometrically) *expanding reproduction* does vindicate Smith's triad in precisely the manner that Dmitriev ([1893] 1974), Leontief (1941), Dorfman, Samuelson and Solow ([1958] 1987), and Sraffa (1960) were to elaborate on. An infinite time-receding matrix multiplier series converges identically to the Dmitriev–Marx simultaneous equation solution to the problem when Marx carries forward at compound interest the earlier-stage factor outlays up to the final date of the present: $\Sigma_0^\infty a^t(1+r)^t \equiv [I - a(1+r)]^{-1}$ in matrix terms, post-multiplied into direct primary factor requirements.[1] The following numerical example elucidates the theorem.

Consider a model with two goods: (subsistence) corn and (luxury) silk. To produce 1 of corn requires 1 acre of direct land and $\frac{1}{2}$ unit of the other good as input; to get 1 of silk requires 1 of direct labour and $\frac{1}{2}$ of the other good as input. Each labourer needs a *subsistence* wage of $\frac{1}{4}$ corn, paid at the beginning of the period, to keep the labour supply stationary. The profit rate is observed to be $33\frac{1}{3}$ per cent per period. Like workers, property owners save nothing, spending all their rent and interest incomes on silk consumption. Suppose the wage is £1 per unit and the rent rate is £1 per acre (both paid *pre factum*). It can be calculated that, by coincidence, both goods have a competitive price of £4 per unit. Only one steady-state reproduction tableau is consistent with our specified data of 200 workers and 150 units of land. The tableau of Marx and bourgeois economics must be as in Table 9.1.

Marx's calculated tableau gives the same tripartite breakdown of income and price(s) as Smith will get from (i) adding up the value-added in all the (infinite) rounds of previous stages of production, taking care (ii) to reckon the compound interest earnable on all the earlier outlays on the primary

Table 9.1 Tableau of stationary reproduction (profit rate = $33\frac{1}{3}\%$)

Departments	*Corn input*	*Silk input*	*Labour (wages)*	*Land (rent)*	*Profit*	*Gross outputs*	*Final outputs*
Corn (150 units @£4)	£0	£300	£0	£150	£150	£600	£200 = £(600–400)
Silk (200 units @£4)	£400	£0	£200	£0	£200	£800	£500 = £(800–300)
	£400	£300	£200	£150	£350		£700

£(200 + 150 + 350) = national income = £(200 + 500)
wages + rent + interest = *NI* $= \Sigma P_j C_j$

inputs from time of purchase to the present day of price reckoning. All this is a routine exercise in Dorfman–Samuelson–Solow ([1958] 1987) and Sraffa (1960) algebra: with W and R being the nominal wage and rent rates, r the profit rate, C_j's the final consumptions, and P_j's the goods' nominal prices, $\Sigma P_j C_j = (W[0\ 1] + R[1\ 0])\ [I + a(1+r) + a^2(1+r)^2 + \ldots]$. Note that this contrived case of equal organic composition of capital carefully avoids any detour into distorting equalized rates of surplus values (percentage mark-ups on *wage outlay alone* to the neglect of return on raw material and/or rent outlays). No wonder Steedman regarded *Marx after Sraffa* (1977a) as properly being where Smith was *before* Marx. Bortkiewicz would concur.

7 *Macroeconomic skirmishing*

My meandering thoughts regress from 1960 to Sraffa's 1932 polemic on Hayek's *Prices and Production* (1931). After a brief period in vogue, in accordance with Oscar Wilde's dictum that 'these days to be understood is to be found out', Hayek's book has earned its benign neglect. As both of the cited *Palgrave* articles aptly pointed out, Sraffa's 1932 article is notable for his defining the concept of an *own-rate of interest in terms of a specified good.* If 100 rice today trade for 106 rice next year, the own-rice-rate of interest is 6 per cent. If the market basket of goods in the price-level index rises in price by 2 per cent in the year and my dollar earns a nominal interest rate of 10 per cent, my real rate (own-rate in terms of the goods basket) is only 8 per cent – 10–2 per cent or, more exactly, [(110/1.02)–100]% = 7.84 . . .%. In the literature on Irving Fisher and Keynes, the own-rate concept lives on purged of some of its *General Theory* ambiguities.

I reread the 1932 item for my *Palgrave* piece but scarcity of space accorded it only perfunctory mention. Let me report here that the allegedly pen-tied scholar, when urged by Keynes to attack Hayek, displayed a brilliant and cutting argumentative style. However, now that the heats of the arguments have cooled down after half a century, the modern reader perceives that Sraffa did not identify the rotten core of the Hayek work but engaged mostly in formalistic word-play concerning such Jesuitical concepts as neutrality of money. Had Sraffa worked the other side of the street, his subtle mind could have formulated for Hayek impeccable descriptions of processes in which, for a time, interest rates are contrived to be lower in real terms than they can remain in the longer run. What was harmful in the Hayek lectures was not their failure to achieve Wittgenstein rigour in formulating their scenarios!

I heard David Laidler in Sweden, during the 1987 meeting celebrating the fiftieth anniversary of the so-called Stockholm School, speculate on why Keynes's *General Theory* had the lasting power that *Prices and Production* and the Ohlin–Myrdal–Lindahl–Lundberg paradigms of the Stockholm School failed to attain. Having lived through those years of yore, I could have told him there was no mystery: the Swedish School messages and paradigms overlapped with, and were dominated by, the post-*General Theory investigations*. Those of them that deserved to live on did and do live on (for example, the Lundberg-like dynamizing of the 1936 statics). The Hayek effort died because, in the midst of a great depression that almost ended capitalism and led down the road to serfdom, it concentrated on parables in which a system must for methodological reasons be started out at full employment and in which the induced shortening of the period of production was non-cogently identified with the depression process then in being. As Lionel Robbins came to regret in reflecting on his misguided *The Great Depression* (1936), every policy insight of the 1931 opus was perverse: with one in four unemployed in Germany and the United States, to regard any expansion of funds for consumption as an evil sin was a programme inviting rejection by good-sense lay people and economists. (Even Hayek had second thoughts.) What died deserved to die. Still, schemata that illuminate how policies that promote over-full employment will entail predictable reactions will Phoenix-like rise from the dead in other times. Science, one hopes, can do better than reel from one non-eclectic exaggeration to another.

8 *The fatal 1926 error*

The two *Palgrave* articles are diametrically different in their evaluation of the 1926 article on competitive returns that brought Sraffa early fame. Both of course agree with his critique of Marshall's attempt to paper over the incompatibility of a firm's falling marginal cost with perfect competition. Helping 1920s Cambridge catch up to 1838 Cournot was a valuable, needed, Sraffian contribution, which did stimulate Joan Robinson and Kahn to those imperfect competition advances that paralleled the contemporary American work of J. M. Clark and Chamberlin. No argument on this.

But on the other half of the 1926 classic – Sraffa's purported demonstration that the category of *constant* competitive cost constitutes the only empirical box with appreciable content – the *Palgrave* articles are 180° apart. I state (Samuelson, 1987a, pp. 458–9), 'This is plain wrong. Sraffa's 1960 book demonstrates that . . . [as does] Joan Robinson's famous 1941 *Economic Journal* article on rising supply price. . . .' As soon as two competitive goods involve different land/labour proportions, the *production possibility* frontier is curved and not straight in the fashion Sraffa needs. A *Palgrave* editor (not Eatwell) in a letter to me suggested in effect that for small (enough) movements the curved frontier would look flat. When I replied that this is an evasion of the question of whether the second derivative is itself zero (or even 'near zero'), he responded by saying that Sraffa was not a trained mathematician – which agrees with my point that Sraffa by pure rhetoric convinced himself and my generation of students of a simple error. I reproach myself that, for a dozen years, I was taken in and passed on to students defective reasoning and conclusions. When I reread the 1926 article with a magnifying glass, I perceived it to be blue smoke: Sraffa does not even purport to provide a cogent proof of anything – by suggestion, and implicit appeal to what is legitimate in (Marshallian) *partial* equilibrium methodology, the cases where alterations in composition of demand alter competitive price ratios are minimized. This is not even good Ricardo! Ricardo never expected Bordeaux wine (*vin ordinaire* or select Chateau) to have a price independent of quantity; and he expected a shift in demand toward goods of high labour intensity (soldiers' services) to raise labour's distributive shares. Eatwell and Panico (1987), p. 448) quote without blushing Sraffa's innocent proposal that, since unit costs of production are (sic) 'constant in respect to small variations in quantity produced, . . . the old and new obsolete theory which makes it [price, under variations in demand] dependent on the cost of production alone appears to hold its ground as the best available.' The issue is not whether small changes in an independent variable induce small changes in a dependent variable, but rather whether the instantaneous derivative of the function is negligibly small. The economics profession, while saluting Sraffa (1926) as a classic, has resolutely ignored its novel supply-curve findings.

To underline that my criticisms are not captious, and that the exceptions to Sraffa's claims cannot be discounted as belonging to some 'peculiar' concatenation of industry and firm 'externalities–internalities', I here present an impeccable Marshallian model in which (a) each of *n* goods is produced by transferable labour and a specialized land specific to itself, (b) every person's demand function for each of the *n* goods is strictly independent of every other good's price or quantity (strongly additive independent utilities), (c) for every person the marginal disutility of labour is a strict constant ('objectively' identifiable from market data). The example glaringly contradicts Sraffa's constancy of costs and obeys *all partial* equilibrium requirements (at the same time that it is a *full* general equilibrium model, a congruence Alfred Marshall never quite achieved). See Samuelson (1971c), for more on such a rigorous partial equilibrium as applied to trade theory. Moreover, in the sense of the mathematicians Smale and Thom, the example's properties are *generic* not singular, persisting when industries use the *same* inputs in varying proportions. At the same time that every firm can be regarded as a price taker, a systematic shift in the composition of demand towards some goods and away from othes will systematically raise the market terms of trade of the newly preferred items. The 1926 attempt to fob off on the twentieth century a value taxonomy that was already obsolete in the early nineteenth century can hardly be termed a brilliant failure.

9 *Demand effects when production is joint*

Smith, Longfield, Cournot, Thünen, Mangoldt and Marshall well understood that joint production makes price ratios depend on the composition of demand (even, I may add, in a timeless technology where labour is the sole factor of production). A new taste for mutton lowers the relative price of wool, etc. In 1926 Sraffa never brought these banalities into doubt.

It is a pity therefore that Eatwell and Panico (1987, pp. 449–50) glean the impression from Part II of Sraffa (1960) that the influence of demand composition on relative prices is absent in Part II in the same way that it can be absent from Part I's model involving labour as the sole factor of production and no jointness of production. (See their exact sentence bridging pages 449 and 450 for explicit utterance of their untruth.) Although Sraffa's 1960 treatment of joint production (1) is quite fragmentary, (2) involves a number of non-optimalities and a few errors, and (3) contemplates *special equalities* cases that bias the reader towards overlooking demand influences, Sraffa, as far as I can remember, never explicitly claims the absence of demand influences.

Let me spell out a few examples that negate the Eatwell–Panico contention. To get 1 corn suppose we need either 5 of labour and 1 of land or 2 of labour and 2 of land. (The reader is licensed in all cases to add the requirement that 1 of corn also requires 1/10 of corn as seed, thereby qualifying corn as a bona fide *basic* good.) Assume the interest rate is always zero. (The reader may put in any other constant for the interest rate that is less than 900 per cent per period.) Assume 1 of cloth is producible out of 1 of labour and 1 of corn. Assume steady-state fixed supply of land; and, for the supply of labour, assume either that it also is fixed or that its supply adjusts to fulfil a subsistence real wage in terms of corn.

This is a joint-product model. Land being permanently durable, our 5 of labour and 1 of land can be thought of as producing along with 1 of corn also 1 of land itself. Etc.

Now we must ask whether the terms of trade between corn and cloth are the same when property owners want to consume those goods in 100-to-1 proportions as in 1-to-100 proportions. The answer is strongly in the negative. It is no defence of error to say that the example violates Sraffa's frequent restriction to equality between the number of goods (three for corn, cloth and land) and the number of processes used (three or two depending upon the exact composition of final demands). On some pages of Sraffa (1960, Part II), moreover, that restriction would be self-contradictory.

A less obvious, and therefore more telling example of the narrowness of Part II's treatment of joint production is the following case: 1 of labour and 1 of corn produces 3 of wool and 1 of mutton; alternatively, 1 of labour and 1 of corn can produce 1 of wool and 3 of mutton. 1 of labour and 1/10 of corn produces 1 of corn. (Remark: instead of wool and mutton, the example can be made to involve machines and raw materials.) Sraffa observes a system in being, with three goods being produced by the three feasible processes: the terms of trade twixt mutton and wool, we see from symmetry without boring calculation, is 1-to-1 when final demands for wool and mutton are in exact balance.

Now shift final demand towards a bit more of wool and a bit less of mutton. What happens to P_{wool}/P_{mutton}? Nothing. It remains at 1/1. Eatwell and Panico are apparently (in *this* case) right? No. Only along a facet of *limited* quantitative magnitude does Sraffa contrive a horizontal, so-called *classical* supply curve ss'. Let the final demand for wool move to more than three times the final demand for mutton and the system will *endogenously* cease to use the process that produces relatively much of mutton. Sraffa *endogenously* loses the equality of number of goods and number of processes he provisionally specified initially. What causes the loss? Shifts in composition of demand, the influence Eatwell and Panico thought to deny.[2]

Can counsel for Sraffa and Eatwell and Panico not find a joint-production case in which demand shifts are powerless to alter cost ratios? Yes, I can contrive a weak jointness case in which a generalization of the no-joint-product 1949 non-substitution theorem does obtain. Let the number of goods and feasible processes be specified as equal (already an arbitrary narrowing of reality). Denote by $[a_{ij}]$ the usual *input* coefficient matrix, in this case specified to be positive and square and obeying familiar Hawkins–Simon conditions for being 'productive'. Write the von Neumann *output* coefficient matrix as $[b_{ij}]$, also square and positive in this case.

Now restrict the $[b_{ij}]$ coefficients by requiring that the off-diagonal coefficients all be 'near' to zero; restrict the diagonal terms so that they are all near to the same positive constant, which might as well be unity. In effect, I am saving the day by weakening the degree of jointness of production as near to the vanishing point as will save the face of the argument.

In this contrived case of *diagonal dominance*, the following inverse matrix exists and has all positive coefficients: $[b_{ij} - a_{ij}]^{-1} = [A_{ij}]$. Then, provided the interest rate is sufficiently near to zero, we can be sure that no shift in (positive) *final* demands can induce a shift out of Sraffa's initial regimen of real individual goods costs calculable *from technology alone*.

The example is beautifully contrived to show how limited, not how universal, the costs alone approach to economics must be. (Added in light of Schefold's Comment: There are also cases where $[b - a]^{-1}$ is positive even though b is not diagonally dominant for any choice of units.)

10 *The irrelevance of Sraffa's 'standard commodity'*

Most sceptics of the microeconomics dominant from Smith and Walras to Debreu (1959) and von Neumann (1935–6), understandably, are not virtuosi of matrix inequalities. It is therefore a natural comfort to them to be told that Sraffa (1960) establishes the concept of a *standard* (or reference) basket of commodities. This helps legitimize Ricardo's hankerings for a labour theory of value, and illuminates Marx's parable concerning how competition exploits workers by making each of them work A hours of the day for themselves and B hours for the capitalists, with the *B/A rate of surplus value* (*mehrwert*) somehow 'revealing' the source of profit and its laws of motion under capitalism.

Alas, this too is blue smoke. No substantive deficiency of the labour theory of value is ameliorated by the *standard* commodity concept pioneered in Sraffa (1960). Eatwell and Panico (1987, p. 450) advance no bold claim for the *standard* commodity, admitting its use is redundant once market competition has established the simultaneous equations of equilibrium, conceding that the concept may be too complex, but concluding lamely that 'It has the virtue, however, of being analytically correct'. The 'it' that is correct is not an existent 'revealer' or 'clarifier'. What is correct is only that a square, non-negative indecomposable matrix possesses a unique right-hand characteristic vector whose elements can be used as weights to form a market basket of goods, in terms of which there is defined a (*post factum*) real wage that has a linear trade-off with the profit rate over any interval of the latter where the matrix in question provides the competitively viable technology for a no-joint-product system. No word in this last sentence is omittable. And from that valid sentence no comfort for the labour theory of value can be gleaned – as I shall demonstrate.

Eatwell (1987) pens a separate *Palgrave* item on the *standard* commodity, calling it an illustrating and clarifying ancilliary device, a *Hilfskonstruktion*. My exposition will explicate why I think it can as aptly be called a *roter* herring.

Now to spell out why the concept of the standard commodity is useless to ameliorate the faults of a labour theory of value or to reveal the essence of labour exploitation. The labour theory of value, let it be agreed, is faultless when profits and land scarcity are ignorable. Smith knew that and was too shrewd to try to explain labour exploitation by a model whose correctness comes only when there is no exploitation.

The faults of the labour theory of value include the following:

A *A change in the composition of demand, towards or away from 'relatively labour – land intensive' goods, in real life alters goods' relative prices.* (Sraffa's failure to single this out for notice is inexplicable: his own 1960 Chapter 8 negates his acceptance of Ricardo's belief that the complications of land rent for relative price can be finessed by concentrating on goods produced at the external margin of no-rent land. Where that margin falls is affected *endogenously* by the composition of demand – as many of Ricardo's own paragraphs reveal.)

Even in the Santa Claus case where Sraffa can define a single standard commodity, this fault of the labour theory is *not in the least bit* touched by any use of the standard commodity. QED.

B The 1867 labour theory of value (cum exploitative mark-ups proportional to wages) fails to analyse how the distribution of income – the relative fractional shares of wages, rents, interest – is dependent on the *composition* of demand. Even when all lands are redundant and all rents are zero, and when the profit rate and the subsistence wage vector are somehow frozen, a shift in the composition of capitalists' demands can be expected to alter the profit/wages distributive share. The *standard* commodity is powerless to paper over all these shortcomings. (One exception: in the singular case of equal organic compositions of capital, all price ratios of goods *happen* to agree with ratios of embodied labour contents; relative factor shares *happen* to be invariant to demand shifts; the rate of surplus value *happens* then to be uniform over industries as a consequence of the empirical uniformity of the profit rate; but, on this razor's edge, the transformation problem evaporates and no scientific novelty is introduced by the *Mehrwert* treatment of surplus. Remark: impeccable Sraffa–Leontief steady-state analyses with the interest rate somehow specified *also* underemphasize the role that *supply* of capital goods can play in determining factors' distributive shares.)

C To determine which technical innovations will be competitively viable, the labour theory of value and the 1867 Marxian paradigm of equalized rates of surplus value provide incorrect policy advice and incorrect predictions. After innovation there are definable as many *different* standard commodities as there are square sub-matrices viably choosable from a rectangular matrix. Now, generally, *the system* has no standard commodity: if the concept were able to help Ricardo's defective labour theory – which it cannot do – it would be helpful only in the unrealistic case where at *all* rates the *same* indecomposable set of techniques were competitively viable. Eatwell's *Palgrave* article on the standard commodity (Eatwell, 1987) needs to be augmented by demonstration of how *limited* the economic domain is in which a *standard* commodity can be defined.

Thus joint-product systems generally do *not* possess a *standard* commodity. Neither do systems that have any viable technologies different from their golden rule zero-interest-rate technology. Nor do simple Ricardo systems that are decomposable (labour hunts deer and labour hunts beaver). If a defence of the labour theory were a valid one, how could it self-destruct when certain input coefficients change from epsilon to zero or when certain characteristic vectors become complex numbers? The *standard* commodity is thus seen to be no saviour of a defective labour theory of value. QED.

To prove my various QED's, the reader need only contemplate one example. 1/10 of wheat and 1 of labour (or it could be 1 of land) produce 1 of wheat. 1 of wheat and 1 of labour produce 1 of bread. We need no matrix algebra to identify Sraffa's *standard* commodity as a basket containing only wheat. Every defect in the labour theory of value remains and cannot be erased by any use of the standard concept. The importance of the concept is especially evident in the plausible case where the subsistence wage involves bread, which is not even in Sraffa's market basket!

For later reference, the reader may contemplate an invention that can produce 1 of bread out of 1/6 of labour, 1/2 of bread, and 1 of wheat. The labour theory of value cannot tell us, what is true, namely that only at interest rates below a critical one will this invention be a viable one. Soon I shall show that this non-esoteric situation refutes the Ricardo–Stigler contention that the defective labour theory of value is 'at least 93 per cent accurate'.

D Present-day sophisticated defenders of Marx's paradigms of the labour theory of value *à la* equalized rates of surplus value admit that the 1867 result differs substantively from competitive reality. But they hope to make the case that, somehow, Marx's approximation yields deep *macro*economic insights and 'understanding'. A patient audit of every different such claim, I and members of my MIT seminars have found, leads only to disappointment. Here is but one sample, a famous case in the post-1867 literature.

Marx refers often to an alleged 'law of the falling rate of profit'. Abstractly put, his attempted *deduction* of this law involves the following factorization of the rate of profit

$$r = \text{total profits/ total capital}$$
$$= (\text{profits/wages})\ (\text{wages/total capital}) = A \times B$$

where total capital is the sum of wages advanced plus non-labour items of capital (called 'constant capital'). The thoughtful reader will note that, if this approach is fruitful, it certainly does not presuppose the validity of the odd 1867 hypothesis that labour-intensive industries have the same (profits/wage) ratio that other industries do. The purpose of rehashing this ancient issue here is to show how Sraffa's 1960 paradigm brings into doubt the fruitfulness of Marx's factorization.

Marx's key notion is that modern times usher in a 'rise in the organic composition of capital', which is interpretable as a decline in the second factor of wages/(wages + constant capital), B. Then, provided we can presume that the first factor of 'exploitation' – profits/wages or A – stays the same, we can deduce that the product – the rate of profit – of the two factors falls.

Let us test the cogency of the crucial *ceteris paribus* clause that Marx invokes almost without realizing what is involved. Sraffian analysis will be our measuring rod. Different cases need analysing.

(i) The class struggle raises the wage rate in a fixed-coefficient Sraffa model that lacks land and joint products. In terms of Sraffa's input/output matrix $\mathbf{a}$ and his row vector of direct labour requirements $\mathbf{a}_0 = [a_{01}, \ldots, a_{0n}] = [a_{0j}]$, Marx's factorization involves a monstrously complicated and ambiguous expression. For this thought experiment, as the rate of profit falls from its Sraffian maximum to zero, the factor A does not stay constant in the fashion Marx needs but rather falls monotonically!

(ii) Suppose the interest rate r is falling because of some possible 'deepening of capital' in the Clark–Solow fashion. Should Marx be given credit for an 1867 anticipation and proof of this process and its effects on the profit rate?

Hardly. Only along the singular Cobb–Douglas razor's edge does his fixed A, falling B story apply. For the case where the elasticity of substitution is greater than unity, Marx's A rises as B falls; for the more realistic case where the elasticity of substitution is fractional, Marx's A falls.

(iii) The case of exogenous technical changes is what Marx and most of us think is the most interesting one. By 1867 unsophisticated observers formed the strong impression that innovation and scientific advance had somehow enlarged the role of non-labour inputs relative to direct labour. An enhanced organic composition of capital due to technical change seemed the natural way to describe this – a greater role for dead labour at the expense of live labour would be the Pickwickian Marxian description of this. (Paradoxically, one of Sraffa's greatest contributions was to demonstrate that it is, in general, *not* possible to associate lower interest rates with 'more roundabout', 'more mechanized', more time-consuming modes of production, a finding as fatal to neoclassical parables as to the notion of recognizable shifts in 'the organic composition of capital'.)

Students of von Neumann, Sraffa and Solow know that technical change can either *raise* competitive profit rates or raise real wage rates (or raise both). No law of the (necessarily) declining rate of profit is factually or deductively true. Even empirical presumptions have not been justified by knowledge of economic history.

The remarkable increase in the system's 'productivity' after the industrial revolution can take place with what Marx calls the organic composition of capital falling rather than rising. Sraffa has taught us to recognize 'Wicksell effects', which can be purely pecuniary effects masquerading as technical changes. Exactly the same thing can be said of 'Marx effects', $C/(C+V)$ changes that occur with the same *technical* coefficients at different profit rates.

Above all, the factorization $A \times B$ kept Marx in darkness about the Sraffa–Samuelson truth concerning a competitive economy sans land and joint products: if the profit rate falls, the real wage cannot fall and create worker immiseration; if the real wage falls for *any* reason, the competitive profit rate must rise. Similar truths concerning the real wage and the 1867 rate of surplus value *cannot* be asserted for a competitive economy.

11 *Hollow victory of standard commodity for the transformation problem*

Suppose by singular chance that the subsistence goods vector, which each worker's real wage must be able to buy if the labour supply is to be in stationary equilibrium, involves the various goods in exactly the same proportions as are involved in the standard commodity market basket – a monstrous assumption; and suppose that by singular chance all non-workers choose to consume goods in those same proportions. Or, alternatively, assume that by fortuitous cancellation the deviation of workers' subsistence from the standard vector happens to be just opposite in sign and of exactly the same magnitude as the deviation of the capitalists' consumption vector from the standard vector; in consequence their sum, the total consumption vector, is to be exactly proportionate to the standard commodity.

In this admittedly academic case, not expected remotely to be encountered in any real-life situation, we can draw up for Marx a tableau of steady reproduction expressed in correct prices of production terms. Presumably, he could draw up for himself an alternative tableau expressed in his 1867–85 marked-up values, obeying his usual Volume II conditions of equalized *rates of surplus value* (*Mehrwert*) and *eschewing any explicit* rate(s) of profit.

To *his* values tableau, Marx could in this specially contrived case apply *his* proposed 1894 Volume III algorithm for the transformation problem. The resulting new tableau – known by us and by him generally *not* to be quite the desired correct tableau expressing the true competitive prices data – happens (in our singular case where the physical consumption vector is exactly proportional to Sraffa's existent standard commodity) to match exactly the correct Smith–Walras–Dmitriev–Bortkiewicz–Seton–Sraffa competitive prices tableau. (Newman, Meek, Burmeister and others have provided proof of this essentially matrix theorem, as described in Eatwell, 1987, pp. 478–80, and mentioned in the *Palgrave* article on the transformation problem – Hunt and Glick, 1987, p. 689 – in connection with the 1972 work of Alfredo Medio.)

This singularity-case defence of Marx is generally recognized to be a hollow defence, belonging to the category of argument: 'If my Aunt Sally had wheels she'd be a stage coach but generally, like most aunts, she's only a biped.'

Equally hollow is Marx's suggested device of concentrating on that particular good whose organic composition happens to be precisely that of the whole system. How does one recognize which of the vast array of industries is at (or really near to, and *stays* near to) the social average? And why think that *its* organic composition ratio is measured in Marxian values, c_j/v_j, rather than C_j/V_j whose capital letters denote the (as yet) unknown cum-profit *prices* magnitudes.

12 *Perhaps unintended Sraffian insights concerning Ricardo and Marx: Ricardo*

Most admirers of Sraffa, one discovers, believe that his 1960 classic (a) lends comfort to a Ricardian labour theory of value, and (b) provides a measure of justification for Marx's surplus value novelties of 1867. I believe that a careful reading of *Production of Commodities by Means of Commodities* and sympathetic mathematical extensions of it and of von Neumann's general equilibrium activity model leads to the reverse.

(a) Sraffian analysis confirms that Ricardo's model, shorn of all gratuitous approximations, has to be a three-component model of value: along with the well-understood labour component, there is the subtle interest-rate component and also the land-requirement component. The lost-Atlantis model of 1815 Ricardo, beloved by Kaldor, Sraffa and Garegnani (1987), bears out this contention of mine.

(b) Had the author chosen to apply himself, not only to a critique of 'the marginal theory of value and distribution', but also to a critique of Marx's paradigm of an equalized rate of surplus value by industries (*Mehrwert*), Sraffa's analysis could provide a sharp Occam's razor of demolition.

If my contentions are demonstrable, why the popular beliefs to the contrary? I abstain from attempting an explanation. However, at least two contributing factors can be identified. Piero Sraffa himself wrote in approval of aspects of Ricardo and Marx that are deemed dubious by mainstream historians of economic thought who write in the vein of what I call the Whig history of science (Samuelson, 1987b). A second factor is that Sraffa was critical of neoclassical marginalism and many of his readers were led by that to discern merit in classicism and in the Marxian alternative to mainstream economics.

This present revisionist exposition concerning Sraffa eschews all defence of neoclassism and intends to couch its every basic argument in terms of von Neumann's discrete activities technology. In this I resemble such post-Marxians as Ian Steedman and John Roemer (and, for that matter, Joan Robinson).

Leaving to the next section what is entailed for the Marxian transformation problem by Sraffa (1960), let me here use my scarce time to explicate the failure of Stigler's defence of Ricardo's so-called *93 per cent labour theory of value.*

Stigler (1958) himself agrees with me that Ricardo knew he had to augment the labour component by an interest component to be generally accurate. (For the 1958 date, Stigler is remarkably tolerant toward Ricardo's belief that he could somehow exclude a rent component.) But he quotes Ricardo's numerical example (Ricardo, [1817–21] 1951, p. 36) of goods that differ in their time-roundaboutness, and accepts uncritically Ricardo's inference from the example that the price ratio of two goods could be affected by a feasible change in the interest rate and the wage rate that 'could not exceed 6 or 7 per cent'.

Two years later, after Stigler could have read Sraffa (1960), he could discover that we can pick for Ricardo a non-bizarre numerical example in which a change in the profit rate from 6 per cent to 6.1 per cent could easily alter P_2/P_1 from 1.0 to 10^6 or to 10^{-6}. Moreover, in Sraffa input/output matrices that look entirely plausible, as the interest drops from its von Neumann maximum to zero, a similar price ratio can oscillate by 70 per cent almost as well as by 7 per cent. Ricardo escaped noticing this because his examples are 'Austrian' rather than 'Leontief'. As soon as outputs require other goods and themselves as inputs, the inverse matrices can become very ill-conditioned indeed.

Here is a horrendous example intended to frighten innocent children. To produce coal 1 period from now takes 1 of labour. To produce 1 of rye takes 9/10 of rye and 1/100 of labour. To produce 1 of corn takes 1/10 of corn and 1 of labour. Ricardo observes a profit rate of 10 per cent per period. Now, for some reason the profit rate rises to 11.1 per cent, surely not a fantastic change. Let Ricardo and Stigler calculate how $P_{\text{rye}}/P_{\text{corn}}$ rises from unity to 100. Shall we coin for Ricardo a belief in a 1 per cent theory of value? (And what does the other 99 per cent refer to?)

Here is the 1815 lost-Atlantis corn-to-corn model attributed to Ricardo. 1 of corn a period from now requires 1/10 of corn, N of labour, $1/N$ of land, where N can be any of 1, 2, . . ., 10, 1/2, 1/4. Cloth requires 1 of labour and 1 of corn. When Garegnani (1987) and I calculate its behaviour under various assumptions about the supply of land, the subsistence wage vector, the capitalists' rates of time preference and/or saving propensities, and when we vary the compositions of capitalists' consumption demands, we see that the resulting behaviour are inconsistent with any Marxian or Ricardian labour theories of distribution. Its price ratios alter with composition of demand as in Walras and Debreu and Solow. Indeed, it behaves like 1960 Sraffa, which is my point about it *and* about Sraffa's system.

13 *How Sraffian analysis debunks proposed Marxian transformation problem solutions*

Trojan horses within the Marxian camp are those who get right the economics of competitive price: namely, John Roemer and Ian Steedman, along with Piero Sraffa and Ladislaus von Bortkiewicz. They not only spot what is erroneous in Marx's transformation treatment (Marx, 1894, ch. 9) but perceive that the correct prices solution is achievable only by solving the high-degree Sraffian equations (a 15th degree polynomial if the system consists of fifteen Sraffian *basic* goods, etc.). This establishes the fundamental futility theorem: first solving the 1867 values tableau problem involving an irrelevant inversion of a 15-by-15 zero-profit matrix, and then solving a 1st degree subsistence wage equation, gets you *nowhere* on your search for correct competitive profit rate and correct real-price and price-wage ratios. When I played the role of the Hans Christian Andersen child (Samuelson, 1970, 1971a) and pointed out that the Emperor wore no clothes – showing that from Dmitriev and Bortkiewicz, through Sweezy, Winternitz, Dobb, Meek, Seton, and the rest, the transformation algorithm from 'values' to 'prices' was an 'erase and replace' procedure – no perceptible dent was made on the stable of *Palgrave* writers on kindred topics.

What I call a 'detour' Garegnani (1987, p. 567) calls a 'mistake' by Marx. Garegnani believes that the mistake was a fruitful one because it led Marx (almost) to a correct Sraffian theory of competitive price. Whether this theory of genesis of progress is accepted or rejected, one erases a recognized mistake and desists from perpetuating it.

Lack of time prevents me from applying Occam's razor to various 'new solutions' to the transformation problem – such as that of Duménil, Foley and Lipietz covered in Hunt and Glick (1987, p. 690) or that of Wolff, Roberts and Callari (1982). One puts to them the question 'Cui bono?', and hopes for a better answer than a quotation from Marx of possible relevance. The search for values tableaux that agree in various scalar totals with prices of production tableaux is a sterile search, as Seton (1957) long ago made clear.

14 *The non-optimality of unequalized profit rates*

Although Sraffa does not investigate the problems of *intertemporal efficiency*, his specification of equalized profit rates – as against, for example, equalized 1867 *Mehrwert* rates – can be shown to be a requirement of intertemporal Pareto optimality under capitalism or socialism. If Nobel Laureate Kantorovich were alive today in the age of Gorbachev, his mathematical proofs of this post-Marxian truth would receive the attention they have always deserved. Any critique of 'marginalism' should not blind us to such truths: that would be a case of throwing out the adult along with the bathwater.

15 *Autonomy of truth*

The ideas of a great mind transcend their creator. I cannot honestly affirm that Piero Sraffa would happily accept my revisionist findings concerning his brain-children. But why should I sell short the subtlety and flexibility of that noble economist?

Notes

1 My explorations in Marx's development do not fully concur with Garegnani's. There is no page on which Marx perceives how to solve the matrix *Mehrwert* relations $p = a_0(1 + \mathrm{m}) + pa = (1 + m)a_0[\mathrm{I} - a]^{-1}$. Such a mode of solving therefore cannot be a springboard to a successful solution of the Sraffa relations $P = a_0(1 + r) + Pa(1 + r) = a_0(1 + r)[I - a(1 + r)]^{-1}$. I hail Marx's numerical tableaux of Volume II, but find it odd that my matter-of-fact erase-and-replace explication of the transformation problem should be considered by Professor Garegnani as being in some sense rebutted by the Sraffa (1951) exposition of what I called in the last section Ricardo's lost-Atlantis 1815 paradigm. The 1815 fabrications are what we get by *not* making any detours or mistakes; the price ratio changes induced in the 1815 model by demand–taste changes are precisely what the *Mehrwert* model mistakenly puts at zero. It is a case of 1960 Sraffa against 1867 Marx.

2 Some continental mathematicians contemplate models in which my two processes are replaced by N processes for wool-or-mutton production: thus, add to (3,1) and (1,3) the new processes (3/4, 25/8) and (1/2, 26/8). Begin say with balanced final demand, so that both (3,1) and (1,3) are initially used equally. 'See,' they say, 'Sraffa has two goods (wool and mutton) and two processes used. After Samuelson alters final demand considerably toward wool, he may induce a competitive shift in the use of processes so that (1,3) and (3/4, 25/8) are solely used: *still*, equality of number of goods and processes is *generically* implied; $2 = 2$. So it goes when the yen for wool goes up further. Sraffa is vindicated.' No. Only the face of the argument is saved. And saved but temporarily. Already demand shifts do *endogenously* shift terms of trade – in negation of 'classical' constancy. Furthermore, with the number of von Neumann activities specified to be finite, for large enough specified taste changes, eventually $2 = 2$ is replaced by $2 > 1$. Furthermore, suppose we choose to measure what is 'generic' by a metric that (say) asks what happens when all people choose to spend the fraction of income c on wool and $(1 - c)$ on mutton. Then the borderline point at which one of the processes begins to be substituted for another does not correspond to an interval that is of mathematical measure zero. So, after all, $2 > 1$ is *not un*generic looked at in this possible and relevant way!

Editorial note

Professor Samuelson had been unable to attend the conference but on later request kindly submitted a paper which arrived when the manuscript of the book was going to the press. The paper therefore could not be discussed by all the participants at the conference. The two main Comments and the Reply here offered all had to be written at short notice. The editors are grateful to John Eatwell for agreeing to submit an additional short Comment although it had to be submitted within less than three weeks because of difficulties in communication on the one hand, and commitments to the publisher on the other. It is hoped that the issues will be taken up in a broader discussion in other publications.

Comment

John Eatwell
Cambridge

Having had very little time for the preparation of this Comment, I must confine myself to answering Professor Samuelson's specific criticisms of the articles by Carlo Panico and me (Eatwell and Panico, 1987; Eatwell, 1987), leaving comment on his wider excursions to another occasion.[1]

I will deal first with Samuelson's reference to an 'explicit utterance of untruth' by Eatwell and Panico concerning the effects, in joint-production models, of changes in the composition of output. Second, I will examine his criticism of the Eatwell and Panico discussion of Sraffa's 1926 critique of Marshallian partial equilibrium. Third, I will turn to Samuelson's comments on my *Palgrave* entry on the standard commodity.

Prices and demand

Samuelson refers repeatedly to the Eatwell–Panico 'error'. The error is our supposed contention that 'the influence of demand composition on relative prices is absent in Part II [of Sraffa's *Production of Commodities*] in the same way that it can be absent from Part I's model involving labour as the sole factor of production and no jointness of production' (page 270).

Samuelson cites, as evidence of our error, a single sentence. If this sentence is restored to the passage from which it has been extracted, it will be seen that our argument is totally different from that which Samuelson represents it to be. To avoid ambiguity it is worth quoting our argument in full:

Considerable puzzlement was engendered by Sraffa's statement in the

Preface of his book that 'The investigation is concerned exclusively with such properties of an economic system as do not depend on changes in the scale of production. . . .' (Sraffa, 1960, p. v). The absence of any reference to demand led unsuspecting readers to equate his results with the non-substitution theorem, and hence with the assumption of constant returns to scale. However, a careful reading of Sraffa's analysis reveals that no knowledge of any relationship between *changes* in outputs and *changes* in inputs, or between price and quantity is *necessary* for the solution of the equations, and hence for the determination of the rate of profit and prices (given the wage). This contrasts with neoclassical theory, in which the determination of prices is dependent upon knowledge of the functional relationships between supply and demand. *If, in Sraffa's analysis, quantities should change, then any consequential change in conditions of production will result in changes in prices.*

In Part II of his book, Sraffa extends his analysis to multi-product industries and fixed capital, and to the analysis of economies with more than one non-reproducible input. As might be expected, the analysis is considerably more complex, and in some cases the results less clearcut (the solution of the system may not, for example, be unique, and the definition of basics and non-basics is more abstract than is the case with single-product industries). Yet the basic structure of classical analysis is preserved – the prices, the rate of profit, and other distributive variables (say, land rents) are determined by the conditions of production, given the wage.

(Eatwell and Panico, 1987, pp. 450–1).

The final sentence of the first paragraph (emphasized here) was apparently overlooked by Samuelson. Perhaps we should have repeated it after the second paragraph too – it is the final sentence of that paragraph that he cites but does not quote. If he had quoted it, it would be evident to the reader that nowhere in that sentence is there any reference to the 'horizontal, so-called classical supply curve' or to the 'costs-alone approach' which Samuelson attempts to foist on us.

In Sraffa's analysis, any change in the composition of output that leads to a change in the conditions of production, for whatever reason, will change relative prices. There is no 'costs-alone approach'.

Sraffa's critique of the Marshallian supply curve

Samuelson argues that Sraffa's critique of the use of diminishing returns in the construction of the partial equilibrium supply curve is flawed, and that Panico and I replicate the flaws without comment. I will not deal with Samuelson's example which, interestingly, fulfils exactly the conditions Sraffa laid down for the construction of a partial equilibrium industry supply curve.

Samuelson does not seem to have grasped that Sraffa's critique is exclusively directed at *partial equilibrium* analysis. Producing general equilibrium examples as a critique of Sraffa is an exercise in irrelevance. Moreover, Samuelson fails to take account of Sraffa's own reference to general equilibrium analysis in the 1926 paper. Panico and I make these points (1987, p. 448).

Apart from his contribution in the *Economic Journal* symposium on increasing returns, Sraffa did not participate further in the debate on the Marshallian theory of cost. The reasons are not hard to seek.

First, imperfect competition theory, instead of providing a new, more concrete approach to the analysis of value and distribution, was simply absorbed into neoclassical theory. The fact that imperfectly competitive models do not provide a foundation for a theory of value seemed to enhance the status of partial equilibrium analysis, rather than hasten its rejection; with the competitive theory of value still holding sway at the level of general equilibrium (a neat rationale is provided by Hicks, 1946, pp. 83–4). The survival of the 'U' shaped cost curve as an analytical tool, constructed from the presumption of increasing, then diminishing returns, is in no small part attributable to the longevity provided by models of the imperfectly competitive firm. Nonetheless, the appearance of the 'U' shaped curve in models of the competitive firm, more than sixty years after Sraffa clearly demonstrated the illegitimacy of the construction, is an indication of just how intellectually disreputable theoretical economics can be.

Second, Sraffa's implicit identification of classical and Marxian theory with the notion that competitive value is 'dependent on the cost of production' is clearly wrong, as examination of neoclassical models which take account of 'simultaneous equilibrium in numerous industries' readily demonstrates. Sraffa had deployed general equilibrium reasoning to demolish the theory of the competitive firm and the industry supply curve. Further criticism of neoclassical theory would require consideration of general equilibrium models of value and distribution. And a constructive rehabilitation of classical theory would require a general analysis too. It would require, that is, an analysis of 'the process of diffusion of profits throughout the various stages of production and of the process of forming a normal level of profits throughout all the industries of a country' – the problem Sraffa acknowledged was 'beyond the scope of this article'. (1926, p. 197)

An example of dubious use of the 'U'-shaped cost curve may be found in Samuelson and Nordhaus (1985, p. 479), together with the discussion of 'long-run breakeven conditions' on p. 480. A more accurate discussion of equilibrium of the competitive firm may be found in Samuelson (1947, pp. 75–80).

The standard commodity

Samuelson criticizes my reference (Eatwell, 1987, p. 476) to the standard commodity as a *Hilfskonstruktion*, i.e. a mathematical technique that aids understanding, that clarifies. He then proceeds to 'spell out why the concept of the standard commodity is useless to ameliorate the faults of the labour theory of value or to reveal the essence of labour exploitation' (p. 272). Since neither the labour theory of value nor exploitation are mentioned in my article at all, it is difficult for me to comment on Samuelson's construction.

Whether use of the physical analogue implicit in the standard commodity clarifies the determination of the rate of profit by the simultaneous solution of n equations in a classical system is, I suppose, a matter of taste. But Samuelson's hostility toward the construction of a *Hilfskonstruktion* is a little odd, when his textbook (Samuelson and Nordhaus, 1985) is littered with simple supply and demand diagrams, which he must know are, in a general equilibrium setting, typically false representations of the characteristics of a market. Why doesn't he draw correspondences? Perhaps they would not 'clarify' the argument?

Conclusion

In his introduction, Samuelson refers to 'ideological jockeyings' within our profession.

Ideological messages are often conveyed by a careful use of language. Hence Panico and I do not simply err, we 'quote without blushing', and indulge in 'explicit utterance of untruth'.

Another powerful ideological device is to remove sentences from their context, to misrepresent arguments, or to erect straw men. Samuelson's paper provides examples of all three of these techniques.

Note

1 The short time-span available for this comment precluded consultation with Carlo Panico; hence he is not responsible for my remarks.

Comment

Pierangelo Garegnani
Rome

1. Professor Samuelson's contribution to the present volume is an excellent example of the difficulty that a present-day theoretical economist has in understanding Sraffa's theoretical enterprise. The theoretical approach of Smith and Ricardo had been so totally 'submerged' (Sraffa, 1960, p. v) – as opposed to criticized and found wanting – that its reappearance in Sraffa's terse lines of his introduction to Ricardo's *Works* (Sraffa, 1951), and in the rigorous modern presentation of *Production of Commodities* (Sraffa, 1960), was bound to raise considerable difficulties of comprehension. And the fact that the approach adopted by Sraffa had been developing for over a century

before Ricardo raises, if anything, additional difficulties. The analysis reappears as a comparatively finished product while the process of its development, which is important to its understanding, has been forgotten or goes unrecognized. Ironically, the difficulties would have been less in the case of a completely new theoretical departure, the germs of which would lie in a literature generally known and understood.

Questions of deadlines will prevent me from going as much as I would like into the issues that Professor Samuelson touches with respect both to pure analysis and to interpretation of the classical economists.

1 *The '1926 error'*

2. In his section on 'the fatal 1926 error', Samuelson attributes to Sraffa's *Economic Journal* article of that date the idea that 'the category of *constant* competitive cost constitutes the only empirical box with appreciable content', and comments:

> This is plain wrong . . . as soon as two competitive goods involve different land/labour proportions, the *production possibility* frontier is curved and not straight in the fashion Sraffa needs.
>
> (pages 268–9)

The idea that Samuelson attributes here to Sraffa is not however the one we find in the article of 1926. There is a subtle but all-important difference. Sraffa's argument was not that the category of constant competitive cost constitutes the only box with empirical content. It was that *among the boxes that the conditions of partial equilibrium allow us to consider,*[1] constant costs constitutes the only box with some content.

As Sraffa himself clearly states at the conclusion of his argument, in the passage quoted (only partially) in the Eatwell–Panico essay (1987, p. 448) to which Samuelson refers,

> In normal cases the cost of production of commodities produced competitively – *as we are not entitled to take into consideration the causes which may make it rise or fall* – must be regarded as constant in respect of small variations in the quantity produced.
>
> (Sraffa, [1926] 1953, pp. 540–1; emphasis added)

and Sraffa leaves little doubt about the fact that decreasing returns would be the typical case in a general equilibrium context.[2]

3. Briefly, Sraffa's 1926 argument starts from the fact that

> the point of view [of 'particular equilibrium'] assumes that the conditions of production and the demand for a commodity can be considered in respect to small variations as being practically independent both in regard to each other and in relation to the supply and demand of all other commodities.
>
> (Sraffa, [1926] 1953, p. 538)

Otherwise, the *ceteris paribus* assumption would be violated and, in the face of a change in supply conditions of the commodity – say, a tax or bounty – we could not assume that the demand will remain fixed or that the converse will be true in the case of a shift in the demand schedule.

Now, with respect to Marshallian decreasing returns (rising long-period costs), Sraffa's argument is that, when they do occur in a particular industry, there will generally be an effect of similar magnitude on the costs of other industries as well (Sraffa, [1926] 1953, p. 539). This leaves only two possibilities: (a) abandoning partial equilibrium when the effect of the increased output of the industry on its own costs cannot be ignored; or (b) assuming constant costs also in the industry in question, when the effect on the costs of the related industries is small enough to be compatible with partial equilibrium.

The first case, Sraffa observes, is the one where the output of the industry requires a *considerable* part of the quantity of the factor 'the total amount of which is fixed, or can be increased only at a more than proportional cost' (Sraffa, [1926] 1953, p. 539). In the language of general equilibrium, this case can be described as one where a large difference exists between the proportions in which the factors are employed in the industry expanding its output and the proportions in which the same factors are employed in the industries that will correspondingly have to contract their output.[3] In this case the increase in costs cannot be ignored in the expanding industry, but for exactly the same reason it will not be possible to ignore it either in those other industries in which the factors are used in a proportion close to that of the expanding industry. This will contradict the *ceteris paribus* condition of partial equilibrium.

The second case is where an industry employs only a small part of the 'constant factor' or, more generally, where the proportions of factors in the expanding industry are almost the same as in the contracting industries. Here, the effect on the costs of other industries using proportions of factors close to those of the expanding industry will be small, and so will be the effect on the costs of the industry in question. Then, to the extent that the former can be ignored, as is required by partial equilibrium, it must be likewise ignored in the expanding industry, where we shall accordingly have to assume constant long-period costs (Sraffa, [1926] 1953, p. 539).

As Sraffa summed up his argument in 1925:

> The substance of the argument rests on the fact that the increase in production of a commodity leads to an increase in the cost both of the commodity itself, and of the other commodities of the group. The variations are of the same order of magnitude, and therefore are to be regarded as being of *equal importance*. Either we take into account these variations for all industries of the group, and we must pass from the consideration of the particular equilibrium of a commodity to that of general equilibrium; or else those variations in all industries are ignored, and the commodity must be considered as produced under constant costs. *What is inadmissible is that the equal effects of a single cause are at the same time considered to be negligible in one case, and of fundamental*

> *importance in the other*. However, it is necessary to accept this absurdity if one wishes to give a general, and not an anomalous character, to the supply curve of a product under conditions of increasing costs.
> (Sraffa, [1925] 1964, p. 324; translated in Sraffa, [1925], 1973; emphasis added)

There remains only a third possibility with respect to decreasing returns – the one in which the industry in question employs *the whole* of a scarce factor. This, Sraffa tells us, is the only case in which we can consistently consider increasing costs in the context of partial equilibrium – a case, however, of unlikely occurrence, in as much as partial equilibrium requires the industry to be small when compared with the whole economy (Sraffa, [1926] 1953, pp. 539–40).

Considerations similar to these (which we need not enter into here) are developed by Sraffa for the case of increasing returns.

4. It is surprising therefore to read in Samuelson's paper:

> Sraffa . . . by . . . *implicit* appeal to what is legitimate in . . . partial equilibrium methodology [minimizes] the cases where alterations in composition of demand alter competitive price ratios.
> (page 269; emphasis added)

One is tempted to interpret the word *implicit* as a misprint: clearly, whatever may be 'implicit' in Sraffa's 1926 article, it is not his appeal to partial equilibrium! However, the misprint interpretation will not do, because Samuelson's argument is in effect based on ignoring that appeal. The 'fatal error of 1926' would in fact exist only if Sraffa had been dealing with the supply schedule in conditions of *general equilibrium*.

No less surprising is the argument with which Samuelson attempts then to take care of Sraffa's 'implicit' appeal to partial equilibrium:

> To underline that my criticisms are not captious . . . I here present an impeccable Marshallian model in which (a) each of *n* goods is produced by transferable labour *and a specialized land specific to itself* . . . The example glaringly contradicts Sraffa's constancy of costs and obeys all *partial* equilibrium requirements (at the same time that it is a full general equilibrium model, a congruence Alfred Marshall never quite achieved).
> (page 269; emphasis added)

Rising costs are undoubtedly compatible with partial equilibrium provided each good is produced by a 'land specific to itself', but is that not exactly what Sraffa argues in his third case above?

It is in any case clear that Marshall's partial equilibrium was never meant to deal only, or even chiefly, with cases like the one described by Samuelson (or with a similar one to which Samuelson refers in another article – 1971c, p. 12). Partial equilibrium was meant to be of *general* applicability: it had therefore to be conceived as a sufficient *approximation* to general equilibrium, and *not* as a special case of the latter. (This incidentally explains why Marshall never 'achieved' Samuelson's congruence between partial and general equilibrium; that congruence was the opposite of what Marshall intended to achieve, as it would have made the partial equilibrium method useless.[4,5])

5. The fact that we can today so lightly dismiss partial equilibrium in scholarly articles (though not in elementary textbooks) is perhaps a sign of the resigned acceptance of the inapplicability of contemporary mainstream pure theory to the concrete problems for which partial equilibrium was designed – it is a sign, that is, of the descent of pure theory towards 'rhetoric', to use Samuelson's word. That was not yet so in 1926, when Sraffa concluded the argument I have reported with:

> If diminishing returns arising from a 'constant factor' are taken into consideration, it becomes necessary to extend the field of investigation so as to examine the conditions of simultaneous equilibrium in numerous industries: *a well-known conception, whose complexity, however, prevents it from bearing fruit, at least in the present state of our knowledge, which does not permit of even much simpler schemata being applied to the study of real conditions.*
>
> Sraffa ([1926] 1953, p. 541; emphasis added)

And in the 1933 *Review of Economic Studies*, Umberto Ricci, a practitioner of general equilibrium who, together with Barone, had accurately studied the mathematical relations between Marshallian partial equilibrium and Walrasian general equilibrium, would still write in an article on 'Pareto and pure economics':

> But when we have . . . paid the tribute due to the authors of one of the most outstanding creations of human thought, we are compelled to limit the field of its application. The whole apparatus gives somewhat the impression of a magic castle, satisfying to the imagination, but of little assistance in solving the housing problem. In more prosaic language the theory remains abstract and without grip . . . Among the theories of equilibrium enshrined in the formidable apparatus of the formulae of [Pareto's] *Manuel d'économie politique*, . . . there is to be found no bridge leading to nine-tenths of the problems which economists set themselves . . . we can by no means afford to put aside the theory of particular equilibrium as developed by Marshall and his many followers . . . Pareto himself, the most jealous custodian of the theory of general economic equilibrium, the most sarcastic belittler of literary economics, the less sarcastic but no less resolute adversary of the theory of particular equilibria, was compelled to forget general equilibrium when he was writing his superb chapters on applied economics.
>
> (Ricci, 1933, pp. 20–1)

Today's intertemporal general equilibrium is surely no less of a 'magic castle' than the Walrasian and Paretian general equilibria of 1933.

2 *Demand and prices*

6. In the article of 1926, Sraffa was in effect still moving largely within the ambit of marginal theory. The classical economists were seen through Marshallian eyes, as assuming horizontal long-period supply functions which allowed them to ignore the effects of demand on prices. This was a misleading picture of classical analysis, as we now know thanks to Sraffa himself. (By that picture, Marshall was in fact attributing to the classical economists an influence of demand on prices *through* distribution and costs, and was therefore taking for granted a demand and supply theory of distribution.)

However, the article needed a follow-up: it had left open the question as to what was to be done beyond that 'first approximation' of constant costs. And the indications given by Sraffa made it difficult to see how further progress could occur within the accepted stream of ideas. Thus, decreasing returns, when important enough, were thought to require turning to general equilibrium – but at the same time that conception was ruled out as being 'too complex to bear fruit'.

In fact, the solution toward which Sraffa was feeling his way lay in a direction entirely different from that of Walras and Pareto: it consisted of a re-examination of the theory of distribution, a line absent from the 1926 article.[6] This re-examination and the associated revival of the classical theory of distribution and relative prices is what emerges in (1951) and (1960).

7. It is not therefore surprising that Samuelson, who looks at *Production of Commodities* (1960) in the terms of marginal theory, should see limitations in Sraffa's treatment of the effects of demand on prices. However what is in fact there is just a *different* way of dealing with the interaction between prices and outputs.

What is perhaps more surprising is that Samuelson should have expected to find there the demand functions of mainstream theory. Had not the criticism of capital theory been promoted by Sraffa and, in particular, by that very book (1960)?[7] And was not that criticism aimed at the explanation of distribution in terms of demand and supply of factors – as Samuelson himself did not fail to see on some occasions?[8] On the other hand, it will be agreed that the mainstream determination of the prices of commodities by their demand and supply functions is one and the same thing as that theory of distribution. (The Samuelson whom we have just seen insisting on increasing costs for commodities – the direct expression of a demand and supply equilibrium in the market for factors – is certainly well aware of this.) It would therefore seem reasonable to expect Sraffa's criticism of the traditional concept of capital (1960) to be accompanied by some different treatment of the interaction between outputs and prices.

8. In my contribution to this volume (Chapter 5), I have in fact attempted to clarify how outputs can influence prices in the context of the theories of the classical economists and Sraffa. I have there pointed out how the principal mechanism by which outputs influence prices in marginal theory – changes in relative outputs giving rise to changes in factor prices and hence in commodity prices – is absent in classical theory. This is because their different theory of the distribution between wages and profits (sketched in section 2 of my

paper) allowed them, and Sraffa, to take the real wage (or the rate of profits) as given when determining prices.[9]

In the classical theories, therefore, demand functions and outputs could be conceived to affect prices *only through variable returns to scale and joint production*. However, the introduction of demand functions for the latter determination meets, among others, the difficulty that the level of individual incomes can no longer be defined by anything like the equilibria of demand and supply for factors. Thus it is difficult to see how commodity demand functions can even be constructed at a general theoretical level. It appears that, as a result, the outputs will have to be dealt with by the different two-stage procedure which was essentially that of the classical economists (see my paper, par. 31). We determine the effect on prices of the change in our independent variable while taking the outputs as given (p. 130) (or as the independent variable in question). Then, at a second logical stage, we can consider the effects on the outputs of the change in both the prices and the independent variable causing them (say a rise in wages). At that second stage we can also consider, where necessary, the effects of those output changes back on the prices, etc.

9. This is the procedure that is reflected in Sraffa's (1960) treatment of the outputs of the several commodities as data. Instead Samuelson reads there an 'inexplicable' failure to single out that 'a change in the composition of demand, towards or away from relatively labour – land intensive goods, in real life alters goods' relative prices', and he continues:

> [Sraffa's] own 1960 Chapter 8 negates his acceptance of Ricardo's belief that the complications of land rent for relative price can be finessed by concentrating on goods produced at the external margin of no-rent land. Where that margin falls is affected *endogenously* by the composition of demand – as many of Ricardo's own paragraphs reveal.
>
> (page 272)

In fact, Ricardo's idea about how to avoid the complications of land rent is irrelevant. What counts is only the possibility of taking outputs as given. When the position of the marginal land depends on distribution and relative prices, prices can be easily determined once outputs are given – just as they can under Ricardo's simplified hypothesis. What is relevant is whether, as a part of the two-stage classical analysis indicated above, outputs can be taken as given when determining prices, or have instead to be determined simultaneously with prices on the basis of the traditional demand functions.

The same considerations apply to the 'narrowness' Samuelson attributes to Sraffa's treatment of joint production (pages 270–1). Sraffa has in fact no need for special cases where prices are independent of outputs. He can quite well take care of how prices change with outputs i.e. with the 'effectual demands' of the classical authors. Of course, joint production raises the additional problem of the equality between the number of processes and the number of commodities. This equality is the normal case, as Schefold (1985a) has argued, and would seem clear once we realize, for example, that highly substitutable commodities should be treated as a single commodity in this respect (the price of mutton in the wool–mutton case certainly has much to do with the price of beef, and therefore with its process of production).

3 *Standard commodity*

10. One of the surprising features of Samuelson's paper is that he seems to view the standard commodity as intended to validate the labour theory of value (page 271) – and not in the sense that the standard commodity allows one to measure the aggregates of commodities entering the determination of the rate of profits independently of distribution, just as the labour theory of value allowed Ricardo and Marx to do. From Samuelson's argument one might gather that the intended validation is that of the principle that commodities exchange according to the quantity of labour required for their production.

Thus, for example, after showing that relative prices do depend on distribution (the rate of profits), contrary to the labour theory of value, Samuelson concludes:

> even . . . where Sraffa can define a single standard commodity, this fault of the labour theory is *not in the least bit* touched by any use of the standard commodity.
>
> (page 272; similar passage on pages 273–4 and *passim*)

The obvious reaction to this statement is: how could the standard commodity touch that? Who said the contrary? (Samuelson gives no precise references). One would imagine that any such error, should anybody have made it, could be quickly disposed of by pointing out that the standard commodity can only do what numéraires can do, that is, modify the absolute expression of prices, and above all, the *shape* of key relations like the wage–profits curve (of which more presently), but certainly not alter the ratios in which commodities exchange.[10]

11. I shall therefore confine myself here to what Samuelson has to say on the standard commodity as such, leaving until later his remarks concerning the labour theory of value.

The starting point here must be that the 'standard system' is not there to validate anything in particular. It is there to render 'more transparent' what is valid independently of it, that is, the properties of the system – just what changes of the 'coordinate system' (of which the standard commodity is one particular instance) are generally intended to do in any science.[11] The standard commodity and system do in fact provide an extremely simple expression of the relationship between wages and profits, and any mathematician would be surprised indeed if that expression were not to make the study of that relationship easier and more complete – whether the measurement of wages in terms of the standard commodity were to be the ultimate one, or only an intermediate step in an analysis where wages are ultimately measured in terms of other commodities.[12]

Moreover, as I have argued (Garegnani, 1987, p. 569, and 1984, p. 312), this expression of the relationship between wages and profits can be obtained by means of the simple mental picture of a known physical net product, to be divided between wages and profits, with the rate of profits originating from the proportion that the corresponding physical share of the net product bears to the equally known physical amount of capital. As a result, the mutual dependence between the wage rate and the rate of profits *is seen at a glance*. And Samuelson is undoubtedly aware of how arriving at known conclusions by a more direct and easily comprehensible route has often been of fundamental importance in science. (Some aspects of analytical geometry reflect the need for a visual representation of mathematical relations that could conceivably be treated independently of it, but I doubt Samuelson would think that these aspects of analytical geometry are useless.)

In that same article (1984), I provided some examples of that increased transparency, and correspondingly better grip over the properties of the system. One example in point was the property stated in a non-substitution theorem by Samuelson himself (Samuelson, 1966a). According to this, in a system of single-product industries, once the rate of interest (profits) is given, the real wage also is: a theorem that would have been unnecessary if the conception of the standard system had been known and in current use.

12. We may now proceed to some of the more detailed points raised by Samuelson on the standard commodity.

A. Contrary to what Samuelson holds (pages 271–3), there appears to be no reason at all why a standard commodity (system) should be said to exist only when the same set of methods of production, one for each commodity (the same 'technique' in the common terminlogy, or the same 'system of production' in Sraffa's own terminology), is in use over the entire range of possible wage and profit rates (pages 271–3) – just as there is no reason at all why we should say that Samuelson's 'factor-price frontier' for one particular technique or system of production exists only under such conditions. These theoretical constructs are intended to exhibit some properties of the system of production to which they relate, and this both in the interval (intervals) of r where the system is the most profitable, and where it is not.[13] The latter intervals are of no less theoretical interest than the former – for example, in ascertaining why the system of production in question is dominated by a second one.[14]

B. The fact that the standard commodity does not coincide with the basket of goods that workers will buy (Samuelson, e.g., page 273) seems to be of little relevance, once the use of that composite commodity is properly understood. It is not only that, owing to Sraffa's treatment of it as dependent variable, the surplus wage can be measured as an abstract value quantity and therefore also in terms of the standard commodity (Sraffa, 1960, p. 33; see also Garegnani, 1984, p. 322). It is above all that the standard commodity and system may be of use even when the wage has ultimately to be measured in a different commodity (just as the treatment of an ellipsis with its centre in the origin of the Cartesian coordinates may be useful for the analysis of an ellipsis in any position whatsoever).

C. Subsistence goods will be present in the standard commodity as soon as we consider the wage variable as consisting only of its surplus element. This takes care of the necessity for an 'indecomposable' matrix of input coefficients, which Professor Samuelson sees as a limitation of the standard commodity (page 272). In fact what is required is not properly the 'indecomposability' of the matrix, but only that such a matrix should possess an irreducible sub-matrix, corresponding to what are in economic terms a group of 'basic' products (entering, that is, directly or indirectly the production of all other commodities). Now, the treatment of subsistence goods as means of production ensures that they all become 'basic commodities', so long as labour directly or indirectly enters the production of all goods.

D. We may, however, conclude our argument on the standard commodity on a lighter tone, by noting how Samuelson ends up by apparently granting to the standard commodity more than its due. He refers (page 275) to a single-product industries case where the actual economy coincides with Sraffa's 'standard system'. The rate of profits can there be reckoned as the ratio between the physical profits and the physical capital, both consisting of standard commodity. It can therefore be also reckoned in terms of the quantities of labour embodied in the two aggregates. This would undoubtedly validate Marx's determination of *the rate of profits* in the so-called 'transformation problem'. However, Samuelson goes further and writes:

> to *his* values tableau, Marx could in this specially contrived case apply *his* proposed 1894 Volume III algorithm for the transformation problem. The resulting new tableau . . . happens (in our singular case . . .) to match exactly the correct Smith–Walras–Dmitriev–Bortkiewicz–Seton–Sraffa competitive prices tableau.
>
> (pages 275–6)

If Samuelson means what he appears to state in the passage, he is not correct: the prices that Marx would obtain by applying the correct rate of profits to the quantities of labour embodied in the variable and constant capitals cannot generally be the correct prices.[15]

4 *The labour theory of value*

13. We may now proceed to Samuelson's remarks on the labour theory of value. His present views are in all essential respects identical to those he expressed a decade and a half ago during a well-known debate in the *Journal of Economic Literature* (1971–74) on Marx's economic theory. At the close of that debate he had thrown a challenge to anybody to offer evidence that

> [Marx's] novel analytical innovations concerning positive equalized rates of surplus value are other than a detour *to one who would understand 19th-century or earlier-century distribution of income* . . . If I am wrong in my answer to this question – which has been *the* number one question among pro- and anti-Marx analysts from 1867 to the present-day – presentation of some new and cogent argumentation controverting my contention can dispose of it.
>
> (1974a, p. 69; emphasis added)

Elsewhere (Garegnani, 1986), I have pointed out that the basis for such a 'cogent argumentation' had in fact been advanced by Piero Sraffa in his 1951 Introduction to Ricardo's *Principles*.[16] There Sraffa (pp. xxx–xxxvii) gave textual and logical evidence to the effect that Ricardo had arrived at the labour theory of value of the *Principles* in order to overcome a central logical error in Adam Smith's *Wealth of Nations*. The error was that, in many parts of his great work, Adam Smith had failed to see the constraint that binds the rates of wages, profits and rents and prevents each such rate from varying without affecting the others.[17] If that is so, it is of course natural to think, and is in fact borne out by considerable evidence both textual and logical,[18] that Marx, who placed that constraint at the centre of his theoretical work, developed Ricardo's 'law of value' for that very same basic analytical purpose (Garegnani, 1987, pp. 567–8; also 1984, pp. 305–9): hardly a 'detour' then.

14. Adam Smith's error emerges when, for example, the real wage is determined by subsistence requirements, as described in Chapter VIII of the *Wealth of Nations*, while the rate of profits is left to be determined (in Chapter IX) by the 'competition' of capitalists.[19] This error appears to be the result of viewing the price of a commodity as somehow capable of accommodating the change in one of those variables without a necessary change in some of the others.[20]

Ricardo was able to see through those misleading appearances, at first by means of the corn wage underlying the principle he used that 'it is the profits of the farmer that regulate the profits of all other trades' (e.g. Ricardo, 1951–73, VI, p. 104, IV, p. 23) – what Samuelson calls the '1815 lost–Atlantis model of Ricardo' (see par. 18 below). As Sraffa has argued, that principle had its rational foundation in the assumption that wages (and therefore, for Ricardo, the entire capital ultimately used there – see Garegnani, 1984, p. 300) consists entirely of corn. Then:

> in agriculture the same commodity, namely corn, forms both the capital (conceived as composed of the subsistence necessary for the workers) and the product; so that the determination of profit by the difference between total product and capital advanced, and also the determination of the rate of this profit to the capital, is done directly between quantities of corn without any question of valuation . . . It follows that if there is to be a uniform rate of profit in all trades it is the exchangeable values of the products of *other* trades relatively to their own capitals (*i.e.* relatively to corn) that must be adjusted so as to yield the same rate of profit as has been established in the growing of corn; since in the latter no value changes can alter the ratio of product to capital, both consisting of the same commodity.
>
> (Sraffa, 1951, p. xxxi)

If we simplify by assuming that capital consists entirely of wages advanced for a single year, we may see the agricultural rate of profits (and therefore the general rate of profits in the economy) as given by

$$r_{\mathrm{A}} = \frac{P - \mathrm{N}}{N} \tag{1}$$

where P is a given amount of corn output and N is the wages (also a quantity of corn) for the quantity of labour required to produce it on the least-fertile land under cultivation (that which yields no rent).[21]

It is then clear that the rate of profits is determined once the real wage (a quantity of corn) is given, since the quantity of labour required to produce the quantity P of corn being given, N will also be given. Smith's 'competition of capitalists', is seen to have no influence at all on the rate of profits. Nor can the rate of profits be raised, as Malthus suggested, by an increased demand for commodities from the landowners. The rate of profits can rise only because of either a reduction in the corn wage or an improvement in the conditions of cultivation of the least fertile land in use.

15. However, it was not long before Malthus pointed out that, once forms of capital other than corn are taken into account, the rate of profits in agriculture must depend on relative prices just as it does in the other sectors. I have dealt elsewhere (Garegnani, 1982c, pp. 76–7) with Ricardo's struggle with that problem in the spring of 1815. The conclusion he reached was that exchange of commodities according to the labour required to produce them could be a reasonable assumption from which to begin. To that extent, both the social product P and the necessary consumption N could be taken as known in terms of labour embodied, and the profit rate could then be calculated according to equation (1) above.

Marx inherited this problem and its difficulties from Ricardo. Ricardo had had to assume that, when measured in terms of a commodity requiring a constant quantity of labour, the value of commodities 'in the production of which no additional quantity of labour is required' remained constant as the wage (or the difficulty of producing the wage goods) increased (Ricardo, 1951–73, I, e.g., pp. 100–103). He had, however, also to admit that the resulting fall in the profit rate would affect the relative prices of all commodities, and, therefore, also their value relative to his standard, thus running the risk of contradicting his very premise and of arguing in a circle.

What Marx attempted was to develop and systematize the procedure by which Ricardo himself had been trying to overcome the difficulty – that is, by measuring 'values' in terms of a commodity that would require a constant quantity of labour to be produced and would be an average (a 'medium') with respect to the proportions of capital to labour it required.[22] Measured in terms of such a commodity, the value of the social product would not change as wages changed and would be equal to the quantity of labour it embodies relative to that embodied in the standard. Ricardo hoped that the change in the general rate of profits might then be determined without reasoning in a circle, and might accordingly be used to ascertain the associated variations in the relative prices of the individual commodities. And this is fundamentally what Marx attempted to do in the so-called transformation problem.

16. The labour theory of value of Ricardo and Marx appears, therefore, to have been the analytical tool that allowed them to arrive at the necessary link that binds, one to another, the rates of renumeration of the productive resources (Garegnani, 1984, pp. 302–3; 1987, pp. 566–7); hardly a detour, therefore, especially '. . . to one who would understand 19th-century or earlier-century distribution of income'. (That link is in fact the same one that

Samuelson was to stress, nearly a century and a half later, in terms of the 'non-substitution theorem' referred to above.)

Equally doubtful appears to be Samuelson's 'erase-and-replace' thesis (page 278) – the one, that is, that he states (1971a, p. 921) when he envisages Marx's 'values' and his 'prices of production' as 'two alternative and discordant systems', and proceeds then to argue that Marx's 'famous transformation problem . . . is seen to involve returning from the unnecessary detour taken in volume I's analysis of values' to what elsewhere in the same article is called 'conventional economic theory' (1971a, p. 399).[23]

Here Samuelson overlooks two important points. The first is that, far from being 'an alternative and discordant system' with respect to 'prices of production', the quantities of labour embodied were seen to be an integral part of the latter system, and as necessary in order to determine the rate of profits without which prices would have remained indeterminate – so far as Marx and Ricardo could see at the time.

The second strictly related point is that Samuelson fails to realize how 'the conventional economic theory' of Marx's time was certainly no more aware than Marx of the fact that the price equations were sufficient to bring out the necessary relation between the real wage and the rate of profits. To the extent that the other authors did not refer to Ricardo's and Marx's labour theory of value (or to the conclusions derived on that basis) and instead confined themselves to prices, they went back to ignoring that necessary relation. Far from providing a more correct theory to which Marx could return after his 'detour' on the labour theory of value, they were in fact providing what Samuelson must admit to have been a logically inconsistent account of prices and distribution. Certainly, after Sraffa, Marx could be anywhere, except back to the point where Smith was (Samuelson, page 264)!

In fact, as I have argued (1987, p. 567; 1984, p. 305), Marx's clarification and development of Ricardo's discussion of the average commodity was an important step forward towards a more exact solution. Marx makes it clear in the manuscripts that became Volume III of *Capital* that he recognized his own arithmetical examples to be inaccurate – in so far as the prices of production are not applied there to the commodity inputs and wages, as well as to the outputs. Thus he anticipated (though he did not himself take) the next necessary step forward, the correctly formulated system of simultaneous price equations (Garegnani, 1984, pp. 307–8).[24]

17. Samuelson is, on the other hand, attempting to crash through a door wide open to welcome him when he tells us of a non-bizarre numerical example in which a small change in distribution causes relative prices to change, quite contrary to what would happen if commodities exchanged according to the quantities of labour embodied. Having dabbled myself with such numerical examples (Garegnani, 1970a, pp. 428–35), I am of course far from surprised. In fact, I greet Samuelson's own example with great pleasure, since the 'innocent children' likely to be frightened by it ought to be those belonging to the stable of the 'MIT writers', rather than to that of the 'Palgrave writers' (Samuelson, page 278).

The fact is that if the relative prices of commodities pertaining to each system of production did not change with distribution, and commodities exchanged in proportion to the quantities of labour required to produce them, the propositions of traditional capital theory associated with the equality between marginal product and rates of remuneration, would all hold.[25] (Indeed, Samuelson himself once argued (1962) for a 'surrogate capital' which rested entirely on the labour theory of value and felt then tempted to assert that the results could be generalized; Garegnani, 1970a, pp. 414–16). Paradoxical as it may at first seem the failure of the principle that commodities exchange according to the quantities of labour embodied is of less consequence for the theory of the classical economists and Marx. In fact, the role of the labour theory of value in Ricardo and Marx was fundamentally that of providing a basis for defining an average commodity by which to bring to light the relation between wages and profits. That role is compatible, in principle, with the individual commodities not exchanging according to the quantities of labour embodied. Indeed, Marx himself would have remained quite unperturbed by Samuelson's 'horrendous' example. The ratios in exchange between the commodities as determined by Marx can also change quite freely with distribution.

18. Before concluding on the labour theory value, let me deal with what Samuelson calls the '1815 lost-Atlantis corn-to-corn model attributed to Ricardo' (page 277 and *passim*). The intended implicit reference is probably to the 'lost papers on . . . capital' to which Sraffa refers in (1951), pp. xxxi–ii. Unfortunately, the romantic aura Samuelson attributes to those papers is spoilt by the fact that, unlike for the Lost Continent, for the Lost Papers we do have a quite down-to-earth record: Trower's letter to Ricardo of 8 March 1814, where Trower says he has seen and read the *actual thing*.

The thesis that seems to underlie Samuelson's references to the 'lost-Atlantis model', or '1815 fabrications' (page 279), so far as I can see, finds little support in the results of the literature on the question. I believe it would be fair to say that Sraffa's textual evidence has been strengthened, if anything, in the course of that discussion.[26] But of course, if Samuelson or others have new textual or logical arguments to the contrary, they would be welcome to come forth in an open discussion on this as well as on other aspects of the interpretation of the classical economists. That discussion, I am sure, would be useful for all concerned.

5 *Conclusions*

19. Finally, before concluding, let me comment on some minor points in Samuelson's paper.

In connection with Sraffa's degree dissertation (which was printed for private circulation, and not 'published'), the statement by Eatwell and Panico, referred to by Samuelson, according to which 'the *normal* value of a currency is completely 'conventional', i.e. it can be at *any* level that common opinion expects it to be' (Eatwell and Panico, 1987, p. 447) needs better focusing. What Sraffa holds to be completely 'arbitrary' (rather than 'conventional') is the *legal* and not the *normal* value of the currency:

> It is suppose that the currency should normally be worth the weight of gold fixed by law . . . but that value is completely arbitrary and . . . is no more normal than any other value the currency may assume.
>
> (Sraffa, 1920, p. 42; my translation)

As for the true normal value of the currency, Sraffa holds it to be that for which 'no force exists tending to make it change' (ibid.).

The dissertation is evidently the work of a brilliant undergraduate (students in Italy were and still are asked to write a dissertation for the BA degree) who, however, has not yet begun his systematic advanced studies of economics and has therefore all the caution that a serious student has in such conditions. Thus, with respect to a role of the government in the distribution of income, what we find in the dissertation is the remark that, in the processes of war inflation considered there, wages adjust more slowly than prices – and the bright student emerges in the less conventional remark that the same need not be the case in a process of deflation. There the initiative for the adjustment rests with the entrepreneurs who, contrary to the workers, whose standard of living has no absolutely rigid lower limit, do have the rigid lower limit of the expenses of production which, if not covered by the sale price, make it convenient for them to suspend production, with the result that they will generally be able to force the workers to accept a cut in their monetary remunerations (Sraffa, 1920, pp. 40–1).

20. For the reasons mentioned at the beginning of this Comment, Sraffa is a very difficult author. The difficulty is made even greater than it needs be, because Sraffa's work has in effect been so little discussed on its own terms. Professor Samuelson is therefore to be thanked for what we must hope will be the beginning of a fuller discussion – a beginning that, like all beginnings, is bound to suffer from the fact that the necessary clearing of the ground has yet to be effected.

Acknowledgements

I wish to thank Dr R. Ciccone, Professors A. Roncaglia, F. Vianello of Rome University, and Dr G. Mongiovi of the New School for Social Research in New York for helpful comments on a first draft of this paper.

Notes

1 Sraffa's expression is 'particular equilibrium'. I have here adopted the more generally accepted, if less exact, denomination of 'partial equilibrium'.

2 In fact, in a letter to Keynes of 8 June 1926 (quoted in Roncaglia 1978, p. 12), Sraffa explicitly rejects the very interpretation we find in Samuelson's paper: '[my] conclusion has been misunderstood and taken to imply that in actual life constant returns prevail . . . of course in reality the connection between cost and quantity produced is obvious. It simply cannot be considered by means of the system of particular equilibria for single commodities in a regime of competition devised by Marshall.'

3 Here a question arises into which it is not possible to go deeper on this occasion. It was generally accepted at the time that the Marshall *ceteris paribus* assumption implied constant quantities produced of the other commodities (e.g. Barone, 1894, reported in Sanger, 1895; also Ricci, 1933). This raises the question of where the factors required for the increased output of the industry we are studying would come from within a theory where the factors are taken to be fully employed. The reply appears to rest largely on the fact that that increase in output is assumed to be small (as stressed by Marshall and recalled by Sraffa in the passage above), so that the decreases in the output of the other industries that do in fact occur are so small (say, about 1/1000 of the already small change in the industry concerned if there were about 1,000 industries) that they can be ignored. The condition about the specialized factor 'causing decreasing returns' can then be translated into the now more familiar form of the *different proportions* in which the quantities of factors will generally be employed in the expanding industry when compared with the contracting industries.

4 I have recalled elsewhere (Garegnani, 1987, para. 6, p. 563) Marshall's basic methodological position according to which 'the function of analysis and deduction in economics is not to forge a few long chains of reasoning . . . but to forge rightly many short chains and single connecting links' (Marshall, 1961, Appendix C).

5 Indeed, Samuelson himself implies a *general* applicability of partial equilibrium when he faces the problem of inducing laymen to accept as plausible the modern apparatus of demand and supply. He does accept there the basis of Sraffa's argumentation: 'other things equal . . . specifically this means that as we change wheat's price, we must not at the same time change family income, or the price of the competing product or anything else that would tend to shift the demand schedule for wheat' (Samuelson, 1973, p. 66).

6 At the end of the 1926 article Sraffa writes: 'the influence [of a normal level of profits throughout all the industries] on the formation of the prices of single commodities is relatively unimportant and [its] consideration is therefore beyond the scope of this article' (Sraffa, [1926] 1953, p. 550). However, where the problem of distribution indirectly emerges, in connection with the influences of the changed outputs on the prices of factor services, the solution remains the received Marshallian one, based on the equilibrium between demand and supply of factors.

7 The first expression of this criticism to appear in print was Joan Robinson's (1953–4); regarding the derivation of that criticism from Sraffa's work, see Robinson (1973), pp. 144–5.

8 For example, with reference to 'reswitching' and 'reverse capital deepening', Samuelson wrote: 'Such perverse effects do have consequences . . . stability and uniqueness problems may be raised for a Solow–Harrod growth model' (Samuelson, 1966b, p. 578), where the model in question, taken in its basic building block affected by these 'perverse' effects, is simply the long-period equilibrium of marginal theory. I cannot enter here into the question of how this criticism also affects, besides that long-period equilibrium, the 'temporary' and 'intertemporal' equilibria of contemporary theory. (It would, however, seem intuitively clear that instabilities of the long-period equilibria will show up in the sequence of the short-period equilibria of the contemporary versions.)

In this connection we may incidentally note how the situation here referred to as 'long-period equilibrium', characterized by a uniform rate of return on the supply prices of capital goods, seems to be taken by Samuelson as equivalent to a 'steady-state analysis' (e.g. page 273), with which it has in fact little in common (on the difference between the two, and on the origin of the present-day tendential identification of the two, see Garegnani, 1976a, pp. 27, 33n). In fact Samuelson appears to view Sraffa's analysis as a steady-state analysis. However, as I have argued in my Comment on Asimakopulos in this volume (Chapter 10), Sraffa's analysis cannot be qualified as relating to an economy stationary or in steady growth, any more than the analyses of Smith, Ricardo and Marx can.

9 We may note in this respect a passage in Samuelson, page 270 above, where he refers to Part I of Sraffa (1960) as a 'model involving labour as the sole factor of production' and he implies that this (together with constant returns to scale) is why demand need not be introduced to determine prices there. This is surprising. Produced means of production are present in Part I of Sraffa (1960), and a positive rate of profits (interest) is paid on them. It is therefore a situation that should be described as one in which there are several factors of production, that is, labour and capital, or labour and the several capital goods, or the several 'dated quantities of labour'. However, what Samuelson may mean is that, since a supply of capital goods is not introduced by Sraffa with a determining role, then it is *as if* there were only one scarce factor – labour (see, for example, Samuelson, page 270 above). If that is what Samuelson means by his 'one-factor' passage, he is incorrect: the 'supply of capital goods' is not present in Sraffa because of the different classical theory of distribution, and not because of any 'underemphasis' of the role of such supply. And the reason why demand does not affect prices is that different theory of distribution, and not any one-factor hypothesis.

10 For the neat criticism of a claim concerning the relations between standard commodity and labour theory of value, advanced in Burmeister (1984), and similar to that by Samuelson I mentioned in the text, see Kurz and Salvadori (1987).

11 See, for example, Rosenbaum (1963), ch. IV, p. 89. I owe the above observation about the generality and importance in mathematics of the method of changes in the coordinates system to Professor Figá Talamanca of Rome University.

12 For instance, I personally found it easy to demonstrate by means of the standard commodity that at any rate of profits *above* the maximum, the wage and prices cannot all be positive (Garegnani, 1976c, p. 427).

13 Cf. the preceding footnote.

14 The fact that the straightline wage–profits curve corresponding to the standard commodities of each alternative system cannot be drawn in the same diagram, whereas the wage–profit curves drawn for a wage measured in a common commodity can, seems hardly relevant. What is relevant is the usefulness of the standard commodity for the analysis *of the system it pertains to*.

15 This can be immediately seen by assuming that constant capital consists of a commodity (a), say 'steel', and variable capital consists of commodity (b), say 'corn'. The relative price p_a/p_b as correctly determined by estimating the capital in price terms is

$$\frac{p_a}{p_b} = \frac{(1+r)\,(c_a p_a + v_a p_b)}{(1+r)\,(c_b p_a + v_b p_b)} = \frac{c_a p_a + v_a p_b}{c_b p_a + v_b p_b} \tag{I}$$

whereas Marx's relative price is

$$\frac{p_a'}{p_b'} = \frac{(1+r)\,(c_a + v_a)}{(1+r)\,(c_b + v_b)} = \frac{c_a + v_a}{c_b + v_b}. \tag{II}$$

Relations (I) and (II) will therefore give the same result only if

$$\frac{c_a + v_a}{c_b + v_b} = \frac{c_a p_a + v_a p_b}{c_b p_a + v_b p_b}$$

i.e. (after simple transformations), only if $c_a/v_a = c_b/v_b$, that is, only with equal organic composition in the production of the two commodities, in which case of course Marx's rate of profits would have been correct even in an economy not coinciding with the standard system and there would have been no transformation problem to deal with.

16 It is in fact to this unpublished paper (Garegnani 1986) that Samuelson appears to refer his comments on page 279, since in Garegnani (1987) there is no reference to Samuelson's 'erase-and-replace' explanation of the transformation problem.

17 'When the stocks of many rich merchants are turned into the same trade, their mutual competition naturally tends to lower its profits, and when there is a . . . like increase of stock in all the different trades carried on in the same society, the same competition must produce the same effect in them all' (Smith, [1776] 1960, p. 105). The passage begins with 'the increase of stock, which raises wages, tends to lower profit', but, as the context of the passage shows, the idea is absent that the lowering of the rate of profits is a *logical implication* of the raising of the wage rate. See also Stigler (1952), p. 203; Hollander (1973b), p. 181.

18 Some of this evidence is given in Garegnani (1984), p. 309.

19 Marginalist theorists avoided the error when with Wicksteed (1894) they faced the problem of the so-called 'exhaustion of the product' once each factor is remunerated at its marginal product.

20 As Sraffa shows (1951, pp. xxxv–vii), Smith's position was in fact connected with his view that a rise in wages would raise all prices.

21 The position of this land is of course given together with the output of corn for the reasons I indicated in par. 8 above.

22 By the time of the third edition of the *Principles*, Ricardo had in fact come to choose as his 'invariable measure of value' a commodity that would constitute a 'medium' such that 'those commodities on one side of this medium, would rise in comparative value with it, with a rise in the price of labour, and a fall in the rate of profits; and those on the other side might fall from the same cause' (Ricardo, 1951–73, VIII, p. 193).

The difficulty of course was that a 'medium' in terms of which the social product would be invariable would not have the same physical composition as the real wage and, therefore, changes of the real wage would not be measured by it before prices are determined.

23 Samuelson makes it clear that the 'conventional economic theory' to which he refers is that of Marx's times, or of 'pre-Marxist' times (see also Samuelson, 1973a, p. 66).

24 Samuelson attributes to me the idea that '[Marx's] mistake was a fruitful one because it led Marx (almost) to a correct Sraffian theory of competitive price'. However, what I stated was that Marx's error of including a rate of profits determined by the ratio of the social surplus value to the social capital was 'suggestive' because '[it] can be envisaged by us as the result of treating as integral parts of a single method . . . what are in fact, when consistently developed, two equivalent methods each of which is sufficient to determine that [rate of profits]' (Garegnani, 1984, pp. 308–9). What is there held to be 'suggestive' is therefore the idea of a rate of profits originating from the distribution of a surplus ascertainable independently of prices, and originating the rate of profits by its uniform distribution over the corresponding capital – the idea that is the basis of the auxiliary constructions of the standard system (Garegnani, 1984, pp. 313–20; 1987, pp. 570–2).

25 In this connection we may refer to Samuelson's argument about an incompatibility between the labour theory of value and the possibility of alternative systems of production coming successively into use as distribution changes (pages 272–5), where Samuelson appears to refer back to his argument in 1974b,

p. 292, according to which 'in a regime of values the technique that minimizes "values" at $r = 0$ will minimize them for all r's – a shortcoming of the value model'. That this is not correct is shown by Samuelson (1962), where, when a 'surrogate production function' exists, the consumption good and the capital good in use always exchange according to the quantities of labour embodied. As I have remarked elsewhere (1984, p. 306n), Samuelson fails here to separate two questions. The first is that of the relative value of commodities pertaining to the *same* system of production, in relation to which the labour theory of value has always been used. The second question is that of the costs, estimated at the prices and profits of the system in use of capital goods specific to systems of production other than that in use (see, for example, Garegnani, 1970, 411n). It is only if the latter costs also happened to be proportional to the quantities of labour embodied, that the relative profitability of alternative systems of production could not change as distribution changes.

26 In the by now abundant literature on the question, see in particular Hollander (1973b); Eatwell (1975b); Hollander (1975); Garegnani (1982c); Langer (1982); Hollander (1983); Garegnani (1983c); de Vivo (1985); Prendergast (1986a, b); Peach (1986); Porta (1986); Groenewegen (1986b).

Comment

Bertram Schefold
Frankfurt am Main

The participants at the conference will be very grateful to Professor Samuelson for having added a major paper to the proceedings, written in a generous spirit of appreciation for an economist of a rather different persuasion. As an editor, directly concerned by some of Samuelson's observations, I take the liberty to offer some comments in an attempt to broaden the consensus in at least some areas, given that this book is dedicated to the memory of Sraffa.

I

'Mainstream economists of the mathematical or literary persuasion can benefit much from Sraffa's contributions', states Professor Samuelson. Indeed, concepts like basics and non-basics, the maximum rate of profit or the treatment of fixed capital as a joint product are now widely used, but there is less readiness to accept Sraffa's method and only limited agreement has been obtained on the extent to which Sraffa's critique of the concept of capital applies. I should like to start my Comment by advancing the latter argument by a small step, since insight into the critique (where much remains to be developed) may help to gain acceptance for the method.

Let us first agree on properties of long run equilibria that are accepted by economists of both classical and neoclassical origin: prices, wage rates, rents for lands of the same quality and the rate of profit are uniform. The uniformity of the rate of profit is a long-run equilibrium condition not only in classical but also in neoclassical theory. It may from the start be assumed to hold as a result of competition. The rate of profit is in general not uniform in this sense in *intertemporal general equilibrium* models, but, to the extent that they are not due to permanent scarcities, the inequalities of different own-rates of interest of different commodities even then tend to disappear as a result of a special form of a competitive process, and a unique uniform rate of profit emerges as the time horizon is shifted towards infinity (Bewley, 1982).

Differing own-rates of interest were introduced in Sraffa's critique of Hayek. I wonder whether it would not have been better if Sraffa had revealed more of his critique of the Austrian theory of capital on that occasion. We do not know how far it had been developed at the time, but he wrote: 'A considerable part of the book is taken up by preliminaries about the relations between the quantity of capital and the length of the process of production and about the proportions in which the flow of money is divided between the purchase of consumer's goods and the purchase of producer's goods. Dr. Hayek as it were builds up a terrific steam-hammer in order to crack a nut – and then he does not crack it. Since we are primarily concerned in this review with the nut that is not cracked, we need not spend time criticizing the hammer' (Sraffa, 1932, p. 45). A critique of Hayek's theory of capital would *eo ipso* also have been one of any supposition of a – barring monetary disturbances, i.e. in the absence of forced saving – spontaneous tendency towards a neoclassical equilibrium at full employment. This might have allowed a more effective attack on the 'rotten core of the Hayek work' than was provided by Sraffa's early critique of the erroneous monetary theory of the cycle.

For those interested in Sraffa's later work the review is important because it helps to elucidate the problematic of the multiplicity of own-rates of interest when relative prices are changing, as in Keynes, where own-rates of interest are used to analyse the short-run equilibrium at less than full employment. I am told that Professor Samuelson, later a pioneer in turnpike theory, dedicated a maiden paper to this connection.

Sraffa interprets inequalities of own-rates of interest of commodities as expressions of differences between the market price and the cost of production (Sraffa, 1932, p. 50). In fact, he considers 'the case of a non-money economy, . . . when equilibrium is disturbed, and during the time of the transition, the "natural" rates of interest on loans in terms of the commodities the output of which is increasing [because an initial deficiency of supply is being made good] must be higher, to various extents, than the "natural" rates on the commodities the output of which is falling; and that there may be as many "natural" rates as there are commodities. It will be noticed that, under free competition, this divergence of rates is as essential to the effecting of the transition as is the divergence of prices from the costs of production; it is, in fact, another aspect of the same thing' (Sraffa, 1932, p. 50).

The formal similarity of a classical equilibrium with a uniform rate of profit and a neoclassical one where own-rates of interest are equal has led to the claim that the world of *Production of Commodities* is only a special case of the Debreu world where divergent own-rates of interest are allowed for. Sraffa is said to deal with that special case in which initial endowments happen to be such that relative prices may remain constant in the intertemporal equilibrium so that own-rates are all equal and we may speak of a uniform rate of profit (Hahn, 1982b).

Against this I have argued elsewhere in this book and in Schefold (1985c) that there are profound differences relating not only to the theories about the genesis of such equilibria, but also to the state that is reached. In fact, the domain of application for such long-run equilibria is larger in the *classical* approach because of the different explanation of distribution and employment and different assumptions about effective demand. In neoclassical equilibrium, prices of goods are determined simultaneously with prices of factors, i.e. with distribution, while classical theory proceeds sequentially: prices of commodities in a classical long-period position are determined on the assumption that the real wage rate or the rate of profits is already exogenously given. Several contributions to this volume discuss alternative theories of distribution: they imply that Sraffa does not refer to a full-employment position.

As to a possible genesis of a neoclassical long-run equlibrium, the divergence of own-rates of interest in a Debreu-type intertemporal equilibrium is proof of a peculiar kind of disequilibrium. It is true that there is an equilibrium in so far as arbitrage would not be profitable: a higher own-rate of interest of a particular commodity does not indicate that one should move into the corresponding industry in order to obtain a higher rate of profit because relative prices change. Rather, it indicates a falling price and that the supply of the commodity is already being increased at a rate that is such that neither excess profits nor losses are being made. But the divergence of the own-rates of interest in the early periods of an intertemporal equilibrium reflects the slowness of the adaptation of production with given endowments – which are employed fully or receive zero prices – to demand, which is ultimately derived from demand for consumer goods. The situation implies a disequilibrium at the beginning in so far as the stocks of endowments of capital goods had once been accumulated to be utilized fully, and equilibrium in the capital goods market must mean not only that capital goods receive a positive price but also that their price corresponds to the cost of production. The prices for endowments of capital goods at the beginning of a Debreu equilibrium are just demand prices; the supply conditions as governed by earlier costs of production are, as it were, simply forgotten when time starts. Viewed as a model describing a process of adaptation, the intertemporal model is deficient in so far as it does not take deceived expectations generated by unused initial endowments into account.

If the Debreu equilibrium is thus understood to start from an initial disequilibrium situation which is, with perfect foresight, transformed into an equilibrium, the proof of the temporary nature of the divergence of own-rates of interest must be that they disappear in the long run – this is precisely what happens according to the results on turnpike properties of intertemporal general equilibria that have been assembled since Bewley's pathbreaking work of 1982. The long-run equilibrium therefore is not only a special case of an intertemporal equilibrium that happens to have endowments in 'correct' proportions, but also the centre of gravitation of an intertemporal equilibrium, if that is formulated as one with a distant time horizon (Duménil and Lévy, 1985), in the special case of permanent market-clearing, full employment and perfect foresight during the process.

Of course, in any neoclassical world with distribution governed by supply and demand for factors of production, relative prices will be constant in the long run only if the relative scarcities of primary factors have no reason to diverge as time goes on – reasons for divergence, which must be excluded, are e.g. the exhaustion of resources (Radner, 1988). Turnpike theorems with recursive utility show that preferences need, on the other hand, not be expressed in terms of discounted utility functions, where the utility function for each period would be assumed to be constant; they are explained directly as evaluations of consumption paths stretching over an infinite horizon, and they are such that the initial endowments of capital goods have no influence on the final stationary state (Epstein, 1987). It has been suggested by Garegnani (1976a) that the old neoclassical notion of long-period equilibrium was replaced, following Hicks and others, by temporal and intertemporal equilibrium concepts. Now, the old concept, in the form of a terminal stationary state with a uniform rate of return, has surfaced again.

What is really at issue is the confrontation of the classical and neoclassical theories of long-period equilibrium themselves (see Garegnani's main paper in this volume – chapter 5); the intertemporal model provides only a special case of a process of convergence to a neoclassical long-period equilibrium, and, if endowments happen to be in 'correct' proportions from the start, there is no problem of convergence.

However, the attempts to show how the neoclassical long-period equilibrium is generated as a terminal state of an intertemporal equilibrium have the merit of clarifying conditions for the convergence, and here I come to my point: as results from Epstein (1987, p. 341), it appears to be necessary, in order to prove the convergence to the long-run equilibrium, to postulate that the economies are 'regular' in the sense of Burmeister (1980). This means, essentially, that reswitching and Wicksell effects have been ruled out by simple assumption. It indicates that the critique of capital concerns all kinds of truly long-run neoclassical equilibria, not only Clarkian parables. It had been claimed that the modern versions of intertemporal equilibrium were immune against the critique; now the task is to show how it extends to neoclassical long-period equilibria as soon as it is asked how they can be attained or be stable.

II

Among the criticisms raised by Samuelson, if not against Sraffa then against some of his followers, one looms particularly large: the neglect of the effect of changes in demand on changes of prices in a system of prices of production with a given rate of profit. Mistaken is the 'impression from Part II of Sraffa (1960) that the influence of demand composition on relative prices is absent in Part II in the same way that it can be absent from Part I's model involving labour as the sole factor of production and no jointness of productions' (see page 270 of Samuelson's paper).

I doubt that many of the relevant authors are really guilty of ignoring such essential relationships; Eatwell has clarified the point concerning his own presentation in his Comment. In order to avoid unnecessary controversy, I shall simply state how I see the problem with regard to land and joint production.

It may be recalled that the conditions of production and the levels of output are regarded as given in the first ten chapters of the book; it is clear that prices of production would change even in the single-product case if returns to scale are not constant and the level of output was varied. In fact, the analysis starts with technology, outputs, employment and distribution *all* taken as determined, and changes of these data are analysed one by one. Sraffa himself never presented an analysis of the interaction of these factors, and it is doubtful whether a complete theory will ever be devised that would explain all their variations in historical conditions.

The properties of prices which may be considered if distribution changes and outputs are kept constant are few, but essential: the best-known example is the change in the value of capital as a consequence of a *hypothetical* change of the distributive variable. The capital controversy has proved that the thought experiment is relevant although one knows that an *actual* change of the distributive variable may cause switches of technique. An actual change in distribution is also likely to affect the composition of output, in particular of investment. There is therefore only limited, but relevant scope for an analysis with changes in distribution and the levels of output taken as given.

The analysis of prices is supported by *hypothetical* alterations of the quantity system (e.g. in the construction of subsystems) which could correspond to real variations of output levels only in the case of constant returns.

If *actual* outputs are assumed to change, with constant returns to scale and with the rate of profit being kept fixed, prices of production remain constant in the single-product case. In joint-production systems and/or if land is considered, such output changes usually induce changes in the method of production (entailing price changes) if they are large, but prices of production will in general stay constant if the changes considered are small. It would perhaps be more straightforward to establish this result by considering changes of given levels of *gross* output to be produced (including investment), but I shall argue in terms of *net* outputs (of consumption goods) because the corresponding model has been thoroughly analysed and is better known. I start with land.

Sraffa, following a long tradition, distinguishes two main types of rent: a familiar example of differential rent of the first kind is the Ricardian cultivation of different lands such that the price of the produce is determined on a marginal no-rent land (which pays no rent because it is not fully utilized). Differential rent of the second kind is illustrated by the use of a well-defined piece of homogeneous land, say the Principality of Monaco, which is used fully by means of two methods, say flats in old villas or in sky-scrapers, such that the combination of the more land-using (villas) and less land-using, but more cost-intensive technique (sky-scrapers) allows the satisfaction of a given demand for the produce (flats for people who want to escape the payment of taxes elsewhere). In both cases, needs and production may rise continuously, with the extension of cultivation on the no-rent land or with the displacement of the more land-using method by the less land-using one, while rents and prices rise spasmodically (as soon as new marginal lands or even less land-using, more cost-intensive techniques have to be brought in). The step function so constructed for either type of rent will be called a normal cost curve. It is clear that the level of output is among the determinants of the step reached, i.e. it codetermines the last land used (first kind of rent) or the methods to be combined (second kind), but only sufficiently large changes of that level lead, with a given spectrum of techniques, to a different step, so that prices remain unchanged with small changes. I want to avoid the possible transition to a continuous change of technique and to non-constant returns in order to focus on this conceptually simplest model.

It has been shown how rents and land may be eliminated in those cases from the system at given levels of output in order to express the prices of basics, either by considering the price at the extensive margin or by combining the two methods in the case of differential rent of the second kind linearly in such a way that rent and land disappear from the combined process ('intensive margin'). By means of this procedure, one can 'get rid of rent' in the consideration of the basis system, *but the exercise is valid only within the stated assumptions*, in particular if only hypothetical price changes are considered and output does not change at all, or little – a familiar application being the proof that taxes on rents fall wholly on landlords (as long as the reduction of the purchasing power of landlords and the increase of that of the state does not affect the methods of production of basics, e.g. through a large change in the composition of output).

In neoclassical theory, land is treated as a primary factor parallel with labour. This leaves room for a determination of rent through demand and supply on land that is cultivated fully by means of one method only, without an explanation of the rent as a differential between the cost of production of this method and some other method, on the same or on some other land. Such a treatment of land also appears in Samuelson's paper, e.g. in his Tableau (p. 267). The assumption seems to be incompatible with a post-Smithian classical theory (leaving aside the special case of monopoly rent and the dubious concept of absolute rent); it would imply that any small change of output may affect rents and prices even if there are constant returns, both for industrial processes and in the expansion of the scale of production on any given piece of land.

I can see two reasons for Samuelson's procedure. One is the repeated combination of a neoclassical approach to rent with Sraffian problems of capital theory in order to extend the critique of the neoclassical theory of capital to the neoclassical hypotheses about land and rent by Metcalfe and Steedman (1972) and other writers.

A more important reason is this. A neoclassical author might cross the normal cost curve with a demand curve falling from the left to the right so that something very similar to the cross of the supply and the demand curve would be obtained. If this intersection was found on a vertically ascending part of the normal cost curve he might say that an equilibrium had been determined such that the price was above the cost of production 'at the margin', and rent or surplus profits correspondingly higher, so that the equilibrium would not be presented by configurations of the Sraffa type. Instead, a separate determination of rent through demand would have been established, as in several of Samuelson's examples. A deeper justification could be based on the following observation: even if we take a classical view of demand, market forces must raise the price of the product, as the expansion of production stops temporarily whenever a new marginal land or a more cost-intensive technique has to be brought in *before* the switch in the methods of production can take place. Should we therefore not say that 'demand' is the true determinant of rents?

What would Sraffa have replied? Thanks to the changes of land with differential rent of the first kind and thanks to the changes of method in the case of differential rent of the second kind, a 'progressive increase of production on the land' is possible and '*output* may increase continuously although the methods of production are changed spasmodically' (Sraffa, 1960, p. 76, emphasis added). Here we have, in chapter 11 an actual change of output levels, but the rate of profit is assumed to stay constant and no theory to explain output is offered. To provide it, many elements would have to be brought in, in particular the principle of *effective* demand in a form compatible with the explanation of distribution; the determination of consumption should not contradict the critique of the neoclassical theory of distribution and employment.

Most contributions to this volume deal with particular aspects of this research programme. It is clear that the level of output affects the level of cultivation, but the influence of demand on rent could not justify the conclusion that rents ought to be explained in terms of supply of and demand for goods and factors in an interdependent full-employment equilibrium, as derived from subjective preferences. Beyond the critique of marginalism, a different theory of demand has to be provided. As is well known, the classical authors interpreted effective demand for each commodity as a specific quantity demanded at the normal prices. But what determines effective demand? In order to face the challenge, I discuss a special and simplified model that relates output to consumption on the assumption that growth rates (investment) and the rate of profit are given. It is further explained in section III on joint production.

First, I have proposed elsewhere in this book (chapter 7) that the demand for consumption goods be dealt with in terms of given needs, as Smith, Ricardo and their followers did, and that the responsiveness of the demand for consumption goods to prices be represented in terms of changes in methods of domestic production for the fulfilment of those given needs. Consumption commodities are means of production for household processes; these are added to the system of industrial processes of production. (The responsiveness of demand to income similarly is related to migration between groups of consumers.) The irreversibility of important demand changes, the impossibility of ascertaining what demand would be at prices significantly different from actual prices, and links between socially determined consumption patterns and economic stratification may thus be taken into account. My discussion of this and of the relative merits of this and of the neoclassical approach to consumer theory cannot be repeated here.

Needs are transformed and distribution changes in the process of development so that our *ceteris paribus* assumptions yield only first approximations, but the formulation of hypotheses concerning the interaction of accumulation, the formation of needs and distribution are beyond the scope of this comment, since Samuelson also takes changes of demand and the rate of profit unexplained as given. This is in keeping with the fact that the discussion is focused on the classical theory of value, but he does not address the question of which theory of demand would be appropriate in the context he considers. Given needs imply that the concept of effective demand is simplified: the normal quantity demanded is determined independently of the price of production, except in so far as there are possibilities of substituting processes and commodities to satisfy the same need.

To the extent that needs are given, the vertical sections of the normal cost curve are then only temporarily met with in the process of accumulation, and this will happen even if the demand for some commodities is price-elastic, provided the explanation of price elasticity of my main paper is used.

The normal or long-period position is found on the horizontal steps. Classical analysis proceeds sequentially. The methods of production are slowest to change. Within that framework, needs and hence normal quantities expand gradually. This is of importance for a (stylized!) interpretation of such an equilibrium as a normal position: actual demand is likely to fluctuate at any time. If the fluctuations are small, they will not lead to a displacement of the equilibrium and a fundamental change in the prices of production. As long as we argue in terms of given needs, whose normal level is fixed or grows slowly relative to rapid fluctuations, positions on the 'steps' are – locally – stable. A major change in effective demand may upset the long-period position itself and cause a change in the course of accumulation.

Second: if demand raises the price beyond the level at which it is 'supported' by the marginal method or combination of methods, the increase is at first to be considered as one of the market price. The normal level of the price of production would then be ill-defined (unless a neoclassical demand curve were used), which is why such a constellation is usually not considered as a long-period position, and a further argument may be advanced to justify Sraffa's assumption. If the constellation is expected to persist for some time, rents are higher than what can be explained through a differential of productivity, and this provides an *incentive* to innovate and to introduce a *new* method of production that allows a profit to be made according to the normal rate of profit at the elevated level of land rent. There may even be an artificial marginal land, as actually happens in the Principality of Monaco where they are filling up the sea on the shore to push out the coast line, or there may be a compromise and the use of old villas is combined not with sky-scrapers but with the construction of intermediate houses. As a result of such an introduction of a new method, the long-period position will again be established on a new horizontal segment of the normal cost curve, eliminating the formal underdeterminacy of the Sraffa system that occurs if the market price raises rent above the normal level.

The picture of a normal cost curve monotonically rising with output does not always hold. Saucier (1981) has shown that the steps may also go down if several lands and agricultural outputs are involved (contrary to Samuelson, 1987a, p. 458).

III

Under classical assumptions, there is a (not complete!) analogy between the contention that the main forms of rent must be explained in terms of the two kinds of differential rent on the one hand and the proposition that joint-production systems will be 'square' on the other. Let us now stick to the model with given needs. In equilibrium, there cannot be more processes than there are commodities produced; otherwise we have an overdetermination of prices at a uniform rate of profit (which corresponds to the competition between different processes of production at unequal rates of profit in the real world). On the other hand, we cannot, except by a fluke, have fewer processes than there are commodities with a positive price, because needs are given in fixed proportions and, with constant returns, fewer than *n* processes will not be sufficient to produce *n* commodities in given proportions. Square systems then emerge if the rule is added that unprofitable activities are not used and overproduced goods receive zero prices (they are not called commodities).

Thus we have the *formal* argument, proposed by Steedman (1976) and rigorously proved by Schefold (1978b and 1988a), using inequalities under general assumptions: a given uniform rate of profit and a, in general lower, rate of growth are imposed. (The two rates need not be close to each other, and the unformity of the rate of growth – analytically convenient but not really classical in spirit – is not essential to the argument; the classical long-period position certainly was not meant as a stationary or steady growth equilibrium.) Then, any vector of final demand will generically result in a long-period position with the number of commodities produced being equal to that of methods used, whatever rectangular array of methods of production is given initially as a book of blueprints. The square system that thus emerges is a long-period position in which, except for flukes, local and small variations of demand are possible, which do not lead to substitutions of methods, whereas larger ones are feasible only if a new equilibrium is reached.

The *substantive* complement to this formal analysis is, on the one hand, that an *overdetermination* of prices is the rule because 'too many' processes compete. Many applications are possible, e.g. to the explanation of patterns of the price determination of obsolescent machines. The question then is which square technique dominates or is socially necessary and determines normal prices relative to which other methods show surplus profits or losses. If, on the other hand, there is an *underdetermination* of prices, the formal argument assures us that competition will eventually result in a square system. But produced goods, available in excess, that are given away free, apart from charges for handling and transportation, are not encountered often. Leaving aside costs of disposal (as considered in my main paper to this volume), the reason, explained elsewhere since Schefold (1977), is that the falling market price of a good that tends to be overproduced is a strong incentive to use that good as an input in the production of new industrial or domestic activities. In consequence, the long-run solution to underdetermination usually is not that of a bottomless fall in some market prices until we get free overproduced goods and a square solution with fewer commodities and processes but, rather, that new methods are introduced through a form of induced technical progress such that an enlarged square system is obtained and becomes the dominant technique of a new normal position.

To show that there are joint-production systems such that processes and prices do not change at all for all variations of the demand vector, Samuelson reverts to systems that I had called 'all-productive' in Schefold (1971). I should like to point out that such systems are not quite as rare as one might think because they do not presuppose diagonal dominance if there are more than two goods and processes and because it is natural to extend them to the consideration of the activity levels, given a vector of a final demand, on balanced growth paths. It can then be shown (see Schefold, 1978a) that a square Sraffa system emerging from an arbitrary technology set will in general have this property as soon as the rate of growth of the system is close to the maximum rate of growth attainable with this technology set. This means that, generically, the inverse of $\mathbf{B} - (1 + g)\mathbf{A}$ will be positive for the Sraffa system emerging from the choice of technique for rates of growth and profit both close to the maximum.

At low rates of growth and profit, all-productive systems are exceptional. But, as a result of the 'squareness' of the solutions, I have found that prices are at least *locally* invariant with respect to output changes in joint-production systems and systems with land: if the classical assumption of a given vector of needs is made, those needs may be varied, with the square solution, prices and distribution unchanged, as long as no activity level turns negative.

Finally, the question should be taken up of whether the 'square solutions' remain generic with other assumptions. In this area, much research remains to be done. Square solutions must result, if needs are different for different classes and if the solution is required to be locally stable with temporary fluctuations in demand, as I have shown in my reply to Salvadori in this volume (chapter 7). The long-run square solutions in themselves are not generic if a neoclassical theory of demand is introduced, as stressed in Schefold (1985a) – I am indebted to Samuelson for this point, which he made on the occasion of a lecture of mine at his Institute. However, there are objections to the non-square solutions even in this case (and in the one of the *ad hoc* example presented in note 2 to Samuelson's paper[1]) if it is assumed to be in the nature of a long-period position that it must accommodate *arbitrary* small short-run changes in the outputs of all commodities. On the one hand, short-run demand changes cannot always be reduced to perturbations of preferences. On the other, there must be room to adapt quantities. Even in Marshall, cattle diseases lead to an increased supply of fish in the market in the short run. With joint production, a sudden demand for mutton would have to be choked off by price rises alone if we did not have, as in Henderson ([1921, 1932] 1968, pp. 54–5), two different methods of raising sheep or if more wool results the expansion of a process – possibly a household activity – to use wool. If effective demand fluctuates, the decisive effect has to be on employment in different industries and in the aggregate; it does not operate on long-run equilibrium prices (although provisional changes in market prices may be necessary to *induce* the changes of output levels). Since it is true that the introduction of neoclassical demand theory generates the possibility of non-square long-period equilibria such that alternative square solutions would be less profitable, a dilemma arises, but it is only another indication that neoclassical demand theory is incompatible with the classical theory of prices – a point that may more forcefully be argued with regard to the theory of distribution (Garegnani, 1983a).

IV

Samuelson's observations on Sraffa's article of 1926 furnish an opportunity to return to the neoclassical interpretation of rent as a factor price. I do not think that Sraffa committed an error in his article of 1926, but he may have been misunderstood by some of his readers, and the relevance of his results may be less obvious to modern Walrasian economists than to a Cambridge Marshallian of the 1920s. First of all, the assessment should be based on Sraffa's article of 1925 (Sraffa, 1925) – which is also available in French, German and other translations (Sraffa, [1925] 1975; [1925] 1986) – since the first pages of the article of 1926 are only a summary of the earlier one. Sraffa's real dilemma was that he felt unable to accept the Walrasian approach in economics when he had found, at the end of his article of 1925, that 'These causes of variations of cost, highly important from the point of view of general economic equilibrium, must of necessity be considered to be negligible in the study of the particular equilibrium of an industry' (quoted in Roncaglia, 1978, p. 12).

The Marshallian apparatus of supply and demand curves seemed applicable only under restrictive conditions, the least implausible of which resulted in the postulate of constant costs in a competitive market. Thus Sraffa did not wish to 'fob off on the twentieth century a value taxonomy that was already obsolete in the early nineteenth century' but wanted to get rid of it altogether – a conclusion to which he came close in his earlier critique and which was openly and defiantly thrown at his opponents after softer means of conveying the message had been exhausted in the course of the debate on increasing returns (Sraffa, 1930).

As a matter of fact, Sraffa himself wrote to Keynes on 6 June 1926:

> This conclusion has been misunderstood and taken to imply that in actual life constant returns prevail . . . in reality the connection between cost and quantity produced is obvious. It simply cannot be considered by means of the system of particular equilibria for single commodities in a regime of competition devised by Marshall.
>
> (Quoted in Roncaglia, 1978, p. 12)

For the neoclassical theory, with full employment, a first dilemma may be presented in the following terms. *Either*, a general equilibrium is assumed, the solution to which consists in one point in the space of prices and quantities if the solution is unique. Without relaxing at least one constraint, changes in costs can then only be observed if the expansion of the industry under consideration is accompanied by a contraction of other industries due to a change of preferences. This is the point of view taken in Joan Robinson's article, referred to by Samuelson. For, although she speaks of a 'supply price', her equilibrium point moves with changes of preferences. Other causes for shifts of equilibrium points, giving rise to equilibrium trajectories, may be changes of technology or of endowments; for example, the changes of prices, and in particular of the wage rate, may be traced as a function of a growing labour force that is always fully employed.

Or the analysis is conducted in terms of demand and supply *curves*. We are here not interested in the demand and supply functions of individual agents or firms that express quantities offered or asked for when all prices vary parametrically, but we are interested in the meaning that can be attached to demand and supply curves in an individual market when other markets are at or near equilibrium, so that an equality of demand and supply in the particular market under consideration implies a general equilibrium. If this approach is chosen, the difficulty is that, as soon as demand and supply are not in equilibrium in the particular market, on points of the supply curve not crossed by the demand curve, there must, because of Walras's law, be at least one other market that is in disequilibrium – a difficulty encountered by Hicks in his stability analysis and dealt with by him using the assumption that the other market in disequilibrium is the money market.

Marshall's assumption, according to Sraffa, is different: he simply assumes that the market under consideration is so small, relative to all others, that a disequilibrium – provided it is not too large – implies disturbances of other markets that are sufficiently small to be ignored. Hence – a point stressed by Marshall and by Sraffa in 1925 – the demand and supply schedules can be drawn only near equilibrium.

Now it is useful to read both articles together. If an expansion of the wheat-growing industry is considered, and if land is not specific to wheat but is also used for other agricultural products, the article of 1926 states on p. 539 (as does, of course, the article of 1925) that, if there are other industries using the same type of land, rents will either not be appreciably affected by the necessary intensification of cultivation in all the industries concerned – this is the case (1) of constant costs, plausible if the other industries are many – or rents rise. In the latter case (2), the change in distribution, if it is sufficiently general, is then susceptible of shifting the demand curves (2a). The article of 1925, however, also stresses another aspect (on p. 324): the supply curves of other industries employing the factor will shift (2b), violating the *ceteris paribus* condition. Joan Robinson's account of the matter in her theory of imperfect competition fails to take the latter point into account, with the result that the argument is not very convincing, and there follows a muddled account of how demand curves might shift with supply (Robinson, 1969, pp. 117–18).

Of course, Sraffa was aware that there were cases in which the use of the Marshallian rising supply curve remained legitimate. It is ironic that the model proposed by Samuelson to provide a meaningful bit of Marshallian analysis in his paper, taken from Samuelson (1971c, p. 367), is precisely the one prescribed by Sraffa in 1925 (but also, more briefly, in 1926): 'These conditions [*ceteris paribus* conditions] reduce the domain to a minimum in which the assumption of rising costs may be applied to a supply curve. They are fulfilled only in those exceptional cases in which all of a factor is employed in the production of an individual commodity' (Sraffa, 1925, p. 323; my translation). In Samuelson's paper there are as many lands as there are commodities, and each land is specialized, each being specifically required for the production of each commodity. This corresponds to Sraffa's assumption that the total amount of a specific factor is used for the production of each commodity.

On the other hand, the example of the paper assumes that each industry uses transferable labour. It is assumed that the labour supply is completely elastic. This could be justified on the ground that the pool of labour used by the group of industries under consideration is small relative to the economy as a whole (this is the assumption proposed in Sraffa, 1925, p. 324). Or there is unemployment, or the disutility of the individual labourer does not change at all with the wage – both not very neoclassical assumptions.

Hence we are, in Samuelson's present paper, exactly where Sraffa stood in 1925. Since the supply of labour has by assumption been made irrelevant to the determination of the supply price, the latter depends only on the degree of intensification of the cultivation of the lands, each of which is specific to the product grown on it. Nobody could deny, least of all Sraffa, that rising supply curves will be so obtained, and Sraffa's error could only consist in his assertion that the situation under consideration is a more special case than that of constant costs. Of constant costs we may simply speak in those cases where a clear tendency to increasing or diminishing returns is absent. A one-to-one assignment of factors to products seems more particular. In this sense, the constant cost box is less empty. But a general theory cannot be so obtained.

In fact, lands tend to be specialized, but this is the result of an economic process that must be analysed, as can be done using Sraffa's (1960) method of counting the equations; it should not be simply presupposed. And complete specialization, as in the Sraffa (1925) – Samuelson (1989) case, will not result often. Thus, if we have twenty lands, the twentieth being marginal, and three products could be grown on each, there will be nineteen rents and three prices to be determined, so that, of sixty feasible processes, only twenty-two coexist in equilibrium, implying that at least eighteen and possibly nineteen, but never all twenty lands will turn out to be specialized (see Sraffa, 1960, p. 77).

V

I have trespassed already on the space rightfully allotted to me, but I want to take up the challenge of the 'red herring'. I think that a more significant meaning can be attached to the standard commodity than emerges from the paper, although it remains an auxiliary construct. To me (Schefold, 1976b, pp. 221–25; Schefold 1986b), Sraffa's standard commodity is interesting not so much because of the *result* (a standard such that the wage curve is linear if wages happen not to be advanced, implying the useful and well-known analogy with the corn model) but because of its *derivation*. In this derivation, the point is not to show that prices of production are equal or close to labour values – something that Sraffa does not contend – but to show how and why prices change with distribution for a given technology. To see this, I focus on chapter III of the book, not on chapter IV.

It is clear to the informed reader that the 'Prelude to a Critique of Economic Theory' cannot be understood independently of the context, i.e. the formal propositions are developed not just in order to obtain abstract propositions but also with a view to questioning traditional economic beliefs, and the formal propositions obtained have, because of their abstract nature, a meaning only within the broader framework of traditional theory, both classical and neoclassical. Chapter III on the proportions between the input of labour to the inputs of means of production (how are they to be measured?) addresses the question of how changes in distribution affect changes in the prices of the outputs of single-product industries. Nowadays, after the introduction of matrix algebra to input–output systems, it is easy to give a formal solution to the apparent problems of circularity that arise where the tools for measuring the amount of inputs, i.e. prices for the given physical quantities, depend on the result of such measurements. The answer is to calculate prices of inputs and outputs simultaneously. But the calculation obliterates the economic processes leading to the formation of such prices and one is tempted to forget the economic tradition that might explain them.

Having considered simple conceptions of the numéraire (a numéraire commodity, then an arbitrary index) and having alluded to different theories of distribution (subsistence wage, given shares of national income) in the opening pages of his book, Sraffa allows the rate of profit to vary and shows that, if prices remain equal to labour values (they are equal if profits are zero), 'deficit' and 'surplus' industries will arise at positive rates of profit, and with a wage reduced from its maximum; therefore he considers a *dis*equilibrium and asks how it might be redressed. If labour values are $\mathbf{u}$, the input–output matrix is $\mathbf{A}$, the labour vector is $\mathbf{l}$, the vector of surpluses and deficits is $\mathbf{z}$, we have

$$\mathbf{u} - \mathbf{A}\mathbf{u} - w\mathbf{l} - r\mathbf{A}\mathbf{u} = \mathbf{z},$$

where w has been lowered a little from its original value of one and r has been raised a little from its original value of zero (there is as yet no wage curve showing which reduction of w would correspond to a given increase of r). Price changes on the input and the output side are found necessary to reduce each component of $\mathbf{z}$ to zero, and 'to achieve this object it is first of all the price ratio between each product and its means of productions that one expects to come into play' (Sraffa, 1960, p. 14). One 'expects' something because there are differing traditions in economic theory. The answer of transforming values into prices of production only on the output side (redistribution of surplus value) is mistaken. (Marx was in fact aware that input prices also ought to have been 'transformed', but he neither had the analytical means to do it, not did he see the implications.)

If Marx's solution does not help, one may turn to the neoclassical view, which here at first sight seems to be confirmed: high rates of return (surplus industries, with the corresponding component of **z** being positive) are associated with low capital intensities. But if the means of production of a capital-intensive industry are produced by labour-intensive industries, the value of the means of production of the capital-intensive industry may *fall* in consequence of the change in prices (when values are being transformed into prices), so that it is not always necessary for a capital-intensive industry to raise its own price. Sraffa therefore here prepares the reader for Wicksell effects, which are presented in a more striking manner in chapter VI.

Sraffa's main point is that the clue to understanding the reaction of prices to changes in distribution lies not only in the proportions of labour to the value of means of production in the industry under consideration, but also in the corresponding proportions in previous industries that produce those means of production, and further on backwards in 'logical' time. The 'invariable' standard of value is therefore one from which the cause of the price changes in consequence of changes in distribution (namely, the unequal proportions of labour to means of production in the industry itself and in the industries producing the means of production of that industry and further backwards) is *absent*. One and only one industry, the one that produces the standard commodity, has this property of (infinite!) recurrence with equal proportions if the system is regular in the sense of Schefold (1971).

The argument cannot be worked out in greater detail here (see Schefold, 1986b, pp. 607–15). Note that causality in this context means that causes are defined relative to traditional explanations in economic theories. *Any* numéraire is invariable in that its price does not change by definition. Sraffa's standard commodity is claimed to be invariable in the more specific sense that the causes that theories of all schools adduce to explain price changes in consequence of changes in distribution are *not* to be found in the standard industry, so that it is appropriate to take the standard commodity as numéraire. It so happens that a linear wage curve results if the wage is not advanced, but, if the wage is advanced, the construction also holds and results in a hyperbola.

The *Hilfskonstruktion* is thus useful for criticizing Marx's attempt to transform values into prices, but it also helps to visualize how prices of production systematically deviate from labour values as the rate of profit is raised from zero to its actual value in a thought experiment. The standard commodity can be constructed only for the system in actual use; it therefore relates actual prices to what prices would be in the same system at a different rate of profit. Since part of its explanatory power is based on the possibility of reduction, it is not only useful for those systems for which a reduction is not possible, i.e. for the majority of joint-production systems (for which it does in fact often not exist). It is obvious that a different standard obtains if the system changes because of technical progress or large alterations in the actual rate of profit or shifts in demand. I regard it mainly as a didactic concept, i.e.

as an introduction to the logic of the classical theory of value and to puzzles of capital theory. Other uses of it can be made. Whether it was of actual help to Cambridge (UK) in the great debate I cannot say.

There are many other points in Samuelson's contribution that might be taken up, especially the transformation problem, but I do not want to defend the labour theory of value as a basis for an accurate modern analysis; the assessment of its historical function in the works of classical economists is a different matter. The real issue concerns the explanatory power of the classical and the neoclassical theories, each taken as a whole, of which the explanation of long-run prices is only a particular aspect. Economists working in the classical tradition should be extremely grateful to Samuelson's inquiring comment, not only because he compels them to deal with questions for which neoclassical theorists have well-practised (though not necessarily correct) answers (such as how the demand for consumer goods is to be modelled), but also because he challenges them to develop the broader perspective of the theory of accumulation. In this field the classical authors developed their splendid vision of the period between the earliest phases of the industrial revolution and the century that followed. The question is what their conceptual tools can contribute to the analysis of a modern world that, it is true, has changed a great deal but that quite obviously is not that of the Walrasian equilibrium either.

Acknowledgements

I should like to thank Krishna Bharadwaj and Piero Garegnani for helpful suggestions concerning my Comment. The responsibility for the final text is mine.

Note

1 According to Samuelson's assumptions, we should have one process, producing all commodities in positive amounts (r given)

$$(1 + r)(a_{11}p_1 + \ldots + a_{1n}p_n) + l_1 = b_{11}p_1 + \ldots + b_{1n}p_n$$

with $g = 0$ and demand functions proportional to income

$$c_j(ra_{11}p_1 + \ldots + ra_{1n}p_n + l_1) = (b_{1j} - a_{1j})p_j$$

where c_j, $c_1 + \ldots + c_n = 1$, indicate the share of income spent on net output of commodity j. Of these $n + 1$ equations, n are seen to be linearly independent; they determine prices in terms of the wage rate. A short-run change in demand could be accommodated only by changing all prices and has no clear effect on employment. If these unit elasticity Engel curves were to be retained, it would be better to assume long-run prices determined by a square system $[\mathbf{B} - (1 + r)\mathbf{A}]p = \mathbf{l}$, long-run relative activity levels $\mathbf{q}$ by

$$(r\mathbf{qAp} + \mathbf{ql})c_j = \mathbf{q}(\mathbf{b}^j - \mathbf{a}^j)p_j;\ j = 1, \ldots, n.$$

If L is employment (how to be derived?), the model might be closed with $\mathbf{ql} = L$. Short-run activity levels $\mathbf{x}$ could deviate from $\mathbf{q}$, and $\mathbf{xl}$ from $\mathbf{ql}$. But, as stated, I should prefer to deduce Engel curves from migrations between groups of consumers with different incomes, with the needs for each group taken as given. A shift of consumers from low- to high-income groups would allow the observation *ex post* of a relationship between a rise in total income and a change in the composition of output (see also Pasinetti, 1981b). The solutions would be square.

Reply

Inside every great scholar is a greater one. Albert Einstein, the stubbornest critic of quantum physics, ranked as a giant with Planck and Bohr in the creation of pre-Heisenberg-Schrödinger-Dirac quantum mechanics. Similarly Piero Sraffa, though it was no part of his intention, was led as if by an invisible hand to perfect time-phased mainstream microeconomics – not of course in the narrow corner of it where reside Clark and Wicksteed.

It is of this greater Sraffa that I sing. At the infancy of classical economics its scientists spoke prose and had equations and unknowns which were equal or unequal in number. When we count the number of Ricardo's equations and unknowns, we verify exactly what kind of a demand and supply system his model is and learn that he can arrive at no determinate distribution of income that can be freed of the 'complications' of consumer tastes, demands, and time preferences. In the Pantheon along with Walras, von Neumann and Arrow-Debreu, Sraffa has earned pride of place. The critique of Marx, begun by Dmitriev and Bortkiewicz, achieves closure with benefits of Sraffian insights – as exemplified in the expositions of Seton, Steedman and Roemer. The fulfilment of Marx's tableaux of steady and expanded reproduction is achieved by the tools and techniques of Leontief, Sraffa, von Neumann and Morishima.

I welcome the uninhibited discussions of John Eatwell, Pierangelo Garegnani and Bertram Schefold. When scholars feel misunderstood, it is natural for them to wonder about motives. Time-consuming discussion is the only way to sort out the areas of disagreement and agreement. My regret is that an overcrowded research schedule and a tight publisher's deadline necessitated a brevity that makes for a tone of dogmatism and unamiability.

Alphabetical order for the authors is appropriate, with some inevitable repetitions. Because I received more than one version to react to, I cannot be sure I have responded to every important point and avoided responding to points later withdrawn.

Eatwell

(1) I had suggested that a revised edition of the *New Palgrave* rewrite the Eatwell–Panico sentence

Yet the basic structure of classical analysis is preserved [in Part II of Sraffa's

> book dealing with joint production and land] – the prices, the rate of profit, distributive variables (say, land rents) are determined by the conditions of production, given the wage.

Eatwell quotes the whole of his earlier paragraphs and declares I have misunderstood the intended meaning. Indeed I have, and a revised text seems to me all the more needed. The reader may judge from my account whether the misunderstanding was an 'ideological device' involving removal of 'sentences from their context', misrepresentation of 'arguments', and 'erection of straw men'. Or whether it was a genuine attempt to isolate what is valid in a 'classical' paradigm as against a post-1870 paradigm.

Can the distribution of income be analysed in some classical fashion independently of the composition of demand? Can relative prices of factors and the profit rate have their equilibrium determined by technology independently of subjectivist utility and time preferences?

The answer given by mainstream economics is No.

The erudite Jacob Viner, my mentor at the University of Chicago, counselled: 'Try to read an author for sense, not for error.' I tried. The indicated Eatwell–Panico sentence, if I extended to the word 'wage' the implicit adjective 'real', could be construed *not* to be an untruth in Part I Sraffa – this by virtue of the 1949 non-substitution theorem. In the face of this non-malicious interpretation, what was I to think of the preceding sentences, which said:

> In Part II . . [of] Sraffa . . [with] multi-product industries and fixed capital, and . . economies with more than one non-reproducible input . . . Yet the basic structure of classical analysis is preserved . . .

and then followed the sentence that I declared to be untrue as applied to Part II.

Was I wrestling with a straw dummy? If readers were to plough through my tedious correspondence files with Sraffians, they would realize how many authors believe that relative prices of joint products are, for a fixed profit rate, invariant to [sufficiently small?] changes in the composition of demand [almost always?].

Since, like Oliver Twist, I am asking for more revisions, I suggest that the two *Palgrave* authors re-examine all these mooted passages. In particular, there will be found to be no valid 'contrast[s] with neoclassical theory, in which determination of prices is dependent upon knowledge of the functional relationships between supply and demand' – in any Sraffa model involving, say, corn produced by labour and land while cloth is produced by labour and corn. When landowners change their tastes for corn and cloth, that changes relative prices and the distribution of rents and wages in Wicksell's demand/supply neoclassical fashion (which is also Smith's and Ricardo's). Etc., etc.

(2) Were generations of readers of Sraffa's 1926 classic right or wrong to believe that the category of increasing cost and rising supply price was demonstrably an empty box? I said they were misled. Eatwell argues that,

in 'general equilibrium', a shift in relative demand toward one good does raise its competitive price, but argues that it is an irrelevancy to bring in general equilibrium since Sraffa's critique is exclusively directed at partial equilibrium.

I agree that it was the fuzzinesses of Marshall's partial equilibrium that Sraffa grappled with – and, I would add, that ultimately mired Sraffa down in a basic non sequitur. But, after I have solved for Marshall and Sraffa *all* the ambiguities of partial equilibrium, why does Mr Eatwell not applaud my debunking Sraffa's claim that 'the old and now obsolete theory which makes it [price] dependent on cost of production alone appears to hold its own as the best available'.

It is not the 'best available'. It was not the best in 1926 (or in 1925). My exact example, which Eatwell says 'fulfils exactly the conditions Sraffa laid down for the construction of a partial equilibrium industry supply curve', refutes Sraffa's attempt to base price on cost alone to the exclusion of *dd* demand curves. Let marginal utility of wine rise relative to that of rye, and the box of rising supply price will be seen to be non-empty – even 'approximately'.

Rereading the *Foundations* (Samuelson, 1947, pp. 75–80) passage Eatwell commends and the Samuelson and Nordhaus (1985, 479–80) passage he finds 'dubious', I find nought to react to in connection with the 1926 Sraffa article or with the expositions themselves.

(3) Eatwell is right that, if textbook writers like me use examples and diagrams that I know to be so oversimplified as to be false representations, it would be churlish to fault him for using Sraffa's *standard commodity* as a simplifying device to explicate how an input–output system with one primary factor has its real prices determined uniquely for each profit rate.

My point is missed. My point is that the *standard commodity* does *not* clarify anything. It does not illuminate 'reswitching'; Wicksell effects; the incidence on relative factor shares of accumulation, innovation, time preference, or tastes changes; the labour theory of value's domain of applicability; the chimera of 'absolute' value; . . . . When more than one technique is competitively viable, no *standard commodity* obtains; under various decomposabilities, none obtains. Its disappearance is no loss; and, in the one-technique, indecomposable single-products case, its appearance is no gain.

My pointing all this out is hardly odd. The reason that the concept does not fade into an appendix on *local* eigenvectors is that Piero Sraffa, late in the task of editing his magisterial Ricardo, bethought to make some sense of notions of *absolute* value: rather than dither between shortest-lived shrimp on the seashore and ancient-trees' masts, or diddle with goods of average time intensity, neo-Ricardians aspired to the objectivity of a Frobenius–Perron matrix's right-hand eigenvector as weights for a market basket. One inessential error in Marx's transformation algorithm could even be lightened when the economy is in a *standard* gross state.

Fun is fun, and heaven knows mathematical economists have their turnpikes and other pebbles on the beach. The only caution is to know the difference between a pebble and a pearl.

Garegnani

(1) I shall concentrate on those points in my critique of Sraffa's classic 1926 paper that have not already been addressed in my reply to Eatwell.

A new point here is that, in Sraffa's longer Italian version of 1925, he is said to have endorsed my position – namely that, as a matter of exact logic, the box of increasing-cost, rising supply is not empty even in an impeccable partial equilibrium model. (Wheat and wine use respective lands specialized for them.) Two people seem to deserve congratulations: Piero Sraffa and I.

How was one to know in the Viner or Schumpeter seminars of 1934–5 that the 1926 author knew better than he wrote? The many merited reprints of the 1926 classic never carried author's alterations to warn of this.

The issue has never been 'Marshall's partial-equilibrium approximations' versus 'classical economics'. It has been Menger and Jevons and Walras versus Ricardo, Mill and Cairnes. It has been Böhm-Bawerk, Wicksteed, Pareto and Wicksell against Marx and Ricardo – with Dmitriev, Bortkiewicz and Seton keeping the score.

What a cleaned-up version of Sraffa (1926) establishes is how *nearly empty* are *all* of Marshall's partial equilibrium boxes. To a logical purist of Wittgenstein and Sraffa class, the *Marshallian partial* equilibrium box of *constant* cost is even more empty than the box of *increasing* cost. I should have said that in *Palgrave* and in my revisionist paper on Sraffa. Piero Sraffa should have said that in 1925 and 1926.

Proof: When all goods use all factors in the same proportions (and a universal non-substitution theorem obtains), which is the most favourable case for 'constant costs', then can Marshall write down *rigorously* a *partial* equilibrium analysis? No. The *ceteris paribus* assumptions he needs do not obtain. QED. As we let Sraffa (1926) fade into history, we are left with no *empirical* primacy for the constant-cost approximation.

(2) Garegnani says I have read Sraffa (1960) with marginalist eyes. I say I have read it with von Neumann eyes, Leontief eyes, Debreu and Koopmans eyes, Dorfman–Samuelson–Solow eyes and Morishima eyes. Later I reread it with Garegnani, Pasinetti and Schefold eyes.

I do reread Ricardo and Smith with all those same eyes and I deny that Ricardo failed to understand how changes in demand and outputs altered factor prices and relative goods prices. The blindness, if any, is in Mr Garegnani's caricature of a classical economist and there is nothing Clarkianly neoclassical about recognition of this pre-marginalist banality. Who begrudges Mr Garegnani *his* two-stage procedures? But why bind *them* on Mr Ricardo or Mr Mill?

When Ricardo addresses a change in tastes toward labour-intensive goods during the Napoleonic War's need for standing armies, he perceives that this raises the intermediate-run real wage relative to real land rents. He perceives that, in *his* longer run, this adds to the equilibrium population. He perceives that this alters the distribution of income in all runs.

Neither in 1814–15, nor 1817 nor 1823, would Ricardo make the elementary mistake of considering the real wage–profit rate trade-off to be independent of the abundance or scarcity of land. Ricardo's glass is alternately half-empty and half-full. Sometimes his real wage rate cleaves to a specified subsistence level; sometimes it evolves downward toward that asymptote; sometimes the industrial revolution is catapulting it upward. Ricardo's long-run profit-rate plateau is even more weakly hypothesized.

My 1959 *QJE* articles on the Ricardian system showed that I have no marginalist qualms about going all the way to extreme long-run Ricardian poles, culminating in his physiocratic *Land* (not Labour) Theory of Value. But why should I or Garegnani saddle this singular case on the general reader in political economy? That seems antiquarian decadence. It is derogatory toward the classical writers and their system, and for no necessary or even useful purpose.

Garegnani's further remarks about 'squareness' of joint-product matrices and *local* price-ratio invariances are taken care of in my discussion of Bertram Schefold's Comment and can be omitted here.

(3) On the *standard commodity* there is overlap between the Eatwell and Garegnani positions. That vectoral concept, Garegnani reassures us, 'is not there to validate anything in particular . . . [but] to render "more transparent" what is valid independently of it . . .' (Garegnani, n. 15, gives as an example the use of x^* in $(1+r^*)Ax^* = x^*$ to demonstrate that, for $r^* < r$, $P = Wa_0(1+r)[I - A(1+r)]^{-1}$ cannot have a positive P/W vectoral solution.)

On p. 291, Garegnani compares the piecewise (real-wage profit-rate) trade-offs over *local* intervals of $1+r$ with piecewise different *standard commodities*. The logic of the two cases is disparate: there is one and only one trade-off locus no matter (1) how variable the techniques, (2) how decomposable or indecomposable the technologies. By contrast, *no* unique market basket defines a real wage linear in the profit rate when techniques are variable or decomposable. A locus that is piecewise linear is *not* linear, and as Garegnani well understands the linear pieces do not even belong on the *same* $W/\Sigma P_j x_j$ vertical axis! It is because, as my critics so well say, the construct does nothing essential for them that its non-existing cases occasion no trouble and so little notice. My Åkerman *Festschrift* positive-profit-rate non-substitution theorem, as I review its explication, does not benefit from Garegnani's proposed vectoral exposition.

I devoted most of my 1983 Alexander Ehrlich *Festschrift* tribute to discussing Marx without matrices, using a one-commodity case to demonstrate how scarcity and plentitude of capital good(s) determine the rate of profit and the real wage. It is a case so singular as to make transparent the superfluousness of the *standard commodity* concept. I therefore am not sure whom the joke can be on if Garegnani somehow infers that I have given the *standard commodity* more than its due. Zero is hardly an excessive rating.[1]

(4) Garegnani's section 4 deals with the labour theory of value. Once again he claims that a corn-only model that Ricardo used in 1814–15 discussions with Trower and Malthus does cogently vindicate the labour theory of value. In this connection Garegnani appeals to Sraffa's 1951 *Introduction* to

Ricardo's *Principles* for an alleged cogent demonstration that Ricardo had detected and overcome a basic Smith flaw and had done so by arriving at the labour theory of value. And, he proclaims, Ricardo's Herculean task was creatively buttressed by Marx's 1867–1885–1894 paradigms of equalized *rate of surplus value* and Marx's successful *Weltanschauung* concerning the 'transformation' problem.

I shall rebut by showing that a corn-only model violates any labour theory of value as fundamentally as the general *n*-good case does. I shall show that Smith's lowering of the profit rate as a result of more capitals competing with each other is transparently vindicated as a logical and empirical possibility against Ricardo's Smithian strictures precisely in the corn-only case! Garegnani's attempt to defend Marx's detours in the transformation problem will be seen to lack cogency.

Samuel Hollander and Garegnani dispute textual matters. Was there an 1814–15 lost-Atlantis model for Trower, Malthus and Ricardo to debate about? Personally, I'd be overjoyed if a manuscript find in some English country home completely vindicated Garegnani. I shall fabricate the find.

Corn and labour and land inputs can produce corn output after one period. (Cloth is similarly producible but by labour and corn as inputs.) With corn Sraffa's only *basic*, if there is to be a steady state, the profit rate that prevails in autonomous agricultural production must be matched by the profit rate elsewhere.

Our 1815 find has Ricardian arithmetic. 1 of corn can be produced on 10 acres with 1 of labour and 1/10 of corn inputs. Or, if we halve the acres, we can double the non-land inputs – and so forth in the continuous land–non-land mode of the classicals. Also, to give Smith his fair chance, the example permits the following alternative techniques to the (1 labour, 1/10 corn) technique: $(\frac{1}{2},\frac{1}{4})$, (2,1/20).

Now we calculate how Ricardo's labour theory of value is neither 100 per cent right, nor 93 per cent right *à la* Stigler. It is simply a wrong one-parameter theory of value when every schoolboy – whether named Adam, David, Léon, Karl or Pierangelo – knows that only a three-parameter theory of value that gives proper scope to rent, wages and interest can properly describe (a) the distribution of income, (b) the interest rate, and (c) the P_{cloth}/P_{food} and $(P_{cloth}/W, P_{food}/W)$ ratios. All this holds in every run. Before population changes, a new accumulation of corn seed will so compete down the P_{corn}/W ratio as to lower the switching-point profit rate *à la* Sraffa. Despite Smith's archaic language – 'more competition of capital' to describe a rise in the competitive supply of corn seed (within the same regimen of non-monopolistic competition) – Smith is right on target. (We are fortunate that Ricardo was such a fuzzy thinker since we owe his valuable *Principles* to his captious critiques of Smith!) Why did Editor Sraffa not stress that Ricardo understood the necessity for a three-parameter theory of value – at least did so more than 7 per cent of his time?

The reader may investigate how a fall or rise in the corn subsistence wage will alter the long-run interest rate, the population, and the goods' terms of trade. Or, how a change in landlords' tastes toward cloth will alter, by supply and demand, short-run P_{cloth}/P_{corn}, until population moves to restore the

P_{corn}/W ratio. When cloth becomes part of the subsistence ration, profit in agriculture no longer unilaterally sets the profit rate. Etc., etc.

Now what besides rhetoric are we offered in the way of insight into our 1815 model by its 1867 *Mehrwert* model? In neither short nor long versions of Marx's transformation problem can I find a cogent core. The 1815 model presents him with his opportunity. I can report to the reader that I put it through the 1867, 1885 and 1894 Marx paces and they failed perfectly to provide a single valid insight. (I wrote down volume II *Mehrwert* tableaux above, below and at switchpoints. Always irrelevancies.) The reader should judge whether Ian Steedman's *Marx after Sraffa* needs any revisions in the light of the Garegnani contentions.

Let me add that I have gone back to reread exactly what Piero Sraffa wrote in 1951 and 1960 and find no words that purport to reduce a three-parameter theory of value down to a one-parameter theory of value (save possibly for the passage in his *Introduction* where he without comment refers to Ricardo's (mistaken) attempt to get rid of the complication of land for exchange theory by considering goods as produced (endogenously?) on marginal zero-rent land.)

(5) Mr Garegnani has served us all well in describing more fully Sraffa's Italian undergraduate thesis.

I completely agree that the merits of a scientist's assertions are independent of the political party he votes for or the Church he attends. When a great scholar has passed into history, those of us who knew him and his works form part of the enterprise that constitutes his scientific biography. If Isaac Newton gave me as a reference for a job at the Mint, I would not deem it necessary to mention his penchant for alchemy; but, if that penchant had aught to suggest for his theory of optics, his scientific biographers will want to weigh contemporaries' impressions of the matter.[2]

Schefold

From no one have I learned more than from Bertram Schefold. At bottom we are in agreement, not disagreement.

(1) Schefold's first comment deals at some length with the undisputed difference between *steady-state* regimens and *transient* regimens when relative prices foreseeably are altered by evolving scarcities of produced-goods endowments (possibly on a rendezvous course with an asymptotic steady state). Mainstream theorists, more lacking in interest in Sraffian matters than I, would recognize all this as part of mainstream economics: Schumpeter, Fisher, Ramsey, von Neumann, Samuelson, Malinvaud, Koopmans, Hicks, Morishima, McKenzie, etc. Dozens of the chapters in *Collected Scientific Papers of Paul A. Samuelson* (1966c, 1966d, 1972, 1978b, 1986) deal with precisely such *transient* and *steady-state* contrasts. I hail Sraffa (1932) for early stimulus, which enabled a maiden paper of mine to identify and correct a *General Theory* blemish on own interest rates by showing that the same

no-excess profits are earned on all goods when relative prices are foreseeably changing – and this *independently* of the numéraire-good used and the choice among heterogenous own-rates of interest. Heady stuff for a 21-year-old old fledgling to correct a Keynes!

Nothing in Schefold's wording should deter his readers from realizing how sharp was my revisionist scalpel and how deep into neo-Ricardian arteries it cut. My censure of the labour theory of value (of Ricardo's editor; of the Garegnani belief that the lost 1815 corn-only model of Ricardo somehow saves the face of the labour theory and defends Marxian uniform-rate-of-*Mehrwert* analysis as a non-detour; and of what I had regarded as the Eatwell–Panico belief that Sraffian joint production leaves relative prices invariant under taste and demand changes) – all these critiques were directed to Schefold's present case of *permanent* rather than transient scarcities.

(2) In a long section, Schefold deals with joint products and with land as a primary factor along with labour. Here is one such permanent scarcities case. Claret is produced by labour largely on cool vineyard lands; vodka by labour largely on potato-bearing plains. Then 1926 Sraffa or 1989 Sraffians will err if they think a shift in tastes from wine to spirits will involve unchanged terms of trade between them in the *longest* run.

Every point in my revisionist critique can be purged of *all* neoclassical elements. Discrete activity analysis *à la* von Neuman and not Clark or Cobb–Douglas marginal products can push my scalpel inward. My contentions do not need to rely on indifference-contour utilitarianism; but like Adam, David and Stuart I would not want to deny that, when goods get dearer, people alter their consumption of them.

Even when the same *permanently* scarce lands can produce all the different goods, Ricardo, his editor and approving reviewers of the editor such as Stigler are simply dead-wrong to think that the complication of Smithian rent can be removed as a deviation from the labour theory of value by utilizing the *no-rent margin* for goods' relative cost comparisons. As Thünen, Wicksell, Frisch, Robbins and I have many times demonstrated, where the 'margin' (extensive or intensive) falls is an *endogenous* unknown dependent on the composition of demand and tastes. Ricardo himself occasionally lapses into good sense on the point: when land comes to be occupied by greater population, corn price rises relative to hair cuts; a permanent state of warfare, with its relative intensification of derived demand for labour-intensive soldiering, raises the population density of a region as the fruits of rent are given over to sustaining more people to be cannon fodder; in any time-run when labour and land are relatively fixed, their factorial terms of trade and shares are demand dependent.

My 1815 example of Garegnani type has already shown that a three-parameter theory of value is irreducibly needed. None of the above facts is possible under a true labour theory of value. Nor are they only 7 per cent possible under realistic conditions, as Ricardo lamely claimed with the support of one arbitrary numerical example that went down better with Stigler's (1958) computer than it did with mine.[3]

(3) Schefold is no dogmatist, and not even much interested in antiquarianism. He has a mathematical point to make in connection with joint products and land-and-labour scenarios. He admits that large enough changes in needs (or in tastes) can invalidate the non-substitution theorems that make equilibrium price ratios independent of the composition of demand. *Globally*, Schefold subscribes to a three-parameter theory of value. But, *locally*, he insists that *ss* supply curves can be regarded generally as flatly horizontal.

Speaking loosely, we can say that shifts in *dd* curves can cause intersections with *ss* curves to occur at different P_i (or P_i/P_j) levels – as the Mill–Ricardo trade theory and the Jevons–Walras paradigm stressed. But, Schefold insists, almost all vertical *dd* curves find their equilibrium intersections on the flats of the *ss* steps and not on the risers. *Locally* [my words, not his], the labour-only invariances do hold.

To a mathematician, the issue involves 'squareness of the effective submatrix', whether it is generally true that the number of goods and processes (counting land as a joint product) endogenously turn out to be equal. Such a contention is almost correct. If it were completely correct, that would not suffice to save the labour theory of value; but it would be an interesting fact.

First, I stress fundamentals. It was a well-known Frank Graham fallacy in the second quarter of this century that *n*-good and two-country comparative advantage models – or *n*-good and *m*-country models – had no need (*No* need? Virtually no need . . .) for demand functions to determine equilibrium terms of trade. The same linear programming calculus of rank of submatrixes of rectangular matrixes was involved. In the end, Graham was seen to be quibbling. The reader can predict that, in the end, just before everyone admits that land rents do affect relative prices, it will be argued that 'At least in proper post-Smith models, such and such holds . . .'.

Thirty years ago in the *QJE* I worked out the linear programming of discrete Ricardian models with differing land qualities. Even in the timeless case or the zero-profit-rate case, the constancy of relative prices entailed by the labour theory of value or the land theory of value was denied. Dantzig's fundamental theorem of linear programming – that extrema can always occur on vertex points – was utilized.

Digression on 'squareness'

We are all in Bertram Schefold's debt since he has been early and preeminent in working out Sraffian joint-production relations. Still that literature has a long way to go to catch up with the general von Neumann–Koopmans inequality–equality analysis of the following type:

$$[P_1 \,..\, P_n]\begin{bmatrix} b_{11} & .. & b_{1m} \\ \cdot & & \cdot \\ b_{n1} & .. & b_{nm} \end{bmatrix} \leqq W[a_{01} \,..\, a_{om}](1+r)$$

$$+ [P_1 \,..\, P_n]\begin{bmatrix} a_{11} & .. & a_{1m} \\ \cdot & & \cdot \\ a_{n1} & .. & a_{nm} \end{bmatrix}(1+r)$$

$$W, P_j \geqq 0, b_{ij} \geqq 0, a_{ij} \geqq 0, 1+r>0, m \gtreqless n \tag{1a}$$

$$[b_{ij}-a_{ij}]\begin{bmatrix} x_1 \\ \cdot \\ x_m \end{bmatrix} = \begin{bmatrix} C_1 \\ \cdot \\ C_n \end{bmatrix} \geqq 0, \qquad [a_{0j}]\begin{bmatrix} x_1 \\ \cdot \\ x_m \end{bmatrix} = L>0$$

$$[P_j][C_i] = WL + r\,[P_j][b_{ij}-a_{ij}][x_i] > 0$$

$$C_i \geqq 0, r \geqq 0, x_i \geqq 0. \tag{1b}$$

Even when generalized Hawkins–Simon conditions are assumed for the (b,a) matrices, we are infinitely far from a determinate unique solution for our steady-state system. Schefold proposes his own version of a theory of consumer 'needs'. Whether a quorum of modern economists will find it of interest and worth does not have to be pronounced on here: it consists of specifying that the (C_i/C_1) ratios be *exogenously* specified at any and all possible non-negative levels; as we shall see, it is a non-generic specification in the sense that it is embeddable in a more general manifold in such a way that (some of) its qualitative properties are lost by an epsilon-small deviation from its Schefold stipulation.

The purpose of all this was to try to show that, *almost always*, the competitive solutions to (1) will involve 'square' Sraffian production: thus, even when $m>>n$, $m-n$ of the x intensity levels will be competitively non-viable and the number of x-activities used positively will equal the number of goods produced positively.

Specify six b_{ij}'s, six a_{ij}'s, three a_{0j}'s, one Schefold's needs variable $C_2/(C_1+C_2)$ or c, and one r, all of which can generically be supposed to be positive. The remaining dozen variables can be specified to obey *any* positive joint-probability density function:

$$(b_{11}, b_{12}, b_{13}, b_{21}, b_{22}, b_{23}, a_{11} \ldots a_{23}, a_{01}, a_{02}, a_{03}, c, r)$$

Schefold's c can take on any value in the [0,1] interval and r any value in a neighbourhood of zero.

I now enumerate the possible results.

First, part of the 17-variable space will not permit of any steady state with positive net consumptions. Never mind: redefine the measure so that the feasible points in the Hawkins–Simon region add up in probability to unity with r permitted to be positive in some interval above zero.

Second, part of the space falls into that 'special domain' where, at $r=0$ and its neighbourhood, one of the three processes is competitively dominated: say, x_3 is the zero one. In the following special domain, Schefold and I are quite agreed that the non-substitution theorem of Sraffa's Part I is in effect satisfied and the C_2/C_1 ratio does *not* affect the P_2/P_1 equilibrium at each specified r. This special domain is where

$$\begin{bmatrix}(b_{11}-a_{11}) & (b_{12}-a_{12})\\(b_{21}-a_{21}) & (b_{22}-a_{22})\end{bmatrix}^{-1}=\begin{bmatrix}J_{11} & J_{12}\\J_{21} & J_{22}\end{bmatrix}>0 \tag{2}$$

Incidentally, Schefold believes I underestimate the 'probability' contained in this special domain: I don't know how to decide whether he should be agreed with in this (in the case of either $n=2$, or $n>2$ where 'diagonal dominance' becomes a more intricate concept).

Third, since the above special domain has only fractional probability, we face positive probability for the traditional cases of joint production described by Smith, Longfield, Mangoldt, Marshall, Hubert Henderson and a horde of pre-Sraffa writers. It is sufficient to contemplate the hoary wool–mutton example, or the taxicab-worked-hard-or-easy-when-new example, to demonstrate the following:

> There is positive-probability measure, not zero-probability measure, that competitive production is *not* 'square' in the Schefold universe. Square production is *not* 'almost always' true.

I have published examples like the following: 1 labour produces 1 red sheep that contains 3 of wool and 3 of mutton. Or: 1 labour produces 1 blue sheep with 4 of wool and 1 of mutton. Or: 1 labour produces 1 green sheep with 1 of wool and 4 of mutton.

When people want wool and mutton in exactly equal Schefold proportions, a singular case that almost never happens, only red sheep are produced. This deviation from squareness is trivially rare and I forbear to count it against Mr Schefold.

Now consider the positive measure in which people 'need' a bit more of wool than of mutton. Mr Schefold gets his squareness. Red and blue sheep are both produced and only them. *Local* swings in his C_2/C_1 ratio leave P_2/P_1 invariant at 1/2. The blade of vertical *dd* demand is weak relative to the *ss* supply blade (on the flat step).

Schefold well understands that a shift of *his* demand to wool being newly needed in fractional amount compared to mutton again produces squareness at first: only red and green sheep are produced; and, so to speak in neoclassical fashion, the newly prized wool has its relative price coaxed up from 1/2 to 2 (the increasing-cost case!).

So far squareness? Yes. But further shifts in the Schefold needs parameter c, below 1/3 or above 3, loses squareness with positive measure.

For C_2/C_1 above 3 only green sheep are competitively producible and we have lost squareness. With similar positive probability C_2/C_1 will be below 1/3, only blue sheep will be producible, and squareness will be lost. With these same probabilities one of the goods will have zero price – or, if disposal costs are unavoidable, even a negative price.[4]

Indeed, if red sheep had their productivities grow from (3 wool, 3 muttons) to above (4,4), for *almost all* Schefold's C_2/C_1 ratios, squareness and all-positive prices would be lost.

Economic squareness's universality is even more limited by the consideration that extreme price changes realistically modify even the neediest of needs. Schefold sees the point, even in exaggerated form, when it is a question of technology and innovation. For him, Necessity is indeed the mother of invention, and Nature indeed abhors the vacuum of a redundant harvest and a free good. But, beyond the thin line of his needs psychology, diplomatic recognition is withheld.

Schefold and I agree that, when C_j demanded is affectable by price, the probability measure of non-square equilibria is definitely positive even when all *P*'s are stipulated to be positive. By stipulating *vertical dd* demand curves, almost all his intersections with the ascending *ss* stairs are on the flat of steps and not on the risers. The Schefold construction is not *generic*, but rather infinitely unrobust. When he lets his *dd*'s be tilted ever so little from the vertical – and whose theory is so exact as to permit no perturbation at all? – Schefold will encounter positive measure of non-squareness cum positive prices and intersections of *dd* on *ss* risers.

Does much of this smack to the reader of Middle Age casuistry concerning how many angels can dance on the end of a pin? If so, join with my complaints and address them to the appropriate post-Sraffian authorities.

In any case the *global* truth that subjectivist demand alters Part II price ratios save in the special domain described above can no longer be in dispute and is independent of the angels-on-pins squareness calculi. Should one laugh or cry when a commentator admits that *local* invariance is compatible with global lack of invariance but excuses not using the local/global distinction because it has become 'controversial in the Sraffian literature'?

Approximation theory can save no argument or the face of any arguer. Consider a Clark–Solow paradigm in which joint production never involves as many techniques as there are goods, in which positive prices are determinable but only by demands–needs considerations, and in which everyone agrees that land invalidates the labour theory of value and *all* non-substitution theorems. Piero Sraffa would turn over in his grave to contemplate such a marginalist's orgy. None the less, Mr Schefold and Mr Garegnani will agree with me that it is a trivial theorem (of approximating an arc by broken line segments) that permits us to specify Sraffa-discrete models that come as closely as we like to having *all* the qualitative and quantitative properties of the Clark–Solow heresy! (As tit for tat, Clark–Solow models come as close as we like to having double-reswitching, 'perverse Wicksell' effects, and plateaus of consumption that both rise and fall with the interest rate. Philip Wicksteed and Bates Clark had a lot to learn from Piero and Joan!)

(4) The reader's patience and my time are by now exhausted. Concerning Schefold's final effort to find a useful role for the *standard commodity*, let me

be over-brief. In the single-products case with a single set of $[a_{ij},a_{0j}]$ coefficients, P_i/P_j ratios are known to be able to vary with $1 + r$ like the ratio of an n'th degree numerator to an n'th degree denominator. Many ups and downs are, in general, possible when n exceeds 2. If the reader learns something further from the *standard commodity* construct that is deemed interesting, I applaud from a distance.

However, as soon as we admit the realism of *alternative* viable techniques at different profit rates, *all is lost*. Literally any (and *all*!) qualitative patterns for P_i/P_j can occur and none of the multiplicity of local-piecewise straight-line-segment loci puts limits on what can qualitatively obtain.

There is a paradoxical turnaround. I used to have to counsel my neoclassical friends to give up the oversimplification that Garegnani, Pasinetti and Morishima showed them does not exist. Now I must nag my Sraffian friends to give up untenable *standard commodity* oversimplifications.

Notes

1 I quite agree with Garegnani that a square $[a_{ij}]$ that is *decomposable* may have associated with it a subsistence wage vector, $0 \leqq [m_i] \neq 0$, such that its associated 1957 Seton matrix, $[s_{ij}] = [a_{ij} + m_i a_{0j}]$ is *in*decomposable and possessive of a unique (normalized) column eigenvector. Such a Seton *standard commodity* is not Sraffa's 1960 *standard commodity*. Sraffa tried to build on the rock of technology. The Ricardo circle knew well that any subsistence wage vector adjusted endogenously to land/labour scarcities: in densely settled Ireland, the potato superseded meat and grain; Ricardo and Mill, along with the later Marx, reduced their *subsistence* model of wage supply to a virtual convention once they divorced subsistence from a hard physiological basis and could make it fit *ex post* any and all observations. Once we augment the direct labour vector $[a_{0j}]$ by a direct land vector $[a_{-1j}]$, the Seton $[s_{ij}]$ matrix and standard commodity lose their autonomous dependence on the (a_0,m,a) coefficients.

2 One of Keynes's biographers, feeling a need to justify his own voyeurism, quoted Schumpeter's disparagement of Keynes as a policy adviser influenced by his childless status. This early instance of Bloomsbury-bashing no doubt plays into the prejudices of conservative anti-Keynesians. But, if it were the case that Schumpeter's arrow hit its target, we could not rule it out of civilized court. Actually, though, as I had to argue at Harvard's 350th gathering, Schumpeter was wrong on this Keynes issue. The man who wrote (in quite another 1923 connection), 'In the long run we are all dead', was a sentimental English patriot in the Edmund Burke style, a loyal son of Eton and King's and of the intellectual middle class, with a concern for posterity that Josef Schumpeter and I could well envy. Sociobiologists like Hamilton and Wilson know that even Popes have nephews and I am not engaging in *double entendre*.

3 Schefold asserts that Saucier (1981) has shown that something I said in 1987 *Palgrave* was wrong. I deny error. The mathematics of maximization endorses what I wrote. The own competitive supply response to a single change in output price can never reverse sign. Not only is this spelled out in the 1983 enlarged edition of *Foundations*, but before the birth of Dantzig's linear programming I had proved in Samuelson (1946) from the logic of maximizing that Giffen sign reversals could not occur in a linear programming problem even more general than Stigler's least-cost diet problem. My *QJE* 1959 Ricardo Appendix, written in

ignorance of Frisch's exploration of the 1930s, showed precisely how many qualities of land affect Ricardo's rents. Whatever Saucier validly established, it was not error in my 1987 sentences. The general supply inequality.

$$0 \leqq (\Delta p_1)(\Delta q_1) + (\Delta p_2)(\Delta q_2) + \ldots$$

is valid and entails, when all Δp_j vanish except for a rise in p_1, that q_1 cannot fall even when (in Schefold's words) 'several lands and agricultural products are involved'.

4 *Editorial note*: After some hesitation, I use my discretion as an editor to clear up a possible misunderstanding. According to the example, we either have an additional disposal process or only one process and one good with a positive price so that the system that actually emerges *is* square according to *my* definition. I have consistently proposed that only goods with non-zero prices and processes with non-zero activity levels should be counted (p. 196, p. 309); my zero-probability theorem rests on this assumption. (BS)

10

Keynes and Sraffa: Visions and Perspectives

Athanasios Asimakopulos
Montreal

Piero Sraffa's *Production of Commodities by Means of Commodities* has stimulated the writing of numerous articles and books, as economic theorists have tried to come to grips with the implications of this seminal work. It has led to the reconsideration of other approaches to economic theory, and the demonstration of the absence of a theoretical basis for '*any* notion of capital as a measurable quantity independent of distribution and prices' (Sraffa, 1960, p. 38) was a critical element in the 'reswitching' arguments of the 1960s (Samuelson *et al.*, 1966; Harcourt, 1972). Sraffa's subtitle for his book was 'Prelude to a critique of economic theory', with the theory referred to being the neoclassical or marginalist explanation of prices and distribution that was developed from the 1870s. Keynes's theory of employment, presented in *The General Theory of Employment, Interest and Money* (1936a), also represents a fundamental criticism of this neoclassical approach,[1] since he tries to establish that the equilibrium position in the economy is not one of full employment. Even though they both provide the basis for fundamental critiques of the neoclassical approach to economics, these works of Sraffa and Keynes focus on different questions. The former is concerned with the determination of relative prices, given technology and final output, and the latter with the factors determining output and employment. On the surface, the two appear to be, at least potentially, compatible, since Sraffa's work leaves open the question of the determination of the level of output (Roncaglia, 1978, p. xviii). It has also been argued (Garegnani, 1979a, p. 79) that the replacement of the marginalist elements in Keynes's analysis by Sraffa's explanation of relative prices will provide a much firmer basis for Keynes's critique of the view that the 'normal' level of employment in a capitalist economy is one of full employment.

Attempts to 'marry' the Sraffa and Keynes approaches to economic theory overlook the fundamental differences between them – the difference in the role of time and the visions of the operations of capitalist economies implicit in these theories. That this is, at least partly, recognized by those who are trying to combine the two theories is evident in the attempt to interpret Keynes's *General Theory* as being concerned with 'long-period' output and employment (Eatwell, 1983; Milgate, 1982). The present paper will deal mainly with Keynes's *General Theory*, and the position taken is that its short-period setting is a critical feature of this theory and must be part of any attempt to consider its implications for developments over time. For purposes of contrast it is useful to begin with a brief statement of what appears to be the economic basis of Sraffa's approach to the determination of prices.

1 *Sraffa's prices of production*

Sraffa's system of production is set in a particular period of time, a year (Sraffa, 1960, p. 3), in which the technical relations of production and the total amount to be produced of each commodity are fixed. These technical relations show (in Part I of the book where there are only single-product industries) the amounts of each of the commodities and labour (which for purposes of simplification is taken to be homogeneous) required to produce the specific output of each commodity. It is assumed in the main body of the book that the system produces a surplus – in the year more is produced of at least one of the commodities than is required as an input, and at least enough is produced of all the other commodities to replace the amounts used as inputs. In order to determine the prices of production in such a system it is necessary to know how the surplus is to be divided between wages and profits. Sraffa asserts that in his system there will be an equal rate of profits in all industries. There is no attempt to justify this assumption; he simply states when setting out his price equations 'we add the rate of profit (which must be uniform for all industries)' (ibid, p. 6). If the share of the surplus going to wages is then given, prices and this equal rate of profits can be determined. For different shares of surplus going to wages, relative prices as well as the rate of profits will, in general, differ.

In this way, Sraffa obtains an explanation of relative prices that depends only on technical relations of production and distributive shares. The commodity composition of the surplus is taken as given in all the comparisons of differences in prices, and there is no investigation of the effect of differences in demand on prices. If the assumption of constant returns to scale in each industry were added, then demand could be said to have no effect on relative prices, but Sraffa makes no such assumption. He notes in his Preface that '[N]o changes in output . . . are considered, so that no question arises as to the variation or constancy of returns' (ibid., p. v). The question of whether demand could affect the prices of production in a complete economic system[2] of which Sraffa's system of production is a part, is thus left formally open, even though the general thrust of Sraffa's work implies that demand is not important in this context or, at least, that its influence on price is 'not comparable' with those of labour and material inputs.[3]

Sraffa writes that the 'standpoint' of his investigation 'is that of the old classical economists from Adam Smith to Ricardo' (ibid.), and his prices of production have thus been identified with the 'natural' or long-period prices of the classical economists (Garegnani, 1979b, p. 185). These prices are viewed as 'centres of gravitation' for actual, market prices (Garegnani, 1976a, pp. 26–9; Milgate, 1982, p. 20). However, Sraffa's system of production and the specification of distributive shares only allow for the mathematical derivation of prices of production; there is nothing in his analysis to justify the treatment of prices of production as values towards which actual prices tend to move. He does not deal with dynamic processes of adjustment.[4] The only 'time' in the system is the 'year' during which production takes place, and there is no linking of 'years' – even in an informal manner – in order to indicate the possible relationship between the prices of production and actual prices.[5]

With Keynes's *General Theory* we are in a very different analytical environment, even though relatively little attention is paid to dynamic processes. The focus is on the factors affecting the determination of output and employment in the short period, with some consideration being given to whether or not there would be reliable forces at work tending to move the economy to a position of full employment over time. The conclusion is negative, with no weight being given to the possibility of attraction being exerted by long-period equilibrium values.

2 *Keynes's theory of employment*

Keynes's analysis of the factors determining the level of output and employment in an economy is set in a Marshallian short period. 'We take as given the existing skill and quantity of available labour, the existing quality and quantity of available equipment, the existing technique . . .' (Keynes, 1936a, p. 245). His theory is concerned, in a formal sense, with the equilibrium level of output and employment in such a period and, in a less formal sense, with whether over time – over a sequence of short periods – automatic forces would be set in motion to move the economy towards a position of full employment. In the one-paragraph first chapter of the *General Theory*, Keynes explains why he is 'placing the emphasis on the prefix *general*' (ibid., p. 3; emphasis in the original) in the title of his book. He states that the postulates of what he calls the 'classical' theory are 'applicable to a special case only and not to the general case, the situation which it assumes being a limiting point of the possible positions of equilibrium' (ibid.). The implication is that his theory is concerned with the general case, where equilibrium with full employment is only one of many possibilities.[6] The term 'equilibrium' as used by Keynes refers to a position of rest for the variable of interest (employment in this case) given the values of the parameters, and not necessarily one where there is no change in the values of other variables (Asimakopulos, 1973; Patinkin, 1982, p. 14). Equilibrium for Keynes in this book does not refer to a situation where prices and quantities transacted are such that all individuals are on their demand and supply curves.

The criticial decision-makers in Keynes's model are the entrepreneurs. They decide on the levels of employment and output in the short period in the light of short-term expectations of prices and costs, and they determine investment on the basis of long-term expectations. The setting for Keynes's model can be viewed as a particular 'moment' in historical time – a 'moment' whose characteristics have been determined by decisions and actions in the past. In fact, this moment is defined by the 'existing quality and quantity of available equipment, the existing technique . . .' (Keynes, 1936a, p. 245). This is one reason for its identification with Marshall's short period, to which a calendar dimension of 'a few months or a year' (Marshall, [1920], 1949, p. 379) is given. Changes in equipment and techniques are, of course, taking place in a progressive economy even within such a period, but the effects of these changes are small relative to those of the initial conditions, and it is not unreasonable to ignore them.[7] Keynes concentrates on equilibrium situations in these short periods; he does not deal with the process of adjustment to equilibrium positions or the time required to reach a new equilibrium position after a change in the values of the parameters. Although Keynes's analysis is in 'historical time' from the point of view of its setting and his emphasis on the expectational basis of decisions and actions, it is 'out of time' in terms of its limitation to situations of equilibrium.[8] With its use of given equipment and techniques, Keynes's short period must occupy a relatively brief span of time in an economy where there is net investment, but the time required to reach a position of equilibrium after a change may be greater than this interval.[9] Keynes simply concentrates on positions of short-period equilibrium, presumably to contrast his conclusions with the equilibrium results of 'classical' theory.[10]

Given his aim of dealing with the factors determining the level of aggregate output, Keynes had to adapt Marshall's short-period supply curves for individual goods to serve this purpose. He distrusts measures and comparisons of aggregate output, because 'the community's output of goods and services is a non-homogenous complex which cannot be measured . . .' (Keynes, 1936a, p. 38). He thus relies 'on the general presumption that the amount of employment associated with a given capital equipment will be a satisfactory index of the amount of resultant output' (ibid., p. 41). The employment in any period is the result of decisions that depend on short-term expectations, which are 'concerned with the price a manufacturer can expect to get for his "finished" output at the time when he commits himself to starting the process which will produce it' (ibid, p. 46). These individual expectations of prices – together with the cost conditions of the individual firms – are then turned into expectations of proceeds for purposes of aggregation. The profit-maximizing competitive firms produce outputs that equate these expected prices and marginal costs, and their short-term expectations of proceeds are the proceeds they would receive if they sold these outputs at the expected prices. Since these proceeds are measured in dollar terms, they can be aggregated over the economy, and for each set of expected prices they provide (once user costs are deducted) a point on the aggregate supply function.[11]

Keynes emphasized the importance of expectations in a theory of employment: 'The *expected* results are not on a par with the *realised* results in a theory of employment. The *realised* results are only relevant in so far as they influence the ensuing expectations in the next production period' (Keynes, 1973b, p. 179; emphasis in original). He could thus have gone on from this perspective to define effective demand as the value of proceeds at the point on the aggregate supply curve corresponding to the short-term expectations of proceeds of entrepreneurs, since in this theory it is this value that determines the amount of employment offered by firms. But Keynes concentrated on situations of short-period equilibrium where the short-term expectations of firms are borne out by events – he identifies the aggregate demand function[12] with the value of proceeds that would be received by firms at alternative levels of employment in the economy, and he defines effective demand as the value 'of the aggregate demand function, where it is intersected by the aggregate supply function . . .' (Keynes, 1936a, p. 25). The proceeds on the aggregate demand function are also taken to be equilibrium values. The consumption expenditures that are included in this function are assumed to be in the desired relation to income, and the investment expenditures are equal to those that firms planned to make in the period.

The factors underlying the aggregate demand and supply functions thus explain the determination of equilibrium employment in the particular short period of the economy. This equilibrium is stable – given the level of investment – because at a value for employment higher (lower) than this equilibrium level, the aggregate supply price would lie above (below) the aggregate demand price. This relationship is assumed to hold because '[T]he psychology of the community is such that when aggregate real income is increased aggregate consumption is increased, but not by so much as income' (ibid., p. 27). Although in the statement of the 'essence' of his general theory of employment,[13] Keynes gives equal emphasis to the role of the propensity to consume and to the volume of investment, it is to the latter that he keeps referring for an explanation of why employment could be less than full. For example, '. . . to justify any given amount of employment there must be an amount of current investment sufficient to absorb the excess of total output over what the community chooses to consume when employment is at the given level . . . It follows . . . that, given what we shall call the community's propensity to consume, the equilibrium level of employment . . . will depend on the amount of current investment' (ibid., p., 27). In his 1937 reply to reviewers of the *General Theory* in the *Quarterly Journal of Economics*, Keynes referred to investment as the '*causa causans*' of the economic system, because of the unreliability of the factors 'which determine the rate of investment . . . since it is they which are influenced by our views of the future about which we know so little' (Keynes, 1973b, p. 121).

Keynes's central message in the *General Theory* is thus two-fold. First, there is the theory of effective demand – output and employment for the economy are determined by the intersection of aggregate demand and supply curves – and, second, there is the unreliability of the factors determining investment, which explains why aggregate demand will be variable and often less than sufficient to ensure full employment.[14]

3 *The determination of investment in Keynes's theory*

Keynes presents two seemingly different approaches to the determination of investment – one in chapter 11 of the *General Theory*, and the other in chapter 12 as well as in his 1937 *Quarterly Journal of Economics* paper. The first approach emphasizes the inverse relationship between the rate of interest and investment, while the second, although not excluding the possibility of such a relationship, looks primarily to states of mind and attitudes in the face of an uncertain future as the major factors underlying investment decisions.[15]

The presentation in chapter 11 implies the existence of a stable, downward-sloping investment demand schedule with investment being pushed to the 'point on the investment demand schedule where the marginal efficiency of capital in general is equal to the market rate of interest' (Keynes, 1936a, p. 137). It is from such a schedule that an IS curve can be derived (Hicks, 1937). The reason Keynes gives for a diminishing marginal efficiency of capital schedule as investment increases is not consistent with the framework of his analysis, as Kalecki pointed out in his 1936 review of the *General Theory* (Targetti and Kinda-Hass, 1982). The marginal efficiency of capital is expected to be lower, the higher the investment in Keynes's short period because of the higher price of capital goods, which are produced under conditions of increasing costs. This argument contains both *ex ante* and *ex post* features. The expectation of profitability, of future quasi-rents from the purchase of capital goods, is *ex ante*, but the higher prices of capital goods, which are required to make the marginal efficiency of capital schedule downward-sloping, would only be experienced as a result of a general increase in investment. If such an increase occurred, prices of other goods and profitability in general would also increase, so that it would not be reasonable to assume that the expectations of future quasi-rents would be unchanged (Asimakopulos, 1971).

In chapter 12, the viewpoint shifts from the dependence on the calculation of yields to recognition of 'the extreme precariousness of the basis of knowledge on which our estimates of prospective yield have to be made. Our knowledge of the factors which will govern the yield of an investment some years hence is usually very slight and often negligible' (Keynes, 1936a, p. 149). Estimates made on such a basis are subject to large margins of error and to substantial change in the light of current events. Keynes thus backs away from the idea of a stable investment demand schedule that can be acted on by monetary policy: '. . . it seems likely that the fluctuations in the market estimation of the marginal efficiency of different types of capital, calculated on the principles I have described above, will be too great to be offset by any practicable changes in the rate of interest' (ibid., p. 164).

With investment being subject to fluctuations for the reasons given above, the short-period equilibrium levels of employment determined by these fluctuating investments will also fluctuate. There is no reason to expect from Keynes's analysis that these fluctuations will be around some full-employment level – there are no 'normal' long-period values that serve as centres of gravitation for actual values in Keynes's theory.[16]

4 *Long-period employment in the General Theory*

The present interpretation of the *General Theory* has emphasized its short-period framework. This theory concentrates on what has been referred to here as 'short-period equilibrium employment'. This is the level of employment corresponding to a situation where actual investment is equal to planned investment, and consumption is in the desired relation to income. In this equilibrium situation the short-term expectations of proceeds held by entrepreneurs are borne out by events in this short period. The proceeds of capital goods producers (equal, in this case, to their short-term expectations) come from investment expenditures, and they thus depend on the long-term expectations of investing firms. These long-term expectations may have been held at different times in the past, since the time-lags in the investment process are such that investment expenditures in any short period are the result of decisions taken at different times. The actual investment in any period is thus, in general, the result of more than one state of long-term expectations. Keynes looks briefly at a very special case where *all* the investment in a short period is the result of a particular state of long-term expectations. The resulting level of employment is 'called the long-period employment corresponding to that state of expectation' (Keynes, 1936a, p. 48). Keynes added a footnote to this definition:

> It is not necessary that the level of long-period employment should be *constant, i.e.* long-period conditions are not necessarily static. For example, a steady increase in wealth or population may constitute a part of the unchanging expectation. The only condition is that the existing expectations should have been foreseen sufficiently far ahead.
>
> (ibid.; emphasis in original)

The level of employment being referred to in all these cases is, of course, short-period employment, but short-period employment based on investment guided by identical long-term expectations. If these expectations are that stationary conditions will prevail, then this employment would be that corresponding to zero net investment.[17] But the unchanging expectations may be of a steady increase in demand over time, with the rates of investment generated by these expectations increasing over time. The corresponding long-period employment would then also be increasing from one short period to the next.

The relationship between Keynes's long-period (equilibrium) employment and his short-period (equilibrium) employment bears a superficial resemblance to the relationship between Marshall's long-period equilibrium and short-period equilibrium for competitive industries (Asimakopulos, 1984-5). A situation of long-period equilibrium must also be one of short-period equilibrium in both cases. For Marshall, long-period equilibrium values tend to attract short-period values,[18] but there is not even a hint in Keynes's presentation of long-period employment serving as a centre of attraction for actual values.[19]

5 Long-period interpretations of the General Theory

Eatwell (1983) and Milgate (1982) have argued for an interpretation of Keynes's theory of output and employment as concerned with 'the long-period level of output' (Eatwell, 1983, p. 98; Milgate, 1982, pp. 84–91). This view differs from the one taken here, which is consistent with statements made by Keynes's close associates. Joan Robinson has always emphasized the short-period framework of Keynes's analysis and she noted, for example, that 'Keynes hardly ever peered over the edge of the short period to see the effect of investment in making additions to the stocks of productive equipment' (Robinson, 1978, p. 14). Lord Kahn has recently reaffirmed this position with his statement: 'The *General Theory* is short-period in the Marshallian sense' (Kahn, 1984, p. 122). The bases for the long-period interpretation advanced by Eatwell and Milgate are a few statements in the *General Theory*. They give a special reading to Keynes's listing of the factors he takes as given when he comes to restate his *General Theory* in chapter 18, and they then attach great weight to Keynes's reference to ' "natural" tendencies' which 'are likely to persist' in the final paragraph of that chapter.

Eatwell argues that 'the fixed composition of the capital stock which defines Marshall's short period plays no role in Keynes's theory of employment – unemployment is, according to Keynes, not due to the shortage of a particular capital good, but to a lack of effective demand' (Eatwell, 1983, p. 97). This position is based on a misinterpretation of the use of Marshall's short period in Keynes's analysis. The composition and quantity of capital equipment are taken as given, with the focus being on the degree of utilization, on average, of that equipment. It is not inconsistent in a macroeconomic analysis to overlook, for purposes of arriving at a general characterization of the situation in the economy, the possibility that an industry may have insufficient productive capacity to meet demand, even though plant in most other industries is operating at less than full capacity. This does not deprive the macroeconomic analysis of its short-period status. Keynes's recognition that, even in a short period, changes in equipment are taking place does not make his analysis a long-period one. The effects of these changes are ignored by Keynes because within the time period of his analysis they are small relative to initial values. Keynes's aggregate supply function, an essential element of his theory of effective demand, is based on the assumption of given productive capacity. Keynes incorporated in his theory the inverse relation between the real wage rate and the level of investment, a relation based on 'the familiar proposition that industry is normally working subject to decreasing returns in the short period during which equipment etc. is assumed to be constant . . .' (Keynes, 1936a, p. 17). If Keynes were dealing with long-period output, as Eatwell and Milgate contend, then he would have had no basis for this inverse relation.

Eatwell interprets Keynes's statement qualifying the assumption of given equipment: 'This does not mean that we assume these factors to be constant; but merely that, in this place and context, we are not considering or taking into account the effects and consequences of changes in them'(Keynes, 1936a, p. 245), as ruling out 'changes in the dominant and persistent forces' (Eatwell, 1983, p. 97) that Marshall classified as affecting secular movements in normal prices.[20] An alternative reading of Keynes's statement that is consistent with Marshall's three periods for the analysis of 'normal' prices – 'short', 'long' and 'secular' – is that Keynes in the *General Theory* was, in the main body of this work, abstracting from the effects of changes in productive capacity that are the concern of long-period analysis. A formal treatment of long-period output would have required the explicit and careful consideration of the effects on productive capacity of investment. Such a treatment – a theory of accumulation – is absent in the *General Theory*.[21]

There is also the matter of the interpretation to be given to Keynes's statement at the end of chapter 18:

> . . . the outstanding features of our actual experience; – namely, that we oscillate, avoiding the gravest extremes of fluctuation in employment and in prices in both directions, round an intermediate position appreciably below full employment and appreciably above the minimum employment a decline below which would endanger life.
>
> But we must not conclude that the mean position thus determined by 'natural' tendencies, namely, by those tendencies which are likely to persist, failing measures expressly designed to correct them, is, therefore, established by laws of necessity. The unimpeded rule of the above conditions is a fact of observation concerning the world as it is or has been, and not a necessary principle which cannot be changed.
>
> (Keynes, 1936a, p. 254)

Eatwell takes these statements to mean that '[T]he *persistent* forces establish the long-period level of output; it is these forces and that level which Keynes's theory is designed to explain' (Eatwell, 1983, p. 98).[22] Keynes's statements should, however, be interpreted in the light of his views on investment. He did not believe that investment, determined by entrepreneurs in a capitalist economy subject to change, would settle down at a level that would result, given the propensity to consume, in full employment. In fact, there is nothing in his vision of the capitalist system that would lead him to believe that the economy would be attracted to some other 'persistent' level of employment. The variability of conditions and uncertainty that affect the outcome of investment decisions would be reflected in the variability of investment, output and employment. The 'intermediate position' around which fluctuations occur, referred to by Keynes, is some average value indicated by 'our actual experience' and 'observation', rather than a 'centre of gravitation'.

For Keynes the time path of output and employment depends on the pattern of long-term expectations held over a sequence of periods, because of their effect on investment. Those who argue 'that the whole of the innovative core of the *General Theory* is best regarded as dealing with the "centre of gravitation" of the system' (Milgate, 1982, p. 90) concentrate on Keynes's theory of effective demand,[23] i.e. the adjustment of desired saving to investment as a result of changes in income. They treat his statements on the importance of the variability of long-term expectations in the face of uncertainty as part of his criticism of the neoclassical theory of interest (Garegnani, 1976a, pp. 39–42), rather than as an integral part of his theory of employment in a capitalist economy. However, in setting out the basis of his theory of employment, Keynes wrote, '[E]xpress reference to current long-term expectations can seldom be avoided' (Keynes, 1936a, p. 50). It is reference to short-term expectations that is often omitted, on the assumption that they are subject to constant revision in the light of realized results, and Keynes tends to identify them with actual values. In the short-period equilibria on which he focussed, the short-term expectations are equal to actual proceeds. It is with reference to this category of expectations that Keynes wrote in his 1937 lecture notes '. . . the theory of effective demand is substantially the same if we assume that short-period expectations are always fulfilled' (Keynes, 1973b, p. 181).[24]

6 *The theory of effective demand in the short and long period*

Production and employment always occur in a short-period context, with given equipment and technique being utilized. This short-period context never disappears, even though the focus of attention is on long-period developments. In considering the latter, one is dealing, at least implicitly, with a succession of short periods as investment and technical progress alter productive capacity and techniques. If, as in the *General Theory*, the analysis concentrates on situations of short-period equilibrium, then employment (in a closed economy, with no government economic activity) in each period will be determined by the level of investment and the economy's propensity to consume.[25] The nature of the theory of effective demand is not altered by extending the analysis to a sequence of short periods. The path traced by the short-period equilibrium output and employment over time depends (assuming that the consumption function is stable) on what happens to investment, that is, on how long-term expectations and financial conditions change. A variety of possible growth paths can be deduced, each reflecting different assumptions about the drive of entrepreneurs, the degree of thriftiness in the economy, financial policies, trade union actions, etc. (Robinson, 1962d, pp. 52–9). Recognition of the infectious nature of good and bad news, and the financial system's propensity to facilitate the capitalization of expected profits (Minsky, 1982), leads to the conclusion that growth paths will be disturbed by cyclical movements and interrupted by crises. In fact, cyclical and long-term factors influence one another and are so intertwined that the separation of the two is problematic. In Kalecki's words, 'the long-run trend is but a slowly changing component of a chain of short-period situations; it has no independent entity . . .' (Kalecki, 1971a, p. 165). There is no reason to expect – certainly in the type of world visualized by Keynes – that 'in the long period', if this is taken to be some time in the future, productive capacity will become adjusted to demand. The consequences of this occurring – and continuing to hold – for a stretch of time can be examined. But in a changing world such a situation would *not* be a 'centre of gravitation' for actual values. In making investment decisions, firms try, of course, to anticipate future demand and not to be caught with too much or too little productive capacity, but this route takes us back to the importance of long-term expectations in determining investment, with employment in any short period then depending on this investment.

Conclusion

Keynes and Sraffa were concerned with very different questions in their two major works under consideration here. Keynes dealt with the factors determining the level of output and employment, and Sraffa with those determining prices of production, given output and employment. A further important difference between them is in the character of the 'equilibrium' implicit in each of their approaches.

Keynes's analysis is centred on a Marshallian short period, and the prices implicit in his model are those determined by the intersection of demand and short-period supply curves. The intersection of his aggregate demand and supply functions is a macroeconomic representation of the intersections of the large number of competitive industry demand and supply curves in his model. Macroeconomic changes would affect the level of costs when, for example, an increase in employment increases money wage rates, and thus the prices of individual commodities, but this could be readily incorporated in a Marshallian short-period analysis. However, Marshall's long-period equilibrium, where productive capacity is adjusted to demand, has no place (even implicitly) in Keynes's analysis. Long-period values can be defined for any given situation of technical knowledge and demand, but in a changing economy such values would be in a continual state of flux, so that they do not serve as the basis of investment decisions and thus do not act as a reliable force of attraction for actual prices. In Keynes's approach, investment decisions are based on expected conditions in future time periods, and in the final analysis, after allowing for all the calculations based on current and past data and informed estimates, these long-term expectations are subjective.

Sraffa's analysis is concerned with the prices of production – prices based on equal rates of profits in all industries – where investment in the different industries has resulted in productive capacity in each that is appropriate to demand. For these prices to serve as centres of gravitation for actual prices, conditions must be changing relatively slowly, so that mistaken investments are relatively minor, with actual prices tending towards the prices of production. Investment decisions in this case – although formally they can be said to be determined by long-term expectations – are basically determined by objective factors. This vision of a capitalist economy in the twentieth century is different from that held by Keynes.

Notes

1. Keynes expected his book to have a profound effect on economic theory. He wrote to George Bernard Shaw at the beginning of 1935 'that I believe myself to be writing a book on economic theory which will largely revolutionise . . . the way the world thinks about economic problems' (Keynes, 1973a, p. 492).
2. As Robinson (1965, p. 9) stated in her 1961 review of this book, 'we are given only half of an equilibrium system to stand on'.
3. I had written to Sraffa in 1971 and had observed that his theoretical framework did not permit any conclusions about the effects of demand on prices unless the

assumption of constant returns to scale were added. He responded in a letter dated 11 July 1971.

> You say 'I don't see how demand can be said to have no influence on ... prices, unless constant returns ...'. I take it that the drama is enacted on Marshall's stage where the claimants for influence are utility and cost of production. Now utility has made little progress (since the 1870s) towards acquiring a tangible existence and survives in textbooks at the purely subjective level. On the other hand, cost of production has successfully survived Marshall's attempt to reduce it to an equally evanescent nature under the name of 'disutility', and is still kicking in the form of hours of labour, tons of raw materials, etc. This, rather than the relative slope of the two curves, is why it seems to me that the 'influence' of the two things on price is not comparable.

4. Newman has written that Sraffa's assumption that the rate of profits should be the same in each industry 'is obviously the equilibrium condition (in a world of certainty) for a dynamic process in which each capitalist tries to maximize his profits' (Newman, 1962, p. 63). Similarly, Carvalho has argued that the view of prices of production as centres of gravitation 'clearly involves the idea of a process and of a time span necessary for the production prices to emerge and assert themselves' (Carvalho, 1983–4, p. 274). In a later work he states that implicit in the view of prices of production as a centre of gravitation is a theory of investment where investments 'must be determined by *current* differences in rates of profit while mistaken investments do not lead to the loss of the capital value invested. Thus, firms are able to reorient their resources from less to more profitable sectors without significant capital loss' (Carvalho, 1984–5, p. 219; emphasis in original).
5. Roncaglia (1978, p. 219) has argued that in contrast to neoclassical theories that 'are placed in an atemporal context as a consequence of the attempt to identify an equilibrium position for the values of the variables of the economic system under consideration ... it would seem more correct to say that Sraffa's analysis is not static, but rather that it represents a "photograph" of a particular moment of a system's development ... time is taken into account by the fact that any particular moment of time is determined by its past history, and serves as the determining factor of the next moment in time.' Prices of production can, of course, be derived for any 'particular moment of time', but there is nothing in Sraffa's analysis to indicate the relationship between actual prices and these prices of production. There is no 'movement' from one 'moment' to the other, or any movement within a 'moment'.
6. Another explanation for the use of the word 'general', a concern with aggregate output, is given by Kahn (1984, p. 121). In support of this explanation rather than the one contained in chapter 1, Kahn refers to Keynes's February 1939 preface to the French edition of the *General Theory* where he wrote, 'I have called my theory a *general* theory. I mean by this that I am chiefly concerned with the behaviour of the economic system as a whole ...'. Kahn concludes that '[T]his is a far more fruitful exposition of the meaning of the word "general" – the result of three years of discussion and thought' (Kahn, 1984, p. 121). But this interpretation is best viewed as an additional justification for the use of the word 'general', since Keynes was not maintaining in his book that the early classical writers had no concern 'with the behaviour of the economic system as a whole'.
7. Keynes notes, when specifying that equipment and technique are taken as given, that '[T]his does not mean that we assume these factors to be constant; but merely that, in this place and context, we are not considering or taking into

account the effects and consequences of changes in them' (Keynes, 1936a, p. 245).

8. 'A state of equilibrium, by definition, is a state in which something, something relevant, is *not* changing; so the use of an equilibrium concept is a signal that time, in some respect at least, has been put to one side' (Hicks, 1976b, p. 140).
9. Hicks has noted the difficulty of reconciling the time intervals implicit in Keynes's analysis.

   It is one of the major difficulties of the Keynes theory (a difficulty that was acutely felt by its first readers, though it has now been lulled to sleep by long familiarity) that it works with a *period* which is taken to be one of equilibrium (investment being equal to saving, saving that is a function of *current* income), and which is nevertheless identified with the Marshallian 'short period', in which capital equipment (now the capital equipment of the whole economy) remains unchanged. The second seems to require that the period should not be too long, but the first requires that it should not be too short; for the *process* of getting into the equilibrium in question (the multiplier process) must occupy a length of time that is by no means negligible. It is not easy to see that there can be any length of time that will adequately satisfy both of these requirements. (Hicks, 1965, pp. 64–6; emphasis in the original)
10. Keynes tended to identify these equilibrium values with actual values. For example, he stated that:

    except in conditions where the consumption industries are already working almost at capacity so that an expansion of output requires an expansion of plant and not merely the more intensive employment of the existing plant, there is no reason to suppose that more than a brief interval of time need elapse before employment in the consumption industries is advancing *pari passu* with employment in the capital-goods industries with the multiplier operating near its normal figure. (Keynes, 1936a, pp. 124–5).

11. For the derivation of the aggregate supply curve from industry short-period supply curves, see Asimakopulos (1982).
12. Parrinello (1980), Casarosa (1981) and Asimakopulos (1982) have pointed out that Keynes's first definition of the aggregate demand function is not consistent with the competitive micro-foundations of his theory. Lord Kahn has reminded us that 'Keynes had no systematic education in economics' (Kahn, 1984, p. 50), and the occasional slip in matters of detail should not be surprising.
13. '. . . the volume of employment in equilibrium depends on (i) the aggregate supply function . . . (ii) the propensity to consume . . . and (iii) the volume of investment . . .' (Keynes, 1936a, p. 29).
14. Patinkin (1982, p. 30) argues that only the first of these two components is Keynes's 'central message', but Kahn (1984, p. 142) is in agreement with the position taken here.
15. Shackle presents the difference between these two approaches as follows:

    Chapter 11 shows us the arithmetic of the marginal efficiency of capital and its relation with interest-rates, a matter for actuaries and slide-rules. Chapter 12 reveals the hollowness of all this. The material for the slide-rules is absent, or arbitrary. Investment is an *irrational* activity, or a non-rational one. Surmise and assumption about what is happening or about to happen are themselves the *source* of these happenings, men make history in seeking to apprehend it. This is the message of the *General Theory*, and that is the only part of it which Keynes troubled to reproduce when in the *Quarterly Journal*

> *of Economics* for February 1937 he brushed aside the painstaking detail of his critics' incomprehension and attempted a final penetration of their minds. (Shackle, 1967, p. 130; emphasis in original)

16. Recall that Keynes did not believe that falling money wages in times of unemployment could be relied on to increase investment and bring about full employment. 'There is . . . no ground for the belief that a flexible wage policy is capable of maintaining a state of continuous full employment' (Keynes, 1936a, p. 267).
17. This is the case examined by Robinson (1937, pp. 105–38).
18. Marshall recognized that this attraction depends on the stationarity of conditions: '. . . the normal, or "natural", value of a commodity is that which economic forces tend to bring about *in the long run*. It is the average value which economic forces would bring about if the general conditions of life were stationary for a run of time long enough to enable them all to work out their full effect' (Marshall, [1920], 1949, p. 347).
19. Vicarelli has emphasized that, in Keynes's view of the capitalist system, 'there is absolutely no mechanism to guarantee that investment will stabilize at some long-term norm, or that its variation over time adheres to a regular law' (Vicarelli, 1984, p. 177).
20. Milgate, in a similar manner, uses a quotation from Keynes's discussion of the factors possibly influencing the propensity to consume to interpret his 'given equipment' assumption as an attempt 'to allow the analysis to proceed without the need to consider [the effects of secular progress]' (Milgate, 1982, p. 90).
21. Garegnani (1979a,b), who has argued for the development of a theory of output in the long period that builds on the critique of the neoclassical conception of capital, recognizes the short-period character of Keynes's writings. Eatwell and Milgate, in their Preface to a collection of papers that includes these and other papers by Garegnani, raise the question '. . . does Keynes's principle of effective demand provide a new long-run theory of output . . .?' (Eatwell and Milgate, 1983). A footnote attached to this question reports on a letter from Garegnani containing an argument with which they are not in agreement. Garegnani writes:

> The meaning of 'long run' cannot but be partly different when used in connection with a theory of aggregate output than when it is used for the theory of relative output. While the meaning of given plant or productive capacity remains, what is relevant for Marshall is the lack of congruence between relative capacity and relative demand in the several industries. What is relevant for a theory of aggregate output like that of Keynes is the lack of congruence between aggregate capacity and aggregate demand . . . When this distinction is made it should be clear that Keynes is concerned with a short period analysis of aggregate output (the determination of the level of capacity utilisation) and that a long period analysis of aggregate output, *i.e.* an analysis of the reciprocal adaptation of aggregate supply and aggregate demand, is one and the same thing as a theory of accumulation. This is absent from Keynes apart from some hints we find in the first two sections of chapter 24 of the *General Theory*.

22. Milgate states that the preceding quotation from Keynes 'bears all the hallmarks of the traditional long-period method: the choice of the term "natural" to describe the tendencies of a market economy and of the term "persist" to describe their long-period character is the standard fare of the traditional

method. The idea that the system oscillates around such a position completes that picture' (Milgate, 1982, p. 88).

23. This view of the theory of effective demand – divorced from his views on the variability and unreliability of investment – as Keynes's 'central message' is, as noted above, shared by Patinkin (1982), but he accepts the short-period nature of Keynes's theory. The theory of effective demand was the *General Theory's* main addition to Keynes's analysis of the determination of employment. But to understand the 'central message' of that work it is important to consider this feature in conjunction with Keynes's views on investment. As Vicarelli wrote, 'the *General Theory* is nothing more than the culmination of Keynes's vision of capitalism' (Vicarelli, 1984, p. 182).
24. Milgate (1982, p. 90) uses this quotation in support of his position that the 'fundamental proposition of the *General Theory* . . . is entirely independent of the existence of uncertainty and expectations', but he omits the adjective 'short-period' that qualifies 'expectations' in the quotation. An unwary reader might be misled by the context to assume that Keynes was referring to long-term expectations (see Harcourt and O'Shaughnessy, 1983, p. 16n).
25. Recall that, for Keynes, 'long-period employment' is not something that tends to occur 'in the long run'. It is employment in a particular short-period situation where all investment expenditures in that period are determined by the same set of long-term expectations.

Comment

Pierangelo Garegnani
Rome

1 *On a long-period analysis of investment and outputs*

1. In his contribution to this volume Professor Asimakopulos writes:

> the short-period equilibrium levels of employment determined by these fluctuating investments will also fluctuate. There is no reason to expect from Keynes's analysis that these fluctuations will be around some full-employment level
>
> (page 336)

In this and similar passages (see also pages 332–3, 337), Asimakopulos is in fact asserting the need for, and possiblity of, a long-period analysis ascertaining, for example, that the cyclical fluctuations of the social product will not be around a full-employment level. It is therefore with a certain surprise that one reads elsewhere in the paper about the irrelevance or impossibility of a long-period analysis (e.g. page 339). And this occurs already when the author continues the above passage as follows: 'there are no "normal" long-period values that serve as centres of gravitation for actual values in Keynes's theory'. However, is not the statement that there is no reason to expect short-period fluctuations around a full-employment level the same as stating a particular, negative, property of the 'normal' long-period level of employment around which the short-period levels fluctuate – namely the property that it will not be a full-employment level?

In fact Asimakopulos goes further than that first negative specification of the 'normal' long-period level of unemployment when he writes on page 340:

> The path traced by the short-period equilibrium output and employment over time depends (assuming that the consumption function is stable) on what happens to investment, that is, on how long-term expectations and financial conditions change. A variety of possible growth paths can be deduced, each reflecting different assumptions about the drive of entrepreneurs, the degree of thriftiness in the economy, financial policies, trade union actions, etc.

This is in fact to specify some further properties of that centre of gravitation of the actual values of outputs and employment, concerning, in particular, the factors governing its change over time. Clearly what Asimakopulos refers to here as 'the path traced' by the short-period equilibrium output, etc., depending on 'the drive of entrepreneurs, the degree of thriftiness in the economy, financial policies, trade unions, etc.', is nothing but the *trend* traced by the sequence of short-period equilibria, which is just what a 'normal' long-period position is meant to explain. In fact the path of the 'short-period equilibria' is the moving long-period position.

2. In fact a misreading of the meaning of a long-period analysis and of the normal positions associated with it seems to underlie the above contradictions. Asimakopulos writes: 'production and employment always occur in a short-period context' (page 340). However, production and employment occur instant by instant in the *actual* economy and, therefore, in the context of neither a short period nor a long period – since both contexts are a matter of *theory* and refer, therefore, to 'normal' and not to *actual* levels of the variables – to centres of gravitation for the actual magnitudes and not to the actual magnitudes themselves.

Accordingly, the distinction between short-period and long-period employment is not, as Asimakopulos seems to think, one between actual magnitudes and a hypothetical 'centre of attraction'. It is the distinction between two kinds of 'centres of attraction' for the actual magnitudes, the first over a period in which productive equipment cannot change appreciably, and the second over a period in which it can so change.[1]

The short-period levels of the variables are therefore centres of attraction for the actual magnitudes – they are in that exact sense 'normal' magnitudes – no less than the long-period ones. This is true to such a degree that Asimakopulos himself refers above to 'short-period *equilibrium* output and employment' and reports elsewhere how Keynes (1936a, pp. 25–7) argued that that equilibrium is 'stable': doesn't this mean that those 'equilibrium', or 'normal', levels of output and employment are (short-period) centres of attraction for the actual levels? It would then seem clear that economic theory, just as it must be concerned with centres of gravitation for the actual magnitudes over a period too short for productive capacity to change appreciably, must also be concerned with the analogous centres of gravitation over a period when those changes *can* occur. Indeed, as is well known, Keynes himself did occasionally refer to such centres, which he called 'long-period positions' (1936a, p. 59), though of course he focused on the short-period centres, which were also more immediately relevant for the economic policies he was concerned with.

3. It appears in fact that a correspondence between theoretical and observable magnitudes can normally be achieved in economics only in the way exemplified by Smith's analysis of the 'natural price', which is the 'central price' to which 'the price of [the commodity is] continually gravitating' (Smith, [1776] 1960, I, p. 5). It is therefore likely to be the price that emerges from some average of the actual prices, since the deviations from it will tend to compensate each other. Smith's metaphor of gravitation is perhaps more compelling when the centre of attraction is itself a spontaneous result and, besides, can be exactly defined in terms of the circumstances determining it, as is the case with the 'natural price'. The metaphor may be less telling when the central magnitude is (in the first instance) the direct result of the decisions of social bodies (e.g., a money wage that results from agreement between trade unions and employers, or a rate of interest fixed by the monetary authorities), or also, when it is less exactly determined (as is likely to be the case for a rate of investment corresponding to the trend described by its oscillations through booms and slumps). However, if what is asserted in the theory about those variables is to be valid, there must ultimately exist some forces that bring the actual magnitudes towards the levels determined in the theory, with which the former magnitudes can in fact never coincide exactly.

4. The reasons why it is difficult for Asimakopulos to recognize this identity between the explanation of an observable economic variable and what Adam Smith described as a centre of gravitation emerge, perhaps, when Asimakopulos approvingly quotes Vicarelli's opinion that, 'in Keynes's view . . . of the capitalist system, "there is absolutely no mechanism to guarantee that investment will *stabilize* at some long-term norm"' (page 344, n 19; emphasis added). This statement, however, can be seen to be almost a contradiction in terms, once it is made clear that the 'long-term norm', there denied, can only be that which emerges from the trend of that fluctuating investment. The question is not whether any variable 'stabilizes' in time, since in fact any moment in the economy is as likely to be affected by disturbances as the preceding one. The question is that, however wildly the actual and the short-period theoretical variable may continue to fluctuate, it inevitably describes a trend.

The question of whether a long-period analysis with the associated long-period normal values is, or is not, possible is therefore really that of whether the corresponding trends are, or are not, explicable in principle. And there is of course no reason why economic phenomena involving changes in aggregate productive equipment should be any less explicable than those that do not (as is shown by Asimakopulos's own passages quoted at the beginning). After all, we do explain and try to forecast the trend of the price of, say, copper, on the basis of the technical changes in its mining, or of the richness of new mines, etc. – in spite of the fact that the prices of copper may fluctuate perhaps as much as 50 per cent on either side of its trend value.

5. This may also explain why Asimakopulos appears to be incorrect in the following passage (where I have distinguished the three propositions occurring there by the letters a, b, and c):

> [a] Sraffa's analysis is concerned with prices of production . . . where investment in the different industries has resulted in productive capacity in each that is appropriate to demand. [b] For these prices to serve as centres of gravitation for actual prices, conditions must be changing relatively slowly, so that mistaken investments are relatively minor, with actual prices tending towards the prices of production. [c] This vision . . . is different from that held by Keynes.
>
> (page 341).

Propositions [b], and hence [c], do not follow from [a] (where 'has resulted' can be taken to mean 'is assumed to have resulted'). Does Asimakopulos really mean to say that prices of production provide no guidance to the behaviour of actual relative prices – that, say, the long-run fall in the price of cars or television sets relative to hotel accommodation cannot be said to be due to different speeds of technical progress in the respective sectors? However, mistaken investments have certainly occurred and are continually occurring in the making of cars, in that of television sets and in the setting up of hotels.

In fact, the conditions that must change *relatively* slowly in order to allow for a long-period analysis are those relating to the trend of prices, outputs, etc., and their 'slowness' is therefore implicit in their very conception, since it is a slowness *relative* to the forces prompting the deviations from the trend. It should then be evident that there is no reason why this slowness should exclude the possibility of major mistaken investment.[2]

6. Professory Minsky seems to me to be similarly incorrect when, in his contribution to the present volume (Chapter 11), he writes:

> The meanings that are normally given to the long run involve some idea of an equilibrium or a centre of gravity towards which [see note on p. 371] it oscillates. . . . But a minimal specification of a monetary production, or better an accumulating capitalist economy with a sophisticated financial system, includes endogenous destabilizing relations.
>
> (page 363)

However, Minsky's 'destabilizing' relations cannot but generate fluctuations, and therefore fluctuations on either side of a *trend*, that is, generate those very oscillations whose possibility he seems to be denying in that passage.

On the other hand, I am sure that Minsky, no less than Asimakopulos, believes that the question of whether economic fluctuations are or are not around full employment is important both for 'the capitalist economies of the twentieth century', and for 'the interpretation of Keynes' (Minsky, page 362). This makes it difficult to understand why the papers in Eatwell and Milgate (1983), which deal, fundamentally, with that issue, should not appear relevant to him (Minsky, page 362; as for Minsky's assimilation of the treatment of money in marginal theory, with that which we find to be implicit in Sraffa and in many of the papers in Eatwell and Milgate, 1983, see my paper, par. 21 p. 124).

In fact, Asimakopulos and Minsky seem at times to juxtapose a long-period analysis of outputs and investment with its marginalist species, as if a rejection of the latter implied a rejection of the former. However, clearly, what is at fault in the traditional analysis is not its reference to long-period centres of gravitation, which appears to be inseparable from economic theorizing and is in fact present also in Keynes. It is, rather, *the particular way* in which those centres are determined. The analysis of the classical economists, which did not postulate any tendency to the full employment of labour, is there to show, were it necessary, how the existence of long-run unemployment can be reconciled with a long-period analysis.

2 *On Sraffa and Keynes*

7. However, Asimakopulos is not likely to find universal agreement on the *content* of the claim I quoted at the very beginning of my Comment, according to which Keynes's own analysis is sufficient to exclude that fluctuations of income and employment occur 'around some full-employment level'. In fact, while Keynes clearly believed that deficiencies of effective demand would affect the long-period development of the economy, his analysis remained confined to the short period characterized by a given productive equipment, and its extension beyond that context clearly raises new problems.

This can be seen in particular in his analysis of the effects on the interest rate and investment of a flexibility of the ratio between the money wage rate and the quantity of money – the point on which all attempted rehabilitations of orthodox theory have essentially relied. Keynes's denial that that flexibility would entail a tendency to full employment – based as it was, in chapter 19 of the *General Theory*, on the psychological factors summed up in the 'state of confidence' – inevitably loses much of its force when the *long-period* issue of keeping the average level of investment and output sufficiently close to their full-employment levels displaces the *short-period* issue of the recovery from a depression (Garegnani, 1979a, pp. 72–3). And this weakness in Keynes's argument has certainly been an important element in the success of the attempted rehabilitations mentioned above.

This brings me to why I believe the 'marriage of Keynes and Sraffa', as Asimakopulos puts it (page 331), not only is possible but is already present in the facts. Before explaining what I mean by this, it may, however, be necessary to clear up some frequent misreadings of Sraffa's work, traces of which may also be found in Asimakopulos's contribution. These misreadings, I believe, are a result of the elliptic character of *Production of Commodities*, and of the deep differences between the classical economists' approach and that of our contemporaries.

8. The misreadings centre on the meaning of prices in Sraffa's book. Asimakopulos writes (page 332): 'Sraffa's system of production is set in a particular period of time, a year (Sraffa, 1960, p. 3), in which the technical relations of production and the total amount to be produced of each commodity are fixed.' However, Sraffa's system of production cannot be properly said to be set in a 'particular year' (the *actual* magnitudes corresponding to it, would, if anything, be a moving average calculated over *several* years). The year comes in Sraffa, just as a week or a day might, as the duration of a cycle of production, or – had he assumed continuous production – merely as the arbitrary period of time over which the input and output flows are reckoned. The year, that is, comes in only to give definiteness to the representation of the process of production. Correspondingly, the technical conditions of production are not assumed to be 'fixed' any more than they are in, say, Keynes's *General Theory* or Marshall's *Principles*. And no greater invariability is of course assumed for the outputs.

Asimakopulos comes closer to facing the true meaning of the prices in Sraffa – though by denying it – when he writes (pp. 332–3):

> Sraffa writes that the 'standpoint' of his investigation 'is that of the old classical economists from Adam Smith to Ricardo' . . . [but] there is nothing in his analysis to justify the treatment of prices of production as values towards which actual prices tend to move. He does not deal with dynamic processes of adjustment. The only 'time' in the system is the 'year' during which production takes place, and there is no linking of 'years' – even in an informal manner – in order to indicate the possible relationship between the prices of production and actual prices.

However, Sraffa has in fact written (1960, p. 9) that 'such classical terms as necessary price, natural price or price of production', as distinct from the equally classical term of "market price", would exactly describe the prices he determines. And the basic argument about such 'prices of production' as the centre of attraction for actual or 'market' prices – hadn't this been put forward by Adam Smith, together with many of his predecessors and successors without any need for Sraffa to repeat it?

This, I believe, also takes care of the objection Asimakopulos seems to be raising on p. 332:

> Sraffa asserts that in his system there will be an equal rate of profits in all industries. There is no attempt to justify this assumption; he simply states when setting out his price equations 'we add the rate of profit (which must be uniform for all industries)'.

Again, hasn't that assumption been generally held as the necessary implication of the hypothesis of free competition?[3]

9. It should now begin to be clear why I believe that what Asimakopulos describes as 'the fundamental differences between [Keynes and Sraffa] – the

difference in the role of time and the visions of the operation of capitalist economies implicit in these theories' (p. 331) is an optical illusion, generated partly by the terseness of Sraffa's argument, and partly by Keynes's attempt to reach his conclusions about labour unemployment *within* a marginalist context – with the consequent need to rely on the psychological factors of incorrect expectations and uncertainty.

No doubt Keynes and Sraffa primarily address themselves to different problems, but the difference is ultimately that between analyses that do *complement* each other. As I have argued elsewhere (1978a, 1979a), the limitations of Keynes's criticism of some of the basic propositions of marginal theory prevented the long-period implications he attributed to his conclusions from being developed in a conclusive manner on the basis he had provided – though the need for such a development was clearly felt at the time by Keynes and his circle (see, for example, Robinson, 1936). Now, it appears that Sraffa's analysis may provide the two essential elements that had been missing from Keynes and that are necessary 'to exclude that fluctuations . . . occur around some full-employment level'.

The first element is a more conclusive criticism of the traditional theory of interest than we find in Keynes's treatment of liquidity preference. Once that theory of interest is recognized as invalid for the long period no less than for the short period, the adjustment of decisions to save to decisions to invest through changes in output is an inevitable consequence, as is the possibility of deficiencies of aggregate demand, in the long period no less than in the short period.

When that criticism is effected, it will also become evident that the resulting theoretical loose end – the behaviour of wages in the presence of unemployment – is, in effect, as I argued in my paper (Chapter 5 above, par. 14), a creation of post-classical theory and of its idea (of course by now deeply ingrained) of a 'full-employment real wage'. And that loose end can accordingly be resolved by going back to the conception of the labour market of the classical economists up to Ricardo who never had the idea of such a wage.

This leads us naturally to the second element that Sraffa can provide in order to support Asimakopulos's initial claim. This second element is a basis from which to start in order to construct a theory of distribution and outputs alternative to the dominant one, incompatible as the latter is with the recognition of the role of effective demand in the long period. This basis is in fact provided by Sraffa's rediscovery and revival of the approach of the classical economists.

It is in this specific sense that I believe the 'marriage of Keynes and Sraffa', or, more exactly, of Keynes and the old classical economists, to be 'in the facts' – in the fact, that is, that aggregate demand controls the speed of capitalist accumulation and not just the temporary underutilization of productive capacity characteristic of the trade cycle.

Editorial Note

Part of this comment is also directed to the subsequent contribution by H. Minsky (Chapter 11).

Notes

1. I might incidentally make clear here that I do not in the least believe that 'the only objects of economic analysis are the "long-run positions" of the system . . . [and that] short-run behaviour [is] irrelevant' (Carvalho, 1984–5, p. 220; passim). As I have often argued (e.g. 1978a, 1979a) the short-period outputs and employment are not only amenable to analysis, but Keynes's analysis of the degree of utilization of capacity is obviously of the greatest importance. The question is whether we need nothing else. And once the terms of the question are correctly understood, everybody will agree that we do need something else, as the passages by Asimakopulos quoted at the beginning show.
2. Investment by the individual entrepreneur is largely motivated by the hope of enlarging one's share of the market at the expense of other firms, and the entrepreneur is always likely to make mistakes in guessing the growth of his own market, whether the growth of the overall market of the commodity is slow or fast.
3. The rate of profits is relevant only for new investment (old plant gets quasi-rents), and there the investor plans the size of his equipment relative to expected demand so that it might have a 'normal' degree of utilization. He therefore expects the rate of profits corresponding to that degree of capacity utilization, which is traditionally referred to in economic analysis. The importance of the assumption of a uniform rate of profits for a correspondence between theory and observable facts is argued in Garegnani (1976a, pp. 38–9, 1989, pp. 355, 356n).

Comment

Edward Nell
New York

Keynes and Sraffa: Marshallian or classical foundations?

In his contribution Asimakopulos gives some telling reasons for believing that, even if a marriage between Sraffa and Keynes could be arranged, it couldn't be consummated. Keynes's *General Theory* rests firmly on Marshallian foundations, which Sraffa rejected. Sraffa's prices are long period, whereas Keynes's concern is with employment and output in the short run. Long-run equilibrium can only be reached in tranquil conditions; Keynes emphasizes the volatility of capitalism and the uncertainty inherent in planning.

I shall argue that matchmakers need not give up hope – a more fertile union is possible, between Marx (extended and corrected by Sraffa) and Kalecki. For the real question is how to find a proper setting for the theory of effective demand. This theory states that in the short run the utilization of labour and current productive capacity will be adapted to the current and immediately expected level of sales, while in the long run the construction of capacity will be adapted to the anticipated growth of markets. Yet the main elements of the theory, its building blocks, so to speak, are various kinds of revenue flows, which, of course, depend on there being an established system of prices. Hence the theory of effective demand may be said to presuppose a theory of prices. Moreover, the prices in question must be relatively insensitive to changes in effective demand. As Asimakopulos points out, and as Hicks remarked almost twenty years ago, Sraffian prices, being determined by the rate of profit, are independent of supply and demand, and so can provide the setting for the study of short-period fluctuations.

However, Keynes presented his treatment of the problem of the utilization of labour and productive capacity in a Marshallian setting. His aggregate supply and aggregate demand functions are derived along Marshallian lines, and his definition of short and long periods is apparently adopted directly from the master. Each of these creates problems, the first of a technical kind, the second a matter of the basic vision and approach.

The aggregate demand–aggregate supply analysis runs into difficulties because it is modelled on the partial equilibrium determination of the outcome of market behaviour. The partial equilibrium approach tends to neglect the implications of changes in costs, as output is varied, for the distribution of income. But when distribution changes, aggregate demand will be affected. Let us consider this in the Keynesian case. The aggregate supply function is constructed by considering various alternative prices: for a given price, output will be adjusted until marginal cost equals price; but this means (with given capital stock) adjusting employment. Thus each price is associated with a level of output and of employment. So, the function is constructed by multiplying the prices by the corresponding outputs and associating the resulting 'proceeds' with the corresponding levels of employment. In general, following the partial equilibrium supply curve, higher prices mean higher outputs and higher employment; hence the 'proceeds–employment' function will have a positive slope. The aggregate demand function is constructed by considering the proceeds that firms could expect to receive as the result of alternative levels of overall employment. (It is *not* the function showing the employment required to generate alternative levels of output; that would just be another form of the aggregate supply function.) The aggregate supply function slopes upwards at an increasing rate, reflecting diminishing marginal productivity, while the aggregate demand function slopes upwards at a decreasing rate, reflecting the diminishing marginal propensity to consume. The intersection of the two is termed the point of effective demand, and, as Asimakopulos points out, will normally be stable.

This construction is flawed by the fact that the implications for distribution have been neglected. Each point on the aggregate demand function associates a level of spending with a level of employment; but the propensity to spend out of wages will normally be greater than the propensity to spend out of profits. Hence, for any given level of employment, the corresponding level of receipts will be greater, the higher the share of wages in the output generated by that employment. Thus the position of the aggregate demand function depends on the distribution of income, and will shift with changes in that distribution.

Now consider the aggregate supply function. Following standard Marshallian thinking, Keynes held that, for offers of employment to increase, the competitive real wage would have to fall since, with a given capital stock, higher employment would result in diminished marginal output. Thus, comparing two points on the aggregate supply function, the point with higher employment (and higher output) will be associated with a lower real wage. But will the proportional decline in the wage be equal to or greater or lesser than the proportional rise in employment? If it is less, then the wage bill will increase, but will the proportional increase be equal to or greater or less than the proportional increase in output? If it is equal, then relative shares remain constant; otherwise they change.

However, if relative shares change from one point to another on the aggregate supply function, then moving along that function will cause the aggregate demand function to shift. To put it another way, the level of employment cannot be determined by the intersection of these two aggregate functions, because that intersection point is not determinate; additional information is needed concerning the distribution of income.

A simple way around this difficulty is to assume a Cobb–Douglas aggregate production function; then relative shares will always be the same. But this amounts to admitting that the aggregate supply–aggregate demand analysis works only in special cases. Even so there is still a problem. Since the stock of capital is fixed, changes in employment must change the marginal product of the existing capital stock in just the way required to keep shares constant. (How this will work out in competitive markets in the short run is not easy to see.) But what is the relation, then, of this marginal product of existing capital to the rate of interest and to the marginal efficiency of (new) capital? As takeovers and mergers show us daily, there is as active a market for existing capital as for new. But if a movement from one point to another on the aggregate supply function, for example, raises the profitability of existing capital relative to new capital and to the cost of money, then investible funds will be shifted from constructing new plant to acquiring existing firms, and the aggregate demand function will shift down, since the latter expenditure has no multiplier effects.

Keynes's construction, then, is flawed. To repair it we would have to reconsider its marginalist foundations, in particular the idea of rising supply price, based on diminishing marginal productivity. Once we do this, we are outside the Marshallian framework, and in need of a new approach to prices.

The same conclusion can be reached by another route, by considering Keynes's adoption of Marshall's distinction between the short and the long run. For Marshall this was based on the ability to vary the way factors of production were used. In the very short run, almost nothing could be varied; so output was fixed – the supply curve vertical – and price therefore depended entirely on demand. In the normal short run, some but not all factors could be varied; the supply curve therefore rose from left to right, and price depended on both the curves. In the long run, however, all factors are variable, and so the supply curve will tend to be flat, or even declining if there are economies of scale, so that price will be set by long-run marginal cost, while the influence of demand will be confined to determining output. Thus the long run is classical – price is determined by cost of production, output by demand – while the market period is the predecessor of the modern notion of temporary equilibrium. But the short run is taken as the norm, where both prices and quantities adjust, and supply and demand conditions influence both variables. As Asimakopulos argues, this is the framework in which Keynes chooses to set his problem.

Yet it is a highly inappropriate framework. In the Marshallian short period demand is governed by preferences and depends on prices, while supply responds to price signals and is constrained by diminishing productivity at the margin. Both prices and outputs are considered to be flexible, and to mutually influence one another, within the period. Under these conditions it is difficult to see how any factor could remain unemployed in equilibrium; if it were, its price would fall until demand increased and supply contracted sufficiently to eliminate the excess supply.

Keynes knew that this was not how things worked, but he was not able to express his new vision adequately within the Marshallian framework. There is, I think, a good reason for this, which is that the problem of effective demand is a matter not only of theory, but also of history.

In the early stages of capitalism the unit that held capital and organized production was the family: the economy consisted of family firms and family farms. Workers were members of the family, apprentices and hired hands who very often lived with the family. In such conditions the question of employment is not whether to hire or to lay off workers, but how best to allocate the given amount of labour – time among the various possible tasks. The supply of work effort in a particular line will then be governed by its relative marginal disutility compared to its reward; the demand by its relative marginal productivity compared to its cost. Output and employment are fixed in the market period, but relative outputs and employment can be changed in the short run, by reallocating labour and supplies. Overall employment, however, will be fixed, except in the long run as capital accumulates.

Such a system is characterized by the use of predominantly small-scale technology, in which most costs are current, rather than capital, but where a high proportion of current costs are fixed, being the costs of supporting the family. Moreover, these costs will be fixed in real, not monetary, terms. Under these conditions a firm facing a decline in the demand for its products will cut prices in order to sell as much as possible. Only when prices have fallen to the level of variable costs will it close down production, and then it will shut down totally. If the lower demand persists it will be forced to reduce the size of its operations on a permanent basis. So, in the long run, supply adapts to demand, while prices are governed by costs, but, in the short term, prices are flexible and output and employment are fixed. (With prices more flexible than money wages, a fall in demand will lead to a rise in the real wage, which will tend to raise consumption, tending to restore the initial position.) This is very close to Marshall, and it makes sense for a system of independent small farms and family-based craft businesses.

(Even Sraffa's famous critique of Marshall looks weak when we treat the theory as describing a system of small family farms and firms. Sraffa contended that (1) moving along a supply curve will cause the demand curve to shift, unless all or most of the economy's fixed factor is used by (only by) the industry in question, and (2) increasing returns must be external to the firm but internal to the industry, otherwise the size of the firm will be indeterminate. Clearly these are very special cases, and quite implausible for modern industry – but they fit the traditional farming and craft economy quite well. Land is the chief fixed factor in agriculture, and traditional skill, passed on from father to son, is the fixed factor in most crafts. As for increasing returns external to the firm, when agricultural output rises sufficiently in an area, new forms of storage and transport will be introduced – the railroad, grain elevators, new roads, etc. Similarly, when crafts develop to a certain size, bulk buying and bulk storage can be introduced.)

Now contrast this with modern capitalist industry, operating large-scale mass production technology. A large proportion of total costs will be capital costs, and these will be amortized and will therefore be expressed in monetary terms. As for current costs, the bulk of these will be labour costs, and these will be variable because the plant will be designed to run at varying speeds or levels of operation, in order to be able to adapt output to the pace of current or expected sales. Now consider a shortfall of demand. With modern technology, goods can be stored at low cost with minimal loss; hence even in the market period there is no necessity to cut prices. Since mass production industrial processes are designed to operate at varying degrees of intensity, production can be adapted to the pace of sales, so labour can be laid off or put on short time, reducing variable costs, which are a high proportion of current costs. Laying off or short-timing labour tends to reduce consumer spending, which in turn has multiplier repercussions on other industries.

Why not cut prices? Surely each firm in a competitive industry will try to attract demand from the others? But price cutting is dangerous. When sales have slowed down, fixed costs per period of time are a higher percentage of total monetary revenue per period. To cut price is *certainly* to reduce unit revenue even further, in the *hope* of selling more units. If competitors do not follow suit then perhaps more sales will be attracted, but if they do, then no one will gain. (Note that, because they tend to be complementary, industrial products are characteristically price inelastic but income elastic.) If it is known that sales have fallen off because bad times have reduced incomes, or because unfavourable expectations have reduced investment, then it will also be known that a general fall in price will not stimulate sales that much.

Moreover, in a mass production economy, prices have to be planned over the lifetime of the investment, since its cost has to be amortized, which means that returns have to be planned many periods ahead. One way to interpret the marginal efficiency of capital calculation is to see it as a *plan* for future pricing and sales: the pricing policy will be chosen so as to keep prices low enough to help the sales division penetrate new markets at appropriate times, while at other times keeping them high enough to obtain an adequate profit. Prices will thus be planned over time, in terms of the expected balance between the need to finance new capacity and the ability to penetrate new markets. These are long-term considerations, part of the process of accumulation. Of course short-term matters could affect pricing policies, but it would be because they affected the expectations of market development.

In short, there can be no 'Marshallian foundations' for the theory of effective demand. If there is a problem of effective demand, the economy has an institutional and technological nature that precludes the applicability of the Marshallian framework. Conversely, if the economy is describable in Marshallian terms, it cannot experience problems of effective demand. (Of course, this refers to pure cases: actual economies will normally be a mixture of corporate mass production and family-based small business.)

Keynes opened a door, but he didn't actually make it through to the other side. He was too heavily burdened with traditional baggage. We can discard that baggage – the supply and demand approach to the understanding of prices – and begin to look at the modern economy as it is – a capitalist mass production system, financed by a banking system that amortizes fixed costs in monetary terms. Pricing must therefore be studied as part of the problem of recouping investments over time, so it is a part of the theory of accumulation. Employment, and the multiplier, on the other hand, depend on the way current production is managed. They arise from the operation of the industrial system, and concern its short-term behaviour.

To try to rescue Keynes, and connect effective demand to Sraffian prices by interpreting him as a 'long-run' theorist, is simply misconceived. The long-run problem of effective demand concerns the adjustment of capacity to demand; it is a branch of the theory of investment and accumulation. Asimakopulos is surely right that Keynes never dealt with this.

There is, however, a connection between the short-run problem of effective demand and Sraffa's pricing approach. Short-run changes must take place in the setting of an actual, previously constructed system. This system embodies certain expectations and commitments, namely those that inspired its construction. We can then ask: what would prices and revenue flows be if this system operated as it was expected to when it was constructed? These can be considered the prices and valuations 'inherent' in the system, and embodied, for example, in its monetary constructs. These prices are therefore the appropriate ones to use in forming the aggregates that figure in the theory of effective demand. We can ask an even more refined question: what would prices and revenue flows be if the system operated according, not to the actual expectations, but to those expectations modified by strict competition, so that the wage rate, all prices and the rate of profit will be uniform? Such prices and valuations would constitute an idealized and simplified picture of the system, a norm against which to judge the actual inherent or embodied values. And these prices – Sraffa prices – are the ones to use in developing the *theory*, bearing in mind that actual prices will deviate from them in all kinds of unpredictable but easily calculable ways.

Reply

Some of the criticisms of my paper made by Garegnani are based on a misreading of it, while others may be due to the difference we attached to the term 'long-period analysis'. I view it as being concerned with the examination of a sequence of short periods, while he apparently identifies it with the view that long-period equilibrium values serve as strong centres of attraction for actual values. Keynes's analysis, even though it is only concerned with short-period equilibrium values, does have long-period implications. He considered the factors that determine investment to be 'most unreliable', a condition that continued over a sequence of short periods. He judged experience to show that these factors result in fluctuations 'round an intermediate position appreciably below full employment and appreciably above the minimum employment a decline below which would endanger life' (Keynes 1936a, p. 254).

Garegnani agrees with my position on the nature of Keynes's formal analysis. It is concerned with short-period equilibrium employment. In Keynes's model this equilibrium value serves as a centre of gravitation for the actual level of employment, which is implicitly assumed to be sufficiently close to the equilibrium value that it can be represented by it. Keynes thus begins his chapter on the trade cycle as follows: 'Since we claim to have shown in the preceding chapters what determines the volume of employment *at any time* . . .' (Keynes 1936a, p. 313; emphasis added). The level of employment in any actual, historical, short interval of time is unlikely to be equal to the short-period equilibrium level of employment for that interval, because entrepreneurs' short-term expectations that determine employment are likely to be disappointed by unforeseen changes. Keynes states that entrepreneurs 'endeavour to approximate to the true position by a method of trial and error. . . . It corresponds precisely to the higgling of the market by means of which buyers and sellers endeavour to discover the true equilibrium position of supply and demand' (Keynes 1973b, p. 182). But it is with this 'true position' of short-period equilibrium that his analysis is concerned, since he believed that 'the theory of effective demand is substantially the same if we assume that short-period expectations are always fulfilled' (*ibid.*, p. 181), and the 'higgling of the market' is ignored.

This attribution of strong powers of attraction to short-period equilibrium values, which leads to the identification of actual and short-period equilibrium values, is made by Keynes, and not by me. (See my critical presentation of Keynes's implicit assumption that the full multiplier effects of changes in investment were completed within the short period, and my reference to Hicks in note 9). Garegnani's comments on page 346 are thus misplaced. The quotation he gives there from my paper is incomplete. It should read: 'Production and employment always occur in a short-period context, *with given equipment and technique being utilized*' (emphasis added). Reference here is being made to actual production and employment, and the italicized words (which Garegnani omits) make clear what is meant by 'short-period context'. There is nothing in my text that should have led him to assume that I consider short-period equilibrium employment to be anything but a theoretical construct. The difference between it and long-period equilibrium employment – and it is a significant difference – is that, for long-period values to be 'centres of attraction', conditions must be stationary for long periods of time. Marshall (1920, p. 347) pointed out that stationarity is required for the

> doctrine of Adam Smith and other economists that the normal, or 'natural', value of a commodity is that which economic forces tend to bring about *in the long run*. It is the average value which economic forces would bring about if the general conditions of life were stationary for a run of time long enough to enable them all to work out their full effect.
>
> But we cannot foresee the future perfectly. The unexpected may happen; and the existing tendencies may be modified before they have had time to accomplish what appears now to be their full and complete work. The fact that the general conditions of life are not stationary is the source of many of the difficulties that are met with in applying economic doctrines to practical problems.

It is with 'practical problems' that Keynes was concerned in his theory of employment, and, given his vision of irregularly changing capitalist economies, he made no use of long-period equilibrium. Garegnani points out that Keynes defined 'long-period employment', but this was no more than an 'aside'. Its definition follows his explanation of short-term and long-term expectations, and represents the very special situation where all the employment at a point in time is consistent with the long-term (and short-term) expectations at that point in time. For this to be the case a state of long-term expectations had 'to continue for a sufficient length of time for the effect on employment to have worked itself out so completely that there is, broadly speaking, no piece of employment going on which would not have taken place if the new state of expectation had always existed . . .' (Keynes 1936a, p. 48). This constancy of long-term expectations over a lengthy interval of time was recognized as a *logical* possibility, and thus Keynes referred to it. But it was not seen as a *practical* possibility, and it had no place in his analysis.

Some indication of how Keynes saw employment and output evolving over time, based on his short-period analysis, is to be found at the end of chapter 18 of *The General Theory*, following his summary of the General Theory, and in his notes on the trade cycle. The latter was not intended to be more than a preliminary consideration of the trade cycle, but taken in conjunction with the chapter 18 material it seems clear that Keynes considered his theory as being capable of sketching out some of the outlines of a time path that combines trend and cycle. In discussing this path, Keynes recognized that the 'independent variables' of his analysis, such as the 'psychological expectation of future yield from capital assets', would be affected by changes occurring in the economy. The last part of Garegnani's final sentence can be restated to accommodate what I see as Keynes's position. Aggregate demand affects the speed of capitalist accumulation, because it affects economic activity and the 'climate' in which long-term expectations are formed and investment decisions are made. But investment expenditures are, of course, an important component of this aggregate demand. This interrelation over time between aggregate demand and investment activity, and the consequent changes in productive capacity, lead to growth and cyclical fluctuations. The difference with Garegnani is that he appears to see the trend as independent of the cycle. This is the implication (given his surrounding comments) of the statement that 'however wildly the actual and the short-period theoretical variable may continue to fluctuate, it inevitably describes a trend' (page 347). The ability mechanically to decompose any time series into 'trend' and 'cycle' components does *not* make them independent.

There is a similar, after the event, breakdown into components in Garegnani's treatment of prices. Important elements in the observed changes in the relative prices of commodities, over long intervals of time, are the differences in the rates of technical progress in their production. These rates are not independent of other changes occurring in the economy, and the investment expenditures that helped give rise to them were not necessarily based on the expectations of these prices. It is the expectations of prices, which enter into expected returns, that are relevant for a theory of investment, and they cannot be reduced to some mechanical average of past data. (Garegnani's initial reference to the 'rate of profits' in note 3, should be preceded by the adjective 'expected'.) The use of 'copper' by Garegnani to illustrate the forecasting of the trend price is probably not accidental (see Keynes 1973b, p. 113). He refers to 'technical changes in its mining, or . . . the richness of new mines, etc.' (page 348) as 'means' used in this process. There are many important factors covered by this 'etc.', such as the unforeseen technical changes that affect the production and the suitability of substitutes for copper, with possible feedback effects on the two items noted by Garegnani. Forecasting a trend – as opposed to 'explaining' a trend line drawn through historical data – can be very difficult and subject to large margins of error.

Garegnani's proposed 'marriage' of Keynes and Sraffa is really a proposed marriage between Sraffa and some (still to be developed?) theory of the determination of aggregate demand that is compatible with Sraffa's prices of production. Considerable confusion will be eliminated if Keynes's name is dropped from this 'union'. The attempts to extend Keynes's theory to deal with accumulation, which tried to observe the fundamentals of that theory (Harrod, 1939, 1948; Robinson, 1956), failed because of the incompatibility of this theory and use of the long-period equilibrium values to be found on Harrod's warranted growth path and Robinson's desired rate of growth (Asimakopulos, 1984, 1985).

Nell does not disagree with the main theme of my paper that there are fundamental differences between the theories of Keynes and Sraffa – reflecting the treatment of time and their visions of the operation of capitalist economies – which make them incompatible. It is not possible to judge the merits of his proposed union 'between Marx (extended and corrected by Sraffa) and Kalecki' (page 352) because there is no further mention of Marx or Kalecki. Nell's criticism of Keynes's theory of effective demand exaggerates the problems with that theory, and his denial of the possibility of Marshallian foundations for a theory of effective demand is mistaken. One may prefer alternative (e.g. Kaleckian or Sraffian) foundations, but the presentation of Keynes's theory in my paper makes clear that Marshallian foundations are possible.

Nell's statement of 'the theory of effective demand' (it is presented as some 'absolute' or 'ideal' notion) ignores the problems caused in any real economy by the passage of historical time. He writes: 'This theory states that in the short run the utilization of labour and current productive capacity will be adapted to the current and immediately expected level of sales, while in the long run the construction of capacity will be adapted to the anticipated growth of markets' (pages 352–3). Firms always try to plan their investment expenditures so that the resulting productive capacity will anticipate the growth of markets and be appropriate for future demand, but they will not usually succeed in an irregularly changing world. Short-run problems concerning the utilization of existing productive capacity do not disappear with the passage of time; they will still be present even after a 'long run of time' in the type of world we inhabit.

Keynes did not examine the implications for his theory of the change in the distribution of income that occurs when there is a change in employment, but this can be readily done within the Marshallian framework. Employment is determined in his model by the short-term expectations of prices of entrepreneurs, and effective demand is the point on the aggregate supply curve corresponding to these expenditures (Asimakopulos, 1982). This is the short-period equilibrium level of employment if the aggregate demand function that reflects the distribution of income corresponding to this employment intersects the aggregate supply function at this point. This equilibrium position is stable, even if the offer of more or less employment leads to a changed distribution of income, because the effects of any such changes will not be destabilizing. For example, if firms mistakenly offer employment greater than the short-period equilibrium level, their short-term expectations of proceeds will be disappointed, and they will decrease their offers. This 'disappointment' is due not only to Keynes's assumption of a marginal propensity to consume of less than unity, but also to the fall in real wage rates, which reduces total consumption expenditures as a fraction of total income.

The aggregate demand function is based on given long-term expectations, and Keynes implicitly assumed that, when alternative points on the aggregate supply function are being considered, long-term expectations, and thus investment expenditures, are unaffected. The analysis would certainly be much more complex if a 'movement' along an aggregate supply function could change the long-term expectation on which the aggregate demand functions are based, and there is immediate repercussion on investment expenditures. But Nell has provided no evidence that this is likely to be the case. He simply proceeds by considering some of the implications if this is the case (page 354). Similarly, his conclusion that 'there can be no "Marshallian foundations" for the theory of effective demand' (page 357) follows a fanciful description of Marshallian economics that robs it of essential elements. It is a 'straw man' that neither Marshall nor Keynes would recognize.

11

Sraffa and Keynes: Effective Demand in the Long Run

Hyman P. Minsky
Washington University St Louis

Given my interpretation of Keynes (Minsky, 1975, 1986) and my view of the problems that economists need to address as the twentieth century draws to a close, the substance of the papers in Eatwell and Milgate (1983) and the neoclassical synthesis are (1) equally irrelevant to the understanding of modern capitalist economies and (2) equally foreign to essential facets of Keynes's thought. It is more important for an economic theory to be relevant for an understanding of economies than for it to be true to the thought of Keynes, Sraffa, Ricardo or Marx. The only significance Keynes's thought has in this context is that it contains the beginnings of an economic theory that is especially relevant to understanding capitalist economies. This relevance is due to the monetary nature of Keynes's theory.

Modern capitalist economies are intensely financial. Money in these economies is endogenously determined as activity and asset holdings are financed and commitments on prior contracts are fulfilled. In truth, every economic unit can create money – this property is not restricted to banks. The main problem a 'money creator' faces is getting his 'money' accepted.

Almost all money creation at some date involves promises to pay the same or some other money at some later date. Therefore money creation is tied into economic processes and transactions by which debtor units acquire what they promise to pay. Endogenous money implies both that money is destroyed when debtors pay banks and the existence of a hierarchy of monies. The obvious example of a hierarchy of monies is the relation between bank money and reserve money. In the taking over of businesses – a major activity in the United States – the liabilities used are often characterized as 'funny monies'. (Since this was written the rapid development of securitization has opened the possibility of public money that does not depend upon the proximate intermediation of a bank or a central bank.)

None of the endogenously determined variables in a modern capitalist economy is independent of monetary variables. Keynes's reply to Leontief about the 'homogeneity postulate' with respect to money wages and money in neoclassical theory is especially relevant (Keynes, 1937b; the homogeneity postulate is also a characteristic of Sraffian theory). Keynes is important because he taught us how to approach and analyse an intensely financial capitalist economy. He gave us an investment theory of effective demand and a financial theory of investment on which we can build.

Furthermore the investment–saving relation that appears in the determination of effective demand can be used to yield the aggregate profits in the economy. In the simplest skeletal model, the system of prices is such that the sum of profits over all outputs equals the investment determined aggregate profits. The price system of a capitalist economy is a mechanism that forces 'a surplus' (savings) that equals financed investment.

The keys to understanding capitalist economies lie in the answers to the following questions:

(1) How is activity, especially investment activity, financed?
(2) How are positions in capital assets financed? and
(3) What determines the price system of assets?

The title of this session, 'Sraffa and Keynes: Effective Demand in the Long Run', puzzles me. Sraffa says little or nothing about effective demand and Keynes's *General Theory* can be viewed as holding that the long run is not a fit subject for study. At the arid level of Sraffa, the Keynesian view that effective demand reflects financial and monetary variables has no meaning, for there is no monetary or financial system in Sraffa. At the concrete level of Keynes, the technical conditions of production, which are the essential constructs of Sraffa, are dominated by profit expectations and financing conditions.

The meanings that are normally given to the long run involve some idea of an equilibrium or centre of gravity towards which the system tends or around which it oscillates. (It can be a static or a growth equilibrium or centre of gravity.) But a minimal specification of a monetary production, or better an accumulating capitalist economy with a sophisticated financial system, includes endogenous destabilizing relations. The ideas of chapter 3 ('Credit and Capital') of Schumpeter's *The Theory of Economic Development* (Schumpeter, 1934) are an essential input to an understanding of a capitalist economy: the early monetary theory of Schumpeter integrates well with Keynes.

Instead of thinking about equilibrium and disequilibrating developments it may be better to think of tranquil and turbulent system behaviour. The same profit-seeking, product market, 'factor' market and financing behaviour ruled in the tranquil era of the 1950s as in the turbulent era of the 1970s. The end result of market behaviour was different. Somehow the environment within which activity takes place was sufficiently different that the overall system behaviour was different.

Therefore, as economists, we have to explain:

(1) why systems of interrelated markets, with no apparent coordinator, can for substantial stretches of time yield coherent or tranquil results.
(2) why such tranquility gives way to turbulence and even periods of apparently incoherent behaviour,
(3) why non-market interventions seem to be necessary to contain emerging incoherence and sustain a semblance of tranquility.

An essentially Keynesian view is that, whereas economists may explain the apparent coherence of the details of a decentralized market economy by constructs that ignore money, it is necessary to introduce and understand a monetary system that finances both positions in capital assets and investment in order to understand the variety of ways in which an accumulating capitalist economy behaves. Economic theory therefore must begin by specifying the essential characteristics of the monetary and financial system.

It follows that Keynesian economic theory starts with:

(1) Chapter 17, 'The essential properties of interest and money', in *The General Theory* (Keynes, 1936a);
(2) Keynes's contribution 'The theory of the rate of interest' (Keynes, 1937a);
(3) Keynes's rebuttal of Viner (having been an undergraduate at Chicago, I think of it as an answer to Viner), 'The general theory of employment' (Keynes, 1937b).

Formal theorizing begins with the (q, c, l) analysis of the determination of asset prices and then goes on to examine how asset prices, output prices and financing relations determine investment and therefore output. Money is not neutral because it is an essential determinant of asset prices. A capitalist economy has two sets of prices, those of assets and output, which are formed on quite different principles. Asset prices are a capitalization of prospective yields allowing for carrying costs and the value of liquidity, whereas output prices, including those of investment goods, are means of recovering costs, mainly wage costs.

The two sets of prices reflect different parts of the economic universe and their immediate determinants are quite different. As a result they can vary with respect to one another. Capitalist economies have two price levels, the price level of capital asset, P_k, and of output, P_o.

Each asset or bundle of assets has a yield, q, a carrying cost, c, and a liquidity premium, l. 'It follows that the total return expected from the ownership of an asset over a period is equal to its yield *minus* its carrying costs *plus* its liquidity premium, i.e., to $q - c + l$' (Keynes, 1936a, p. 226). The yield, q, of an asset, or of a collection of assets, is a cash flow; it is most truly identified as gross capital income net of the taxes. In short hand we will call q profits. In *The General Theory*, Keynes identifies c with wastage (time depreciation and storage costs) but we can extend the idea of c to include the costs of financing the position in the assets that yield q. By this extension, c is a cash flow – the gross payment commitments on debts. By making q and c cash flows, they are dimensionally commensurate.

Keynes introduces the concept of the liquidity premium l in the following passage.

> Finally, *the power of disposal over an asset during a period* may offer a potential convenience or security, which is not equal for assets of different kinds, though the assets themselves are of equal initial value. There is, so to speak, nothing to show for this at the end of the period in the shape of output; yet it is something for which people are ready to pay something. The amount (measured in terms of itself) which they are willing to pay for the *potential convenience of security given by this power of disposal* (exclusive of yield or carrying cost attaching to the asset), we shall call its liquidity-premium l.
>
> (Keynes, 1936a, p. 226; emphasis added)

The liquidity premium, l, is a 'potential' cash flow as an asset is sold or 'incorporated' into output that is sold. The ease with which an asset can be sold or can be pledged for a loan yields a 'potential convenience or security' and will therefore carry a premium market price that varies with the 'ease'. This liquidity characteristic of an asset protects its owner against contingencies; it has the attributes of an insurance policy. As is well known, units will willingly pay a premium over the 'fair bet' value for insurance (Friedman and Savage, 1948).

Either in terms of a 'potential' cash flow when the asset is disposed of or as an 'in kind' premium for an insurance policy, 'l' is a cash flow; it is dimensionally equivalent to the q and the c even though q and c may be actual expected receipts and spending while l is the receipts equivalent of an insurance policy.

It is worth noting that this argument tranforms every capital-asset-owning business into the equivalent of a bank. The capital asset organized into plants and owned and operated by firms are not readily marketable but yield incomes: they are equivalent to non-marketable loans that a bank might own. The liabilities of businesses and banks are the interest, dividend and repayment of principal cash flows; as a result, businesses as well as banks hold assets because of 'l' to allow for shortfall of 'q'.

Every bundle of assets has a price, P_k. Money, the unit in which the q's are earned and in which payments c are committed, always has a price of 1: a dollar is a dollar. As the virtue of being readily transformed into cash changes, as the likelihood of the need to fall back on the insurance changes, the price of any bundle of assets, or any particular asset which is not money, will change. Relative asset prices will change depending on the weight of q, c and l in determining their value. 'Money' in this argument is an asset whose price is determined solely by the value of l. As the price of money is always 1, the prices of assets whose value is derived in all or in part from q and c will change relative to the price of money as the value of l changes.

There is a price system, that of capital assets, which is determined by capitalizing q, c and l. This price system reflects the subjective value placed on l. As l is an attribute of money, the greater the quantity of money the more abundant l and therefore the lower the relative price of assets that are valuable because of l. But, as the price of money and near monies is always 1, the lower relative price of money means a higher nominal price of q-yielding assets. There is a Keynesian quantity theory of money that is radically different from the quantity theory based upon equations of exchange.

The route from the nominal prices of q-yielding assets to output, prices and money wages is through investment, aggregate demand and labour market conditions at inherited money wage rates. Changes in the money supply will affect the price level of output as mark-ups per unit of output change, as aggregate profits change, as market power changes with aggregate demand changes or as labour market conditions lead to changes in money wages.

If this were a fully independent paper and not derived from a discussant's intervention, at this point I would introduce section II of Keynes (1937b, pp. 112–19) as a basis for reasoning about the relation between uncertainty and asset values. It is in this section that Keynes remarks 'why should anyone outside a lunatic asylum wish to use money as a store of value?' (pp. 115–16).

Uncertainty in the sense of matters for which 'there is no scientific basis on which to form any calculable probability whatever' (p. 114) is introduced as a basic concept for the analysis of the accumulation of wealth, which aims 'to produce results, or potential results, at a comparatively distant, and sometimes at an *indefinitely* distant, date'. Money in this argument is valuable because it embodies protection against unfavourable contingencies that are not reducible to insurable risks. To a great extent, money is valuable because the carrying costs, c, which are largely a time series of payment commitments, are usually denominated in money.

Even so, with a well-functioning money market, the assets held for insurance can and do differ from demand deposits and currency as long as units assume that the market will function so that the assets held for insurance can be cheaply exchanged or pledged for money. In complex financial markets such exchanges may at times be possible only with the support of the central bank. The Lender of Last Resort function of the central bank reflects a recognition by the political authorities that a situation can arise in which the exchange of financial assets for money may be so difficult or so expensive that the funds that can be raised in a market without intervention fall short of the amount needed to validate payment commitments. Assets that are held because market participants are not inmates of lunatic asylum may require the protection of central bank which stands ready to exchange its 'money' for such assets.

In Keynes, uncertainty is not an imperfection of markets. It is a fundamental aspect of nature in an accumulating capitalist economy. Accumulation cannot be understood, and why booms and busts accompany the process of accumulation under capitalist conditions cannot be understood, without introducing uncertainty. Keynes without uncertainty is like Hamlet without the Prince, and the role of money, liability structure and various systems of intervention in a capitalist economy cannot be studied without introducing uncertainty.

If we consider 'The general theory of employment' (Keynes, 1937b) as offering a guide to the understanding of *The General Theory*, then asset prices, uncertainty, financing condition (both internal flows and external transactions) and the supply price of investment output combine to generate investment. The Keynesian theory of investment not only shows that there is a relation between investment, uncertainty and financing but also shows why investment is given to fluctuation. In particular, the fluctuation of investment is affected by the payment commitments that go under the general heading of '*c*', carrying costs.

Economies are systems with yesterdays, todays and tomorrows. A great American philosopher and football coach, George Allen, once said that 'The future is now'. The *q*'s are cash flows that are currently anticipated; the *q*'s stretch out over time. The existing financial liabilities, the in-place '*c*'s', represent contracts that are already signed and that call for payments 'now' and in the future. The structure of interest rates on various instruments that can be used to finance positions in assets and investment demand reflect the value placed upon liquidity, *l*, because of the uncertainty that surrounds *q*'s and *c*'s, and terms on which money can be obtained by issuing instruments that promise future *c*'s. An economist studying capitalist accumulation needs to amend Allen by recognizing that in both capital assets and liability structures 'The future, the past and now are all now'.

Over each period of time there are cash payments, *c*, that have to be made because of maturing dated contracts and because asset holders are exercising rights to demand payment. These payment commitments are on account of both principal and interest. These commitments can be fulfilled because either the *q*'s being earned are large enough or borrowing to repay debt and even to pay interest takes place. I have called the commitment–receipt structure hedge, speculative and Ponzi finance, where Ponzi is a scheme in which interest payments are financed by debts. Although Ponzi was a Boston swindler, Ponzi finance can be honest and above board; the IMF has been sponsoring Ponzi financing for heavily indebted countries.

The investment activity that is financed leads to variation in effective demand, which leads to profits and to savings that are equal to investment. Financed investment activity depends upon current expectations of future profits and the new financing that is forthcoming. If the proportion of the *q*'s that go to *c*'s increases, then the likelihood increases that new financing will not be forthcoming. In particular, if a sufficient shortfall of cash payments to financial institutions (including banks) occurs, financed investment will decrease. The willingness and the ability to finance and to commit financing depends upon the extent to which currently and recently due payments because of financial commitments have in fact been made. A sufficient repudiation or non-validation of commitments on liabilities will have a disastrous effect on new commitments.

The links between accumulation, the debt structure, investment and profits are the keys to an understanding of the behaviour of accumulating capitalist economies. These links are nowhere examined in Eatwell and Milgate (1983).

Both the neoclassical synthesis and the substance of the content of Eatwell and Milgate are similar in that they ignore money. The first sentence in Frank Hahn's *Money and Inflation* (1983) is: 'The most serious challenge that the existence of money poses to the theorist is this: the best developed model of the economy cannot find room for it.' John Eatwell and Murray Milgate write:

> the essays assembled in this volume provide the essential ingredients of a framework for demonstrating the manner in which the classical theory of value may be regarded as being congruent with Keynes's principle of effective demand. . . . Of course, many difficult analytical problems remain to be settled, not the least of which are to be found in the important areas of the theory of money and the theory of capitalist accumulation.
>
> (Eatwell and Milgate, 1983, p. 15)

Both neoclassical and Sraffian theory stand mute when it comes to money and accumulation under capitalist conditions. In *both* frameworks the central areas of 'the theory of money and the theory of capitalist accumulation' are among the 'difficult analytical problems' that 'remain to be settled'.

Once we integrate money into the accumulation process, we have a theory of money for a capitalist economy which, when combined with the way effective demand yields profits, tells us the total of the profits that individual productions will generate. Profits are in no way a reflection of a marginal productivity of 'capital' but rather a return that reflects the financed demand for investments (along with the other determinants of profit that follow from Kalecki's structure); aggregate profits result from the scarcity of output capacity and distribution of profits reflects the structure of total demand.

In a capitalist economy, output supply prices are means of recapturing costs. The Sraffa–Leontief equation schemes can be viewed as specifying the total costs that must be recovered for production to take place: the competition for profits by producers leads to the realized mark-up.

The neoclassical synthesis, by using preferences and production functions to determine a labour market equilibrium, employment and output, proves too much and cannot explain coherence in the price structure with excess supply. The Sraffian system is able to show that coherence of markets is possible at various levels of employment, even as the Keynesian analysis is able to show why normal market reaction to excess supplies may make things worse not better. There is a possible link between Sraffa and Keynes in which the Keynes aggregate demand is transformed into a vector of outputs, which in turn leads to gross outputs and the distribution of gross output into 'inputs' and 'final outputs'.

Such a system would not be one in which equality of the rate of profit plays any role: realized profit flows would be a distribution among outputs of the aggregate but the distribution will not be an equilibrium rate. In fact, the 'rate of profit' disappears from such an analysis as there is no well-defined denominator, for the historic costs of capital assets disappear from the determination of any economic variable. All that remains from the past is the physical capabilities of the machines and the mass of financial obligations embodied in the structure of liabilities and intermediation.

This is not to dispute the insight that the relevant jiggling of the system reflects the profit drives of accumulators, of those who order investment outputs. But there is no process in Sraffian analysis to explain this phenomenon. Seeking profits through investments and controlling capital is the subject of the negotiations between bankers and businessmen. A profit-flows-based analysis of an accumulating capitalist economy requires that the analysis include money and banking from the very beginning. This is the meaning of Keynes and why Keynes is incompatible with neoclassical theory and only marginally compatible with Sraffian theory.

Another great American philosopher, Vincent Lombardi, who, like George Allen, was a successful football coach, once said 'Winning isn't everything, it is the only thing'. I would like to paraphrase this sage and make the radical statement that for an analysis of capitalist economies 'Money isn't everything, it is the only thing'.

Note

What follows originated as a discussant's intervention at the Sraffa conference. However, it was prepared without the constraints imposed by having a paper to discuss: that paper never materialized. The editors of this conference volume asked to publish my informal remarks as a paper. With this history the reader will appreciate that what follows is largely a restatement of views I have expressed at other times and places, modified by my using Eatwell's contributions to Eatwell and Milgate (1983) as, so to speak, a proxy for the paper that never was and as a 'centre of gravity' for my remarks.

Reply

In his comment on Asimakopulos's paper (chapter 10), Garegnani takes exception to a statement I make in my contribution (chapter 11). Garegnani has me stating that:

> The meanings that are normally given to the long run involve some idea of an equilibrium or a center of gravity towards which it oscillates. . . . But a minimal specification of a monetary production or better an accumulating capitalist economy with sophisticated financial system includes endogenous destabilizing relations (p. 348).

In truth I state that

> The meanings that are normally given to the long run involves some idea of an equilibrium or center of gravity towards *which the system tends or around* which it oscillates. (It can be a static or a growth equilibrium or a center of gravity.) But a minimal specification of a monetary production or better an accumulating capitalist economy with a sophisticated financial system includes endogenous destabilizing relations (p. 363, emphasis added).

After the citation Garegnani states that 'However, Minsky's "destabilizing" relations cannot but generate fluctuations, and therefore fluctuations on either side of a trend, that is, generate those very oscillations whose possibility he seems to be denying in that passage' (p. 348). Garegnani's 'cannot but' phrase has to be amended, as all such assertions must be, to *cannot but within a specified analytical framework*. Garegnani's 'cannot but' is not valid to statements made within an analytical framework that differs from his.

The analytical framework within which my remarks are made is one in which money, in the sense of the money that emerges within a full-bodied capitalist financial structure, is there at the beginning. Money is not added onto an analysis that derives its essential propositions in a framework that abstracts from money and hopes that these propositions have some relevance for a monetary economy.

This distinction between analytical frameworks that integrate money and those that add on money is of particular importance when we recognize that within a capitalist economy at any moment the prices of capital assets are not closely connected to the prices of production of investment output and that the difference between these two sets of prices is essential in determining investment. The fundamental contribution of Keynes is that he fully integrated money into the determination of the prices of capital assets and thus into the determination of employment, outut and distribution.

Garegnani works within a framework set up to demonstrate that markets achieve and sustain an equilibrium. Orthodox neoclassical theorists work within a framework set up to demonstrate that markets achieve and sustain an equilibrium. In such set-ups, outside disturbances can only move the economy from an equilibrium. Cycles are generated because overshoots occur in the process of returning to the assumed unique equilibrium or centre of gravity. To Garegnani and neoclassical theorists the business cycle is analogous to a pendulum.

In a parenthetical remark Garegnani states, 'as for Minsky's assimilation of the treatment of money in marginal theory, with that which we find to be implicit in Sraffa and in many of the papers in Eatwell and Milgate, 1983'. I assume this to mean that Garegnani recognizes that Sraffian theory has no explicit treatment of money. From the point of view from which I approach problems of accumulation in a capitalist framework, he has to stand mute when problems of the path of the economy through time are addressed. If one does not postulate the existence of an equilibrium or a centre of gravity to which the economy tends, and if one explicitly models money and finance within an accumulating capitalist economy so that strong endogenous destabilizing forces appear from time to time, then the path through time of the economy is generated by the combination of market forces with strong disequilibrating properties and the constraints and interventions that contain the disequilibrating forces.

Inasmuch as endogenous relations within a monetary economy are nonlinear and the constraints and interventions needed to achieve coherence are logically equivalent to the introduction of new initial conditions, the path of the system is sensitive to the (imposed) intermittent initial conditions. Within the general pattern of expansion implied by accumulation and innovations that lead to technical dynamism, the result of endogenous instability and a structure of constraints and interventions is a path without an equilibrium or a centre of gravity.

Of course, the time series that result can be decomposed into a trend and fluctuations around the trend, but this is arithmetic not economics. Keynes and Kalecki offered economists frameworks that could enable us to escape from the constructs of physicists. If I decipher Garegnani correctly, he prefers being a prisoner of pre-Keynesian analytical structures.

Note by P. Garegnani

The words 'the system tends or around which', missed by the typist (who mistook the first 'which' in the full sentence for the second), should have been inserted here. Professor Minsky has however centred his answer on those missing words. Apart from the difficulty which the inexplicable 'it', and the oscillations 'towards', may cause to an attentive reader – I fail to see how missing those words could in any way have altered Minsky's thesis in the passage, which is *both* against the tendency to an 'equilibrium', and (therefore) against the idea of oscillations around it.

PART III

ROUND TABLE 1

Accumulation, Effective Demand and Distribution

12

Sraffa: Measurement and Aggregation

Josef Steindl
Vienna

1 *Sraffa and macroeconomics*

My purpose is not an appraisal of Sraffa's work or a probing into his aims or philosophy. I want to deal with a particular aspect. Sraffa's book is concerned with measurement, concepts, aggregation. Indeed, a good deal of the intellectual difficulties that he has mastered are precisely in this field. He had to find a concept that would make it possible to deal with a multi-commodity economy in the same way as if it were Ricardo's corn economy (one-commodity economy). He found the concept in the standard commodity. It is an aggregate and yet a physical measure like corn, independent of prices and distribution. It may serve to measure consumption and investment, wages and profits alike. It is a macroeconomic concept derived from data for the individual commodities.

I wonder whether macroeconomists should not be interested in this side of Sraffa, since measurement and aggregation must ultimately be of concern to them. Indeed, macroeconomics generally works with real values (real wages, real investment or consumption, productivity, etc.), which are ill-defined aggregates. It is just assumed that these 'real values' have meaning and that for practical purposes they can be approximated by working with aggregate consumption, etc., at constant prices. In most cases, this is quite satisfactory for the short run, where the changes over a business cycle are studied. It becomes more and more unsatisfactory when longer series of data are used, where the underlying commodity pattern changes more and more in the course of time.

It might be said that the success of macroeconomics is based on the decision to sweep the problem of aggregation (in the above sense) under the carpet. If Kalecki and Keynes had waited for a meticulous treatment of this problem they would never have got on with their work. Sooner or later, however, the neglected problems may become relevant. It is for this reason that I want to raise the question how far Sraffa's work is relevant to this problem. It should be understood that the question of measurement and definition of 'real' values is to be dealt with merely on a conceptual level here. The practical application can come only much later; but it is obvious that the general question of definition and measuring must precede it.

2 *Duality*

Although a knowledge of Sraffa's book is assumed here, it will be useful to remind the reader of certain features of his solution, in particular of the duality aspect. (For the mathematical background see, for example, Nikaido, 1972.)

Sraffa's starting point is a competitive closed system with a uniform rate of profit, occasionally referred to by him as the original system to distinguish it from the transformations derived from it later. This system is described by two sets of equations.

The typical equation of the one set describes how the total output of a commodity is allocated to various industries (each of which produces one particular commodity):

$$a'_{k1}\, q_1 + a'_{k2}\, q_2 + \ldots + a'_{k,n+m} q_{n+m} = q_k \qquad (1)$$
$$k = 1, \ldots, n$$

$q_v a'_{kv}$ is the amount of commodity k going into the production of commodity v. The total of these inputs of commodity k, q_k, must again be equal to the output of this commodity.[1] The q's are the weights of the various industries. To give them a concrete dimension they are measured in terms of direct labour, so that an equation for the allocation of labour to the various industries has to be added:

$$l'_1\, q_1 + l'_2\, q_2 + \ldots + l'_{n+m}\, q_{n+m} = L. \qquad (1a)$$

The typical equation of the second set describes the amounts of the various commodities going into the production of one particular commodity, as well as the amount of direct labour used; together with the prices, the wage and the rate of profit, this determines the value of output of the commodity in question:

$$(a'_{1v}\, p_1 + a'_{2v}\, p_2 + \ldots + a'_{n,v}\, p_n)(1 + r) + +l'_v\, w = p_v. \qquad (2)$$
$$v = 1, \ldots, n$$

The skeleton in each of the systems is formed by the input coefficients a'_{kv}. It is important that these coefficients are the same in both sets of equations; they just appear in a different order.

To elaborate on this I had better introduce immediately Sraffa's important distinction between basic commodities – those that directly or indirectly enter as inputs into the production of all other commodities – and non-basics –all commodities that are not basic. The basic commodities reproduce themselves, each appears both as input and as output. It is a fundamental assumption that the basic sector as a whole, given appropriate proportions of the commodities, produces either a surplus or at least reproduces itself (viability condition).

I shall now use matrix notation. The input coefficients will be expressed as fractions of the total input for each commodity, i.e. each of the coefficients a'_{kv} will be divided by the input $\Sigma a'_{kv} = q_k$.

Thus

$$a'_{kv} / \Sigma a'_{kv} = a_{kv}.$$

We define the technology matrix A of basic commodities as follows:

$$A = \begin{bmatrix} a_{11} & a_{12} & \cdots\cdots & a_{1n} \\ a_{21} & a_{22} & \cdots\cdots & a_{2n} \\ a_{31} & & \cdots\cdots\cdot & \\ \cdot & & & \\ \cdot & & & \\ \cdot & & & \\ a_{n1} & & \cdots\cdots\cdots & a_{nn} \end{bmatrix}$$

The rows of this matrix appear in equation (1), the columns in equation (2). The rows, weighted with q's, sum to the total inputs; the columns, priced with p's, sum to output value. Since input must be equal to output for each commodity, there is a close relation between the two equation systems.

An element of A, say a_{kv} represents the input of commodity k per unit of commodity v.

The system represented by A is supposed to be viable, that is, capable of at least replacing itself or producing a surplus, which is assured by the Simon-Hawkins conditions (upper left corner principal minors of A must be positive).

The system of equations (1) and (2) can be represented in matrix form as follows (where A_1 is the matrix of non-basics that appear only as outputs, while A_2 is the less important matrix of those non-basics that enter into their own production):

$$\begin{bmatrix} A & A_1 \\ 0 & A_2 \end{bmatrix} q = q. \tag{3}$$

$$p' \begin{bmatrix} A & A_1 \\ 0 & A_2 \end{bmatrix} (1 + r) + lw = p'. \tag{4}$$

$$A\colon n \times n; \quad A_1\colon n \times m; \quad A_2\colon m \times m;$$

$$q\colon n + m; \quad l\colon n + m; \quad p\colon n + m.$$

I pass now from Sraffa's original system to a reference system constructed by means of the technology matrix A.

By choice of the appropriate weights q Sraffa wants to make the surplus ratio s the same for all commodities. Thus

$$A\ (1 + s)\ q = q.$$

$$(A - \lambda I)q = 0. \tag{5}$$

where $\lambda = 1 / (1 + s)$.

Since A is a matrix of non-negative elements, the largest of the eigenvalues λ, the Frobenius root of the characteristic equation,

$$|A - \lambda I| = 0 \tag{6}$$

will guarantee that the eigenvector q is positive, provided the matrix A is indecomposable. This solution q^* is the standard commodity (more precisely, the vector of proportions in which the various commodities are represented in the standard commodity). The surplus ratio s corresponding to the largest eigenvalue λ is uniform for all commodities, which implies that the structure of input and output of the basics is the same.

Another problem Sraffa set turns out to be closely related to the above one. If in the price-determining equations the wage is put equal to zero, all the surplus will go to profits. The profit rate will be a maximum, say R, and there will be a price system corresponding to it. Restricting the argument again to the basics, i.e. to the matrix A, the matrix equation is

$$\begin{aligned} p'A(1+R) &= p' \\ p'(A-\lambda I) &= 0 \\ \lambda &= 1/(1+R) \\ R &= s. \end{aligned} \tag{7}$$

The maximum rate of profit R is equal to the physical surplus ratio s, because the Frobenius root of the characteristic equation (7) is the same as before. The prices p^* are the left-hand eigenvector corresponding to this eigenvalue; the vector is positive, provided the matrix A is indecomposable.

The dual relation between the two aspects – physical surplus and standard commodity here, and maximum profit rate and prices p^* there – has already become apparent. It remains to complement the above equation systems (5) and (7). Since the eigenvectors are determined by the n equations (one of which is dependent on the n–1 others) only up to a scalar factor, we have still to determine this absolute level. Sraffa uses for this the direct labour employed in the n industries:

$$l'_1q_1^* + l'_2q_2^* + \ldots + l'_nq_n^* = L,$$

where L is the total labour employed in the original system. Putting this equal to one, we have

$$l_1q_1^* + l_2q_2^* + \ldots + l_nq_n^* = 1, \qquad l = l'/L. \tag{8}$$

This determines the weights q^* as fractions of the total labour employed in the system.

It remains to determine the absolute level in the case of the price vector. For this purpose Sraffa puts the net product of the system equal to unity.

This brings us to the question that is the actual subject of this chapter: the definition and measurement of the net product. For Sraffa it is important that this measure, as well as the prices p^*, be independent of distribution. A measure of the net product that is invariant with respect to distribution can be obtained in two ways, starting from the one or the other of the two eigenvectors of the technology matrix A, i.e. either from the 'multipliers' q^* – the standard commodity – or from the prices calculated with maximum profit rate, p^*. The two definitions are related in so far as the two eigenvectors belong to the same eigenvalue of the matrix A.

According to the first method the net product will be the difference between the output of each commodity and its inputs going into other industries, measured in the proportions of the standard product:

$$(I - A)\, q^* = \tilde{q}. \tag{9}$$

Now $Aq^* = \lambda I q^*$ from (5), so that we have

$$\tilde{q} = \frac{R}{1+R} I q^* \tag{10}$$

as an expression for the net product in terms of the standard commodity. Since the unit of standard commodity has been linked to the amount of direct labour used in the economy, we can also define the net product in terms of labour as

$$\frac{R}{1+R} L. \tag{11}$$

To get a measure in terms of money value we have to introduce a price vector. We are, in principle, free to choose any price system we want, the essential properties of the standard commodity being preserved in whatever terms of money we express it.

For example, we may choose the prices corresponding to the maximum rate of profit p^* (the left-hand eigenvector of A). We obtain the net product in terms of p^* prices, which, following Sraffa, we equate to unity, making it thereby the unit of the pricing system:[2]

$$p^{*\prime}\, (I - A)\, q^* = 1. \tag{12}$$

Note that the non-basics do not explicitly occur in this product because A refers only to basics. The non-basics are taken account of by equation (1a), which allocates the total labour of the original system (which contains the non-basics) to the basics only. That means that a hypothetical shift of labour from the non-basics to the basics is assumed, and the net product is then measured in terms of the latter. (One might say that in this form 'labour value' still plays a role!)

According to the second method of measuring the net product we make use of the maximum profit rate and of the prices p^* based thereupon. The idea must clearly be that we ascertain the net product in physical terms, and price each item of it with the maximum profit prices p^*. We obtain then a system of prices and we have only to find weights for the commodities to define the net product.

It will be natural to try and proceed in a manner analogous or symmetric to the first method above. Analogy is found in the following: We have to introduce quantities for the various industries. We are in principle free to choose these weights q as we please because the resulting measure of the net product will always be invariant with respect to distribution. But we have now to choose between two different ways of doing it.

We may confine ourselves to the basics, in perfect symmetry to the former method. In this case we shall apply the weights q^* obtained by the former method, because these weights together with the condition $lq^* = 1$ will be a guarantee that the equivalent of the resources absorbed by the non-basics is absorbed by the basics. It follows that the solution of the problem, i.e. the expression for the net product

$$p^{*\prime} (I - A) \, q^* = 1, \tag{12}$$

will be exactly the same as by the former method.

The alternative way is to take into account the non-basics explicitly, which we can do very well in this case since their prices can be determined by means of the prices of basic goods. We are here quite naturally led to apply the actual quantities of the original system because it is they, non-basics and basics together, that form the equivalent of the standard weights q^* of basic goods (which result from shifting the resources of the non-basic sector into the basic sector). We shall therefore have for the net product

$$p^{*\prime} \begin{bmatrix} I - A & A_1 \\ 0 & 0 \end{bmatrix} q, \tag{13}$$

where A_1 is the matrix of coefficients of the non-basics (we neglect the unimportant A_2 here) and q is the vector of the actual quantities of the original system.

The net product of the non-basics $\bar{p}^{*\prime} A_1 \bar{q}$ (bars denote truncated vectors) must be regarded as the equivalent of the part of the standard product that owes its existence merely to the (hypothetical) shift of labour from the non-basic to the basic sector; this equivalence was used to justify the calculation of the standard product in the first place.

From this it follows that the definition of the net product according to (13) is equivalent to that according to (12). We are then able to measure the net product in terms of the standard commodity by pricing its components on the basis of the maximum profit rate, using the quantities in which they are actually produced in the original system.

This method makes it possible to evaluate not only the net product but also any part of it in terms of a share in the net product. Thus, if we evaluate the luxury goods at prices p^* (i.e. with maximum profit rate R), the resulting value will directly give their share in the net product (since this has been given unity value). For this computation we have only to take equation (9) and change the vector of weights q in such a way that all commodities except the luxuries get zero weight.

Addendum

Sraffa's definition of the net product differs from the one given in equation (12) above (see Sraffa, 1960, pp. 24–5) because Sraffa uses a price vector that does not correspond either to the original system's prices or to the maximum profit prices. He uses the production equations of the original system, inserts in them for q the standard multipliers (q^*in the notation of this paper) and leaves the prices to be determined from this system of equations. This definition is not suitable for the study of duality. Sraffa seems to have been aware of duality, but for a further definition of the net product he looked for a different way.

He states that any system that would obey the relation

$$r = R\ (1 - w) \tag{14}$$

(w = share of wages in the net product, r = rate of profit)
will imply that wage and prices are measured in standard product (Sraffa, 1960, p. 31). He proposes therefore to substitute (14) for the equation (on p. 24–5) that defines the net product and equates it to unity. If I understand Sraffa rightly, he would then recalculate prices in the original system as follows: Starting, say, from a given rate of profit r and having calculated R from the eigenvalue of A, he would determine w from (14) and subsequently all prices on the basis of r and w. In this way 'the commodity prices are expressed, in terms of the standard net product' even without our knowing what it consists of (Sraffa, 1960, p. 32).

As a further alternative, the net product is defined in terms of labour, i.e. as the amount of manpower that can be bought by the net product, at the given rate of profit. As the relation

$$\frac{1}{w} = \frac{R}{R - \mathrm{r}} \tag{15}$$

(both net product and total labour are equal to unity) shows, this amount of 'labour commanded by the net product' will vary from one, with a zero profit rate, to infinity, with a profit rate approaching the maximum R. The increase in the so-defined net product with increasing profit rate is of course only a reflection of the decreasing share of wages.

3 *The subsistence wage*

Sraffa mentions two alternative ways of dealing with wages in his system of equations. Either they could be regarded as consisting of two parts: (a) a subsistence wage given exogenously as a vector of quantities of goods required for the upkeep of the workers and (b) a part of the net product (surplus) that goes to the workers on the basis of their bargaining strength. Or else wages could be regarded in their entirety as a part of the surplus.

Sraffa chose the second alternative in order to present the essence of his method, but he admits that this has disadvantages. It means that most of the mass consumption goods are no more included in the basic goods sector than are luxury goods (exceptions would be only goods like coal, which also enter as inputs in production). In consequence, the coefficients of production, i.e. productivity in most industries producing consumption goods, would not affect the rate of profit, prices and the surplus ratio of the whole system (Sraffa, 1960, p. 10).

In fact, however, this is not even the whole objection. In the treatment chosen by Sraffa, neither labour nor, in principle, subsistence goods enter the basic goods sector, from which it follows that economy in the use of labour – labour productivity – does not affect the surplus ratio (= maximum rate of profit R), which we should expect to reflect the productivity of the system. In fact, the measure R reflects economy only in the use of raw materials and energy or in the use of fixed capital (production per machine hour). What becomes of the productivity of labour? It enters the system simply via the relation of total labour L to the net product.

Indeed, the labour input coefficients l_k for the various commodities occur only in the equation

$$q_1^* l_1 + q_2^* l_2 + \ldots + q_n^* l_n = 1$$

(where the total labour is put equal to unity), which is outside the matrix A of basic goods.

If there is a linear reduction in all labour requirements l_k without any change in the technology matrix A, then the amount of labour employed in the whole system with unchanged net product will be lower, while R, r and prices will remain unchanged. (Employment in this new system will again be set equal to unity, i.e. the unit of labour will be debased as it were.) The distribution of the surplus between wage and profit may, of course, be affected; the question will be whether or not the fewer workers, on account of their greater productivity, will obtain the same share as before.

The conclusion to be drawn from the above argument is that we have to include workers' subsistence in the basic goods sector, especially since productivity measurement is a topic of this paper. At first sight it would appear simplest to introduce a commodity labour power, which is produced by the various subsistence goods, and to introduce both into the basic goods sector. The introduction of labour power as a basic good, however, raises the question of whether it should yield a surplus (Roncaglia, 1978, p. 87). Moreover, if we try to do it this way, we risk making the matrix A decomposable, which is not a happy arrangement.[3] The best way seems to me to introduce the subsistence requirements directly in place of labour into the equations of production. The input coefficient for each subsistence good will be the product of two coefficients: the input coefficient of labour, and the required amount of subsistence goods for a unit of labour. In this way we can ensure that the resulting Frobenius root R will take due account of labour productivity in general and of the conditions of production in the mass consumption goods industries in particular.

4 *The reference system*

Sraffa's analysis is strictly confined to the values taken by a number of variables in one given period. Roncaglia (1978, p. 21) in this context speaks of 'a photograph of the system at an instant of time' and of the relations between variables 'as if they were being considered "isolated in a vacuum"'. The past is felt in the system only in so far as it has left certain endowments at the beginning of the period; the link to the future is established only by the stocks that are left at the end.

The legitimate method in the circumstances is what is sometimes called 'comparative statics'. For example, the relation established by Sraffa between the profit rate r, the maximum profit rate R, and the proportion of wage in the net product w,

$$r = R\ (1 - w),$$

refers to a comparison of two separate systems with the same technology, neither of which influences the other. In another example we may compare two independent systems with different technology matrices and establish the consequences for the maximum profit rate R.

It may well be asked now how these static methods could ever be of use for the measurement of change. In fact, it is possible to take account of change without touching the static character of Sraffa's picture. We can do it in the same way as a film is made – by a succession of static pictures it is possible to represent change. We shall then have two representations running side by side, one the continuous process of the 'original economy' from which Sraffa starts, the other a succession of static pictures, which I shall call the reference system (Sraffa speaks of an auxiliary system in referring to his standard commodity).

The two representations have the same technology. The reference system receives data from the original system, especially the amount of labour employed and the technology matrix. The reference system merely carries out certain operations on these data (it has, as it were, no life of its own). (An 'explanation' of the process going on in the continuous system could, of course, not be given by comparative statics; it would require a dynamic treatment, for example difference equations starting from given initial conditions.) Let us put it in more concrete terms.

There are two kinds of activity going on in the real economy, one concerned with reproduction of basic goods, the other with production of non-basic goods. Sraffa usually talks of luxury goods only in connection with non-basics, which would imply 'simple reproduction' in the sense of Marx. There is not the slightest reason, however, why the non-basics should not (in part) take the form of investment goods, and, moreover, of new goods embodying new technology. Accumulation and technological change would then take place in the reference system as follows: the net investment and new technology would emerge in the non-basic sector while it was being created; in the following period the new investment goods would be included among the basic goods, to be reproduced like the others. Thus, the change takes place behind the scenes, leaving the static character of the auxiliary system untouched. The technology matrix, correspondingly, will be different in the second period from what it was in the first; in consequence, the surplus ratio will be different as well.

The link between two adjacent periods of the reference system will be provided by the physical identity of the goods that in the second period will be inputs of basic goods and those goods that are produced but not consumed in the previous period. The signals for the various dispositions come from the real system, where the acts of investment, consumption, etc. actually take place.

The dichotomy of the economy according to basic and non-basic goods is vaguely connected with a fundamental charactertistic of our economic system. To a large extent it is devoted to producing the same things all over again, a system of reproduction; a minor part of it, however, is engaged in the production of new goods. It is like in nature where the species on the whole only reproduces itself, but on the edge throws out some mutations.

It is this practical importance of reproduction that justifies Sraffa's way of measuring the productivity of the system by the following calculation. Imagine that the resources of the economy are all shifted to the reproduction of the same basic goods, in the same proportions for input and output, so that physical 'reproduction on an extended scale' (Marx) takes place. This will yield a physical measure of the productivity or surplus ratio of the system. Sraffa thus measures the reproductive potential of a given economy, which is analogous to the net reproduction rate of a species of animals or plants. The measurement is made possible by an imagined shift of resources, taking the coefficients of the technology matrix as a basis for the calculated transformation of output.

This implies, *inter alia*, basing the input coefficients on full utilization (or a uniform constant utilization) of capacity. It also justifies disregarding economies of scale. The imagined transformation presupposes simple linear relations. The transformation of the original ('real') economy into the auxiliary system of reproduction with uniform surplus ratio has again to be viewed in terms of comparative statics.

5 *Commodities and money*

We now have to leave the main thread of the argument in order to discuss a question that has puzzled many readers of Sraffa. His book is concerned with commodities and prices of production. Money does not come into those problems – essential money, that is. Credit, financial assets, interest, uncertainty, have no place in the 'auxiliary system'. Because of the absence of money, the realization problem plays no role in the reference system. The utilization of capacity is implicitly assumed to be full or at a uniform constant level. In a word, it is a Ricardian world.

Yet money exists in the real world. It is for this reason that, when Sraffa wants to apply the distribution relation he established for the auxiliary system (equation (14))to the actual world, money wages and interest appear on the scene in § 44 (Sraffa, 1960, p. 33) – and the reader gets a jolt.

Finding distribution data in terms of money, Sraffa is faced with the difficulty of translating a money language into a commodity language and vice versa. His own solution of using the profit rate (ultimately the interest rate) for the translation is not quite convincing. He discards the method of measuring the wage by evaluating wage goods in terms of the standard commodity, because this is not applicable when the worker receives a money wage and we do not know what he spends it on (possibly he may save it in part). But if we were to assume the case of a pure commodity world we could evaluate the share of wages in the net standard product. The profit rate would result then from what was left over according to the formula (14).

How can it be proved that this profit rate in terms of standard product is actually the same as the profit rate in terms of production prices given in the real price and wage system? Actually it is quite a trivial matter that distribution in a money economy is more complicated than in Ricardo's world. The capitalist's profit is based on expectation, expressed in the valuations of his balance sheet; it is a matter of speculation. The worker's wage, if he saves part of it, depends on future prices.

Before such difficulties it is better to capitulate and confine the analysis to the commodity world. Let me assume that in our real economy workers do not save. It is then possible, in principle, to identify wages and profits in terms of physical commodities consumed or received by the two classes (household budgets could, in principle, establish what the workers and what the capitalists have consumed in physical terms). This will, on the basis of valuation at R prices, give the shares of wages and profit. If we go further and assume that capitalists invest all their profits, then the dichotomy according to wages and profits will coincide with the dichotomy according to consumption and investment. In this way we shall, by sheer force of assumption, remain in the commodity world.

6 *Measurement of productivity and real wages*

After so much preparation, the stage is now set and the discussion of the main issue can begin. Can the 'film' – the reference system – be used, together with Sraffa's surplus ratio (s or R), to measure changes in productivity over time?

Let us consider the changes that the technology matrix A undergoes in the course of development. Technical progress will lead to a reduction in the input coefficients a_{kv} in many industries. It is quite true, though, that in many other cases the input coefficients will rise at certain stages of development. Thus the input of energy increased in the course of the industrial revolution (while nowadays the tendency to save energy has gained the upper hand). But we usually take it for granted that this has been offset, and more than offset, by a saving in direct labour, so that R will rise as a consequence of the technical change provided that we include the direct cost of labour, in the form of subsistence requirements, in the matrix of basic goods. There will, however, be a complication. As has been stated before, the input coefficients for the means of subsistence will be products of the input coefficients of labour and the requirement of the subsistence good per unit of labour c_v:

$$l_k \begin{bmatrix} c_1 \\ c_2 \\ c_3 \\ \cdot \\ \cdot \\ \cdot \end{bmatrix} k = 1, \ldots, n$$

Now the input coefficients of labour l_k will be reduced by technical progress, but the same cannot be said of the vector of requirements c of various subsistence goods per unit of labour. If the subsistence wage (the price of labour power) is regarded as a conventional measure subject to historical change, then it will increase with economic development. In other words, the coefficients c will tend to move in the direction opposite to the labour input coefficents l and most of the other input coefficients a. To measure the growth in productivity it will therefore be necessary to disentangle these two countervailing tendencies.

We may write

$$\Delta R = \Delta R^* - \Delta W^*, \tag{16}$$

where R^* is productivity and W^* is the subsistence wage. We imagine that accounting takes place at the end of each period. The surplus ratio R is then computed for the period in two ways: First, it is assumed that the subsistence wage has remained at the same level as it was the year before. Thus $\Delta W^* = O$. We obtain then, comparing the surplus ratio R with that in the year before, a measure of the change in productivity ΔR^*. In the second stage we compute R on the basis of the actual subsistence wage of the year just ended (which presumably has increased in relation to the preceding year). We obtain a lower value of R than in the first place, and from the two estimates we obtain the increase in the subsistence wage:

$$\Delta W^* = \Delta R^* - \Delta R. \tag{17}$$

Thus, the increase in the real subsistence wage is defined as the weakening of the productive potential of the economy by the increased standard of living of the workers. This, needless to say, is a rather mechanical way of looking at it.

A word now has to be said on the underlying philosophy, the crucial question. Is it meaningful to compare the reproductive potential of two economies with different technologies and different standard commodities? I think it is, both for the comparison of one economy over time, and for the comparison of entirely different economies. It has as much meaning as the comparison of net reproduction rates for men or for animals. Most economists do not hesitate to compare growth rates in India and in Europe, although they know very well that the same things are not grown here and there.

It has to be mentioned now that the above measure of the real subsistence wage has a remarkable property. It will take account of improvements in the quality of goods and of the introduction of new goods into the usual subsistence of the workers. Indeed, both of these will weaken the reproductive potential because they will absorb resources. The new goods will be included in the basic sector as additional inputs for each unit of labour, and will therefore reduce the surplus.

I have shown how we could compare productivity and the real subsistence wage for two successive years. The method chosen above is, however, not unique. We may either keep the productivity constant in the two years, or keep the subsistence wage constant. Further, we may choose for this purpose the level of productivity or subsistence wage respectively of year one or year two, so that we obtain four alternative measures. We get involved again in the classical problem of index numbers – the difference between Laspeyre and Paasche, which will only disappear if we compare very short periods. This problem of changing weights (represented by the coefficients of the standard commodity) are, however, less troublesome here than usually, because we base ourselves on technology matrices which are not affected by changes in utilisation of capacity.

7 *The accumulation process*

The net product can be divided into investment and consumption, and I shall suppose it is possible to identify the two in terms of physical goods.[4] These can then be valued in terms of R prices (at maximum profit rate). As explained further above (page 382) we need only use the equation

$$p^{*\prime}\left[(I-A)\ \mathrm{A}_1\right]\tilde{q}=\mu, \tag{18}$$

where $\tilde{q}$ is a vector in which the quantities $\tilde{q}_V$ of all commodities except luxuries or investment, respectively, are made equal to zero. The expression (18) then states the share of luxuries or investment, respectively, in the net product.

In the case of investment, we should also like to know its relation to the capital stock. This capital stock, in Sraffa's system, is represented by the inputs of basic goods to which the profit rate is applied. The relation of the net product to the capital is the 'standard ratio' R. The relation of investment to the capital, that is, the rate of accumulation, is known immediately: if we know that the share of investment in the net product is μ, then it follows that the rate of accumulation will be μR.

Are we justified in adding up these growth rates of capital μR over time? A certain plausible justification is the fact that we have a link between one period and the next in the physical identity of the capital goods bequeathed by the preceding period and those received by the following period. The former passes on its basic goods (except in so far as they are discarded for being obsolete) and the new investment goods that have so far been non-basics. The latter receives exactly those physical goods and includes them in its basic goods sector, to be reproduced in the same period. This, I think, may lend meaning to the idea that real capital, even though it is changing in physical content, can be regarded as a steadily growing entity. We might express the share of profits in the net product, in the same way as the share of investment, if we can identify the physical goods consumed by the capitalists and add them to the investment goods, assuming all along that workers do not save and capitalists do not borrow. In fact, we have here, intriguingly enough, the conceptual material for the 'Cambridge theory' of distribution.

8 *Remarks on distribution*

The following remarks are not an interpretation of Sraffa. I do not claim that his book contains this or that theory of distribution; I merely note down some ideas that came to me while writing this paper.

Sraffa's suggestion (made for the very special reason that it is impossible to express money wages in terms of a standard commodity) of prior determination of the profit rate, which leaves the wage as a residual, is the same as the 'Cambridge theory'. This is, of course, the classical subsistence theory stood on its head. Instead of profits, the wages are what is left over.

A slightly more complicated approach is suggested by Sraffa's idea of the split wage (used in this paper), consisting of a price of labour power based on the cost of subsistence, and a share in the surplus. Now this implies that both the classical theory and the Cambridge theory are relevant. The former determines a rock bottom for the real wage based on conventional means of subsistence, which is defended very strongly and on the whole recognized by the employers themselves. The share of wages in the surplus, on the other hand, is determined by the growth requirements of capital, which determine the rate of profit, leaving the remainder of the surplus to wages.

For the arguments of the preceding pages of this paper, such a conception would be very convenient, because it would reduce a source of dissatisfaction: namely, the fact that the subsistence wage, being conventional and historical, is a little vague. If, however, the surplus wage is a residual, then it will matter less whether we overestimate or underestimate the subsistence wage. The error will be compensated in part by an opposite move in the surplus wage.

Finally, a remark on the profit rate being determined by the money rate of interest. This fits in with Keynesian ideas of a long-run character (the euthanasia of the rentier): if interest disappeared then the profit would become merely an entrepreneurial wage. It probably also has an application to the conditions of extraordinary high interest rates in recent years, which can plausibly be assumed to have been shifted at least in part onto profit rates. Yet it is difficult to believe in a general theory of interest dominating distribution in an economy in which monopolistic power based on impediments to free entry in the commodity markets accounts for a large part of profits.

Notes

1. This will evidently be true if the last m commodities embody the surplus while the first n are just reproducing themselves. This is the distinction between basics and non-basics (see below). But the surplus may also (perhaps partly) take the form of basic commodities, as Kurz has pointed out to me. We could represent this as an input of, say, commodity k, etc., into a special industry, called 'storage of basic surplus commodities' which would be included among the m non-basic industries (commodities). Alternatively we could multiply the whole of the left side of the equation, i.e. the inputs of (1), by $(1 + s_k)$, where s_k is the surplus ratio in so far as the surplus takes the form of basic commodities, in relation to the total input of k. In the sequel this problem will solve itself because the surplus ratio will take care of the equality of input and output of each commodity.
2. It should be noted that this definition of the net product is not the same as Sraffa's, because he uses a different price system.
3. Most subsistence goods will be inputs only in the production of labour power and there will therefore appear a large block of zero input coefficients.

4. Actually the means of subsistence that are put aside as additions to stocks have also to be counted as investment goods to enable us to measure accumulation.

Comment

Heinz D. Kurz
Graz

Measurement and Aggregation

In his paper Professor Steindl raises the question whether macroeconomists should be interested in Sraffa's standard commodity, 'since measurement and aggregation must ultimately be of concern to them', particularly 'when longer series of data are used.' The answer he gives is in the affirmative: in section 6 of the paper it is contended that Sraffa's concept has meaning 'both for the comparison of one economy over time, and for the comparison of entirely different economies'. In this brief comment I shall not enter into a discussion of the more technical parts of Steindl's argument and especially his elaboration on the standard system. I shall rather focus attention on some conceptual issues and point out differences between Steindl's reading of Sraffa and mine.

In my opinion, the key to a proper understanding of the concept of the standard commodity can be found in an oral intervention by Sraffa at the 1958 Corfu conference on the theory of capital. There Sraffa argued:

> one should emphasize the distinction between two types of measurement. First, there was the one in which the statisticians were mainly interested. Second, there was measurement in theory. The statistician's measures were only *approximate* and provided a suitable field for work in solving index number problems. The theoretical measures required *absolute precision* . . . If we found contradictions, then these pointed to defects in the theory, and an inability to define measures of capital accurately.
> (See Lutz and Hague, 1961, pp. 305–6; emphasis added)

This distinction appears to be also lurking in the background in the following passage taken from Sraffa's Introduction to Ricardo's *Works*:

> The search for what has been called 'the chimera of an invariable standard of value' preoccupied Ricardo to the end of his life. However, the problem which mainly interested him was not that of finding an actual commodity which would accurately measure the value of *corn or silver at different*

> *times and places*; but rather that of finding the conditions which a commodity would have to satisfy in order to be invariable in value – *and this came close to identifying the problem of a measure with that of the law of value.*
> (Sraffa, 1951, pp. xl–xli; emphasis added)

Ricardo's unfortunate tendency to confound these two radically different issues caused a lot of confusion and turned out to be an obstacle in the way of a proper understanding of the role of the standard commodity in Sraffa's approach to the theory of value and distribution. Indeed, many interpreters wrongly considered Sraffa's ingenious concept an attempted solution to 'the' Ricardian problem.

However, as should be clear from the foregoing, there are *two* distinct Ricardian problems, only one of which is addressed by Sraffa in his celebrated book: he is exclusively concerned with the theoretical measure, or, to use his above phrasing, 'the law of value'. The standard commodity proves to be a powerful tool in the theory of value and distribution of classical derivation; it simplifies the analysis of the mathematical properties of the system of normal competitive prices. It deserves mentioning that the results derived by Sraffa can also be obtained by using the Perron–Frobenius theorem. In fact, Sraffa's demonstration of the existence and uniqueness of the standard commodity (in the case of single production) can be regarded as a (not fully complete) proof of this theorem. For a more detailed exposition of this view, see Kurz and Salvadori (1987).

If this interpretation is accepted then there would seem to be no room for attributing to the standard commodity the entirely different role of providing a measure that can be used in intertemporal or interspatial comparisons. In fact, as Steindl points out, different technologies, either of the same economy at different times or of different economies at the same time, generally have different standard commodities. Which of the standard commodities should then be adopted as the common standard, and why? To take an extreme case, imagine that two systems of production have no single commodity in common. In this case it is all too obvious that the idea under consideration is bound to founder.

So far it has been assumed that a standard commodity always exists and that it is unique. However, this need not be the case. In particular, it is well known that for systems with some jointness of production (including the case of intensive diminishing returns on homogeneous land, fixed capital and joint production proper) a standard commodity may or may not exist (see again Kurz and Salvadori, 1987, pp. 878–9). Since joint production is to be considered the general case, and is empirically very common indeed (see Steedman, 1984b), it cannot be presumed that a standard commodity always exists.

After these more general remarks on the role of the standard commodity in Sraffa's analysis I shall, in what follows, comment on some particular aspects of Steindl's investigation.

Scrutiny shows that in the discussion of what he calls 'the main issue' of his paper (commencing with section 6), Steindl is in fact pre-eminently concerned with comparisons of different economic systems in terms of their maximum growth potentials, whereas the standard commodity plays a subordinate role only. The maximum rate of growth, G, is the rate that solves the quantity system

$$q = (1 + G)Aq,$$

where A is the augmented matrix including the necessary subsistence for the workers. Since actual wages may include a share of the surplus product, it is not clear how the subsistence component is ascertained. Indeed, as Joan Robinson pointed out in her review of Sraffa's book, it can hardly be imagined that 'when workers had a surplus to spend on beef, their physical need for wheat was unchanged' (1961, p. 54). Further on, Steindl's measure of changes in the system's 'productivity' in terms of changes in the maximum possible growth rate crucially depends on a hypothesis of how technological change affects the subsistence component, both directly and indirectly, via its impact on the general level of wages. It would be interesting to hear more about the kind of hypothesis Steindl has in mind.

According to Steindl, Sraffa starts from the assumption of given 'endowments at the beginning of the period', i.e. 'stocks that are left at the end' of the previous period. To avoid possible misunderstandings, it is perhaps worthwhile stressing that the capital stocks contemplated in Sraffa's analysis are those necessary to produce the given levels of output of the different commodities at minimum costs. In contradistinction to the neoclassical approach, which starts from the familiar assumption of an arbitrarily given endowment vector, Sraffa takes plant and equipment to be fully adjusted to effectual demand. Obviously, the capital stocks inherited from the past will generally not be consistent with a normal or long-period position of the economy characterized by a uniform rate of profit.

This leads to a final observation. Steindl maintains that 'Sraffa's way of measuring the productivity of the system . . . is made possible by an imagined shift of resources'. Clearly, the only resource to which the idea of an 'imagined shift' could perhaps be applied is the quantity of labour employed, whereas the capital stocks required for the standard system need not and in general will not coincide with the stocks of the actual system. (This is immediately obvious in the case of non-basics that serve as means of production.) However, even with regard to labour, the idea of a hypothetical redistribution of the given labour force employed in the actual system is dubious. Since Sraffa allows for heterogeneous labour (1960, p. 10), there is no presumption that the same quantities of the different kinds of labour employed in the actual system will also be required in the standard system. This reveals again the purely *auxiliary* character of the standard system.

Reply

There are two different attitudes towards Sraffa: either you want to put his work under glass and contemplate it from the outside or you want to do something with it. I do not suggest that Professor Kurz represents the first attitude: in fact he does not. I suspect, however, that he would suffer my irresponsible gambolling much more gladly if I pursued it like Francis Seton, who considered similar ideas (unknown to me when I wrote my paper) without any reference to Sraffa at all (Seton, 1985). Unfortunately I cannot do that because, as far as I am concerned, my ideas come from Sraffa.

Kurz is in a very strong position when he attacks my failings and weaknesses, but he does not seem to be quite as fully aware of the weaknesses of the alternative positions which I chose not to take. He stresses the ubiquity of joint production and implicitly blames me for failing to take that problem into account. But is he not sitting in a glass house? Is not the generality of Sraffa's analysis itself reduced to the same extent to which joint production prevails in reality, since we have hardly found a completely satisfactory answer to these problems? Again, he implicitly blames me for neglecting heterogeneity of labour, which, he says, Sraffa 'allows for'. But this is just not true. The whole of Sraffa's analysis is based on the assumption of homogeneous labour.

The concept of a subsistence wage is difficult to swallow for anybody. But the alternative chosen by Sraffa (considering wage as a part of the surplus) implies that the surplus ratio is not affected by economy in the use of direct labour; it takes account only of economy in the use of commodities (raw materials and energy). Also it is not at all influenced by conditions in the wage goods industries. One can't just brush this off like a bit of dust. It limits drastically the practical relevance of a surplus ratio calculated in this way. The classicals were more consistent than their present-day followers, who discard the subsistence wage as an outdated piece of the classical *ameublement* although this damages to some extent the importance of the surplus concept itself.

In fact my subsistence wage, although very fuzzy, is not entirely without basis. It is the standard of living that workers have already achieved in recent years. This is a matter of reproduction of basically the same wage goods. Anything newly gained in addition will in principle involve non-basic goods and belong therefore to the surplus, because it is not merely a reproduction of an accustomed real wage. The surplus part of the wage and the commodities that represent it become gradually included in the subsistence wage in the course of history and the subsistence wage correspondingly changes in composition.

Kurz is right to stress my main problem – the comparison of different periods with different technology and different subsistence wages. He understands me correctly when he says that I use the surplus ratio as the measure of comparison when trying to evaluate changes in the efficiency of the system. In trying to take account both of the change in technology and of the change in real wage I cannot avoid being finally faced with the problem that the index makers have, the alternative between Laspeyre and Paasche. This again involves fuzziness, but I hope less than the ordinary index numbers. In any case, I can take account of new goods without any special tricks.

I do not understand why Kurz objects to my contention that Sraffa's reference system is derived from his original system by a shift of resources. In the original system, non-basics are produced, while in the reference system there is room only for basics. How can that happen without a shift of resources? I think Kurz must suspect something sinister behind a completely harmless statement.

13

Accumulation, Distribution and the 'Keynesian Hypothesis'

Heinz D. Kurz
Graz

We have come to praise Sraffa's *Production of Commodities by Means of Commodities*, not to bury it. However, one may wonder whether the theme of this round table lends itself to this honourable task. In what respect, if at all, can Sraffa's book be considered relevant for a probing into the formidable problem of 'Accumulation, Effective Demand and Distribution'? Many would question the usefulness of Sraffa's approach for an analysis of this problem. They could point out that his 'investigation is concerned exclusively with such properties of an economic system as do not depend on changes in the scale of production' (Sraffa, 1960, p. v); and that the problem of effective demand is entirely left out of consideration. The contrast with our theme could hardly be more pronounced.

The purpose of this paper will be to provide some arguments in support of the view that Sraffa's analysis may be considered an adequate starting point of an investigation of accumulation and effective demand. Indeed, if the 'normal' or 'long-period positions' of the economy Sraffa is concerned with are to be regarded as the centres around which the actual economy is gravitating, then the study of 'normalcy' appears to be a prerequisite to a study of the actual path of capital accumulation and the long-run impact of effective demand on the economic performance of the system.

The structure of the paper is as follows. Section 1 is devoted to a discussion of the concept of normal positions, with particular emphasis on the problem of normal utilization of plant and equipment. Section 2 contains some observations on the relationship between accumulation and income distribution. It is argued that the neo-Keynesian approach to the problem does not provide a proper generalization to the long period of the so-called 'Keynesian hypothesis' that investment can be taken as the independent variable. In section 3 the question is raised whether or not the normal position of an economy at a given moment of time depends on the path of accumulation that the economy followed in the past.

Unless otherwise stated, the argument is developed in terms of the following simplifying assumptions. There are constant returns to scale throughout the economy, in particular, there are no scarce natural resources, such as land; there is no joint production proper; the items of fixed capital exhibit constant efficiency over their lifetime; all commodities are basic (excluding old items of fixed capital); the set of alternative techniques of production is given; there is free competition. It will be shown that even under these premises the output produced from normal capital utilization will typically fall short of the potential maximum output. Additional output could therefore be produced to match higher levels of effective demand by a higher degree of capital utilization, provided it is profitable to do so. The difference between normal capacity and maximum capacity contributes to an explanation of the elasticity of the industrial system, i.e. its potential to absorb significant fluctuations in the rate of net accumulation.

1 *'Normal' capital utilization*

According to the principle of effective demand, as it will be understood in this paper, actual production is regulated by aggregate demand, which may fall short of, or exceed, the output produced from 'normal' utilization of the capital stock. Hence we are in need of a proper specification of what we mean by normal capital utilization. The answer to this question is implicit in Sraffa's approach to the problem of the choice of technique (1960, part III).

Choice of technique and capital utilization

When a producer plans to build a new plant, this involves some decision as to the desired normal rates of utilization of the various items of fixed capital. Otherwise it would not be possible to decide how much of these items to install in order to match the average expected demand for the product. Under competitive conditions this decision 'will be exclusively grounded on cheapness' (Sraffa, 1960, p. 83), i.e. the producer will choose the cost-minimizing method of production. However, with fixed capital a full characterization of a 'method of production' includes a description not only of the quantities of the different kinds of means of production used up (i.e. circulating capital), the quantities of the different kinds of labour employed and the quantity of the respective product produced, but also of the quantities and rates of utilization of the different items of fixed capital operated.

The rate of utilization of an item of durable capital depends on the intensity of operation per unit of active time (hour) and on the number of time units within a given time period (year) during which the item is actually operated. Hence capital utilization per time period can be increased by speeding up the rate of operation of the durable capital good or by stretching out the duration of its operation. The different feasible modes of operation of plant and equipment may be conceived as different methods of production.

We now have to take into consideration the all-important fact that the prices of the different inputs into the production process behave differently over unit time. While some prices are time-invariant, others are *time-*

specific.[1] As regards the latter, the most important example is perhaps the wage rate, a characteristic feature of which is that it varies regularly by time of day (or day or week). Thus, in order to utilize plant and equipment outside of 'ordinary working hours',[2] by scheduling work at night or at weekends or holidays, firms must generally pay higher wages to workers: they must pay the going basic wage rate and a wage premium or differential to compensate workers for their work during abnormal hours (or days). The levels of the basic wage and the wage differentials may be envisaged as reflecting the going balance of power of the two parties involved in the conflict over the distribution of the product.

We may now illustrate the principle of the choice of the cost-minimizing system of operation of plant and equipment in terms of an exceedingly simple example (see also Kurz, 1986). The case under discussion is *shift work*.

Suppose that a producer has the choice of operating a 'machine' (a plant) under a single- or a double-shift system. Suppose that under the second (night) shift the quantities of the means of production used up per unit of output are the same as under the first ('day') shift. Hence, under the double-shift system the same daily output could be produced by working half of the machinery twice as long each day as under the single-shift system. Assume for simplicity that the machine's lifetime lasts two years under the single and one year under the double-shift system.

Obviously, the producer is confronted with three alternatives: single 'day' or night shifts or double shifts. He can compare the cheapness of these alternatives only for given prices and wage rates. I shall assume that the comparison is carried out in terms of the set of prices that obtains when the pure 'day'-shift system is in use. Let p_M^d be the price of the new plant required to produce annually the quantity Q of a commodity 'q', the unit price of which is p_Q^d, K_Q^d the value of the means of production used up (circulating capital), r the rate of profits and W_Q^d the corresponding wages bill. Then, under the 'day'-shift system, the price equation representing the production of commodity 'q' will be (see Sraffa, 1960, p. 66)

$$p_M^d \frac{r(1+r)^2}{(1+r)^2-1} + K_Q^d(1+r) + W_Q^d = Qp_Q^d \tag{1}$$

Under the conditions specified, the question of whether or not it would be profitable to schedule work regularly at night instead of at 'day' is easily decided. All that matters is how the 'day'-shift and night-shift wages bills compare. Let π denote the extra profits the producer could make when scheduling work at night and W_Q^n the corresponding wages bill. Hence

$$\pi \gtreqless 0 \quad \text{if} \quad W_Q^n \lesseqgtr W_Q^d. \tag{2}$$

The difference in the wages bills can generally be related to differences in 'day' and night wage rates, w^d and w^n, and in the respective quantities of labour employed, L_Q^d and L_Q^n. Since in general both the wage rate and the labour input will be larger on the late shift,[3] work will not be scheduled exclusively at night.

There remains the alternative of adopting the double-shift system. By doing so the entrepreneur could economize on his plant by one-half. On the other hand, he would incur a larger wages bill, W_Q, which would amount to

$$W_Q = \tfrac{1}{2}(W_Q^d + W_Q^n) = \tfrac{1}{2}(w^d L_Q^d + w^n L_Q^n). \tag{3}$$

The extra profits he could make are determined by

$$\tfrac{1}{2} p_M^d(1+r) + K_Q^d(1+r) + W_Q + \pi = Qp_Q^d. \tag{4}$$

Subtracting equation (1) from (4) gives

$$\pi = \tfrac{1}{2} p_M^d \left[\frac{r(1+r)}{2+r}\right] - (W_Q - W_Q^d) \tag{5}$$

or

$$\pi = \tfrac{1}{2} p_M^d \left[\frac{r(1+r)}{2+r}\right] - \tfrac{1}{2}(\Delta_w L_Q^d + \Delta_L w^n), \tag{5'}$$

where $\Delta_w = w^n - w^d$ is the wage differential and $\Delta_L = L_Q^n - L_Q^d$ is the labour input differential. The first term in equations (5) and (5′) indicates the annual charge on the plant on which the producer could economize by adopting the double-shift system, while the second term indicates the additional wages he would have to pay. Clearly

$$\pi \gtreqless 0 \quad \text{if} \quad p_M^d \left[\frac{r(1+r)}{2+r}\right] \gtreqless \Delta_w L_Q^d + \Delta_L w^n. \tag{6}$$

Double shifts would be adopted if $\pi > 0$; for $\pi = 0$ producers would be indifferent, while for $\pi < 0$ they would maintain single ('day') shifts.[4]

Some further considerations

While the example given may suffice to illustrate the choice of technique problem at issue and to explain why rhythmic labour costs can induce firms optimally to schedule the work process intermittently – shutting down regularly despite the increased fixed capital charge that incurs – it hides of course many of the complications involved. In what follows, some of these will be briefly mentioned.

The first thing to be noticed is that, in general, different modes of operation of plant and equipment will differ in several or all of the physical characteristics of the respective processes of production (and not just in their respective labour inputs). An increase in the rate of utilization may increase or even decrease the wear and tear of some or all of the fixed capital items, it may change the pattern of maintenance and repair activities, it may affect the amounts used up of circulating means of production per unit of output, etc. For a detailed account of the various possibilities the reader is referred to the vast, mainly neoclassical, literature on the subject; see in particular the survey by Betancourt and Clague (1981) and Winston (1983), who analyses both aspects of capital utilization, i.e. duration and intensity. However, since these contributions use essentially a partial equilibrium framework, they fail to notice the possibility of a variant of the famous phenomenon of the reswitching of techniques: *the return of the same system of operation of plant and equipment*. Indeed, it cannot be ruled out that the same pattern of capital utilization is superior at disconnected ranges of the basic wage rate, given the wage differential whereas some other system(s) is (are) optimal at ranges of the wage rate in between.

We have seen that the optimal duration of a firm's production, and hence its utilization of plant and equipment, depends on the wage rhythm over the unit time. Essentially the same argument applies to time-specific prices in general, each of which tends to discourage the continuous operation of machinery, etc., and thus contributes to an explanation of intentionally idle capacity. As to the combined effect of several rhythmically varying prices of inputs on the schedule of production in time in a given industry, little definite can be said without detailed knowledge of the technical alternatives. Here it suffices to draw attention to the fact that there is the possibility of two time-specific prices both reinforcing each other and counteracting the other's impact. An example to illustrate the second case are high wages at night that are partly or completely offset by cheap off-peak electricity.[5]

While the time-specificity of some prices can legitimately be taken as an exogenous datum in a first step of the analysis of planned idle capacity, this 'datum' itself needs to be explained. Interestingly, the explanation has to be sought in an analysis of the very problem we are concerned with, i.e. the determination of the optimal size and utilization of plant and equipment. More precisely, the time-specificity of certain prices can be traced back to the difficulty of synchronizing the rates of output and demand, which derives from the fact that each of them is subject to more or less autonomous fluctuations. For example, seasonal variations in the rate of production are ubiquitous in primary production and other outdoor activities such as construction. Rhythmic variations in demand are experienced by virtually all industries, particularly by services, and reflect, among other things, the time pattern of consumption activities of households, which in turn depends on a variety of customary and institutional factors. These fluctuations involve the temporal mismatch of productive capacity and demand. The introduction of time-specific prices, by exerting some influence on the time profiles of both output and demand, may effectively contribute to keeping this mismatch within limits and thus improve the conditions for higher rates of profitably utilized capacity.

Clearly, whether or not a product is storable is of great importance to the entire discussion of temporally idle capacity. Where the storage of the product is possible, normal fluctuations in demand can be matched by contrary fluctuations in inventories, while production may be carried out at a fairly steady rate. Whether it is economical to do so is again a question that, in competitive conditions, will be decided on the grounds of cheapness.

In this context we may briefly turn to an interesting argument put forward by Kalecki (1965) and Steindl (1952), which is referred to again in more recent contributions. Reference is to various attempts first to explain the remarkable elasticity of the capitalist economy and then to draw the implications of this fact for the theory of accumulation. This elasticity, which consists in the capacity of the system to translate variations in the pace of accumulation into substantial variations in the rates of expansion of output and productive capacity, is basically explained by these authors in terms of reserves of plant firms are assumed to hold in order to be able to meet peak expected rates of demand.

While this argument may add to the better understanding of the phenomenon under consideration, its importance should be seen in perspective. Indeed, carrying a reserve of capacity that is for the most part idle both day and night is but one among several other alternatives for meeting peak orders. Working overtime, adding an extra (second or third) shift, running down inventories or increasing the intensity of work and capital utilization may equally serve the purpose. Which of these alternatives (or combinations among them) will turn out to be the most economical cannot be answered in a simple, straightforward manner in other than very special cases. However, two results reported in Marris (1964) deserve mentioning. Comparing the holding of a reserve of machinery to the possibility of adding an extra shift, Marris concludes, first, if the proportion of total output over the whole life of the plant that will be produced at the peak rate is small, 'it is more likely, other things being equal, that a firm would plan to meet the peak output by adding an extra shift rather than by activating a daytime reserve of capacity'. He continues: 'This is an important result, since it implies that a large portion of observed multiple-shift working will be *occasioned* by short-run increases in demand' (Marris, 1964, p. 96). Second, 'the more variable the expected future demand, the more likely it is to seem best to plan to meet periods of high demand by shift-work' (ibid., p. 97).[6]

In the discussion so far emphasis has been on the problem of the optimal duration of production while, apart from incidental mentioning, the problem of the intensity of production has not been dealt with. This must not be mistaken as implying that the intensity dimension is considered to be of only secondary importance. It is rather to be interpreted as an indication of the inherent extreme complexity of the issue at hand, which in general does not allow simple, clear-cut answers. A few remarks must suffice.

The possibility of varying the intensity of production appears to play an important role in the short period, when with a given size and composition of productive capacity any adjustment of output to demand is to be effected in terms of variations in the intensity (or duration) of its utilization per unit time. In this connection it is to be noted that there appears to exist a close relationship between the way in which plant and equipment is operated and the intensity of work of those who operate it. Indeed, a fundamental precondition of the short-run elasticity of the system is to be seen in the fact that the labour contract is, within limits, 'open' as regards the intensity of work performed. Hence, in the short run the intensity of work can generally be adjusted so as to generate the required speed of production without necessitating a reconsideration of the labour contract, in particular the level of the going wage rate.

As to the determination of the normal or long-period intensity of work and, implicitly, of capital utilization, it is again cost-minimization that, under conditions of free competition, has to be considered the ruling criterion. Thus, on the simplifying assumption that the real wage is given and constant while the intensity of work is variable, the entrepreneur will increase intensity up to the point where the rate of profit attains its maximum level. A higher intensity would involve sub-normal profitability owing to, for example, an increase in the use of material inputs per unit of output, an increase in the proportion of low-quality output that is non-vendible or vendible only at a reduced price, and more rapid wear and tear of fixed capital. For an analysis of the effects of various changes in the labour process on the normal rate of profit and prices of production, see Steedman (1977a, ch. 6 and pp. 175–8).

Having sketched what in my view is the appropriate concept of normal capital utilization, let us now turn to a brief discussion of the problem of accumulation, effective demand and income distribution.

2 *Accumulation and effective demand*

In order to focus attention on the central problem addressed by the principle of effective demand, I shall for most of the following discussion set aside all questions related to possible discrepancies between the composition of productive capacity on the one hand and that of effective demand on the other. Moreover, I shall for simplicity assume that the utilization of social capital can be expressed in an unambiguous way in terms of a single variable: 'the' rate of capital utilization.

The warranted rate of capital accumulation

In accordance with traditional long-period analysis I have assumed so far that the size and composition of the capital stock are fully adapted to (i) the levels of output or 'requirements for use' (Sraffa), and (ii) the dominant, i.e. cost-minimizing, methods of production, given the going normal distribution of income. The factors determining the capital stock may be envisaged as reflecting the current 'state of improvement' (Adam Smith) attained by society.

Yet, as has been emphasized already in the foregoing, it cannot be presumed that the actual economy will ever be *in* a normal position. It is rather to be assumed that in any 'short period' the capital stock inherited from the past will generally not be the one best suited to effective demand. These incongruities between productive capacity and effective demand will be reflected in rates of utilization of plant and equipment and in levels of prices, real wages and profits actually realized that deviate from their normal values.

The classical economists were well aware of the possibility of incongruities of the sort described. However, because of their identification of decisions to save with those to invest, the only discrepancies between productive capacity and the demand for commodities they were willing to admit were those relating to 'particular employments of capital' (Ricardo, [1817–21] 1951, p. 91). For the economy *as a whole* these discrepancies were regarded as roughly compensating each other in their effect on the 'general price of commodities, wages, or profits'; the conclusion that they were best left 'entirely out of consideration' was close at hand (ibid., pp. 91–2). Hence, for the central part of their analyses the classical economists proceeded *as if* the path the economy follows consists of a succession of normal positions, the comparison of which is the object of the long-period method.

Once it is admitted that the economy is subject to the principle of effective demand, this premise can no longer be sustained. The path the economy actually takes will generally be different from the one that would be characterized by the continuous normal utilization of plant and equipment. Accordingly, the role of the normal position as the centre of gravitation can make itself felt only over a succession of 'short periods', allowing the reciprocal adjustment of productive capacity and effective demand. This is illustrated schematically in Figure 13.1, which plots ln K, where K is the capital stock, against time. Let BB' indicate the path of capital accumulation corresponding to an economy that persistently realizes the normal level of capital utilization, or, to use Harrod's term, the *warranted* path. Clearly, starting from a position P at time t_o, the position T at time t_2 on that path could be arrived at over a succession of boom and slump (or of a number of booms and slumps), extending from t_o to t_1 and from t_1 to t_2, respectively. In Figure 13.1 two such possibilities are depicted. While the path PRT exhibits positive rates of growth of the capital stock throughout the business cycle under consideration, the path PST illustrates a pattern of growth with rapid capital accumulation in the upswing and capital decumulation in the downswing. (For simplicity it has been assumed that the growth rates are constant in each of the two phases; the growth rates are given by the slopes of the lines connecting the points corresponding to the two types of cyclical behaviour.)

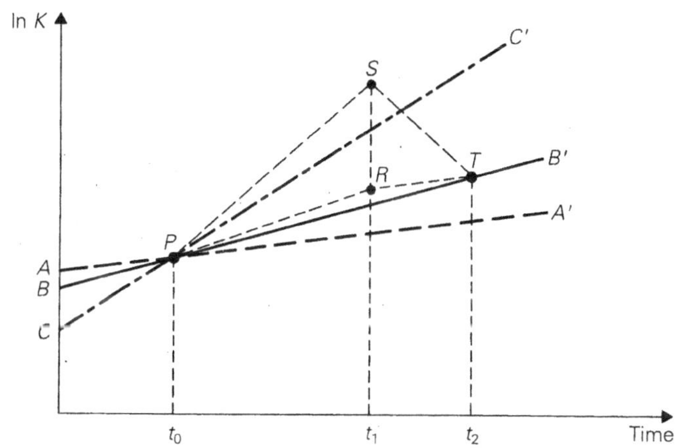

Figure 13.1

However, there is no reason to suppose that averaging out between any pair (or a number) of successive booms and slumps will generate a trend that approximates with sufficient precision the warranted path of capital accumulation. In other words, the latter cannot simply be taken to emerge as some kind of statistical average of the actual path the economy takes. Thus, if in

Figure 13.1 the warranted path in question were in fact AA' instead of BB', the economy would on average (over a single or several cycles) display an above-normal degree of capital utilization, while, with CC' as the warranted path, utilization would be below normal. The implication of this would generally be that the 'realized rate of profit', to use Joan Robinson's term (1962d, p. 29), deviates from the normal rate of profit.[7]

The possibility of a difference between the trend of the actual path and the warranted path raises several closely related questions, the following two of which will be discussed. First, what is the long-run impact of capital accumulation and effective demand on income distribution? Second, is it at all possible to conceive the normal position of an economy at a given moment in time as independent of the actual path the economy followed in the past, or, put differently, is the centre of gravitation path-dependent? Before proceeding with these questions, however, let us briefly consider two well-known approaches that try to deal with the problem of accumulation and distribution in terms of steady-state analysis.

Accumulation and income distribution: steady-state analysis

As is well known, the relation between accumulation and income distribution is a major concern of alternative theories of economic growth developed in the late 1950s and early 1960s in reaction to the earlier work by Harrod.

According to the neoclassical approach, the trend of capital accumulation is determined by society's saving propensity, which in turn is shaped by the preferences of utility-maximizing individuals. The accumulation of capital together with the exogenously given growth of the labour force and the increase in technical knowledge then determine the growth of output. In short, the pace and direction of economic expansion is seen to be governed by 'preferences, biology and technology' (Marglin, 1984a, p. 23). The 'opposing forces of demand and supply' in markets for commodities and factor services are envisaged to bring about a set of relative prices and rates of remuneration of 'factors of production' that tend to clear all markets. In the orthodox view, distribution is a special application of neoclassical price theory. Flexible prices and factor rewards are considered a necessary and sufficient condition for the assumed gravitation of the economy around a position sufficiently close to full employment and normal utilization of plant and equipment in the long run. However, by invalidating the neoclassical notions of 'capital' and 'substitutability between factors', Sraffa's critique of the 'marginal theory of value and distribution' (Sraffa, 1960, p. vi) succeeded in removing the basis of any attempt to explain normal distribution, prices and quantities in terms of supply and demand.

Whereas in orthodox theory investment is governed by the propensity to save, in the alternative 'neo-Keynesian' theory it is taken to be independent of savings. It is rather the autonomously determined volume of investment that via the multiplier process is seen to generate the corresponding volume of savings. The treatment of investment as an independent variable was called the 'Keynesian hypothesis' by Kaldor (1955/6, p. 95).

It was also Kaldor who contended that the corresponding volume of savings could be generated in two different ways: either via a change in the level of output as a whole, given the propensity to save, or via a change in the overall propensity to save through a change in income distribution, given the level of output. Accordingly, in Kaldor's view two notions of the multiplier must be distinguished. While the first notion is conceived as a theory of the short run, the second provides a theory of the long run, 'or rather, the one is used in the framework of a static model, and the other in the framework of a dynamic growth model' (ibid., p. 94).[8]

We know the result of Kaldor's approach (and of parallel efforts by Joan Robinson) to generalize the 'Keynesian hypothesis' to the long run. For given propensities to save out of profits and wages, s_P and s_W, a given capital output ratio $v^* = K/Y$, and a given 'rate of growth of output capacity' $g = I/K$, the rate of profit $r = P/K$ is 'determined' by

$$r = \frac{g - s_W/v^*}{s_P - s_W} \tag{7}$$

$(1 > s_P \geq s_W \geq 0)$. In the case in which workers do not save $(s_W = 0)$, equation (7) simplifies to

$$r = g/s_P. \tag{8}$$

Hence the application of the 'Keynesian hypothesis' to the long run appears to confirm Kaldor's view that the principle of the multiplier can be used as a theory of distribution demonstrating that in the long run the rate of profit is governed by the rate of net capital accumulation. Marglin summarizes the essence of the neo-Keynesian approach to the theory of accumulation and distribution:

> [I]n the long run, the period with which neo-Keynesian analysis concerns itself, there is no excess capacity to accommodate investment demand. Distribution must bear the brunt of adjusting aggregate demand to supply. In contrast with the short period, the long-run conflict is a zero-sum game – at least in the absence of technological substitution or technological change.
>
> (Marglin, 1984a, pp. 474–5)

The neo-Keynesian theory of economic growth and distribution exhibits several shortcomings. While the following objections are levelled at Kaldor's version, most of them equally apply to similar approaches advocated by other authors, most notably Joan Robinson.

First, as both Keynes's attack on the orthodox theory of output and employment and the recent capital-theoretic critique of the demand and supply approach have shown and as the facts suggest, there is no automatic mechanism in a private-enterprise economy to keep accumulation going at the right rate for full employment in the long run. The assumed tendency towards normal utilization of capital, every so often thwarted by a variety of factors of a more or less long-lived nature, must therefore not be confounded with an alleged tendency towards full employment of labour. Kaldor's opinion 'that a theory of growth should be based on the hypothesis of full employment' (Kaldor, 1960, p. 12), and his consequent inclination to identify the rate of accumulation g with the 'natural' rate of growth λ, can at best be considered an illegitimate generalization of a particular historical experience.

Second, according to Kaldor the 'Keynesian hypothesis' purports that 'the ratio of investment to output can be treated as an independent variable' (Kaldor, 1955/6, p. 95). Two objections can be raised against this. First, there are good reasons to suppose that entrepreneurs control only the flow or volume of investment, whereas the share of investment in income depends on the income effect of the multiplier process and is thus the result of a multiplicity of factors that exert their influence, so to speak, behind the back of investors (see Kurz, 1984 and 1985b). A second deficiency concerns the necessary independence of the investment–output ratio from the distribution of income between wages and profits. For, unless this ratio is itself independent of the rate of profits, the suggested determination of distribution would result in circular reasoning. The two most important cases in which the approach is not threatened in this way are: first, the one in which relative prices are independent of distribution, i.e. prices are proportional to quantities of labour embodied; and second, the one in which the economy is in a steady-state equilibrium. Clearly, neither case provides a solid basis for the theory of accumulation and distribution to stand on.

Finally, it is worth pointing out that the savings ratios need not be constant but may themselves depend on the rate of accumulation. There is the purely hypothetical case in which the impact of a change in the rate of accumulation g on the rate of profit r is exactly offset by corresponding changes in s_P and s_W. The impact of g on r may at any rate be mitigated by variations in the savings ratios. Thus, if in times of relatively high rates of accumulation firms tend to increase the proportion of retained profits, then, other things being equal, the rise in profits realized per unit of capital will correspondingly be smaller.

We may conclude that the neo-Keynesian view according to which accumulation generates the corresponding growth in the volume of savings through a change in the normal level of the rate of profit (the real wage rate) is difficult to sustain. The necessity to retreat to steady-state analysis in order to preserve the causal structure of the basic argument entails the danger that one loses sight of important features of the functioning of the capitalist economy. In particular, there is no presumption that the actual trend of capital accumulation follows the warranted path. What are the implications of this for the distribution of income between wages and profits?

The realized rate of profit

The lack of an *ex ante* co-ordination of investment decisions is incompatible with the idea that labour could be continuously fully employed and plant and equipment continuously utilized at the normal level. It is essentially this consideration that is at the bottom of the notion of the instability of the capitalist economy. Before proceeding with the main argument, an observation must be made on the meaning of this notion in Keynes and his major successors, in particular Harrod.

In the *General Theory*, Keynes's major concern was with demonstrating that the economy need not gravitate around a full-employment equilibrium, as traditional theory maintains, but may get stuck in an underemployment equilibrium. Hence, the system is envisaged to be unstable in the sense that deviations from full-employment equilibrium will not be automatically corrected by endogenous forces that come into play as soon as such deviations occur. Moreover, there is a second aspect of instability to be noted, which draws on the fact that the economy is subject to fluctuations. Both aspects are well expressed in Keynes's observation 'that we oscillate, avoiding the gravest extremes of fluctuation in employment and in prices in both directions, round an intermediate position appreciably below full employment' (Keynes, 1973c, p. 254). In fact, in Keynes's view the economy 'is not violently unstable' (ibid., p. 249). The concept of a centre of gravitation of prices and quantities is clearly discernible in his characterization of 'the mean position' as being 'determined by "natural" tendencies, namely, by those tendencies which are likely to persist' (ibid., p. 254).

Interestingly enough, similar views were advocated by major authors who elaborated on Keynes's contribution to the theory of effective demand, in particular Harrod, who was concerned with generalizing Keynes's short-period analysis of the saving–investment mechanism to the long period and to whom we owe the famous Instability Principle. The unmodified version of it suggests that once the actual rate of capital accumulation has departed from the warranted rate this departure will tend to be ever-increasing: in the case of a downward departure the result will be an ever-deepening depression, in the case of an upward departure an ever-amplifying inflationary pressure. It must not be overlooked, however, that Harrod supplemented the Instability Principle with an analysis of turning points and thus provided a theory of cyclical movements about the warranted growth path. In his analysis of turning-points, regular cyclical fluctuations of income distribution, the average propensity to save and the capital–output ratio play an important role; for a summary statement see Harrod (1959, pp. 460–2).

Let us now have a closer look at the impact of accumulation on the realized rate of profit and the realized real wage rate. To begin with, it is useful to point out a change of opinion by Keynes subsequent to the publication of the *General Theory*.

As is well known, Keynes in the *General Theory* retained what he called the first 'classical' postulate, i.e. the marginalist proposition that the real wage rate is equal to the marginal product of labour. On the further assumption that in the short run the returns to labour are decreasing, an increase in aggregate demand would entail an increase not only in output and employment but also in the relation between prices and money wages, i.e. a decrease in real wages.

In 1939, in a reply to Dunlop, Tarshis and Kalecki, Keynes retracted his previous opinion and agreed 'that if we start from a level of output very greatly below capacity, so that even the most efficient plant and labour are only partially employed, marginal real cost may be expected to decline with increasing output, or, at the worst, remain constant' (Keynes, 1973c, p. 405). The politically important conclusion was close at hand:

If we can advance farther on the road towards full employment than I had

> previously supposed *without seriously affecting real hourly wages* or the rate of profits per unit of output, the warnings of the anti-expansionists need cause us less anxiety.
>
> (ibid., p. 401; emphasis added)

However, he added:

> But a point must surely come, long before plant and labour are fully employed, when less efficient plant and labour have to be brought into commission or the efficient organisation employed beyond the optimum degree of intensiveness.
>
> (ibid., p. 405)

Thus, starting from a situation of high unemployment and a low degree of capital utilization, a variation in the rate of investment can safely be assumed to be reflected in the first place in a change in the *realized* rate of profit. The volume of savings corresponding to a higher volume of investment will be generated by raising *both* the level of output via an increase in the utilization of productive capacity in existence and, possibly, employment, *and* by raising the overall savings ratio through an increase in the share of profits in total income.

Hence, assuming prices to correspond to prices of production and dividing both sides of the $I = S$ condition by the value of social capital in existence, $\bar{K}$, we obtain

$$\frac{I}{\bar{K}} = \frac{s(\theta)Y}{\bar{K}} = s(\theta)\frac{Y^*}{\bar{K}}\frac{Y}{Y^*} \tag{9}$$

or

$$\gamma = \frac{s(\theta)}{v^*}u, \tag{10}$$

where s is the overall savings ratio, θ the share of profits, Y total net output (income), Y^* potential output attainable with the normal utilization of the given capital stock, γ the rate of accumulation in the period under consideration, v^* the normal capital–output ratio and u the degree of utilization ($u = 1$ indicates normal utilization). In the case in which workers do not save we would have

$$\gamma = \frac{s_p\theta}{v^*}u = s_p\tilde{r}(u), \tag{11}$$

where $\tilde{r}(u)$ is the realized rate of profit, which is seen to depend on the degree of utilization, given the real wage rate.

Clearly, starting from a 'Keynesian situation' with the level of output substantially below normal capacity output, rates of expansion of output that are largely independent of the real wage rate may be realized until normal utilization is approached. Further on, looking at the problem from a long-run perspective, an increase in the pace of accumulation widens the margin for further expansions in output in response to expansions in aggregate effective demand because of the 'capacity effect' of net investment (see Garegnani, 1982b). Thus, interpreting γ in equations (10) and (11) as referring to the proportional rate of growth of the capital stock, a higher γ will be associated with a higher u, a lower capital–output ratio $v = v^*/u$, a higher rate of growth of output, and a higher $\tilde{r}$.

The question now is what are the implications of a situation in which the stimuli for an increase in the pace of accumulation are strong enough and sufficiently long-lived that the economy would sooner or later have to realize and then preserve for some time an above-normal degree of capital utilization. In particular, does this mean that the real wage rate has to fall?

Some authors tend to answer this question in the negative. In their view an above-normal degree of capital utilization is perfectly compatible with and will indeed generally be associated with an above-normal ratio of actual profits to capital in existence, even if real wages happen to remain at their normal level (see Vianello, 1985, and Ciccone's contribution to this volume). The 'source', so to speak, of supernormal profits to be realized per unit of capital is traced back to the reserves of idle capacity that firms are assumed to hold in order to be able to meet peak expected orders and unexpected increases in demand (see section 1 above). With a rise in the pace of accumulation and thus a more rapid expansion of aggregate demand, these reserves will be activated, thereby increasing the profitability of business without necessitating a fall in real wages. Furthermore, it is argued that the constellation depicted need not be short-lived but may last for a long period of time.

Clearly, this proposition deserves careful scrutiny. Here it suffices to note some scepticism on my part as to the bearing on the argument under discussion. While it cannot be ruled out that under conditions to be specified in detail there may exist margins for the realized rate of profit to rise above the normal rate (given the real wage), these margins seem to be small rather than large. Since the tendency to hold reserves of idle capacity can be assumed to differ between industries, with some industries holding very little or no extra reserves at all, a speed-up of accumulation beyond the warranted rate would soon run into bottlenecks.[9] Consequently, a situation favourable to a rise in the money prices of some commodities would develop. With capacity constraints becoming effective in the wage goods industries themselves or because of rising prices of some of the inputs used, there will be a tendency for wage goods prices to rise relative to money wages, i.e. for the real wage rate to fall. This tendency, i.e. the departure of actual from normal distribution to the detriment of labour, may then render it profitable for entrepreneurs to add extra shifts or to work plant and equipment more intensively. Hence, in the purely hypothetical case with no technological innovations, a more rapid pace of accumulation can be expected sooner or later to be reflected not only in a realized rate of profit that is above normal, but also in an actual real wage rate that is below normal.

On the assumption that the fundamental causes of the long-period position of the economy, in particular the balance of power in the conflict over distribution, happen to remain the same, then *by definition* accumulation can have no impact on *normal* distribution. This means that in the case discussed workers will eventually be successful in re-establishing the normal level of real wages, which of necessity entails a reduction in the ratio of profits to capital. This, in turn, implies that, contrary to what Kaldor had argued in his approach to the theory of accumulation and distribution, the route of savings adjusting to investment *via* changes in income distribution, or, more precisely, deviations from normal distribution, is much less important in the long run than it is in the short run. In the long run the adjustment is effectuated predominantly through changes in the level of output produced from changing levels of productive capacity, whereas changes in the share of savings in net income due to a change in distribution are of secondary importance only.[10]

3 *Accumulation and long-period conditions*

So far the investigation has pre-eminently been concerned with the problem of the working of the investment–savings mechanism in the long run on the explicit assumption that the long-period conditions remain the same. Obviously, there is nothing wrong with this 'innocent exercise' if it does not mislead one into disregarding the fact that in general these conditions will be altered by accumulation. To study the impact of accumulation on these conditions and the feedback on the pace and pattern of accumulation is the major task of an analysis of accumulation.

The significance of accumulation for the normal conditions of production and distribution is immediately obvious in the case where returns to scale are not constant everywhere. Variations in the levels of output would of necessity be accompanied by changes in relative prices and in the general rate of profits (or the real wage rate).

The classical economists deserve the credit for having developed a powerful framework for the analysis within which the effects of increasing and decreasing returns can be studied. Some form of increasing returns is dealt with by Adam Smith in his investigation of the division of labour. In his view the extent of this division is limited by 'the extent of the market', which in turn is seen to depend on accumulation. A standard case of decreasing returns is analysed in classical rent theory. It is shown that, with a constant real wage rate and in the absence of technological progress, the accumulation of capital entails a tendency for the rate of profits to fall. More recently, Kaldor (1966) tried to demonstrate the presence of static and dynamic economies of scale. The rate at which these economies of scale can be exploited depends on the growth of output, which in turn is governed by the pace of accumulation.

(Gross) investment is the vehicle by means of which new products and new processes of production are introduced into the economy. Investment expenditures in research and development generate inventions, some of which will become innovations, i.e. will be used commercially. By means of introducing better products and new methods of production that economize on costs, firms endeavour to survive the competitive struggle. At the same time, many innovations are designed to render possible a more intensive use of labour power and a better control of the labour process. Technological and organizational changes tend to alter the balance of power between capital owners and workers.

Since there exist good reasons to suppose that up to a point an increase in the rate of accumulation tends to increase the rate of diffusion of new methods of production and the rate of induced innovations, the speed of change in the dominant technique is positively related to the rate of accumulation. The associated growth in productivity increases the margin for the level of output to rise in response to a rise in aggregate demand. It is *this* effect of accumulation that in the long run appears to be most important. A change in the dominant technique necessarily involves a change in the normal rate of profits or the real wage rate.

The impact of accumulation and the accompanying improvements in the methods of production on the ordinary wage rate was a major issue in classical political economy. Ricardo, for example, stressed that 'with every improvement of society, with every increase in its capital, the market wages of labour will rise; but the permanence of their rise will depend on the question, whether the natural price of labour has also risen' (Ricardo, [1817–21] 1951, p. 96). And a few lines before he maintained that the market rate may, 'for an indefinite period, be constantly above [the natural rate]' (ibid., p. 95). In such a situation there may develop 'comforts which custom renders absolute necessaries' (ibid., p. 94). Accordingly, the normal wage rate is envisaged to depend on the pace of accumulation, i.e. the normal position to be path-dependent.

We may conclude by saying that the constraint binding changes in the normal level of the real wage and the rate of profits remains effective over time. However, it has to be taken into account that this constraint, i.e. the w–r relationship, continuously changes its location and shape, thereby shifting the centre around which the economy is assumed to gravitate.

Acknowledgements

The present paper is a revised version of my contribution to the Sraffa conference. I am grateful to K. Bharadwaj, C. Bidard, P. Garegnani, H. Hagemann, P. Kalmbach, D. Kattermann, N. Salvadori, I. Steedman and G. Vaggi for helpful discussions of some of the questions raised in this paper. It goes without saying that the responsibility for any misconceptions rests entirely with me.

Notes

1 See Winston (1983, pp. 54–9). Winston deals with a third type of price behaviour, i.e. duration-specificity. The example he gives is the price of the capital services used in production, which is seen to be inversely dependent on the rate of utilization of the capital stock. I shall come back to this below.

2 What in a given historical situation are to be considered 'ordinary working hours' in a given line of employment is itself an institutional datum that plays some role in defining the normal position of the respective economy.

3 See, for example, the empirical evidence reported in the session 'Economics of Slack Capacity' of the 1980 meeting of the American Economic Association (*American Economic Review*, Papers and Proceedings, vol. 71, 1981, pp. 48–69).

4 Clearly, for a particular system of operation of plant and equipment to be cost-minimizing it has to turn out to be so at any set of prices associated with the alternative systems at which the comparison can be carried out (see Sraffa, 1960, p. 83).

5 In some industries the time-specificity of certain input prices and wages does not deter firms from nearly continuous utilization of capital. Apparently, the extra costs incurred are more than compensated by economies in fixed capital charges and in raw materials and fuel. Thus Foss (1981, p. 59) reports that in the United States in 1976 the average work-week of fixed capital in the paper, primary metals and petroleum industries was 139.6, 142.4 and 162.9 hours, respectively. This can perhaps be considered as indirect evidence of the inverse relationship between unit costs and daily duration of the production process in these industries.

6 The second observation may also have some bearing on an attempt to explain the existence of excess capacity in terms of firms' fear of losing customers in the case of an unexpected increase in demand. In the light of what has been said in the above it would seem that even in the absence of extra reserves of idle capacity the existing margins for an expansion of output together with the option to run down inventories are often sufficient to take care of unforeseen peaks of demand. However, a proper answer to the problem under discussion would require an explicit modelling of competitive decisions in markets with stochastic demand.

7 As Joan Robinson has already observed, the 'realized rate of profit' is vague and difficult to define with sufficient precision to render it useful as a theoretical concept. The best definition available appears to be the one that uses normal prices to evaluate the surplus product actually realized and the social capital in existence; see also Kurz (1984, p. 178). It goes without saying that, outside the normal position, profit rates will generally differ between industries; for some industries the profits actually realized may temporarily even become negative. The realized rate of profit therefore is some kind of average rate for the economy as a whole.

8 It is worth mentioning that, contrary to Kaldor's interpretation, a given and constant real wage rate was assumed neither by Kahn in his original 1931 formulation of the multiplier (Kahn, 1972b) nor by Keynes in his discussion in the *General Theory* (Keynes, 1973c, especially ch. 10). Both authors started from the premises that in short-period analysis it is reasonable to assume that money wages are not changed as a consequence of a variation in the level of employment or of any variation in prices that may accompany the change in the level of employment. And even if money wages were to change it cannot be presumed that the relation between wages and the level of prices remains constant. Hence, the traditional version of the multiplier as it is to be found in these authors does not rule out short-run distributive effects. (See also Harrod, [1936] 1965, p. 71.)

It is of course an entirely different matter whether Keynes' particular view of the distributive effects associated with changes in the overall level of activity holds good. As has been pointed out by his critics, the assumption of decreasing returns to labour in the short run upon which his view of the determination of the real wage is based is dubious. For Keynes's reaction, see his 1939 article 'Relative movements of real wages and output' (Keynes, 1973c, pp. 394–412). I shall come back to this in section 2.

9 In an open economy these bottlenecks could be overcome by imports, which however could lead to balance-of-payment problems.

10 One of the first authors to criticize Kaldor's claim that his theory was appropriate to deal with the long period was Preiser (1961). Instead Preiser used Kaldor's approach to explain oscillations of actual income distribution about normal distribution, which itself was seen to express what Preiser called the going 'structural degree of monopoly'.

Comment

Roberto Ciccone
Rome

In his paper (see in particular pp. 409–10), Professor Kurz objects to my contention that an increase in the realized rate of profit above the normal rate can be obtained through an increase in above-normal capacity utilization, at a constant real wage. He stresses that firms may find it profitable to plan to meet the expected peaks of demand by starting extra shifts of works – typically, night shifts – rather than by installing margins of capacity to be kept idle when demand is lower. In Kurz's view, therefore, an above-normal degree of capacity utilization may well imply a rise in the unit cost of output, due to the higher hourly wage rates to be paid to extra shift-workers. Consequently, for an increase (above the normal degree) of capacity utilization to be actually obtained, an increase in prices relative to wages would be required, so that the increase in the realized profit rate would also involve a fall in the (basic) real wage rate.

In my view, the following points may weaken Kurz's argument.

First, the planning of extra work-shifts to meet the expected peaks of demand does not in fact appear to be very common. This might be due to relatively high wage differentials, which make shift-work unprofitable. But other reasons may prevent the planning of shift-work even in cases in which it would appear to be the most profitable choice according to Kurz's analysis.

A first reason can be found in the social and institutional obstacles to night work, as Marris himself (whose book Kurz refers to) notes at the beginning of his work: 'In practice, most societies do collectively decide . . . to live with a fairly low rate of capital utilisation, and thus ensure that shift-work is a minority experience' (Marris, 1964, p. 22).

A second reason, of a strictly economic nature, might be found in the consideration of the additional costs (besides those Kurz takes into account) that the planning of shift work may involve. As is obvious, firms cannot be absolutely certain about what the future levels of demand will be. One can presume, therefore, that they will not limit themselves to the consideration of a single distribution of frequencies of demand levels, but will take into account different distributions with different degrees of probability. In this perspective, the size of capacity that appears to be the most profitable at a particular distribution of demand levels need not be so in absolute sense if it causes the firm to run the risk of large additional costs or losses should the effective distribution of demand levels be different. It is precisely the planning of shift work to meet demand peaks that seems to provide an example of this kind, because it makes the firm less and less competitive as high levels of demand last longer than expected. And since situations of lasting booms of demand can be particularly favourable to the entry of new firms in the market, the resort to shift work might cause losses due to the need of not raising (or even of lowering) the price in the face of higher costs, or to the loss of market shares which might not be easily regained. The consideration of such a risk could then induce the firm to meet the highest levels of demand by greater capacity rather than by additional shifts of work. Indeed, contrary to this latter option, greater capacity seems generally to ensure a decrease in unit costs as the highest levels of demand turn out to be more frequent and lasting than was expected as most probable.

A second point, related to the first, is that if the resort to shift work is limited to relatively few industries, its direct and indirect effects on unit costs in the economic system as a whole can be more than compensated by the higher level of output per unit of capital. Consequently, a fall in the real wage would not be needed for a higher-than-normal utilization of capacity to be globally profitable. This does not exclude a change in *relative* prices in favour of the industries where unit costs have actually risen: for instance, such a change could occur through proportionally different increases in money prices, while money wage rates rise in the *average* proportion needed to keep the real rates unvaried.

Further, it must be noted that even if the resort to shift work were sufficiently generalized in the economy, this would not exclude the possibility of a rise in the realized profit rate above the normal rate due only to a higher-than-normal utilization of capacity. Although it would be quite restricted, this possibility would still exist, depending on the way in which the actual fluctuations of output would cause the average utilization of equipment to be higher than normal. It suffices to remember here that a higher average degree of utilization can derive from less deep and/or less frequent slumps, and not only from higher and/or more frequent booms.

Finally, it is worth emphasizing that the possible changes in the real wage to which Kurz refers cannot support a theory of the *normal* level of the real wage, and therefore of normal distribution. The question is not merely that normal distribution is *assumed* to be differently determined, as Kurz seems to think; rather, those variations are by their own nature unable to play such a fundamental role. First, those changes in the real wage would be needed, if at all, only for *increases* in actual above-normal capacity utilization, while no need of changes arises in the opposite case. Second, the question is precisely about *changes* in the real wage, and not about its *level*: in order to determine the latter, one should also know its pre-change value, which therefore would still need explaining. Thus, the possible falls in the real wage considered by

Kurz might at most explain some deviations of the real wage from its normal level, while they cannot throw any light on what that level is.

Comment

Josef Steindl
Vienna

Professor Kurz, starting from a 'Ricardian' position, endeavours to refute the idea that the pace of accumulation determines the profit rate. This endeavour is perhaps from the beginning the fruit of a misunderstanding. A theory that – in spite of the context in which it was presented by Joan Robinson – is essentially dynamic in character is, one suspects, being measured and judged on the basis of an essentially static position of long-term equilibrium (it was Sraffa who presented it as essentially static). There is hardly any common ground and no bridge ('traverse') between two theories dealing with different problems.

It should be noted at the outset that the theory in question was presented by Joan Robinson and Nicholas Kaldor, the only authors considered by Kurz, on a high level of abstraction, without explanation of how the adjustment actually works and leaving it somewhat uncertain how far the arguments can actually be applied to the historical process of accumulation. Kurz chooses Kaldor as the text for his criticism (pp. 405–6). He is on fairly firm ground when he questions the role that the full-employment assumption plays in Kaldor's presentation. One of Kaldor's contentions is that a flexible profit margin will make it possible for the warranted rate of growth to adjust to the natural rate of growth so that a smooth growth rate with full employment will be realized.

I may try to interpret this in more concrete terms. What Kaldor really wants to show is that on the one hand, a flexible margin will prevent the system from running into excess demand and inflation when the rate of accumulation increases (subject to certain limits: the real wage cannot be compressed beyond a certain limit), and on the other hand it will prevent the system from running into lower and lower utilization leading to perpetual decline in the case of an initial fall in the rate of accumulation.

The whole argument is extremely abstract, but it is clear that the essential question to which the theory is directed is the possible consequence of a *change in the rate of accumulation* – which is what I should call an essentially dynamic problem. The assumption of full employment does not seem to be relevant to the question. If Kurz had turned to my own version of the theory, recently restated in Steindl (1985) he would not have met the features that have disturbed him. When he stresses, in contrast to the smooth growth at full employment, the instability of capitalism, referring himself to Keynes, I could not agree more – though in fairness to Kaldor it ought to be added that he did not deny the instability but wanted to attribute it to other reasons (see the text quoted by Kurz).

On the other hand, Kurz is undoubtedly a victim of misunderstanding when he talks of circular reasoning. In the text quoted Kaldor is perfectly aware that the ratio of investment to national income is actually the proportion of saving in national income, which in the equation he uses there plays the passive role of adjusting itself to the growth rate of capacity on the right-hand side of the equation.

Kurz then turns to his own view of the problem. At the outset he sounds terribly orthodox: '*by definition* accumulation can have no impact on *normal* distribution' (p. 409). But he goes further and does not even approve of Ciccone's position that it is the change in utilization that brings about the adjustment of ('realized') profits to the rate of accumulation in the long run (as it undoubtedly does in the short run). He argues that an increase in the rate of accumulation will lead to a rate of profit above normal and a real wage rate below normal, but 'workers will eventually be successful in re-establishing the normal level of real wages' (p. 410). How they will do it he does not say (it would not be obvious in a closed system, at any rate). In the end, Kurz rather darkly alludes to the theory that the problem of an increasing rate of accumulation would solve itself by means of the increased output capacity that it would bring about in due course (pp. 409–10). He seems to forget that the increased output capacity materializes only *after* the investment has been completed, that is, with a considerable time-lag, and that saving is necessary precisely to bridge this gap. If the additional capacity could be created *simultaneously* with the spending on the investment goods there would be no limit to accumulation at all, and we could turn the whole of the third world into an enormous Manhattan or Hong Kong in no time!

In his final section Kurz takes a remarkable step in a direction where, who knows, we might finally meet. He is considering the question whether 'the normal position of an economy at a given moment of time depends on the path of accumulation that the economy followed in the past' (p. 398). His answer is that the conditions that determine the long-run equilibrium position are continuously changing in time and that they depend *inter alia* also on accumulation. He illustrates this by reference to economies of scale, R&D, innovations, technology and organization. He might very well have added 'the balance of power in the conflict over distribution' (p. 409), which is historically determined, as the classicals would have stressed.

But, if the long-run position is continuously moving in response to all these dynamic factors, is it not the case that interest must necessarily shift to them and to the question of how the changes in these determinants of the long-run equilibrium can themselves be explained?

14

Accumulation, and Capacity Utilization: Some Critical Considerations on Joan Robinsons's Theory of Distribution

Roberto Ciccone
Rome

This paper is intended to be a critical discussion of the theory of distribution that Joan Robinson put forward mainly in Robinson (1956) and (1962d). In particular, the paper will question the conception, which appears to be essential to this theory, that the flexibility of the degree of capacity utilization is limited to the short period only.

According to Robinson's theory, the normal distribution of income is determined by the strength of accumulation. Particularly in Robinson (1962d), this explanation of distribution is based on the direct relationship between the rate of accumulation and the rate of profit, which apparently derives from the equality condition of net investment and saving, once these are expressed in proportion to the value of the capital stock. Under the assumption that saving out of wages is nil, that equality may in fact be written as the well-known relation

$$I/K = s_c P/K,$$

where I, P and K represent the values at normal prices, respectively, of net investment, net profits and the stock of capital, and s_c is the (normal) propensity to save out of net profits.

On the basis of the 'Keynesian conceptions' according to which it is saving that adjusts to investment, the relation here referred to implies, in Robinson's view, that (with a given propensity to save out of profits) the rate of accumulation I/K determines both the general rate of profit P/K and the normal distribution of income.[1] In its turn, the rate of accumulation is seen by

Robinson as a fundamentally exogenous magnitude: conceived as an expression of the strength of accumulation, its determinants should be sought precisely in the circumstances that govern accumulation, and that, in her view, fall for the most part outside the sphere of economic analysis (see Robinson, 1956, pp. 55–6, and 1962d, pp. 15–16).

Thus Robinson considers that savings adjust to investment through income distribution,[2] and therefore in a radically different way from the traditional Keynesian mechanism, which is based on variations in the level of income. The following passage seems intended to explain this basic difference:

> In the short period, to which the formal argument of the *General Theory* was confined, the equalization of saving to investment comes about mainly through varying the level of utilization of given capital equipment; that is, through varying the level of total income. In long-run competitive equilibrium the relation of total income to the stock of capital is determined within certain limits by technical conditions. . . . The distribution of income, however, is strongly influenced by the rate of investment.
>
> (Robinson, 1962d, p. 11)

So although variations in the degree of utilization of capacity are admitted for the short period, Robinson excludes them as far as the long period is concerned. The rigidity thus attributed to the utilization of equipment, and hence to the level of income produced per unit of capital, seems therefore to have an essential role in the conception that in the long period it is distribution, rather than the level of income, that adjusts saving to investment.

1 *The utilization of capacity in the long period*

The idea that with reference to the long period the degree of utilization of capacity must necessarily be considered as inflexible does not appear well founded, despite the sureness with which it is asserted by Robinson, as by other writers.

At the root of this conception there seems to be the very notion of long-period prices. As is generally recognized, these are the prices determined on the basis of conditions of production that can be defined as normal, and hence of a particular degree of utilization of capacity, which we can also indicate as 'normal'. Deviations in the actual degree of utilization with respect to the 'normal' degree are of course admitted, just as with divergences of actual prices from long-period values. However, just as these divergences are limited to the short period – and indeed they characterize the very notion of short period – the same is implicitly or explicitly asserted for the divergences of actual from 'normal' utilization. In other words, the gravitation of prices around their long-period values is thought to be associated with the gravitation of the actual degree of utilization of capacity around the 'normal' degree, so that in the long period there is room for only a single ratio of the level of demand to the stock of existing capacity.

If this reconstruction is valid, the conclusion now stressed does not appear, on close examination, to be sufficiently justified. The tendency towards long-period prices does not in fact seem to require the simultaneous gravitation of the effective utilization of capacity around its 'normal' level – i.e. the level of utilization implicit in those prices. As will be seen below, the degree of utilization of capacity that is relevant for long-period prices seems to be that expected for newly installed capacity, which need not necessarily coincide with the degree of utilization actually realized with the existing stock of capacity. Nor on the other hand does the effective utilization of capacity to a 'normal' extent appear to be necessary for the uniformity of the rate of profit that (in conditions of free competition) characterizes long-period prices. What the uniformity in question seems to require is that, for given levels of demand, the *relative* sizes of the industries be such that (gross) investment is not more profitable in one industry than in another, and not also that the *absolute* size of overall capacity should be in a particular relation to aggregate demand; the presence of generalized excesses or deficiencies of capacity with respect to the size compatible with its normal utilization would not prevent transfers of capital from one industry to another from making relative prices tend towards the values corresponding to a uniform rate of profit.[3]

This does not exclude the possibility that a tendency of capacity to assume a particular size relative to demand is constantly at work. There is no evident reason, however, for thinking that an adjustment of this type must take place 'simultaneously' with the gravitation of prices towards their long-period values; the tendency to that adjustment seems rather to give rise to a slower and more complex process, which implies net accumulation (positive or negative) for the economy as a whole. In this connection, a significant distinction appears to be that traditionally made in economic analysis between the question of accumulation and that of the tendency of prices towards their normal values, also with regard to the length of the time periods concerned.[4] In any case, a general accumulation or decumulation of capital cannot fail to have a wide-reaching influence on aggregate demand itself, and the achievement of a particular size of capacity *relative* to that of demand appears in itself to be a process that is liable to be frustrated for long periods of time. It is then conceivable that these periods may be longer than those required for normal prices to show themselves as the central positions of actual prices – longer, that is, than the 'long period' itself.

From the foregoing it follows that the reference to the long period does not necessarily imply the utilization of the existing stock of capacity to the normal extent, i.e. to the extent implicit in long-period prices. Divergences of actual utilization from that particular level therefore also appear conceivable beyond the short period.

The 'normal' utilization of capacity has already been indicated as that which enters into the determination of the normal prices of commodities, but which, in accordance with the conclusion reached above, is not necessarily to be identified with the actual utilization realized, in the long period, with the existing stock of capacity. It now becomes imperative to specify better this notion of 'normal' utilization.

It seems, first of all, possible to state that the costs of production including profits at the general rate towards which competition pushes prices are those that may be calculated with reference to gross investment – i.e. with reference to the productive processes into which capital flows can be 'incorporated' in the different industries. When and if the prices of commodities became adjusted to those costs, there would not in fact be any more reason why competition, which precisely operates through the investment and disinvestment in the various branches of production, should tend to modify them further. The costs already mentioned therefore appear as the values towards which prices tend, and hence as the values representing long-period prices.

It follows from this that the degree of utilization of capacity that contributes to determining the costs in question, and hence the long-period prices of commodities, must be understood as referring to equipment that constitutes or might constitute gross investment, and not necessarily to that which constitutes the existing stock of capacity.[5] In particular, this degree of utilization appears specific to *newly* installed equipment.

The 'normal' utilization of capacity (as the utilization implicit in long-period prices has been defined) seems therefore identifiable in the *expected* utilization of new plant that has been or might be installed. The size of this plant would be of course what entrepreneurs would consider most appropriate in relation to the expected demand for products – which would constitute an expression of the tendency, already discussed, for capacity to adjust to demand – and the character of *normality* attributed to the expected utilization of the capacity in question appears therefore to be justified.

We must now consider the circumstances that can determine the *level* of normal utilization of capacity, by influencing the size of plant that appears profitable for given levels of expected demand. At the same time it will be observed that these circumstances seem to guarantee, in the long period, considerable flexibility in the actual utilization of capacity when responding to levels of demand that are different from those expected.

The first circumstance whose influence on the desired size of capacity it is as well to consider, consists in the fluctuations that, in a market economy, generally characterize demand and hence, more or less closely, production.[6] As is generally recognized, these fluctuations are largely resolved into variations in the utilization of fixed capital. Indeed, what is observed in reality is a utilization of capacity that varies from relatively high levels, corresponding to the peaks reached by production in boom periods, to relatively low levels, corresponding to times of recession.

This simple ascertainment gives us reason to think that the size of capacity installed is commensurate with the relatively higher levels of demand that entrepreneurs expect to encounter, with a certain frequency, during the economic life of their plant. Its volume would therefore be considerably larger than the expected average levels of production, and of course larger still than the troughs of production that can be foreseen. The conclusion thus suggested by observation of the facts seems moreover to find an explanation in the need of the individual firm not to lose market shares when demand goes up – and so, ultimately, in the pressure of competition (see Steindl, 1952, pp. 8 and 10; Marris, 1964, p. 95).

On the basis of these considerations it seems possible to conceive the 'normal' utilization of capacity as that which entrepreneurs expect to realize on average, over long periods of time, as a result of fluctuations in the degree of utilization. Leaving aside for the moment other circumstances that can influence the desired size of capacity, this average degree of utilization will therefore be the smaller, the larger are the breadth and frequency of the expected falls in production with respect to the peaks for which capacity is adequate.[7] In general it will therefore be considerably lower than the full utilization apparently referred to in the passage from Robinson (1962d) quoted above; and it is moreover evident that, even if effective levels of demand do happen to coincide with expected levels, the 'normal' utilization of capacity thus understood would not necessarily be realized at any particular moment in time.

But what counts most, for our purpose, is that the notion of 'normal' utilization thus identified appears compatible with a wide flexibility of the actual utilization of capacity that is not limited to short periods of time. To support this let me begin by supposing that the relatively higher levels of demand that do effectively occur correspond to expected levels, i.e. to the levels for which the installed capacity is adequate. The average utilization of the equipment may however turn out to be greater or less than 'normal' utilization according to the effective extent and duration of demand levels that are *below* the peaks. Thus, in Figures 14.1 and 14.2 the 'normal' utilization of capacity is represented as the average utilization corresponding to regular oscillations in the degree of utilization (the dotted curves). The actual utilization may turn out to be higher than the 'normal' if, on average, the falls in production with respect to the expected peaks are less deep and/or less frequent compared to those corresponding to 'normal' utilization; this is the case exemplified in Figure 14.1. An average utilization below the 'normal' level would occur in the opposite case, i.e. if the drops in production with respect to the expected peaks turned out to be deeper and/or more frequent than those implicit in 'normal' utilization, as exemplified in Figure 14.2.

Average levels of demand that, relative to productive capacity, turn out to be higher or lower than those expected can in this way give rise to average degrees of utilization that are respectively greater or less than 'normal'. It follows from this that, even considering long periods of time, the adjustment of the (average) savings/capital ratio to the (average) investment/capital ratio can take place through differences in the (average) level of income produced per unit of capital – corresponding to differences in the (average) utilization of capacity. The presumed necessity that differences in the value of the accumulation rate should imply, in the long period, an adjustment of savings per unit of capital obtained via the distribution of income thus seems to receive a first disavowal.

The conclusions now reached have been obtained by assuming that the highest levels of aggregate demand correspond, in any case, to those for which the installed capacity is adequate. This hypothesis has served to show how, over long periods, the actual utilization of capacity can turn out to be different from 'normal' utilization without the size of the capacity being seen as 'wrong' with respect to what entrepreneurs would have found profitable to install. In other words, this hypothesis has enabled us to verify the existence

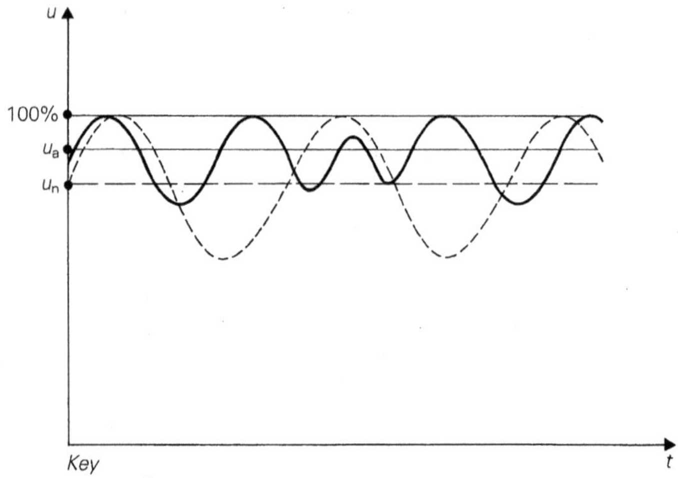

Key
t = time
u = average degree of capacity utilization
u_n = 'normal' utilization
u_a = actual utilization

Figure 14.1

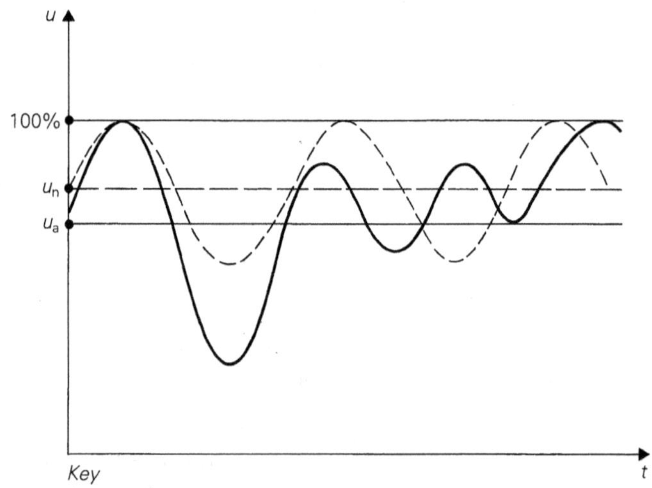

Key
t = time
u = average degree of capacity utilization
u_n = 'normal' utilization
u_a = actual utilization

Figure 14.2

of margins within which deviations, not limited to the short period, in the utilization of capacity with respect to 'normal' utilization do not resolve into undesired excesses or deficiencies of capacity.

The possibility that over long periods the actual utilization of capacity should turn out to be different from 'normal' does not however seem to be avoided if the hypothesis in question is put aside. This appears immediately evident for the case in which the effective levels of demand do not reach the expected peaks, or reach them less frequently than would be necessary to make the existing volume of capacity profitable. In this case we would have an actual excess of capacity over the size that it would have been profitable to install; and, for reasons that in part have already been mentioned, this excess would not necessarily be eliminated quickly enough. The durability and indivisibility of fixed capital constitute a first, evident obstacle to its reduction; but above all the negative effects, on the level of aggregate demand itself, of the disinvestments or lower levels of investment tending to that effect leave us to presume that the attempt to reduce the size of capacity *relative* to demand may turn out to be unfruitful even over long periods of time. Falls in the average utilization of capacity with respect to 'normal' utilization therefore appear possible, over long periods, even to the extent that they imply the persistence of undesired excess capacity.

A symmetrical possibility would appear not to exist, at first sight, for levels of demand that *exceed* the expected peaks and hence, in accordance with my present assumptions, the size of existing capacity.

In order to give better consideration to this case, it is opportune to distinguish the demand for investment from the aggregate demand that the former generates via the multiplier. It can thus be seen that excess demand for capital goods with respect to the capacity of the relative industries, which is the most immediately relevant problem for my concerns, does not necessarily extend to the whole of aggregate demand. The multiplier in fact can feed global demand only to the extent that demand for capital goods is translated into an effective production of income in the industries directly concerned, and therefore not beyond the threshold of the full utilization of the capacity of those industries.[8] Investment demand therefore seems to be able to cause an *excess* of aggregate demand only in the case where in the rest of the economy the full utilization of capacity is generally reached *before* it is reached in capital goods industries; in other words, if we are faced with disproportions in the size of consumer good industries with respect to the capacity of capital good industries.

The possibility that disproportions of this type may occur, especially in conjunction with 'high' levels of investment, certainly cannot be ruled out, nor, for reasons that are by now well known, is it certain that they represent a phenomenon limited to short periods.[9] On the other hand, it is evident that they cannot constitute the starting point for reaching sufficiently general conclusions. It therefore appears legitimate here to abstract from the possibility of these disproportions – assuming, for example that the sizes of the different industries are such that the full utilization of their respective capacities is reached simultaneously.[10]

Since it is thus limited to the demand for capital goods alone, an excess with respect to productive capacity appears capable of being 'redistributed', as it were, over a longer time-span by the formation of backlogs of orders – which would obviously be less plausible for most of consumer demand. The constraint imposed by existing capacity in capital goods industries could therefore modify the *form* otherwise taken by the fluctuations in the demand for these goods, in fact by 'squashing' their excesses at levels that would be lower but more extended over time.

By means of this mechanism the excesses of demand for capital goods with respect to the capacity of the relative industries would resolve themselves into the maintenance over periods longer than those expected of a full or at any rate high utilization of this capacity, and, by the working of the multiplier, of overall capacity; other conditions being equal, this would contribute to raising the average effective utilization of capacity with respect to 'normal' utilization. Contrary to what appearances seem to suggest, deviations from the 'normal' utilization of capacity could therefore exhaust even possible deficiencies of existing capacity with respect to the potential peaks of demand.

The possibility that higher peaks of demand than those expected may produce a higher average utilization of capacity than 'normal' would naturally be even stronger if the size of capacity were greater than the peaks of demand foreseen by entrepreneurs. And in effect it is not hard to identify reasons to justify the profitability of such excess margins of capacity.

The expectation of a growth in demand, together with the economic indivisibility that may characterize fixed capital, already constitutes an evident reason why it may be profitable to install a capacity greater than the peaks expected for the most immediate future (see Steindl, 1952, pp. 9–11).

The choice of excess volumes of capacity in regard to the highest expected levels of demand may furthermore follow from the relation existing, for given levels of output, between the size of the plant and the production costs obtainable. Thus, if equipment of greater capacity permitted the adoption of more economical methods of production, their employment could turn out to be profitable even for production levels that stayed permanently below their potential. Or, again, excess capacity could be profitable if the unit costs of production increased as the degree of utilization of the plant increased beyond certain limits: this could occur, for example, as an effect of the higher hourly wage rates that generally have to be paid for work done outside normal working hours (see Marris, 1964, ch. 1).

The 'normal' utilization of capacity can therefore imply not only the expectation of a certain breadth and frequency of the fluctuations in demand, but also the expectation of the idleness of the excess capacity deliberately chosen by the entrepreneurs; on the other hand, these margins of (intended) excess capacity seem to increase the elasticity that the actual utilization of capacity can show in response to higher than expected demand levels.

2 *Rate of accumulation, normal distribution and profits per unit of capital*

As has already been mentioned in the previous section, the flexibility shown by the actual utilization of capacity even over long periods of time seems to rule out the necessity for any influence of the rate of accumulation on the normal distribution of income. If, as in general it appears reasonable to suppose, total saving varies in direct relation to the level of total income, different (average) values of the investment/capital stock ratio can generate adequate savings per unit of capital via a greater or lesser average utilization of capacity, and hence through differences in the average level of income produced per unit of capital. In other words, given the rate of saving per unit of capital corresponding to *normal* distribution of income and utilization of capacity, average investment and savings per unit of capital that are greater or lesser than this value may be realized through average degrees of capacity that turn out to be, respectively, higher or lower than 'normal' utilization. The analysis carried out in the previous section has shown in what way this could actually occur.

Thus, in contrast to what is maintained by Joan Robinson's theory, normal distribution does not seem to be necessarily involved in the adjustment of savings per unit of capital to a given long-period value of the rate of accumulation. This result can be seen as immediately evident if, as in Robinson (1956), the influence of the rate of accumulation on distribution is represented by the presumed inverse relation between the rate of accumulation and the real wage. Thanks to the flexibility of the actual utilization of capacity, the differences in the (average) ratio of demand to productive capacity of consumer goods, generated by different (average) levels of investment per unit of capital, can be satisfied by correspondingly different (average) levels of production of those goods. In consequence, differences in the (average) rate of accumulation do not imply necessary differences in the ratio of the production of consumer goods to the total quantity of labour employed in the economy, and so do not require changes in the real wage.

The implications for the theory under discussion deriving from the analysis conducted so far may be less transparent when we look at the presumed direct relation between the rate of accumulation and the (normal) profit rate. In effect, the necessary validity – in the hypothesis that only profits are saved – of the relation between investment and profits per unit of capital makes the question to some extent more problematical; as can be guessed, the conclusions I shall reach will, however, be symmetrical with those obtained for the relation between rate of accumulation and (normal) wage rate.

A first, crucial result seems in any case to follow immediately from the above analysis. Owing to the flexibility that, as has been argued, characterizes (also in the long period) the actual utilization of capacity, and hence the level of income produced per unit of capital, the necessary direct relation between investment and profits per unit of capital seems capable of being satisfied independently from changes in the real wage. Assuming that this be given at its 'natural' level, the average value of the profits obtained relative to capital could, in other words, take on different values corresponding to different values of the average accumulation rate, as an effect of a greater or lesser level of output realized per unit of capital;[11] the level of the normal wage rate, therefore, could not be traced back unequivocally to the value of the rate of accumulation.[12]

In short, the profits realized per unit of capital depend not only on the level of the real wage and on technical conditions, but also on the actual utilization of capacity. This seems to open up a further question, in particular since the profits I am referring to are those realized, on average, over *long* periods of time: the question is whether these profits can be identified with the *normal* rate of profit, that is with the rate generally taken into consideration in distribution theories. The answer to this question evidently has a certain interest in itself, and is in any case relevant to establish if, from the direct relation between rate of accumulation and profits per unit of capital, there may follow at least a determination of the normal rate of profit, if not the normal real wage rate.

To pose this problem is equivalent to asking oneself if, given the wage at its 'natural' level, the value of the normal rate of profit depends on the utilization of capacity that has effectively been made over the long period; or, in more general terms, which is the utilization of capacity that together with the technical conditions establishes the relation between the (normal) values of the two distributive variables.

It seems that a solution to this question must be found in what I said in the preceding section about the utilization of capacity implicit in the long-period prices of products. Indeed, the degree of utilization that for a given wage rate and for given productive methods determines the normal rate of profit can only be the same as that which determines, simultaneously, the normal values of commodities. It was then argued that this utilization of capacity, in its turn defined as 'normal', appears as that expected for the *newly* installed equipment, from which the actual utilization of the stock of capacity can differ even for long periods of time.

For a given real wage rate and for given technical conditions, the normal rate of profit therefore appears to be determined in correspondence with the 'normal' degree of utilization of capacity. From the possibility that in the long period the actual utilization of capacity turns out to be different from 'normal' utilization, it therefore seems to follow that it is necessary to keep the profits realized per unit of capital distinct from the normal rate of profit[13] – which is shown, according to what I have said above, in the expected yield on investment, rather than in that on the existing stock of capital.

The further question that must lastly be considered concerns the legitimacy of the distinction between the actual utilization of capacity obtained over long periods and the 'normal' utilization – a distinction underlying the other distinction, just delineated, between profits realized per unit of capital and the normal rate of profit. Against the first distinction it could be maintained that 'normal' utilization, i.e. the utilization expected for the newly installed plant, derives plausibly from the observation of the utilization of capacity that has actually taken place, on average, over long periods of time. A clear distinction between the two notions of utilization would therefore be meaningful in the short period, but could be held to be much less so in the long period, in which 'normal' utilization would adjust, as it were, to the utilization of capacity effectively realized.

A first, immediate answer to this possible objection is that, to the extent that effective long-period utilization of capacity implies undesired excesses or deficiencies of capacity, it cannot influence the utilization expected for the newly installed equipment – the size of which will be, as is obvious, what appears most suited for expected levels of demand.

It has, however, been stressed in the previous section that the average utilization of capacity can be considerably different according to the effective breadth and frequency of fluctuations in demand, and this even in the absence of undesired excesses or deficiencies of capacity. It is therefore reasonable to refer to these margins of flexibility in the discussion of the influence that the actual utilization of capacity may have on what is considered 'normal' utilization.

In effect, within those limits it does not seem possible to deny the existence of a relation between 'normal' and actual utilization of capacity. Since the future fluctuations of demand (relative to capacity) cannot in general be known in advance, it is plausible that the average expected utilization of equipment of the desired size is to a large extent estimated on the basis of the utilization of capacity experienced in the past. However, precisely the variability of fluctuations in demand, which on the one hand prevents forecasts of their breadth and frequency, on the other leads us to suppose that the determination of 'normal' utilization of capacity refers to the average utilization observed over very long periods of time – long enough, for example, to include several economic cycles. It consequently seems possible to maintain that the effectively experienced utilization of capacity influences the utilization considered normal only very slowly, and the distinction between the two notions therefore appears justified when the temporal dimension of the analysis is the one usually referred to as 'long period'.

Acknowledgement

This is a later version of the paper originally presented at the Sraffa conference. The work was rendered possible by a contribution from the Italian Ministry of Education.

Notes

1 See Robinson (1962d), pp. 11–12. In Robinson (1956) the link between the rate of accumulation and income distribution is mainly referred to as an inverse relation between the former and the real wage (see pp. 77 and 83–4). The (corresponding) direct relation between the rate of accumulation and the rate of profit is also mentioned, however, in this book (see, for instance, p. 76), although with a lesser emphasis than in Robinson (1962d).

2 'The main weight of the equalization of saving to investment (at normal prices) falls upon the distribution of income between classes' (Robinson, 1962d, p. 12).

3 In conditions of this type the transfers of capital could of course take place simultaneously with variations in the absolute size of the stock of capacity, thus assuming the form of proportionately different contractions or expansions of the capital invested in the different industries.

4 See, for example, Marshall (1961, Bk v, ch. v, sec. 8, p. 379), where, with regard to normal prices, he refers to '*long* periods of several years', and then distinguishes the 'very gradual or *Secular* movements of normal prices, caused by gradual growth of knowledge, of population and of *capital*' (last emphasis added).

5 An analogous distinction can be made with regard to the techniques of production that are relevant for the determination of normal prices. These techniques are not necessarily those incorporated in the existing stock of capital or in a particularly large portion of it, but rather are those that, as an effect of competition, are currently introduced (to a sufficient extent to influence prices) via gross investment. In this connection, see also Roncaglia (1978), ch. 2, para. 4, pp. 27–9.

6 Obviously, to the extent to which they give rise to variations in stocks, fluctuations in demand do not determine fluctuations in production. The fact that the latter do, however, occur seems to show that in general the accumulation and depletion of stocks (which in any case does not constitute a cost-free option) cannot eliminate the need for variations in output; on the contrary, it is sometimes maintained that the management of stocks has pro-cyclical rather than anti-cyclical effects (see Zarnowitz, 1985, p. 527).

7 The breadth and frequency mentioned in the text can constitute purely *implicit* connotations of the normal level of utilization if, as appears plausible, this is to a large extent determined on the basis of observation.

8 A mechanism that can arrest the expansionary phases of the economic cycle – i.e. determine the *ceiling* reached during booms is identified in the fact that the multiplier cannot operate beyond the full utilization of capacity in capital goods industries; see, for example, Matthews (1959), pp. 155–6. Robinson herself seems to hold an opinion of this kind (see Robinson, 1956, pp. 200–1).

9 This in fact would be a case of deficiencies of capacity extended to a considerable number of industries, the investment of which would presumably have large effects on aggregate demand itself.

10 This is equivalent to supposing that the composition of the capital stock is adjusted to the composition that aggregate demand assumes in correspondence with the full utilization of capacity in capital goods industries.

11 If a degree of utilization of capacity higher than 'normal' implies, on average, higher unit costs – for example, as an effect of higher wage rates owing to overtime work – it could happen that the lower (net) profit per product unit were not compensated by the greater average level of output, and that, for the same (basic) real wage rate the average profits/capital ratio actually realized might not increase, and might even decrease, with respect to that corresponding to the 'normal' utilization of capacity. In this case the realization of higher average profits per unit of capital could not be ensured simply by a higher utilization of capacity, and would require the (basic) real wage to be somewhat lower. The existence of an inverse relation between the rate of accumulation and the *normal* level of the real wage could not, however, be revived on this ground. First of all, the need for a fall in the real wage cannot be explained, in the case under consideration, by the need to adjust saving to investment per unit of capital: it is sufficient to abandon the assumption that savings are drawn only from profits to obtain the result that their ratio to the stock of capital may increase as income per unit of capital increases – even if the ratio of profits to capital is not increasing. That fall in the real wage should rather be justified by the consideration that, for a higher degree of capacity utilization to be realized, entrepreneurs must have an interest in it, and this reasonably means obtaining higher profits per unit of capital. But, as has already been said, a fall in the real wage becomes necessary, in this connection, only if unit costs increase as capacity utilization turns out to be higher than normal and, moreover, they increase so much that the lower profits per unit of capital are not compensated by the higher levels of output. In my view, none of these conditions necessarily occurs when capacity utilization is higher than 'normal' (for a different opinion, see Kurz's contribution to this volume – ch. 13) the size, as well as the algebraic sign, of the differences in unit costs

would be different according to several circumstances, including the 'shape' of the fluctuations that would bring about the higher-than-normal utilization of capacity.

Thus, the influence that the rate of accumulation may exert in this way on the real wage does not seem to be sufficiently general for the determination of the normal wage rate to be based on it – as is confirmed by the absence of a symmetrical need for changes in the real wage in the case of falls in the utilization of capacity with respect to the 'normal' degree. That influence, I believe, should rather be put at the origin of possible *deviations* of the real wage from its normal value, and this conclusion seems to be reinforced by the consideration that what that influence would express is not the need for a particular *level* of the real wage, but only the need for particular *variations* in it. The level to which that influence could bring the real wage would therefore be undetermined, since it would depend on the starting level of the wage itself.

12 Of course, the impossibility of determining the normal real wage rate also prevents us from determining the corresponding relative shares of wages and profits.

13 A similar distinction is, in contrast, absent in for example Steindl's analysis, where the rate of profit is solely identified with the profits realized relative to the capital stock, and hence depends on the effective degree of utilization of capacity (see Steindl, 1952, p. 122; see also Steindl, 1985, in particular pp. 53–5).

Comment

Josef Steindl
Vienna

I may perhaps at the outset state my position: I think it is perfectly true that, as Professor Ciccone argues, utilization is flexible not only in the short but also in the long run. This does not, however, necesarily exclude the alternative method of adjusting saving to a change in accumulation, namely a shift to or from profits (what he calls a change in normal profits), from also playing a role. Ultimately this seems to me to be a question of facts, but Ciccone tends to make it an issue of high doctrine. Thus he is very concerned to deny that accumulation may have an influence on the real wage (pp. 425–6); his argument is that, owing to flexible utilization, an increase in accumulation could always be accommodated by increased output from the given capital stock, which would obviate a decline in real wages. But in the context of a growing economy the real wage (also the subsistence wage in a conventional historical interpretation) will presumably be expected to rise, and the question will be how much or how little it will be permitted to rise by the pace of accumulation. In other words, even with all the flexibility in the world, the pace of accumulation will not be irrelevant for the development of the real wage.

Strictly speaking, Joan Robinson's arguments were concerned not with historical developments but with a 'long run competitive equilibrium', and quite logically Ciccone tries to refute her on this ground. He immediately meets the difficulty that for a price equilibrium (Sraffa's system, though not mentioned, is always in the background) we have to assume some sort of 'normal' capacity utilization. However, since Ciccone's utilization has to serve the demon accumulation, it cannot at the same time serve as a basis for the determination of normal prices. He tries to resolve this difficulty by assuming that normal prices are determined independently of *actual* utilization on the basis of a different value of utilization, namely the utilization that investors in new equipment expect to realize with their new equipment in the future (pp. 418–19ff). Now this implies that the profit rate calculated on the basis of this 'normal' expected rate of utilization will be different from the profit rate that is necessary to make the given pace of accumulation possible. Ciccone has a way out again: he has two different profit rates – the normal profit rate and one that he calls 'profit realized per unit of capital' (p. 426). The distinction is quite legitimate analytically. But do managers live with such a dichotomy? It would rather seem that they cannot have much interest in calculating, on the basis of a normal profit rate, normal prices that will never become reality however long the run.

To my mind what all this amounts to is only the recognition that there is never a long-run equilibrium in an economy with changing accumulation rates (and there is no gravity either). It is possible to arrive at this conclusion in other ways, but in any case I could hardly dissent.

On the other hand, I have seen no convincing proof that accumulation could not affect 'normal profit rates'. It might do so if a high long-run average of utilization relaxed the aggressive competitive spirit (Joan Robinson did not use this argument, though).

Reply

Although Professor Steindl agrees about the flexibility of capacity utilization in the long run (about which he wrote long before I did), he maintains that the possibility still exists that saving adjusts to investment through the distribution, rather than through the level, of income: this, in his view, is 'a question of facts'. However, this does not seem to be a real objection to my argument, any more than the other question, also raised by Steindl, concerning the possible influence of accumulation on the real wage. What my paper tried to show is that there is no *necessity* that a different ratio of saving to capital should be obtained, in the long period, through a change in the real wage (and the normal profit rate), since changes in the level of income per unit of capital can generally bring about this result. This does not mean that changes in the pace of accumulation cannot be accompanied by, or even be the ultimate cause of, changes in normal distribution: indeed, accumulation can have an influence on the circumstances that govern the latter. But even in cases in which those changes in distribution would actually help to adjust saving to investment, this would not imply that such an adjustment plays any role in *determining* distribution: for that contribution to the equalization of saving to investment can simply be an 'incidental' effect of the change in distribution, whose causes should be sought elsewhere.

Another question raised by Steindl concerns the distinction between the normal and realized profit rate, which in my paper parallels the corresponding distinction between normal and actual capacity utilization. Although he considers it as 'analytically legitimate', Steindl seems to think of the first distinction as irrelevant. The argument he develops in this regard can be separated into two stages:

(1) the possibility that the realized profit rate persistently diverges from the normal rate implies that normal prices 'never become reality';
(2) consequently, entrepreneurs cannot be interested in calculating such normal prices, or in knowing the profit rate and the utilization of capacity on which the determination of those prices is based.

Now, one of the points for my paper is precisely that, although normal prices are determined on the basis of normal capacity utilization and the normal profit rate, the tendency towards them does not require that the actual degree of utilization of the existing stock of capacity should gravitate around the normal (i.e. expected) degree. Therefore, normal prices can still be referred to as long-period centres of gravitation, although the actual degree of capacity utilization and the profits realized on the existing capital stock persistently diverge from, respectively, the normal degree of utilization and the normal rate of profit.

Further, it must be observed that in any case, if normal prices are conceived of as gravitation centres, they need not 'become reality' at any particular moment of time; for the same reason they need not result from entrepreneurs' actual calculations. This does not exclude the possibility, however, that, when forming prices, entrepreneurs refer to some condition of 'normality' of costs, market situations, etc., as is maintained in some recent work.

15

On the Monetary Explanation of Distribution

Massimo Pivetti
Naples

In the classical–Marxian approach to distribution the real wage rate and the rate of profit are not symmetrically and simultaneously determined; on the contrary, after either one of these two variables has been explained independently from both the social product and the other distributive variable, then the other one is determined as a residue. Once the view is abandoned that real wages consist of the worker's necessary subsistence, and the possibility of variations in the division of the social surplus is admitted, a theory of distribution on these lines requires a solution to the question of which of the two distributive variables should be regarded as independent or 'given' in the present reality of the capitalist economy, and through which social–institutional channels the distribution between profits and wages is actually arrived at. As is well known, the rate of profit is treated as the independent variable for much of Sraffa's *Production of Commodities by Means of Commodities* – the choice resting upon the idea that the rate of profit is 'susceptible of being determined from outside the system of production, in particular by the level of the money rates of interest' (Sraffa, 1960, p. 33).[1]

This paper deals with that idea, with a view to taking some steps forward in the direction suggested by Sraffa for explaining the distribution of income between capitalists and workers.

It is perhaps worth starting by recalling that economic theory is in substantial agreement in recognizing that there is a connection between the rate of profit on the one hand and the money rate of interest on the other; that these two tend to move in sympathy, that is, when a sufficiently long period of time is taken into consideration. The significant theoretical question is rather the nature of the connection between the two rates: which of the two ultimately governs the other.

Section 1 of this paper will briefly consider Marx's and Keynes's critical positions on the commonly received conception of the money rate of interest as a magnitude subordinate to the normal rate of profit; I then examine what I regard as the main circumstances supporting a 'prior' determination of interest in actual experience. Section 2 will deal with the actual mechanism by which the long-term interest rate governs the rate of profit – how the rate of interest can be arrived at as the regulator of the ratio of prices to money wages. The question of the excess of profit over interest is then considered in section 3, where the normal rate of profit in each particular sphere of production will be arrived at by a process of adding up two autonomous components: the long-term rate of interest plus the normal profit of enterprise. This conception of profits will be compared in section 4 with the classical–Marxian conception, with particular reference to the role played by competition among capitalists in determining the distribution of income. Sections 5 and 6 will focus on a few significant implications of regarding the rate of interest as 'setting the pace' in its connection with the rate of profit. The main questions that will be considered are: the effects of wage bargaining on distribution; the explanation of the price level – in particular the question of the influence of the rate of interest on the price level; the effects of changes in interest rates on the inducement to invest. Section 7 finally distinguishes between the nominal rate of interest and the real rate (the money rate corrected by reference to any change in the value of money) and tries to point out some interesting results of postulating equalization of the rate of profit with the real interest rate.

1 *The rate of interest as a 'monetary phenomenon'*

According to both classical and marginalist economists the money rate of interest is ultimately determined by those 'real forces' that explain the course of the normal rate of profit: the 'fundamental phenomena of Productivity and Thrift' (Robertson, 1940, p. 25), as far as marginalism is concerned; the real wage rate and production techniques in the classical theory of distribution up to Ricardo.

An important implication is the denial of any substantial power for the monetary authorities, in the sense that, given the state of the real forces governing the 'natural real rate', the impact on the price level or on real output and accumulation of any lasting discrepancy between the courses of the two rates would force them so to act as to make the rate of interest move in sympathy with the rate of profit. It seems, then, that Sraffa's suggestion is in sharp contrast with both main streams of economic theorizing.

However, somewhat dissenting views had already been expressed concerning the commonly received conception of the money rate of interest as a subordinate phenomenon, both before and after the inception of maginalism. The two most outstanding cases are those represented by Marx and Keynes; let us briefly consider their positions, before looking at concrete reality.

Marx does not appear to share Smith's and Ricardo's view that lasting changes in the rate of interest must reflect changes in the normal rate of profit. In fact, his position on the relation between profit and interest is much nearer to that of J. S. Mill, who argues that the rate of interest 'is also acted upon by causes particular to itself, and may either rise or fall, both temporarily and permanently, while the general rate of profits remains unchanged' (Mill,

[1874] 1974, p. 114).[2] For Marx, too, the rate of interest is influenced but not exclusively governed by the general rate of profit – the latter having rather to be regarded, in his view, as 'the maximum limit of interest' (Marx, [1894] 1977, p. 360). He maintains that 'The average rate of interest prevailing in a certain country – as distinct from the continually fluctuating market rates – cannot be determined by any law. In this sphere there is no such thing as a natural rate of interest in the sense in which economists speak of a natural rate of profit and a natural rate of wages' (ibid., p. 362).

The main point Marx endeavours to highlight by insisting on the absence of a general law in the determination of the rate of interest is the latter's marked degree of autonomy from the rate of profit. The main socioeconomic and institutional circumstances that, according to Marx, combine to militate in favour of an 'autonomous determination' of the rate of interest are: the fact that 'many borrow without any view to productive employment' (ibid.); the existence of a developed credit system (ibid.); the discount rate policy of the Bank of England and 'the direct influence exerted by the world market on establishing the rate of interest' (ibid., p. 364, n68; p. 367); finally, the fact that 'Customs, juristic traditions, etc. have . . . much to do with determining the average rate of interest' (ibid., p. 364). As I have argued elsewhere (Pivetti, 1983, pp. 16–17), such a conception of the rate of interest cannot easily be reconciled with the Marxian (and Ricardian) conception of the real wage as the independent or given variable in the relation between profits and wages. There remains however the suggestion – of particular interest to us here, and which Marx seems to derive from an unprejudiced observation of facts – of 'the average rate of interest prevailing in a certain country' as a magnitude determined by influences unrelated to those real forces governing in his analysis the ordinary rate of profit.

The unprejudiced observation of concrete reality clearly also plays a significant part in Keynes's interpretation of the rate of interest as a 'monetary phenomenon' (Keynes, 1973b, pp. 80, 206, 229 and 231). The fact that Keynes is far from being entirely happy with his monetary explanation of interest (ibid., p. 213; see also p. 215), does not shake his conviction that the rate of interest is not determined by the real forces envisaged by traditional theory. Accordingly, he maintains that it is the profitability of capital that tends to adapt itself to the rate of interest, and not vice versa: 'instead of the marginal efficiency of capital determining the rate of interest, it is truer . . . to say that it is the rate of interest which determines the marginal efficiency of capital' (ibid., p. 123; see on this point pp. 444–6 below). As has been argued (Garegnani, 1979a, pp. 78–9), the persistence in Keynes's analysis of some traditional premises seriously weakens his conception of the rate of interest as a magnitude determined by monetary factors. But, again, what is of interest to us here is that, notwithstanding those traditional theoretical premises, Keynes is led to regard the rate of interest as the regulator of the rate of profit, rather than the other way round.

It would of course be most desirable for us to be able directly to verify by experience which of the two rates should be regarded as 'setting the pace' in the causal relationship connecting them. Unfortunately, it is extremely difficult to establish precise causation in complicated economic phenomena like the one we are dealing with. As Wicksell says, 'concrete reality is altogether too shifting and complex for us to be able directly to appeal to its testimony: an isolation of the phenomena is both difficult and doubtful'; moreover, whereas 'the level of the rate of interest on money . . . [is] just known to economic statistics, about the magnitude of the natural rate on capital nothing is really known at all' (Wicksell, [1906] 1962, p. 90; see also [1898] 1958, p. 85). We must try, then, some indirect appeal to concrete reality, and content ourselves with a judgement less 'quantitative' and clear-cut in character. The question is ultimately that of deriving from actual experience elements capable of showing that the interest rate policy of any one country, both in the short and in the long run, is susceptible of being explained on the basis of circumstances that are clearly independent of the factors regarded by the two alternative theoretical approaches as the determinants of the profitability of capital. It seems to me that two sets of such circumstances are particularly well-suited to illustrate the autonomous or 'prior' determination of the rate of interest: those connected with the management of government debt, and those connected with any one country's position *vis-à-vis* the rest of the world.

As the *Radcliffe Report* endeavoured to make clear more than twenty-five years ago, the size that government debt has historically acquired, in relation to the other financial assets of the private sector, makes it impossible for the authorities to adopt a passive or neutral policy with respect to interest rates – leaving them to be determined 'by market forces' – even if they wanted to do so. 'Such a policy of neutrality is ruled out by the facts that, in our economies nowadays, the Government is the largest borrower and that certain forms of government debt are the ultimate means of payment. . . . In present circumstances – and all foreseeable circumstances . . . the authorities must have a positive policy on interest rates, because debt operations are inescapable' (Committee on the Working of the Monetary System, 1959, para. 492).

Naturally, among such 'inescapable operations' there is the servicing of the debt; the question of the cost of debt service, and of its fiscal implications, can actually be singled out as the most important factor behind the debt management and interest rate policies followed over long periods in this century. Thus the origin of the 1932–51 period of cheap money policy can be traced to the purpose of reducing the charges for interest in the national budget, and making room for other expenditures. As far as England is concerned, the cheap money programme was inaugurated in the summer of 1932 by the Great War Loan conversion operation, which firmly established 3½ per cent as the gilt-edged long-term rate. As has been argued, the manner in which the conversion operation was carried out, the series of measures by which it was accompanied (a substantial credit expansion among them), and the published beliefs of the Treasury and the Bank of England that cheap money would continue, all succeeded in convincing investors that the fall in interest rates was a long-term phenomenon – so that 'the belief in cheap money helped to make it effective' (Morton, 1943, p. 248; see also Nevin, 1955, pp. 92–107). Basically that experience and that combination of manoeuvres are what Keynes had in mind when he wrote that 'the rate of interest is a highly conventional phenomenon', and that the level of the long-term rate of interest established by convention 'will not be always unduly resistant to a modest measure of persistence and consistency of purpose by the monetary authority' (Keynes, 1936a, pp. 203 and 204).

Besides the pressure for the minimum cost of debt service, the second important motive behind debt management and the long-term behaviour of interest rates has historically been the desire to lengthen the average life of the securities outstanding – more generally, to ensure a debt structure more consonant with the need not to lose control of the general liquidity of the economy.[3] This second motive is generally in contrast with the aim of holding interest rates down so as to get the new debt placed as cheaply as possible – the desired structure of the debt requiring that the long-term rate be pushed to a level that is high enough to attract sufficient firm holders for it. In periods of rapidly rising government debt, the debt manager's aim to avoid the growth of its liquidity to a degree thought dangerous from the point of view of keeping control of the monetary situation is bound to entail a marked and lasting rise in interest rates, as shown by the experience of the United States economy during the first half of the 1980s.

In addition to debt management and its motives, the level of interest rates in any one country is clearly influenced by its relations with the rest of the world. Low rates of interest, for example, simply cannot be a long-term phenomenon in a relatively small and internationally integrated economy unless low interest rates prevail and persist in the rest of the world. If a persistent cheapening of money is hindered by external constraints, then, given the generally acknowledged long-period connection between the rate of interest and the rate of profit, a persistent lowering of the rate of profit cannot take place either – even if domestic circumstances were such as to favour a change in the normal distribution of income. It is worth stressing here that the weight of external influences in the determination of the rate of interest may be significant also for the large and dominant economy. Thus it is difficult to conceive how, in the conditions of the 1980s, the authorities of the United States could have managed a relatively rapid growth of domestic demand without the strengthening of the dollar achieved through their policy of high and rising interest rates.[4]

It seems, then, that the level of the rate of interest in any one country is strongly influenced by circumstances that have nothing to do with those different 'real forces' regarded by the classical and marginalist economists as the determinants of the normal rate of profit. Actual experience, in other words, seems to validate Marx's (and J. S. Mill's) idea of an 'autonomous' determination of the money rate of interest – autonomous in the sense that interest rates do experience lasting changes that are very reasonably explainable without any need to refer to a *primum movens* represented by changes in the normal profit rate.

As should be clear from what has been said, I do not think that interest rate policies are unconstrained – i.e. that monetary authorities can always bring the rate of interest to whatever level they deem desirable. The disposition or will may not be accompanied by the necessary power, owing to obstacles of a monetary nature,[5] to external constraints, to the distributive implications of their actions (see pp. 440–3 below). The upshot of my argument is rather that interest rate policy, both in the short and in the long run, does not appear to be constrained by a somehow predetermined normal profitability of capital. My view then is that the rate of interest should be regarded as a 'monetary phenomenon', meaning however by this that in the causal relationship between the rate of interest and the rate of profit it is the former that 'sets the pace'. In the following sections I shall basically endeavour to explain the actual mechanism whereby lasting changes in interest rates must be followed by corresponding changes in normal profit rates, and to point out some significant aspects of this causation.

Before so doing, let me be explicit about what I understand by 'normal rate of profit'. By this concept I simply mean what the theories of distribution endeavour to explain: classical and Marxian expressions such as 'natural rate of profit', 'permanent rate of profit' or 'general rate of profit', and marginalist expressions such as 'natural or real rate of interest' and 'equilibrium or full-employment rate of interest', never refer to actual or effective profits but refer to normal profits. The latter, reckoned gross of interest,[6] correspond to the rate of return on capital that would be obtained by firms using dominant or generally accessible techniques, and producing output at levels regarded as normal at the time the capacity was installed. As actual profits always deviate from normal profits, economic theory is in substantial agreement in regarding the normal rate of profit as a magnitude that cannot be arrived at statistically and empirically. Thus, as we saw above, Wicksell says that 'nothing is really known at all' about 'the magnitude of the natural rate on capital', so that 'the only escape is to appeal to generally accepted economic principles'; and Marx says that 'the general rate of profit appears blurred and hazy' (Marx, [1894] 1977, p. 368), a magnitude that can be arrived at only through analysis. Now, the reason why it is this 'blurred and hazy' magnitude that has always been taken into consideration by economic theory remains that given by Smith in the *Wealth of Nations*: though actual profits are always deviating from normal profits, they are constantly tending towards them.

2 *The rate of interest as the regulator of the ratio of prices to money wages*

To understand the actual mechanism by which changes in the long-term rate of interest are susceptible of causing corresponding changes in the rate of profit, it is perhaps convenient for us to follow a three-stage line of reasoning.

The first stage simply consists in regarding competition as the mechanism by which prices tend to be equated to normal costs. This role of competition is generally acknowledged by economic theory. The second stage of the reasoning consists in looking at the rate of interest as a determinant of production costs, together with money wages and production techniques. Thus, lasting changes in interest rates constitute changes in normal costs, which, *ceteris paribus*, will result in corresponding changes in the price level. The third stage of the reasoning comes about as a consequence of the first two: because of the competition among firms within each industry, a lasting change in interest rates causes a change in the same direction in the level of prices in relation to the level of money wages, thereby generating changes in income distribution. So, a persistent fall in interest rates causes a fall in prices relative to the wage level, and thereby brings about a lower rate of profit and a higher real wage.[7]

The notion that lasting changes in interest rates constitute changes in normal costs does not rest on the assumption that all capital employed in production is borrowed capital. Interest (as economic theory has always looked at it) is the price for the use of capital – the 'pure' remuneration of capital, whatever the form of its employment, whether financial or real. If production is carried on with the firm's own capital, interest constitutes its opportunity cost, and as such will enter into the normal cost that in the long run tends to be equated with the unit price. Firms would not continue to replace plant that is wearing out unless the prices for their commodities were such that they could not do better for themselves by investing their depreciation funds in gilt-edged securities; conversely, commodity prices could not permanently involve rates of return on the firms' funds exceeding the relevant rates of interest by more than a normal remuneration for the 'risk and trouble' of productively employing capital.

The case of share capital does not alter the fundamentals of the picture. It may be presumed that the nearest competing alternative to shares are long-term bonds, and that ordinary shares will be held only if the expected yield on them exceeds the yield on long-term bonds. As there is a significant section of the investing public ready to switch from one kind of investment to the other, this tends to maintain their respective yields at a steady level. That is to say, at any given time there will be a certain relationship between the prices of the various classes of securities: a shift in the price of one large class must be followed by a general shift in the whole range of prices (Sayers, 1964, p. 210). Thus, a rise in prices for long-term government bonds – a fall in the 'pure' long-term rate of interest resulting from the pursuit of a cheap money policy – will be followed by a rise in prices for securities generally.[8] But a higher quotation for existing equities implies that companies can raise capital by issuing shares on more favourable terms; in the words of Keynes (1936a, p. 151, n1): a high quotation for existing equities has 'the same effect as if [companies] could borrow at a low rate of interest'. We may therefore conclude that the issue of common stocks, as a method of financing investment available to joint-stock companies (corporations), will also become cheaper (or dearer) in the face of a persistent fall (or rise) in interest rates.

The upshot of the entire argument developed so far is the singling out of the rate of interest as the regulator of the ratio of prices to money wages. To help crystallize my ideas, it may be worth calling attention to the main difference between this view and the familiar post-Keynesian theory of distribution: one may say that whilst in that theory changes in the level of prices in relation to the level of money wages are determined by changes in aggregate demand, according to my view they are determined by lasting changes in interest rates.[9]

3 *On the excess of profit over interest*

As was hinted above, profits on capital employed in production will normally include, besides interest (what I called the 'pure' remuneration of capital), also a remuneration for the 'risk and trouble' of productively employing it – what may be termed a normal profit of enterprise. How does this excess of profit over interest affect my conception of the rate of interest as the regulator of the ratio of prices to money wages? When the profit of enterprise is taken into consideration, such a conception implies assuming that the remuneration for the 'risk and trouble' is independent of the rate of interest and is a sufficiently stable magnitude.[10]

It would seem that these are quite reasonable assumptions. If profit does normally exceed interest – i.e. if competition does not tend to equalize profit and interest – then the excess must cover objective elements of 'risk and trouble' or elements that are regarded as objective by the majority of the investing public.[11] Such elements, moreover, must have been present for a sufficiently long period of time for a certain profit of enterprise to have come to be regarded as normal. In addition, when conventional factors play an important part in determining the normal profit of enterprise in a particular production sphere, the convention itself will generally be rooted in some persistent facts and will not tend to change except in the face of lasting changes in those facts.

Actually, these views about the normal profit of enterprise are largely consistent with classical conceptions: production and accumulation would not continue, Ricardo argues, if the profits of the farmers and manufacturers were 'so low as not to afford them an adequate compensation for their trouble and the risk which they must necessarily encounter in employing their capital productively'. Such 'adequate compensation' will be different in the various employments of capital, according to 'any real or fancied advantage which one employment may possess over another'; and, once so adjusted as to reflect those relative advantages, 'the profits of stock would probably continue permanently with that relative difference, and with that difference only' – so that, if we 'suppose that all commodities are at their natural price, . . . profits of capital in all employments . . . [will] differ only so much as, in the estimation of the parties, is equivalent to any real or fancied advantage which they possess or forgo' (Ricardo, [1817–21] 1951, pp. 90 and 122).[12]

There remains, however, the most important difference between my view and the Ricardian conception. Interest is viewed by Ricardo (and Smith) as a residue, or what remains of profits once the normal remuneration for the 'risk and trouble' has been deducted.[13] Interest and profit of enterprise are thus conceived by Ricardo, as by the whole classical–Marxian approach, as the two magnitudes into which normal profits – determined by real wages and production techniques – resolve themselves;[14] whereas, according to my view, the same two magnitudes should rather be regarded as the autonomous determinants of the rate of profit. The normal rate of profit in each particular production sphere (r_a) is arrived at by adding up two autonomous components: the long-term rate of interest (i) or 'pure' remuneration of capital, plus the normal profit of enterprise (npe_a) or the remuneration for the 'risk and trouble' of productively employing capital in that particular production sphere. In symbols:

$$r_a = i + npe_a.$$

Provided that npe_a is a sufficiently stable magnitude, and one that is independent of i and of lasting changes in i, the picture given above remains substantially unaffected: lasting changes in the rate of interest will cause corresponding changes in profit rates, and inverse changes in the real wage.[15]

4 *Competition and distribution*

The difference pointed out between my conception of normal profits and the classical–Marxian conception has important bearings upon the question of the role and scope of competition among capitalists in determining the distribution of income between profits and wages. I shall focus on this question in this section, starting with the views of the classical economists and Marx.

In classical and Marxian theory competition is envisaged essentially as the mechanism whereby, in each sphere of production, a single price tends to be established – the price that enables the means of production to be reintegrated on the basis of the dominant production techniques, and wages and profits to be paid at their normal rates. Normal wages and profits must be explained independently from competition, and, in Marx's words, *it is they that regulate competition*, rather than being regulated by it.[16]

Within this conception, the conditions of competition – for example, the presence of monopoly elements in this or that sphere of production – will affect the division of profits amongst the particular stocks making up social capital, but not the normal distribution of net output between profits and wages (see ibid., p. 861). Given the dominant methods of production, the normal rate of profit depends exclusively on wages. If real wages, as determined by historical and social conditions independently from prices and from the rate of profit,[17] absorb only a part of the net product of the economy, it is simply impossible for competition, however intense it may be, to determine prices such as to render nil or 'as low as possible' what remains of the value of the product after the means of production have been reintegrated and the wages paid.[18]

Let us now attempt to focus on the possible role of competition with respect to the explanation of distribution based on the notion I have put forward that the normal rate of profit consists of the sum of two autonomous components: the long-term rate of interest plus the normal profit of enterprise. Given the money wage, the real wage appears here as a residue on the basis of the price level reflecting the dominant techniques in the different spheres of production and the normal profit rate determined in each sphere in the way I have just indicated.

Analogously to the classical analysis considered above, greater (or lesser) profits than normal will reflect more advanced (or more backward) techniques than the dominant ones. Effectively greater or lesser profits than normal will also be obtained each time 'effectual demand' is greater or smaller than the volume of production that was considered normal when the productive capacity was installed.

In contrast to the classical analysis, however, since in this approach the real wage constitutes the residual variable, the presence of monopoly elements in this or that sphere of production may affect not only the division of profits amongst the different employments of capital, but also the distribution between profits and wages. Given in fact the money wage, the possibility for some commodities to obtain a monopoly price that rises above the 'price of production' will translate into a price level/money wage ratio that will be higher than it would if there were no monopoly elements, and hence into a lower real wage.

If we thus assume, to start with, that the presence of monopoly elements exerts no influence on the long-term interest rate, it follows that lasting effects of the conditions of competition on distribution may be obtained in one direction only: higher profits than normal. For the long-term interest rate and the normal remuneration of 'risk and trouble' establish, in each sphere of production, the minimum or 'necessary' level below which the profit rate cannot go, over the long run, however intense one may suppose the forces of competition to be.[19]

In any case, I believe that the possibilities of distribution being more favourable to profits as a result of the presence of monopoly elements should not be overrated. Even in spheres where the entire production is carried on by a small number of firms, any agreements they may make – aimed, for example, at avoiding price-cutting when normal costs go down – will tend to be inhibited by the freedom of capital movement and hence by the fear that new firms might move into the market.[20] It appears to me to be probable that, apart from situations of natural monopoly, the 'monopoly elements' most easily encountered in reality are those arising from forms of institutional protection granted to particular firms or industries.[21]

We must lastly consider the possibility that the conditions of competition influence the normal profit rate via the long-term interest rate. Amongst the main factors of a possible influence on the rate of interest is the level of the real wage. Let us see why.

In my approach it has been said that the real wage is the residual variable in the relation between wages and profits, since the normal profit rate is arrived at by adding up the rate of interest and the normal profit of enterprise. However, to acknowledge that lasting variations in the interest rate determine variations in normal distribution is not to concede that the real wage may move to any level whatsoever. Thus, in each concrete situation, it would be hard to carry on the productive process in an orderly manner if the real wage were lower than certain levels reflecting institutional and historical as well as economic circumstances, such as the degree of organization of the workers, the levels of employment, the strength of the unions, etc. So let us imagine that the profits of enterprise within the different spheres of production are kept abnormally high by the widespread presence of 'monopoly elements', and/or that a protectionist policy keeps the price level/money wage ratio high via backward techniques and a low productivity of labour. In these conditions, efforts to ensure standards of living (i.e. real wages) considered indispensable for social stability could lead to a policy of low interest rates.

In short, underlying the case of a possible influence of competition which I have just considered there is the fact that the level of the real wage constitutes in any case an important constraint on the freedom of monetary policy to establish the level of interest rates.

5 *Wage bargaining, distribution and the price level*

Let us now proceed to the following question: if changes in normal profits are governed by lasting changes in long-term interest rates, real wages being a residue, does wage bargaining have any effects on distribution between wages and profits? According to the view expounded above, this question amounts to one of the influence of wage bargaining on monetary policy. In fact, if the notion of the rate of profit as a sum of the two autonomous components is founded – considering that the normal profit of enterprise must be regarded as independent of the behaviour of any other component of total unit cost (see section 3 above) – then wage bargaining, in order to have any persistent effect on income distribution, will ultimately have to exert some influence on the level of the rate of interest. It seems, then, that wage bargaining will not have 'direct' effects on normal distribution, but will possibly have 'indirect' effects, via monetary policy on the latter, depending directly on the level of the rates of interest.

Let us consider, for example, a marked rise in money wages. If interest rates were kept unchanged, prices would rise (unless the increase in money wages was compensated for by a growth in productivity). Assuming a closed economy, the main shortcoming of the rise in prices would probably be its impact on the real income of social classes and groups other than the capitalists and the wage-earners. This impact, in situations where the economic and political weight of the injured social categories is significant, could then constitute an obstacle to a policy of unchanged interest rates – particularly if an unchanged ratio of prices to money wages caused strong unions to ask for and obtain new wage increases.

If an open economy is assumed, the freedom of the monetary authorities to establish interest rates is further restricted by foreign competition. In the face of strong unions and a relatively rapid growth in money wages, sticking to high interest rates could impair the competitiveness of domestic products and lead to lower output levels. It is true that if interest rates are kept at sufficiently high levels, balance-of-payments problems arising from current accounts could be compensated for by net capital inflows, but this might simply enable domestic demand to be sustained in the face of lower growth rates of domestic output. Over the short run, firms might decide to content themselves with lower than normal prices, in order not to lose shares of the domestic and external markets and so as to prevent capacity utilization from falling; but sooner or later capacity and output would tend to be adjusted downwards – unless there occurred a lasting lowering of interest rates, and hence a persistent redistribution of income from profits to wages.

A relatively small and internationally integrated economy, however, will generally not be able to keep the rate of interest at low levels if the other countries do not follow the same policy. A lowering of interest rates in such cases will usually be of too short a duration to influence the production costs of goods, and hence normal prices. This seems to imply that income distribution, in a relatively small and internationally integrated economy, will largely be affected by the long-term monetary policy followed by the major economies. Other considerations of this kind could be developed; other types of obstacles to the ability and freedom of monetary policy to establish the level of the rates of interest can be pointed out (see pp. 435–7 above). All of them, I believe, would go to show that the question of the impact of wage bargaining on income distribution cannot be decided on an *a priori* basis – the power of the unions, as reflected in the behaviour of money wages, being one of the circumstances upon which distribution ultimately depends.

According to my view, then, the money rate of interest should be looked upon as the magnitude in which the respective powers of capitalists and workers manifest themselves *in the first place*. Wage bargaining and monetary policy are regarded as the main channels through which class relations act in determining distribution, and those relations are seen as tending to act primarily upon the profit rate, via the monetary rate of interest, rather than upon the real wage rate, as maintained by both the classical economists and Marx. The level of the real wage prevailing in any given situation is the *final* result of the whole process by which the distribution of income between workers and capitalists is actually arrived at.

It seems to me that in the conditions of modern capitalism it is difficult to conceive of the real wage rate as the independent or given variable in the relationship between wages and profits. The difficulty, as I see it, arises from the fact that the direct outcome of wage bargaining is a certain level of the money wage, while the price level cannot be determined before and independently from money wages. Let us briefly consider this question, before I proceed with the development of my argument.

Given the distribution between profits and wages, and given the methods of production, the level of prices simply depends on the level of money wages. Thus, in my picture, the long-term rate of interest enters into the determination of the price level because it contributes to the regulation of the ratio of the price level to the money wage – i.e. of the distribution between profits and wages.

If, instead, the real wage rate is taken as given, the ratio of prices to money wages will be determined by the condition that it must be such as to ensure the given level of the real wage; on this basis, wage bargaining (in determining money wages) can be thought of as determining also the price level. In such a picture monetary policy plays a purely passive role – the level of the rate of interest having to accommodate to lasting changes in the ratio of prices to money wages, rather than governing that ratio. Now, what we are ultimately facing here is a conception of the ratio of prices to money wages as being determined by a magnitude – the real wage rate – that is not actually known before that ratio is known. This explains, in my opinion, why of the two alternative propositions – that the ratio of prices to money wages depends on the real wage rate, or that the real wage rate depends on the ratio of the price level to the money wage – the latter is easier to digest: in actual fact, no circumstances determine real wages that are distinct from those acting through money wages, the level of prices and the ratio of prices to money wages.[22]

What in my picture appears to be in sharp contrast with commonly received opinion is the influence of the rate of interest on prices. According to traditional views, low and decreasing interest rates would be accompanied by high and rising prices, and vice versa; whereas, according to the explanation of distribution under discussion (given money wages and production techniques), a lowering of the rate of interest, provided it were not of a temporary nature, would bring about lower prices – there would be, in other words, a direct relationship between the rate of interest and the price level.

If one looks back into economic literature, the first outstanding author who strongly sustained such a relationship between the rate of interest and the price level was the nineteenth-century English economist Thomas Tooke, the leader of the Banking School. Arguing against the dominant opinion that a low rate of interest raises prices and that a high rate depresses them, Tooke ([1844] 1959, p. 81) actually maintained that a persistent reduction in the rate of interest constitutes a diminution of the cost of production, which could not fail, through competition among the producers, to bring about a fall in prices.[23] He went so far as to state that it is difficult to find evidence of facts more in contrast with the influence ascribed to a low rate of interest in raising prices, and vice versa: 'The theory is not only not true', he wrote in 1844, 'but the reverse of the truth' (ibid., p. 84). Strictly connected with the influence ascribed to a low rate of interest in lowering prices (and vice versa) are Tooke's views about money and prices – his main contention being 'that the prices of the commodities do not depend upon the quantity of money . . .; but that, on the contrary, the amount of the circulating medium is the consequence of prices' (ibid., p. 123). It seems, then, that we owe to Tooke's unprejudiced observation of facts the first conception of 'endogenous money' in the history of economic analysis.[24]

But if the idea is agreed upon that commodity prices do not depend on the quantity of money, and a produced money commodity world is not assumed, then the question arises of what determines the price level. My answer is already contained in my explanation of distribution: the price level depends on the level of the money wage (on the socioeconomic and institutional circumstances governing money wages), given the level of the money rate of interest – given the magnitude, that is to say, governing the distribution of income between profits and wages.

6 *The rate of interest and the inducement to invest*

Let me now point out how the conception of the rate of interest as an autonomous determinant of normal profits and normal costs may lead to a view of the influence of the rate of interest on spending decisions that is very different from the commonly received one.

What is ultimately in question when discussing the two connected topics of the relation between money and prices and of the influence of the rate of interest on the price level are the effects of changes in interest rates on the inducement to purchase commodities. Thus Tooke, consistently with his position, criticizes the notion that the facility of borrowing at a low rate of interest not only confers the power of purchasing commodities, but also affords the motive, the inducement to do it. 'The error', he says ([1844] 1959, p. 79), 'is in supposing the disposition or will to be co-extensive with the power.'[25] And Wicksell, for his part, bases both his view of the influence of the loan rate on prices and his criticisms of Tooke's view upon the interest elasticity of the demand for loan capital (see [1898] 1965, ch. 7; and [1906] 1962, pp. 175–208).[26]

Now the notion, sustained here, that the rate of profit moves in sympathy with the rate of interest (through changes in prices relative to money wages) may help to explain the lack of sensitivity of investment decisions to lasting changes in the long-term rate of interest that is pointed out by so many contributions, starting from the famous 'Oxford inquiry' at the end of the 1930s (see Wilson and Andrews, 1951). Let us consider a very simple example, taken from Wicksell ([1898] 1958, p. 79), where capital is committed for an 'infinite period', as in building activity.

Consider a house that, given production techniques and money wages, can be built for 100 million and that brings in 4 million net in rent. At a rate of interest, i, of 4 per cent the capital value of the house will also be 100 million and this kind of investment would just be profitable at $i = 4\%$. Imagine now, always following Wicksell, that i falls to 3%, while a similar house can still be built for 100 millions. Then, according to both Wicksell and Keynes, the purchase of such a house would have become an extremely profitable investment, the capital value (or demand price) of the house having risen to 133 millions – much higher than its supply price. (In the case of Wicksell, since the normal situation of the economy is characterized by the full employment of all productive factors, the increased monetary spending will result in a rise in prices; in the case of Keynes, it could bring about a rise in income and employment.)

The important point here is that both authors' ways of thinking are based on the idea that the rate of return on the real asset in question (more generally, on the existing stock of capital goods) is unaffected by the assumed change in the rate of interest. If instead it is acknowledged that, in the face of a lasting lowering of the rate of interest, competition among firms within the house-letting industry will bring about a lowering of rents,[27] then no increase in building activity (in investment in houses) should be expected as a consequence of a lower rate of interest: the demand price of houses would not increase relative to their supply price. Note that we do not need to say anything about what happens to the level and composition of output: such gravitation of the rates of return toward the level of the money rate of interest, I have repeatedly referred to, is independent of the level and compostion of output, and would occur even if they remained the same. In Keynes, on the other hand, the rates of return on the various types of capital assets will eventually adapt themselves to the new lower level of the money rate, but through increases in the capital stock due to net investments, and the consequent changes in the level and composition of output.[28]

What I have been saying about the role of monetary policy and the rate of interest in determining distribution does not rule out any traditional-type influence of the rate of interest on activity and prices. In considering the influence of the money rate on distribution and the price level, I have always been referring to *lasting* changes in interest rates. The effects of changes of a temporary nature may be altogether different. A lowering of the long-term rate, for example, regarded as temporary is likely to induce an expansion of significant expenditure categories where capital is committed for very long periods, such as house purchases and capital expenditures by state and local governments, thereby exerting a temporary pressure also on the price level. The reason for this expansion can be found, in the light of my theory, in the fact that the corresponding investment projects will tend to be anticipated so as to take advantage of the cheap money situation, which, being regarded as temporary, is not expected to affect their rates of return. If, however, the opinion should spread that low (high) interest rates have come to stay, no positive (negative) impact on such expenditures would occur.[29]

According to my way of thinking, then, the little weight of such factors as depreciation and obsolescence allowances would explain the sensitivity of investment spending on long-lived capital goods (e.g. houses) to *temporary* changes in interest rates. As far as the influence of lasting changes in interest rates is concerned, however, there would be no difference between this kind of investment and investment of machinery and equipment.

Finally, to regard the rate of interest as 'setting the pace' in its connection with the rate of profit has another implication that is worth indicating here. This is that changes in interest rates will tend to be associated with changes in aggregate demand, but by a different route from the one traditionally envisaged. Both the propensity to consume and the inducement to invest, it will be acknowledged, are most likely to be affected by changes in the normal distribution of income between profits and wages. Indeed, *this* is the route by which I envisage the rate of interest influencing the level of output and its composition. The directions of such influence, however, cannot be predicted on the basis of some *a priori* functional link, ultimately because the impact of changes in distribution on the inducement to invest is bound to be different in each different concrete situation, and may go either way. If, for example, a lasting lowering of interest rates is assumed, then, according to my view, there will be a fall in normal profit rates; the negative impact of this fall on the inducement to invest may or may not be counter-balanced by a rise in effective profit rates (i.e. higher utilization rates of existing capacity resulting from the rise in real wages) and/or by investment decisions intended to restore normal profit rates to their former levels by the introduction of new productive processes. But although the weight of all such elements will have to be separately studied in each case – in order to appraise the impact of a change in distribution on activity levels – it can still be concluded, on the basis of the explanation of distribution under discussion, that both the level and composition of output will be affected by changes in money rates of interest.

These considerations hint at the question of the importance of money in long-period analysis of output levels. In traditional long-period analysis – in both the monetarist and the 'neoclassical synthesis' version – the relationship between the rate of interest and the rate of profit (Wicksell's 'natural real rate') does not play any role in the explanation of output levels. The process of gravitation of the money rate towards the normal rate of profit is significant for explaining changes in the price level and/or fluctuations of output around its normal or full-employment level. Money, that is to say, may be important to the gravitation of the economy towards its full-employment output; but money and the money rate of interest do not have any role to play with respect to the full-employment output and to its composition and changes. Things are likely to be very different within the alternative theoretical approach to value and distribution, if the notion that the normal rate of profit is governed by the money rate of interest is well founded. The point, of course, is the significance of income distribution for effective demand: if money plays an important role in determining income distribution, it will also play an important role in the determination of the level and composition of output.

7 *Nominal and real rates of interest*

In discussing the influence of the rate of interest on the rate of profit, I made no distinction between the nominal rate of interest and the real rate – the money rate corrected by reference to any change in the value of money between a loan being advanced and its being repaid. In fact, competition among firms within each industry should tend to cause the rate of profit to move in sympathy with the real rate of interest, rather than with the nominal rate – the former constituting the actual price for the use of capital in production, or its opportunity cost.

The real rate of interest depends on the nominal rate and on the rate of increase in prices: if nominal interest is 20 per cent per annum and the value of money is falling by 20 per cent per annum, the repayment of 120 a year hence in return for 100 loaned today will leave the lender with a sum of the same real value and with zero real interest. For simplicity, let us now make the following assumptions: normal profits of enterprise are absent, so that the rate of profit can be regarded as being strictly determined by the rate of interest; capital employed in production is only circulating capital; a year is the period of turnover of circulating capital in the production of the various commodities; there are no changes in productivity.

If nominal interest is 20 per cent per annum and 100 is the amount of capital (the price of the capital goods) employed in production at the beginning of the year, equalization of the rate of profit with the real rate of interest by competition among firms simply implies that, whatever the change in prices during the year, firms should be left at the end of the year with 120 after having paid wages.[30] The magnitudes of both the real rate of interest and the rate of profit will depend on the change in prices necessary to bring about this result: the higher the rate of increase in prices, the lower will these magnitudes be. Thus, if 10 per cent is the rise in prices necessary to leave firms with 120 after having paid wages, 9 per cent (10/110) would be the rate of profit = the real rate interest; it would be zero with a 20 per cent rise in prices, and 20 per cent if there was no change in prices during the year.

But what does govern the change in prices in the conditions assumed? If equalization of the profit rate with the real interest rate requires that firms be left with '120' after wage payments, then the change in prices will, at first, exclusively reflect the change in money wages: following an increase in money wages, Δw, the nominal rate of interest, r_n, remaining the same, prices would rise at first in a lesser proportion than money wages; the real rate of interest and of profit falls and the real wage rises – the more so, the higher the rate of increase in money wages and the consequent increase in prices. After this first increase, prices would keep on gradually rising year after year till both the prices of all capital goods and profits at the given r_n have risen in the same proportion as money wages. At that point prices would cease to rise, and the real rate r_r would have risen back to r_n – the level at which r_r was before Δw. But throughout the inflationary process following the assumed Δw (i.e. during each of the yearly production cycles making up the whole period of transition to the new equilibrium price level), r_r would have remained below the given r_n.

It seems, then, that as far the influence of wage bargaining on the distribution between wages and profits is concerned, the notion that the rate of profit tends to gravitate towards the real level of the money rate of interest has the following implication: rising money wages, if nominal interest is kept unchanged, tend to result in a temporary redistribution of income in favour of workers.[31] In order to keep distribution constantly unaffected, the nominal rate of interest would have to be varied by reference to any change in the rate of inflation. *Given* a certain (desired) level of r_r – the real rate of interest and of profit – the nominal rate r_n required to validate $\bar{r}_r$ is an increasing function of the rate of inflation, $\frac{\Delta p}{p}$:

$$r_n = \bar{r}_r + (1 + \bar{r}_r)\frac{\Delta p}{p}. \tag{1}$$

This is shown graphically in Figure 15.1.

This relation provides us with a simple short-cut to determining the level of r_n necessary to maintain $\bar{r}_r$ in the face of any rate of increase in money wages, $\frac{\Delta w}{w}$. What one actually wants to know is the level of r_n that, given a new higher level of money wages, will bring about 'at once' the appropriate level of prices. Since, for distribution to remain unchanged, prices must rise in the same proportion as money wages, i.e.

$$\frac{\Delta p}{p} = \frac{\Delta w}{w}, \tag{2}$$

then the nominal rate of interest required to keep a certain pattern of distribution unchanged in the face of any rate of increase in money wages can be obtained from equations (1) and (2).[32]

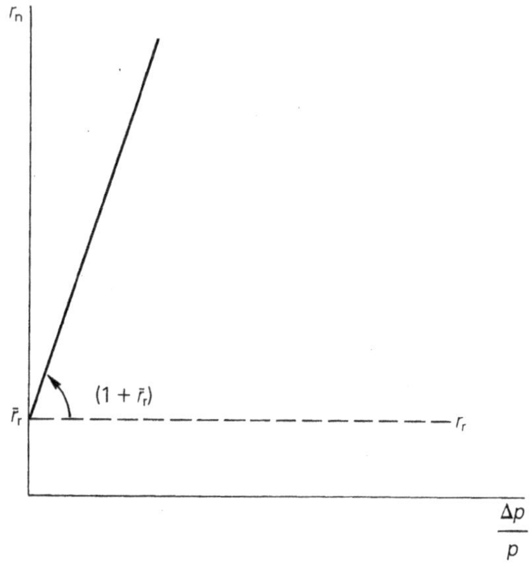

Figure 15.1

Acknowledgements

I should like to thank P. Garegnani and G. De Vivo for helpful suggestions and comments on earlier drafts of this paper. I wish to thank also E. Nell and D. Foley who commented on some of the main propositions developed here, which were contained in the text of a lecture on T. Tooke and K. Wicksell delivered at the second 'International Summer School of Economics' held in Trieste in 1982.

Notes

1 For a reconstruction of the analytical setting of the classical–Marxian approach, see Garegnani (1984), *passim.*

2 Note the difference with respect to Ricardo, who maintains that 'The rate of interest, though *ultimately and permanently* governed by the rate of profit, is however subject to *temporary* variations from other causes' (Ricardo, [1817–21] 1951, p. 297; emphasis added).

3 On this 'monetary' aspect of debt management, see in particular the *Radcliffe Report* (Committee on the Working of the Monetary System, 1959), para. 603.

4 The influence of the country's position *vis-à-vis* the rest of the world in the determination of interest rates must have also been very significant in the days when Great Britain was the dominant capitalist economy. Think of the interest due to Great Britain (as a major lender country) from abroad, and the importance of its level from the point of view both of interest recipients (British firms and citizens) and of Britain's balance of payments. Think also of the dear money policy over a large part of the 1920s, a necessary counterpart of the restoration of

the pound to its pre-war parity with gold. It is worth noting here that in the *Treatise*, at a time when Keynes still regarded Wicksell's 'natural rate of interest' as a very useful and significant concept, the general British-led return to the Gold Standard round about the mid-1920s is referred to as an event 'which served to maintain the market rate of interest somewhat regardless of the underlying realities of the natural rate' (Keynes, [1930] 1965, p. 379); on Keynes's change of view about the significance of the 'natural rate' concept, see Keynes (1936a), pp. 242–4. On the British experience with the restoration of the pre-war parity, see Moggridge (1972), *passim.*

5 Thus Sayers (1964, p. 318), in illustrating the UK government's failure to enforce an 'ultra-cheap' money policy in 1945–7, points out that, 'given market sentiment' as to future prices of government securities, 'creation of bank deposits on an enormous scale would have been necessary for holding the 2½ per cent line: the only alternative was retreat'.

6
> The 'classical' concept of profit related to the incomes derived from the ownership and management of capital by a group of people known as capitalist; . . . Ideally, it was the income of the owner–manager of a firm. If a farmer, manufacturer or merchant employed borrowed funds, his profits were always reckoned gross of the interest that he paid out.
>
> (Tucker, 1960, p. 77)

As for marginalism, in Wicksell's long-period equilibrium the 'normal or natural rate' corresponds to 'the expected yield on the newly created capital', which tends to exceed loan interest ('the money rate') to compensate for 'the risk attached to every productive undertaking' (Wicksell, [1906] 1962, pp. 191, 193).

7 Given the level of the money wage, the change in the price level resulting from a lasting change in the rate of interest would also be necessarily accompanied by a change in relative prices – owing to the different weight of interest in the production costs of the different commodities. It follows that the real wage, whilst rising or falling in terms of any commodity, will rise or fall to a different extent in terms of each different commodity. It is possible, then, to distinguish between two effects on prices of a persistent change in the rate of interest: a change in the price level, and a change in relative prices. Both effects would follow from intra-industrial competition causing the rate of profit to move in sympathy with the predetermined rate of interest.

Given the money wage and production techniques, the so-called 'reduction to dated quantities of labour' – when it can be applied – provides the simplest way to calculate the effects on money prices and on the real wage of changes in the rate of profit brought about by changes in the rate of interest. With the reduction to dated labour terms it can be easily seen, in particular, that reasoning in terms of money prices, for a given level of the money wage, amounts to a reasoning in terms of 'labour commanded' (to a given change in the rate of profit, there will correspond in both cases the same change in relative prices and in the real wage).

8 On the general cheapening of the raising of funds in the capital market by British industry after the inception of cheap money in 1932, see Nevin (1955), ch. VI.

9 Unless one *assumes* situations of full utilization of existing capacity, there appears in fact to be no analytical reason (outside an orthodox approach to value and distribution) why changes in aggregate demand should be associated with changes in distribution; they will rather tend to be associated with changes in output, and, in long-run analysis, also with changes in productive capacity. See in this connection Ciccone's contribution to this volume (ch. 14).

10 It is also necessary not to conceive the normal profit of enterprise as a magnitude given in absolute terms; on this question, see note 15 below.

11 As an important example of one such element one may refer to the illiquidity risk. The additional yield of investment in real assets (such as factories or houses), in relation to gilt-edged securities,

> is a reflection, not mainly of the uncertainty concerning the future level of (say) rents, but of the easy marketability of gilt-edged in relation to house property, which makes it possible for the investor to consider gilt-edged holdings as a form of reserve that can be readily 'switched' into other forms as and when profitable investment opportunities present themselves; this easy marketability is certainly absent in investment in real property (or plant and equipment).
>
> (Kaldor, 1959, p. 288)

Needless to say, different investments in real assets may present very different illiquidity risks, owing to various factors: the higher the degree of specialization of a certain plant or factory, for example, the less 'marketable' the corresponding investment and the higher (given all the other elements of 'risk and trouble') the normal profit of enterprise.

12 The classical conception of the normal excess of profit over interest has little in common with the views one finds in Knight's *Risk, Uncertainty and Profit*. This author distinguishes between 'a measurable uncertainty, or risk proper' and a 'true or unmeasurable uncertainty', and contends that it is the latter that gives rise to 'pure profit' (i.e. the excess of profit over interest) regarded as an aspect of 'the divergence between actual and theoretical competition' (Knight, [1921] 1933, pp. 18–21 and ch. VII). Even more distant from the classical conception is Schumpeter's 'entrepreneurial profit' – a temporary surplus over costs, accruing to the innovating entrepreneur (see Schumpeter, 1934, ch. IV).

13 Natural prices, on the basis of this conception, will have to be such as to ensure that, in each production sphere, what remains of the value of the product, after deducting wages and the replacement of the means of production, is sufficient to 'adequately' remunerate the 'risk and trouble' and pay interest at a uniform rate.

14 Of the two magnitudes into which the normal rate of profit resolves itself, Marx tends to regard profit of enterprise (*Unternehmergewinn*) as the residual one. This arises from the fact that, as we saw on pp. 433–4 above, in Marx's analysis the rate of interest is regarded as a largely autonomous magnitude with respect to the rate of profit. On the differences between the classical economists and Marx in the analysis of the interest–profit relationship, see Pivetti (1983), *passim*.

15 npe_a has been conceived in the text as a magnitude proportional to capital employed in production. This is also the conception of Adam Smith: given the recompense for the risk and trouble in percentage terms, a rise in the 'ordinary rate of profit' will result, in his view, in a rise in the rate of interest, which will consequently account for a larger proportion of the ordinary rate of profit (see Smith, [1776] 1961, vol. 1, p. 109).

But the 'real or fancied advantages' possessed by the various capital employments could also be thought of as tending to resolve themselves in given proportions between interest and normal profits of enterprise (for example: $npe_a = 1/2i$; $npe_b = 3/2i, \ldots, npe_k = 2i; \ldots$). This appears to be Ricardo's conception: from a consideration of those advantages, he refers to given and stable proportions between the normal rates of profit in the various trades (Ricardo, [1817–21] 1951, p. 90). Even this way of interpreting the normal profit of enterprise, however, is compatible with my conception of the rate of interest as the regulator of the ratio of prices to money wages. As was said at the beginning of this section, such a conception requires lasting movements in interest rates not to be associated with contrary movements in normal profits of enterprise as percentages of capital employed.

The possibility of such contrary movements should instead be acknowledged within an interpretation of normal profits of enterprise as magnitudes given in absolute terms. It seems to me very unlikely, however, that a careful review of the main elements of 'risk and trouble' would support a view of the normal excess of profit over interest in any particular trade as an absolute magnitude, independent of the value of capital employed in production; the more so, if one considers that in the conditions of modern capitalism the 'risk' elements covered by the remuneration under discussion largely outweigh the 'trouble' elements of the farmer and manufacturer considered by the classical economists.

16 And when we speak of a necessary rate of profit, what we wish to know is precisely the rate of profit independent of the movements of competition, which in turn regulates competition itself. The average rate of profit sets in when there is an equilibrium among the competing capitalists . . . When this equilibrium is established, why is the general rate of profit now 10, or 20, or 100%? Because of competition? No, on the contrary, competition has eliminated the causes producing deviations from 10, 20, or 100%. . . . The magnitude of this profit itself is independent of competition.

(Marx, [1894] 1977, p. 865)

17 The actual value of the labour-power . . . depends not merely upon the physical, but also upon the historically developed social needs, which become second nature. But in every country, at a given time, this regulating average wage is a given magnitude.

(Marx, [1894] 1977, p. 859).

18 On the basis of Sraffa's price equations (Sraffa, 1960, paras 1–4) it is easy to see that, given the wage in terms of specified necessaries and the methods of production, if there is a surplus product in the economy then the system necessarily determines, together with prices, also a positive general rate of profit, which no competition whatsoever among capitalists can eliminate or change.

19 Indeed, in this lies the fundamental difference with respect to the explanations of industrial profits in terms of the greater or lesser strength of the forces of competition: in the present approach the positive level of profit is explained that, when established, brings to an end any action by competition. For the chief explanations of industrial profits in terms of the strength or weakness of the forces of competition, I refer to those contributed by Kalecki (1943a and 1971b), *passim*; and Steindl (1952), chs 4 (sec. 3), 5 and 7.

20 Already at the end of the 1940s Andrews (1949, p. 24) was maintaining that 'competition is much more important than modern economists tend to recognize'. More recently (Clifton, 1977, pp. 143 *et seq.*), much the same thesis has been maintained on the basis of the growing adherence to reality, in modern capitalism, of the hypothesis of the free mobility of capital.

21 An important case of institutional protection against competition is that provided by patents. Referring however to such legal restrictions on freedom of entry, Andrews observes that 'even when he has a firm patent for a new, indispensable and unique article, the business man's pricing policy will still be affected by the knowledge that some potential competition always exists' (Andrews 1949, p. 173). It may be added that a particularly high profit of enterprise for the period of validity of the patent is ultimately the reward for the 'risk and trouble' of developing and applying new knowledge.

22 This argument does not apply to situations where real wages consist of a specified bundle of consumption goods determined by the workers' necessary subsistence, so that they can be treated 'on the same footing as the fuel for the engines or the feed for the cattle' (Sraffa, 1960, p. 9). Apart from such situations, the conception of the real wage as the given variable – i.e. the idea that class relations tend to act primarily upon the real wage rate – does not raise the above difficulties if a produced money commodity is assumed within a labour theory of value framework: with given methods of production, there would be under such conditions a perfect correspondence between changes in the 'money' wage and changes in the real wage measured in terms of any commodities.

23 Although Tooke does not develop the distribution theory implications of this view of the influence of the rate of interest on prices, it follows from what has been said so far that there is implicit in it a causal relationship between the rate of interest and the rate of profit going from the former to the latter. The significant point is the inclusion of the money rate of interest among the autonomous determinants of normal production costs, together with money wages and production techniques. The ratio of the price level to the money wage then becomes the connecting link between the rate of interest and the rate of profit: a lower rate of interest causes a lowering of that ratio, hence bringing a lower rate of profit.

24 The expression 'endogenous money' is used by Kaldor in his well-known 1970 article, in which he argues that the money supply tends to accommodate itself to the needs of trade. (Other examples of very similar ways of thinking by modern economists can be found in Hinshaw, 1972; see in particular the positions of Harrod and Rueff on the relation between money and prices, pp. 51, 99, 109 and 147.)

The thesis 'that prices are not high or low because much money circulates, but that much or little money circulates because prices are high or low. is expressed by Marx in the *Grundrisse* ([1857–58], 1973, p. 195); it is also present in the chapter on money in *Capital* (vol. 1), but without any reference to Tooke. Marx's debt to Tooke and the Banking School, however, is substantially acknowledged in *A Contribution to the Critique of Political Economy* ([1859] 1978, pp. 185–6); moreover, in a letter to Engels (5 March 1858, a few days after Tooke's death), he refers to Tooke as to 'the last English economist of any value' (Marx, [1858] 1983, p. 284).

25 Tooke is perfectly aware of the important permissive role played by money: given the inducement to purchase commodities, 'given the force of the motive', he writes in the *History of Prices*, 'the extent to which it can be acted upon is doubtless affected as regards persons who can buy only on credit, or who must borrow in order to be able to buy, by the greater or less facility of borrowing' (Tooke, 1840, p. 154).

26 For a criticism of the Friedman School's contention that changes in the money supply have a 'direct effect' on the demand for goods, and not only an 'indirect effect' via the rate of interest, see Kaldor (1970), p. 9n. On the classical economists' views about the sensitivity of aggregate expenditure with respect to the rate of interest, see Caminati (1981), pp. 83–7.

27 A lowering of the long-term rate constitutes a lowering of the normal production costs of residential services, to which their prices (hence rents) will tend to accommodate.

28 For a particularly concise and clear-cut account of this latter way of postulating the relation between the rate of profit and the rate of interest, see Robinson (1938), pp. 80. 81.

29 It may be added that to acknowledge that lasting dear money policies represent,

by themselves, an inflationary factor does not lead to the exclusion of any effect of such policies on prices in the commonly expected direction. Thus, to the extent to which a dear money policy is associated with lasting programmes of credit restrictions, a check on the rise in prices might come about through the negative impact of the restrictions (on the availability of funds, in relation to the demand for them) on activity levels, hence on the level of employment and of money wages.

30 This amounts to saying that, in the presence of inflation and of an unchanged nominal interest rate, firms are led by competition to use in their calculation the 'historical' purchase price (the price of the capital goods at the beginning of each yearly production cycle), rather than the current reproduction prices of capital goods.

31 The redistribution of income need not be just a short-run phenomenon, if, starting from an equilibrium situation with no inflation and $r_r = r_n$, a series of yearly increases in money wages is assumed, instead of a single $\triangle w$. With a given r_n, the yearly increases in money wages could prevent the ratio of prices to money wages from rising back to its starting level.

32 Naturally, rising money wages do not constitute the only circumstance that may result in high nominal interest rates and rates of inflation through the policy aim of maintaining r_r. The process could originate also in rising prices of imported inputs due to devaluation (though the determination of r_n in such a case is more complicated than in the case considered in the text). For example, the very high nominal interest rates and rates of inflation experienced by the Brazilian economy over the 1970s and 1980s might be explained in my theory by a government policy of maintaining r_r in the face of a continuous process of devaluation of the cruzeiro – with the burden of the adjustment falling on real wages. The matter of general interest ultimately is that by manipulating r_n it should be possible, in the face of any initial agent of price changes, to bring about 'at once' the corresponding equilibrium price level, so as to avoid any more or less prolonged change in the real profitability of capital.

Comment

Robert Ciccone
Rome

The last section of Professor Pivetti's paper may at first appear to be somewhat alien, and even contradictory, to the rest of the work. Actually, a close examination reveals that no incongruity necessarily exists between that section and the previous part of the paper. It may be useful, however to indicate some difficulties that in my opinion are possibly encountered in connecting that section with the main body of Pivetti's analysis, and to single out what I believe to be the source of such apparent inconsistencies.

On the basis of the previous part of the paper, one arrives at the last section with one's mind on the *nominal* interest rate – the only notion of interest rate so far met with in the analysis – as the 'independent variable' that governs the ratio of prices to money wages. This clear picture seems to collapse in section 7. On the one hand, although the (nominal) interest rate is assumed to be constant, increases in the money wage rate are here able to affect, temporarily or permanently, income distribution. On the other hand, in the face of increases in the price level the profit rate is said to adjust not to the nominal but to the *real* rate of interest – i.e. the interest rate net of inflation. Thus, a double-sided perplexity arises. First, distribution no longer appears to be governed by the behaviour of the monetary authorities, since it can be directly influenced by wage bargaining. Second, it is not easy to see how the real rate of interest can be substituted for the nominal rate as the relevant 'independent variable', given its obvious dependence on the rate of increase in money prices.

Let us consider the first problem just mentioned – that is, the admitted possibility that rising money wages affect distribution. Since the influence at issue is a *direct* one, it seems to be in conflict with what Pivetti argues in section 5 of his paper. Consistently with his main thesis, he maintains there that wage bargaining can affect distribution only in an indirect way, by influencing the behaviour of the monetary authorities with regard to the level of the interest rate. It is true that in Pivetti's analysis the influence of wage bargaining on distribution is merely temporary, and therefore does not represent a real problem for his long-period argument, if the increase in money wages occurs once and for all. In this case, with a constant nominal interest rate, the price level would progressively increase until the original ratio of prices to money wages had been restored. But, as Pivetti himself notes, wage bargaining can have a permanent influence on distribution if, always with a constant nominal interest rate, money wages increase in each period in response to increases in the price level. This contrasts with the determination of distribution put forward in the rest of the paper. Nor does there seem to be any easy way out of the problem in the following analysis of what change in the nominal rate of interest is needed in order to keep the real interest and profit rates unaffected in the face of a given change in the money wage rate. On the contrary, this may cause further perplexities to the reader, since at first sight the link between the profit rate and the nominal rate of interest seems to have been reversed, with the latter being managed in order to obtain a *given* profit rate.

On closer consideration, however, it is precisely in this final point of the paper – where Pivetti deals with the maintenance of a particular real interest rate through suitable changes in the nominal rate of interest – that one can find the key for a re-examination and solution of most of the apparent incongruities that have been outlined here. The fundamental issue, as I understand it, concerns what, in Pivetti's analysis, the monetary authorities have as a target. What they are assumed to control, *through* the nominal interest rate, is precisely the real rate of interest. Once this qualification is made, what happens (at least over long periods) to that rate, and therefore to the rate of profit, in the face of rising money wages is to be considered a conscious choice of the monetary authorities, in whose hands the determination of distribution ultimately lies.

Obviously, this qualification should also be extended to the previous sections of the paper; indeed, the reader would have been greatly helped if Pivetti had made it clear from the beginning that the focus of his analysis is the real, rather than the nominal, interest rate. Of course, nothing prevents him, in so far this is useful, from assuming constant money wages and prices, so that the nominal and the real rate of interest are numerically equal; still, the qualification should be made explicit. What should be checked, in this regard, is whether the circumstances that in Pivetti's analysis are strongly connected with nominal interest rates (public debt management, the international position of the country), can be more generally related to real interest rates. Furthermore, and I thus come to the second problem mentioned at the beginning of this comment, it should be considered whether the monetary authorities can actually be successful in managing the real rates of interest in the face of an increasing price level – i.e. whether the real rate of interest can be generally taken as the 'independent variable' in the determination of distribution.

Comment

Josef Steindl
Vienna

Professor Pivetti's paper is admirably suited to bring into focus the differences among us between various lines of thinking (tentatively identified as neo-Ricardian as against post-Keynesian or Kaleckian). To go to the heart of the matter, these differences concern the role that we attribute to the actual importance of monopoly elements in our twentieth-century society. A further difference is the question whether we can use equilibrium relations to draw conclusions about the response of the economic system to changes imposed on it.

In certain other respects ideas from the various strands of thought seem to overlap. That the profit rate, and not (as Marx and the classics wanted) the real wage, is subject to prior determination and the share of the wage is left as a residual – the inversion of Marx as it were – is shared also by post-Keynesian writers. It is only when we ask what determines the profit rate that opinions divide. That the determination should come from the rate of interest is an opinion found in Keynes, only, again, the mechanism of the influence is different: with Keynes, the influence would come about in so far as a discrepancy between profit and interest would act on investment. How does this influence of interest on profit work according to Pivetti?

He refers to the equilibrium system of prices of production based on normal cost and a uniform rate of profit, equal to interest. But can these equilibrium relations be used to draw conclusions about a process of adjustment? In actual fact, there is a jumble of capital assets from different periods with different techniques and different costs of output. If there is anything that empirical study can show it is that there are vast differences in costs of production between different firms (not temporary or accidental but systematic!). How can a calculation of normal cost and uniform rate of profit be applied under such circumstances? In fact, new techniques are emerging all the time, upsetting all chance of equilibrium ever being reached, and producers will be modest or ambitious in their profit requirements according to their circumstances. Surely Schumpeter was just a little nearer to the truth when he related profits to these dynamic considerations?

Pivetti has carefully analysed the dilemma that might arise if we assumed an automatic adjustment of profit rate to interest: it would preclude any effect of interest changes on investment. His solution: short-run changes in interest will affect investment, but once they are regarded as permanent the price adjustment occurs and there can be no further effect on quantities. The necessary condition for this 'price effect' is competition – no impediments to free entry and mobility. Pivetti is perfectly aware of the importance of this assumption (pp. 440–2) and he tries very hard to play down these disturbing elements.

While I fundamentally disagree with this attitude I would not at all exclude an influence of interest on the profit rate. As far as the extraordinary high rates of interest in recent years in the US are concerned, one may suspect that they have partly been shifted to prices, otherwise one should have thought the frequency of bankruptcies would have been greater and the effect on investment more pronounced than was actually the case. The motive might have been the common experience of the pressure of debt, and the low real wage and material prices would have favoured the shift.

In the last part of his paper (which is rather hard to follow) Pivetti tries to apply his theory where it would seem to have the least chance of fitting – to the case of inflation. This is a hardy undertaking. One would have thought that in an inflation it would be the profit rate that would pull the interest rate up (by competition between the real and the financial investments) and not the other way round, i.e. the interest pulling the profit rate down. But Pivetti suggests exactly this. He maintains that it is the *real* rate of interest to which profit rate will adjust, because, he says, the real interest is the opportunity cost for the use of capital in production (pp. 447–8). But since the real rate of interest is what the holder of a bond gets *in real terms*, an entrepreneur who equated his profit rate to it would not be able to maintain his capital intact unless he used his profits (provided they were sufficient) for this purpose.

And the reader is further puzzled because on page 448 it is shown that, in order to maintain a certain ('desired') level of the real rate of interest (which equals the rate of profit), the nominal rate of interest has to exceed the real rate by the growth rate of prices (which in his example is equal to the growth rate of money wages). So it appears that the two main actors have changed places and the rate of profit is now acting on the nominal rate of interest! In note 32 this is underlined by reference to circumstances 'that may result in high nominal interest rates and rate of inflation through the policy aim of maintaining r_r' [r_r is the real rate of interest).

This gives me the cue for what I really want to say. The rate of interest is a matter of institutions and of policy. This, at least, is an opinion on which Sraffa and Keynes would have agreed! It is therefore not possible to make sweeping generalizations about the direction of the influence. Whether you can regard interest as an autonomous force unilaterally acting on the profit rate, or whether you have to admit that the influence may work just as well in the opposite direction, depends not on the working of an invisible hand but on the decisions of human policy-makers. These vary according to circumstances, and they are liable to institutional change. Traditional central banking policy would follow the course of the rate of profit, increasing interest in the boom and lowering it in the later phases of the recession. A Keynesian policy-maker might make a more autonomous policy. That is short run, Pivetti would answer. But the long run is not independent of it. And if the policy-maker should by any chance get it into his head to aim, for example, at a long-run stability of the rate of profit, then, exactly in accordance with Pivetti's own demonstration above (pp. 444–8), his interest policy would have to take account of the rate of profit.

Reply

Professor Steindl's critical comments on my paper are centred upon three questions. The first two concern monopoly and the dynamic character of the economy: according to Steindl, the importance of both is denied by the explanation of distribution put forward in my paper. Finally, Steindl criticizes as somewhat puzzling and confusing the formulation of the issue of real vs. nominal interest in the last section of my paper.

Concerning monopoly elements in our twentieth-century society, I certainly share Andrews (1949) view that 'competition is much more important than modern economists tend to realize'. The relevant point, however, is that, contrary to what Steindl says in his comment, the explanation of distribution advanced in my paper does not, in itself, deny the importance of monopoly; rather it tries to furnish a firm basis upon which to study also the possible influence of monopoly elements on the distribution between profits and wages (see section 4). I put forward an explanation of the minimum or necessary long-run level of the rate of profit, assuming, in the first place, competition amongst firms within each sphere of production and free transferability of capital from one sphere to another. The long-term interest rate and the normal remuneration of 'risk and trouble' are regarded as determining, in each sphere of production, the *positive* level of profit that, when established, brings to an end any action by competition. Normal profits having thus been explained, it then becomes possible to realize that any lasting effects on distribution of the conditions of competition may be obtained in only one direction: higher profits than normal. The presence of monopoly elements in this or that sphere of production will translate into a price level/money wage ratio that will be higher than it would be if there were no monopoly elements, and hence into a lower real wage.

This picture is certainly different from the view of those scholars who, like Kalecki and Steindl, tend to identify the circumstances governing distribution with the greater or lesser strength of the forces of competition. Because of this identification, the existence of a positive profit in long-run conditions seems ultimately to be attributed to the circumstance that competition is not sufficiently strong to bring it down to zero (for Steindl's explanation of industrial profits as differential rents, see my citations in note 19).

As for the question of 'the dynamic character of the economy' and its consequences, I confess that it is not clear to me why the fact that 'new techniques are emerging all the time' and the 'existence of a jumble of capital assets from different periods with different techniques and different costs of output' must be denied by the explanation of profits put forward in my paper. On the one hand, the question of the connection between the rate of profit and the money rate of interest – which of the two governs the other – is quite independent of the question of the dynamic character of the economy: if the rate of interest does 'set the pace', as is argued in the paper, then a lasting rise in interest rates will result in a distribution of income more favourable to profits than it would otherwise have been, quite irrespective of the stationary or dynamic character of the economy. On the other hand, economic theory has always considered the notions of normal profits and normal costs to be fully compatible with the fact of vast differences in costs of production between different firms; such differences – more precisely, the employment by different firms of more advanced or more backward techniques than the (ever-changing) dominant (generally accessible) ones – are regarded as a source of discrepancies at any one time between actual and normal profits, the latter being explained *independently* of those differences in costs. Quite on the contrary, Professor Steindl seems to believe that the very existence of profits should be related to differences in costs of production between different firms (so that all profits would disappear if the dynamic circumstances that account for those differences disappear).

Finally, we come to the question of real interest in the last section of my paper. My point is that competition amongst firms within each industry should cause the rate of profit to be governed by the real cost of capital (real interest), which is lower than nominal interest when the rate of inflation is positive. Given then the nominal rate of interest and of profit, the higher the rate of inflation the lower the real rate both of interest and of profit. In the paper, I assume an increase in money wages and tried to argue that in order for the real profitability of capital to remain unaffected, nominal interest must be adjusted upwards – taking into account that any adjustment in nominal interest affects in its turn prices and hence real interest. Thus the problem on which I actually focused my attention was that of finding the level of the nominal rate of interest necessary to leave distribution unaffected in the face of any initial agent of price changes.

According to Steindl, 'it appears that the two main actors have changed places and the rate of profit is now acting on the nominal rate of interest!'. In fact, no such change has occurred: my argument is that there will always exist a value for the nominal rate of interest, such that the prices resulting from the calculation at that nominal rate will keep the real rate at a given (desired) level r_r. One may say with Steindl that in this argument 'the rate of profit is acting on the nominal rate of interest' – but not in the sense that the latter is adjusting to a normal rate of profit that is predetermined by other forces in the economic system (whether these forces are the real wage, competition between firms or the rate of growth of the economy). The notion that normal profit is governed by money interest has amongst its significant implications that, to the extent to which policy-makers possess the power of establishing the level of the money rates of interest, they can influence the distribution of income accordingly – i.e. keep the profitability of capital 'at a given (desired) level'. So my example is intended to show that, by manipulating nominal interest, it should be possible, in the face of any change in money wages, to avoid any more or less prolonged change in the real profitability of capital.

Comment

Luigi L. Pasinetti
Milan

Does Sraffa's *Production of Commodities* contain a specific theory of income distribution? Several authors presenting papers, or participating in discussions, at this conference take it for granted that it does. They attribute to Sraffa the 'theory' that the distribution of income between wages and profits is determined by the forces operating on the money markets, which determine the money rate of interest and hence, through it, the rate of profits.

I should like to express dissent with this view.

My understanding of Sraffa's attitude in *Production of Commodities* (Sraffa, 1960) is that he is concerned with the *foundations* of a theory of income distribution, not with any specific theory that may be laid on those foundations. More specifically, my understanding is that Sraffa is basically concerned with rejecting the marginalist approach to income distribution, which had been prevalent for almost a century, and with going back to the 'standpoint of the old Classical economists', who considered the net product as a surplus that – after deduction of rent – is divided between profits and wages, by forces that operate 'outside the system of production'. This means that either the wage rate or the rate of profit is '"given" before the prices are fixed' (Sraffa, 1960, p. 33). This is the really basic point.

The problem of *which* forces, outside the production system, determine *which* independent variable remains secondary, and is actually open to alternative solutions, each of which may be appropriate to particular historical situations and each of which is perfectly compatible with the classical foundations. Sraffa himself opens his *Production of Commodities* by following the strictly classical 'practice' of considering the wage rate as 'given'. Then he changes over to the rate of profits in chapter V and, on p. 33, concludes the chapter with a section that is worth reproducing in full:

> The last steps of the preceding argument have led us to reverse the practice, followed from the outset, of treating the wage rather than the rate of profits as the independent variable or 'given' quantity.
>
> The choice of the wage as the independent variable in the preliminary stages was due to its being there regarded as consisting of specified necessaries determined by physiological or social conditions which are independent of prices or the rate of profits. But as soon as the possibility of variations in the division of the product is admitted, this consideration loses much of its force. And when the wage is to be regarded as 'given' in terms of a more or less abstract standard, and does not acquire a definite meaning until the prices of commodities are determined, the position is reversed. The rate of profits, as a ratio, has a significance which is independent of any prices, and can well be 'given' before the prices are fixed. It is accordingly susceptible of being determined from outside the system of production, in particular by the level of the money rates of interest.
>
> In the following sections the rate of profits will therefore be treated as the independent variable.

The authors I am criticizing concentrate all their attention on that short phrase 'in particular by the level of the money rates of interest'; and by taking it out of its context, they attribute to it the role of a 'theory' of income distribution. This is what I am objecting to.

It seems clear to me that, if one reads the whole section, this half-line phrase could not be taken as a 'theory' of income distribution, to the exclusion of others. The short phrase is purely incidental: it begins 'in particular', an expression that seems to suggest that 'in general' it is not so. The phrase, moreover, remains entirely isolated. Sraffa does not take it up anywhere else in the whole book – not even in the Index. We know that Sraffa devoted great care to the compilation of the indexes of his works. But we find no entry for 'rate of interest' in the Index of *Production of Commodities*. We do not even find the term 'rate of interest'. Still more importantly, there *is* an entry in the Index that refers to the arguments of p. 33. This entry is under 'rate of profits'. It reads: 'rate of profits . . . as independent variable, p. 33'. Sraffa does *not* add: 'rate of profits . . . as determined by the level of the money rates of interest', as he surely would have done had he attributed any, even slight, importance to that incidental phrase. We must therefore take what he writes at face value. The substance of the arguments on p. 33 is that he is taking the rate of profits as the independent variable.

The curiosity may remain as to why Sraffa should have introduced that incidental phrase at all. On this, one can only speculate. To me that incidental phrase sounds like an aside. If one considers that this part of the book was developed in the 1930s, it may well have been a concession to Keynes's liquidity preference theory, which Sraffa must have discussed at length – the meaning being that Keynes's theory of the rate of interest is, after all, not incompatible with his theoretical framework. This is perfectly in line with the interpretation given above. One might then ask why, by the same token, Sraffa did not make a similar concession, in the 1950s, to Joan Robinson and Nicholas Kaldor, by adding, for example, at the end of the same incidental phrase 'or by the rate of growth of the economic system'. Slight reflection immediately reveals, however, that Sraffa could not do that. He would have gone beyond his initial assumptions of taking the physical quantities as given.

Postscript

A few lines to eliminate a possible misunderstanding. I have no objections to the development of a theory of rate-of-profit determination based on the working of monetary markets. My objection is to presenting such a theory as Sraffa's theory of income distribution. Sraffa explicitly mentions at least another (alternative) way of closing the distribution degree of freedom in his model, namely exogenous determination of the wage rate. I have mentioned a third one (i.e. Kaldor's rate-of-profit determination through the rate of growth). The relevant point I want to stress is that each one of these three ways (but of course not all of them, or any two of them, at the same time: they are *alternative*) is *compatible* with Sraffa's system, in striking contrast with marginal productivity theory, which is incompatible.

Reply

In his Comment on Sraffa and the theory of income distribution, Professor Pasinetti criticizes 'several authors presenting papers at this conference' for not understanding that Sraffa's *Production of Commodities* is concerned with the *foundations* of a theory of distribution, rather than with any specific theory that may be laid on those foundations. As the author of a paper on the 'monetary explanation' of distribution, I would like to observe, first of all, that it is precisely because Sraffa's book does not contain an explanation of the forces actually governing the division of income that one may feel a need to try to develop such an explanation on the classical foundations that Sraffa reinforced.

The passage in which Sraffa explains why he is reversing the classical practice and is taking the rate of profit as the independent variable in the relationship between profits and wages certainly does not constitute a 'theory' of income distribution; it *suggests* a specific direction in which to develop a theory of distribution.

If one considers the problem of *which* forces, 'outside the system of production', determine *which* independent variable to be an important problem, then two courses of action seem open in the face of Sraffa's suggestion.

A first course is to take it seriously and see if a full explanation of income distribution between profits and wages can be developed from it that is both coherent and supported by reality. Empirical support is in fact what will lead one to take Sraffa's suggestion seriously in the first place. It here means that actual experience should present elements capable of showing an autonomous or 'prior' determination of the money rate of interest – i.e. that interest rate policy, both in the short and in the long run, does not appear to be constrained by a somehow predetermined normal profitablility of capital.

The second course is that followed by Pasinetti: the passage stating that the rate of profit is susceptible of being determined by the money rate of interest is no more then a 'purely incidental phrase' – 'an aside', to which its author surely did not attribute 'any, even slight, importance', and at the end of which he might perfectly well have added 'or by the rate of growth of the economic system', were it not for 'his initial assumptions of taking the physical quantities as given'.

I find it hard to believe in such a casual and easy attitude on Sraffa's part on the question of the forces actually governing the division of income. Following Pasinetti's own invitation, let us 'take what he writes at face value'. Sraffa write that the rate of profit is 'susceptible of being determined from outside the system of production, in particular by the level of the money rates of interest.' This points to a concept of the rate of interest as a magnitude governed by circumstances that have nothing to do with a pre-determined normal profitability of capital – i.e. as a 'monetary phenomenon', to use Keynes's expression. Such a concept of the rate of interest is clearly incompatible with the idea that the normal rate of profit is determined by the rate of growth of the economic system, unless one is prepared to deny any long-run connection between the rate of interest and the rate of profit. With that concept of interest in mind, therefore, Sraffa could not make that 'concession to Joan Robinson and Nicholas Kaldor', quite independently of his assumptions concerning the physical quantities. It may be added that it would have required a huge amount of good-will on the part of the reader to regard a rate of profit determined by the rate of growth of the economic system as a magnitude 'determined from outside the system of production', which can be taken as '"given" before the prices are fixed'.

Pasinetti appears also to believe that the problem of which forces determine which independent variable in the present reality of the capitalist economy is, after all, secondary. I take it, on the contrary, to be crucial for a thorough understanding of the functioning of the system, as is shown by the discussion in my paper of some implications of the theory that can be developed on Sraffa's suggestion. Indeed, if well founded, the notion that the money rates of interest govern the ratio of prices to money wages must lead one to hold very different views from the commonly accepted ones on such questions as the influence of wage bargaining on distribution; the influence of the rate of interest on the price level and on the inducement to invest; and the impact of money (and monetary factors) on physical quantities.

ROUND TABLE 2

Development and Policy

16

Some Remarks on the Relevance of Sraffa's Analysis for Economic Policy

Alessandro Roncaglia
Rome

There are three routes by which theory exerts its influence over economic policy: (i) by the development of new analytical tools or results, which throw new light on the interpretation of economic reality, and suggest new ways of dealing with economic policy problems; (ii) by the critique of old theories, since this may imply discarding old analytical tools or results as being misleading in interpreting economic reality or in suggesting solutions for economic policy problems; (iii) by the proposal of a shift in the research programme, suggesting a new way of looking at economic problems, and possibly giving rise to the very development of new analytical tools and results for specific fields of inquiry referred to in (i) above.

Here I shall consider these three aspects (respectively in sections 1, 3 and 4) with respect to Sraffa's analysis. My contention is that there is a danger of overestimating the first and underestimating the second and, especially, the third aspect. These last two aspects are respectively connected with the critical side and the constructive side of the 'Sraffian revolution', briefly discussed in section 2. The conclusion will be that Sraffa's analysis could have a decisive impact on economic policy, if considered as a basic contribution to the reconstruction of the classical approach.

1

Three analytical tools developed in Sraffa's 1960 book are generally considered relevant from the point of view of economic policy: the basic–non-basic dichotomy, the wage-profit relationship, and the subsystem. Some other aspects of Sraffa's analysis were also attributed, more doubtfully, direct relevance for applied economics: the prices of production for economic planning, the standard commodity and the standard system for economic growth.[1]

Basic–non-basic dichotomy
Sraffa (1960, p. 7) defines basics as commodities that enter directly or indirectly as means of production in all processes of production, while non-basics are commodities that do not serve as means of production or that are used, directly or indirectly, in the production of non-basics only. This distinction has often been related to the classical distinction between 'necessaries' and 'luxuries', mainly used for the analysis of tax incidence. A tax on 'necessaries' has general repercussions – bringing about a general increase in prices according to Smith, and a fall in the general rate of profits according to Ricardo; a tax on luxuries, in contrast, would increase only the price of those goods actually taxed (Smith [1776] 1976, pp. 869ff., Ricardo [1815] 1951). Analogously for sectoral technical change: again, a technical improvement in the production of necessaries has a general impact, while the impact of a technical improvement in the production of luxuries is limited to their prices.

Smith ([1776] 1976) and Ricardo in *Essay on Profits* ([1815] 1951] consider 'necessaries' as equivalent to 'wage goods'. Under Malthus's criticism, Ricardo moves on (in his *Principles*, [1817–21] 1951) to consider as 'necessaries' also the commodities required for the production of wage goods. In Torrens's 1821 *Essay* there are two distinct necessary commodities, agricultural product and manufacturing product, each of which is in fact an aggregate of heterogeneous goods required as an input both in its own production and in the production of the other composite commodity, either directly as means of production or indirectly as a wage good.[2] Hence originally the distinction between necessaries and luxuries was founded on the central role of workers (considered in fact as the only real basic commodity, directly required in all processes of production) and on their subsistence requirements. Later on, 'technologically basic status' becomes relevant, side by side with subsistence requirements. Finally, in Sraffa's analysis 'technologically basic status' remains alone at the centre of the stage; more precisely, this happens as soon as Sraffa assumes that the wage rate includes a non-subsistence element, so that workers participate in the distribution of the surplus (Sraffa, 1960, p. 9ff).[3]

Accepting Sraffa's definition, wage goods become non-basics:[4] a change in their methods of production or a specific tax levied on them do not affect the rate of profits or the whole system of relative prices (when we use a basic commodity as our unit of measure). However, the whole system of relative prices is affected when the change in the price of the specific wage good provokes a change in the wage rate, so that there is a shift along the wage–profit curve. Thus, using a basic commodity as the unit of measure, we reach a tripartite classification:

(a) *'technological' basics* (like steel or oil) – a change in their conditions of production implies a shift of the whole wage–profit curve, and a change in the whole system of relative prices;
(b) *wage goods* (like milk, corn and bread, meat, cows, etc.)[5] – a change in their conditions of production does not provoke a shift of the wage–profit curve, but may lead to a movement along the curve, which in turn affects the whole system of relative prices;

(c) *luxury goods* (such as racehorses, sailing boats, jewels, etc.) and the goods required for their production that do not already belong to the previous two groups – a change in the conditions of production of any of these goods does not affect the wage–profit relationship and the whole system of relative prices, but affects only the price of the specific commodity involved or of 'related' luxuries.

This tripartition is subtler than the classical dichotomy, and is more relevant in present-day conditions when the money wage rate cannot be considered as dependent on (equal to) the price of any specific set of wage goods;[6] while its use is the same as that of the classical dichotomy – for an analysis of the effects of taxes levied on specific goods, or of sectoral technical change, or of sectoral differences in market forms.

However, the fact that Sraffa's (1960) analysis refers to an economic system *at a point in time* (in the sense specified later, in section 4) should be kept in mind, calling as it does for a great deal of caution when one applies the tripartite classification in practice. For example, technical change may imply the introduction of new basic commodities (say, computers), which are non-basics when they are first produced; while old basic commodities may lose their relevance and become non-basics (say, coal). Moreover, since the transition from the old to the new technology takes time, we will have commodities 'in transition' from basic to non-basic status, or the other way round. Since concrete policy issues involve consideration of historical time, these aspects cannot be ignored. Yet the need for caution should not be exaggerated: for most purposes, the tripartition examined above remains useful, though not as clear-cut as we might wish.

Wage–profit relationship

This analytical tool has been used for two purposes: for stressing the role of class conflict in income distribution, and for the analysis of technical change.

With respect to class conflict over income distribution, what is relevant is not so much the inverse relationship connecting the wage rate to the rate of profits, which is accepted by marginalist economists as well.[7] The relevance of Sraffa's analysis lies rather in the critique of the marginalist traditional conception of distributive variables as 'scarcity prices' of the so-called 'factors of production', capital and labour. According to that conception, only one specific point on the wage–profit frontier would represent an equilibrium position:[8] market forces would solve the distributive conflict by pushing the economic system towards those values of the distributive variables that correspond to full employment of both capital and labour. The critique of this conception opens the way to an interpretation of the wage rate as 'the independent variable' (Napoleoni, 1963, p. 170), implying a degree of freedom for trade unions' wage bargaining policy. In Italy 'the wage as the independent variable' became a widely accepted slogan, often used in newspaper articles and in political speeches, as implying theoretical support for trade unions' increased combativeness.[9]

The wage–profit curve has also been used for distinguishing various concepts of 'neutrality' of technical change.[10] Empirical analysis of historical tendencies has also been attempted, but the difficulties due to the lack of data necessary for the computation of actual wage–profit frontiers have only been circumvented in a rather careless way.[11]

Subsystem

Sraffa's subsystems (Sraffa, 1960, Appendix A, p. 89) are artificial 'miniature systems' that may be derived from the economic system under consideration, for any commodity included in the net product, so as to obtain 'a smaller self-replacing system the net product of which consists of only one kind of commodity'. Thus subsystems take into account the whole set of productive activities directly and indirectly used for obtaining each commodity or any given net product.

The subsystem methodology has been developed by Pasinetti's notion of 'vertically integrated sectors', in such a way as to allow its use for analyses of the production and employment structure of contemporary economies. Thus Momigliano and Siniscalco (1982, 1984) used it to analyse the factors explaining the increase in the share of services in national income and employment, and the R&D content of Italian foreign trade. This line of analysis, focusing as it does on the production interrelations connecting the different sectors of the economy, promises to be a very fruitful one.

Some authors (e.g. Mathur 1963, 1965; Sinha, 1974; Finoia, 1979) also consider the prices of production and/or the distinction between basics and non-basics as directly relevant for planned economies. Dobb (1969, ch. 8) and Abdel-Fadil (1975) also discuss this point. However, there is no reason to consider the prices of production to be the optimal solution for price planning. The use of prices of production as exchange ratios in a centrally planned economy, where means of production are owned by the state, simply implies that all industries receive from the sale of their products an amount of finance proportional to the value of their means of production, so that all industries can grow at the same pace, with investments wholly financed from internal sources. However, in a changing environment (different sectoral rates of technical progress, changes in the structure of consumption, whether resulting from changes in preferences or from 'Engel curve effects') proportional growth need not be the optimal solution. Moreover, proportional growth may be compatible with exchange ratios different from prices of production, when external sources of finance are considered. (These elements do not constitute objections to Levine's provocative proposal to use Sraffa's analysis as a basis for prices and incomes policy, using vectors of sectoral wage and profit rates: see Levine, 1983.)

Sraffa's standard commodity and standard system were also attributed empirical relevance (for example, by Mathur, 1962, p. 128n; Steenge, 1980) in the analysis of economic growth. As we know, Sraffa's standard commodity is a composite commodity having the property that its means of production are but a given quantity of this same composite commodity, so that the maximum profit rate (and the profit rate corresponding to each wage rate, when the wage rate is measured in terms of the standard commodity itself) can be obtained as ratios of physical quantities. Both the standard commodity and the standard system (the production system that produces the standard commodity) are hypothetical constructs, with purely analytical value. Since the wage rate is neither paid nor consumed in terms of the standard commodity, it cannot be used as an 'invariant standard of measure' in any concrete problem. Moreover, the standard commodity should not be confused with any sort of 'average' for actual economic systems, such as the Marxian 'average commodity' produced by a sector with an average 'organic composition of capital'.

The formal similarity between the standard system and von Neumann's (1945–46) system might suggest some use of Sraffa's analysis for price planning in the context of proportional growth (i.e. when the 'turnpike theorem' applies and the system is made to grow along the 'von Neumann ray'). However, this use of the standard system implies the assumptions of a given and unchanged technology and of constant returns to scale; while, on the contrary, Sraffa concentrates his analysis on a given moment of time, thus avoiding the need for any assumption on technological change over time or on returns to scale. Furthermore the status of non-basic wage goods is different in Sraffa's analysis in comparison to von Neumann's (Roncaglia, 1978, pp. 59–61). In short, both the standard commodity and the standard system appear to have very little application in dealing with concrete problems of applied economics. In fact, the idea of proportional growth in a given technological environment may actually be misleading when applied to development policy issues; see, for example, Hirshman's (1958) well-argued case in favour of non-proportional growth.

In summary, Sraffa's (1960) analysis provides analytical tools that may have *some* relevance for applied policy problems, but a great deal of caution is necessary in order to avoid misusing them. The fact that Sraffa's analysis refers to a given moment in time, thus avoiding the need for assumptions on technical change and returns to scale, strongly limit its *direct* use for policy issues, which necessarily involve consideration of changes (or potential changes) of an economy over time.

2

This rather negative conclusion, however, should not be considered as a conclusive statement on the relevance of Sraffa's analysis for economic policy. As I shall try to argue, Sraffa's analysis is in fact *very* relevant, but in a *more general* and *indirect* way. It is relevant because it provides the background for a drastic shift in the 'research programme' of economic science – away from the dominant marginalist approach towards the so-called surplus approach rooted in the classical tradition.

A number of papers at the conference dealt with the nature of this shift (for my own interpretation, see Roncaglia, 1978 or 1983). Let me summarize here the main characteristics of the marginalist tradition that Sraffa criticizes and of the classical tradition that Sraffa re-proposes. This kind of dichotomy implies drastic simplifications, which become apparent when we try to apply it to specific authors; however, it is useful in recalling the presence of some conception of the main forces at work in economic reality lying behind any specific theory. In fact, models expressing the relationships connecting specific groups of variables cannot *prove* that the forces under consideration are the most important ones, but rather serve to express the implications of our selection of such forces. Even if this selection cannot be evaluated on the basis of the logical consistency of the models alone, economists should be as explicit as possible about their conception of economic reality – namely about the selection of the most relevant forces active in reality, to be captured and expressed in analytical models, and about the reasons justifying this selection.

In this vein Sraffa (1960, p. 93) points to the 'striking contrast' between the classical 'picture of the system of production and consumption as a circular process' and the marginalist 'view . . . of a one-way avenue that leads from "Factors of production" to "Consumption goods"'. Here Sraffa hints at a difference in the basic conception of the economy, which is reflected in a basic difference concerning the choice of the data and the variables to be explained in the area of value theory, commonly regarded as the foundation for other aspects of economic analysis. On the one side, classical economists do not commonly consider as an analytical necessity the simultaneous determination of relative prices, relative activity levels and income distribution. Thus the analytical relationship between 'natural' prices and income distribution, expressing the conditions allowing for the 'regular' repetition of the production process, can be determined on the basis of the technology corresponding to a given set of activity levels. On the other side, marginalist economists search for equilibrium prices and quantities stemming from the confrontation of initial resources endowments (which in some models – mainly the so-called temporary equilibrium models – include produced means of production side by side with primary inputs) and economic agents' preferences (generally mediated not only through exchange, but also through production).

A related difference concerns the problem of income distribution. In the classical approach, distributive variables – wage and profit rates – are determined not through the equilibrium condition between supply of and demand for 'factors of production', but instead through a process of haggling and fighting for a larger share by each group, so that the analysis of distribution involves socio-political aspects alongside the purely economic ones. Rather than locating an 'equilibrium' point on the wage–profit frontier for any given set of conditions, we should assume as given the levels reached at some moment in time by the distributive variables, and then look at how and why these variables move over time (see Roncaglia, 1986a).

Sraffa's (1960) analysis is framed in such a way as to provide both an internal criticism of the traditional marginalist theories of value and distribution based on the notion of 'capital' as a 'factor of production', and a solution to the problem of the relationship connecting relative prices and income distribution, which classical economists had been unable to solve. Thus Sraffa (1960, p. v) points out that his analysis of prices and distribution (leaving aside the problem of the choice of techniques, as treated in Part III of the book) does not require any specific assumption about returns to scale, though 'anyone accustomed to think in terms of the equilibrium of demand and supply [i.e. any economist trained in the marginalist tradition] may be inclined . . . to suppose that the argument rests on a tacit assumption of constant returns in all industries'. In other words, if we *introduce* some additional elements – such as the assumption of constant returns to scale and the assumption of equality between endowments and demand of 'factors of production' – *into* Sraffa's formal analysis, we can consider it as a special case of general equilibrium analysis. We can then attribute general relevance to the criticism, drawn from this special case, concerning the internal inconsistency of some basic tenets of the traditional marginalist theory of value and distribution when it is considered as directly applicable to a multi-commodity world or as a simplified 'parable' providing the same results as the more complex 'general' analysis. However, as Sraffa points out – both in the Preface and, more explicitly, in Appendix D of his book – his analysis stems from the classical tradition.

3

The marginalist approach that Sraffa criticizes interprets economic reality through the idea of the market as a self-regulatory automatic mechanism that provides solutions to the problem of allocating scarce resources among alternative uses. From this idea the marginalist tradition derived specific theories asserting, under perfect competition, the tendency of distributive variables to an equilibrium level, which expresses the relative scarcity of the so-called factors of production in comparison to final consumers' needs and desires, and implies full utilization of the factors of production and, specifically, full employment of the available labour force. These theories had obvious policy implications, such as that the existence of trade unions pressing for real wage rates higher than the equilibrium level causes unemployment. These policy implications have been refuted, together with the underlying theory, on the basis of Sraffa's analysis. It would be very difficult to exaggerate the relevance of Sraffa's analysis for economic policy in this respect.[12]

Marginalist theories and their policy implications have been refuted by means of Sraffa's analysis in other, more specific, fields of enquiry. Most relevant among these is the theory of international trade, where Heckscher–Ohlin–Samuelson (HOS) theorems affirmed a tendency of each country to specialize in the production of those goods and/or in the use of those techniques that require relatively larger amounts of the factors of production relatively more abundant in those countries. Those theorems were refuted in the 1970s utilizing the Sraffian analysis of prices of production (see, for example, Parrinello, 1970, and the essays collected in Steedman, 1977b, 1979b).[13]

4

In his 1960 book, Sraffa isolates *in vacuo* a specific problem, that of the relation between relative prices and distributive variables, and considers only the factors that are directly relevant to the problem being examined. The levels of production of the various sectors are among the data of the problem, so that the analysis concerns the 'photograph' of an economic system at a given moment of its development. The specific problem considered is thus isolated from the other traditional problems of economic theory, such as those concerning the decisions regarding the levels of production, the sale of the amounts produced, technological change, and so on. We might interpret it as suggesting that these problems are better tackled separately (even if not along completely independent lines), on the basis of different sets of assumptions and possibly also with different analytical instruments.

This opens the way to an approach to policy problems that is more complex but more open than that stemming from the traditional marginalist approach, where each problem is subjected to translation in terms of maximization (or minimization) under constraint. Here I shall discuss this 'classical' approach to policy issues in very general terms, referring to what we might call 'main lines of causality', namely the identification of links between economic variables, which allow us to locate actions conducive to certain policy objectives.[14]

In discussing this aspect, I need to stress the purely analytical role that should be attributed to what Garegnani (1984) calls the 'core' of the classical system, namely the relationship between relative prices and income distribution, assuming technology, the level and composition of output, and (assuming a uniform wage rate and rate of profits) one distributive variable as exogenously given: analytical representations of other aspects of economic reality must be consistent with it – at least conceptually.[15] This 'analytical core', however, cannot be used as a justification, even less as a *proof*, of a main line of causality in the development of an economic system going *from* any specific group of variables *to* any other specific group of variables – say, from income distribution to technical choice. Nor should the analytical importance of the 'core' suggest that problems other than the relationship between relative prices and distributive variables should be tackled by *starting from* the core and enlarging on it.

Even as far as prices are concerned, we should be careful not to interpret in too strict a way the idea that technology and distribution 'determine' relative prices. Prices of production provide 'only' the theoretical representation of the main forces affecting, in a systematic way, the exchange relationships between sectors, *at a point in time* (i.e. given the productive structure of the economic system under consideration). This in itself does not necessarily imply a 'gravitation' *over time* of market (actual) prices towards sufficiently stable natural prices.[16]

The reconstruction of the analytical foundations of classical political economy accomplished by Sraffa provides a connected 'vision' within which specific 'pieces' of non-neoclassical analysis may find their place. The classical tradition provides a rich crop of such analyses; moreover, widespread dissatisfaction with the concrete implications of the various specific parts of neoclassical theory (from employment theory to the theory of international trade, from distribution to market forms, and so on) provides a rich crop of specific non-neoclassical analyses in contemporary economics, even if not directly connected to the classical tradition.[17] If we accept the idea of different kinds (or 'levels') of analysis for dealing with different aspects of economic reality, provided that there is conceptual consistency with a basic general view of the functioning of the economic system, there is a large wealth of analyses of specific issues compatible with the classical approach, even if often framed in marginalist terminology. (I am not assuming that the economists quoted in note 17, or others who might have been quoted there, are 'Sraffians' without knowing it; I am assuming only that we can *use* their analyses, perhaps with slight modifications, within the framework of the classical approach re-proposed by Sraffa.)

Moreover, the classical tradition is rich in suggestions concerning important economic issues that were largely lost from sight in the period of dominance of the marginalist approach. In this respect, we may recall briefly what is perhaps the main line of causality of the classical tradition, which centres around the study of the wealth of nations and its development. This line of causality goes from the developments in the division of labour (or, in a less general sense, from technological change), to changes in market forms and in power relationships within society, and hence to distribution and prices. It was dominant in classical authors such as Smith and Babbage, and was also central in the Marxian vision of the 'laws of motion' of the capitalist system; while it appears in contrast to the line of causality implicit in the marginalist approach criticized by Sraffa, which goes *from* original endowments of resources and consumers' preferences *to* prices and technical choice. Turning away from the marginalist approach and towards the classical approach as proposed by Sraffa brings this line of causality back to the fore (see Sylos Labini, 1984a; Roncaglia, 1986b).

(I might add that the somewhat sparse applied work stemming directly from Sraffa's analysis is perhaps due to the fact that attention has been concentrated on what Garegnani calls the 'core' of classical analysis, to the detriment of other lines of causality prominent in the writings of classical economists and of contemporary economists working along classical lines though not referring directly to Sraffa's analysis.)

5 *Conclusion*

My rather impressionistic survey of works related to Sraffa's *Production of Commodities by Means of Commodities* and bearing on economic policy issues has been based on the following (i) tripartition: application of the analytical tools developed by Sraffa to specific economic policy issues; (ii) implications of the Sraffian criticisms of traditional marginalist theories of value and distribution; (iii) implications of the Sraffian reconstruction of the classical approach. Each of these headings – as well as each of the specific economic policy issues touched on in each case – would deserve separate detailed consideration. However, my purpose here was simply to suggest that the relevance of Sraffa's analysis for economic policy lies not so much in the specific analytical tools developed in his 1960 book (since great caution is required for their use outside Sraffa's specific field of enquiry), as in his contribution to a shift in the research programme from the marginalist approach to the classical one. It has been suggested that such a shift may have deep implications for the whole range of economic policy issues, taking the ground from under traditional marginalist replies and offering new foundations for a fruitful reappraisal of lines of enquiry stemming from the classical vision of the economy.

Acknowledgements

For comments on a previous draft, thanks (but no implication) are due to M. Amendola, P. Garegnani, J. Kregel, D. Siniscalco, L. Spaventa, M. Tonveronachi and especially I. Steedman.

Notes

1 Economists trained in the neo-classical tradition are often better acquainted with Sraffa's (1926) contribution to the theory of imperfect competition than with the analytics of Sraffa's (1960) book. However very early – around 1928 – Sraffa took a fully negative attitude towards the development of a theory of imperfect competition within a Marshallian conceptual and analytical apparatus. In fact, Sraffa rejects the very idea of a functional relationship connecting costs to quantity produced, which is *the* architrave of the neoclassical analysis of the firm – and thus of the theory of product supply and input demand, and all that flows from this – so that Sraffa's attitude in this respect has an obvious negative impact on the still widely accepted neoclassical theory of the firm (on this see Roncaglia, 1978, ch. 1, and 1983).

2 Torrens (1821, pp. 43–5) also suggests that the distinction between 'necessaries' and 'luxuries' is helpful for analysing the impact on prices of non-competitive market situations.

3 Sraffa's first two systems (Sraffa, 1960, pp. 3–5 and 6–8), in which workers' subsistence is included among the required means of production and the wage rate is limited to the subsistence level, are equivalent to the second classical position, in which 'necessaries' – or 'basics', in Sraffa's terminology – include wage goods and the commodities directly or indirectly necessary to their production.

4 Except for wage goods that are also 'technologically' basics.

5 This second group also includes all commodites that are directly or indirectly required for the production of wage goods and that are not already included in the first group.

6 However, when money wage rates are 100 per cent indexed to the money prices of a specific basket of wage goods, these goods are equivalent to classical 'necessaries'. The wage can then be considered as fixed in real terms at the subsistence level, and workers' subsistence can be included among the required means of production in place of labour requirements (see note 3 above).

7 Furthermore, under joint production the wage–profit curve may exhibit 'bumps', i.e. intervals in which both the wage rate and the rate of profits may move in the same direction.

8 On multiple equilibria, see note 12 below.

9 However, Sraffa's analysis is based on the assumption of given levels of output, which has to be abandoned when we consider the effects on employment of

changes in the real wage rate. Even discarding the traditional neoclassical mechanism of substitution of capital for labour, changes in the real wage rate affect employment through their (Keynesian) effects on entrepreneurs' expectations and expenditure and production decisions (and, in open economies, through international competitiveness). The possibility of feedback effects on the wage rate must then be recognized. These elements, though recognized by Napoleoni, were often lost from sight in the ensuing political debate.

10 See, for example, Montani (1975), Schefold (1976a, 1979), Varri (1982). These analyses should be compared with those conducted along traditional lines, such as Hahn and Matthews (1964).

11 For example, Marzi and Varri (1977) and Krelle (1977), seem to be unaware of the fact that the actual shape of wage–profit frontiers depends on sectoral ratios of fixed to variable capital, on the life expectancy of each specific capital good, and on the length of the period of production (generally different from one sector to another). Leontief (1984) takes account of fixed capital goods, but not of sectoral differences in the period of production (and refers to a modified version of his input–output analysis rather than to Sraffian wage–profit frontiers directly, though the analytical resemblance is striking).

12 For an account of the debates centred on the criticism of the marginalist theory of value and distribution, see Harcourt (1972). On their implications for employment theory, see Roncaglia and Tonveronachi (1983).

Modern general equilibrium theory (see, for example, Hahn, 1982c) admits the possibility of multiple equilibria, of underemployment equilibria, or of unstable equilibria. However, even when admitted, these cases have often been downplayed (as a 'curiosum') by marginalist economists, especially prior to the capital theory debates of the 1960s stemming from Sraffa's contribution. Yet, statements referring to 'the' Walrasian full-employment equilibrium still abound in the literature: see, for example, Friedman (1970) or the rational expectations models of the new classical macroeconomics. (The shift to the 'natural rate of unemployment' notion does not imply a change in the basic theoretical structure.)

In fact, when Hahn criticizes Friedman and new classical macroeconomics for their appeal to general equilibrium theory as the basis for the uniqueness of full-employment equilibrium, he is, as it were, affected by the spirit of the Cambridge debates, joining forces with the critical tradition stemming from Sraffa's analysis. In this respect, it should be noted that, unlike Sraffa, Hahn does not accompany his critiques with the proposal of a positive approach, alternative to the marginalist one, for the analysis of concrete economic policy issues. (In fact, Hahn himself often recognizes the sterility of general equilibrium theory, recalling among other things the difficulty of considering the case of increasing returns to scale.)

13 HOS theorems with multi-commodity, multi-factor models could not be used as an adequate reply to these criticisms, because of the possibility that then arises of multiple equilibria, instability, etc., even more than because of the difficulty of finding adequate data.

14 Thus I shall not discuss specific instances of analysis of concrete policy problems conducted within the framework of the classical approach. Some examples are Garegnani's analysis of the development problem of Southern Italy (Garegnani, 1962), or Schefold's analyses of ecological problems and the energy issue (Schefold, 1977, 1983), or my own analysis of the international oil market (Roncaglia, 1985). Bose (1975) also uses Sraffa's 1960 contribution as a starting point for his analysis of different modes of production – perhaps with insufficient caution as to the limits of this procedure. Much applied work, though not

directly referring to Sraffa, is clearly embedded in the classical tradition. A few examples: Kalecki's analysis of the political aspects of full employment (Kalecki, 1943b), Goodwin's analysis of the trade cycle (Goodwin, 1967), Bharadwaj's analyses of the Indian economy (Bharadwaj, 1974, 1979), Sylos Labini's analyses of oligopoly and social classes (Sylos Labini, [1956] 1962 and 1974).

15 Formal consistency is required only when two different problems are analysed 'at the same analytical level'. When the 'analytical level' most appropriate to the analysis of each problem is different, formal consistency cannot even be verified. There is, however, a wider notion of consistency, which refers to the basic conception of the working of an economic system. This kind of consistency is necessary in order to consider the set of specific theories about specific aspects of economic reality as a (loosely) unified building of economic science; and this is one of the main 'security systems' against possible abuses of the idea of 'different analytical levels'.

The idea of different analytical levels is common in modern science. For some applications of this idea (for example to the analysis of human and artificial intelligence), see Hofstadter (1979), who also provides some examples of the kind of 'loose consistency' hinted at above: for example, our interpretation of how symbols interact in the human mind cannot be inconsistent with our interpretation of the interaction of neurons in the human brain, even though the two analyses are conducted at different 'analytical levels'.

16 In this regard we may recall that, in open economies, internal technology and international prices and financial conditions may 'determine' internal income distribution.

17 A few examples: Kaldor's analysis of UK economic growth (Kaldor, 1966), Hirsch's analysis of the social limits to growth (Hirsch, 1976), Minsky's analysis of the instability of capitalist economies (Minsky, 1980), Hirshman's analysis of issues relating to underdeveloped countries (Hirshman, 1958), or Biasco's analysis of international financial relations (Biasco, 1979).

17

Trade, Growth and the Pattern of Specialization

Jaime Ros
Geneva

The analysis of international trade within a Sraffian theoretical framework has led to a reconsideration of the determinants of the pattern of specialization and has produced some new results in the analysis of the gains from international trade in the context of growing economies (see, for example, Parrinello, 1973; Steedman, 1979a; Levy, 1980). Among these results there is the possibility of losses from trade arising from the non-optimality of the choice of specialisation or from a temporary fall in employment in the trading economy. However, in the absence of a divergence between the rate of profit and the rate of growth (which is the source for the possibility of a non-optimal choice of specialisation) and abstracting from the possibility of temporary falls in employment, the longer term effects of international trade are clearly positive, leading to an outward shift in the wage-profit and consumption-growth frontiers. The effects of specialization are analogous to technical progress (or, rather, to a once and for all technical improvement).[1]

The main reason for this conclusion is that in these models, as one author puts it:

> Economies are indifferent whether in the equilibrium solution they produce commodities 1 through h or commodities $h + 1$ through n. In more pedestrian terms, from the point of view of the model, it does not matter whether in the equilibrium solution you produce bananas or computers.
> (Levy, 1980, pp. 119–20)

The purpose of this paper is two-fold. First, I show that the pattern of specialization can be said to have no important implications on the growth path of the economy only when one adopts the commonly made assumptions of no differential rates of technical progress, constant returns to scale and uniform income and price elasticities of demand for the different commodities. Second, I shall claim that, when we abandon these unrealistic assumptions, the long-term effects of international trade may or may not be positive for the trading economy, depending on the pattern of specialization and on the resulting growth path of the economy.

1 *A simple model of a growing economy: the static gains from trade*

These propositions may be illustrated by means of a very simple model. Let us consider an autarkic economy producing two commodities (1 and 2) by means of labour alone. The rate of profit is, implicitly, zero and the wage rate is uniform across the two industries. Although there is no capital accumulation, the economy expands through time as the employed labour force grows exogenously at a constant rate g. At any time, all wage income is completely spent on the two commodities. At time t, the economy may be described by the following system of equations:

$$p_1(t) \cdot Q_1(t) = L_1(t) \cdot w(t) \tag{1}$$

$$p_2(t) \cdot Q_2(t) = L_2(t) \cdot w(t) \tag{2}$$

$$p_1(t) \cdot Q_1(t) = \alpha(t) \cdot L(t) \cdot w(t) \tag{3}$$

$$p_2(t) \cdot Q_2(t) = [1 - \alpha(t)] \cdot L(t) \cdot w(t) \tag{4}$$

$$L_1(t) = a_1(t) \cdot Q_1(t) \tag{5}$$

$$L_2(t) = a_2(t) \cdot Q_2(t) \tag{6}$$

$$L(t) = L_1(t) + L_2(t) \tag{7}$$

$$L(t) = L(0) \cdot e^{gt} \tag{8}$$

$$w^*(t) = \frac{p_1(0) \cdot Q_1(t) + p_2(0) \cdot Q_2(t)}{L(t)} \tag{9}$$

where p_1 and p_2 are the prices of commodities 1 and 2, Q_1 and Q_2 the quantities produced and consumed of the two commodities, L_1 and L_2 the levels of employment in the two industries, L is total employment and w the wage rate. $\alpha(t)$ is the fraction of income spent on commodity 1 and therefore, when relative prices change, a given and constant α implies a unitary price elasticity for both commodities. $w^*(t)$ is the real wage measured at prices of the initial period and, under my assumption, it is also a measure of real income per employee.

I shall compare the growth path of the autarkic economy with that of an economy that, starting at time 0, is open to international trade. I shall make the assumption (until the last section) of a small open economy facing given terms of trade and no demand constraints on the quantities exported and also that the level of total employment is the same, at any time, as in the autarkic economy. Thus, when the economy opens to trade in period 0, the industry in which the economy specializes absorbs instantaneously the labour force that was employed in the industry that disappears.

Let $P_2(t)$ be the international price of commodity 2 (in terms of commodity 1) and let us assume that when the economy opens up to trade $p_2(0) > P_2(0)$.

Comparative advantage leads the economy to complete specialization in commodity 1. At time t, the economy may be described by the following system of equations:

$$p_1(t) \cdot Q_1(t) = L_1(t) \cdot w(t) \quad (1')$$

$$P_2(t) = P_2(0) \cdot e^{\beta t} \quad (2')$$

$$p_1(t) \cdot C_1(t) = \alpha(t) \cdot L(t) \cdot w(t) \quad (3')$$

$$p_1(t) \cdot X_1(t) = p_1(t) \cdot Q_1(t) - p_1(t) \cdot C_1(t) \quad (4')$$

$$P_2(t) \cdot C_2(t) = [1 - \alpha(t)] \cdot L(t) \cdot w(t) \quad (5')$$

$$L(t) = a_1(t) \cdot Q_1(t) \quad (6')$$

$$L(t) = L(0) \cdot e^{gt} \quad (7')$$

$$w^*(t) = \frac{p_1(0) \cdot C_1(t) + p_2(0) \cdot C_2(t)}{L(t)} \quad (8')$$

where C_1 and X_1 are the levels of internal consumption and exports of commodity 1, C_2 is the level of consumption and imports of commodity 2, w^* is again the real wage measured at the pre-trade initial prices. Notice that equations (1′), (3′) and (4′) imply that, at any time, the value of imports is equal to the value of exports. The international price P_2 of commodity 2 is assumed to change at a constant rate β. This rate may be zero, in which case the terms of trade for the economy considered remain constant through time.

Taking commodity 1 as the numéraire and assuming the labour coefficients a_1 and a_2 as well as the demand coefficient α as known, the solutions for prices, quantities and the real wage in the two economies are as follows:

Autarky

$$p_2(t) = a_2(t)/a_1(t) \quad (1.1)$$

$$Q_1(t) = \frac{\alpha(t) \cdot L(0) \cdot e^{gt}}{a_1(t)} \quad (2.1)$$

$$Q_2(t) = \frac{[1 - \alpha(t)] \cdot L(0) \cdot e^{gt}}{a^2(t)} \quad (3.1)$$

$$w^*(t) = \frac{\alpha(t)}{a_1(t)} + \frac{a_2(0)}{a_1(0)} \cdot \frac{[1 - \alpha(t)]}{a_2(t)} \quad (4.1)$$

Free trade

$$P_2(t) = P_2(0) \cdot e^{\beta t} \tag{1.1'}$$

$$Q_1(t) = \frac{L(0) \cdot e^{gt}}{a_1(t)} \tag{2.1'}$$

$$C_1(t) = \frac{\alpha(t) \cdot L(0) \cdot e^{gt}}{a_1(t)} \tag{3.1'}$$

$$C_2(t) = \frac{[1 - \alpha(t)] \cdot L(0) \cdot e^{gt}}{a_1(t) \cdot P_2(0) \cdot e^{\beta t}} \tag{4.1'}$$

$$X_1(t) = \frac{[1 - \alpha(t)] \cdot L(0) \cdot e^{gt}}{a_1(t)} \tag{5.1'}$$

$$w^*(t) = \frac{\alpha(t) + [1 - \alpha(t)]\, p_2(0)/P_2(0) \cdot e^{\beta t}}{a_1(t)}. \tag{6.1'}$$

Let us consider the static effects of trade in the initial period when the economy considered opens up to international trade. In time $t = 0$, the total level of employment will be the same, by assumption, under autarky and free trade. In the trading economy, the employment in the production of industry 1 for internal consumption will be the same as the overall employment in industry 1 under autarky (see equations (3) and (3′) for $t = 0$). But now the additional production for exports of industry 1, due to the absorption of the labour force previously employed in industry 2, will be able to purchase, through trade, a larger quantity of commodity 2 than was previously produced and consumed under autarky, due to the lower relative price of commodity 2 under free trade. Real income, total and per capita, will thus be larger, in period 0, under free trade than under autarky. This is the static positive gain from trade due to specialization in the industry showing a comparative advantage in international trade.

This gain may be seen, more formally, by comparing the real wage in the initial period in the two economies. For $t = 0$, the real wages under autarky $[w_A^*(0)]$ and under free trade $[w_{FT}^*(0)]$ are:

$$w_A^*(0) = \frac{\alpha(0) + [1 - \alpha(0)]}{a_1(0)}$$

$$w_{FT}^*(0) = \frac{\alpha(0) + [1 - \alpha(0)]\, p_2(0)/P_2(0)}{a_1(0)}$$

and since:

$$\frac{p_2(0)}{P_2(0)} > 1, \qquad w_{FT}^*(0) > w_A^*(0).$$

As can also be seen from this comparison, the static gain from trade will be larger: (*a*) the lower the relative international price of the imported commodity with respect to the relative price of that commodity under autarky; (*b*) the larger the fraction of income consumed in the imported commodity.

Under the assumptions of no technical progress, constant returns to scale and uniform income elasticities of demand for the two commodities, the static gain from trade just mentioned will be the only effect of international trade (assuming constant terms of trade through time). What I shall now do is to abandon, step by step, those assumptions and investigate the implications of this abandonment. It will be seen that dynamic effects of international trade appear, owing to the implications of the pattern of specialization on the growth path of the economy. These dynamic effects may be in the same or in an opposite direction to the initial static gain from trade and may actually be the most important ones in the longer term.

2 *The case of non-uniform technical progress*

I shall now keep the assumption of constant shares of the two commodities in consumption but introduce different rates of labour productivity growth in the two industries. In this section, I shall take these rates of growth as constant and independent of the growth of output. I shall also assume, as a first step, that the trading economy faces constant terms of trade through time so that $\beta = 0$. The above assumptions may be expressed as follows:

$$\alpha\ (t) = \alpha \tag{10.2}$$

$$a_1\ (t) = a_1\ (0) \cdot e^{-\rho_1 t} \tag{11.2}$$

$$a_2\ (t) = a_2\ (0) \cdot e^{-\rho_2 t} \tag{12.2}$$

$$P_2\ (\mathrm{t}) = P_2\ (0) \tag{13.2}$$

where ρ_1 and ρ_2 are the rates of growth of labour productivity in industries 1 and 2. Under free trade, since the economy specializes in industry 1, the rate of growth of productivity in industry 2 is only a potential rate.

Substituting now expressions (10.2)–(13.2) in the equations of pages 481–2, we obtain the following solutions for prices, quantities and the real wage under autarky and free trade:

Autarky

$$p_2\ (t) = \frac{a_2\ (0)}{a_1\ (0)} \cdot e^{(\rho_1 - \rho_2)t} \tag{1.2}$$

$$Q_1\ (t) = \frac{\alpha \cdot L\ (0)}{a_1\ (0)} \cdot e^{(g + \rho_1)t} \tag{2.2}$$

$$Q_2\ (t) = \frac{(1 - \alpha) \cdot L\ (0)}{a_2\ (0)} \cdot e^{(g + \rho_2)t} \tag{3.2}$$

$$w^*\ (\mathrm{t}) = \frac{\alpha \cdot e^{\rho_1 t} + (1 - \alpha)\ e^{\rho_2 t}}{a_1\ (0)} \tag{4.2}$$

Free trade

$$P_2(t) = P_2(0) \tag{1.2'}$$

$$Q_1(t) = \frac{L(0)}{a_1(0)} \cdot e^{(g+\rho_1)t} \tag{2.2'}$$

$$C_1(t) = \frac{\alpha \cdot L(0)}{a_1(0)} \cdot e^{(g+\rho_1)t} \tag{3.2'}$$

$$C_2(t) = \frac{(1-\alpha) \cdot L(0)}{a_1(0) \cdot P_2(0)} \cdot e^{(g+\rho_1)t} \tag{4.2'}$$

$$X_1(t) = \frac{(1-\alpha) \cdot L(0)}{a_1(0)} \cdot e^{(g+\rho_1)t} \tag{5.2'}$$

$$w^*(t) = \frac{\alpha \cdot e^{\rho_1 \cdot t} + (1-\alpha)\,[p_2(0)/P_2(0)] \cdot e^{\rho_1 t}}{a_1(0)} \tag{6.2'}$$

The consideration of non-uniform technical progress introduces dynamic effects of trade on the growth path of the economy, which lead to gains or losses from international trade in addition to the initial static gain.

The solution of the model shows that the growth path of the autarkic economy is characterized by the following features: (*a*) a changing structure of relative prices reflecting the different rates of technical change in the two industries; (*b*) a changing structure of output, each industry growing at a rate that is the sum of the growth rate of the total labour force and the rate of growth of productivity in the industry considered (given the assumptions of unitary income and price elasticities of demand); (*c*) a changing real wage at a rate that is a weighted average of the rates of growth of productivity in the two industries.

In the trading economy, the growth path shows: (*a*) a constant structure of relative prices, given the assumption of constant terms of trade; (*b*) a growing level of output at a rate equal to the sum of the growth rate of the labour force and the rate of productivity growth in industry 1, with exports, consumption and imports growing at this same rate; (*c*) a changing real wage (starting from a higher level than in the autarkic economy, due to the static gain from trade) at a rate equal to the rate of productivity growth in industry 1.

A comparison of the paths of the real wage in the two economies shows the presence of additional dynamic gains (or losses) from international trade that depend on the comparative rate of productivity growth in the industry in which the economy specializes under free trade. If $\rho_1 > \rho_2$, the real wage (and total output) will grow faster under free trade than under autarky. The economy has specialized in the technologically more progressive industry and the dynamic effects of trade are in the same direction as the initial static gains.

However, if $\rho_2 > \rho_1$, the real wage (and total output) will grow at a lower rate in the trading economy than in the autarkic economy. Free trade and static comparative advantage have led the economy to specialize in the technologically less progressive industry and this has the effect of retarding (relative to autarky) the overall rate of technical progress in the economy. Having started from an initially higher level, the real wage in the trading economy will, after a certain period, fall below the level that it would have had in the autarkic economy. The dynamic effects of trade will completely offset the initial static gain and the economy will suffer dynamic losses arising from the pattern of specialization adopted.

So far I have assumed that the trading economy faces constant terms of trade through time. In the general case, however, the rate of change of the international relative price P_2 will be different from zero. Assuming that this rate of change reflects the difference between the productivity growth rates ($\overset{*}{\rho}_1$ and $\overset{*}{\rho}_2$) of industries 1 and 2 in the rest of the world, so that $\beta = \overset{*}{\rho}_1 - \overset{*}{\rho}_2$, the expressions for the real wage under autarky and free trade become:

$$\textit{Autarky:} \quad w^*(t) = \frac{\alpha \cdot e^{\rho_1 t} + (1-\alpha)\, e^{\rho_2 t}}{a_1(0)}$$

$$\textit{Free trade:} \quad w^*(t) = \frac{\alpha \cdot e^{\rho_1 t}}{a_1(0)} + \frac{(1-\alpha)}{a_1(0)} \cdot \frac{p_2(0)}{P_2(0)} \cdot e^{(\rho_1 + \overset{*}{\rho}_2 - \overset{*}{\rho}_1)t}.$$

Comparing these two expressions, it becomes clear that the long-term advantage of the economy will coincide with static comparative advantage (specialization in industry 1) if:

$$\rho_1 + \overset{*}{\rho}_2 - \overset{*}{\rho}_1 > \rho_2 \Rightarrow \rho_1 - \overset{*}{\rho}_1 > \rho_2 - \overset{*}{\rho}_2 \quad \text{or} \quad \rho_1 - \rho_2 > \overset{*}{\rho}_1 - \overset{*}{\rho}_2\,,$$

i.e. when the economy specializes in the industry having the comparatively larger potential rate of productivity growth.

If, however, $\rho_2 - \rho_1 > \overset{*}{\rho}_2 - \overset{*}{\rho}_1$, the economy would benefit in the long term from specializing in industry 2, while static comparative advantage leads to specialization in industry 1.

These results have striking similarities with Pasinetti's analysis of 'comparative productivity-change advantage': 'in order to obtain the highest possible gains from international trade, a country should specialise in producing those commodities for which it can achieve, over the relevant period of time, the highest comparative rates of growth of productivity' (Pasinetti, 1981b, p. 274).

The point to stress, as Pasinetti also does, is that free trade may or may not lead to the specialization that is to the longer term advantage of the economy; and that, when it does not, the economy may actually suffer dynamic losses from its participation in international trade.

3 *The case of variable returns to scale*

We shall here continue to keep the assumption of constant consumption shares but abandon the assumption of constant returns to scale by introducing different rates of growth of labour productivity that are a function of the growth of industrial output. I shall start by assuming, as in the beginning of section 2, that the trading economy faces constant terms of trade through time. The following expressions summarize my assumptions:

$$\alpha(t) = \alpha \tag{10.3}$$

$$a_1(t) = a_1 \cdot Q_1^{-\lambda_1}(t) \tag{11.3}$$

$$a_2(t) = a_2 \cdot Q_2^{-\lambda_2}(t) \tag{12.3}$$

$$P_2(t) = P_2(0). \tag{13.3}$$

The coefficients λ_1 and λ_2 reflect the type of returns to scale considered. For:

$0 < \lambda < 1$, we have increasing returns to scale

$\lambda = 0$, we have constant returns to scale

$0 > \lambda > -1$, we have decreasing returns to scale.[2]

Substituting now expressions (10.3)–(13.3) in the equations of pages 481–2, we obtain the solutions for prices, quantities and the real wage under autarky and free trade for the present case:

Autarky

$$p_2(t) = \frac{a_2}{a_1} \cdot \frac{\left(\frac{\alpha \cdot L(0)}{a_1}\right)^{\frac{\lambda_1}{1-\lambda_1}}}{\left[\frac{(1-\alpha) \cdot L(0)}{a_2}\right]^{\frac{\lambda_2}{1-\lambda_2}}} \cdot e^{\left(\frac{g\lambda_1}{1-\lambda_1} - \frac{g\lambda_2}{1-\lambda_2}\right)t} \tag{1.3}$$

$$Q_1(t) = \left(\frac{\alpha \cdot L(0)}{a_1}\right)^{\frac{1}{1-\lambda_1}} \cdot e^{\left(\frac{g}{1-\lambda_1}\right)t} \tag{2.3}$$

$$Q_2(t) = \left[\frac{(1-\alpha) \cdot L(0)}{a_2}\right]^{\frac{1}{1-\lambda_2}} \cdot e^{\left(\frac{g}{1-\lambda_2}\right)t} \tag{3.3}$$

$$w^*(t) = \frac{[\alpha \cdot L(0)]^{\frac{\lambda_1}{1-\lambda_1}}}{a_1^{\frac{1}{1-\lambda_1}}} \cdot \left[\alpha \cdot e^{\left(\frac{g\lambda_1}{1-\lambda_1}\right)t} + (1-\alpha)\, e^{\left(\frac{g\lambda_2}{1-\lambda_2}\right)t}\right] \tag{4.3}$$

Free trade

$$P_2(t) = P_2(0) \tag{1.3'}$$

$$Q_1(t) = \left(\frac{L(0)}{a_1}\right)^{\frac{1}{1-\lambda_1}} \cdot e^{\left(\frac{g}{1-\lambda_1}\right)t} \tag{2.3'}$$

$$C_1(t) = \alpha \left(\frac{L(0)}{a_1}\right)^{\frac{1}{1-\lambda_1}} \cdot e^{\left(\frac{g}{1-\lambda_1}\right)t} \tag{3.3'}$$

$$C_2(t) = \frac{(1-\alpha)}{P_2(0)} \cdot \left(\frac{L(0)}{a_1}\right)^{\frac{1}{1-\lambda_1}} \cdot e^{\left(\frac{g}{1-\lambda_1}\right)t} \tag{4.3'}$$

$$X_1(t) = (1-\alpha)\left(\frac{L(0)}{a_1}\right)^{\frac{1}{1-\lambda_1}} \cdot e^{\left(\frac{g}{1-\lambda_1}\right)t} \tag{5.3'}$$

$$w^*(t) = \frac{L(0)^{\frac{\lambda_1}{1-\lambda_1}}}{a_1^{\frac{1}{1-\lambda_1}}} \cdot \left[\alpha \cdot e^{\left(\frac{g\lambda_1}{1-\lambda_1}\right)t} + (1-\alpha)\frac{p_2(0)}{P_2(0)} \cdot e^{\left(\frac{g\lambda_1}{1-\lambda_1}\right)t}\right] \tag{6.3'}$$

Before considering the growth paths of the autarkic and the trading economies, it is worth observing that the presence of variable returns to scale introduces a static gain (or loss) from trade, additional to the one analysed in section 2. Indeed, solving the equation of the real wage under autarky and free trade for $t = 0$, we have:

Autarky: $$w_A^*(0) = \alpha^{\frac{\lambda_1}{1-\lambda_1}} \cdot \left[\frac{L(0)^{\lambda_1}}{a_1}\right]^{\frac{\lambda_1}{1-\lambda_1}}$$

Free trade: $$w_{FT}^*(0) = \left[\frac{L(0)^{\lambda_1}}{a_1}\right]^{\frac{1}{1-\lambda_1}} \left[\alpha + (1-\alpha)\frac{p_2(0)}{P_2(0)}\right].$$

Now the initial real wage under free trade is different from the initial real wage under autarky not only because the relative price of the imported commodity is lower than under autarky ($\frac{p_2(0)}{P_2(0)} > 1$, which gives rise to the static gain from trade already discussed) but also because the absorption of employment in industry 1, from industry 2, changes, under variable returns to scale, the productivity level of industry 1 (this difference is reflected in the term $\alpha^{\frac{\lambda_1}{1-\lambda_1}}$). Whether this second effect of trade on the initial real wage is positive or negative will depend on the type of returns to scale in industry 1.

If returns to scale in industry 1 are increasing ($\lambda_1 > 0$), the increase in employment in industry 1 will increase labour productivity in industry 1 and the initial real wage under free trade over and above the increase due to the lower relative price of commodity 2. This additional positive gain from trade is:

$$\left[\frac{L(0)^{\lambda_1}}{a_1}\right]^{\frac{1}{1-\lambda_1}} (1 - \alpha^{\lambda_1/1-\lambda_1})$$

(which is $w_{FT}^*(0) - w_A^*(0)$ assuming $\frac{p_2(0)}{P_2(0)} = 1$). Since $\alpha < 1$, this gain from trade will be larger: (*a*) the higher the returns to scale in industry 1 (the larger λ_1 is); (*b*) the lower the consumption share of commodity 1 (the lower α is) since then for a given overall labour force, the productivity gains of absorbing employment in industry 1 from industry 2 are larger; and (*c*) the larger the size of the labour force ($L(0)$), since then the larger will be the increase in employment in industry 1 and the resulting productivity gains.

If, however, returns to scale in industry 1 are decreasing ($\lambda_1 < 0$), the increase in employment in industry 1 reduces labour productivity in industry 1. The additional effect on the initial real wage is then negative and tends to offset the static gain from trade derived from the lower relative price of commodity 2.

The net gain from trade:

$$w^*_{FT}(0) - w^*_A(0) = \left[\frac{L(0)^{\lambda_1}}{a_1}\right]^{\frac{1}{1-\lambda_1}} \left[\alpha + (1-\alpha)\frac{p_2(0)}{P_2(0)} - \alpha^{\frac{\lambda_1}{1-\lambda_1}}\right]$$

will be larger (*a*) the larger the difference between the international relative price of commodity 2 and the autarky relative price of this commodity; (*b*) the less the returns to scale in industry 1 decrease; (*c*) the smaller the size of the labour force ($L(0)$) since then the smaller will be the increase in employment and the fall in productivity in industry 1.[3] The influence of the consumption share on the net gain from trade is ambiguous since it has opposite effects on the two elements of the net gain.

I turn now to a comparison of the growth paths of the autarkic and trading economies. This comparison yields similar results to those analysed in the previous case of different rates of technical progress in the two industries, the main difference being that the productivity growth rates $(\frac{g\lambda_1}{1-\lambda_1})$ and $\frac{g\lambda_2}{(1-\lambda_2)}$ are now dependent on the rate of growth of the labour force and the type of returns to scale in each industry.

The above implies that the dynamic gains or losses from international trade will depend now on the comparative returns to scale in the industry in which the economy specializes under free trade. If $\frac{g\lambda_1}{(1-\lambda_1)} > \frac{g\lambda_2}{(1-\lambda_2)}$, which implies that $\lambda_1 > \lambda_2$, the economy, by specializing in industry 1, which has the highest returns to scale, will have a faster growth of the real wage and total output under free trade than under autarky.

If, on the contrary, $\lambda_2 > \lambda_1$, the trading economy specializes in the industry that has the lowest returns to scale and this pattern of specialization will produce a retardation of the rate of growth of overall labour productivity, total output and real wages. The economy under free trade then suffers dynamic losses that tend to offset the initial static gains from trade.

I shall now abandon the assumption of constant terms of trade through time and consider a changing relative international price P_2. Assuming that the sources of productivity change are the same (variable returns to scale) in the rest of the world as in our economy, the rate of change of P_2 is $\beta = \frac{[g^* \lambda_1^*]}{(1-\lambda_1^*)} - \frac{[g^* \lambda_2^*]}{(1-\lambda_2^*)}$ where g^* is the rate of growth of the labour force in the rest of the world and λ_1^*, λ_2^* are the returns to scale coefficients in industries 1 and 2 in the rest of the world.

With $\beta \neq 0$, the expressions for the real wage under autarky and free trade become:

Autarky:

$$w^*(t) = \left[\frac{\alpha \cdot L(0)^{\lambda_1}}{a_1}\right]^{\frac{1}{1-\lambda_1}} \cdot \left[\alpha \cdot e^{\left(\frac{g\lambda_1}{1-\lambda_1}\right)t} + (1-\alpha) \cdot e^{\left(\frac{g\lambda_2}{1-\lambda_2}\right)t}\right]$$

Free trade:

$$w^*(t)=\left[\frac{L(0)^{\lambda_1}}{a_1}\right]^{\frac{1}{1-\lambda_1}}\cdot\left[\alpha\cdot e^{\left(\frac{g\lambda_1}{1-\lambda_1}\right)t}+(1-\alpha)\frac{p_2(0)}{P_2(0)}\cdot e^{\left(\frac{g\lambda_1}{1-\lambda_1}+\frac{g^*\lambda_2^*}{1-\lambda_2^*}-\frac{g^*\lambda_1^*}{1-\lambda_1^*}\right)t}\right].$$

Comparing these two expressions, it is clear that the long-term advantage of the trading economy will be to specialize in industry 1 when:

$$\frac{g\lambda_1}{1-\lambda_1}+\frac{g^*\lambda_2^*}{1-\lambda_2^*}-\frac{g^*\lambda_1^*}{1-\lambda_1^*}>\frac{g\lambda_2}{1-\lambda_2}$$

$$\Rightarrow g\left(\frac{\lambda_1}{1-\lambda_1}-\frac{\lambda_2}{1-\lambda_2}\right)>g^*\left(\frac{\lambda_1^*}{1-\lambda_1^*}-\frac{\lambda_2^*}{1-\lambda_2^*}\right),$$

while the long-term advantage will be specialization in industry 2 when:

$$g\left(\frac{\lambda_2}{1-\lambda_2}-\frac{\lambda_1}{1-\lambda_1}\right)>g^*\left(\frac{\lambda_2^*}{1-\lambda_2^*}-\frac{\lambda_1^*}{1-\lambda_1^*}\right).$$

The point again is that the best pattern of specialization may or may not coincide with the pattern of trade induced by static comparative advantage under free trade.

It is worth noting that the best pattern of specialization depends not only on comparative returns to scale but also on the rate of growth of the labour force relative to the growth of the labour force in the rest of the world. To see the influence of the latter let us consider the case where $\lambda_1=\lambda_1^*$ and $\lambda_2=\lambda_2^*$ with $\lambda_2>\lambda_1$. Then, for a fast-growing economy ($g>g^*$), the dynamic long-term advantage will be to specialize in the industry having the highest returns to scale (industry 2), even if the economy does not have a comparative returns to scale advantage in that industry. On the contrary, for a slow-growing economy ($g<g^*$), the best pattern of trade will be to specialize in the industry having the lowest returns to scale (industry 1) while taking advantage of the productivity gains in industry 2 in the rest of the world through a falling relative price of commodity 2 in the international economy.

4 *The case of different income elasticities of demand and the role of effective demand*

In this section, I shall abandon two assumptions that I have so far maintained throughout this paper. The first change concerns the assumption of a small open economy facing no demand constraints on its volume of exports. Instead, I shall assume that, at given and constant terms of trade, the volume of exports is constrained by demand and grows at a given constant rate x. This change implies that, under the assumption of balanced trade, the model of the trading economy (see section 1) cannot now be closed by postulating an exogenously given growth rate of the employed labour force. Under the assumptions now introduced, the growth of the economy is demand-constrained by the rate of growth of exports together with the condition of balanced trade, and therefore, the growth of employment is endogenous to the model and must be consistent with the exogenously given growth of exports.

The second assumption I shall drop refers to the constancy of consumption shares. Instead, I shall assume that consumer tastes change in such a way that the share of one of the commodities (commodity 1 in my example) increases through time from an initial level $\alpha\ (0)\ (>0)$ to a final level $\alpha\ (\infty)\ (<1)$ according to the following expression:

$$\alpha\ (t)=\frac{\gamma_1}{\gamma_2+\gamma_3\cdot e^{-rt}}\quad \text{where } r>0,\quad \alpha\ (0)=\frac{\gamma_1}{\gamma_2+\gamma_3}\quad \text{and}\quad \alpha(\infty)=\frac{\gamma_1}{\gamma_2}.$$

In order to isolate the effects of the changes introduced, I shall assume, as I did in section 1, that there is no technical progress and that returns to scale are constant. Thus $a_1\ (t)=a_1\ (0)$ and $a_2\ (t)=a_2\ (0)$. Under these assumptions, the trading economy, with a specialization in industry 1, may be described by the following system of equations:

$$p_1\ (t)\cdot Q_1\ (t)=L\ (t)\cdot w\ (t) \tag{1}$$

$$P_2\ (t)=P_2\ (0) \tag{2}$$

$$p_1\ (t)\cdot C_1\ (t)=\left(\frac{\gamma_1}{\gamma_2+\gamma_3\ e^{-rt}}\right)\cdot L\ (t)\cdot w\ (t) \tag{3}$$

$$X_1\ (t)=X_1\ (0)\cdot e^{xt} \tag{4}$$

$$P_2\ (t)\cdot C_2\ (t)=\left(1-\frac{\gamma_1}{\gamma_2+\gamma_3\ e^{-rt}}\right)\cdot L\ (t)\cdot w\ (t) \tag{5}$$

$$Q_1\ (t)=X_1\ (t)+C_1\ (t) \tag{6}$$

$$L\ (t)=a_1\ (0)\cdot Q_1\ (t) \tag{7}$$

$$w^*\ (t)=\frac{p_1\ (0)\cdot C_1\ (t)+p_2\ (0)\cdot C_2\ (t)}{L\ (t)}. \tag{8}$$

The solutions for prices, quantities and the real wage under free trade are:

$$P_2\ (t)=P_2\ (0) \tag{1}$$

$$Q_1\ (t)=X_1\ (0)\ .\ e^{xt}/\left(1-\frac{\gamma_1}{\gamma_2+\gamma_3\ e^{-rt}}\right)\cdot L\ (t)\cdot w\ (t) \tag{2}$$

$$C_1\ (t)=\frac{X_1\ (0)\cdot\gamma_1\cdot e^{xt}}{\gamma_2-\gamma_1+\gamma_3\cdot e^{-rt}} \tag{3}$$

$$C_2\ (t)=X_1\ (0)\cdot e^{-xt}/P_2\ (0) \tag{4}$$

$$X_1\ (\mathrm{t})=X_1\ (0)\cdot e^{xt} \tag{5}$$

$$w^*\ (t)=\frac{\alpha\ (t)+[1-\alpha\ (t)]\cdot p_2\ (0)/P_2\ (0)}{a_1\ (0)}. \tag{6}$$

It is worth making several observations on the initial and long-term effects of free trade on the economy. The first is that, in the presence of demand constraints on the levels of output and employment, and in contrast to previous sections, the industry in which the economy specializes will not completely absorb the employment of the disappearing industry. There may now be an overall fall in employment, which may or may not be reversed depending on the long-term rate of growth of the economy. When it occurs, this reduction in employment is an initial loss from trade, which has to be compared with the improvement in the real wage resulting from the lower relative price of commodity 2 under free trade.

Second, the growth of output and employment is determined, under free trade, by the growth of exports and the rate of change of the consumption share of the commodity in which the economy specializes (or its income elasticity of demand). The overall growth rate is higher: (*a*) the higher the rate of growth of exports (x); and (*b*) the higher the income elasticity of the internal demand for the commodity in which the economy specializes (the higher r is). For $r > 0$, the rate of growth of the economy g_{FT} will be higher than x, approaching x as $\alpha(t)$ tends to its final value $\alpha(\infty)$. While for $r < 0$, g_{FT} will be lower than x, approaching x as $\alpha(t)$ tends to $\alpha(\infty)$.

Thus, depending on the growth of exports and the internal income elasticity of demand for commodity 1, the growth of employment and output may fall short of the growth corresponding to the autarkic economy. If this is the case, the trading economy will suffer dynamic losses over time.[4]

The analysis of the rate of growth of output and employment in the trading economy leads to a third observation. Considering the alternative patterns of specialization, and assuming that they share the same rate of growth of exports, the long-term advantage of the trading economy will be to specialize in that commodity having the highest income elasticity of internal demand (the imported commodity having, then, the lowest income elasticity of demand) since this is the pattern of specialization that yields the highest growth of output and employment. When the growth rate of exports is different among industries, the best pattern of specialization will be that for which the growth of exports and the internal income elasticity of demand are such as to maximize the growth of output and employment.

The final point is that, again in this case, static comparative advantage under free trade may or may not lead to the best pattern of specialization for the trading economy.

5 *Final comments*

The analysis presented has shown that the abandonment of the traditional assumptions of no differential technical progress, constant returns to scale and uniform income elasticities of demand has far-reaching implications for the analysis of the long-term effects of international trade. Free trade may appear then, under certain conditions, as an inferior alternative to autarky, implying dynamic losses for the trading economy. At the same time, my analysis suggests that, in the absence of demand constraints on growth, there is a pattern of specialization (not necessarily induced by free trade) that is in the best long-term advantage of the economy. This best pattern of specialization depends not only on static comparative advantage but also on such factors as the comparative potential for technical progress among industries, the type of returns to scale, the growth of the labour force and the income elasticities of demand internally and abroad.

The analysis implies, then, that the free operation of the market does not lead, except by coincidence, to the best possible allocation of resources in the international economy, and it also suggests that the allocation of resources that is in the best interests of one country may be very different from that which is in the best interests of another country (particularly when demand constraints are present). This recognition may provide a way to link the theory of international trade with the real workings of the international economy.

To develop more fully the policy implications of the present analysis would need further research. As I have hinted in the text, some of these implications may be different for small and for large countries as well as for fast-growing and slow-growing economies. And some will probably coincide with those reached previously by other schools of thought (such as the Latin American structuralist school or the theories of economic growth with a balance of payments constraint) as well as with the common sense of policy-makers facing real and complex policy issues. In this latter respect, it may be worth quoting, as a final comment, the rationale of Japan's industrial policy given by vice-minister Ojimi, of the Japanese Ministry of International Trade and Industry (MITI), whose views were one of the starting points for the analysis presented in this paper:

> The MITI decided to establish in Japan industries which require intensive employment of capital and technology, industries that in consideration of comparative cost of production should be the most inappropriate for Japan, industries such as steel, oil-refining, petro-chemicals, automobiles, aircraft, industrial machinery of all sorts, and electronics, including electronic computers. From a short-run static viewpoint, encouragement of such industries would seem to conflict with economic rationalism. But, from a long-range viewpoint, these are precisely the industries where income elasticity of demand is high, technological progress is rapid, and labour productivity rises fast. It was clear that without these industries it would be difficult to employ a population of 100 million and raise their standard of living to that of Europe and America. . . .
>
> (quoted by Singh, 1982, pp. 8–9)

Notes

1 One important exception to this view is Pasinetti (1981b), ch. XI. The similarities between this analysis and the results in section 2 of my paper will become clear in the text.

2 I use the term 'decreasing returns to scale' in an informal way to indicate an inverse relationship between labour productivity and the level of output.

3 Thus, with respect to the static effects of trade, when specialization occurs in an increasing returns industry a large economy will gain more from trade than a small economy (given $p_2(0)/P_2(0)$). And when specialization is in a decreasing returns industry, it is the small economy that will gain more.

4 These dynamic losses will be larger under increasing returns to scale since then not only the growth of output and employment but also the growth of labour productivity and real wages will be negatively affected.

18

The IMF View of International Economic Policy and the Relevance of Sraffa's Critique of economic theory

Amiya K. Bagchi
Calcutta

I

Any dominant class or coalition of classes needs an ideology to justify its dominance or rule. When that ideology serves the interests of a class that happens to move the wheels of history forward, it comes out probably in its clearest form without any mincing of words or concepts. Adam Smith or David Ricardo could be ruthlessly objective about the origin of capitalist profit and the real nature of capitalist dominance in an economy where both land and labour power were taking on the nature of commodities because capitalist growth was creating a new world that was in many ways superior to the older world of dominance by feudal magnates. When this world view and the dominance of capitalist rule came to be challenged, Nassau Senior, Henry Carey and Frederic Bastiat emerged to obfuscate classical economic analysis (see Marx, [1862–3] 1968; [1862–3] 1971). Real and imagined difficulties with classical economic analysis combined with the self-interest of academic economists to generate the neoclassical 'revolution' in economic theory, which fought a highly successful battle to rid economics of such inconvenient associations as classes and production relations (see Bharadwaj, 1978b). There was some kind of refurbishing of economics as an approach to objective analysis during the post-Second World War period when successful demand management seemed to provide a justification for both Keynesian policies and ameliorative capitalism. Even during that period, for the underworld of the underdeveloped countries, the role of economics as mystifying ideology remained dominant.

The collapse of the near consensus on Keynesianism (or rather on the 'neoclassical synthesis' presented by Hicks, 1937, and Modigliani, 1944) among academic economists has been accompanied by a series of somersaults and other acrobatics among academic economists. From economics as a series of operational postulates to 'explain' any isolated series data the theorist chose to pick out (see Friedman, 1953), a group of economists retreated to a position where they would liken economics to the 'Sciences of the Artificial' *à la* Herbert Simon (1969). In this view, 'realism' is no longer a valid criterion of judging economic theory either at the level of assumptions or at the level of the inferences (Lucas, 1980). Economic theory is literally reduced to 'games people play'. However, one of the practitioners of such games has recently confessed: 'Most of us have long realized that game theory and the "real world" (it might be better called the complex world) have a relationship that is not entirely comfortable; that it is not clear just what it is that we are trying to do when we build a game-theoretic model and then apply solution concepts to it' (Aumann, 1985). So a large part of economic theory is no longer even 'vulgar economics' – a rationalization at however far a remove of the dominance of a particular kind of class rule in the real world – but 'fantasy economics' – a denial that there is any reality to be explained, any dominance to be rationalized. By denying the relevance of reality, the fact of dominance is excised from the minds of the theorists and their self-satisfied audience.[1]

But, of course, there has long existed a dissonance between the 'theoretical practice' of the high priests and their acolytes who have after all to bully the ordinary people to accept the false gods in the temple. The economists associated with the International Monetary Fund (IMF) as advisers, staff members or as ideologues have to explain the work of that Mammon to the governments and the people that they coerce into making the appropriate sacrifices. Such explanations cannot take the form of fantasies that produce only distant 'analogues' of the world of the senses. So they have to resort to some version of neoclassical theory. Such theorizing may be denounced by a purist such as Frank Hahn (1981) or Rudiger Dornbusch (1982, 1983, 1985). But the IMF view of the world survives such denunciations and is sought to be justified by such prolific rationalizers as Bela Balassa (1971, 1978) and Anne Krueger (1978, 1981). The view is churned out in numerous publications and internal policy documents of the IMF and the World Bank. The vision of the capitalist world embedded in these studies and theories can be dubbed as the IMF view, and it is a sub-class of those studies that I shall take up for critical analysis.

II

The typical IMF view has as its centre of discourse a community of savers, whose intentions are continually frustrated by governments stupidly trying to control prices, including wages, interest rates and exchange rates, instead of allowing market forces to work themselves out. In the work of McKinnon (1973) and Shaw (1973) the usual Friedman-style tirade against the maleficient influence of activist government policies was further reinforced with a theory of financial intermediation in which free credit markets do their job not only of allocating a given amount of savings as between different uses but also of eliciting the required volume of savings.

This vision of the economy denies the existence of most of the problems that have provided the rationale of Marxian, Keynesian or Kaleckian economics or the theorizing about problems of long-period growth that have explicitly or implicitly figured in the work of the classical political economists, Marx, Nicholas Kaldor, Joan Robinson, Piero Sraffa and their followers, who take their problematics and methods of analysis seriously. This denial extends to the following issues: (1) problems caused by the lack of prior co-ordination of activities by atomistic individuals in a capitalist economy; (2) problems arising from the essential unknowability of the future; which in the view of many theorists provides the rationale for the holding of money and credit instruments as assets in a capitalist economy; (3) problems caused by the mobility of capital and changes in techniques and products in response to changes in wages and profit rates; (4) problems caused by the inequality in the power exercised by different groups of capitalists or firms (only a subset of which is captured by the conceptualizations in terms of 'imperfections' in product and factor markets). It follows that the IMF view denies the existence of the problems of deficiency of effective demand and involuntary unemployment except in so far as they are attributed to the consequences of actions of governments, trade unions or particular firms – actions that all invite the prescription of freeing the markets from non-market interference.

In a paper by Khan and Knight (1982), for example, we get a simple cross of the supply of savings and demand for investment on the part of the private sector plotted against the rate of interest, and the putative effects of various policies are discussed with the help of such diagrams. The analysis is no different from what one would consider to be appropriate for, say, the market for apples in Switzerland. If apples are sold at a price fixed by some public agency or trade cartel, and if the price is below that necessary to clear the market, an excess demand for apples develops. If the price of apples is allowed then to rise, this would not only augment the supply of home-grown apples (which would come out of inventories and a lower-level consumption of apples by the growers), it would also encourage the inflow of apples into Switzerland from Germany, Austria, Italy, France and countries further out. According to Khan and Knight, in less developed countries (LDCs) the officially regulated rate of interest is typically below the level that would equalize savings and investment, that is, the supply of, and demand for, capital (in a flow, not a stock, sense). If the rate of interest were increased, this would stimulate the flow of domestic savings and inflow of foreign capital, analogously to the working of the market mechanism in the case of apples. Even a Marshallian economist writing before Khan and Knight would consider factors other than price in finding out how to stimulate the growth of capacity for producing apples or augmenting the long-run supply of apples. Khan and Knight are not bothered by such complications and their bold prescription for stimulating the growth of the economy by raising the rate of interest is about the only item considered under a subsection headed 'Policies to stimulate the growth of capacity output'.

It is obvious that Khan and Knight's paper disregards the repercussions that changes in income and income distribution might have on the rate of savings or, for that matter, on the rate of investment. Their analysis of stimulation of foreign capital flows in response to changes in rates of interest also disregards differences in the geopolitical situation of different countries as possible havens for capital. The same rise in the rate of interest from the same levels would not, for example, attract the same inflows of capital into India and the USA. Nineteenth-century policy-makers and economists were aware of such facts (see, for example, Goschen, 1905), but not so the resident economists of the IMF. (There are other, more sophisticated, analysts of international capital flows, but even they tend to shy away from some of the most basic issues, as we shall see later.)

In the Khan and Knight analysis the short period is stretched to cover long-period changes, the possibility of deficiency of effective demand is disregarded and changes in income distribution are supposed to have an unambiguous relationship to the stimulation of saving and enterprise (the possibility of a more unequal distribution of income depressing the level of effective demand and, hence, the propensity to invest is disregarded). A similarly pre-Sraffian, pre-Keynesian and, in some respects, pre-Marshallian framework provides the core of the analysis of 'financially repressed markets' by McKinnon (1973) and Shaw (1973). They start out from a loanable funds theory of interest and saving.[2] But their quarry is not short-period income alone, but the long-period evolution of the economy. And they seek to understand this evolution entirely on the basis of the working of the capital markets and the behaviour of the government budget deficit. It is *par excellence* a theory that owes its origin and popularity to the financial mushrooming of advanced capitalism and the fiscal crisis of the modern state. McKinnon and Shaw concentrate their attention on the consequences of regulating the lending (deposit) or borrowing (loan) rate of interest. These models have provided the rationale for the high-interest regimes prescribed by the IMF–World Bank theorists and many other conservative theorists in the advanced capitalist countries as well as in the third world. According to this line of thinking,

> The real rate of interest as the return to savers is the key to a higher level of investment and, as a rationing device, to greater investment efficiency. The impacts on growth are multiplicative. Growth in the financially repressed economy is constrained by saving; investment opportunities abound.
>
> (Fry, 1982a, p. 733)

Here we again find an explicit denial of the problem of deficiency of effective demand. It is strange to meet this kind of modelling as serious theory in a period of global recession, but the explanation for its fame is to be sought in the fact that it serves the purpose of those who stand to gain from an inflationary recession, so long as it does not get out of hand. Particular attention is paid in these models to the deficit of the government and public sector enterprises. Such deficits are invariably supposed to crowd out private saving and investment irrespective of the degree of underutilization of capacity and propensity to invest on the part of private investors. For some reason, private investment is *ipso facto* considered to be more productive than public investment. Thus an unargued, ideological bias is displayed towards what is in many cases a purely institutional division between spheres of government and private business – both representing the same interests and both subject to some of the same problems of inefficiency. One explanation for this is that, in a situation of inflationary expectations, financiers and speculators of all kinds hope to benefit by trading in the unregulated credit markets and by wheeling and dealing in the denationalized public enterprises. Where there is a large service sector, the group of potential operators in free-wheeling credit and asset markets may well be large. Another factor may be the desire to impose the ideology of 'nominal' government espoused by ruling groups in the UK and the USA on the rest of world, so that the business environment may be more welcome everywhere to transnational capital.

Such political issues are germane to the discussion of the theory and the practice of international economic policy: only ideological factors and considerations of a desire for political harmony in the long run can explain why policies of high interest rates of monetarism or supply-side economics are espoused by many watchdogs of international capitalism even when such policies or doctrines have been found to be unsound and positively inimical to sustain growth in the major capitalist economies.

Of course, there are differences of opinion and interest as between different groups striving for hegemony within the capitalist world. High interest rates and large budget deficits have long been regarded as inimical to the health of the world economy and even of the US economy in the long run by many official organizations such as the Bank for International Settlements (see, for example, BIS, 1983) and US bankers such as Felix Rohatyn (1984). A stage has been reached for some time when even the staff of IMF recognize the harmful effects of high interest rates all round but are unable to do much about it because the US government and the major transnational banks (TNBs) are yet to reverse their policies in this regard.[3]

Many of the spokesmen of the IMF and the World Bank are wringing their hands publicly about the high interest rates in the USA, the fatal attraction the United States has as a sink for the capital flowing out of most market economies of the world, and the alarmingly large budget deficits of the USA. They are also stressing the need for larger inflows of aid and loans to support what are euphemistically termed adjustment policies in countries of the third world caught in a debt trap.[4] But the changes that are contemplated within the limits of choices that are considered feasible by the financial watchdogs of the OECD countries will leave the order of international inequality unchanged – and what is more, are unlikely to reverse the trend towards a regressive redistribution of the real resources of the world through the working of the international trade and payments mechanism.

III

Not all theorists espousing the IMF view are pre-Keynesian in the sense that they completely deny the problem of deficiency of demand under capitalism. In order to analyse the consequences of various government policies, many of them utilize the so-called neoclassical synthesis effected by Hicks (1937), Patinkin (1966), Samuelson (1947) and others to discuss the consequences of an increase in 'money supply', a budgetary deficit or a change in private investment intentions. A straightforward conflict between the goal of economic expansion and equilibrium in the balance of payments often emerges from such analyses (Swan, 1963).

Many of these analyses utilize either the original IS–LM apparatus of Hicks, or the IS–LM variant of it (as given, for example, in Hansen, 1949, ch. 12). The IS–LM apparatus was very useful for capturing some of the characteristics of the advanced capitalist economies in the post-war period, as Solow has recently claimed (Solow, 1984). However, from the very beginning, Joan Robinson and other economists who had followed the development of Keynesian macroeconomics closely had found the IS–LM apparatus a hindrance rather than a help in thinking about the manifold problems of a functioning capitalist economy. Hicks has himself pointed to some of the most important problems in dealing with the IS–LM apparatus (Hicks, 1983b). First, it compels the theorist to assume that some of the major markets are in 'equilibrium', at least in the neighbourhood of the particular point in the space of interest rate and national income at which the economy is supposed to be operating. Only some markets are allowed to be out of equilibrium. Secondly, the relationship between output and employment cannot be clarified with the apparatus without making particular assumptions about the length of the time period over which the relevant interactions are to take place – assumptions that are somewhat inconsistent with one another. In particular, the market for output is supposed to have a very short duration, so that investment and consumption plans can be taken to be frozen for the period in question. On the other hand, unless we rule out the possibility of firms meeting excess demands by drawing down stocks, we cannot get any positive relationship between changes in output and changes in employment. Thirdly, if neither the labour market nor the output market is cleared through price adjustments, then prices must be set by some rules of thumb or conventions such as mark-up pricing; the relationship between changes in money and real product in the interest–income graph is not then always unambiguous. Moreover, the rule of thumb about mark-up pricing can hardly be justified within the theoretical framework that is used to support the IS–LM analysis.

There are yet other problems associated with the use of the IS–LM apparatus for the analysis of a capitalist economy, some of which have been set out in a paper by Leijonhufvud (1983). These have to do with the lack of justification for collapsing individual investment decisions in an atomistic market system into an aggregate investment function with properties of self-fulfilment, the inability to find a place for money as a hedge against uncertainty (and not just as an accounting unit or a medium of exchange) and the invalid separation of the product market and asset market repercussions of government expenditures.[5] The demonstration of capital theoretic paradoxes in the work of Joan Robinson (1953–4) and Sraffa (1960) has put a question-mark over the construction of smoothly monotonic investment demand schedules. For, if higher present values of capital are not necessarily associated with lower interest rates, then we cannot unambiguously construct a schedule of marginal efficiency of investment that declines with a rise in the interest rate. This problem remains even if we refrain from asking inconvenient questions about aggregation of individual marginal efficiency schedules into an investment demand function for the economy as a whole (see Garegnani, 1983b).

Despite all these limitations, the IS–LM apparatus lives on in textbook accounts. In recent years, analysts with 'radical' intentions have even tried to use it to show the paradoxical results of policies of adjustment prescribed and enforced by the IMF and transnational banks to cure the ills of third world countries plagued with chronic balance-of-payments problems (see, for example, Taylor, 1981, 1983). However, such applications are fraught with analytical pitfalls. For example, Taylor (1981) distinguishes between so-called 'Keynesian' shifts and 'Fisherian shifts' of the IS curve. In the case of the former, when output rises, investment is unresponsive but savings respond positively. In this case, in order to bring about a savings–investment balance, the interest rate must fall, and the price level also rise, presumably in order to generate a higher volume of savings.

This seems to be garbling the short-run IS–LM analysis. In that analysis, it is either the money supply or the liquidity preference or investment schedules that are variable, and output is the *resultant*. Nothing can be said about the effects of an increase in output that is somehow anterior to changes in any of the basic schedules. A shift in the savings rate as a result of a change in the price level belongs to the theoretical domain of the neo-Cambridge (or Kaleckian) growth theory, and cannot be incorporated in the short-run IS–LM framework without exploding it altogether. In Taylor's analysis, as in much other work on third world problems, there is a tendency to confound long-period and short-period problems, and to deny either that effective demand can be at all deficient in the long run, or that long-period problems of growth and of the degree of robustness of investment demand are connected in any essential manner. Of course, there is no simple way of resolving the issue of how to situate short-run effective demand problems of a typical third world economy in the context of the long-period investment behaviour of such an economy. (For an attempt to relate the two types of problems, see Bagchi, 1988.) But to deny the importance of the problem of the determinants of accumulation by the capitalist class, except in the context of the short-run management of balance of payments or the price level, is to miss the essence of the reality of uneven development of international capitalism and the under-development of a major part of the third world, which seems to be an inevitable facet of such unequal development (see Bagchi, 1982, chs 2, 5 and 9). The 'structuralist' problem stressed by many Latin American economists, which Taylor (1981) seeks to capture, is a part of such long-period distortions caused by the development of capitalism the world over.[6]

IV

Focusing on the long-period problems of unequal development and underdevelopment should form a central part of a reasoned critique of the IMF view of international economic policy. For the classical economists, for Marx and for Sraffa, explaining the *modus operandi* of the generation of surplus within a capitalist mode of production and its accumulation formed a major part of their theoretical concerns. As is well known, Sraffa's *Production of Commodities by Means of Commodities* (1960) was, on the face of it, concerned with the logical working out of the impact of the generation of a surplus (in a self-reproducing or an expanding system) on relative prices; his system simultaneously tackled the issue of changes in the distribution of incomes between wages and profits – that is, the distribution of the net product between the two major contending classes under capitalism.

However, if we postulate that one of the major forces spurring capital accumulation is competition between capitalists and that such competition tends to equalize profit rates as between different sectors of the economy, then we arrive at a dynamic version of Sraffa's theory (see Garegnani, 1978a, 1979a). The way in which techniques change, so changing the input–output coefficients in the matrixes underlying the process of reproduction of commodities and capital, would be part of that dynamic version. Similarly, if profit rates are found to differ systematically between different sectors of the economy, however defined, the dynamic story would also have to attempt to explain such differentials. Such 'dynamization' has further to be embedded in a theory of capitalist competition and social relations. Attempts are now being made to construct such theories and derive their implications (see, for example, Semmler, 1984; Flaschel and Semmler 1986). It is necessary to extend such work to the international arena and to take into account many so-called pre-capitalist features of third world countries in order to understand the dynamics of capital. Theories of imperialism and transnationalization of capital would enter into such a construct. Nothing so ambitious is attempted in this paper. Instead, I shall try to delineate some of the international political processes that shape the fates of the economies of third world countries (TWCs) and suggest that IMF policies generally buttress the dominance of transnational capital over the capitalists of TWCs, and at the same time perpetuate many of the features of underdevelopment that characterize the latter.

When we fix on distributive parameters as being an integral part of this income determination process, we see that the Sraffa critique of neoclassical economic theory directs our attention (as Kalecki's work did in a different way) to the institutional mechanisms keeping particular distributive arrangements in place. What determines the average rate of profit in a modern, capitalist economy? In an economy with a well-developed system of capital markets it might be monetary policy that, in combination with investment and saving propensities, determines the rate of profit and the share of profits in national income. But in economies where capital markets are not well developed or where drastic changes in the share of wage incomes are resisted by the profit-earners and rentiers, many legal, regulatory and coercive instruments are used to keep up the share of non-wage income in total income. When we transfer our attention from an essentially closed economy to an international economy, we can see that movements of capital between different economies are influenced by many political factors and factors governing the behaviour of such actors as transnational manufacturing, mining and banking firms, and the IMF and the World Bank. If the method of division of the total product and the surplus within a country is a political process, then the division of the total product and the surplus in the international economy is even more emphatically a political process. Factor prices, and factor movements are as much shaped by that process as they determine the limits and character of the process. Paradoxically enough, the severely structuralist work of Sraffa has helped greatly to pinpoint this fact, which seems at first to lie outside his domain of discourse altogether.

The Sraffa critique has been extended to the area of international trade theory by Steedman, Metcalfe (Steedman, 1979b) and other economists. From their analysis it follows that most of the propositions of the Heckscher–Ohlin–Samuelson theory of international trade fall by the wayside when we take account of the fact that traded products are produced by means of other products, and therefore rates of profit earned at different stages of production of the product enter integrally into the relative prices earned in the international market.

The Steedman–Metcalfe results in international trade theory are derived on the basis of completely equalized profit rates. However, systematic differentials in profit rates as between countries or sectors would strengthen rather than weaken those results as far as they constitute a refutation of the folklore of neoclassical theories of international trade. Systematic differences in the mechanisms determining the international prices of primary products sold by LDCs and manufactured products sold by the advanced capitalist countries have long been recognized (see Kalecki, 1954, ch. 1). Empirically it has been found furthermore that there are systematic and persisting differences in the prices of the same commodites as between different advanced countries linked by international trade (Encauoua and Geroski, 1986). These findings run directly counter to the policy of making internal prices conform to 'world market prices', which is a major constituent of the IMF prescriptions. They also necessitate a direct investigation of the political and social factors influencing the actual international economic policies that the IMF view seeks to rationalize. I turn now to an investigation of these factors.

V

It has been recognized since 1982, when Mexico appeared to be on the point of defaulting in her external debt obligations, that a major part of the third world – including many of the countries that had been hailed as showing the path of development via exports and liberal trade policies – has been passing through a debt crisis of unparalleled dimensions.[7] The solution to the debt crisis is nowhere in sight. Debt reschedulings have only postponed the day of reckoning, literally, for many countries and many TNBs. This has been recognized by the World Bank (1985a), which has pontificated:

> An inherent property of durable structures is that they flex, and do not break. That property was evident in the financial markets during 1984, as participants responded positively and flexibly in coping with the debt-servicing problems of the developing countries.

What are the factors that endow the debt-servicing problems with the property of durability? What are the essential features of the structure that the TNBs, the IMF, the World Bank or the OECD governments try to protect while they negotiate 'flexibly' with the heavily indebted LDCs about debt rescheduling?

As a mnemonic device for summarizing the factors governing the origins and persistence of third world debt problems, we can say that they are caused by misfortunes, mismanagement and machinations (three Ms). The first refers to the fact that most of the third world countries started their development effort with adverse initial conditions in respect of development of productive forces, endowments of mineral and other natural resources, composition of aggregate and of industrial output, and, above all, social structures and political conditions. This combination of adverse factors can be summarized as the state of being underdeveloped or retarded (Bagchi, 1982, ch. 2).

The initial problems of the non-socialist third world countries were compounded by the mismanagement of their economies by their ruling classes. Many orthodox economists have focused on the policies that have caused macroeconomic imbalances in the economy.[8] However, few of them have tried to find out what might have been the long-term alternative to the policies pursued by third world governments and entrepreneurs, and fewer still have enquired closely into the predisposing causes of the widespread 'mismanagement' of the economies by the politicians and the businessmen.

There is a third group of causes responsible for the deepening of the debt crisis of the third world. This is the deliberate manipulation of the difficulties of the debt-ridden countries by TNBs and other TNCs, by policy-makers in OECD countries and by the IMF and the World Bank. In such manipulation, these bodies have generally had the willing collaboration of ruling groups in the third world, but in some cases, as in Tanzania, they have also faced resistance. It should be obvious that misfortunes, mismanagement and machinations are intimately related to one another. The third world economies could not have been so easily manipulated if their mismanagement by domestic rulers had not delivered them into the hands of the IMF and the TNBs, nor would mismanagement have been so pervasive if the ruling groups had been aligned differently with the actual producers in these countries or with the ruling classes of the advanced capitalist countries. It is analytically expedient none the less to take the three Ms separately for an initial foray.

While the three Ms comprehend the major aspects of the internal social and political dynamics of the third world countries and their interaction with the advanced capitalist countries, policies pursued within the latter and competition between the countries belonging to the OECD also have serious implications for the development of the external debt positions of the third world. In particular, deflationary monetary policies pursued by leading OECD countries, the emergence of Japan as the country enjoying the largest payments surpluses for several years running, and protectionist policies pursued by practically all OECD nations have aggravated the debt problems of the third world. They have also quickened the process of transfer of real resources from the third world to the first, and increased the costs of that transfer; it is one of the ironies of the situation that such changes have not benefited the major part of the population of the first world either.

VI

The vast majority of TWCs are exporters of primary products and importers of manufactured goods. The demand for most of the products exported by these countries is inelastic with respect to changes in world income and, in particular, the incomes of the OECD countries that are their main customers. A handful of countries such as Brazil, Mexico, Argentina, South Korea, Hong Kong, Singapore and Taiwan (the so-called newly industrializing countries – NICs) managed to expand their exports of manufactures by sizeable amounts in the 1970s. But some of them, such as Brazil, Mexico and Argentina, became enmeshed in severe debt-servicing problems from 1981 onwards.

The terms of trade of most of the TWCs had sagged in the post-war period mainly because of the structure of their exports and imports (Bairoch, 1975; UNCTAD, 1982, Part II; Spraos, 1982). The steep rise in oil prices after 1978, the rise in interest rates in the international economy, and the enormous appreciation of the US dollar further accentuated the decline in terms of trade of those countries – and these included some of the major NICs, which imported large quantities of oil and capital goods, and had their imports denominated in US dollars even when these imports did not originate in the US (see World Bank, 1985c, ch. 3). The appreciation of the US dollar in relation to most TWC currencies has directly added to the debt burden of these countries, since the debt was often denominated in dollars.

The structure of production and the tendency of spurts of growth in the NICs to be accompanied by balance-of-payments difficulties because of the income–inelastic nature of their imports (Taylor, 1982) have contributed to stop–go cycles in these countries (Bagchi, 1982, ch. 5). They also nullified the attempts of the OPEC countries to raise long-term oil prices in 1973 and 1978. On the one hand, some of the producing countries such as Saudi Arabia and Kuwait, because of their archaic social structures and their refusal to permit immigration of foreign workers, have been unable fruitfully to utilize their surpluses and have used them to build up assets in advanced capitalist countries, to construct luxury housing of all kinds and to import armaments on a massive scale. Other countries such as Nigeria, Iran under the Shah and Venezuela, to a greater or lesser extent, have embarked on capital expenditures on a large scale without taking care to see that such expenditures added to the productive capacity of the economy: the precondition for effective absorption of foreign technology was a change in social structure so as to diffuse literacy and purchasing power as widely as possible, and the ruling classes stood squarely against permitting any such social change.

I have imperceptibly shifted from a consideration of misfortunes to a consideration of the type and effects of mismanagement of economies by the rulers and policy-makers in the third world. The 'mismanagement' of third world economies by their ruling classes also inheres largely in their class structure. The typical lapses on the part of these rulers that have been shown up in the orthodox analysis of their record of macroeconomic management are an inadequate rate of saving, failure to get markets to work so as to bring about an efficient allocation and use of resources, a tendency to foster import substitution irrespective of its costs, and a corresponding failure to take advantage of opportunities provided by the growth of world trade. However, the criticism rarely takes account of the constraints on the rulers' decision-making processes imposed by their heterogeneity – landlords, petty chieftains, merchants, bankers and industrialists are all in the ruling coalition – and by their inability to be rid of the influence of foreign capital in some of the most vital decisions affecting the economic and social well-being of their societies. Nor is there any discussion of the longer-term issues of decision-making. Orthodox analysts of policy-making have advanced to the point where they talk about the need to adopt 'positive adjustment policies' (OECD, 1983). By such policies they mostly mean the need to shift resources out of uncompetitive sectors to internationally competitive sectors, the need to cut down burgeoning government deficits, and the need to improve the working of labour and credit markets.

But, in fact, a country that had earlier been plagued by underdevelopment needs to practise considerable social engineering in order to enforce 'positive adjustment policies'. Land reforms to minimize the non-market power of landlords, to increase the attractiveness of investment in assets other than land and real estate, and to improve the distribution of incomes and the educational level of workers are a minimum condition for effecting structural change. In the field of industry, with a fast-changing technology, the need is to adopt an 'active adjustment policy', 'wherein the policy-makers look ahead to future comparative costs, based on the removal of structural bottlenecks, and on long-term real resource availabilities . . .'. An 'active adjustment policy' is no different from a dynamic policy of self-reliance based on the endowment of resources, including human resources, of a country (Bagchi, Ghosh and Dasgupta, 1985, p. 5). The Japanese, who have successively ridden one external shock after another and have emerged as world leaders in such diverse fields of production and export as finished steel, consumer electronics, automobiles and industrial robots, have always believed in planning ahead and have created their own dynamic comparative advantage rather than allow their economy to be buffeted by arbitrary changes in the direction of world trade.[9]

The heterogeneity of the ruling classes of many TWCs, their total unwillingness to effect any major social changes lest they get out of hand and their dependence on TNBs, the IMF, the World Bank and the OECD governments for financial flows, all combine to make their policies *ad hoc* and myopic. (An agreement between coalition partners with divergent interests has to be short term, for one partner is always hoping to do better than the others with any possible change in the parameters that are relevant to their decision.) With a greater degree of internationalization of world production and consumption patterns, the rich in the third world generally imitate the consumption styles of the rich and the not-so-rich in the first world. Often they live ostentatiously in order to show their own people that they are as good as the colonial rulers they have displaced or the native aristocracy they hope to be co-opted into. When they try to foster domestic industry, the effort is often bedevilled by lack of experience leading to excessive costs, by failure to build up to a scale that might allow the firms or the plants to break even, and by restrictive practices of all kinds. The so-called import substitution route to industrialization seemed to be the only one available to many, if not most, of the TWCs, for it seemed to provide a respite from endemic balance-of-payments crises. However, high tariffs and quotas are not the only factors pushing up costs in import-substituting industries. Since many TNCs build up factories under high tariff barriers in these countries, the transfer pricing practised by them pushes up the costs of TNC-affiliated enterprises. High turnover margins are charged as a 'normal' trade practice in these countries. Moreover, there are often formal or informal rings ensuring stability of market shares, erecting impediments against the entry of new firms, and pushing up prices all round.

When such macro-social processes impeding mobility and growth work together with an agrarian property structure that is holding up the growth of agriculture and marketed surplus, the income levels of the ordinary people are depressed and bottlenecks against the fuller utilization of capacity multiply in the form of shortages of domestic and importable inputs (since there is an endemic foreign exchange shortage). Under these circumstances, the policy-makers have to resort to foreign loans on an unsustainable scale and their economies fall a ready victim to the deflationary policies enforced by the IMF and its backers and collaborators.

However, the machinations of the TNBs and TNCs, the governments of the dominant OECD countries, their financial agencies and the indigenous collaborators of foreign capital, of course, do not begin at the point where a TWC is already strapped for debt and appears to be unable to meet its debt-service obligations. Soon after the first oil shock of 1973, TNBs and financial markets in the West in general were flush with OPEC funds, which were recycled in a multitude of ways. The advanced capitalist countries, of course, were the first targets of their TNBs, but as recession gathered strength in such countries, while some of the NICs seemed to be eager to borrow money, the TNBs directed increasing proportions of their funds to the major NICs of Latin America and, to a lesser extent, of Asia. This was also the period when official aid from the Development Assistance Committee (DAC) countries to the LDCs either declined absolutely or stagnated. As a result, the proportion of official flows to net financial flows of DAC countries to the LDCs declined from 49.1 per cent in 1970 to 35.1 per cent in 1978, and the financial flow from banks based in the DAC countries to the LDCs increased from 4.4 per cent to 29.89 per cent between 1970 and 1978 (UNCTAD,

1980, ch. III). These developments became even more pronounced after 1978; by 1981 new lending by TNBs amounted to US$ 195 billion, of which the LDCs accounted for 32 per cent (World Bank, 1985c, p. 110).

Many of these were syndicated loans and an increasing proportion was officially guaranteed. It has been noted that these procedures created moral hazard problems, and banks lent increasing amounts without a proper assessment of the repaying ability of the borrowing countries, and especially of those countries that were supposed to be favoured politically by the USA (Gersovitz, 1985; Harberger, 1985; Nunnenkamp, 1985). More than four-fifths of the external debt of such countries as Argentina, Brazil, Mexico and Venezuela came to be owed to a handful of US-based TNBs. An increasing proportion of the debt of the LDCs was contracted at floating interest rates with short maturities (five to seven years in the case of the so-called long-term loans). The upward trend in interest rates combined with a shortening of the repayment period enormously increased the debt-servicing problems of the LDCs.

One aspect of the flows of loans from TNBs and, to a much lesser extent, of official aid flows from DACs that has escaped attention is the outflow of private capital from the LDCs to the financial centres of the world, and in particular to Switzerland, the UK and the USA. Long before the debt crisis erupted, capital had been transferred from most LDCs to these financial centres by TNCs, private capitalists and others, and there had not been any proper accounting for such outflows. Some idea of the magnitude of transfer effected can be gauged from the fact that the former Shah of Iran is reputed to have accumulated a personal wealth of at least US$ 25 billion when he had to flee the country in the wake of the fundamentalist take-over in Iran. Some semi-official estimates have been made of the private capital outflows from the heavily indebted countries of Latin America. According to these estimates, over the period 1974–82, capital flight from Mexico amounted to US$ 32.7 billion, that from Venezuela amounted to $10.8 billion, and from Argentina to $15.3 billion. Over the same period, the external debts of Mexico, Venezuela and Argentina increased by $82.6 billion, $27 billion and $32.6 billion, respectively (World Bank, 1985b).

Thus, it would appear that, as official aid or officially guaranteed bank loans were flowing into the country by one window, private capital (naturally belonging to the rich and the powerful) was flowing out by another window. This suited the interest of the US government, which had turned its home base into the biggest absorber of capital from all over the world through its policy of high interest rates and encouragement of uninhibited private enterprise. The TNBs and the ruling groups of the LDCs joined together in pursuing a policy that would keep up the official exchange rate, allow the transfer of capital abroad on favourable terms, and facilitate the import of goods in the profits of which TNBs, other TNCs and domestic capital, and the rulers would all have a share. The stashing away of capital abroad by the indigenous ruling groups of LDCs partly explains why they were so eager to co-operate with the IMF and TNBs in executing policies that would effectively damage their economies and make them even more dependent on international trade and international financial organizations. (Enormous amounts of capital are reputed to have been removed to the US and other financial centres by Marcos, the ex-President, and his cronies, from the Philippines, which had been bankrupted and badly impoverished by the policies pursued by the dictator.)

The objective collaboration between the rulers of most LDCs, the DAC countries and the IMF and World Bank took other forms which had the immediate effect of increasing the outflows of resources of the LDCs and their external indebtedness.[10] Some of the major oil-producing countries such as Saudi Arabia and Iran under the Shah, were induced to go in for arms expenditures – mostly bought from the OECD countries – on a massive scale so that much, if not most, of their surpluses were gobbled up this way. Iran and Iraq were locked in a disastrous war for more than eight years, and much of their national income has been squandered in that war. The aggressive posture of Israel, backed by major OECD governments, has kept the military expenditures of most West Asian and North African governments at a very high level, while Israel herself has been badly affected by the global recession and the war-related drain of resources. Many other countries, such as India and Pakistan, that can ill afford to waste their surpluses on military expenditures have been pressurized into competitive arms-buying from the OECD countries and the Soviet Union because of superpower competition for hegemony in every region of the world.

The oil price hikes in 1973–4 and 1978–9 by OPEC countries and other oil producers have brought only transient benefits to the oil-producing LDCs. Besides military expenditures, the rise in the prices of manufactured and, especially, capital goods exported by OECD countries to the oil-producing LDCs soon ate up their trade surpluses. Then commercial bank loans, at higher interest rates and with shorter periods of repayment, often turned some of the oil producers such as Mexico, Nigeria and Venezuela into heavily indebted countries. The refusal of non-OPEC producers to join the oil cartel, the success of Western economies in cutting down the use of oil, and continued recession of the global economy have led to a continuous decline in the price of oil in recent years. It has now reached levels that prevailed in 1974 or so. This slide in oil prices has enormously aggravated the balance-of-payments problems and indebtedness of oil-producing LDCs or NICs such as Nigeria, Mexico and Indonesia.

Meanwhile, the recession raging in practically all the major OECD countries (except Japan) and the deflationary monetary policies pursued at first in the US and UK and then in all the other major DAC countries made the prospects of expansion of trade by the LDCs (for which the OECD remained the biggest trade partners) extremely bleak. The crunch in the international debt situation came in 1982, with the threat of Mexican default. This led to a drastic fall in bank lending by the TNBs to the heavily indebted LDCs. One result was a major recession in the LDCs induced both by IMF-imposed adjustment policies and by their inability to buy imports that were essential for carrying on production in these economies. They found themselves at the short end of an intensified international division of labour.

The IMF, often prodded by consortia of TNBs, has carried out 'rescue operations' for many of the LDCs that were plagued by balance-of-payments difficulties. It has generally imposed 'conditionality' clauses of an increasingly severe nature in an effort to bring about 'structural adjustment' in these countries. These comprise rigorous limits on public expenditure (including spending by public sector enterprises) and on the expansion of money supply, curtailment of subsidies (especially those that are meant to benefit consumers rather than producers), wage restraint, raising of interest rates, abolition or lowering of quantitative restrictions on imports (and exports), relaxation of price and exchange controls and a host of similar conservative measures (Guitian, 1981; Bagchi, 1981). As the international liquidity position became tighter after 1980, the TNBs themselves sought IMF clearance before lending to third world countries. Increasingly, conditions very similar to those required by the IMF as adjustment policies from prospective borrowers were imposed on the latter by the TNBs themselves. Moreover, the differences between the various tiers of conditionality clauses became blurred in IMF policy-making, and progressively tougher conditions were imposed even when the IMF granted loans for meeting short-term balance-of-payments crises (Dell, 1982).

The fiat of the IMF, TNBs and their collaborators in the LDCs has not gone unchallenged. In Jamaica, Tunisia, Brazil and many other countries there have been popular protests and revolts against the economically and politically repressive measure that the IMF and the TNBs have sought to impose. In rare cases, such as the government of Tanzania and some democratically elected governments in Latin America, there have also been official denunciations of the IMF-imposed policies. So the contradictions in the international economic arena have evoked resistance at various levels; it would therefore be wrong to view the reactionary version of international economic policy-making as an all-conquering force, even in this period of global economic crisis.

VII

In countries such as the UK and the US, and other OECD countries taking their cue from the UK, one argument for following deflationary policies was that, if they were pursued long enough, they would lead to better functioning markets and structural adjustment of the kind needed to stimulate productivity growth all round. The recovery of US economic activity in 1983 and 1984 and resumption of growth in Japan seemed to give support to this view. Furthermore, the rate of inflation in the major industrial countries also decelerated considerably, coming down to 4.1 per cent per year (IMF, 1985a, ch. II). However, US economic recovery was propelled not by deflationary policies but by a high-interest policy combined with a strongly expansionary fiscal policy. It took place at the cost of widening balance-of-payments deficits, which converted the US from a net international creditor to the biggest absorber of funds in the international capital market – funds that were often sucked from the drastically impoverished NICs of Latin America. Moreover, the spread effect of the US recovery was much weaker than expected. As the Bank for International Settlements remarked in the Annual Report for 1984–5:

> Two disturbing facts should serve as a starting point for the badly needed innovative thinking in both fields [of economic analysis and policy]. The first is that macroeconomic anti-inflationary policies have now been in place in most western countries for almost five years without having succeeded in eradicating inflation. The second is that recovery has progressed far without having done more than halt the unemployment in Europe and bring only partial and unevenly distributed relief in the United States. Worse still, in Europe there is little prospect of any really substantial reduction in unemployment even if growth were to continue at a moderate pace for some years to come.
>
> (BIS, 1985, p. 4)

In fact, most projections for the remaining part of the 1980s did not hold out prospects of substantial growth in either the industrial countries or the majority of the LDCs. To take just one example, in April 1985 the IMF published a scenario for both short-term and medium-term prospects of growth. At that time it predicted a rate of growth of 4.5 per cent in the output of the LDCs ('developing countries') in 1986 compared with 1985 and of 4.0 per cent in 1985 as compared with 1984 (IMF, 1985a, p. 205). Six months later, in October 1985, these figures were revised downward to 4.1 per cent and 3.5 per cent, respectively (IMF, 1985b, p. 43). Even with rather optimistic assumptions, the IMF (1985a) could only project a rate of growth of a little over 3 per cent per year in the output of the industrial countries until 1990, with only marginal declines in the proportion of the population unemployed.

In spite of the official preaching of the virtues of free trade, strong protectionist barriers against the entry of goods from the third world had been erected by most of the OECD countries. The continuing recession in these countries and mounting levels of unemployment have strengthened the protectionist tendencies. While nominal tariff rates have come down in some cases as a result of multilateral trade negotiations and a generalized system of preferences has been extended to imports from many LDCs, much of the presumed benefits derivable from these changes have been nullified by the multiplication of non-tariff barriers against imports from LDCs and all trade partners in general (UNCTAD, 1982, pp. 25–7). The so-called multifibre agreement, which governs the imports of textiles from the LDCs, is one of the most blatant examples of non-price discrimination.

Besides such general problems of recession and discrimination obstructing the process of recovery in the heavily indebted LDCs and increasing their debt-repayment burden, competition between, and changes in the relative positions of, the leading OECD countries have introduced further elements of instability in the patterns of international commodity and capital flows. In particular, while the USA has emerged as the leading borrower country, Japan has surfaced as the country with the largest surpluses in her trade and balance of payments. Furthermore, in recent years the major part of Japanese investment overseas has flowed towards the USA. This has created severe problems for the LDCs, for unlike in the era when the USA and other North Atlantic countries channelled part of their surpluses towards the LDCs, the latter now have only an uncertain flow of loans from TNBs marginally augmented by semi-official and official 'aid' to depend on to meet their balance-of-payments deficits.

The nature of the contradiction inherent in the situation can be clearly grasped if we look briefly at the relations of Japan with her East Asian neighbours. It has been claimed that the Asian NICs 'have been catching up with Japan by manufacturing labour-intensive, technologically standardized textile products and electrical and electronic machinery, and thereby gaining the edge in the world export market, while they themselves are in turn being pursued by the ASEAN countries.[11] Furthermore, it is even possible to surmise that this multiple catch-up process is about to extend from the labour-intensive, technologically standardized to the capital- and technology-intensive industrial subsectors (Watanabe and Kajiwara, 1983, p. 37). However, this catching-up process is not at all smooth. First of all, Japan is unwilling to open her markets to more labour-intensive products from either the Asian NICs or the ASEAN countries. As has been pointed out by a Japanese economist:

> Product differentiation will lead to a pattern of export of higher-quality goods from the industrial countries and lower-quality goods from Asia. As Japanese incomes increase, their tastes become more sophisticated whereas the income elasticity for higher-quality goods is relatively higher, the demand for lower-quality goods is subjected to price competitiveness in the market. The price effect tends to be depressed, however, by the complicated distribution system indigenous to Japan.
>
> (Tanaka, 1980, p. 417)

The same economist writes, elaborating the last point:

> Japan's product distribution system involves the addition of commercial margins at each of the complicated wholesale stages before the products reach the consumer so that the competitive advantage of low prices that would otherwise be enjoyed by NIC products is obliterated.
>
> (Tanaka, 1980, p. 432)

In addition, the MITI and other official and semi-official agencies have imposed various straightforward and non-transparent barriers against the import of labour-intensive products from the LDCs (FEER, 1984, pp. 81–3). While Japan complains about protectionism in the USA, NICs and other countries in East Asia complain about Japanese protectionism. The problems of the East Asian countries are rendered acute by the fact that they are heavily dependent on Japan for imports of capital goods and, to a lesser extent, intermediate products. Some of the high-performing Asian NICs such as South Korea and Singapore were badly affected by global recession and protectionism (FEER, 1985a). In this context, the channelling of most Japanese foreign investment to the USA and other OECD countries rather than to the LDCs can only have further destablizing effects. The continued pursuit of orthodox fiscal policies by Japan does not augur well either for the reflation of the Japanese economy or for the East Asian economies or for the world economy as a whole (FEER, 1985b).

Behind Japanese policies, of course, lie the military-political relations between Japan and the USA, her relations with the two major socialist countries, namely, the Soviet Union and China, and the determination of her ruling class to keep labour on a tight leash. Such issues cannot be fully explored here. But probing into one segment of inter-capitalist relations in East Asia has been enough to show that a solution of the debt problem of the LDCs is not likely to be found by tinkering with the financial mechanism alone. Overhauling the financial mechanism and bringing down the absurdly inflated interest burdens (see, for example, Avramovic, 1983), if necessary through the declared intention of all LDCs to repudiate their debts, would be a necessary condition. The numerous rescheduling operations mounted under the leadership of the aid consortia, TNB consortia and the IMF can be seen as attempts to perpetuate the old financial order and extract as much surplus out of the LDCS for the benefit of TNBs and their associates.

Redressal of this situation will require major political initiatives both inside the LDCs and on the international plane. The orthodox theory of international economic policy-making tries to avoid all such issues.

VII

My road from Sraffa's critique of neoclassical economic theory to the intricacies of international economic policy has in some ways been exactly the reverse of the direction of the intellectual journey undertaken by Sraffa. He had started by studying wartime inflation in Italy, and conducted further studies on banking and monetary policies,[12] and then turned to a project of rejuvenation of classical theory as a method of understanding the processes of income distribution in a commodity-producing economy. But the reverse journey also has to be undertaken by later researchers who would want to relate this knowledge recovered to the processes in the real world. In summing up my extremely sketchy outline of the issues under enquiry I would like to reiterate the following points.

First, international economic policy-making *à la* IMF and World Bank really boils down to internal policy-making for the TWCs. It involves detailed and systematic interference in practically all aspects of economic policy; moreover, the IMF–World Bank authorities can rarely, if ever, exact any *quid pro quo* from the advanced capitalist countries. They can do little to change the large and continuing balance-of-payments surpluses of such countries as Japan and Western Germany, the huge budget deficits of the US, the protectionist tendencies in most of the OECD countries, or the high interest rates and the high costs of imports from the OECD countries.

Secondly, the internal policies recommended for the borrowing countries are meant to increase the surpluses in the hands of private profit-earners in those countries. The class bias of such policies is made brutally clear in most of the policy statements of the IMF, the World Bank and their spokesmen.

Thirdly, the policies pursued by the TWCs in the 1970s and the subsequent policies imposed on them by the financial system result in transfers of large surpluses to the developed capitalist countries and the financial markets centring on them. When a poor, third world country, reeling under recession, has to transfer anywhere up to 5–6 per cent of her national income as debt- and investment-servicing costs, it naturally results in further cutback in domestic activities and further deformation of the domestic economic system.

Fourthly, political factors play a direct and, very often, a decisive role, in the policies and mechanisms leading to the redistribution of incomes towards profit-earners in TWCs, and the transfer of a significant proportion of the surplus towards the developed capitalist countries. It is not very fruitful under these circumstances to try to separate the role of 'unequal exchange' or the tendency of rates of profit to be equalized across sectors and countries. Even if interest rates are equalized across countries, this equalization is itself orchestrated within a vertically ordered international financial and economic order. Sraffa's framework could be used to find out the implications of the equalization of rates of profit (including interest) within each tier of the vertically ordered world system over a short interval of time. But one would have also to enquire into the mechanisms that perpetuate the large differentials in nominal interest rates paid, let us say, by financiers or bankers or conglomerate firms and petty traders, artisans, poor peasants and share-croppers in the third world. If we want to explain how a vertically ordered system is maintained and how the different tiers of the system are articulated, we have to take into account variables and relations that go well beyond the confines of pure economic theory. Likewise, conflicts within the system and breaks in the system would also need to be explained by taking class structures, group conflict and international political realities into account. We owe it to the legacy of Sraffa and Marx that we can raise and discuss such issues without encountering any insuperable barriers between one mode of discourse and another.

Acknowledgement

I am indebted to Krishna Bharadwaj and to participants at the Sraffa conference for stimulating comments.

Notes

1 The 'rational expectations' episode in economic theory can be regarded as a warning against regarding either expectations of business firms or government policies as a *deus ex machina* that can be externally coupled to the play of the structure which is regarded as being independent of investors' (or asset-holders') expectations and of government policies. The possibility of a change in the mode of interplay of social structures and state policy can be provisionally denied for carrying out comparative static exercises in the short run, but to do so in either a

predictive or a prescriptive model seems to be nothing less than stupid. Few economic theorists seem yet to be aware of the need to take such 'complications' into account.

2 For a summary of these models of financial repression or disequilibrium and appropriate policies in their presence, see Fry (1982a,b).

3 In IMF (1985a, p. 2), we read:

> A welcome development in late 1984 and the early part of 1985 was the easing in short-term interest rates in the United States. This change reversed the rise in rates that had occurred from early in 1983 up to the middle of last year and appears to have reflected shifts in asset preferences as well as a slackening in the pace of demand growth and diminished near-term inflationary expectations. Interest rates in the other major countries (except the United Kingdom) have generally been steadier and lower in real terms than those in the United States.
>
> Despite the downward trend in US interest rates and the lower rates prevailing in other financial centres, real yields remain surprisingly high in a historical perspective. In January 1985 the average of short-term rates in the five principal financial centres, after adjustment for current inflation was 4½ per cent, while the corresponding long-term rate was over 6 per cent. These yields are 3½ percentage points and 4 percentage points, respectively, above the average for 1960–80. While interest rates are expected to fall gradually in the medium term, no decline (and even some increase) is assured in the near-term forecast.

4 For a short account of the ideology informing the typical 'structural adjustment' policies recommended by the IMF, the World Bank and the major commercial banks, see Bagchi (1981). For accounts of the conditionality clauses imposed by the IMF, see Gold (1979) and Guitian (1981). For a discussion of alternatives to IMF-style policies, see Singh (1985).

5 The invalidity of this separation was exploited by Milton Friedman and other monetarists to put forward their policy prescription for the functioning of a capitalist economy.

6 These comments are not meant to deny the reality of the paradox and difficulties – such as contractionary effects of devaluation, stop–go cycles caused by balance-of-payments deficits, and continuing stagflation – that Taylor seeks to analyse. For an analysis of some of these problems and references to the pioneering work of R.N. Cooper and Carlos Diaz Alejandro, see Bagchi (1982, esp. ch. 5).

7 According to the figures published by the World Bank in 1985, the external long-term debt of 104 'developing countries' (a bitter euphemism for most of the African countries south of the Sahara and many other countries as well) came to US$ 655 billion. This does not cover the short-term debt of many of the countries nor does it cover most of the loans without public guarantees of repayment. The ratio of debt-service payments to GNP in 1983 exceeded 3 per cent for such countries as Brazil and Turkey and 5 per cent for Chile. Similar figures could be quoted for many countries whose total debts are small but whose total GNPs are also small. See World Bank (1985a).

8 See, for example, the introductory summary by Cuddington and Smith and papers by Dornbusch and Harberger in Smith and Cuddington (1985). See also World Bank (1985, chs 4 and 5).

9 See, in this connection, two issues of *The Developing Economies* (Institute of Developing Economies, 1972 and 1980) concerned specifically with the structural adjustment problems of the Japanese economy. In December 1972, Ichiro and other economists saw overseas Japanese investment (mainly in the 'developing countries') as the way to increase Japan's resource base and at the same time

tackle emerging problems of environmental pollution in that small island-country. In December 1980, Hiroshi Kitamura and others emphasized the inadequacy of a trade-policy-centred approach in solving structural adjustment problems, and emphasized innovations in technology, marketing organizations, co-operative organizations for development at the municipal level, the creation of new needs and product diversification – all supported by deliberate government policies. These prescriptions derive importance from the fact that Japanese public authorities and firms have actually carried out many of these policies with resounding success.

10 It should be pointed out that, although the IMF was supposed to guard the interests of all member countries equally, it in fact consistently discriminated against LDCs, denying them loans at critical times or imposing unnecessarily harsh conditions (Gulati, 1980).

11 In this context, Asian NICs include South Korea, Taiwan, Hong Kong and Singapore, while ASEAN countries include Thailand, Malaysia, Indonesia and the Philippines.

12 See, for example, the bibliography of Piero Sraffa's published writings to 1976 in Roncaglia (1978, pp. 151–3).

19

Clearing the Path for 'Production of Commodities by Means of Commodities': Notes on the Collaboration of Maurice Dobb in Piero Sraffa's Edition of the 'Works and Correspondence of David Ricardo'

Brian H. Pollitt
Glasgow

The first ten volumes of Sraffa's edition of the *Works and Correspondence of David Ricardo* were published for the Royal Economic Society by the Cambridge University Press over the years 1951–5. After the publication of Vol. X, Sraffa began to 'put together out of a mass of old notes' the pages published in 1960 as *Production of Commodities by Means of Commodities*. This was an assembly of cogitations from earlier decades to which 'little was added, apart from filling gaps which had become apparent in the process (such as the adapting of the distinction between "basics" and "non-basics" to the case of joint products)' (Sraffa, 1960, p. vi). The task occupied Sraffa for some five years but was only a fraction of what he himself described as 'the disproportionate length of time over which so short a work has been in preparation' (ibid).

The small number and sparse length of Sraffa's lifelong publications have been the subject of wry, affectionate, admiring or exasperated comment over the years. The dearth of formal publications over the period 1932–51 was especially conspicuous[1] and has been explained principally in terms of the magnitude of the tasks relating to his edition of Ricardo. To this has been added observation of Sraffa's extreme 'perfectionism'. The trait is illuminated by his pursuit of an impeccable reproduction of Ricardo's published works and manuscripts and of the correspondence to and from Ricardo's contemporaries. But the term also embraces his painful difficulties in distilling his own thoughts and writings into formulations he felt able to commit to the printed page. These seem to have originated in the finely honed power of his own mind to perceive ambiguities of meaning or logical flaws in the sequences of words assembled for diverse purposes by others. When turned in upon its own product, this same power checked and sometimes paralysed his capacity to expound via the printed word both his own lines of thought and those of Ricardo. What follows is a brief explanation of the role played by Maurice Dobb in making it possible for Piero Sraffa to publish his edition of Ricardo and thereby to proceed to the publication of *Production of Commodities by Means of Commodities*.

Illumination of the origins and nature of the Dobb–Sraffa collaboration is not greatly aided by the reproduction of their published accounts of it. These were in both cases succinct. In his 'Random biographical notes', written for a Polish readership in 1965, Dobb recorded that in 1948 – the year in which he was elected a Fellow and Lecturer of Trinity College and in which his teaching duties consequentially increased – he 'started collaborating with P. Sraffa in completing the editing of the 10-volume edition of the *Works and Correspondence of David Ricardo* and in writing several editorial Notes and Introductions (including the Introduction to vol. I)' (Dobb, 1978, p. 119). For his part, in the General Preface to the edition, dated December 1950, Sraffa wrote that: 'In 1948 Mr Maurice Dobb came in to assist with the editorial work, in particular being associated in the writing of the Introductions to vols. I, II, V and VI' (Sraffa, 1951, p. x). The dates and planned length of all joint working sessions on the Ricardo edition were recorded by Dobb in his Cambridge University Diaries (MHD–A). These report that the initiation of collaborative effort began on 5 February 1948 and concluded on 28 June 1954. The entries are a useful guide to the duration of the endeavour and more especially to its intensity over particular periods within it. Dobb's comments to correspondents on its progress over these years are also instructive. But a much broader contextualization of the enterprise is necessary and this must include (albeit in compressed form) some account of earlier personal, political and intellectual events of salient importance to either Dobb, Sraffa or both. The brief historical narrative required for this purpose inevitably covers ground that for many is well trodden. Even so, some incidents (which may be considered variably as of major or trivial importance) are unlikely to be generally known and this must serve to justify the more familiar historical recapitulation.

Sraffa was born in 1898 and Dobb in 1900 and their common early transitions from youthful pacifism to revolutionary socialism were shaped by the same cataclysmic events: the First World War and the Bolshevik Revolution. Both events were witnessed in contrasting contexts. The difference in their ages was small but signified that Dobb escaped direct participation in the Great War while Sraffa did not; and the repercussions of the Russian Revolution upon Sraffa's Italian milieu were far sharper than upon Dobb's England.[2] When the two men first met, and in respects perhaps more readily understood by their contemporaries, Sraffa was thus 'older' than Dobb in more than simple years. Even so, Dobb then (as later) was a most unusual Englishman for Sraffa to meet. Professor E. J. Hobsbawm has referred to the 'Siberian climate in which the plant of intellectual Marxism then attempted to put out its feeble shoots' in Britain, and in which Cambridge, even in the 1930s, was 'an exaggerated example of avoidable Anglo-Saxon insularity' (Hobsbawm, 1967). In September 1920, none the less, Dobb had concluded his first year as a student of economics at Cambridge with an attack on Professor Achille Loria's endeavour to detach Marx from the labour theory of value (Dobb, 1920a); and he followed this with a trenchant critical deployment of the concept of surplus value that can be read with appreciation to this day (Dobb, 1920b). An attempt to resolve Böhm-Bawerk's 'great contradiction' was offered in February 1921 (Dobb, 1921). When he graduated from Cambridge in 1922, he joined the Communist Party in London as a Marxist and an economist (itself a rare combination at that time), and one influenced moreover in his broader political and philosophical readings by writers such as Croce and Labriola.[3]

While there is no certainty as to the year and place of their first meeting, it substantially antedated both Sraffa's removal to Cambridge in 1927 and the publication in the *Economic Journal* in 1926 of 'The laws of returns under competitive conditions' (Sraffa, 1926). In the spring of 1925, for example, Dobb was Sraffa's guest at Rapallo and the context of Dobb's report of this suggested yet earlier contact (Correspondence, Dobb to R. Palme Dutt, Cambridge, 20 May 1925; MHD-A and Archives of the CPGB, London). It was during this visit that Dobb saw the manuscript (which he cited in *Capitalist Enterprise and Social Progress* – Dobb, 1925, p. 88) that Sraffa was to publish later that year as 'Sulle relazioni fra costo e quantità prodottà' (Sraffa, 1925). It was quite evident that both men stood at the same (and in Cambridge quite isolated) point of entry from which Sraffa probed his 'dark spot' in 'the tranquil view which the modern theory of value presents us'. At root, this was a shared enthusiasm for the 'controversies on the theory of value by which political economy was characterised during the past century' and a shared opposition to the 'indifference' of their contemporaries towards this realm of theory – for Sraffa an indifference perhaps explicable because it had 'lost much of its direct bearing upon practical politics, and particularly in regard to doctrines of social changes, which had formerly been conferred upon it by Ricardo and afterwards by Marx, and in opposition to them by the bourgeois economists' (Sraffa, 1926, pp. 535–6).

Such indicators of early personal, political and intellectual affinity are important but should not of course be distorted into any claim for total congruity in interest and approach. Dobb reported that he had read Marshall in his student days with little liking (Dobb, 1978, p. 117). Whether he liked him or not, Marshall's influence upon him was perceptible throughout the 1920s and was not comprehensively rejected until his publication of *Political Economy and Capitalism* in 1937 (Dobb, 1937). Dobb was unable to find in Marx a 'tool-box' sufficiently complete for the analysis of detailed features of capitalist economy. In 1922, the imagery he drew upon to express himself on this subject was that of map-making. Marx's achievement, he suggested, was that he had drawn a small-scale map of capitalist economy as a whole.

'Orthodox' economics, by contrast, drew very large-scale maps but these were solely of part of the terrain – and the parts omitted were more important for Marx and Marxists than those they included. The problem, essentially, was that Marx's 'map' enabled you to find your way around the country but not from street to street in a particular town. 'Orthodox' economics, on the other hand, supplied a town street-guide but told you nothing of the country you were in. Street-guides were none the less valuable and elements of 'orthodox' economics, properly shorn of class bias, could and should be used to enrich Marxist analysis. It is easy to sympathize with Dobb's problem and his metaphor was not without attraction, but he proceeded to suggest that: 'We must use conceptions such as Marginal Utility to measure short-period fluctuations of Price, and in cases where, owing to concrete circumstances, purposely 'disregarded' by Marx . . . labour-value is not fully realised in the concrete world' (Dobb, 1922). In 1925 he still argued that the flaws in utility theory were sins of omission rather than commission. He wrote that it omitted crucial subjects such as the class struggle and imperialism – subjects that *determined* the margin – but that 'the theory of marginal utility seems to me logically perfectly sound, & as an explanation of prices & price changes quite a helpful advance on the classical doctrine, framing it more precisely & forging a more exact tool of analysis'.[4] Sraffa, of course, did not share this view at that time but, as is well known, the elaboration of his personal assault on Marshallian doctrine in lecture form in Cambridge from 1927 proved too taxing for him and he sought (and, with Keynes's collaboration, secured) relief from this burden. With hindsight, perhaps, the episodes foreshadowed difficulties that became more familiar in later years.

In any event, in the second half of the 1920s Dobb was not primarily concerned with theoretical problems in prevailing bourgeois economic doctrine. His energies were principally directed at the study and description, in both academic and popular form, of the political economy of the Russian Revolution. He spent the summer months of 1925 in the USSR and his major work entitled *Russian Economic Development since the Revolution* appeared in 1928 (Dobb, 1928a). He returned to Russia in 1929 and, in a pamphlet, reported with pleasure that: 'The Marx–Engels Institute recently published complete editions of the works of Hegel and Ricardo and sold 8,000 of one and 5,000 of the other on advance orders alone' (Dobb, 1930). A reviewer was in tune with the opinions of many of Dobb's British contemporaries when he remarked: 'If the Russian Revolution achieves nothing else, it will have succeeded in dragging one economist at least from a well-deserved obscurity' (d'A-G., 1930). In 1930 Dobb visited the USSR once more and was joined in Moscow in August of that year by Sraffa. This seems to have been the occasion when Sraffa carried personal and political tidings to the wife of the imprisoned Gramsci (see Napolitano *et al.*, 1978, p. 64), and in September Dobb briefly chronicled their plans to visit Soviet industrial and agricultural enterprises in Leningrad, the North Caucasus and the Ukraine (Correspondence, Dobb to E.A.G. and J. V. Robinson, Leningrad, 4 September 1930, MHD–A).

It was on his return from Russia in 1930 that Sraffa immersed himself fully in the edition of the works of Ricardo. Some years before, in 1922, the

Economic Journal had reported the discovery of Ricardo's long-lost 'Notes on Malthus' and announced their forthcoming publication 'with convenient apparatus' under 'the editorial care of Professor J. H. Hollander, of the Johns Hopkins University, and Dr. T. E. Gregory, of the London School of Economics' (Royal Economic Society, 1922). In 1928, as is well known, the Royal Economic Society, of which Keynes was Secretary, assigned a complete edition of the works of Ricardo to (now Professor) Gregory at the LSE. By then, however, Sraffa had removed to Cambridge at Keynes's urging and, since he was both attached to and accommodated by King's College, Keynes had full scope to appreciate his deep interest in the classical economists in general and in Ricardo in particular. Moreover, the two were great bibliophiles and Keynes both understood and shared Sraffa's passion for the pursuit of rare editions and the perusal of aged manuscripts. In 1929 Sraffa indicated his unwillingness to continue with the lectures he had been appointed to give in 1927 and 'intimated his wish to resign' from his Cambridge Lectureship in Economics (King's College, Cambridge, 1984, p. 75). The invention of a post as Librarian of the Marshall Library and, more importantly, the transfer, with Gregory's assent, of the RES's project for the Ricardo edition from London to Sraffa's care in King's College emerge as Keynes's astute strategems for binding Sraffa to Cambridge.

Of Keynes's involvement in his edition of Ricardo, Sraffa was later to write: 'The initiative in launching this enterprise was due to the late Lord Keynes, who to the end of his life showed the closest interest and lent his active support, particularly in the search for unpublished material and in advising on the planning and annotation of the volumes' (Sraffa, 1951, p. x). Little will be added here to Sraffa's account of his relationship with Keynes, except to stress what is well known but sometimes understated. This is that, whatever common body of interests and opinions Keynes and Sraffa might have shared, it quite excluded that point of entry into the arena of political economy and politics in which the isolation of Sraffa and Dobb was in Cambridge economic circles virtually complete. In particular, Keynes's intellectual antipathy towards Marx, Marxian socialism and even Ricardo could hardly have been expressed in more extreme terms and hence the gulf between himself, Sraffa and Dobb on such subjects been etched more widely or clearly.[5] More germane to the purpose of this account is that it was Keynes (in the context of damning Ricardo's approach while exhalting that of Malthus) who announced in 1933 that Sraffa's 'complete and definitive edition' of Ricardo would be published for the Royal Economic Society 'in the course of the present year' (Keynes, 1933, p. 96). Although it was based on propinquity with the materials as then assembled, his judgement was proved to be spectacularly in error.

In King's College in the 1930s it was a talking point that Sraffa's work on Ricardo kept the Library lights burning into the small hours of the morning. It was later observed that it was work that 'gave full scope for his fastidious scholarship', but it was also noted that: 'Perhaps he was too meticulous: at any rate he was very slow . . .' (King's College, Cambridge, 1984, p. 75). It was in the hope of accelerating his progress that Mrs. A. B. Lowe was contracted in 1936 as Sraffa's editorial assistant. She worked with him until

1939 (returning to Cambridge in 1969 to complete with him the preparation of the General Index) and Keynes enjoined her that of all the qualities she might be called upon to display in her labours the cardinal one was that of 'patience' (interviews with the late Mrs. A. B. Lowe, Cambridge, March–April 1983). This was a quality also required in high measure of Keynes himself, of the RES Council and, on a more taxing day-to-day basis, of the printers.

The Second World War disrupted the enterprise, the manuscripts being lodged for safety for some time in the vaults of King's College and Sraffa, having retained his Italian citizenship, being for some time interned. He could later report, none the less, that by the summer of 1940 'six volumes of the present edition had been set up in page-proof, while the volume of Speeches and Evidence had reached the stage of galley-proofs' (Sraffa, 1951, p. ix). Furthermore, with the fortuitous discovery in Ireland in 1943 of Ricardo's letters to James Mill together with others of his manuscripts including the uncompleted final essay 'on absolute value and exchangeable value', the delays in the pre-war publications of the edition were converted from vices into virtues. The post-1945 editorial task seemed largely to be the laborious but quite finite one of integrating the new discoveries into the corpus of volumes already in page- or galley-proof and of expanding the number of these appropriately. This is certainly the impression to be derived from Sraffa's formal account of the varying stages of the edition (Sraffa, 1951, pp. ix–x). In the years immediately following the war, however, there was mounting and well-justified apprehension that what seemed finite to others could in Sraffa's care become infinite.

In the summer of 1947, Lucy Munby, then a 20-year-old graduate of St Hugh's College, Oxford, was appointed as research assistant to Sraffa. The manuscripts were now lodged in his rooms at Trinity College, to which he had removed as a Fellow in 1939. These became her place of work. It was hoped that her appointment would quicken proceedings, principally by liberating Sraffa from the more mundane editorial tasks not the least of which was by that time the reading and checking of proofs. So that she might appreciate the urgency of the work in hand, Sraffa required her to read the extensive correspondence to him from Brooke Crutchley of the Cambridge University Press. Its tone had become increasingly anxious and impatient over the years. Notwithstanding, the salient feature of her experience in work with Sraffa was his total inability to delegate responsibility for the most menial editorial chore. Fearful of error, he re-checked all the proofs that she had read and corrected, usually in her company, greatly compounding the time taken up in this laborious process by his enthusiastic discussion of every item they read together. His enjoyment of teaching (at least on an individual basis) extended more widely than the confines of the edition: if she raised any point of economics with him 'he would gladly suspend everything to explain it'. There was also much discussion of politics, in which 'he treated [her] like a one-woman Gallup Poll – "what do young people think of this or that?" '. She found all this fascinating but somewhat 'remote from the job'. Within the detail of work on the edition, her most vivid recollection was of a protracted discussion on whether or not a comma was appropriate in a particular sentence. A decision was reached, but the next morning Sraffa 'came in looking worried and said that, on balance, he had decided that we'd made the wrong decision and we then reversed the previous day's "work".' Lucy Munby resigned in January 1948 and took up a post teaching history (interviews with Mrs. Lucy Munby, Cambridge, January 1983, and her written report to me of 10 February 1983, MHD–A).

In 1945, Austin Robinson succeeded Keynes as Secretary of the Royal Economic Society. At the time it was assumed that Keynes would continue to oversee the Ricardo edition as the Society's President, but this ended with his death in 1946. The very slow progress on the edition in the years that followed became an increasing source of worry, not least because Robinson was well aware of delays that could be attributable (as in Lucy Munby's account) to doubts as to a point of punctuation in a faded mansucript. He recalled an occasion at that time on which Sraffa successfully attempted to convince him of the case for inserting a comma. When the case for its inclusion was conceded, Sraffa then argued equally convincingly for its omission. Sraffa himself was quite unable to decide on the matter. If everything was indeed equal, Robinson suggested, it could be decided by the spin of a coin. Sraffa, he reported, 'was profoundly shocked' (Correspondence from Professor Sir E. A. G. Robinson to me, Cambridge, 4 March 1983; MHD–A). Perhaps philosophers and lawyers are most alive to the ambiguities of meaning that can be imparted or removed by the placement or omission of a mark of punctuation. The matter is not unimportant. It was very obvious, however, that if Sraffa's energies were at least partly to be absorbed in protracted and indecisive agonizing over problems such as these, then no reasonable time-scale for completion of the edition could realistically be promised by anyone. It was in this context that, on Lucy Munby's resignation, Austin Robinson asked Dobb if he could assist Sraffa with the edition.

By the beginning of 1948, Dobb had just completed what he described as a period of 'intense' academic activity that yielded *Studies in the Development of Capitalism* in 1946 (Dobb, 1946) and his revised and updated *Soviet Economic Development since 1917*, completed in 1947 and published in 1948 (Dobb, 1948). In combination in particular with his *Political Economy and Capitalism* of 1937 (Dobb, 1937) these works consolidated and further established his international reputation as a major – and for many, at that time and later, the foremost – figure in Western Marxian political economy and areas of economic history. Dobb produced numerous articles, notes or comments over the period 1948–54, but these were by his prolific standards limited. More significantly, he did not publish another book (excluding a collection of essays) until *An Essay on Economic Growth and Planning* appeared in 1960 (Dobb, 1960). There is little doubt that the primary cause of this was the duration and depth of his immersion in his collaboration with Sraffa in the edition of Ricardo.

The assistance proffered by Dobb was initially informal, but the scope and practical impact of his commitment was apparent to Sraffa after joint activity during the vacation of Easter and a spell of solitary labour by Dobb over the summer of 1948. Austin Robinson responded to an account of progress over this period sent to him by Dobb and wrote on 10 September 1948 that he had

had 'a long talk with Piero . . . about the general basis of the help that you are giving him. He is most anxious (and I share his anxiety) that we should find some way of formalizing the help, both in terms of credit for the ultimate results and of finance.' He continued:

> Meanwhile I do want to say how grateful I feel to you, because these protracted delays have become exceedingly discouraging to the R.E.S. Council, and I inherit Maynard's worries. From the talk I had with Piero it does seem that he has become stuck psychologically as much as technically, and that the sort of low-grade assistance that we have been trying to offer him really produced no effective result. I do hope that you can find it possible to help him through to the end. I am sure nothing in the world could make more difference to Piero's happiness.

He concluded that, after the press had been provided with 'something substantial for them to get on with during the autumn', 'there will remain the two major jobs of the introduction to the *Principles* and the preface to the whole thing' (Correspondence, E. A. G. Robinson to Dobb, Cambridge, 10 September 1948; MHD–A.)

A full year later, none the less, Dobb's opinion on the prospects of early publication was very cautious. Steady work over the winter of 1948–9 was disrupted by Sraffa's switch of College rooms and was fitful thereafter.[6] No progress was reported on the introduction to the *Principles*. One (albeit not the crucial) impediment to progress was conflict in the time periods available to each for collaborative endeavour. After the Second World War, Sraffa was anxious to renew his personal and cultural ties with Italy and university vacations supplied him with opportunity. Dobb, by contrast, with a heavy teaching load in term-time, was freed for exclusive activity on Ricardo only during vacations. Sraffa spent much of the summer of 1948 in Italy and returned there once more in the summer of 1949. Dobb reported the outcome of the Italian elections of the time to have been 'rather a sore blow to him; sending him back in his disappointment to his Ricardo manuscripts'. With the latter, Dobb added, 'I've been trying to help him of late – with the result that I have *some*, but no *firm*, hopes that two volumes of the long-awaited R.E.S. edition of Ricardo's Works may be ready soon' (Correspondence, Dobb to Th. Prager, Cambridge, 6 September 1949; MHD–A).[7]

By late spring of 1950, however, the tempo of their work together picked up markedly and, with a short break in August, was sustained through to the end of the year. This was the period in which the writing of the Introduction to the *Principles* was completed in its final form and then that of the General Preface to the edition. These were written to meet a deadline, but it was not one imposed by the Royal Economic Society or by the Cambridge University Press. It was imposed instead by the Delhi School of Economics. Earlier in that year, Dobb accepted an invitation to be Visiting Professor at Delhi and to lecture extensively in India on the history of economic thought, problems of development and planning, and the process of Russian post-war reconstruction. He was to sail from England in late December 1950 and would not return before the Easter of 1951. In the event, Dobb's prospective absence from Cambridge proved to be a far more potent stimulus for completing work on the first volumes than any expression of anxiety or menace emanating from elsewhere. The two men had, of course, already hit on the method by which the Introduction to the *Principles* would be written, since those to volumes II, V and VI had already been completed in similar fashion. Both Barbara Lowe and Lucy Munby had been recipients of Sraffa's innumerable disquisitions on the meaning and significance of items encountered in Ricardo's texts or manuscripts. While educational, the words were simply spoken and 'lost'. Dobb, by contrast, noted them down, probed further, wrote them up and returned them to Sraffa for him to cogitate upon whether or not they constituted accurate expression of his thought. As it finally emerged, after much drafting and redrafting, the Introduction to the *Principles* was primarily the product of Dobb's pen but without doubt was also primarily the product of Sraffa's mind.[8] It was for this reason, of course, that Dobb invariably referred in publications or lectures to 'Mr Sraffa's Introduction'.[9]

On 23 December 1950, Dobb, on board the P&O liner *Stratheden* en route for India, wrote to Theodor Prager in Vienna. He feared that the news he gave him concerning the Ricardo edition was 'academic trifles, which must seem from your central European angle of very little moment with things as they are'. None the less, he reported:

> Sraffa's edition of Ricardo's works and correspondence (on which as you probably know he has been engaged since 1930, and on which I have come in since 1948 to help him finish it) is, I'm glad to say, nearing completion; at least so far as the first 4 volumes are concerned, and it looks as though these may come out this spring or summer. The great bottle-neck holding the thing back was the Introduction to the 'Principles'. This is now complete and past the galley-proof stage. I think you will find in it some things of interest. In particular I think we conclusively establish (in opposition to the traditional Hollander–Marshall–Cannan view) that there was no 'weakening' of Ricardo's enunciation of the labour theory as time went on: that in fact he reached at the end of his life a position rather close to that of Marx, so that the true line of descent is certainly from Ricardo to Marx, and *not* from Ricardo to cost-of-production theory as in Mill to Marshall as the bourgeois tradition has it. A minor scoop is the unpublished (and unfinished) final paper which he was writing just before his death on 'Absolute Value and Exchangeable Value', showing that he was at the last still exercised with a notion of an Absolute Value (= embodied labour) as something distinct from, but underlying, exchange-value: in fact the notion and the distinction is *more* explicit in this last paper than in the 'Principles' (Correspondence, Dobb to Th. Prager, Port Said, 23 December 1950; MHD–A).[10]

On 8 February 1951, Sraffa teased Dobb from Cambridge with a suggestion that if he returned to England late he would bear some responsibility for delay in the publication of volume V (Correspondence, Sraffa to Dobb, Cambridge, 8 February 1951; MHD–A). Dobb did not delay his return from

India; resumed joint activity with Sraffa in May and June; and the Prefatory Note to volume V was dated August 1951. On 4 December 1951, Austin Robinson wrote to Dobb on behalf of the Council of the Royal Economic Society and referred to 'all the immense labour you have done on Ricardo'. He said:

> I was asked . . . to tell you officially what I think I have already told you unofficially, that we are tremendously in your debt for all you have done to get Ricardo to the point of publication and that we are most sincerely grateful to you. (Correspondence E. A. G. Robinson to Dobb, Cambridge, 4 December 1951; MHD–A).

However, while the back of the editorial work had long since been broken, first by Sraffa alone and then by Dobb and Sraffa in tandem, a substantial burden still remained to be shouldered, especially with regard to the 'Biographical Miscellany' of which volume X was comprised. This was work, moreover, that in its wider implications lacked much of the intellectual excitement associated with interpretation of the *Principles* and of certain of the discoveries of 1943. This had spiced the often infinitely tedious processes of proof-checking, pursuing obscure references, reconciling recondite points of notation and order, constructing indices and the like. Volumes V–IX all appeared in 1952 but volume X was not committed to the press until April 1954. Rudolph Schlesinger was besieging Dobb in this period with requests for reviews, comments or articles on Soviet economic history and planning. On 25 June 1952 Dobb responded to one such request for book reviews that: 'Tied hand & foot to Ricardo VOL 10, as I am, until end of July I couldn't possibly tackle them myself . . .' (Correspondence, Dobb to R. Schlesinger, Cambridge, 25 June 1952; MHD–A). (Some months earlier, in an uncharacteristic moment of asperity, he had noted his summer commitments to 'the damned Ricardo!' Correspondence, Dobb to R. Schlesinger, Cambridge, 8 March 1952; MHD–A.)[11] In the autumn and winter of 1952–3, work on volume X was disrupted in consequence of injuries sustained by Sraffa during a walking holiday in Norway in the summer of 1952. By January 1953, however, the likely scale of renewed activity on Ricardo once more dominated Dobb's plans for his own work. The scope and deadline of a proposed contribution to *Soviet Studies*, for example, 'all depends on how deeply I have to get implicated (a) in Ricardo VOL X over Easter & in the summer (b) in examining in June' (Correspondence, Dobb to R. Schlesinger, Cambridge, 3 January 1953; MHD–A). Perhaps the best of all indications of Dobb's commitment to the final stages of the Ricardo edition is a draft of a letter written for Sraffa on 11 March 1953. In the hope – a premature one in the event – that volume X would be ready for the press earlier than it was in fact to be, Sraffa had asked Dobb how much time he could devote in the summer vacations to planning the General Index. Dobb replied:

> As regards the planning of the index: although I had been looking forward to a breathing-space this summer after VOL. X had gone to press, and still feel, as I told you, most reluctant to be involved in the bewildering

> quicksands of the Index, I will do my best to give assistance with it between June 28th (this allows for a short rest-up after the Tripos & the Scholarship Elections) and the middle of August (say Aug. 15th). I won't guarantee to do an 8 hour day on it every day of this period, or to live in college the whole of this period; but I will so far as is possible give it priority over anything else and devote most of each weekday to it over these seven weeks. I shall then fervently hope and trust that you will allow it, after this preliminary model-building, to go to some professional – if one can be found – and both of us be rid of it. (Draft of correspondence, Dobb to Sraffa, Cambridge, 11 March 1953; MHD–A.)[12]

In practice, work on volume X absorbed the bulk of their collective energies until June 1954 and by then the thing was done.

On 3 January 1955 Dobb reported that: 'Piero is just back from interesting voyagings on the other side of the world; Ricardo Vol. X shd be out about Feb; and he's now off for a stay in Majorca – hoping to do some work (non-Ricardo) of his own, tho' not *too* hopeful that he actually will. (Correspondence, Dobb to R. Schlesinger, Cambridge, 3 January 1955; MHD–A.) The work that Sraffa hoped to do in Majorca, of course, was to begin the process of thought and assembly of past thoughts that eventually emerged as *Production of Commodities by means of Commodities*. That he would have felt able to do this before publication of his edition of Ricardo seems unthinkable.

Diverse opinions have been offered over the years as to quite what Sraffa required in order for him to publish his own work or that of Ricardo in a form that fitted his excessively exacting standards. Mrs Barbara Lowe did not know Dobb and spoke from her own experience to say that Sraffa needed someone 'to give him the words and make him make up his mind' (Interviews with Mrs. A. B. Lowe, Cambridge, March–April 1983). For the Ricardo edition he certainly needed this and much more. He needed to have sufficient confidence in the quality of his collaborator as to permit a division of labour. He needed someone with the patience that Keynes had stressed. He needed someone who understood his thoughts as he spoke them (or who could come to understand them in the course of writing them down and discussing them). He needed someone whose commitment to the most tedious editorial chores was as great as to the elucidation and elaboration of grand matters of theory. He needed someone of a general capability that reflected possession of substantial independent creative powers – but he also needed someone who would suppress their exercise over protracted periods. For all this he needed someone who perceived a higher interest to be at issue: an interest, in the final analysis, to be located in a shared, isolated and unfashionable point of entry into the entire arena of political economy and politics. On 18 January 1956, Austin Robinson wrote to Dobb reiterating the gratitude of the RES Council for his work on Ricardo the edition of which was 'now . . . regarded as one of the great triumphs of economic scholarship'. He reported the 'national pride' he had found among Italian ministers in Rome – a pride expressed with particular enthusiasm by President Einaudi – in Sraffa's role in it. He delivered himself also of the judgement that: 'Without your obstetrical assistance I do not believe that Ricardo would ever have been born' (Correspondence, E. A. G. Robinson to Dobb, Cambridge, 18 January 1956; MHD–A). We cannot, of course, know with certainty whether this would or would not have been the case. We do know, however, that the qualities required of Dobb to be the midwife of Piero Sraffa's intellectual child were exceedingly rare.

Notes

In 1982–83, I was a Visiting Fellow Commoner at Trinity College, Cambridge, sponsored by Dr. J. Eatwell. The year was spent gathering and giving preliminary order to the papers of Maurice H. Dobb. These were later given to Trinity College and will in due course constitute the Dobb Archive, which is currently in formation at Cambridge and the University of Glasgow. The primary sources upon which this paper draws were mostly assembled and discussed in 1982–3 in the company of Professor B. J. MacFarlane of the University of Adelaide. References to the Dobb Archives are abbreviated 'MHD–A'.

1 The exception was his edition with Keynes of David Hume's *An Abstract of a Treatise on Human Nature* (1938).
2 The most accessible biographical introductions to P. Sraffa and M. H. Dobb are: the 'special Dossier' published in honour of Sraffa's 80th birthday by *Rinascita*, translated and published in the *New Left Review* (Napolitano *et al.*, 1978); E. J. Hobsbawm's 'Maurice Dobb' in *Socialism, Capitalism and Economic Growth* (Hobsbawm, 1967); and Dobb's 'Random Biographical Notes' (Dobb, 1978).
3 See Dobb (1978), p. 117. The influence of Croce, Labriola, Sorel and Sombart, among others, is most clearly acknowledged in an unpublished paper on Marx's method written in 1925 with J. G. Crowther (MHD–A).
4 Correspondence, M. H. Dobb to R. Palme Dutt, 20 May 1925; MHD–A. The impact of such a view is apparent in Dobb's earlier works, particularly in *Capitalist Enterprise and Social Progress* (1925) and in his Cambridge Economic Handbook on *Wages* (1928a).
5 Keynes visited Russia in 1925 (where Dobb, *inter alia*, witnessed some of his exchanges with Soviet economists) and his reaction to the Russian Revolution was ambivalent. He stated a preference for Soviet over Tsarist Russia and an inclination 'to help and not to hinder'. But he exclaimed:

> How can I accept a doctrine which sets up as its bible, above and beyond criticism, an absolete economic textbook which I know to be not only scientifically erroneous but without interest or application for the modern world? How can I adopt a creed which, prefering the mud to the fish, exhalts the boorish proletariat above the bourgeois and the intelligentsia, who, with whatever faults, are the quality in life and surely carry the seeds of all human advancement? Even if we need a religion, how can we find it in the turbid rubbish of the Red bookshops? It is hard for an educated, decent, intelligent son of Western Europe to find his ideals here, unless he has first suffered some strange and horrid process of conversion which has changed all his values (Keynes, 1925).

His hostility towards Ricardo's approach to economics is most clearly expressed in his essay on 'Thomas Robert Malthus' (Keynes, 1933, pp. 97–8).

6 On taking up his Fellowship at Trinity College in October 1948, Dobb occupied rooms in the same Court as Sraffa's. Sraffa moved from one set of rooms to others nearby during the Christmas vacation of 1948–9.

7 In the Italian elections of April 1949, to which Dobb refers, the Popular Democratic Front of Communists and Socialists secured 31 per cent of the vote but did not improve on their positions of 1946. By contrast, the Christian Democrats increased their share of the vote to 48.5 per cent and secured an absolute majority in the Chamber of Deputies.

8 In 1963, I questioned Dobb concerning the writing of the Introduction to the *Principles*. Several years later, both Dobb and Sraffa were questioned on the same subject by Dr. J. Eatwell. All the accounts tally. For Eatwell's version, see Eatwell (1979), pp. 143–4.

9 See, for example, Dobb's treatment of the edition of Ricardo in Dobb (1973). When delivering a lecture on 'Ricardo and economic policy' to the Annual General Meeting of the Royal Economic Society in July 1972 (Sraffa having declined to contribute) Dobb introduced himself as 'a second-class understudy for the real star of this occasion' (MHD–A).

10 A minor modification to Dobb's hyphenation has been made in the interest of clarity.

11 Dobb and Sraffa worked together during the Easter vacation of 1952 but this concerned the participation of the British delegation to the International Economic Conference then held in Moscow. Their 1952 visit to Russia was for both men their first since their joint travels of 1930.

12 This is not the place to recount the saga of the General Index. Suffice it to note that the 'bewildering quicksands' that Dobb feared swallowed up him and others in later years. Sraffa emerged from them exhausted in Barbara Lowe's company only in 1972.

Bibliography

Abdel-Fadil, M. (1975), *La planification des prix en économie socialiste* (Paris: Presses Universitaires de France).

Abramovitz, M. *et al.* (1959), *The Allocation of Economic Resources* (Stanford: Stanford University Press).

Alchian, A. A. (1959), 'Costs and outputs', in M. Abramovitz *et al.* (1959), pp. 23–40.

Allen, R. G. D. (1965), *Mathematical Economics*, 2nd edn (London: Macmillan).

Andrews, P. W. S. (1949), *Manufacturing Business* (London: Macmillan).

Arena, R. (1982), 'Réflexions sur la compatibilité des approches ricardienne et keynésienne du fonctionnement de l'activité économique', *Économie Appliquée*, vol. 35(3), pp. 405–48.

Arena, R. (1988), 'La dynamique économique: nouveaux débats, nouvelles perspectives', *L'Actualité Economique.*

Arena, R. and Froeschlée, C. (1986), 'Formes de progrès technique, séquences d'équilibres temporaires et stabilité économique', *Économie Appliquée*, vol. 39(3), pp. 415–47.

Arena, R. and Torre, D. (1986), 'Approche sraffaienne et théorie de la gravitation', *Economie Appliquée*, vol. 39(1), pp. 61–86.

Armstrong, P., Glyn, A. and Harrison, I. (1984), *Capitalism since World War II: The Making and Breakings of the Great Boom* (London: Fontana).

Arrow, K. J. ([1951] 1963), *Social Choice and Individual Values*, 2nd edn (New York, London, Sydney: Wiley).

Arrow, K. J. (1974), 'General economic equilibrium: Purpose, analytic techniques, collective choice', *American Economic Review*, vol. 64, June, pp. 253–72.

Arrow, K. J. and Hahn, F. H. (1971), *General Competitive Analysis* (San Francisco: Holden-Day; Edinburgh: Oliver & Boyd).

Arrow, K. J. and Intriligator, M. D.(eds) (1981–6), *Handbook of Mathematical Economics*, vols 1–3 (Amsterdam: North-Holland).

Asimakopulos, A. (1971), 'The determination of investment in Keynes's Model', *Canadian Journal of Economics*, vol. 4, August, pp. 382–8.

Asimakopulos, A. (1973), 'Keynes, Patinkin, historical time, and equilibrium analysis', *Canadian Journal of Economics*, vol. 6, May, pp. 179–88.

Asimakopulos, A. (1982), 'Keynes' theory of effective demand revisited', *Australian Economic Papers*, vol. 21, June, pp. 18–36.

Asimakopulos, A. (1984), 'Joan Robinson and economic theory', *Banca Nazionale del Lavoro Quarterly Review*, December, pp. 381–409.

Asimakopulos, A. (1984–5), 'Long-period employment, in the "*General Theory*"', *Journal of Post Keynesian Economics*, vol. 7, Winter, pp. 207–13.

Asimakopulos, A. (1985), 'Harrod on Harrod: the evolution of "a line of steady growth"', *History of Political Economy*, vol. 17, Winter, pp. 619–35.

Asimakopulos, A. and Burbidge, J. B. (1974), 'The short-period incidence of taxation', *Economic Journal*, vol. 84, June, pp. 267–88.

Asimakopulos, A. and Burbidge, J. B. (1979), 'Harberger and Kalecki on the incidence of taxation: A critical comparison', *Greek Economic Review*, vol. 1(2), pp. 70–81.

Aspramourgos, T. (1986), 'On the origins of the term "neoclassical"', *Cambridge Journal of Economics*, vol. 10(3), pp. 265–70.

Aumann, R. I. (1985), 'What is game theory trying to accomplish?', in K. P. Arrow, and S. Honkapohja (eds), *Frontiers of Economics* (Oxford: Basil Blackwell), pp. 28–76.

Avramovic, D. (1983), *International Financial Cooperation: Problems and Prospects* (Bombay: Indian Institute of Bankers).

Bagchi, A. K. (1981), 'The ideology behind the maximum conditionality demanded by the IMF and its implications', *The IMF Loan: Facts and Issues* (Calcutta: Government of West Bengal).

Bagchi, A. K. (1982), *The Political Economy of Underdevelopment* (Cambridge: Cambridge University Press).

Bagchi, A. K. (1987), *Public Intervention and Industrial Restructuring in China, India, and Republic of Korea* (New Delhi: ILO (ARTEP)).

Bagchi, A. K. (1988), 'Problems of effective demand and contradictions of planning in India', in A. K. Bagchi (ed.), *Economy, Policy and Society: Essays in Honour of Professor Bhabatosh Dutta*, (Calcutta: Oxford University Press).

Bagchi, A. K., Ghosh, A. and Dasgupta, S. (1985), 'Industrial policy and the economy'. *Social Scientist*, no. 148, September, pp. 3–15.

Bailey, S. (1837), *Money and its Vicissitudes in Value: As They Affect National Industry and Pecuniary Contracts, by the Author of The Rationale of Political Representation, A Critical Dissertation on Value* (London: Effingham Wilson, Royal Exchange).

Bairoch, P. (1975), *The Economic Development of the Third World since 1900* (London: Methuen).

Balassa, B. *et al.* (1971), *The Structure of Protection in Developing Countries* (Baltimore: Johns Hopkins University Press).

Balassa, B. (1978), 'Export incentives and export performance in developing countries: a comparative analysis', *Weltwirtschaftliches Archiv*, vol. 114(1), pp. 24–61.

Baran, P. A. (1957), *The Political Economy of Growth* (New York: Monthly Review Press).

Baranzini, M. and Scazzieri, R. (1986a), 'Knowledge in economics: a framework', in M. Baranzini and R. Scazzieri (eds) (1986b), pp. 1–87.

Baranzini, M. and Scazzieri, R. (eds) (1986b), *Foundations of Economics* (Oxford: Blackwell).

Barone, E. (1894), 'Sulla "consumers rent"', *Giornale degli Economisti.*

Baumol, W. J. (1959), *Business Behavior, Value and Growth* (New York: Macmillan).

Becker, G. (1976), *The Economic Approach to Human Behavior* (Chicago: Chicago University Press).

Beer, M. (1929), *A History of British Socialism*, vol. II: *Chartism to the Present Day* (London: Bell).

Bell, O. and Kristol, I. (eds) (1981), *The Crisis in Economic Theory* (New York: Basic Books).

Bernstein, E. ([1899] 1909), *Evolutionary Socialism* (London: I.L.P.).

Bernstein, E. ([1915] 1921), *My Years of Exile, Reminiscences of a Socialist* (London: Parsons).

Betancourt, R. R. and Clague, Ch. K. (1981), *Capital Utilization – A Theoretical and Empirical Analysis* (Cambridge: Cambridge University Press).

Bewley, T. (1982), 'An integration of equilibrium theory and turnpike theory', *Journal of Mathematical Economics*, vol. 10(2/3), pp. 233–67.

Bharadwaj, K. (1972), 'Marshall on Pigou's *"Wealth and Welfare"*,' *Economica* (new series), vol. 39, February, pp. 32–46.

Bharadwaj, K. (1974), *Production Conditions in Indian Agriculture* (Cambridge: Cambridge University Press).

Bharadwaj, K. (1976), *Classical Political Economy and Rise to Dominance of Supply and Demand Theories*, Dutt Lectures (Calcutta: Orient Longman). 2nd revised edn, 1986.

Bharadwaj, K. (1978a), 'The subversion of classical analysis: Alfred Marshall's early writing on value', *Cambridge Journal of Economics*, vol. 2(3), pp. 253–71.

Bharadwaj, K. (1978b), 'Maurice Dobb's critique of theories of value and distribution', *Cambridge Journal of Economics*, vol. 2, pp. 153–74.

Bharadwaj, K. (1979), 'Towards a macroeconomic framework for a developing economy: the Indian case', *The Manchester School*, September, pp. 270–302.

Bharadwaj, K. (1983a), 'On a controversy over Ricardo's theory of distribution', *Cambridge Journal of Economics*, vol. 7(1), pp. 11–36.

Bharadwaj, K. (1983b), 'Ricardian theory and ricardianism', *Contributions to Political Economy*, vol. 2, pp. 49–77.

Bharadwaj, K. (1984), 'Piero Sraffa: the man and the scholar: a tribute', *Economic and Political Weekly*, vol. 19(31–33), pp. 1236–51.

Bharadwaj, K. (1986), 'Production and exchange in theories of price formation and economic transition', in M. Baranzini and R. Scazzieri (eds), (1986b), pp. 339–60.

Biasco, S. (1979), *L'inflazione nei paesi capitalistici industrializzati* (Milan: Feltrinelli).

Bidard, C. (ed.) (1984), *La production jointe Nouveaux débats.* (Paris: Economica).

BIS (1983), *Fifty-third Annual Report, April 1, 1982 – March 31, 1983* (Basle: Bank for International Settlements).

BIS (1985), *Fifty-fifth Annual Report, April 1, 1984 – March 31, 1985* (Basle: Bank for International Settlements).

Bladen, V. (1975), 'Command over labour: a study in misrepresentation', *Canadian Journal of Economics*, vol. 8(4), pp. 504–19.

Blaug, M. (1974), *The Cambridge Revolution. Success or Failure?* Institute of Economic Affairs (London: Hobart Paperback).

Blaug, M. (1980), *The Methodology of Economics* (Cambridge: Cambridge University Press).

Bliss, C. J. (1970), 'Comment on Garegnani', *Review of Economic Studies*, vol. 37(3), pp. 437–8.

Böhm-Bawerk, E. v. ([1884] 1890), *Capital and Interest. A Critical History of Economical Theory* (London: Macmillan).

Böhm-Bawerk, E. v. ([1895] 1949), 'Karl Marx and the close of his system', in P. Sweezy (ed.) (1949), pp. 3–118.

Böhm-Bawerk, E. v. ([1914] 1959), *Capital and Interest. History and Critique of Interest Theories* 3rd edn (South-Holland, Ill.: Libertarian Press).

Bortkiewicz, L. v. ([1907] 1949), 'Zur Berichtigung der grundlegenden theoretischen Konstruktionen von Marx im dritten Band des "Kapital"', *Jahrbücher für nationalökonomie und Statistik*, vol. 34(3), pp. 370–85.

Bortkiewicz, L. v. ([1907] 1949), 'On the correction of Marx's fundamental theoretical construction in the third volume of *Capital*', in P. Sweezy (ed.) (1949).

Bose, A. (1965), 'Consumers' demand, distributive shares and prices', *Economic Journal*, vol. 75, December, pp. 771–86.

Bose, A. (1975), *Marxian and Post-Marxian Political Economy* (Harmondsworth: Penguin).

Bradley, J. and Howard, M. (eds) (1982), *Classical and Marxian Political Economy. Essays in Honour of R. Meek* (London: Macmillan).

Brown, M., Sato, K. and Zarembka, P. (eds) (1976), *Essays in Modern Capital Theory* (Amsterdam: North-Holland).

Bruno, M. (1967), 'Optimal accumulation in discrete capital models', in K. Shell (ed.) (1967), pp. 181–218.
Bucharin, N. ([1919] 1966), *L'économie politique du rentier. Critique de l'économie marginaliste* (Paris: E.D.I.).
Bücher, K. ([1893] 1926), *Die Entstehung der Volkswirtschaft*, 17th edn (Tübingen: Laupp).
Burmeister, E. (1968), 'On a theorem of Sraffa', *Economica*, vol. 35(137), pp. 83–7.
Burmeister, E. (1974), 'Synthesizing the neo-Austrian and alternative approaches to capital theory: A survey', *Journal of Economic Literature*, vol. 12(2), pp. 413–56.
Burmeister, E. (1975), 'Comment: This age of Leontief . . . and who?', *Journal of Economic Literature*, vol. 13(2), pp. 453–7.
Burmeister, E. (1977), 'The irrelevance of Sraffa's analysis without constant returns to scale', *Journal of Economic Literature*, vol. 15(1), pp. 68–70.
Burmeister, E. (1980), *Capital Theory and Dynamics* (New York: Cambridge University Press).
Burmeister, E. (1984), 'Sraffa, labor theories of value, and the economics of real wage rate determination', *Journal of Political Economy*, vol. 92(3), p. 508–26.

Caminati, M. (1981), 'The theory of interest in the classical economists', *Metroeconomica*, vol. 33(1–3), pp. 79–104.
Cannan, E. ([1929] 1964), *A Review of Economic Theory* (London: Cass).
Cannan, E. (1967), *A History of the Theories of Production and Distribution 1776 to 1848* (New York: Kelley).
Caravale, G. (ed.) (1985), *The Legacy of Ricardo* (Oxford: Blackwell).
Carvalho, F. (1983–4), On the concept of time in Shacklean and Sraffian economics'. *Journal of Post Keynesian Economics*, vol. 6, Winter, pp. 265–80.
Carvalho, F. (1984–5), 'Alternative analyses of short and long run in post Keynesian economics', *Journal of Post Keynesian Economics*, vol. 7, Winter, pp. 214–34.
Casarosa, C. (1981), 'The microfoundations of Keynes's aggregate supply and expected demand analysis', *Economic Journal*, vol. 91, March, pp. 188–94.
Chamberlin, E. H. ([1933] 1947), *The Theory of Monopolistic Competition*, 5th edn (Cambridge, Mass.: Harvard University Press).
Clark, J. M. (1931), 'Distribution', in *Encyclopædia of the Social Sciences* (New York: Macmillan).
Clifton, J. A. (1977), 'Competition and the evolution of the capitalist mode of production', *Cambridge Journal of Economics*, vol. 1(2), pp. 137–51.
Coddington, A. (1976), 'Keynesian economics: The search for first principles', *Journal of Economic Literature*, vol. 14(4), pp. 1258–73.
Collard, D. A. (1963), 'The production of commodities', *Economic Journal*, vol. 73, March, pp. 144–6.
Collard, D. A. (1964), 'The production of commodities – a rejoinder', *Economic Journal*, vol. 74, September, pp. 726–7.
Committee on the Working of the Monetary System (1959), *Radcliffe Report* (London: HMSO).
Cyert, R. M. and March, J. G. (1963), *A Behavioral Theory of the Firm* (Englewood Cliffs: Prentice-Hall).

d'A-G., H. J. (1930), 'Russia to-day and to-morrow – a Review', *The Cherwell*, November.
Agata, A. d' (1983) 'The existence and uniqueness of cost-minimizing systems', *Metroeconomica*, vol. 35(1/2), pp. 147–58.
Debreu, G. (1959), *The Theory of Value* (New York: Wiley).

Debreu, G. (1974), 'Excess demand functions', *Journal of Mathematical Economics*, vol. 1(1), pp. 15–21.

Dell, S. (1982), 'Stabilisation: The political economy of overkill', *World Development*, vol. 10(8).

Vivo, G. de (1982), 'Notes on Marx's critique of Ricardo', *Contributions to Political Economy*, vol. 1(1), March, pp. 87–99.

Vivo, G. de (1984), '*Ricardo and his Critics. A Study of Classical Theories of Value and Distribution*', (Modena).

Vivo, G. de (1985), 'R. Torrens and Ricardo's "corn ratio" theory of profits', *Cambridge Journal of Economics*, vol. 9(1), pp. 89–92.

Vivo, G. de (1987), 'David Ricardo', in J. Eatwell, M. Milgate and P. Newman (eds) (1987), pp. 183–98.

Dickler, R. A. (1983), 'Exogene Vorgaben des Szenarios "Wertewandel"', *Anlagenband I zum Bericht der Arbeitsgruppe Modelle*, Enquête-Kommission 'Zukünftige Kernenergiepolitik', Deutscher Bundestag, 9. Wahlperiode, pp. 106–35.

Divisia, F. (1925), 'L'indice monétaire et la théorie de la monnaie', *Revue d'Économie Politique*, vol. 29, July/August, pp. 842–61.

Dmitriev, V. K. ([1898] 1974), 'First essay: The theory of value of D. Ricardo – an attempt at a rigorous analysis', in V. K. Dmitriev, *Economic Essays on Value, Competition and Utility* (Cambridge: Cambridge University Press), pp. 37–95.

Dobb, M. H. (1920a), 'The importance of the labour theory of value', *The Plebs* (London), September.

Dobb, M. H. (1920b), 'The problem of surplus value', *Youth* (London), November.

Dobb, M. H. (1921), 'The great contradiction', *The Plebs*, (London), February.

Dobb, M. H. (1922), 'Marx and Marshall – a study of the relation of bourgeois and working-class economics', *The Plebs* (London), April.

Dobb, M. H. (1925), *Capitalist Enterprise and Social Progress* (London: Routledge).

Dobb, M. H. (1928a), *Russian Economic Development since the Revolution*, assisted by H. C. Stevens (London: Routledge).

Dobb, M. H. (1928b), *Wages* (Cambridge: Cambridge University Press).

Dobb, M. H. (1930), *Russia To-day and To-morrow* (London: Hogarth Press).

Dobb, M. H. (1937), *Political Economy and Capitalism – Some Essays in Economic Tradition* (London: Routledge).

Dobb, M. H. (1946), *Studies in the Development of Capitalism* (London: Routledge).

Dobb, M. H. (1948), *Soviet Economic Development since 1917* (London: Routledge).

Dobb, M. H. (1960), *An Essay on Economic Growth and Planning* (London: Routledge).

Dobb, M. H. (1969), *Welfare Economics and the Economics of Socialism* (Cambridge: Cambridge University Press).

Dobb, M. H. (1970), 'The Sraffa system and critique of the neo-classical theory of distribution', *De Economist*, vol. 118(4), pp. 347–62.

Dobb, M. H. (1973), *Theories of Value and Distribution since Adam Smith* (Cambridge: Cambridge University Press).

Dobb, M. H. (1978), 'Random biographical notes', *Cambridge Journal of Economics*, vol. 2(2), pp. 115–20.

Dorfman, R., Samuelson, P. A. and Solow, R. M. (1958), *Linear Programming and Economic Analysis* (New York: McGraw Hill).

Dorfman, R., Samuelson, P. A. and Solow, R. M. ([1958] 1987), *Linear Programming and Economic Analysis* (New York: Dover).

Dornbusch, R. (1982), 'Stabilisation policies in developing countries: What have we learned?' *World Development*, vol. 10(9), pp. 701–8.

Dornbusch, R. (1983), 'Flexible exchange rates and interdependence', *IMF Staff Papers*, vol. 30(1).

Dornbusch, R. (1985), 'External debt, budget deficits and disequilibrium exchange rates', in G. W. Smith and J. T. Cuddington (eds) (1985), pp. 213–35.

Duménil, G. and Lévy, D. (1985), 'The classicals and the neoclassicals: a rejoinder to Frank Hahn', *Cambridge Journal of Economics*, vol. 9(4), pp. 327–45.

Dunlop, J. G. (1938), 'The movement of real and money wage rates', *Economic Journal*, vol. 48, September, pp. 413–34.

Eatwell, J. (1975a), 'Scarce and Produced Commodities', PhD dissertation, Cambridge, Mass.: Harvard University.

Eatwell, J. (1975b), 'The interpretation of Ricardo's Essay on Profits', *Economica*, vol. 42, May.

Eatwell, J. (1977), 'The irrelevance of returns to scale in Sraffa's analysis', *Journal of Economic Literature*, vol. 15(1), pp. 61–8.

Eatwell, J. (1979), 'Maurice Dobb', in D. L. Sills (ed.), *Biographical Supplement to the International Encyclopædia of the Social Sciences* (New York: The Free Press & Macmillan), vol. 18, pp. 142–4.

Eatwell, J. (1980), 'A framework for the analysis of taxation, distribution and effective demand', in E. J. Nell (ed.) (1980), *Growth, Profits and Property. Essays in the Revival of Political Economy* (Cambridge: Cambridge University Press).

Eatwell, J. (1982a), *Whatever Happened to Britain?* (London: Duckworth and the BBC).

Eatwell, J. (1982b), 'Competition in classical and Marxist political economy', in J. Bradley and M. Howard (eds) (1982), pp. 203–28.

Eatwell, J. (1983), 'Theories of value, output and employment', in J. Eatwell and M. Milgate (eds) (1983), pp. 93–128.

Eatwell, J. (1987), 'Standard commodity', in J. Eatwell, M. Milgate and P. Newman (eds) (1987), vol. 4, pp. 476–8.

Eatwell, J. and Panico, C. (1987), 'Sraffa, Piero (1898 – 1983)', in J. Eatwell, M. Milgate and P. Newman (eds) (1987), vol. 4, pp. 445–52.

Eatwell, J. and Milgate, M. (eds) (1983), *Keynes's Economics and the Theory of Value and Distribution* (London: Duckworth).

Eatwell, J., Milgate, M. and Newman P. (eds) (1987), *The New Palgrave. A Dictionary of Economics*, vols 1–4 (London: Macmillan).

Encauoua, D. and Geroski, P. (1986), 'Price dynamics and competition in five OECD countries', *OECD Economic Studies*, no. 5.

Engels, F. ([1885] 1977), 'Preface', in K. Marx, *Capital. A Critique of Political Economy*, vol. 2 (London: Lawrence & Wishart).

Engels, F. ([1891] 1977), 'Introduction' to K. Marx, *Wage Labour and Capital*, in Marx–Engels, *Collected Works*, vol. 9 (London: Lawrence & Wishart).

Engels, F. ([1894] 1977), 'Preface', in K. Marx, *Capital. A Critique of Political Economy*, vol. 3 (London: Lawrence & Wishart).

Epstein, L. G. (1987), 'The global stability of efficient intertemporal allocations', *Econometrica*, vol. 55(2), pp. 329–55.

FEER (1984), 'The protection racket', *Far Eastern Economic Review*, 25 October.

FEER (1985a), 'Export-led slowdown; The crunch has come for trade-oriented NICs', *Far Eastern Economic Review*, 24 October.

FEER (1985b), 'Export-led growth: Japan faces a policy dilemma', *Far Eastern Economic Review*, 26 December.

Feinstein, C. H. (ed.) (1967), *Capitalism and Economic Growth* (Cambridge, Cambridge University Press).

Finoia, M. (1979), *Guida a "produzione di merci a mezzo di merci" di Piero Sraffa* (Bologna: Cappelli).
Fisher, I. (1906), *The Nature of Capital and Income* (New York: Kelley).
Fisher, I. (1930), *The Theory of Interest* (New York: Kelley).
Fitoussi, J. P. (ed.) (1983), *Modern Macroeconomic Theory* (Oxford: Blackwell).
Flaschel, P. and Semmler, W. (1986), 'The dynamic equalization of profit rates for input–output models with fixed capital', in W. Semmler (ed.), *Competition, Instability, and Nonlinear Cycles* (Berlin: Springer-Verlag), pp. 1–34.
Foley, D. K. (1986), 'Say's law in Marx and Keynes', *Cahiers d'Économie Politique*, vol. 10/11, pp. 183–94.
Foss, M. F. (1981), 'Long-run changes in the workweek of fixed capital', *American Economic Review, Papers and Proceedings*, vol. 71, May, pp. 58–63.
Foxwell, H. S. ([1899] 1962), 'Introduction' to A. Menger, *The Right to the Whole Produce of Labor* (New York: Kelley).
Frankel, M. (1955), 'Obsolescence and technological change in a maturing economy', *American Economic Review*, vol. 34(3), pp. 296–319.
Friedman, M. (1953), 'The methodology of positive economics', in M. Friedman, *Essays in Positive Economics* (Chicago: Chicago University Press), pp. 3–43.
Friedman, M. (1955), 'Leon Walras and his economic system. A review article', *American Economic Review*, vol. 45(5), pp. 900–9.
Friedman, M. (1970), 'A theoretical framework for monetary analysis', *Journal of Political Economy*, vol. 78, March–April, pp. 193–238.
Friedman, M. and Savage, L. J. (1948), 'The utility analysis of choices involving risk', *Journal of Political Economy*, vol. 56, pp. 279–304.
Frisch, R. (1936), 'Annual survey of economic theory: the problem of index numbers', *Econometrica*, vol. 4, pp. 1–38.
Fry, M. J. (1982a), 'Models of financially repressed developing economies', *World Development*, vol. 10(9), pp. 731–50.
Fry, M. J. (1982b), 'Analysing disequilibrium interest rate systems in developing economies', *World Development*, vol. 10(12), pp. 1025–6.

Garegnani, P. (1960), *Il capitale nelle teorie della distribuzione* (Milan: Giuffrè).
Garegnani, P. (1962), *Il problema della domanda effettiva nello sviluppo economico italiano* (Rome: SVIMEZ).
Garegnani, P. (1966), 'Switching of techniques', *Quarterly Journal of Economics*, vol. 80, November, pp 555–67.
Garegnani, P. (1970a), 'Heterogenous capital, the production function and the theory of distribution', *Review of Economic Studies*, vol. 37(3), pp. 407–436; repr. in E. K. Hunt and J. G. Schwartz (eds) (1972), pp. 254–91.
Garegnani, P. (1970b), 'A reply', *Review of Economic Studies*, vol. 37(3), p. 439.
Garegnani, P. (1976a), 'On a change in the notion of equilibrium in recent work on value and distribution', in: M. Brown, K. Sato and P. Zarembka (eds) (1976), pp. 25–45.
Garegnani, P. (1976b), 'On a change in the notion of equilibrium in recent work on value and distribution', repr. in J. Eatwell and M. Milgate (eds) (1983), pp. 129–45.
Garegnani, P. (1976c), 'The neoclassical production function: comment', *American Economic Review*, vol. 66(3), June, pp. 424–7.
Garegnani, P. (1978a), 'Notes on consumption, investment, and effective demand I', *Cambridge Journal of Economics*, vol. 2(4), pp. 335–53.
Garegnani, P. (1978b), 'Changes and comparisons: A reply' (to Joan Robinson), mimeo, published in Italian: *Valore e Domanda Effectiva* (1979), (Turin: Einaudi).
Garegnani, P. (1979a), 'Notes on consumption, investment and effective demand II', *Cambridge Journal of Economics*, vol. 3, March, pp. 63–82.

Garegnani, P. (1979b), 'Notes on consumption, investment and effective demand: a reply to Joan Robinson', *Cambridge Journal of Economics*, vol. 3, March, pp. 181–7.

Garegnani, P. (1981), *Marx e gli economisti classici* (Turin: Einaudi).

Garegnani, P. (1982a), 'The classical theory of wages and the role of demand schedules in determination of relative prices' (read at AEA conference meeting), mimeo.

Garegnani, P. (1982b), 'Una polemica su Sraffa', *Rinascita*, no. 25.

Garegnani, P. (1982c), 'On Hollander's interpretation of Ricardo's early theory of profits', *Cambridge Journal of Economics*, vol. 6(1), pp. 65–77.

Garegnani, P. (1982d), Summary of the paper 'Some notes for an analysis of accumulation', mimeo.

Garegnani, P. (1983a), 'The classical theory of wages and the role of demand schedules in the determination of relative prices', *American Economic Review, Papers and Proceedings*, vol. 73(2), pp. 309–13.

Garegnani, P. (1983b), 'Two routes to effective demand: Comment on Kregel', in J. Kregel (ed.) (1983b), pp. 69–80.

Garegnani, P. (1983c), 'Ricardo's early theory of profit and its "rational foundation": a reply to Professor Hollander', *Cambridge Journal of Economics*, vol. 7(2), pp. 175–8.

Garegnani, P. (1984), 'Value and distribution in the classical economists and Marx', *Oxford Economic Papers*, vol. 36(2), pp. 291–325.

Garegnani, P. (1986), 'The labour theory of value: detour or analytical advance?' paper presented at the conference of History of Economics, 1986, mimeo; also deposited at the Marshall Library, Cambridge University, England.

Garegnani, P. (1987), 'Surplus approach to value and distribution', in J. Eatwell, M. Milgate and P. Newman (1987), vol. 4, pp. 560–74.

Garegnani, P. (1989), 'Some notes on capital, expectation and the analysis of change' in G. Feiwell (ed.) *Joan Robinson and Modern Economics* (London: Macmillan).

Georgescu-Roegen, N. (1966), *Analytical Economics: Issues and Problems* (Cambridge, Mass.: Harvard University Press).

Gershuny, J. (1981), *Die Ökonomie der nachindustriellen Gesellschaft. Produktion und Verbrauch von Dienstleistungen* (Frankfurt, New York: Campus).

Gersovitz, M. (1985), 'Banks' international lending decisions: What we know, and implications for future research', in G. W. Smith and J. T. Cuddington (eds) (1985), pp. 61–78.

Gold, J. (1979), *Conditionality* (Washington, DC: International Monetary Fund).

Goodwin, R. (1967), 'A growth cycle', in C. H. Feinstein (ed.) (1967), pp. 54–8.

Goschen, G. J. (1905), *Essays and Addresses on Economic Questions* (London: Edward Arnold).

Grandmont, J. M. (1982), 'Temporary general equilibrium theory', in K. J. Arrow and M. D. Intriligator (eds) (1981–6), vol., 2 pp. 879–922.

Grandmont, J. M. (1983), *Money and Value, A Reconsideration of Classical and Neoclassical Monetary Theories* (Cambridge: Cambridge University Press).

Groenewegen, P. D. (1977), 'Adam Smith and the division of labour: a bi-centenary estimate', *Australian Economic Papers*, vol. 16(29), pp. 151–74.

Groenewegen, P. D. (1982), 'History and political economy: Smith, Marx and Marshall', *Australian Economic Papers*, vol. 21(38), pp. 1–17.

Groenewegen, P. D. (1986), 'Professor Porta on the significance of understanding Sraffa's standard commodity and the Marxian theory of surplus: a comment', *History of Political Economy*, vol. 18(3), pp. 455–62.

Groenewegen, P. D. (1988a), 'Rehabilitating the classical notions of 'productive' and 'unproductive' with special reference to their relevance to taxation' in G. H.

Brennan, B. S. Grewal and P. D. Groenewegen (eds), *Taxation and Fiscal Federalism: Essays in Honour of Russell Mathews*, chapter 6 (Canberra: Australian National University Press).
Guitian, M. (1981), *Fund Conditionality: Evolution of Principles and Practices* (Washington, DC: International Monetary Fund).
Gulati, I. S. (1980), *International Monetary Development and the Third World* (Calcutta: Orient Longman).

Hahn, F. H. (1973), *On the Notion of Equilibrium in Economics* (London: Cambridge University Press).
Hahn, F. H. (1975), 'Review of political economy: The wrong issues and the wrong argument', *Economic Record*, vol. 51, September, pp. 360–4.
Hahn, F. H. (1981), 'Review of M. Beenstock: a neoclassical analysis of macroeconomic policy', *Economic Journal*, vol. 91, December, pp. 1036–9.
Hahn, F. H. (1982a), 'Stability', in K. J. Arrow and M. D. Intriligator (eds) (1981–6), vol. 2, pp. 745–93.
Hahn, F. H. (1982b), 'The neo-Ricardians', *Cambridge Journal of Economics*, vol. 6(4), pp. 353–74.
Hahn, F. H. (1982c), *Money and Inflation* (Oxford: Blackwell).
Hahn, F. H. (1983), *Money and Inflation* (Cambridge, Mass.: MIT Press).
Hahn, F. H. (1984a), *Equilibrium and Macroeconomics* (Cambridge, Mass.: MIT Press and Oxford: Blackwell).
Hahn, F. H. and Matthews, R. C. O. (1964), 'The theory of economic growth: a survey', *Economic Journal*, vol. 74, December, pp. 779–902.
Hall, R. L. and Hitch, C. J. (1939), 'Price theory and business behaviour' *Oxford Economic Papers*; repr. in T. W. Wilson and P. W. S. Andrews (eds) (1952), pp. 107–38.
Hansen, A. H. (1949), *Monetary Theory and Fiscal Policy* (New York: McGraw Hill).
Harberger, A. C. (1985), 'Lessons for debtor-country managers and policy makers', in G. W. Smith and J. T. Cuddington (eds) (1985), pp. 236–57.
Harcourt, G. C. (1972), *Some Cambridge Controversies in the Theory of Capital* (Cambridge: Cambridge University Press).
Harcourt, G. C. (1975), 'Revival of political economy: a further comment', *Economic Record*, vol. 51, September, pp. 368–71.
Harcourt, G. C. (1982), 'The Sraffian contribution: an evaluation', in I. Bradley and M. Howard (eds) (1982), pp. 255–75.
Harcourt, G. C. and O'Shaughnessy, T. J. (1983), 'Keynes's unemployment equilibrium: some insights from Joan Robinson, Piero Sraffa and Richard Kahn', University of Cambridge, Faculty of Economics and Politics, Research Paper Series 30; published in G. C. Harcourt (ed.) (1985), *Keynes and his contemporaries* (London: Macmillan), pp. 3–41.
Harrod, R. F. ([1936] 1965), *The Trade Cycle* (New York: Kelley).
Harrod, R. F. (1939), 'An essay in dynamic theory', *Economic Journal*, vol. 49, March, pp. 14–33.
Harrod, R. F. (1948), *Towards a Dynamic Economics* (London: Macmillan).
Harrod, R. F. (1959), 'Domar and dynamic economics', *Economic Journal*, vol. 69, September, pp. 451–64.
Harrod, R. F. (1961), 'Review of Piero Sraffa, *Production of Commodities by Means of Commodities* (1960)', *Economic Journal*, vol. 71, December, pp. 783–7.
Hayek, F. A. v. (1931), *Prices and Production* (London: Routledge & Kegan).
Henderson, H. ([1921, 1932] 1968), *Supply and Demand*, (Cambridge: Cambridge University Press).
Herford, C. H. (1931), *Philip Henry Wicksteed, His Life and Work* (London and Toronto: Dent).

Hicks, J. R. (1937), 'Mr. Keynes and the "classics": a suggested interpretation', *Econometrica*, vol. 5(2), pp. 147–59.
Hicks, J. R. ([1939] 1946), *Value and Capital*, 2nd edn (London: Oxford University Press).
Hicks, J. R. ([1939] 1962), *Value and Capital* (London: Oxford University Press).
Hicks, J. R. (1965), *Capital and Growth* (London: Oxford University Press).
Hicks, J. R. (1976a), 'Revolution in economics', in S. Latsis (ed.), *Method and Appraisal in Economics* (Cambridge: Cambridge University Press), pp. 207–18.
Hicks, J. R. (1976b), 'Some questions of time in economics', in A. M. Tang, F. M. Westfield and J. S. Worley (eds) *Evolution, Welfare, and Time in Economics: Essays in Honor of Nicholas Georgescu-Roegen* (Lexington, Mass.: Lexington Books), pp. 135–51.
Hicks, J. R. (1979), *Causality in Economics* (Oxford: Blackwell).
Hicks, J. R. (1982), *Money, Interest and Wages, Collected Essays on Economic Theory*, vol. II (Oxford: Blackwell).
Hicks, J. R. (1983a), *Classics and Moderns* (Oxford: Blackwell).
Hicks, J. R. (1983b), IS–LM: an explanation', in J. P. Fitoussi (ed.) (1983), pp. 49–63.
Hicks, J. R. (1985a), 'Sraffa and Ricardo: A critical view', in G. Caravale (ed.) (1985), pp. 305–19.
Hicks, J. R. (1985b), *Methods of Dynamic Economics* (Oxford: Clarendon Press).
Hicks, J. R. and Hollander, S. (1977), 'Mr. Ricardo and the moderns', *Quarterly Journal of Economics*, vol. 9(3), pp. 351–69.
Hilferding, R. ([1904] 1949), 'Böhm-Bawerk's criticism of Marx', in P. Sweezy (ed.) (1949), pp. 119–96.
Hilferding, R. ([1910] 1981), *Finance Capital* (London: Routledge & Kegan).
Hinshaw, R. (ed.) (1972), *Inflation as a Global Problem* (London: Johns Hopkins Press).
Hirsh, F. (1976), *Social Limits to Growth* (Cambridge, Mass.: Harvard University Press).
Hirshman, A. O. (1958), *The Strategy of Economic Development* (New Haven: Yale University Press).
Hobsbawn, E. J. ([1956] 1964), 'Doctor Marx and the Victorian critics', *Labouring Men. Studies in the History of Labour* (London: Weidenfeld & Nicolson).
Hobsbawm, E. J. (1967), 'Maurice Dobb', in D. Feinstein (ed.), *Socialism, Capitalism and Economic Growth* (Cambridge: Cambridge University Press), pp. 1–9.
Hofstaedter, D. R. (1979), *Goedel, Escher, Bach* (New York: Basic Books).
Hollander, S. (1973a), *The Economics of Adam Smith* (London: Heinemann).
Hollander, S. (1973b), 'Ricardo's analysis of the profit rate, 1813–15', *Economica*, vol. 40, August, pp. 260–82.
Hollander, S. (1975), 'Ricardo and the corn profit model: reply to Eatwell', *Economica*, vol. 42, May, pp. 188–202.
Hollander, S. (1979), *The Economics of David Ricardo* (Toronto: Hinneman).
Hollander, S. (1983), 'Professor Garegnani's defence of Sraffa on the material rate of profit', *Cambridge Journal of Economics*, vol. 7(2), pp. 167–74.
Hollander, S. (1986), 'Comment on Peach', *Economic Journal*, vol. 96, December, pp. 1091–7.
Hume, D. ([1739] 1938), *An Abstract of a Treatise on Human Nature*, edited by J. M. Keynes and P. Sraffa (Cambridge: Cambridge University Press).
Hunt, E. K. and Glick, M. (1987), 'Transformation problem', in J. Eatwell, M. Milgate and P. Newman (eds) (1987), vol. 4, pp. 688–91.
Hunt, E. K. and Schwartz, J. G. (eds) (1972), *A Critique of Economic Theory* (London: Penguin Books).
Hutchison, T. W. (1953), *A Review of Economic Doctrines, 1870–1929* (Oxford: Clarendon Press).

IMF (1981), *Annual Report of the Executive Board for the Financial Year, ended April 30* (Washington, DC: IMF).
IMF (1985a), *World Economic Outlook*; April (Washington, DC: IMF).
IMF (1985b), *World Economic Outlook*, October (Washington, DC: IMF).
Institute of Developing Economies (1972), *The Developing Economies*, December (Tokyo).
Institute of Developing Economies (1980), *The Developing Economies*, December (Tokyo).

Jevons, W. S. ([1871] 1971), *The Theory of Political Economy* (Harmondsworth: Penguin).
Johnson, H. G. (1976), *The Theory of Distribution* (London: Gray-Mills).

Kahn, R. F. (1931), 'The relation of home investment to unemployment', *Economic Journal*, vol. 41(2), pp. 173–98.
Kahn, R. F. (1972a), *Essay on Employment and Growth* (Cambridge: Cambridge University Press).
Kahn, R. F. ([1931] 1972b), 'The relation of home investment to unemployment', in R. F. Kahn (1972a), pp. 1–27.
Kahn, R. F. (1984), *The Making of Keynes' General Theory* (Cambridge: Cambridge University Press).
Kaiser, B. (ed.) (1967), *Ex Libris. Karl Marx und Friedrich Engels – Schicksal und Verzeichnis einer Bibliothek* (Berlin: Dietz Verlag).
Kaldor, N. (1955–6), 'Alternative theories of distribution,' *Review of Economic Studies*, vol. 23(1 and 2), pp. 83–100.
Kaldor, N. (1959), 'Economic growth and the problem of inflation', *Economica*, vol. 26, Part 1 (August), pp. 212–27; Part 2 (November), pp. 287–98.
Kaldor, N. (1960), *Essays on Economic Stability and Growth* (London: Duckworth).
Kaldor, N. (1961), 'Capital accumulation and economic growth', in F. A. Lutz and D. C. Hague (eds) (1961), pp. 177–222.
Kaldor, N. (1964), 'Will underdeveloped countries learn to tax?' in *Essays in Economic Policy*, vol. 1 (London: Duckworth), pp. 255–65.
Kaldor, N. (1966), *Causes of the Slow Rate of Growth of the United Kingdom* (Cambridge: Cambridge University Press).
Kaldor, N. (1970), 'The new monetarism', *The Lloyds Bank Review*, vol. 97, pp. 1–17.
Kaldor, N. (1972), 'The irrelevance of equilibrium economics', *Economic Journal*, vol. 82, December, pp. 1237–55.
Kaldor, N. (1980), 'The economics of the selective employment tax', in *Reports on Taxation*, vol. 1 (London: Duckworth).
Kaldor, N. (1985), 'Obituary on Sraffa', *Proceedings of the British Academy.*
Kalecki, M. (1937), 'Principle of increasing risk', *Economica*, vol. 4(16), pp. 440–7; repr. in M. Kalecki (1939).
Kalecki, M. (1938), 'The determinants of the distribution of national income', *Econometrica* vol. 6(2), April pp. 97–112; repr. in M. Kalecki (1971a), pp. 62–77.
Kalecki, M. (1939), *Essays in the Theory of Economic Fluctuations* (London: Allen & Unwin).
Kalecki, M. (1943a), 'Cost and prices'; repr. in M. Kalecki (1971a), pp. 43–61.
Kalecki, M. (1943b), 'Political aspects of full employment'; repr. in M. Kalecki (1971a), pp. 138–145.
Kalecki, M. (1954), *Theory of Economic Dynamics* (London: Allen & Unwin).
Kalecki, M. ([1954] 1965), *Theory of Economic Dynamics*, 2nd edn (London: Allen & Unwin).

Kalecki, M. (1971a), *Selected Essays on the Dynamics of the Capitalist Economy, 1933–1970* (Cambridge: Cambridge University Press).
Kalecki, M. (1971b), 'The class struggle and the distribution of national income', in M. Kalecki (1971a), pp. 156–64.
Kehoe, T. J. (1985), Multiplicity of equilibria and comparative statics', *Quarterly Journal of Economics*, vol. 100(1), pp. 119–47.
Keynes, J. M. (1923), *Tract on Monetary Reform* (London: Macmillan).
Keynes, J. M. (1925), 'A short view of Russia', *The Nation and Atheneum*, vol. 1, 17 and 25 October, Hogarth Essay; repr. in J. M. Keynes (1971–9), pp. 253–71.
Keynes, J. M. (1930), *Treatise on Money* (New York: Harcourt Brace).
Keynes, J. M. ([1930] 1965), *A Treatise on Money*, vols 1 and 2 (London: Macmillan).
Keynes, J. M. (1931), *Essays in Persuasion* (London: Hart-Davis), pp. 297–311.
Keynes, J. M. (1933), 'Thomas Robert Malthus', *Essays in Biography* (London: Macmillan), pp. 95–149; repr. in J. M. Keynes (1971–9), vol. 10, pp. 71–108.
Keynes, J. M. (1936a), *The General Theory of Employment, Interest and Money* (London: Macmillan).
Keynes, J. M. (1936b), 'Relative movements of real wage and output', *Economic Journal*, vol. 46, March, pp. 34–51.
Keynes, J. M. ([1937a] 1973,), 'The theory of the rate of interest', in A. Gayer (ed.), *Lessons of Monetary Experience: Essays in Honour of Irving Fisher*; repr. in J. M. Keynes (1971–9), vol. 14, pp. 101–8.
Keynes, J. M. ([1937b] 1973), 'The general theory of employment', *Quarterly Journal of Economics*, vol. 51, February; repr. in J. M. Keynes (1973b), pp. 109–23.
Keynes, J. M. ([1937c] 1973), 'Some economic consequences of a declining population'; repr. in J. M. Keynes (1973b), pp. 124–33.
Keynes, J. M. (1971–79), *The Collected Writings of John Maynard Keynes*, vols 1–29, edited by D. Moggridge (London: Macmillan).
Keynes, J. M. (1973a), *The General Theory and After: Part I Preparation*, in J. M. Keynes (1971–9), vol. 13.
Keynes, J. M. (1973b), *The General Theory and After: Part II Defence and Development*, in J. M. Keynes (1971–9), vol. 14.
Keynes, J. M. (1973c), *The General Theory of Employment, Interest and Money*, in J. M. Keynes (1971–9), vol. 7.
Keynes, J. M. (1979), *The General Theory and After: A Supplement*, in J. M. Keynes (1971–9), vol. 29.
Khan, M. S. and Knight, M. D. (1982), 'Some theoretical and empirical issues relating to economic stabilization in developing countries', *World Development*, vol. 10(9), pp. 709–30.
King's College, Cambridge (1984), 'Piero Sraffa, obituary', in *Annual Report of the Council* (Cambridge: Cambridge University Press), October, pp. 74–6.
Knight, F. H. ([1921] 1933), *Risk, Uncertainty and Profit*, Series of Reprints of Scarce Tracts in Economic and Political Science, no. 16 (London: The London School of Economics and Political Science).
Knight, F. H. (1956), *On the History and Method of Economics* (Chicago: University of Chicago Press).
Koppmans. T. C. (1957), *Three Essays on the State of Economic Science* (London: McGraw Hill).
Kraft, J. (1984), *The Mexican Rescue* (New York: Group of Thirty).
Krause, U. and Steedman, I. (1984), 'Goethe's Faust, Arrow's possibility theorem and the individual decision taker', mimeo, 51 pp.
Kregel, J. (1983a), 'The microfoundations of the "generalization of *The General Theory*" and "bastard Keynesianism": Keynes's theory of employment in the long and the short period', *Cambridge Journal of Economics*, vol. 7(3/4), pp. 343–61.

Kregel, J. (ed.) (1983b), *Distribution, Effective Demand and International Economic Relations* (London: Macmillan).

Krelle, W. (1977), 'Basic facts in capital theory: some lessons from the controversy in capital theory', *Revue d'Économie Politique*, vol. 87(2), pp. 282–329.

Krueger, A. O. (1978), *Foreign Trade Regimes and Economic Development: Liberalization Attempts and Consequences* (Cambridge, Mass.: Ballinger Press).

Krueger, A. O. (1981), 'Export-led industrial growth reconsidered', in W. Hong and L. Krause (eds), *Trade and Growth of the Advanced Developing Countries in the Pacific Basin* (Seoul: Korea Development Institute).

Kurz, H.D. (1984), 'Akkumulation, Einkommensverteilung und effektive Nachfrage', in H. Hagemann and H. D. Kurz (eds), *Beschäftigung, Verteilung und Konjunktur – Zur Politischen Ökonomik der modernen Gesellschaft* (Bremen: Bremen University Press).

Kurz, H. D. (1985a), 'Sraffa's contribution to the debate in capital theory', *Contributions to Political Economy*, vol. 4, March, pp. 3–24.

Kurz, H. D. (1985b), 'Effective demand in a "classical" model of value and distribution: The multiplier in a Sraffian framework', *The Manchester School*, vol. 53(2), pp. 121–37.

Kurz, H. D. (1986), 'Normal positions and capital utilisation', *Political Economy*, vol. 2(1), pp. 37–45.

Kurz, H. D. and Salvadori, N. (1987), 'Burmeister on Sraffa and the labor theory of value: a comment', *Journal of Political Economy*, vol. 95(4), pp. 870–81.

Lancaster, K. (1966), 'A new approach to consumer theory', *Journal of Political Economy*, vol. 74(2), pp. 132–57.

Langer, (1982), 'Further evidence for Sraffa's interpretation of Ricardo's early theory of profits', *Cambridge Journal of Economics*, vol. 6(4), December, pp. 397–400.

Leijonhufvud, A. (1983), 'What was the matter with IS–LM?' in J. P. Fitoussi (ed.) (1983), pp. 64–90.

Leontief, W. W. (1941), *The Structure of American Economy, 1919 – 1929* (Cambridge, Mass.: Harvard University Press).

Leontief, W. W. ([1941] 1951), *The Structure of American Economy 1919–1939* (New York: Oxford University Press).

Leontief, W. W. (1953), 'Static and dynamic theory', in W. W. Leontief (ed.), (1953). *Studies in the Structure of the American Economy* (New York: Oxford University Press).

Leontief, W. W. (1971), 'Theoretical assumptions and nonobserved facts', *American Economic Review*, vol. 61, March, pp. 1–7.

Leontief, W. W. (1984), 'Technological change, prices, wages and rates of return on capital in the US economy', mimeo (New York University).

Levine, A. L. (1974), 'The age of Leontief . . . and who? An interpretation', *Journal of Economic Literature*, vol. 12(3), pp. 872–81.

Levine, A. L. (1975), 'This age of Leontief . . . and who? A reply', *Journal of Economic Literature*, vol. 13(2), pp. 457–61.

Levine, A. L. (1977), 'The irrelevance of returns to scale in Sraffa's analysis: a comment', *Journal of Economic Literature*, vol. 15(1), pp. 70–2.

Levine, A. L. (1982), 'Marshall and the classical tradition', *Journal of Post Keynesian Economics*, vol. 4(4), pp. 565–73.

Levine, A. L. (1983), 'Price and incomes policy: a "Sraffian" perspective', *Mathematical Social Sciences*, no. 2, pp. 215–25.

Levine, A. L. (1985), 'Sraffa's *Production of Commodities by Means of Commodities*, returns to scale, relevance, and other matters: a note', *Journal of Post-Keynesian Economics*, vol. 7(3), pp. 342–9.

Levy, S. (1980), 'Towards a "Sraffian" approach to the theory of international trade', PhD thesis, Boston University.

Loasby, B. J. (1978), 'Whatever happened to Marshall's theory of value?' *Scottish Journal of Political Economy*, vol. 25(1), pp. 1–12.

Loria, A. ([1883] 1902), 'Karl Marx', in A. Loria (1902).

Loria, A. ([1895] 1902), 'Intorno ad alcune critiche dell'Engels', in A. Loria (1902).

Loria, A. (1902), *Marx e la sua dottrina* (Palermo: Sandron).

Lowe, A. ([1965] 1983), *On Economic Knowledge. Toward a Science of Political Economics* (London, New York: Sharpe).

Lucas, R. E. (1980), 'Methods and problems in business cycle theory', *Journal of Money, Credit and Banking*, vol. 12(4), Part 2, pp. 696–715.

Lutz, F. A. and Hague, D. C. (eds) (1961), *The Theory of Capital* (London: Macmillan).

McKinnon, R. I. (1973), *Money and Capital in Economic Development* (Washington, DC: Brookings Institutions).

McNulty, P. J. (1968), 'Economic theory and the meaning of competition', *Quarterly Journal of Economics*, vol. 82(4), pp. 639–56.

Mair, D. (1984), 'Towards a Kaleckian theory of the short period incidence of the property tax', *Government and Policy*, vol. 2(2), May, pp. 117–34.

Malinvaud, E. (1977), *The Theory of Unemployment Reconsidered* (Oxford: Blackwell).

Mandel, E. ([1962] 1968), *Marxist Economic Theory* (London: Merlin Press).

Mandel, E. ([1967] 1971), *The Formation of the Economic Thought of Karl Marx* (London: New Left Books).

Mansfield, E. (1975), *Macroeconomics. Theory and Application* (New York: W. W. Norton).

Marcuzzo, M. C. (1986), 'Introduction', in N. Kaldor (1986), *Ricordi di un economista* (Italy: Garzanti).

Marglin, S. (1984a), *Growth, Distribution and Prices* (Cambridge, Mass. and London: Harvard University Press).

Marglin, S. (1984b), 'Growth, distribution and inflation: a centennial synthesis', *Cambridge Journal of Economics*, vol. 8(2), pp. 115–44.

Marglin, S. (1987), 'Investment and accumulation', in J. Eatwell, M. Milgate and P. Newman (eds) (1987), vol. 2, pp. 986–91.

Marris, R. (1964), *The Economics of Capital Utilization* (Cambridge: Cambridge University Press).

Marshall, A. ([1879] 1930), *The Pure Theory of Domestic Values*, Series of Reprints of Scarce Works on Political Economy, no. 1 (London: London School of Economics and Political Science).

Marshall, A. (1890), *Principles of Economics*, 1st edn (London: Macmillan).

Marshall, A. (1920), *Principles of Economics*, 8th edn (London: Macmillan).

Marshall, A. ([1920] 1949), *Principles of Economics* (London: Macmillan).

Marshall, A. ([1920] 1961), *Principles of Economics*, 9th enlarged edition by C. W. Guillebaud (London: Macmillan).

Marshall, A. and Marshall, M. P. (1881), *The Economics of Industry* (London: Macmillan).

Marx, K. ([1847] 1978), *The Poverty of Philosophy. Answer to the "Philosophy of Poverty" by M. Proudhon* (Peking: Foreign Languages Press).

Marx, K. ([1857–58] 1973), *Grundrisse* (Harmondsworth: The Pelican Marx Library, Penguin). Translated and Foreword by M. Nicolaus.

Marx, K. ([1858] 1983), Letter to Engels of 5 March 1858, in Marx-Engels, *Collected Works*, vol. 40 (London: Lawrence & Wishart).

Marx, K. ([1859] 1977), *A Contribution to the Critique of Political Economy* (Moscow: Progress Publishers).
Marx, K. ([1862–3] 1968), *Theories of Surplus Value*, Part 2 (Moscow: Progress Publishers).
Marx, K. ([1862–3] 1969–72), *Theories of Surplus Value*, vols 1–3 (London: Lawrence & Wishart).
Marx, K. ([1862–63] 1971), *Theories of Surplus Value*, Part 3 (Moscow: Progress Publishers).
Marx, K. (1867), *Das Kapital*, vol. 1, 1st edn (Hamburg: O. Meissner).
Marx, K. ([1867] 1954), *Capital*, vol. 1 (London: Lawrence & Wishart).
Marx, K. ([1867] 1967a), *Capital*, vol. 1 (New York: International Publishers).
Marx, K. ([1867] 1967b), *Capital*, vol. 1 (London: Lawrence & Wishart).
Marx, K. (1885), *Das Kapital*, vol. 2, 1st edn (Hamburg: O. Meissner).
Marx, K. ([1885] 1956), *Capital*, vol. 2 (London: Lawrence & Wishart).
Marx, K. (1894), *Das Kapital*, vol. 3, edited by F. Engels, 1st edn (Hamburg: O. Meissner).
Marx, K. ([1894] 1967a), *Capital*, vol. 3 (New York: International Publishers).
Marx, K. ([1894] 1967b), *Das Kapital*, vol. 3 (East Berlin: Dietz-Verlag).
Marx, K. ([1894] 1977), *Capital*, vol. 3 (London: Lawrence & Wishart).
Marx, K. (1974), *Karl Marx – Friedrich Engels Werke*, vols 1–39, Ergänzungsbände 1, 2 (East Berlin: Dietz-Verlag).
Marx, K. and Engels, F. (1983), *Letters on 'Capital'* (London: New Park Publications).
Marzi, G. and Varri, P. (1977), *Variazioni di produttività nell'economia italiana: 1959 – 1967* (Bologna: Mulino).
Maslow, A. H. (1970), *Motivation and Personality*, 2nd edn (New York and London: Evanston).
Mathur, G. (1962), 'Il progresso tecnico e la funzione di produzione', in L. Spaventa (ed.), *Nuovi problemi di sviluppo economico* (Turin: Boringhieri), pp. 118–87.
Mathur, G. (1963), 'The classification of basics and nonbasics', *Economic Weekly*, 29 June, pp. 1039–41.
Mathur, G. (1965), *Planning for Steady Growth* (Oxford: Blackwell).
Matthews, R. C. O. (1959), *Trade Cycle* (Digswell Place: Nisbet, and Cambridge: Cambridge University Press).
Medio, A. (1972), 'Profits and surplus value: appearance and reality in capitalist production', in E. K. Hunt and J. G. Schwartz (eds) (1972), pp. 312–46.
Meek, R. L. (1961), 'Mr. Sraffa's rehabilitation of classical economics', *Scottish Journal of Political Economy*, vol. 8(2), pp. 119–36.
Metcalfe, J. S. and Steedman, I. (1972), 'Reswitching and primary input use', *Economic Journal*, vol. 82, March, pp. 140–57.
Milgate, M. (1982), *Capital and Employment: A Study of Keynes's Economics* (London: Academic Press).
Mill, J. S. (1844), *Essays on Some Unsettled Questions of Political Economy*, 1st edn (London: Longmans).
Mill, J. S. ([1848] 1965), *Principles of Political Economy with Some of their Applications to Social Philosophy* (Toronto).
Mill, J. S. ([1871] 1909), *Principles of Political Economy, with Some of their Applications to Social Philosophy*, edited with an Introduction by W. Ashley (New York: Kelley).
Mill, J. S. ([1874] 1974), *Essays on Some Unsettled Questions of Political Economy*, 2nd edn (Clifton, NJ: Kelley)
Minsky, H. P. (1975), *John Maynard Keynes* (New York: Columbia University Press).

Minsky, H. P. (1986), *Stabilizing an Unstable Economy* (New Haven: Yale University Press).
Minsky, H. P. (1980), 'Finance and profits: the changing nature of American business cycles', *The Business Cycle and Public Policy, 1929–80* (Washington: US Government Printing Office).
Minsky, H. P. (1982), *Can 'It' Happen Again?: Essays on Instability and Finance* (Armonk, NY: Sharpe).
Mitchell, W. C. (ed.) (1947), *What Veblen Taught: Selected Writings of Thorstein Veblen* (New York: Viking).
Modigliani, F. (1944), 'Liquidity preference and the theory of interest and money', *Econometrica*, vol. 12, pp. 45–88.
Moggridge, D. E. (1972), *British Monetary Policy 1924–1931* (Cambridge: Cambridge University Press).
Momigliano, F. and Siniscalco, D. (1982), 'The growth of service employment: a reappraisal', *BNL Quarterly Review*, no. 142, pp. 269–306.
Momigliano, F. and Siniscalco, D. (1984), 'Technology and international specialization', *BNL Quarterly Review*, no. 150, pp. 257–84.
Montani, G. (1975), 'La teoria della compensazione', *Giornale degli economisti*, January–February, pp. 159–92.
Morgenstern, O. (1972), 'Thirteen critical points in contemporary economic theory: an interpretation', *Journal of Economic Literature*, vol. 10(4), pp. 1163–89.
Morishima, M. (1964), *Equilibrium, Stability and Growth* (Oxford: Clarendon).
Morishma, M. (1970), 'A generalization of the gross substitute system', *Review of Economic Studies*, vol. 37(2), pp. 177–86.
Morishima, M. (1973), *Marx's Economics: A Dual Theory of Growth* (Cambridge: Cambridge University Press).
Morton, W. A. (1943), *British Finance 1930–1940* (Madison, Wis.: University of Wisconsin Press).

Napoleoni, C. (1963), 'Salari e politica sindacale nella relazione Carli', *Rivista Trimestrale*, vols 5–6, pp. 157–73.
Napolitano, G. *et al.* (1978), 'Special dossier', *New Left Review*, no. 112, November–December, pp. 62–83. Transl. from the original publication in *Rinascita*, vol. 4.
Nell, E. J. (1967), 'Theories of growth and theories of value', *Economic Development and Cultural Change*, vol. 16(1), pp. 15–26.
Neumann, J. v. (1935/6), 'Über ein ökonomisches Gleichungssystem und eine Verallgemeinerung des Brouwerschen Fixpunktsatzes'; in K. Menger (ed.) (1937), *Ergebnisse eines mathematischen Kolloquiums* (Leipzig: Deuticke), pp. 73–83.
Neumann, J. v. (1945–6), 'A model of general economic equilibrium', *Review of Economic Studies*, vol. 13(1), pp. 1–9.
Nevin, E. (1955), *The Mechanism of Cheap Money; A Study of British Monetary Policy, 1931–1939* (Cardiff: University of Wales Press).
Newman, P. (1962), 'Production of commodities by means of commodities', *Schweizerische Zeitschrift für Volkswirtschaft und Statistik*, vol. 98(1), pp. 58–75.
Nikaido, N. (1972), *Introduction to Sets and Mappings in Modern Economics* (Amsterdam: North-Holland).
Novshek, W. and Sonnenschein, W. (1987), 'General equilibrium with free entry: a synthetic approach to the theory of perfect competition', *Journal of Economic Literature*, vol. 25(3), pp. 1281–306.
Nunnenkamp, P. (1985), 'Bank lending to developing countries and possible solutions to international debt problems', *Kyklos*, vol. 38(4), pp. 555–77.

OECD (1983), *Positive Adjustment Policies: Managing Structural Change* (Paris: OECD).

Okun, A. M. (1981), *Prices and Quantities* (Washington, DC: Brookings).

Panico, C. (1980), 'Marx's analysis of the rates of interest and profit', *Cambridge Journal of Economics*, vol. 4(4), pp. 363–78.

Panico, C. (1985), 'Market forces and the relation between the rates of interest and profit', *Contributions to Political Economy*, vol. 4, March, pp. 37–60.

Parrinello, S. (1970), 'Introduzione ad una teoria ricardiana del commercio internazionale', *Studi economici*, vol. 25 (3–4), pp. 267–321.

Parrinello, S. (1973), 'Distribuzione, sviluppo e commercio internazionale', *Economica Internazionale*, vol. 26(2), pp. 197–226.

Parrinello, S. (1980), 'The price level in Keynes' effective demand', *Journal of Post Keynesian Economics*, vol. 3, Fall, pp. 63–78.

Parrinello, S. (1982), 'Flexibility of choice and the theory of consumption', *Metroeconomica*, vol. 34(1–3), pp. 1–10.

Pasinetti, L. L. (1959–60), 'A mathematical formulation of the Ricardian system', *Review of Economic Studies*, vol. 27(2), pp. 78–98.

Pasinetti, L. L. (1965), 'A new theoretical approach to the problems of economic growth', *Pontificiae Academiae Scientiarum Scripta Varia*,no. 28, Proceedings of a Study Week on The Econometric Approach to Development Planning (Vatican City; repr. Amsterdam: North-Holland), pp. 572–696.

Pasinetti, L. L. (1969), 'Switches of technique and the "rate of return" in capital theory', *Economic Journal*, vol. 79, September, pp. 508–25.

Pasinetti, L. L. (1973), 'The notion of vertical integration in economic analysis', *Metroeconomica*, vol. 25, pp. 1–29; repr. in L. L. Pasinetti (ed.) (1980), pp. 16–43.

Pasinetti, L. L. (1977), *Lectures on the Theory of Production* (London: Macmillan and New York: Columbia University Press).

Pasinetti, L. L. (ed.) (1980), *Essays on the Theory of Joint Production* (London: Macmillan).

Pasinetti, L. L. ([1975] 1981a), *Lezioni di teoria della produzione*, 2nd edn (Bologna: Il Mulino).

Pasinetti, L. L. (1981b), *Structural Change and Economic Growth – A Theoretical Essay on the Dynamics of the Wealth of Nations* (Cambridge: Cambridge University Press).

Pasinetti, L. L. (1985), 'Sraffa's circular process and the concepts of vertical integration', *Political Economy. Studies in the Surplus Approach*, vol. 1(3), pp. 3–16.

Pasinetti, L. L. (1986), 'Theory of value – a source of alternative paradigms in economic analysis', in M. Baranzini and R. Scazzieri (eds) (1986b), pp. 409–31.

Patinkin, D. (1966), *Money, Interest and Prices: An Integration of Monetary and Value Theory*, 2nd edn (New York: Harper & Row).

Patinkin, D. (1982), *Anticipations of the General Theory? And Other Essays on Keynes* (Chicago: University of Chicago Press).

Peach, T. (1984), 'David Ricardo's early treatment of profitability', *Economic Journal*, vol. 94.

Peach, T. (1986), 'Ricardo's early treatment of profitability: reply to Hollander and Prendergast', *Economic Journal*, vol. 96, December.

Pease, E. R. (ed.) (1913), *A History of Socialism*, 5th edn, revised and largely rewritten by T. Kirkup (London: Black).

Phelps-Brown, E. (1972), 'The underdevelopment of economics', *Economic Journal*, vol. 82, March, pp. 1–10.

Pigou, A. C. (1925), *Memorials of Alfred Marshall* (London: Macmillan).

Pigou, A. C. (1933), *The Theory of Unemployment* (London: Macmillan).

Pivetti, M. (1983), 'Interesse e profitto d'impresa: parti in cui il profitto si risolve o *determinanti* del profitto?', paper given at the Conference 'Karl Marx, 1883–1983', organized by the Istituto Gramsci, Rome, November.
Porta, P. (1986), 'Understanding the significance of Piero Sraffa's standard commodity: a note on the Marxian notion of surplus value', *History of Political Economy*, Fall, pp. 443–54.
Preiser, E. (1961), *Wachstum und Einkommensverteilung* (Heidelberg: Carl Winter Universitätsverlag).
Prendergast, R. (1986a), 'Comment on Peach', *Economic Journal*, vol. 96, December, pp. 1098–1104.
Prendergast, R. (1986b), 'Malthus' discussion of the corn ratio theory of profits', *Cambridge Journal of Economics*, vol. 10(1), pp. 187–9.

Quadrio-Curzio, A. and Scazzieri, R. (1986), 'The exchange production duality and the dynamics of economic knowledge', in M. Baranzini, and R. Scazzieri (eds) (1986b), pp. 377–407.

Radner, R. (1988), 'Intertemporal general equilibrium', IEA Conference 'Value and Distribution', mimeo (Bologna).
Ricardo, D. ([1815] 1951), 'An essay on the influence of a low price of corn on the profits of stock'; repr. in D. Ricardo (1951–73), vol. 4, pp. 9–41.
Ricardo, D. ([1817–21] 1951), *On the Principles of Political Economy and Taxation*; repr. in D. Ricardo (1951–73), vol. 1.
Ricardo, D. ([1823] 1951), 'Absolute value and exchangeable value'; repr. in D. Ricardo (1951–73), vol. 4, pp. 358–412.
Ricardo, D. (1951–73), *The Works and Correspondence of David Ricardo*, edited by P. Sraffa with the collaboration of M. H. Dobb, vols. 1–11 (Cambridge: Cambridge University Press).
Ricci, U. (1933), 'Pareto and pure economics', *Review of Economic Studies*, vol. 1.
Robbins, L. (1935), *An Essay on the Nature and Significance of Economic Science*, 2nd edn (London: Macmillan).
Robbins, L. ([1935] 1962), *An Essay on the Nature and Significance of Economic Science* (London: Macmillan).
Robbins, L. (1936), *The Great Depression* (London: Macmillan).
Robertson, D. H. (1940), *Essays in Monetary Theory* (London: Staples Press).
Robertson, D. H. (1957), *Lectures on Economic Principles* (London: Fontana).
Robertson, D. H. (1957–9), *Lectures on Economic Principles*, vols 1–3. (London: Staple Press).
Robinson, J. V. (1933), *The Theory of Imperfect Competition* (London: Macmillan).
Robinson, J. V. (1936), 'The long period theory of employment', *Zeitschrift für Nationalökonomie*, vol. 7(1), pp. 74–93.
Robinson, J. V. (1937), *Essays in the Theory of Employment* (London: Macmillan).
Robinson, J. V. (1938), *Introduction to the Theory of Employment* (London: Macmillan).
Robinson, J. V. (1941), 'Rising supply price', *Economica*, New Series, vol. 8(29), pp. 1–8.
Robinson, J. V. (1942), *Essay on Marx* (London: Macmillan).
Robinson, J. V. (1953–4), 'Production function and the theory of capital', *Review of Economic Studies*, vol. 21(2), pp. 81–106.
Robinson, J. V. (1956), *The Accumulation of Capital* (London: Macmillan).
Robinson, J. V. (1959), *Collected Economic Papers*, vol. 3 (Oxford: Blackwell).
Robinson, J. V. (1961), 'Prelude to a critique of economic theory', *Oxford Economic Papers*, vol. 13(1), pp. 53–8.

Robinson, J. V. (1962a), *Collected Economic Papers*, vol. 2 (Oxford: Blackwell).
Robinson, J. V. (1962b), 'Review of H. G. Johnson: *Money, Trade and Economic Growth*', *Economic Journal*, vol. 72, September, pp. 690–2.
Robinson, J. V. (1962c), 'Review of Sraffa's *Production of Commodities by Means of Commodities*', *Oxford Economic Papers*, vol. 3, pp. 53–8.
Robinson, J. V. (1962d), *Essays in the Theory of Economic Growth* (London: Macmillan).
Robinson, J. V. (1965), *Collected Economic Papers*, vol. 3 (Oxford: Blackwell).
Robinson, J. V. (1969), *The Economics of Imperfect Competition*, 2nd edn (London: Macmillan).
Robinson, J. V. (1970), 'Capital theory up to date', *Canadian Journal of Economics*, vol. 3, May, pp. 309–17.
Robinson, J. V. (1971), *Economic Heresies* (New York: Basic Books).
Robinson, J. V. (1973), *Collected Economic Papers*, vol. 4 (Oxford: Blackwell).
Robinson, J. V. (1978), 'Keynes and Ricardo', *Journal of Post Keynesian Economics*, vol. 1, Autumn, pp. 12–18.
Robinson, J. V. (1980a), *Collected Economic Papers*, vol. 5 (Oxford: Blackwell).
Robinson, J. V. (1980b), *What are the Questions and Other Essays* (New York: M. E. Sharpe).
Robinson, J. V. (1982), *Essays in the Theory of Economic Growth* (New York: St Martin's Press).
Rohatyn, F. (1984), 'The debtor economy: a proposal', *The New York Review of Books*, vol. 8, November.
Roncaglia, A. (1978), *Sraffa and the Theory of Prices* (Chichester, New York: Wiley).
Roncaglia, A. (1983), 'Piero Sraffa and the reconstruction of political economy', *BNL Quarterly Review*, no. 147, pp. 337–50.
Roncaglia, A. (1985), *The International Oil Market* (London: Macmillan).
Roncaglia, A. (1986a), 'The neo-Ricardian approach and the distribution of income', in A. Asimakopulos (1988) (ed.), *Theories of Income Distribution* (Boston: Kluwer), pp. 159–80.
Roncaglia, A. (1986b), 'Le scuole sraffiane', mimeo: forthcoming in G. Becattini (ed.), *Il Pensiero economico* (Turin: UTET).
Roncaglia, A. and Tonveronachi, M. (1983), 'Raices prekeynesianas de la sintesis neoclassica', *Hacienda Publica Española*, no. 83, pp. 219–29.
Rosenbaum, R. (1963), *Introduction to Projective Geometry and Mathematical Analysis* (London: Wesley).
Rowthorn, B. ([1974] 1980), 'Neo-classicism, neo-Ricardianism and Marxism', *Capitalism, Conflict and Inflation. Essays in Political Economy* (London: Lawrence & Wishart).
Royal Economic Society (1922), 'Current topics', *Economic Journal*, vol. 32, June, pp. 131–3.

Salvadori, N. (1982), 'Existence of cost minimizing systems within the Sraffa framework', *Zeitschrift für Nationalökonomie*, vol. 42(3), pp. 281–98.
Samuelson, P. A. (1946–47), 'Comparative statics and logic of Economic Maximizing', *Review of Economic Studies*, vol. 14, pp. 41–3, repr. in (1966c), pp. 54–6.
Samuelson, P. A. (1947), *Foundations of Economic Analysis* (Cambridge, Mass.: Harvard University Press).
Samuelson, P. A. (1957), 'Wages and interest: a modern dissection of Marxian economic models', *American Economic Review*, vol. 37, December, pp. 884–912.
Samuelson, P. A. (1959), 'A modern treatment of Ricardian economy', *Quarterly Journal of Economics*, vol. 76, February, pp. 1–35, and May, pp. 217–31.
Samuelson, P. A. (1966a), 'A new theorem on nonsubstitution', in (1966c) edited by

J. E. Stiglitz, *The Collected Scientific Papers of Paul A. Samuelson*, vol. 1 (Cambridge, Mass.: MIT Press), pp. 520–36.

Samuelson, P. A. (1966b), 'A summing up', *Quarterly Journal of Economics*, vol. 81, November, pp. 568–83.

Samuelson, P. A. (1966c, 1966d, 1972, 1978b, 1986), *Collected Scientific Papers of Paul A. Samuelson*, vols. I–V (Cambridge, MA: MIT Press).

Samuelson, P. A. (1967), 'Indeterminacy of development in a heterogeneous capital model with constant saving propensity', in K. Shell (ed.) (1967), pp. 219–31.

Samuelson, P. A. (1970), 'The "transformation" from Marxian "value" to "competitive" prices: a process of replacement and rejection', *Proceedings of the National Academy of Sciences*, vol. 67 (September), pp. 423–5; repr. in (1972), pp. 268–75.

Samuelson, P. A. (1971a), 'Understanding the Marxian notion of exploitation: A summary of the so-called transformation problem between Marxian values and competitive prices', *Journal of Economic Literature*, vol. 9(2), pp. 399–431; repr. in (1972), pp. 276–308.

Samuelson, P. A. (1971b), 'Sraffa's returns and post-Ricardian analysis', mimeo, M.I.T.

Samuelson, P. A. (1971c), 'An exact Hume–Ricardo–Marshall model of international trade', *Journal of International Economics*, vol. 1(1), February, pp. 1–18; repr. in (1972), pp. 356–73.

Samuelson, P. A. (1973a), 'Reply on Marxian matters', *Journal of Economic Literature*, vol. 11(1), pp. 64–8.

Samuelson, P. A. (1973b), *Economics* (New York: McGraw-Hill).

Samuelson, P. A. (1974a), 'Insight and detour in the theory of exploitation', *Journal of Economic Literature*, vol. 12(1), pp. 62–70.

Samuelson, P. A. (1974b), 'Marx as mathematical economist: steady-state and exponential growth equilibrium', in G. Horowich and P. A. Samuelson (eds), *Trade, Stability and macroeconomics: Essays in Honor of Lloyd A. Metzler* (New York: Academic Press), pp. 269–307.

Samuelson, P. A. (1977), 'A Modern theorist's vindication of Adam Smith' *American Economic Review*, vol. 67, pp. 42–9.

Samuelson, P. A. (1978), 'The canonical classical model of political economy', *Journal of Economic Literature*, vol. 16, December, pp. 1415–34.

Samuelson, P. A. (1982a), 'Quesnay's "Tableau Economique" as a theorist would formulate it today', in I. Bradley and M. Howard (eds), *Classical and Marxian Political Economy: Essays in Honor of Ronald L. Meek* (New York: St Martin's Press), pp. 45–78.

Samuelson, P. A. (1982b), 'The normative and positivistic inferiority of Marx's values paradigm', *Southern Economic Journal*, vol. 49(1), pp. 11–18.

Samuelson, P. A. (1987a), 'Sraffian economics', in J. Eatwell, M. Milgate, and P. Newman (eds) (1987), vol. 4, pp. 452–61.

Samuelson, P. A. (1987b), 'Out of the closet: a program for the Whig history of economic science', Keynote address at History of Economics Society Boston Meeting; 20 June, (published in *H. E. S. Bulletin*, vol. 9(1), 1987).

Samuelson, P. A. and Nordhaus, W. D. (1985), *Economics* (New York: McGraw-Hill).

Samuelson, P. A. *et al.* (1966), 'Paradoxes in capital theory: a symposium', *Quarterly Journal of Economics*, vol. 80, November, pp. 503–83.

Sanger, C. P. (1895), 'Recent contributions to mathematical economics', *Economic Journal*, vol. 5, March, pp. 113–28.

Saucier, P. (1981), 'Le choix de techniques en situation de limitations de ressources', doctoral thesis, University of Paris II.

Sayers, R. S. (1964), *Modern Banking*, 6th edn (Oxford: Clarendon Press).

Schefold, B. (1971), *Piero Sraffas Theorie der Kuppelproduktion, des Kapitals und der Rente*, dissertation (English title: *Mr Sraffa on Joint Production*) (Basle: private print, 2nd edn in Schefold (1989)).
Schefold, B. (1976a), 'Different forms of technical progress', *Economic Journal*, vol. 86, December, pp. 806–19.
Schefold, B. (1976b), 'Nachworte', in P. Sraffa (1976), *Warenproduktion mittels Waren* (Frankfurt/M.: Suhrkamp), pp. 129–226.
Schefold, B. (1977), 'Energy and economic theory', *Zeitschrift für Wirtschafts- und Sozialwissenschaften*, vol. 97, pp. 227–49.
Schefold, B. (1978a), 'Multiple product techniques with properties of single product systems', *Zeitschrift für Nationalökonomie*, vol. 38 (1–2), pp. 29–53.
Schefold, B. (1978b), 'On counting equations', *Zeitschrift für Nationalökonomie*, vol. 38(3–4), pp. 253–85.
Schefold, B. (1979), 'Capital, growth, and definitions of technical progress', *Kyklos*, vol. 32(1/2), pp. 236–50.
Schefold, B. (1980), 'Von Neumann and Sraffa – mathematical equivalence and conceptual difference', *Economic Journal*, vol. 90, March, pp. 140–56.
Schefold, B. (1981), 'Nachfrage und Zufuhr in der Klassischen Ökonomie', in F. Neumark (ed.) (1981) *Studien zur Entwicklung der ökonomischen Theorie I* (Berlin: Duncker and Humblot), pp. 53–91.
Schefold, B. (1983), 'Ecological problems as a challenge to classical and Keynesian economics', *Metroeconomica*, vol. 37(1), pp. 21–61.
Schefold, B. (1985a), 'Sraffa and applied economics: Joint production', *Political Economy*, vol. 1(1), pp. 17–40.
Schefold, B. (1985b), 'Cambridge price theory. Special model or general theory of value', *American Economic Review, Papers and Proceedings*, vol. 75(2), pp. 140–5.
Schefold, B. (1985c), 'On changes in the composition of output', in *Political Economy – The Surplus Approach*, vol. 1(2), pp. 105–42.
Schefold, B. (1986a), 'Schumpeter as a Walrasian austrian and Keynes as a classical marshallian', in H. J. Wagener and J. W. Drukker (eds) (1986), *The Economic Laws of Motion of Modern Society – a Marx-Keynes–Schumpeter Centennial* (Cambridge: Cambridge University Press), pp. 93–111.
Schefold, B. (1986b), 'The standard commodity as a tool of economic analysis: a comment on Flaschel', *Journal of Institutional and Theoretical Economics – Zeitschrift für die gesamte Staatswissenschaft*, vol. 142, pp. 603–22.
Schefold, B. (1988a), 'The dominant technique in joint production systems', *Cambridge Journal of Economics*, vol. 12(1), pp. 97–123.
Schefold, B. (1988b), 'Platon und Aristoteles', in J. Starbatty (ed.) (1988), *Klassiker des ökonomischen Denkens* (München: Beck).
Schefold, B. (1989), *Mr Sraffa on Joint Production and Other Essays* (London: Unwin and Hyman).
Scherhorn, G. (1984), 'Ökonomie und Ökologie', mimeo (Stuttgart).
Schumpeter, J. A. ([1912] 1961) *The Theory of Economic Development* (New York: Oxford University Press).
Schumpeter, J. A. (1934), *The Theory of Economic Development* (Cambridge, Mass.: Harvard University Press).
Schumpeter, J. A. (1954), *History of Economic Analysis* (New York: Oxford University Press).
Semmler, W. (1984), *Competition, Monopoly and Differential Profit Rates* (New York: Columbia University Press).
Sen, A. K. (1978), 'On the labour theory of value: some methodological issues', *Cambridge Journal of Economics*, vol. 2(2), pp. 175–90.

Seton, F. (1957), 'The transformation problem', *Review of Economic Studies*, vol. 24(3), pp. 149–60.
Seton, F. (1985), *Cost, Use and Value. The Evaluation of Performance, Structure and Prices across Time, Space and Economic Systems* (Oxford: Clarendon Press).
Shackle, G. L. S. (1967), *The Years of High Theory: Invention and Tradition in Economic Thought, 1926 – 1939* (Cambridge: Cambridge University Press).
Shackle, G. L. S. (1972), *Epistemics and Economics* (Cambridge: Cambridge University Press).
Shaw, E. S. (1973), *Financial Deepening in Economic Development* (New York: Oxford University Press).
Shaw, G. B. (1884), 'Who is the thief? by G. B. S. Larking', *Justice*, 15 March.
Shaw, G. B. ([1885] 1944), 'The Jevonian criticism of Marx', in P. H. Wicksteed (1944), pp. 724–30.
Shaw, G. B. (1925), 'Memorandum on The History of Fabian Economics' App. I/A to E. R. Pease, *The History of the Fabian Society*, 2nd edn, (London: Fabian Society, and Allen & Unwin).
Shell, K. (ed.) (1967), *Essays on the Theory of Optimal Economic Growth* (Cambridge, Mass.: MIT Press).
Shove, G. F. (1942), 'The place of Marshall's *Principles* in the development of economic theory', *Economic Journal*, vol. 52(4), pp. 294–329.
Simon, H. (1969), *The Sciences of the Artificial* (Cambridge, Mass.: MIT Press).
Singh, A. (1982), *Latin America and the World Economy in the 1980s: Reflections on Issues of Economic Policy* (Dept. of Applied Economics, University of Cambridge).
Singh, A. (1985), 'The world economy and the comparative performance of large semi-industrial economies', mimeo (Bangkok: ILO–ARTEP).
Sinha, L. (1974), *Value and Growth* (Derbhange, India: Mithila Mandal).
Smith, A. ([1776] 1960), *The Wealth of Nations*, 2 vols (London: Dent and Sons).
Smith, A. ([1776] 1961), *An Inquiry into the Nature and Causes of the Wealth of Nations*, Cannan edn (London: Methuen).
Smith, A. ([1776] 1976), *The Wealth of Nations*, edited by R. H. Campbell and A. S. Skinner (Oxford: Oxford University Press).
Smith, G. W. and Cuddington, J. T. (eds) (1985), *International Debt and Developing Countries* (Washington, DC: The International Bank for Reconstruction and Development).
Solow, R. M. (1979), 'Alternative approaches to macroeconomic theory: a partial view', *Canadian Journal of Economics*, vol. 12(3), pp. 339–54.
Solow, R. M. (1980), 'On theories of unemployment', *American Economic Review*, vol. 70, March, pp. 1–11.
Solow, R. M. (1984), 'Mr. Hicks and the classics', in D. A. Colard, D. R. Helm, M. F. G. Scott and A. K. Sen (eds) (1984), *Economic Theory and Hicksian Themes* (Oxford: Oxford University), pp. 13–25.
Solow, R. M. (1985), 'Towards a theory of unemployment equilibrium', mimeo (Birmingham).
Sonnenschein, H. (1972), 'Market excess demand functions', *Econometrica*, vol. 40, pp. 549–63.
Spengler, J. J. (1959), 'Adam Smith's theory of economic growth', parts 1 and 2, *Southern Economic Journal*, vol. 25(4), pp. 397–415; vol. 26(1), pp. 1–12.
Spraos, J. (1982), 'Deteriorating terms of trade and beyond', *Trade and Development, An UNCTAD Review*, Winter.
Sraffa, P. (1920), *L'inflazione monetaria in Italia durante e dopo la guerra* (Milan).
Sraffa, P. (1925), 'Sulle relazioni fra costo e quantità prodotta', *Annali di Economia*, 2(1), pp. 277–328.

Sraffa, P. ([1925] 1964), 'Sulle relazioni fra costo e quantità prodotta', *La Rivista Trimestrale*, March, pp. 177–213.
Sraffa, P. ([1925] 1973), translation of 'Sulle relazioni fra costo e quantità prodotta' by J. Eatwell and A. Roncaglia, mimeo.
Sraffa, P. ([1925] 1975), 'Sur les relations entre coût et quantité produite', in P. Sraffa (1975), *Ecrits d'économie politique* (Paris: Economica), pp. 1–49.
Sraffa, P. ([1925] 1986), 'Über die Beziehungen zwischen Kosten und produzierter Menge', in B. Schefold (ed.) (1986), *Ökonomische Klassik im Umbruch – Theoretische Aufsätze von David Ricardo, Alfred Marshall, Vladimir K. Dmitriev und Piero Sraffa* (Frankfurt/M.: Suhrkamp), pp. 137–93.
Sraffa, P. (1926), 'The laws of returns under competitive conditions', *Economic Journal*, vol. 36, December, pp. 535–50.
Sraffa, P. ([1926] 1953), 'The laws of returns under competitive conditions', in G. J. Stigler and K. E. Boulding (eds), *Readings in Price Theory* (London: Allen & Unwin).
Sraffa, P. (1930), '"A critique" and "A rejoinder" in "Increasing returns and the representative firm": A symposium', *Economic Journal*, vol. 40(1), pp. 89–92, 93.
Sraffa, P. (1932), 'Dr. Hayek on money and capital', *Economic Journal*, vol. 42(1), pp. 42–53.
Sraffa, P. (1951), 'Introduction', in D. Ricardo (1951–73), vol. 1, pp. xiii–lxii.
Sraffa, P. (1960), *Production of Commodities by Means of Commodities. Prelude to a Critique of Economic Theory* (Cambridge: Cambridge University Press).
Sraffa, P. (1962), 'Production of Commodities: a comment', *Economic Journal*, vol. 72, June, 477–9.
Steedman, I. (1976), 'Positive profits with negative surplus value: a reply', *Economic Journal*, vol. 86, December, pp. 873–6.
Steedman, I. (1977a), *Marx after Sraffa* (London: New Left Books; repr. London: Verso, 1981).
Steedman, I. (ed.) (1977b), *Saggi sulla teoria del commercio internazionale* (Venice: Marsilio).
Steedman, I. (1979a), *Trade amongst Growing Economies* (Cambridge: Cambridge University Press).
Steedman, I. (ed.) (1979b), *Fundamental Issues in Trade Theory* (London: Macmillan).
Steedman, I. (1984a), 'Natural prices, differential profit rates and the classical competitive process', *Manchester School*, vol. 52, June, pp. 123–40.
Steedman, I. (1984b), 'L'importance empirique de la production jointe', in C. Bidard (ed.) (1984), pp. 5–20.
Steedman, I. (1985), 'Heterogeneous labour, money wages and Marx's theory', *History of Political Economy*, vol. 17(4), pp. 551–74.
Steenge, A. E. (1980), *Stability and Standard Commodities* (Rijksuniversiteit te Groningen).
Steindl, J. (1952), *Maturity and Stagnation in American Capitalism* (Oxford: Blackwell).
Steindl, J. (1957), 'Zur Berechnung von Indices der Produktivität', *Monatsberichte des österreichischen Instituts für Wirtschaftsforschung*, special issue 11.
Steindl, J. (1981), 'Ideas and concepts of long run growth', *Banca Nazionale del Lavoro Quarterly Review*, vol. 34(136), pp. 35–48.
Steindl, J. (1982), 'The control of the economy', Banca Nazionale del Lavoro.
Steindl, J. (1985), 'Distribution and growth', *Political Economy*, vol. 1(1), pp. 53–68.
Stigler, G. J. (1952), 'The Ricardian theory of value and distribution', *Journal of Political Economy*, vol. 60, June.
Stigler, G. J. (1958), 'Ricardo and the 93% labor theory of value', *American Economic Review*, vol. 48(3), pp. 357–68.

Stigler, G. J. ([1959] 1965), 'Bernard Shaw, Sidney Webb, and the theory of Fabian socialism', *Essays in the History of Economics* (Chicago and London: University of Chicago Press), pp. 268–86.
Swan, T. (1963), 'Longer-run problems of the balance of payments', in H. W. Arndt and W. M. Corden (eds) (1963), *The Australian Economy: A Book of Readings* (Melbourne: Cheshire Press).
Sweezy, P. M. (ed.) (1949), *Karl Marx and the Close of His System by Eugen von Böhm-Bawerk, and Böhm-Bawerk's Criticism of Marx by Rudolf Hilferding*, with an appendix by L. v. Bortkiewicz (New York: Kelley).
Sweezy, P. M. ([1942] 1968), *The Theory of Capitalist Development* (New York: Monthly Review Press).
Sylos Labini, P. ([1956] 1962), *Oligopoly and Technical Progress* (Cambridge, Mass.: Harvard University Press).
Sylos Labini, P. (1968), 'Introduzione di forme di mercato non concorrenziali nello schema di Sraffa e passagio alla riproduzione su scala allargata: appunti preli minari e provvisori', mimeo (Rome: Istituto di Economia della Facoltà di Science Statistiche), September.
Sylos Labini, P. ([1956] 1969), *Oligopoly and Technical Progress*, translated from the Italian by E. Henderson, revised edn (Cambridge, Mass.: Harvard University Press).
Sylos Labini, P. (1971), 'La théorie des prix en régime d'oligopole et la théorie du dévelopment', *Revue d'économie Politique*, vol. 81, March–April, pp. 244–72.
Sylos Labini, P. (1974), *Saggio sulle classi sociali* (Rome–Bari: Laterza).
Sylos Labini, P. (1976), 'Competition: The product market', in T. Wilson and A. Skinner (ed.) (1976), *The Market and the State. Essays in Honour of Adam Smith* (Oxford: Clarendon Press), pp. 200–32.
Sylos Labini, P. (1984a), *The Forces of Economic Growth and Decline* (Cambridge, Mass.: MIT Press).
Sylos Labini, P. (1984b), 'The theory of prices in oligopoly and the theory of growth', in P. Sylos Labini (1984a), pp. 123–45.
Sylos Labini, P. (1984c), 'Competition and economic growth in Adam Smith', in P. Sylos Labini (1984a), pp. 3–36.
Sylos Labini, P. (1984d), 'Competition and economic growth in classical theory with an appendix on Ricardo on diminishing returns', in P. Sylos Labini (1984a), pp. 1–36.
Sylos Labini, P. (1985a), 'Sraffa's critique of the Marshallian theory of prices', *Political Economy: Studies in the Surplus Approach*, vol. 1(2), pp. 51–72.
Sylos Labini, P. (1985b), 'La spirale e l'arco', *Economia politica*, vol. 2(1), pp. 3–10.
Symposium (1930) on the representative firm, in *Economic Journal*, vol. 40(1).

Tanaka, T. (1980), 'The pattern of international specialization among Asian countries and the future of Japanese industry', *The Developing Economies*, vol. 18(4).
Targetti, F. and Kinda-Hass, B. (1982), 'Kalecki's review of Keynes' *General Theory*', *Australian Economic Papers*, vol. 21, December, pp. 244–60.
Taylor, L. (1981), 'IS/LM in the tropics: Diagrammatics of the new structuralist macro-critique', in W. R. Cline and S. Weintraub (ed.) (1981), *Economic Stabilization in Developing Countries* (Washington, DC: Brookings Institution), pp. 465–506.
Taylor, L. (1982), 'Back to basics: theory for rhetoric in the north–south round', *World Development*, vol. 10(4), pp. 327–36.
Taylor, L. (1983), *Structuralist Macroeconomics* (New York: Basic Books).
Tooke, T. (1840), *A History of Prices and of the State of the Circulation in 1838 and 1839, with Remarks on the Corn Laws and some of the Alterations in our Banking System* (London: Longman, Orme, Brown, Green & Longmans).

Tooke, T. ([1844] 1959), *An Inquiry into the Currency Principle,* Series of Reprints of Scarce Works on Political Economy, no. 15 (London: The London School of Economics and Political Science).

Torrens, R. (1815), *An Essay on the External Corn Trade* (London).

Torrens, R. (1818), 'Strictures on Mr. Ricardo's doctrine concerning exchangeable values', *Edinburgh Magazine*, October.

Torrens, R. (1821), *An Essay on the Production of Wealth* (London: Longman).

Tucker, G. S. (1960), *Progress and Profits in British Economic Thought, 1650–1850* (Cambridge: Cambridge University Press).

UNCTAD (1980), *Transnational Banks: Operations, Strategies, and their Effects on Developing Countries* (New York: United Nations).

UNCTAD (1982), *Trade and Development Report 1982* (New York: United Nations).

Varri, P. (1982), 'La rilevanza empirica della relazione tra salario unitario e saggio del profitto', *Ricerche economiche*, no. 4, pp. 514–28.

Velupillai, K. (1980), 'Review of Luigi Pasinetti, *Lectures on the theory of production*', *Journal of Economic Studies*, vol. 7(1), pp. 64–5.

Velupillai, K. (1982), 'Methodological morality in the Cambridge controversies: some notes', unpublished.

Vianello, F. (1985), 'The pace of accumulation', *Political Economy*, vol. 1(1), pp. 69–87.

Vicarelli, F. (1984), *Keynes: The Instability of Capitalism* (Philadelphia: University of Pennsylvania Press).

Watanabe, T. and Kajiwara, H. (1983), 'Pacific manufactured trade and Japan's options', *The Developing Economies*, vol. 21(4), December.

Webb, S. and Webb, B. (1920), *The History of Trade Unionism, 1666–1920*, 2nd edn (London).

Weintraub, E. R. (1977), 'The microfoundations of macroeconomics: A critical survey', *Journal of Economic Literature*, vol. 15(1), pp. 1–23.

Weizsäcker, C. C. v. (1983), 'Adaptive preferences', mimeo, 35 pp.

Whitaker F. Z. (ed.) (1975), *The Early Economic Writings of A. Marshall 1867–1890*, 2 vols (London: Macmillan).

Wicksell, K. ([1898] 1958), 'The influence of the rate of interest on commodity prices', *Selected Papers on Economic Theory* (London: Allen & Unwin).

Wicksell, K. ([1898] 1965), *Interest and Prices* (New York: Kelley).

Wicksell, K. ([1906] 1962), *Lectures on Political Economy*, vol. 2 (London: Routledge & Kegan).

Wicksell, K. (1934), *Lectures on Political Economy*, vol. 1 (London: Routledge and Kegan).

Wicksteed, P. H. [1884] 1944), '*Das Kapital:* a criticism', in P. H. Wicksteed (1944), vol. 2, pp. 705–24.

Wicksteed, P. H. ([1894] 1932), *Co-ordination of the Laws of Distribution* (London: London School Reprint, No. 12).

Wicksteed, P. H. (1914), 'Political economy in the light of marginal theory', *Economic Journal*, vol. 24, pp. 18–20.

Wicksteed, P. H. (1944), *The Common Sense of Political Economy and Selected Papers and Reviews on Economic Theory*, edited by L. Robbins (London: Routledge & Kegan).

Wilson, T. and Andrews, P. W. S. (eds) (1952), *Oxford Studies in the Price Mechanism* (Oxford: Oxford University Press).

Winston, G. C. (1983), *The Timing of Economic Activities* (Cambridge: Cambridge University Press).

Wolff, R. D., Roberts, B. and Callari, A. (1982), 'Marx's (not Ricardo's) transformation problem: a radical reconceptualization', *History of Political Economy*, vol. 14(4), pp. 564–82.

World Bank (1985a), *World Debt Tables*, 1984–5 edn (Washington, DC: World Bank, IBRD).

World Bank (1985b), 'The outflow of capital: for some countries it is big', *The World Bank Research News*, 6(1), Summer.

World Bank (1985c), *World Development Report* (Washington, DC: World Bank, IBRD).

Worswick, G. D. N. (1972), 'Is progress in economic science possible?' *Economic Journal*, vol. 82, March, pp. 73–86.

Zamagni, S. (1984), 'Hayek and Ricardo effects in a fix-wage model of traverse', *Oxford Economic Papers*, vol. 36, supplement, pp. 135–51.

Zarnowitz, V. (1955–6), 'Technology and the price structure in general equilibrium systems', *Review of Economic Studies*, vol. 23(2), pp. 109–25.

Zarnowitz, V. (1985), 'Recent work on business cycles in historical perspective: a review of theories and evidence', *Journal of Economic Literature*, vol. 23, June, pp. 523–80.

Appendix II
The extension of Sraffa's model (see ch. 1, p. 19)

Soon after the publication of *Production of Commodities* two opposite dangers became evident. One was that young and impatient economists would have tried to apply prematurely Sraffa's model to the problems of the real world; the other danger was that of concentrating most of the efforts to the defence of the basic approach (which was the classical one) against the foreseeable attacks of the marginalists and to the development of the model on the same highly abstract plane, thus giving rise to the idea that Sraffa's model was good only for pure theorists; in such a case, the problems of the real world have remained largely under the influence of traditional economists – in his comment to my paper Professor Groenewegen points out precisely this situation, with reference to the problems of taxation.

Today, after 25 years, we can say that the first danger has been avoided, but not the second, in spite of several important works, some of them presented here.

Among the most relevant problems of the real world we find those connected with growth processes. The first step to use Sraffa's model in the analysis of such processes, that is, the analysis of proportional growth, is very easy – the limit to such a process being given by the relatively scarce basic commodity entering into the surplus. The problems concerning technical progress, the change in the composition of output, the increase in fixed capital and in capacity utilization: all such problems imply considerable difficulties. But as Pasinetti and Schefold have shown, such difficulties are not insurmountable. The road in front of us, however, is a long one.

Without thinking of impossible marriages between Sraffa and Keynes, it is perfectly possible to make use of the two analyses in a complementary way; but this can be done only after at least the preliminary steps along the path of growth analysis have been made. In fact, the problems of effective demand become relevant precisely in the analysis of growth processes and not in the first approximation, where all quantities are given and reciprocally compatible.

It has been maintained that we have to distinguish between endogenous and exogenous impulses to the expansion of effective demand – technological innovations being the most important endogenous impulse, State expenditure the most important exogenous stimulus. As for the latter, we have to recognize that both Keynes and the Keynesians have neglected two interrelated problems: that of the optimum rate of expansion of total public expenditure and that of the optimum distribution between productive and unproductive expenditure – the former being a special kind of investment, the latter including two important categories of expenditure, one relating to social welfare, the second to military activities. In its turn, the problem of public expenditure is related to that of public receipts, that is, of taxation. In my view, it is perfectly possible to analyze public expenditure and taxation in a 'Sraffa type' of model.

In our time the models that are logically compatible with the classical approach and, therefore, with Sraffa's analysis are quite a few, though the relations are not always obvious. Yet, I believe that if we work out models that adopt the classical approach *and* make use of Sraffa's analysis we can make further important theoretical progress.

Index

* denotes reference to notes on page.

For Product Safety Concerns and Information please contact our EU representative GPSR@taylorandfrancis.com
Taylor & Francis Verlag GmbH, Kaufingerstraße 24, 80331 München, Germany

www.ingramcontent.com/pod-product-compliance
Lightning Source LLC
LaVergne TN
LVHW021003300926
849160LV00007B/233
* 9 7 8 1 1 3 8 2 3 0 1 1 8 *